ELIZABETH THE QUEEN

Alison Weir lives and works in Surrey. Her books include *Britain's Royal Families*, *Mary, Queen of Scots*, *Henry VIII: King and Court*, *Eleanor of Aquitaine* and most recently, *Katherine Swynford*.

ALISON WEIR

Elizabeth the Queen

VINTAGE BOOKS
London

Published by Vintage 2008

4 6 8 10 9 7 5

First published in Great Britain in 1998 by Jonathan Cape

Vintage
Random House, 20 Vauxhall Bridge Road,
London SW1V 2SA

www.vintage-books.co.uk

Addresses for companies within The Random House Group Limited
can be found at: www.randomhouse.co.uk/offices.htm

The Random House Group Limited Reg. No. 954009

A CIP catalogue record for this book
is available from the British Library

ISBN 9780099524250

The Random House Group Limited supports The Forest
Stewardship Council (FSC), the leading international forest
certification organisation. All our titles that are printed on
Greenpeace approved FSC certified paper carry the FSC logo.
Our paper procurement policy can be found at:
www.rbooks.co.uk/environment

Printed and bound in Great Britain by
CPI Cox & Wyman, Reading, RG1 8EX

This book is dedicated to
my very supportive aunt and uncle,
Pauline and John Marston.

And also to
my equally supportive brothers and sisters-in-law,
Ronald and Alison Weir
and
Kenneth and Elizabeth Weir.

With grateful thanks to all.

Contents

Author's Preface   xi
Prologue: 17 November 1558   1
Introduction: Elizabeth's England   2

1   'The Most English Woman in England'   11
2   'God Send Our Mistress a Husband'   35
3   'Disputes over Trifles'   54
4   'Bonny Sweet Robin'   70
5   'Presumptions of Evil'   89
6   'Dishonourable and Naughty Reports'   110
7   'The Daughter of Debate'   124
8   'Without a Certain Heir'   134
9   'A Matter Dangerous to the Common Amity'   154
10   'Things Grievouser and Worse'   169
11   'A Dangerous Person'   185
12   'A Vain Crack of Words'   202
13   'Gloriana'   219
14   'A Court at Once Gay, Decent and Superb'   240
15   'The Axe Must Be the Next Warning'   269
16   'Less Agreeable Things to Think About'   284
17   'Princely Pleasures'   297
18   'Frenzied Wooing'   311
19   'Between Scylla and Charybdis'   331
20   'Practices at Home and Abroad'   349
21   'The Tragical Execution'   360
22   'Eliza Triumphant'   384
23   'Great England's Glory'   401
24   'We Are Evil Served"   424
25   'The Minion of Fortune'   447

26 'The Sun Setteth at Last'   469

Epilogue   485
A Note on Sources   489
Bibliography   491
Genealogical Tables: The Tudors   511
                     The Boleyn and Howard Connections   513
                     The Dudleys   515

Index   517

Illustrations

1 Elizabeth I at her accession. (© Hever Castle Ltd, Hever Castle, Kent)
2 Robert Dudley, Earl of Leicester, attr. to Steven van Meulen. (By courtesy of the Wallace Collection)
3 William Cecil, Lord Burghley. (By courtesy of the Marquess of Salisbury)
4 Lord Darnley and Mary Queen of Scots. (By courtesy of the National Trust)
5 Philip II of Spain and Mary. (By courtesy of Woburn Abbey)
6 Lettice Knollys, Countess of Leicester. (By courtesy of the Marquess of Bath and the Courtauld Institute)
7 Sir Christopher Hatton by Nicholas Hilliard. (By courtesy of the Victoria and Albert Museum)
8 Sir Francis Walsingham by John de Critz the Elder. (By courtesy of the National Portrait Gallery, London)
9 Francis Duke of Alençon. (By courtesy of the Mary Evans Picture Library)
10 Sir Philip Sidney. (From the collection at Parham Park, West Sussex)
11 Sir Walter Raleigh. (By courtesy of the Mary Evans picture Library)
12 Sir Francis Drake. (By courtesy of the Mary Evans Picture Library)
13 Elizabeth I: the Armada Portrait. (By courtesy of Woburn Abbbey)
14 Sir Robert Cecil. (By courtesy of the Marquess of Salisbury)
15 Robert Devereux, Earl of Essex. (By courtesy of Woburn Abbey)
16 James VI of Scotland and I of England. (From the collection at Parham Park, West Sussex)
17 Elizabeth I in old age. (By courtesy of the Methuen Collection)
18 The funeral procession of Elizabeth I. (By courtesy of the British Library)

Author's Preface

Elizabeth the Queen is the third volume in my series of books on the Tudor monarchs. Having chronicled Elizabeth Tudor's childhood in *The Six Wives of Henry VIII* and her formative years in *Children of England*, I found the prospect of writing about her life as Queen of England irresistible.

This was never meant to be a political biography, nor did I intend to write a social history of the times. My aim has always been to write a history of Elizabeth's personal life within the framework of her reign, drawing on her own extensive literary remains, as well as those of her contemporaries. The manuscript was originally entitled *The Private Life of Elizabeth I*, but it very soon became apparent that Elizabeth's 'private' life was a very public one indeed, hence the change of title. Nor is it possible to write a personal history of her without encompassing the political and social events that made up the fabric of her life. What I have tried to do, therefore, is weave into the narrative enough about them to make sense of the story, and emphasise Elizabeth's reaction to them, showing how she influenced the history of her time.

The Elizabethan Age is a vast canvas, and there are so many aspects to Elizabeth and her reign that the writer's hardest task is choosing what to include and what to leave out. The details I have included are those which best portray Elizabeth as queen and woman, and which illustrate the many facets of her character.

There are many stories threaded through the book: Elizabeth and Leicester, Elizabeth and Mary Stuart, Elizabeth and Philip of Spain, Elizabeth and Essex, and, of course, Elizabeth and her many suitors. In presenting events chronologically, I have woven all these threads together into a single narrative – although, at times, it has felt as if I have been writing four different books!

Queen Elizabeth was such a fascinating and charismatic character that her life as queen merits a book of its own. In her time, monarchs ruled as well as reigned, and the personality of the sovereign could have a profound effect upon the history of the kingdom. This is a study of personal government at its best.

Alison Weir
Carshalton, 1998

Prologue: 17 November 1558

Between eleven and twelve o'clock on the morning of 17 November 1558, large crowds gathered outside the Palace of Westminster and at other places in London. Presently, heralds appeared, announced the death, earlier that morning, of Mary I, and proclaimed her half-sister Elizabeth Queen of England. Even as they spoke, the Lord Chancellor Nicholas Heath, Archbishop of York, was announcing the new monarch's accession to the House of Lords.

As Londoners joyfully celebrated the death of the woman whom they had of late come to regard as a tyrant and her replacement by one widely looked upon as their deliverer, the lords of the Privy Council were arriving at the royal palace at Hatfield in Hertfordshire, where the Lady Elizabeth had been living in judicious obscurity after narrowly evading her half-sister's attempts to deprive her of the crown. Here, as noon approached, the princess, unheeding of the bitter cold, was taking the air in the park surrounding the palace, seated beneath an old oak tree, reading a book.

She was not unaware of her imminent change of status. For several days now, courtiers and councillors with an eye to the future had been deserting the court of the dying Queen Mary and wending their way north to Hatfield to demonstrate their loyalty to her youthful heiress. Yet, when the lords of the Council came and knelt before her in the park, saluting her as their sovereign lady, Elizabeth was for a few moments speechless. Struggling with her emotions, she sank to her knees on the grass, and pronounced in Latin, 'This is the Lord's doing: it is marvellous in our eyes.'

Then she rose and, having recovered her composure, led the way back to the palace to receive the acclaim of her people and begin the business of ruling England.

Introduction
Elizabeth's England

Mary Tudor, the first female English monarch, had reigned for five unhappy years. The daughter of Henry VIII by his first wife, Katherine of Aragon, she had suffered a miserable youth as a result of her father's treatment of her mother, whose marriage had been annulled so that Henry could marry her lady in waiting, Anne Boleyn. A fervent Catholic, Mary had also been appalled by her father's break with Rome and later by the establishment of the Protestant faith in England by her brother, Edward VI, Henry's child by his third wife, Jane Seymour, whom he had married after Anne Boleyn was beheaded for treason. Hence when Edward died prematurely at fifteen in 1553, and Mary, his heiress, having overcome a Protestant plot to replace her with her cousin, Lady Jane Grey, ascended the throne to unprecedented public acclaim, she resolved to restore the Catholic faith. But in order to produce Catholic heirs to carry on her work, she made a fatally ill-judged and unpopular marriage with Europe's premier Catholic ruler, Philip of Spain, and at a stroke lost the love of her subjects. Matters were made worse when she reintroduced the laws against heresy and sanctioned the burning of some three hundred English Protestants – an act that would later earn her the sobriquet 'Bloody Mary' . In the last year of her reign, England lost Calais, the last outpost of her great medieval continental Empire, to the French, and Mary was blamed for it. Having suffered two phantom pregnancies and been deserted by her husband, she sickened and died, a very unhappy woman.

She left England in what her successor would describe as 'a sad state', reduced to the status of a minor power on the edge of a Europe riven by religious and political strife, and a prey to the ambitions of the two major international monarchies, Spain and France. England and Spain were technically allies against France, but the re-establishment by Elizabeth of the Protestant faith in England, which was confidently expected by many of her subjects, could not but cause dangerous discord with King Philip, who saw himself as the leader of the European Counter Reformation and had vowed to stamp out heresy. Backed by the Papacy, the Inquisition, the Jesuits and the wealth of Spain's territories in the New World, there was no doubt that he could prove a very formidable enemy if provoked. France was torn by civil and religious warfare, yet the French King, Henry II, had not only occupied Calais but was also maintaining a threatening military presence in Scotland, whose rulers were his allies. There was no money in the English treasury because much of it had gone to finance Philip of Spain's foreign wars, and the country had been stripped of its arms and munitions; its chief defences and fortresses were ruinous and, had war come, it could not have defended itself.

Internally, there was dissension and dissatisfaction. Many persons had lost confidence in the government, which was in debt to the tune of £266,000 – an enormous sum in those days. The people of England – who numbered between three and four million – having lived through a quarter-century of Reformation and Counter Reformation, were now divided by deep religious differences. The Count de Feria, Philip's ambassador in England at the time of Queen Mary's death, claimed that two thirds of the population was Catholic; he may have been exaggerating, but the fact remained that London, the seat of court and government, was aggressively Protestant and influential in public affairs. Where London led, the rest of the country eventually followed.

On the domestic front, life was not easy. England was not a wealthy country and its people endured relatively poor living standards. The landed classes – many of them enriched by the confiscated wealth of former monasteries – were determined in the interests of profit to convert their arable land into pasture for sheep, so as to produce the wool that supported the country's chief economic asset, the woollen cloth trade. But the enclosing of the land only added to the misery of the poor, many of whom, evicted and displaced, left their decaying villages and gravitated to the towns where they joined the growing army of beggars and vagabonds that would become such a feature of Elizabethan life. Once, the religious houses would have dispensed charity to the destitute, but Henry VIII had dissolved them all in the 1530s, and many former monks and nuns were now themselves beggars. Nor did the civic authorities help: they passed laws in an attempt to ban the poor from towns and cities, but to little avail. It was a common sight to see men and women lying in the dusty streets, often dying in the dirt like dogs or beasts, without human compassion being shown to them.

'Certainly', wrote a Spanish observer in 1558, 'the state of England lay now most afflicted.' And although people looked to the new Queen

Elizabeth to put matters right, there were many who doubted if she could overcome the seemingly insurmountable problems she faced, or even remain queen long enough to begin tackling them. Some, both at home and abroad, were of the opinion that her title to the throne rested on very precarious foundations. Many regarded the daughter of Henry VIII and Anne Boleyn as a bastard from the time of her birth on 7 September 1533, although, ignoring such slurs on the validity of his second marriage, Henry had declared Elizabeth his heir. When, in 1536, Anne Boleyn was found guilty of adultery and treason, her marriage to the King was dissolved and Elizabeth was declared illegitimate and excluded from the succession. Later on, having mellowed towards his younger daughter, Henry VIII named her in his will as his successor, after Edward and Mary, and had the terms of that will enshrined in an Act of Parliament. But his failure to declare her legitimate and Elizabeth's suspected leanings towards Protestantism made her a vulnerable target for ambitious foreign princes and disloyal Englishmen with designs on her throne. Added to this, she was a woman, and England's experience of Mary, its first female sovereign, had not been a happy one. In that patriarchal age, the consensus of opinion held that it was against the laws of God and Nature for a woman to hold dominion over men, for women were seen as weak, frail, inferior creatures who succumbed to temptations and were constitutionally unfit to wield power in a male-dominated world. A woman's role was, as St Paul had decreed, to keep silent in church and learn in humility from her husband at home.

However, respect for the royal bloodline was even more powerful than reservations about a woman exercising sovereign power, and Elizabeth was, after all, great Harry's daughter, who had for some years now enjoyed the affection and loyalty of a people who regarded her as their future liberator and the hope of Protestantism. And what England needed most now was a firm and able hand to guide her on a safe course, provide her with stable government and security, heal her divisions, set her finances on a stable level, and enhance her prestige abroad. It was a seemingly impossible task, but many of her subjects hoped that Elizabeth would be equal to it.

The England that Elizabeth inherited was, on the face of it, a strictly hierarchical society, with each man born to the degree God intended, and each class defined by its style of living, manners and dress. This was the medieval ideal, of which the new Queen heartily approved, yet it masked a new mobility, both social and geographical, given impetus by the burgeoning materialism and competitive spirit that was insidiously pervading all classes and which gathered momentum as the reign progressed and opportunities for self-enrichment widened with a reviving economy. This was in fact no medieval society, but a nation that was to grow increasingly secular, confident and proud of its achievements and its increasing prosperity – a prosperity that would enrich not only the nobility but also the merchants and yeomen who were the backbone of English society. In the 1590s, a Pomeranian visitor observed that many an English yeoman kept greater state and a more opulent table than the nobles of Bohemia.

Elizabeth's subjects were a hard-headed race, largely conservative in their outlook. Superstitious in the extreme, they believed in witches, fairies, goblins and ghosts, and set great store by the predictions of seers, wizards and astrologers. Lives made difficult because of high mortality rates – average life expectancy was around forty years – limited medical knowledge, more severe winters than are usual today, regular epidemics of plague and, for many, the grinding poverty of a daily existence in which starvation might be a very real prospect, bred in these people not only a stoicism and fortitude rare today, but also a morbid preoccupation with death. Life could be short and a wise man prepared himself to meet his Maker at any time.

One of the chief concerns of Elizabethan society was that the Queen's peace should be maintained throughout the kingdom, so that the lives of her subjects could be lived in orderly fashion, yet there was lawlessness and violence both in town and country areas, and it could be dangerous to walk the London streets at night. The roads were the haunt of footpads, and those who could afford to hired bodyguards when they travelled abroad. The law in its full majesty could be very severe on offenders, and the punishments meted out were often savage – more than 6000 persons were executed at Tyburn alone during Elizabeth's reign, and whipping, branding or confinement in the stocks or pillory were common – though these did not always act as a deterrent.

Travelling about sixteenth-century England was not easy at the best of times. The landed classes were supposed to pay for the upkeep of roads in their locality, but few bothered, hence many roads were impassable in bad weather. Most roads were just footpaths or narrow tracks, yet the main roads – the Queen's Highways – did at least have the benefit of a fine assortment of wayside inns, said by foreign visitors to be the best in Europe. Most people got about on foot or on horseback, whilst ladies of quality would travel by horse litter. It was not until later in the reign that horse-drawn carriages – unsprung and very uncomfortable – were used, and then only by the very rich.

London, the capital city, boasted a population of 200,000 by the end of the sixteenth century. It was a crowded, dirty, noisy place where plague was endemic in the summer, but under Elizabeth it became a thriving commercial centre, handling most of England's trade, while at the same time the city boundaries spread beyond the old medieval walls, creating suburbs from the outlying villages. London was not only a great trading centre and port, but also boasted good shops, especially in Cheapside, where goldsmiths sold their wares, and the famous market in the nave of the medieval St Paul's Cathedral. Along the Strand, on the banks of the Thames, the great nobles had their town houses, with gardens sloping to the river. Each had a private jetty, for the narrow streets were so congested that it was quicker and easier to travel by water. South of the Thames, on the Surrey shore, were to be found brothels and, later, the first theatres, among them Shakespeare's Globe. On the opposite bank stood the grim bulk of the Tower of London, which served as palace, prison, armoury and fortress; during the reigns of the Tudors it had acquired a sinister reputation as the scene of royal executions, yet this did not prevent the Londoners from taking their children to visit the famous menagerie which was housed there.

Within the walls of London, rich merchants built themselves fine houses, controlled the craft and trade guilds, and decked themselves and their wives in fine velvets and gold chains in emulation of their betters. Philip Stubbs, a contemporary writer, described the Londoners as 'audacious, bold, puissant and heroical'. Bear-baiting and cock-fighting were their favourite entertainments. London was by far the largest city in England; the next largest and most prosperous cities were Norwich and Bristol.

The English, being an island people and on the periphery of European life, were fiercely insular and patriotic, their new queen being no exception. The Reformation had made them even more so, and had given birth to an age in which map-makers and geographers were recording England's physical features in detail for the first time, and secular historians chronicling her history for an ever-widening audience. The English language, soon to reach its apotheosis in the plays of Shakespeare, was by Englishmen accounted the equal of any other language, classical or modern. Since the introduction of printing in the 1470s, books had become popular with an increasingly literate population whose favourite reading was the Greek and Roman classics, (which were available in many editions, in their original form or in translation) or more modern Italian literature by Castiglione, Boccaccio, Machiavelli (whose books were officially banned) or Ariosto. Poetry, especially erotic verse, was enormously popular. Learning, once the province of the ruling classes and the clergy, was now embraced by the burgeoning middle classes, and from 1550 increasing numbers of grammar schools were founded, many under the auspices of Queen Elizabeth herself, who cared passionately about education. All of this laid the foundations for the flowering of English culture – and, in particular, drama – that took place in the 1580s and 90s, the age of William Shakespeare, Edmund Spenser and Christopher Marlowe.

During the first half of the sixteenth century it had become fashionable for gently-born girls to be educated in the same way as their brothers – Elizabeth herself had benefited enormously from this – but after the publication of Balthasar Castiglione's *The Courtier* in 1561, the trend was towards proficiency in social skills rather than academic ones. Well-reared young ladies were expected to be able to read, write letters, paint, draw, make music, do fine needlework and dance – accomplishments all designed to enhance their chances in the marriage market. Nevertheless, those ladies in attendance on the Queen, who was a formidable intellectual, were expected to be well-read and erudite, for the court was a centre of high culture.

Most arts of the Elizabethan period reflected the domestic tastes of the upper and middle classes. Portraiture flourished, but the vogue was for detailed costume pieces rather than the realistic portrayals by Holbein and Eworth that had inspired an earlier generation. It had been Holbein who gave impetus to miniature painting in England, but it was left to the genius of Nicholas Hilliard to make it popular and start an English tradition that continues to this day.

Architecture flourished: this was an age of aristocratic building, with great houses being either restored or built anew in the English Renaissance style. This was characterised by classical design, sculptured ornaments and friezes, tall chimneys, large mullioned windows, balustrades on the parapets, decorated columns and Italianate facades. Gone were the fortified manor houses and castles of the Middle Ages; if crenellations, gatehouses and moats were included in the Renaissance designs, their purpose was purely decorative.

Inside each mansion was to be found the by now obligatory long gallery with its tapestries and family portraits, and other rooms sumptuously adorned with marble, wall murals, linenfold panelling, decorative plastered ceilings and glass stained and leaded with colourful coats of arms set in large oriel or bay windows. Heraldic or symbolic motifs were incorporated into the decor everywhere. In the rooms might be found furniture of English oak, upholstered with leather or velvet, looking-glasses of silver, great tester beds with embroidered hangings, and often a set of virginals, reflecting the current craze for instrumental chamber music, a fashion set by the Queen herself. Music was one of the great domestic arts of the period, with the ballads and madrigals of Thomas Morley, John Wilbye, Thomas Weelkes and John Dowland rivalling the inspiring devotional anthems and motets written at court by Thomas Tallis and William Byrd.

The gardens that surrounded the stately houses, and also those outside more humble homes, attracted admiring comments from foreign visitors. It is now rare to find an Elizabethan garden in its original state, but what is clear from contemporary records is that vineyards, orchards and flower beds containing rare and unusual plants were considered more important aesthetically than kitchen or herb gardens, although the latter had their practical uses when it came to flavouring food or distilling medicines. The fashionable garden would provide an elegant setting for the house, and would be of formal design, surrounded by stone walls or thick hedges of holly or hornbeam, all set at rigid right angles to each other. Shaded arbours and classically inspired urns or statues completed the scene.

The Elizabethans made costume their own peculiar art form. Never before had fashions been so fantastic. Men wore tight-fitting doublets with high collars and padded shoulders over lawn or cambric shirts with frills that were exposed at the neck. Starched ruffs later replaced this detail. Men's balloon-shaped breeches, which were often stuffed with horsehair and might reach to the knees, sometimes achieved ludicrous proportions and made their hose-clad legs look ridiculously stick-like. Only men with well-turned calves could carry off this fashion well. Cloaks were short and attached to the doublet at the shoulders, whilst hats sported plumes and were set at a jaunty angle. Apart from his sword or dagger, the Elizabethan gentleman of fashion adorned his costume with as much embroidery, braiding and jewellery as there was space for.

Women's dress changed subtly during the period, but still managed to exaggerate the contours of the female shape. The square necklines of earlier decades continued to predominate, but for many years they were worn over embroidered chemises. It was only towards the end of the century that the bosom was again exposed. Like men, women wore ruffs – small frills at first, which later developed into the large pleated cartwheel ruffs of the 1580s and the open-front design of the 1590s, the latter often being worn against a stiffened collar of gauze. Skirts grew ever wider and fuller, supported by the Spanish farthingale, a petticoat stiffened with whalebone or thin steel rods. Above was worn a stiff bodice that tapered to a point over the stomach. One wit remarked that ladies of the court looked like trussed chickens set upon bells.

Sleeves – separate attachments for a gown – were full, and were often richly embroidered or slashed to show puffs of the fine lawn undershirt beneath. Materials were usually silk or velvet, whatever the season, and jewels were worn in abundance – hair ornaments, necklaces, ropes of pearls, bracelets, rings, brooches, pins, pomanders, girdles and even jewelled books to hang at the waist. Many women used cosmetics, often ruining their complexions with concoctions containing lead or arsenic.

Frequently the cosmetics were used to hide the ravages of smallpox, then a common and much-feared disease.

For all their insularity, the Elizabethans did look beyond their island to the new worlds being discovered overseas. The sixteenth century was England's age of exploration and adventure, of speculation in overseas expeditions, of Sir Walter Raleigh, who founded the first English colony in Virginia, named after the Queen, and of Sir Francis Drake, who circumnavigated the world.

At home, as trade flourished, so industry expanded. Protestant refugees from the Continent introduced lace-making, silk weaving, engraving, needle- and thread-making and other skills into England, whilst the woollen cloth industry continued to thrive and bring prosperity to an ever-widening area. The Statute of Apprentices of 1563, by making long indentures mandatory, helped to bring stability to industry and farming.

Yet commercial success had its debit side. The pursuit of wealth and the frantic race to acquire land and power meant that most people cared only for their own interests and not for the public good or the needs of those weaker than themselves. It was a greedy, avaricious age, corrupt in many ways. The court was seen as a magnet for grasping scavengers, and there were many who managed to suborn the laws by bribery.

The rich lived well. The writer Philip Stubbs observed: 'Nowadays, if the table be not covered from the one end to the other with delicate meats of sundry sorts, and to every dish a sauce appropriate to its kind, it is thought unworthy of the name of a dinner.' People were prepared to spend liberally on expensive imported spices, which were often used to disguise the taste of meat that had gone off during winter storage, for most animals were slaughtered in the autumn and their meat salted down and barrelled for use until the spring. Small beer or ale was drunk in preference to water by all ages and classes, and fine wines were imported from the Continent. Drunkenness was common, so it became commonplace to serve drinks from a sideboard rather than at table, in the hope that people would not drink as much.

Although Sir Walter Raleigh is widely credited with introducing tobacco into England from America, it was probably John Hawkins who first imported the weed in 1566. By the 1590s, pipe-smoking was a common, if costly, habit − tobacco cost three shillings an ounce. Everybody, it seemed, was using it − princes, courtiers, noble ladies, soldiers and sailors.

Such was the England of Elizabeth Tudor. When she came to the throne her subjects knew relatively little about her. Nurtured in a hard school, having suffered adversity and uncertainty from her infancy, and having gone in danger of her life on at least two occasions, she had learned to keep her own counsel, hide her feelings and live by her wits. Already, she was a mistress of the arts of deception, dissimulation, prevarication and circumvention, all admired attributes of a true Renaissance ruler. At twenty-five years old, she was at last in control of her destiny, and having lived in one kind of constraint or another for the whole of her existence so far, she was determined to preserve her independence and autonomy. She had learned from her sister's mistakes, and resolved never to repeat them. She would identify herself with her people and work for their common interests. She would bring peace and stability to her troubled kingdom. She would nurture it, as a loving mother nurtures a child. For this, she believed, God had preserved her life.

I
'The Most English Woman in England'

The first act of Queen Elizabeth had been to give thanks to God for her peaceful accession to the throne and, as she later told the Spanish ambassador, to ask Him 'that He would give her grace to govern with clemency and without bloodshed'. With the calamitous example of her sister before her, she had already decided that there should be no foreign interference in the government of England, not from Spain or Rome or anywhere else, and was resolved to be herself a focus for English nationalism – 'the most English woman in England'.

Elizabeth could certainly boast of her English parentage. Her father, Henry VIII, had been of royal Plantagenet stock, with some Welsh blood from his father Henry VII, while Elizabeth's mother, Anne Boleyn, had been an English commoner whose ancestors had been Norfolk farmers and merchants who had risen to prominence through their wealth and a series of advantageous marriages with daughters of the nobility. Through Anne's mother, Elizabeth Howard, Elizabeth was related to the Howards, earls of Surrey and dukes of Norfolk, England's premier peers, and through the Boleyns themselves to many other notable English families such as the Careys and the Sackvilles.

When Henry VIII fell in love with Anne Boleyn in approximately 1526, he had been married for seventeen years to a Spanish princess, Katherine of Aragon, whose maid of honour Anne was. Katherine had failed to provide Henry with the male heir he so desperately needed, and for some years he had entertained doubts about the validity of the marriage, on the grounds that the Bible forbade a man to marry his brother's widow: Katherine had briefly been married to his elder brother Arthur, who died aged fifteen, but she stoutly maintained that the marriage had never been consummated.

Henry had had affairs before, but his passion for Anne Boleyn was all-consuming, and burned ever more fiercely after she made it clear that she would not be his mistress. Her virginity, she declared provocatively, would be the greatest gift she would bring her husband.

By early 1527, Henry VIII had decided to apply to the Pope for an annulment of his marriage. At around the same time, he resolved to have Anne Boleyn for his wife, as soon as he was free. But the Pope, scared of Katherine's powerful nephew, the Holy Roman Emperor Charles V, refused to co-operate. The King's 'Great Matter' dragged on for six years, by the end of which time the English Church had been severed from the Church of Rome, and Henry VIII had declared himself its Supreme Head. Thus liberated, he was able to have his marriage to Katherine declared null and void, and marry Anne, which he did as soon as she became pregnant in 1533. The new Queen was vastly unpopular among his subjects.

Henry and Anne had confidently anticipated that their child would be a son, and were disappointed when it turned out to be a girl. Named after both her grandmothers, Elizabeth of York and Elizabeth Howard, the Princess Elizabeth was nevertheless a healthy baby, and her parents were hopeful of providing her with a brother shortly.

This was not to be. Two, possibly three unsuccessful pregnancies followed, during which time Henry fell out of love with Anne and began paying court to one of her ladies, Jane Seymour. He had realised also that Anne was entirely unsuitable as queen, since she was over-flirtatious, immoderate in her public behaviour, and vengeful towards her enemies. She was, in the brief time allowed her, a good mother, incurring her husband's displeasure by insisting on breastfeeding Elizabeth herself, which high-born mothers never did, and choosing pretty clothes for the child. She rarely saw her, however, for the Princess was given her own household at Hatfield House at three months old, and thereafter her mother could only visit when her other duties permitted.

The loss of a stillborn son in January 1536, on the day of Katherine of Aragon's funeral, sealed Anne's fate. Arrested with five men, one her brother, she was charged with plotting to murder the King and twenty-two counts of adultery – eleven of which have since been proved false, which suggests that the rest, for which there is no corroborative evidence, are equally unlikely. Anne was taken to the Tower, tried and condemned to death. After her marriage had been annulled and her daughter declared a bastard, she was beheaded on 19 May 1536.

Elizabeth was not yet three when her mother was executed, and no one knows when or how or what she found out about that tragic event. She was a precocious child, and soon noticed the change in her life, asking her governor why she had been addressed as my Lady Princess one day and merely as my Lady Elizabeth the next. The loss of her father's favour can only have led to more awkward questions, so it is reasonable to suppose that she found out what had happened to her mother sooner rather than later. The effect on her emotional development can only be guessed at, but it must have been profound.

Nor do we know whether or not she believed in her mother's guilt. She made only two references in adult life to Anne Boleyn, neither of them particularly revealing, although she was close to, and promoted the interests of, several relatives on her mother's side. What is clear is that throughout her life she revered the memory of her sometimes terrifying father, who had had her declared baseborn and could not bear to have much contact with her in the years following Anne Boleyn's disgrace. Those years brought a succession of stepmothers, all of whom took pity on the motherless child and did their best to restore her to favour.

Perhaps the worst episode in her childhood occurred when Elizabeth was eight. The King's fifth wife, Katherine Howard, a cousin of Anne Boleyn, was a giddy young girl who unwisely admitted former lovers into her household and – it was later alleged – into her bed. Late in 1541 her crimes were discovered. The King wept when told, but would not see her. In February 1542, she met the same fate as Anne Boleyn.

It was around this time that Elizabeth told her friend, young Robert Dudley, son of the Earl of Warwick, 'I will never marry.' Some writers have suggested that the events of her childhood led her to equate marriage with death, and although there is no evidence to support this theory, there can be little doubt that this was a traumatic time for Elizabeth, with Katherine Howard's execution reviving painful thoughts of what had happened to her mother.

It was not until Henry married Katherine Parr in 1543 that Elizabeth came to enjoy a semblance of family life, as the Tudors understood it, and even then she incurred her father's displeasure for an unknown offence and was banned from seeing him for a year. They were reconciled before his death in January 1547, when his nine-year-old son Edward VI succeeded to the throne and Elizabeth went to live under the guardianship of Katherine Parr at the latter's dower palace at Chelsea.

Henry VIII may have neglected his younger daughter in many ways, but he did ensure that from the age of six she should be educated as befitted a Renaissance prince. Katherine Parr made it her business to supervise the education of her stepchildren and engaged the best tutors for Elizabeth, among them William Grindal and the celebrated Cambridge scholar, Roger Ascham. Ascham and his circle were not only humanists, dedicated to the study of the ancient Greek and Latin classics and to the education of women, but also converts to the reformed faith, or Protestants, as such people were now known, and it is almost certain that Elizabeth was fired by their ideals at an impressionable age.

She had a formidable intelligence, an acute mind and a remarkably good memory. Ascham declared he had never known a woman with a quicker apprehension or a more retentive memory. Her mind, he enthused, was seemingly free from all female weakness, and she was 'endued with a masculine power of application'; he delighted in the fact that she could discourse intelligently on any intellectual subject. There were many learned ladies in England, but Ascham was not exaggerating when he claimed that 'the brightest star is my illustrious Lady Elizabeth'.

Like most educated gentlewomen of her day, Elizabeth was encouraged to become the equal of men in learning and to outdo 'the vaunted paragons of Greece and Rome'. The curriculum devised for her was punishing by today's standards, but she thrived on intellectual exercises and had a particular gift for languages, which she enjoyed showing off. As queen, she read and conversed fluently in Latin, French, Greek, Spanish, Italian and Welsh. She had read the New Testament in Greek, the orations of Isocrates and the tragedies of Sophocles, amongst other works. Her interest in philosophy and history was enduring, and throughout her life she would try to set aside three hours each day to read historical books.

Elizabeth was also skilled at many of the traditional feminine pursuits of the English gentlewoman. In youth, she was adept at needlework and is known to have embroidered bookbindings. Ascham testifies to the beauty of her work and the hours she spent engaged upon it. Her talent as a calligrapher is evident in the many surviving examples of her 'sweet Roman [italic] hand' that survive. 'Nothing can be more elegant than her handwriting,' commented Ascham. She had inherited her parents' passion for music, and could play the lute and virginals with virtuosity, as well as sing and write music. She was an excellent horsewoman and one of her favourite forms of exercise was to go hunting. At other times she enjoyed walking outdoors, or shooting with a crossbow. Above all, she passionately loved dancing, although prior to her accession she had had little opportunity to indulge in this pastime.

Elizabeth's education continued at Chelsea under the auspices of Katherine Parr, but there was also learning of a very different kind, for Katherine had taken, with almost indecent haste, a new husband, the Admiral Thomas Seymour, brother of the late Queen Jane. The Admiral was a shallow, ambitious man and jealous of the power enjoyed by his elder brother, Edward Seymour, Duke of Somerset and Lord Protector of England during the King's minority. Anxious to increase his influence at court, Seymour had entertained the idea of marrying one of the old King's daughters, but had been firmly warned off by the Council. Now, a newly-married man, this swashbuckling Lothario indulged in daily romps with the adolescent Elizabeth, tickling and slapping her as she lay in her bed, or coming into her room in his nightclothes. Her governess, Katherine Ashley, thought this scandalous, and reported it to Queen Katherine, although the Dowager Queen dismissed the Admiral's behaviour as innocent fun, and even joined in the romps on a few occasions.

Then Katherine became pregnant, and Seymour's flirtation with Elizabeth grew more serious. How far he became involved with her is not known, but his activities aroused sufficient concern for Katherine to send Elizabeth away from her household in order to preserve not only her own marriage but also the girl's honour. After Katherine died in childbirth in 1548, the Council found out how Seymour had behaved towards Elizabeth, who was second in line of succession after her sister Mary by the terms of both her father's will and an Act of Parliament, and could not marry without the sovereign's consent. The Admiral was suspected of having secretly plotted once more to make her his wife. In fact, he was plotting the overthrow of his brother, and was soon afterwards arrested after having been caught with a loaded pistol outside the young King's bedroom. He was charged with treason and executed, Elizabeth commenting with commendable control, for there is little doubt that she had been strongly attracted to him, 'This day died a man of much wit and very little judgement.' Again, she may have made the equation that sexual involvement was inextricably linked with death.

Subsequently, Elizabeth's servants were questioned, as was she herself, and the sordid details of Seymour's behaviour were exposed, almost ruining Elizabeth's reputation and placing her life in danger. Nevertheless, she defended herself most ably, despite her youth and the intolerable pressure put upon her by her interrogators to confess. Although he was fond of his sister, the young King was powerless to help her, and it was only by adopting the dullest and most circumspect way of life, as well as the sober mode of dress so beloved by her brother and his religious reformers, that Elizabeth eventually managed to salvage her good name.

After Edward died of tuberculosis in 1553, John Dudley, formerly Earl of Warwick and now Duke of Northumberland, staged an abortive coup to place Lady Jane Grey on the throne. Lady Jane Grey was Henry VIII's great-niece, the granddaughter of his favourite sister Mary, to whose heirs he had willed the succession of the crown after the lines of Edward, Mary and Elizabeth had died out. Northumberland, who had ousted and replaced Somerset as *de facto* ruler of England during the young King's minority, was anxious to remain in power and determined that the Lady Mary, an ardent Catholic, should never have the opportunity of overthrowing the Protestant religion established under Edward VI. To this end, he married Lady Jane to his son Guilford and persuaded Edward to sign an illegal device altering the succession. The people of England, however, rose in Mary's favour, and she succeeded to the throne on a tide of popular approval. Northumberland, convicted of treason, and Lady Jane Grey, his innocent victim, later went to the block.

Elizabeth took no part in Northumberland's coup, wisely remaining in the country. When her sister Mary emerged triumphantly as queen, Elizabeth rode to London to greet her. But relations between the half-sisters had never been easy, and they soon deteriorated when Mary began to suspect Elizabeth of being a secret Protestant. Accused of complicity in Sir Thomas Wyatt's rebellion of 1554, which began as a protest against Mary's plans to marry Philip of Spain, Elizabeth spent three months in the Tower, expecting daily to be executed. Nothing could be proved against her, yet although she was eventually freed without charge, Mary remained convinced of her guilt. By Elizabeth's own later admission, her spell in the Tower was the most traumatic event of her youth; in a speech to Parliament, she recalled, 'I stood in danger of my life; my sister was so incensed against me.' She never ceased to render thanks to God for her deliverance, and often spoke of it as a miracle. Thanks were due in fact to Philip of Spain, who had interceded with Mary on her behalf, but Elizabeth had prayed for God's help, and believed He had answered her, thus confirming her belief in the efficacy of prayer. As late as 1579, she was still composing private prayers of praise to the Almighty for 'pulling me from the prison to the palace'.

After her release, Elizabeth lived quietly in the country, evading involvement in plots against her sister, whilst Mary made a disastrous marriage with Philip.

Elizabeth was twenty-five years old at her accession. She was tall and very slender, with a tiny waist, small bosom and beautiful, long-fingered hands, which it pleased her vanity to display to advantage in a variety of affected poses. She had a swarthy, 'olive' complexion like that of her mother, although she made a habit of whitening it with a lotion made up of egg-whites, powdered eggshell, poppy seeds, borax and alum, which made her face appear white and luminous. She had inherited also Anne Boleyn's long, thin face, high cheekbones and pointed chin. From her father she had her red, naturally curly hair and high, hooked nose. In 1557, a Venetian envoy had written: 'Her face is comely rather than handsome, but she is well-formed and has fine eyes.' They were bright and piercing, beneath thin, arched brows, but their colour is still a matter for dispute. If she was not conventionally attractive, she certainly had a definite charm that attracted men: not all her courtiers' flattery proceeded from sycophancy. Above all, wrote one ambassador, 'Such an air of dignified majesty pervades all her actions that no one can fail to suppose she is a queen.'

Elizabeth's character was something of a mystery to most people in 1558. She had learned early on to keep her own counsel, control her emotions, and to behave circumspectly in public, thus giving the lie to any adverse rumours about her. Although she had lived most of her life away from the public gaze, she had cleverly managed to convey to her future subjects – without making any public declaration of the fact – that she identified their interests with her own and that she would be the champion of the true religion, Protestantism.

Always dignified and stately in her bearing, she could also be vain, wilful, dictatorial, temperamental and imperious. Her sense of humour sometimes had a malicious edge to it, and she was capable of making sharp, cutting remarks, yet she could be warm and compassionate when occasion demanded, particularly towards the old and the sick, the bereaved and those who had suffered misfortune. She had courage, both in her convictions and in the face of danger, and was not above metaphorically thumbing her nose at her enemies. Possessing an innate humanity, she was not normally cruel – unlike most rulers of her day – and many regarded her as being unusually tolerant in that age of religious dogmatism. She saw herself as a paragon of 'honour and honesty' who dealt with others in a straightforward manner and would stand by 'the word of a prince', but the reality was somewhat different. She could prevaricate, dissemble and deceive as well as any other ruler of her time. The need constantly to economise had made her so careful with money as to appear parsimonious, and to the end of her life she would avoid spending it if she could. Caution was her watchword in all her dealings: she took no more risks than she had to. She had learned in a hard school.

She had also learned to use her femininity to advantage, artfully stressing her womanly weaknesses and shortcomings, even idulging in effective storms of weeping, whilst at the same time displaying many of the qualities most admired in men. She had wisdom, common-sense, staying power, integrity and tenacity, which, along with the ability to compromise, a hard-headed sense of realism, and a devious, subtle brain, would make her a monarch worthy of respect. Men might despise her sex, and they might mistake her finely-calculated sense of timing for dithering, but they learned to appreciate her abilities, even if they did not always understand how her mind worked, her unpredictability, her tendency to unconventional behaviour, and – above all – her ability to change her mind far more than they deemed necessary, or put off making decisions for what seemed an inordinate length of time.

Elizabeth's physical health was robust, and she had boundless energy, but her troubled adolescence had made her neurotic and she suffered intermittent panic attacks, irrational fears and bouts of emotional paralysis, when she was incapable of knowing what to do. She could not tolerate loud noises, although she had a quick temper and was not above shouting and swearing at her hapless advisers.

There is no doubt that she found it an advantage being a young, marriageable female in a court of men: flirtation was her life blood, and she was well aware that her attraction for men was not entirely due to her exalted status. Like her mother, she knew how to charm the opposite sex into thinking her beautiful by her wit and vivacity, her lively conversation and her expressive eyes. Her personality was compelling and charismatic: she was, as one courtier claimed, at once 'so effervescent, so intimate and so regal'. She was far more at ease in the company of men than in that of women, and was never happier than when indulging in the games of courtly love. Throughout her life, it pleased her to believe that the male courtiers who flattered her and fawned upon her – as she expected them to do – were in love with her. Because of this, she viewed most other women as a threat..

On the afternoon of her accession day, 17 November 1558, the new Queen summoned those councillors who had arrived at Hatfield to attend her to discuss her immediate plans. Dressed in the demure black and white garments so applauded by her Protestant admirers, she presided over the meeting with a self possession and business acumen that surprised those who had felt concern at her lack of political experience. One man, however, who had known Elizabeth since her early teens and had long been one of her foremost supporters, had no doubts about her ability to rule her people. His name was William Cecil, and for the next forty years he was to be her chief adviser and dear friend.

Cecil was now thirty-eight. The only son of a Northamptonshire squire who had served Henry VIII, he had – like Roger Ascham – been educated at Cambridge and similarly influenced by the humanist-reformist movement which flourished there. After university, he was sent by his father to Grays Inn to study law, and within a short time he was offered a handsomely remunerated position in the Court of Common Pleas. His first wife was Mary, sister of Edward VI's tutor John Cheke, another Cambridge humanist, but she died young, and William married secondly another bluestocking, Mildred, eldest of the four highly-educated daughters of Sir Anthony Cooke, Edward VI's governor. Mildred was plain and long-faced, but the marriage was happy and fruitful, and Cecil came to revel in the delights of fatherhood. According to John Clapham, who served in his household and became his biographer, 'If he could get his table set round with his little children he was then in his kingdom.' Although he loved simple pleasures, the family was wealthy and had residences at Stamford in Lincolnshire – he began the building of the palatial Burghley House in 1553 – and Wimbledon in Surrey.

Under Edward VI, Cecil prospered; he became Master of the Court of Requests, Member of Parliament for Stamford, secretary to the Lord Protector Somerset, a member of the Privy Council and Secretary of State, before being knighted in 1551. He achieved this meteoric rise through sheer hard work and integrity, proving to his masters that he was discreet, learned, trustworthy and a statesman of the highest order. Conservative in his views, he would throughout his life share Elizabeth's belief in the time-honoured medieval ideals of social hierarchy. He was also a patriot and a realist, who reluctantly acknowledged the need for reform, was prepared to put his country's needs before his own, and would not scruple to use ruthless and underhand methods in the national interest. It was his supreme caution that was his greatest strength, and it would be the single most important influence upon the affairs of England during the years to come.

Cecil was a fervent Protestant, and although he concealed his true leanings when Mary came to the throne, his career suffered a period of stagnation; he held no court office during her reign, although he retained his post at the Court of Common Pleas.

John Clapham described Cecil as having 'a well-tempered constitution of body, of stature rather comely than tall, in countenance grave, but without authority'. His portraits – and there are more extant of him than of any other of Elizabeth's subjects – portray him as a great statesman, a man with grey eyes, a pink complexion, greying hair and moustache (his hair was white from about 1572), a brown beard and three warts on his right cheek. As a commoner, he certainly felt at a disadvantage amongst the noble lords of the court, and some of them would indeed resent him in the years to come.

During Edward's reign, and then Mary's, Cecil had advised Elizabeth on financial matters and later used his influence and political experience to counteract the machinations of her enemies. It did not take her long to recognise his worth, nor for him to appreciate her unique qualities, and so began one of the most remarkable partnerships in English history. Before long, she was calling him her Spirit – her bestowal of nicknames on those close to her came to be recognised as a signal mark of favour – and once wrote to him, when he doubted that favour, as he periodically had cause to do:

Sir Spirit, I doubt I do nickname you, for those of your kind (they say) have no sense; but I have of late seen an *ecce signum*, that if an ass kick you, you feel it too soon. I will recant you from being my Spirit if ever I perceive that you disdain not such a feeling. Serve God, fear the King, and be a good fellow to the rest. Do not be so silly a soul as not to regard her trust who puts it in you. God bless you, and long may you last.

Thus it was that Cecil was seated beside Elizabeth when her councillors met on the afternoon of 17 November, when the formal announcement of her accession was issued to foreign courts and English embassies abroad. Three days of mourning for Queen Mary were proclaimed, and then the meeting broke up, although the new Queen would continue to consult individual councillors in private. Meanwhile, so many courtiers and loyal supporters were arriving at Hatfield that it was impossible to find lodgings for them all.

The next morning, Queen and councillors met informally again to make arrangements for the royal household, and later that day the appointment of Lord Robert Dudley as Master of the Horse was announced. There was some murmuring about this, for Dudley was the son of the traitor Northumberland, who in 1553 had unsuccessfully plotted to oust Mary and Elizabeth from the succession in favour of Lady Jane Grey. Both Northumberland and Jane had gone to the block, and Dudley, with his surviving brothers, had spent some time in the Tower. Later he was released and during Mary's reign saw active service in the armies of his patron and friend, Philip of Spain, distinguishing himself at the Battle of San Quentin in 1557. Back at court, he earned himself the reputation of being a superb horseman and accomplished jouster; but the taint of treason still clung to the Dudley name, and there were many who were wary of him.

For Elizabeth, Dudley was the obvious choice to be Master of the Horse, a post which had to be filled with the utmost urgency if arrangements for her court to proceed to London were to be made in good time. To begin with, his eldest brother, John, Earl of Warwick, now dead, had held it under Edward VI, so Robert was his natural successor. More importantly, he was particularly skilled in equine matters, and he had been Elizabeth's friend since childhood; they were almost of an age. Born on 24 June 1533 he had spent time at court as a child, and may have been one of that select group of aristocratic children chosen to share lessons with the royal siblings Edward and Elizabeth, becoming particularly close to the latter. Later in life he would write: 'I have known her better than any man alive since she was eight years old.'

In 1550 Dudley had been appointed Master of the Buckhounds, and that same year he married Amy, daughter and heiress of Sir John Robsart of Syderstone in Norfolk. Edward VI was a guest at the wedding. This marriage made Robert a wealthy landowner in Norfolk, and to begin with at least it brought him personal happiness: it was, remembered William Cecil, 'a carnal marriage, begun for pleasure'.

In 1553 he became a Member of Parliament and supported his father's abortive coup. He was still a prisoner in the Tower under sentence of death when Elizabeth was confined there in 1554, and although there is no evidence that they met within those grim walls, many writers have speculated that they might indeed have done so, and even that their romance began at that time. This is unlikely, as Elizabeth was held under the strictest security and Dudley had requested and obtained permission for his wife to visit him 'at any convenient time'. All we can surmise is that Robert and Elizabeth's separate experiences of imprisonment under the shadow of the axe forged a common bond between them. After his return from the Continent in 1557, Robert settled in Norfolk, but he did not forget Elizabeth and at one time 'sold a good piece of land to aid her'. As soon as he heard of her accession, he came post haste to Hatfield, symbolically mounted on the proverbial white charger, to offer his loyalty and his services, and Elizabeth found that offer irresistible.

As Master of the Horse, Dudley's annual salary was £1500 along with various perks including a suite of rooms at court. He was permitted to be waited on by his own servants, who had permission to wear the green and white household livery of the Tudors. Four horses were allocated for his personal use. The post was no sinecure, requiring him to purchase, breed, train and maintain horses for the use of the Queen and her court. Dudley attended to his duties with panache, improving the standards at the royal studs, one of which he founded himself at Greenwich for the purpose of breeding barbary horses. He was also responsible for organising state processions and courtly entertainments such as tournaments, masques, plays and banquets, tasks to which he was ideally suited with his flair for organisation and showmanship and his vast knowledge of heraldry and the rules of chivalry. In royal processions, it was his privilege to ride immediately behind the Queen. As Elizabeth took 'great pleasure in good horses', she and Dudley were to be in each other's company almost on a daily basis, and before the court left Hatfield they were seen riding out together in the park; Elizabeth loved nothing more than to be out of doors on a horse, especially in the company of this handsome young man who urged her to regard regular exercise as a necessary escape from her state duties. It was not long before these rides with her Master of Horse became a regular habit.

Dudley was almost six feet tall and very attractive; his skin was so dark as to earn him the nickname of 'the Gypsy', a name used by some to refer to his moral character rather than his face. Sir Robert Naunton described him as 'a very goodly person and singular well-featured, and all his youth well-favoured, but high-foreheaded.' He had red-brown hair, a reddish beard and moustache, a high-bridged nose and sardonic, heavy-lidded eyes. Elizabeth much admired his long, slender fingers. As a young man he was lean and muscular, with long, shapely legs, and showed his physique off to advantage in fine and fashionable clothes. He was dynamic and energetic: he jousted, rode, played tennis and archery, and enjoyed fishing. He could also dance and sing well, and was an excellent conversationalist. A true Renaissance man, he was fascinated by science, mathematics, geometry, astronomy, cartography and navigation, had read many classical authors and could speak both French and Italian fluently. It is possible that Dr John Dee, the notable scientist, astrologer and reputed magician, had been his tutor, for Dee had once been a member of Northumberland's household, and it was not long before Dudley would introduce Dee to Queen Elizabeth, who came to set great store by the doctor's wisdom and knowledge and would often accompany Dudley to his house at Mortlake.

Dudley's appointment and his obvious favour with the young Queen dismayed those at court who feared a revival of his family's ambitions. Some remembered that not only his father but also his grandfather, Edmund Dudley, had gone to the block for treason, the latter at the beginning of Henry VIII's reign, although it now seems likely that Edmund was merely a scapegoat for Henry VII's unpopular financial policies. Yet it was not long before Elizabeth's favour extended to other members of the Dudley family, notably Robert's brother Ambrose and his sister Mary, the wife of Sir Henry Sidney of Penshurst, who became one of the Ladies of the Bedchamber to whom the Queen was most devoted.

Throughout the 18th and 19th of November Elizabeth worked with her advisers to form a new administration, and on 20 November the Privy Council and a large section of the peerage, come to make obeisance to the Queen, met formally in the great hall at Hatfield to hear Elizabeth name the men she had chosen as her chief advisers and make her first public speech.

First, Sir William Cecil's appointment as Secretary of State was announced, and he took the oath of office. The office of Secretary was not the greatest that the Queen could bestow, but it would enable her to form a close working relationship with Cecil, whom she trusted above all other men. He, however, had his misgivings, for he subscribed to the almost universal masculine view that women, being wayward, emotional, weak and vacillating creatures, were unfit to govern and incapable of running an administration. Elizabeth, who was in time to prove him wrong, now displayed for the first time as queen the regal command and dignified style of oration that was to characterise her public appearances, and told him: 'I give you this charge that you shall be of my Privy Council and content to take pains for me and my realm. This judgement I have of you, that you will not be corrupted with any manner of gifts, and that you will be faithful to the state; and that, without respect of my private will, you will give me that counsel which you think best; and if you shall know anything necessary to be declared to me of secrecy, you shall show it to myself only; and assure yourself I will not fail to keep taciturnity therein.'

The rotund and amiable lawyer Sir Nicholas Bacon was then sworn in as Lord Keeper of the Great Seal, the office of Lord Chancellor being then temporarily in abeyance, then other appointments were announced. Katherine Parr's brother William, out of favour under Mary, was restored to the Marquessate of Northampton and made a Privy Councillor; Sir Nicholas Throckmorton, a zealous and vocal Protestant, became Chamberlain of the Exchequer. Sir Francis Knollys, another fanatical Protestant who was hurrying home from exile upon receiving news of Elizabeth's accession, was the husband of the Queen's cousin Katherine Carey, daughter of Anne Boleyn's sister Mary, and was made a Privy Councillor. Ten of the councillors who had served under Mary were retained, including the Marquess of Winchester and the Earls of Shrewsbury, Derby, Arundel and Pembroke; most were middle-aged men of considerable experience, whose conspiracies against her in the previous reign Elizabeth was prepared to overlook, although she could never bring herself to like Arundel or Pembroke. Those of Mary's councillors who had displayed strong Catholic loyalties were dismissed and replaced with Protestant lords of Elizabeth's own choosing, but the new Privy Council was to be smaller than it had been under Mary, Elizabeth believing, with reason, that forty-four 'councillors would make rather discord and confusion than good counsel'.

Elizabeth then addressed the assembly from her throne under the canopy of estate.

The law of Nature moves me to sorrow for my sister. The burthen that is fallen upon me maketh me amazed; and yet, considering that I am God's creature, ordained to obey His appointment, I will yield thereto, desiring from the bottom of my heart that I may have assistance of His grace to be the minister of His heavenly will in this office now committed to me. And as I am but one body, so I shall require you all, my lords, to be assistant to me, that I with my ruling, and you with your service, may make a good account to Almighty God, and leave some comfort to our posterity on Earth.

I mean to direct all mine actions by good advice and counsel. My meaning is to require of you all nothing more but faithful hearts, and of my good will you shall not doubt, using yourselves as good and loving subjects.

For the next three days she was busy, drawing up lists of councillors, formulating policies, cranking the machinery of government into action, and planning her household appointments. First to be promoted were those who had served her faithfully as princess. Her former governess, Katherine Ashley, was made Mistress of the Robes and First Lady of the Bedchamber with responsibility for the maids of honour, who were all young girls from noble families. Ashley's husband John was to be Master of the Jewel House, while Elizabeth's former treasurer, Thomas Parry, was knighted and made Comptroller of the Household. Her old Welsh nurse, Blanche Parry, who had served her since birth and taught her the Welsh language, was appointed Keeper of the Queen's Books. Sir Francis Knollys became Vice-Chamberlain of the Household; his daughter Laetitia, known as Lettice, was one of the Queen's first maids of honour. Another of Elizabeth's cousins, Henry Carey, Mary Boleyn's son and a man of great abilities, was raised to the peerage as Baron Hunsdon.

Several of those Catholic ladies who had served Queen Mary were dismissed and replaced with ladies who professed Protestant beliefs. The Queen was an exacting and demanding mistress who expected high standards to prevail in her household. She disliked employing anyone who was ugly, and once turned down an application for a position from a man whose handsome face was marred by a missing tooth. Yet those who were lucky enough to secure places in the royal household were well looked after, even when they became old or sick. Then the Queen would ensure that they received 'good pensions'.

When Queen Mary lay dying, King Philip had sent an ambassador, the Count de Feria, to England, to present his master's congratulations to his wife's successor and ensure the continuance of the Anglo-Habsburg alliance, which united England and Spain against France and protected the valuable trading markets of the Habsburg-owned Low Countries from French harrassment. The alliance was very important to Philip, and he was prepared to overlook Elizabeth's suspected heretical tendencies in the interests of their common friendship. There had even been rumours, current in Mary's lifetime, that he meant to marry Elizabeth.

De Feria had an audience with Elizabeth at Hatfield, at which his claim that she owed her throne to Philip's influence had met with the contempt it deserved; in this matter, she told him tartly, her gratitude was due solely to her people. But she knew it was not in her interests to alienate Spain, for she needed Philip's friendship as much as he needed hers. On the day of her accession, the Catholic Henry II of France had publicly declared that, as a bastard, Elizabeth was unfit to be Queen of England, and proclaimed as the true queen his daughter-in-law, Mary, Queen of Scots, great-niece of Henry VIII.

Mary and her husband, the Dauphin Francis, were already displaying the royal arms of England quartered on their own of Scotland and France. Many Catholics had not acknowledged Henry VIII's divorce from Katherine of Aragon, mother of Mary I, nor his marriage to Anne Boleyn, and to them Mary, Queen of Scots was the rightful Queen of England. Elizabeth could not know that Henry II's actions were merely mischievous, and she was angered and immensely troubled by them, becoming even more so when she heard rumours that he intended to persuade the Pope to have her formally proclaimed 'a bastard and a heretic and ineligible to the Crown'. If Spain remained allied to England, the Pope would hardly wish to offend Philip by insulting England's Queen. Moreover, Elizabeth was resolved to win Calais back from the French, and hoped that Philip would help her; she did not yet comprehend that the French were too deeply entrenched in Calais for its recovery ever to be a realistic prospect.

Naturally, de Feria, like most other people, expected the Queen to marry. It was unthinkable that a woman would attempt to rule alone without a man to guide and protect her; he could also father her children and so ensure the continuance of the dynasty and the future security of the realm. Marriage, as Cecil later told the Queen, was her 'only known and likely surety, at home and abroad', and, as she herself acknowledged, 'There is a strong idea in the world that a woman cannot live unless she is married.'

That November, a German envoy observed, 'The Queen is of an age when she should in reason, and – as is woman's way – be eager to marry and be provided for. For that she should wish to remain a maid and never marry is inconceivable.' A husband could share 'the cares, the labours and fatigues of her government'. Although several times during Mary's reign Elizabeth had expressed her desire to remain single, most people put this down to maidenly modesty. Hardly anyone took her at her word. Besides, it was seen as unhealthy for a woman to remain unwed: marriage could provide her with the emotional and sexual satisfaction that brought physical and mental fulfilment. It was acknowledged that women who remained single were sexually frustrated, given to fantasies and lust, and had unstable minds.

In de Feria's opinion, there was only one suitable match for Elizabeth, and that was King Philip himself. The advantages of such a union would be manifold on both sides. On 21 November the Count wrote to his master: 'The more I think about this business, the more certain I am that everything depends upon the husband this woman may take.' There was little doubt in his mind that, if King Philip proposed, Elizabeth would accept him. 'If she decides to marry out of the country, she will at once fix her eyes on Your Majesty.'

Nevertheless, the Queen had been expressing some disturbingly independent views. Whereas both Philip and de Feria had counted upon her relying on her brother-in-law's advice, both she 'and her people hold themselves free from Your Majesty, and will listen to any ambassadors who may come to treat of marriage'. There was no time to lose, for people were already talking of a marriage with the Austrian branch of the Habsburg family, which would not at present be in Spain's interests. That there would be difficulties in arranging a marriage between Elizabeth and Philip, de Feria anticipated, but 'with great negotiation and money' it might be accomplished. The ambassador went on to give his impressions of the new Queen: he thought her

> sharp, without prudence. She is a very vain and clever woman. She must have been thoroughly schooled in the manner in which her father conducted his affairs. She is determined to be governed by no one.

He had been at once intrigued and baffled by her, being disconcerted by her relaxed manner during the audience and her habit of laughing meaningfully, as if she knew what he was thinking. 'She is a very strange sort of woman,' he concluded.

Rumours about his impending match with Elizabeth were rife at Philip's court at Brussels, yet for the present the King refused to acknowledge them, nor did he instruct de Feria to propose marriage. In truth, he had little inclination to marry again in England, and even less to be united with the heretical Elizabeth, whom he suspected would be less tractable than her sister.

On 23 November, Elizabeth left Hatfield with a retinue of over one thousand courtiers and travelled through Hertfordshire and Middlesex to London for her official reception as Queen. She was cheered along the way by crowds lining the streets to see her, and was received outside the City walls by the Lord Mayor, who made a speech of welcome and presented his aldermen and sheriffs to her. As, smiling, she extended her hand to each to be kissed, she saw the advancing figure of Edmund Bonner, Bishop of London – 'Bloody Bonner', who had been responsible in Mary's reign for the burning of many Protestants. As the Bishop knelt, the Queen withdrew her hand and moved away.

She then entered London and, because Whitehall Palace was not ready to receive her, took up her lodging at the Charterhouse near Smithfield, a former monastery that was now the residence of Lord North. Here she stayed for five days, receiving visitors, presiding over meetings of the Council and attending to matters of state.

On 28 November, Elizabeth, again attended by her thousand-strong retinue, removed to the royal apartments in the Tower of London. Choosing a different route from the traditional one that she would follow on the day of her coronation, she emerged sumptuously attired in purple velvet with a rich scarf around her neck, and went in procession through the packed, newly-gravelled, banner-bedecked streets of the capital to Cripplegate and Tower Hill, revelling in the acclaim of her subjects, the pretty speeches delivered by children at various places along her route, the music and singing of the City waits, the pealing of the bells of a hundred churches, and the fanfares of trumpets that announced her coming. The procession was led by the Lord Mayor of London and Garter King of Arms, with Pembroke bearing the Sword of State and Lord Robert Dudley, on a black charger, riding behind the Queen's horse. As she approached the Tower via Fenchurch Street and Gracechurch Street, 'there was great shooting of guns, the like was never heard before', which lasted half an hour.

The whole of London, it seemed, had turned out to watch her arrival, and was entranced, especially when the Queen displayed an inclination for 'stately stooping to the meanest sort' of commoner. Sir John Hayward wrote:

> If ever any person had either the gift or the style to win the hearts of the people, it was this Queen. All her faculties were in motion, and every motion seemed a well-guided action; her eye was set upon one, her ear listened to another, her judgement ran upon a third, to a fourth she addressed her speech; her spirit seemed to be everywhere. Some she pitied, some she commended, some she thanked, at others she pleasantly and wittily jested, condemning no person, neglecting no office, and distributing her smiles, looks and graces so artfully that thereupon the people again redoubled the testimony of their joys, and afterwards, raising everything to the highest strain, filled the ears of all men with immoderate extolling of their prince.

The dignified de Feria was shocked at such condescension to her subjects, but the citizens of London would not have agreed with him: they had already embarked upon their love affair with Elizabeth, and they applauded her common touch, which she contrived to exercise 'by coupling mildness with majesty' without any loss of dignity. Touched by her care for them and her vibrant youth and gracious smiles, they cried out their greetings and blessings with gusto.

As she neared the Tower, Elizabeth reined her horse to a standstill, reflecting that when she had last come here it had been as a prisoner in fear of execution. Now she expressed gratitude for her deliverance before the watching crowds: 'O Lord, Almighty and Everlasting God, I give Thee most hearty thanks that Thou hast been so merciful unto me as to spare me to behold this day.' Then, to her people:

> Some have fallen from being princes of this land to be prisoners in this place. I am raised from being a prisoner in this place to be a prince of this land. That dejection was a work of God's justice. This advancement is a work of His mercy.

She then rode into the Tower precincts and entered the royal apartments, summoning the Lieutenant of the Tower to attend her. He was Sir Henry Bedingfield, her former gaoler. Graciously, she thanked him for his services to the late queen and informed him that he was to be relieved of his duties. Yet there was no animosity in her.

'God forgive you the past, as I do,' she told him, then added mischievously, 'Whenever I have one who requires to be safely and straitly kept, I will send him to you!'

After lodging a week in the Tower, Queen and court went by river, 'with trumpets playing and melody and joy', to take up residence in Somerset House on the Strand, Elizabeth's town house when she was princess. During the winter evenings, she could be seen in her barge, being rowed along the Thames to the sound of music, attended by a host of little boats, and the Londoners grew used to her daily appearances in the streets of the capital, usually en route to dine with various courtiers. She knew well that, to retain her people's love, she had to remain visible.

On 23 December, she moved to Whitehall Palace, which was to be her principal, if not her favourite, residence. Here, the court gave itself up to daily entertainments and celebrations, its members being 'intent on amusing themselves and on dancing till after midnight', following the lead of their mistress, who was determined to enjoy her new-found freedom. Liberated from the fear of danger that had stalked her since early youth, she was thrilled to be not only the centre of attention and flattery, but also the supreme power in the land.

Arriving at Whitehall, Feria was put out to discover that, contrary to the usual custom, no room had been allocated to him; nor could he obtain an audience with the Queen or speak with her councillors – he noticed the latter trying to avoid him, 'as if I were the Devil'. Elizabeth was already making it clear that she would rule without guidance from any foreign power.

Unlike Henry VIII, who had given all his time over to pleasure during the early years of his reign and left the business of governing to others, Elizabeth worked hard every day, finalising plans for her household and attending to state business. She insisted that every letter arriving at court be brought for her inspection, much to Cecil's dismay, for he believed that a woman had no business poking her nose into matters that were properly the concern of the Council. When he found out that an ambassadorial dispatch from overseas had been taken straight to Elizabeth without first being shown to him as Secretary of State, his irritation increased, and he was further aggravated when the Queen blithely revealed that she had discussed the contents of the letter with the messenger who delivered it. Later, Cecil lectured the poor fellow, saying he had had no right to take it to Her Majesty, 'a matter of such weight being too much for a woman's knowledge'.

The young Queen had from the first established a set daily routine. She rose early and went in all but the worst weather for a brisk walk in the palace gardens. She then had breakfast served to her in her Privy Chamber, where she would remain while she attended to the day's business, summoning her secretaries, who would kneel before her to present letters and documents that needed the royal signature. She might then preside over a meeting of the Privy Council. At noon, dinner was served to her, again in her Privy Chamber, for she rarely ate in public. In the afternoon she might hold formal receptions in her Presence Chamber for foreign ambassadors and other visitors, remaining standing for hours on end and conversing in fluent Latin. Usually, she would set aside time in which to indulge her passion for dancing: it was not unusual for her to dance six spirited galliards in the Presence Chamber. This exercise invariably had a beneficial effect on her mercurial temper.

In the evenings there were state banquets or courtly entertainments to attend. Elizabeth loved music of all kinds, and welcomed many performers at her court. Sometimes she herself would play on the lute or virginals. Later in the evening, after supper, she would play cards with her courtiers, but she usually worked for an hour or so on state papers before retiring to bed, and was not above summoning Cecil and other councillors at all hours of the night if she wanted some advice. Often, she would make a decision at midnight, but change her mind in the morning. Needless to say, this kind of behaviour drove her advisers to near distraction.

On 14 December, Queen Mary was buried in Westminster Abbey, and the requiem mass sung for her conformed to the traditional Catholic ritual at the new Queen's command. Elizabeth had as yet said little on the crucial matter of religion, yet few people doubted which way she meant to follow. On the day of the funeral, de Feria wrote gloomily to King Philip:

> The kingdom is entirely in the hands of young folks, heretics and traitors. The old people and the Catholics are dissatisfied, but dare not open their lips. Her Majesty seems to me incomparably more feared than her sister, and gives her orders and has her way as absolutely as her father did. We have lost a kingdom, body and soul.

It seemed to de Feria that his mission was hopeless. The precious English alliance seemed now to be in jeopardy, and he had still not been granted an audience. He could not imagine how he was to influence Elizabeth in her choice of husband, and was alarmed by what people were saying at court. 'Everybody thinks that she will not marry a foreigner, and they cannot make out whom she favours, so that nearly every day some new cry is raised about a husband.' Already, Elizabeth had discovered the pleasures and advantages of keeping everyone guessing, a game at which she was to become maddeningly adept. De Feria feared that neither the Queen nor her councillors would consider 'any proposal on Your Majesty's behalf'. His only hope lay in trying to persuade the councillors that an English match would have many drawbacks. If he saw the Queen, he would 'begin by getting her to talk about Your Majesty, and run down the idea of her marrying an Englishman, and thus to hold herself less than her sister, who would never marry a subject'. There were no English suitors worth speaking of, and it would look bad if she married a mere nobleman when there were great princes on the Continent waiting to offer themselves and protect her from the pretensions of Mary, Queen of Scots.

But Philip had not as yet proposed, and de Feria was becoming daily more anxious that he would not. He pressed the matter as much as he dared: 'If she inclines to Your Majesty, it will be necessary for you to send me orders whether I am to carry it any further or throw cold water on it and set up the Archduke Ferdinand [of Austria], because I do not see what other person we can propose to whom she would agree. I am afraid', he added bitterly, 'that one fine day we shall find this woman married, and I shall be the last man in the place to know anything about it.'

On Christmas Day 1558, Queen Elizabeth gave an inkling of her future religious policy. Normally, the Archbishop of Canterbury would have celebrated mass in her private chapel on Christmas morning, but the primacy was vacant, the last Archbishop, Cardinal Pole, having died on the same day as Queen Mary. Several of the Catholic bishops who had held office under Mary were suspicious of Elizabeth's supposed Protestant leanings, and Nicholas Heath, Archbishop of York, who should have deputised in the absence of a Primate, had made it clear that he would not crown a heretical Queen. Hence it was Owen Oglethorpe, Bishop of Carlisle, who was celebrating the Christmas mass in the Queen's chapel at Whitehall. Prior to the service, Elizabeth had sent a message commanding him to omit the elevation of the Host – for Catholics, the most sacred element of the mass, but for Protestants, the symbol of the miracle of transubstantiation that they denied. Oglethorpe, however, decided to proceed as normal, according to his convictions. When the Gospel had been read, and the Bishop started to raise the bread and wine before the congregation, the Queen loudly ordered him to desist, to the astonishment of those present. But Oglethorpe merely frowned at her and went on with what he was doing, whereupon Elizabeth, in a fury, rose and withdrew from the chapel, determined not to witness what was offensive to her.

Two days later she issued a proclamation decreeing that parts of the mass might be said in English rather than Latin, and forbidding all preaching until further notice. This injunction, she hoped, would deter the fanatics on either side of the religious divide from engaging in a verbal power struggle and inciting unrest. When Parliament met after the coronation, planned for January, the religious issue would be decided.

The twelve days of Christmas festivities that year were lavish and very merry indeed. Lord Robert Dudley was in charge of the court entertainments, which included balls, banquets and masques. One of the latter, staged on Twelfth Night, had a decidedly anti-clerical theme, as Il Schifanoya, a shocked agent of the Duke of Mantua, reported to his master:

> Your lordship will have heard of the farce performed in the presence of Her Majesty on Epiphany Day, and the mummery performed after supper, of crows in the habits of cardinals, of asses habited as bishops, and of wolves representing abbots. I will consign it to silence. Nor will I record the levities and unusual licentiousness practised at the court.

As was customary, gifts were exchanged on Twelfth Night, and it was on this occasion that Elizabeth was presented with her first ever pair of the new – and expensive – silk stockings. She was delighted with them, and vowed never again to wear cloth stockings.

De Feria's last despondent dispatch had had the effect of prompting King Philip to action, and on 10 January 1559 he informed the ambassador: 'I have decided to place on one side all other considerations which might be urged against it, and am resolved to sacrifice my private inclination and render this service to God and offer to marry the Queen of England.' When de Feria was able to obtain a private audience with Elizabeth, he was formally to propose marriage on Philip's behalf.

But the King was no joyous wooer: 'Believe me', he confided, 'if it was not to serve God, I would not have got into this. Nothing would make me do it except the clear knowledge that it would gain the kingdom for His service and faith.' Despite such a union being of 'enormous importance to Christianity', he felt 'like a condemned man awaiting his fate'. However, as ruler of Spain, Portugal, the Low Countries and much of the New World, he saw himself, as he was in truth, as the champion of Catholicism in Europe, and felt he had no option but to do his best to save England from a downward slide into heresy. He did not want to achieve this by violence, or by papal anathema, but by diplomacy; the truth was that, with his treasury drained by years of war with France, he was in no position to enter into an armed religious conflict, and he needed England's friendship for commercial reasons. If Elizabeth consented to his proposal and undertook to remain, as she had professed to be for the past few years, a devout Catholic, and 'maintain and uphold' the Roman faith in her kingdom, then Philip was prepared to help her regain Calais.

However, as he confided to de Feria on 10 January, he felt there would be 'many great difficulties'. His royal duties would require him to be often absent from England, which had caused great distress to Queen Mary. Because of Elizabeth's suspected heretical beliefs, he could foresee Mary, Queen of Scots's claim to the throne being pressed, and his war with France becoming 'perpetual'. He could not afford to maintain an English household to the standard that he had done in the previous reign. He was only marrying Elizabeth as a service to God, and only on condition that she would abjure her Protestant beliefs, declare herself a Catholic, and obtain absolution from the Pope for her former error. By doing these things she would proclaim that it was Philip who had saved her and England from eternal damnation, and 'it will be evident and manifest that I am serving the Lord in marrying her'.

What Philip failed to take into account was the attitude of the English people towards another Spanish marriage. Many of them had risen in rebellion in 1554 when his betrothal to Mary was announced, and most blamed his influence for the burnings of her reign, notwithstanding the fact that he had done his best to curb Mary's fanatical enthusiasm for saving souls, knowing what it was doing to her reputation – and his. For Elizabeth to marry the King of Spain now might well cost her the loyalty of her people and even her throne.

There was also the little matter of near affinity: the Church forbade a man to marry his dead wife's sister, yet Philip did not doubt that the Pope would feel the circumstances justified the issuing of a Bull of Dispensation permitting the marriage.

De Feria was relieved and pleased that his master had finally proposed, and felt certain that Elizabeth would be sensible of the great honour being done to her, the ruler of a small island, by the greatest prince in Europe. He had forgotten that prior to her accession she had told him that Queen Mary had lost the love of her people by marrying a foreign prince. He hoped she would now appreciate that there were very many good reasons for the marriage to take place.

His first step was to see her alone, for such a matter must be broached with the utmost delicacy. This proved impossible for the time being, as Elizabeth was much preoccupied just then with plans for her imminent coronation.

She had wanted the ceremony to take place on a propitious date, and – at Robert Dudley's suggestion – had consulted Dr John Dee, who studied his astrological charts and told her that, if she were crowned on 15 January, her reign would be glorious and prosperous. The date being set, Dudley was put in charge of the arrangements and began discussions with the Lord Mayor of London about the lavish pageants and welcoming ceremonies that would be staged by the City in the Queen's honour. Elizabeth had insisted that her coronation and its attendant celebrations be as magnificent as possible, so as to make an indelible impression upon those who had cast doubts on her legitimacy and her title to the throne. The appearance of splendour and majesty meant a great deal in an age that equated greatness with lavish outward show, and so the Queen meant to use her coronation to make a political statement.

By the end of December, preparations were well advanced, with people working 'both day and night, on holidays and weekdays'. Cloth of gold and silver, silks, velvets and satins were imported from Antwerp at a cost to the Exchequer of £4000 and made into liveries, hangings, banners, and clothing for those who were to take part in the processions and ceremonies. Trumpeters and heralds received new tabards, and even the royal jester, Will Somers, and minor officials such as Joan Hilton the laundress and William Toothe, the royal fishmonger, were given new outfits. The royal tailors altered Queen Mary's coronation robes to fit her taller and slimmer sister, and orders were given that the Queen should have first choice of all crimson silk arriving at the Port of

London. Extra seating was erected in Westminster Abbey, and triumphal arches set up in the City streets. Householders hung tapestries and painted cloths from their windows, and the streets through which the Queen would pass were strewn with fresh gravel. Seven hundred yards of blue cloth were purchased to make a carpet that would stretch from the Abbey to Westminster Hall. No detail was omitted, even the purchase of cotton wool 'to dry up the oil after the Queen's anointing'. The total expenditure would add up to £16,741.

However, after Elizabeth's contretemps with Bishop Oglethorpe at Christmas, no bishop showed himself willing to perform the ceremony. Archbishop Heath of York had candidly told the Queen that, since she had refused to witness the elevation of the Host, she could be no other than a heretic, and he would not crown her. Other bishops, most of them Catholics, followed his lead, and only Oglethorpe – after much persuasion had been applied – could be prevailed upon to officiate.

At last, everything was ready, and on Thursday, 12 January 1559, the Queen boarded her barge at Whitehall and travelled along the Thames to the Tower, where English monarchs traditionally spent a night before their coronations. She was escorted by 'the Mayor and aldermen in their barge, and all the crafts [guilds] in their barges, decked and trimmed with the banners of their mysteries'. A Venetian envoy stated that the sight reminded him of Ascension Day in Venice, when the Doge and Signory were symbolically wedded to the sea.

At the Tower, the Queen was formally welcomed by her chief officers of state, and entered the royal apartments to a 'great and pleasant melody of instruments, which played in most sweet and heavenly manner'. The next day, she created several Knights of the Bath, and on the Saturday morning she left the Tower to make her ceremonial progress through London.

2

'God Send Our Mistress a Husband'

On the morning of her coronation eve, Queen Elizabeth was attired in a robe made from twenty-three yards of cloth of gold and silver, trimmed with ermine and overlaid with gold lace – one of four she had ordered for her coronation, and on her head was set a golden cap ringed with a princess's crown. Outside, light flakes of snow were drifting down and the sky was leaden, but the courtiers in the Queen's vast retinue glowed in their rich satins and velvets and glittered with jewels. The magnificent procession formed, with over a thousand mounted dignitaries, and Elizabeth walked to her waiting litter, which was lined with white satin, trimmed with gold damask and drawn by two 'very handsome mules'.

Before climbing in, she prayed aloud, 'O Almighty and Everlasting God, I give Thee most hearty thanks that Thou hast been so merciful unto me to spare me to behold this joyful day. Thou hast dealt as wonderfully and as mercifully with me as Thou didst with Daniel, whom Thou delivered out of the den from the cruelty of the raging lions. Even so was I overwhelmed, and only by Thee delivered.' This was an apt prayer, as the lions in the Tower menagerie were just then making their presence known by roars and growls and the bystanders applauded warmly.

Having reiterated her conviction that God Himself had brought her to her throne, the Queen entered her litter, made herself comfortable on eight enormous satin cushions, and with a canopy of estate borne above her head, was carried in state, 'with great majesty', through four miles of London's streets to a tumultuous welcome. The whole event had been planned as a propaganda exercise, intended to cement the harmonious relationship between Elizabeth and her people and herald the new age that was beginning.

Alongside the Queen's litter walked her personal guard, the

Gentlemen Pensioners, wearing their livery of crimson damask and carrying ceremonial gilt battleaxes. She was attended also by many footmen in jerkins of crimson velvet studded with gilt and silver buttons and embroidered with the red and white rose of the Tudors and the initials E R. Before the Queen marched her trumpeters in scarlet, while behind her rode Robert Dudley as Master of the Horse, leading the Queen's palfrey, followed by thirty-nine ladies, all in crimson velvet gowns with cloth of gold sleeves. The Privy Councillors also rode in the procession, bravely decked out in splendid robes of satin.

The City had made great efforts, the Mayor and aldermen having commissioned and spent large sums on a series of five 'stately pageants [and] sumptuous shows and devices' at strategic points along the route, which was packed with sightseers, many of whom had camped out overnight to get a good view of the Queen. Behind wooden rails draped with painted cloths and tapestries stood the members of the City guilds, important in their fur-lined gowns and company liveries. The City was a bastion of Protestantism, and its pageants and tableaux all incorporated meaningful references to the bad days of Queen Mary that were now past and the good things that were hoped for from her successor. Chief among them was the establishment of true religion, and when the Queen heard references to this, she raised her eyes and hands heavenwards and called upon her subjects to repeat 'Amen'.

The City's celebrations began at Fenchurch Street, where a little child attempted to recite welcoming verses against the roar of the crowd. The Queen begged for quiet, and listened 'with a perpetual attentiveness in her face and a marvellous change of look, as if the child's words touched her person'.

The first pageant, 'The Pageant of the Roses', was in Gracechurch Street, and it displayed, on a three-tiered platform, persons representing the Tudor dynasty, supported by Unity and Concord. On the lowest tier were shown – together for the first time in twenty-five years – Henry VIII and Anne Boleyn, and on the highest tier Elizabeth herself appeared.

Next to the conduit in Cornhill, a child representing the Queen sat enthroned on the Seat of Worthy Governance, supported by four allegorical figures of the Virtues, including one called Good Religion, who trod the Vices, among them Superstition and Ignorance, underfoot.

Cheapside was noisy with fanfares of trumpets and the singing of the City waits, who stood beside the Eleanor Cross, which had been decorated for the occasion. Here, as custom decreed, the City Recorder presented the Queen with 1000 gold marks (£666) in a purse of crimson satin. She accepted it graciously, saying,

I thank my Lord Mayor, his brethren and you all. And whereas your request is that I should continue your good lady and queen, be ye assured that I will be as good unto you as ever queen was to her people. And persuade yourselves that for the safety and quietness of you all, I will not spare, if need be, to spend my blood. God thank you all.

Her speech prompted a 'marvellous shout and rejoicing' from the bystanders, who were 'wonderfully ravished' by it.

The pageant at Little Conduit had as its centrepiece Time. The Queen gazed at it and mused, 'Time! And Time hath brought me hither.' The pageant depicted two pastoral scenes representing a flourishing commonwealth and a decayed one. A figure representing Truth emerged from between the two, led by Time, and received from Heaven an English Bible. A child explained in pretty verses that the Bible taught how to change a decayed state into a flourishing empire. Truth presented the Bible to the Queen, who kissed it and held it to her heart, thanking the City most warmly for it and 'promising to be a diligent reader thereof'.

Outside St Paul's Cathedral, a scholar of St Paul's School made a speech in Latin extolling Elizabeth's wisdom, learning and other virtues. Music played as she passed through Ludgate into Fleet Street, where she watched the final pageant, which portrayed Deborah, 'the judge and restorer of the House of Israel', who had been sent by God to rule His people wisely for forty years. Deborah was depicted wearing Parliament robes and sitting on a throne, consulting with the three estates of the realm as to how best to provide good government. A poem was presented to the Queen reminding her how Deborah had restored Truth in place of Error.

Elizabeth exhibited great interest and delight in the pageants, and constantly expressed her gratitude to her subjects, being genuinely touched by the welcome afforded her. When the crowds cheered, she waved at them with 'a merry countenance', repeating again and again, 'God save them all!' Several times along the way she demonstrated her humanity by stopping her litter to speak in the most 'tender and gentle language' to humble folk, or accept small gifts, such as posies of flowers offered by poor women. She kept a spray of rosemary, given by a woman supplicant at Fleet Bridge, beside her in the litter all the way to Westminster. Some foreign observers felt that she was over-familiar with her subjects and exceeded the bounds of decorum that preserved a monarch's dignity, but Elizabeth knew her people better. They were responding to her common touch, and if this was the way to win and retain their favour, then she would follow her instincts. Her father had

had such a way with him, and one person, seeing the resemblance, cried out, 'Remember old King Harry the Eighth?' Elizabeth was seen to smile at this.

'Be ye well assured, I will stand your good Queen. I wish neither prosperity nor safety to myself which might not be for our common good,' she declared to her people, and they knew she meant it. An old man turned away, but not before she had espied him weeping. 'I warrant you it is for gladness,' she told those close by.

At Temple Bar, which was surmounted for the occasion by two huge statues of figures from London mythology – Gogmagog the Albion and Corineus the Briton – the City authorities formally took their leave of Elizabeth, and a little child recited a poem, 'Farewell, O worthy Queen!' A pamphlet describing the events of the day came off the publisher Richard Tothill's press ten days later, and was much sought after as a souvenir of the occasion, running into three editions.

At the end of this long and triumphant day, Elizabeth came to the Palace of Westminster, where she lay that night.

Sunday, 15 January – Elizabeth's coronation day – was frosty and crisp, with a light covering of snow on the ground. The Queen emerged from Westminster Hall, wearing her coronation robes beneath a swirling mantle of embroidered silk lined with ermine, with fine silk and gold stockings and a crimson velvet cap adorned with Venice gold and pearls. To the joyous sound of fifes, drums, portable organs and all the bells of London's churches, she went in procession from Westminster Hall to the Abbey along a blue carpet beneath a canopy borne by the Barons of the Cinque Ports; she was followed by the Duchess of Norfolk, who bore her train. No sooner had Elizabeth passed than the crowds fell upon the carpet, tearing off pieces as souvenirs, and almost knocking over the hapless Duchess in the process.

Westminster Abbey glowed with the light of hundreds of torches and candles, which illumined the rich tapestries that had been hung on its walls, tapestries that had been commissioned by Henry VIII and based on designs by Raphael. Elizabeth's magnificent coronation service was notable not only for its glorious music, but also because it was the last in England to be conducted – at Bishop Oglethorpe's insistence – according to the medieval Latin rubric, although parts of it – the Epistle and Gospel – were read in English as well. Oglethorpe officiated, assisted by Dr Feckenham, the last Abbot of Westminster. During the mass, the Queen refused to be present at the elevation of the Host, and retired to a curtained pew in St Edward's Chapel until that part of the ritual was over, a gesture applauded by her hopeful Protestant subjects. Her coronation oath was administered from an English Bible held aloft by

William Cecil, although she was nevertheless proclaimed 'Defender of the True, Ancient, Catholic Faith'.

Nearly the whole peerage was present in the Abbey, and when the Queen was presented for her subjects' acceptance, there were such shouts of acclaim, and such thundering and crashing of organs, trumpets and bells that it seemed to some as if the end of the world had arrived. Elizabeth retired to change her gown during the lengthy ceremonies that followed, emerging after her anointing in crimson velvet surmounted by a mantle of cloth of gold. In this she sat enthroned, as the ring that symbolically wedded her to her people was placed upon the fourth finger of her right hand to the sound of trumpets. Then came the climax of the ceremonies, the crowning itself, when first St Edward's crown and then the imperial crown of England, weighing seven pounds, were placed in turn on Elizabeth's red head.

After the ceremonies were ended, Elizabeth, in full regalia and wearing a smaller crown – perhaps that made for Anne Boleyn in 1533 – and carrying the orb and sceptre, walked in procession back the way she had come, smiling broadly and shouting greetings to the enthusiastic crowds lining her way. 'In my opinion', sniffed the Mantuan ambassador, 'she exceeded the bounds of gravity and decorum.'

There followed the traditional lavish coronation banquet in Westminster Hall, a custom that ended with George IV in 1821. This lasted from three in the afternoon until one o'clock the next morning, and during it, as was customary, the Queen's Champion, Sir Edward Dymoke, rode into the Hall in full armour, daring any to challenge her title. The Queen presided from the high table, beneath a canopy of estate, having changed into yet another gown, this one of purple velvet. Music played throughout, and a delicious variety of dishes were served to her on bended knee by her great-uncle, Lord William Howard, and the Earl of Sussex. The nobility were permitted to keep their coronets on during the feasting, only uncovering when the Queen rose to drink their health, thanking them for all the trouble they had taken on her behalf.

On 16 January, because 'Her Majesty was feeling rather tired' and was suffering from a heavy cold, she postponed the tournament planned for that day, remaining in her Privy Chamber to sleep and attend to state business. The celebrations continued with banquets, masques, and a series of jousts held over the next few days, Robert Dudley being prominent among the contestants. Foreign observers were unanimously impressed with the coronation and its attendant festivities, which had been lavishly staged in order to give the impression that England was a land of great wealth and power. A full-faced portrait, which is no longer extant, of Elizabeth in coronation robes was painted, which was used as a model for the image on her first Great Seal and early official documents; a later copy, dating from around 1600 and once at Warwick Castle, is now in the National Portrait Gallery.

Now that she was firmly established on her throne, Elizabeth turned her attention to the urgent matters of state that would be debated in her first Parliament. Two issues seemed likely to dominate the session: the controversial subject of religion, and the more delicate matter of the Queen's marriage. For most people, it was not a question of whether she would marry, but whom she would marry. Linked to this was the ongoing problem of the Tudor succession, which had exercised politicians' minds for four decades now; it was not clear who would succeed in the event of Elizabeth's early death.

On the political front there were hopes that a peace would be concluded with France, thereby frustrating those who wished to support the Dauphine Mary Stuart's dynastic claims and removing the necessity for French troops to remain in Scotland. Such a peace was rendered all the more necessary by the news that on 16 January Mary and her husband had begun styling themselves King and Queen of England. Yet it was also imperative that England maintain her friendship with Spain in order to safeguard the lucrative trading links between the two powers and perhaps obtain protection against French ambitions. It was obvious to the Queen from the first that her success in the field of diplomacy would depend upon playing off those bitter enemies France and Spain one against the other.

Lack of money was a major problem that would have to be addressed. Elizabeth's annual income was about £250,000, out of which she had to finance the needs of court and government and pay off Queen Mary's debts of £266,000. Prices were rising all the time, yet Elizabeth set herself to live within her means by practising the most stringent economies and selling off Crown lands. As a result, her annual expenditure never exceeded £300,000 throughout her reign.

Elizabeth went in state wearing her coronation robes, attended by forty-six peers, to open her first Parliament on 25 January 1559, after postponing the ceremony for two days because of her cold and the atrocious weather, which had delayed the arrival in London of many MPs. De Feria informed King Philip that 'the Catholics are very fearful of the measures to be taken in this Parliament' and Elizabeth's own behaviour gave a hint of what was to come. On her way to the House of Lords for the opening of the new session she was met by the Abbot of Westminster at the head of his monks, all carrying lighted tapers, symbols of the old faith that were frowned upon by Protestant divines.

'Away with those tapers!' snapped the Queen tartly. 'We see well enough!' As she was standing on sanctified ground, the Abbot was profoundly shocked by her words. Still in a bad mood, she stamped to her throne by the high altar in the Abbey, and was only partially mollified when she heard Dr Richard Cox, formerly tutor to King Edward VI, preach a vituperative sermon against monks in general, accusing them of participating in the burning of Protestants. God, he thundered, had raised His servant Elizabeth to the dignity of Queen that she might put an end to the Catholic practices restored by Queen Mary, and he urged her to cast down all images of the saints, to purify her churches of idolatry, and dissolve all religious houses re-established by Mary. Cox ranted on for an hour and a half, while the Queen, who hated sermons, fidgeted and became increasingly irritated, and the peers stood sweating in their robes.

Once enthroned in Parliament in a chair padded with gold cushions, Elizabeth made it clear that she would not brook any presumptuous behaviour from members of the Commons, many of whom expected a female sovereign to be tractable and easily manipulated.

One of the first Acts passed by Queen Mary had been one declaring herself legitimate, Henry VIII having decreed that his marriage to her mother had never been lawful. Elizabeth was in a similar situation: bastardised in 1536, she had been 'excluded and barred' by statute from the succession. This had never been repealed, although in his 1544 Act of Succession Henry named her as his heir after Edward and Mary. Hence Elizabeth's title to the throne was open to question, and she consulted Sir Nicholas Bacon as to whether she should take steps to legitimise herself. His advice was to let sleeping dogs lie, and she took it, but the taint of her bastardy, and its implications for the security of her throne, was to remain a sensitive subject with her to the end of her days.

The succession was another sensitive issue. The Tudors were not a fertile family and there was a dearth of suitable heirs to replace the Queen should she die childless. The 1544 Act and Henry VIII's will provided that, after Elizabeth, the crown should pass to the heirs of his younger sister Mary, Duchess of Suffolk. Mary had left two daughters, Frances and Eleanor Brandon. The elder, Frances, had produced three daughters, one of whom had been the ill-fated Lady Jane Grey. The two other daughters were Lady Katherine and Lady Mary Grey, aged nineteen and fourteen respectively in 1559.

Both were Protestants but Elizabeth heartily disliked them, especially Katherine – 'the Queen could not abide the sight of her'. She was particularly suspicious of their dynastic pretensions, and perhaps with cause, for in 1559 there were rumours that King Philip, aware that Lady Katherine Grey had the strongest claim to the English succession, was plotting to abduct her and make her the wife of his heir, the degenerate

Don Carlos. Katherine was aware of Elizabeth's dislike, and in March 1559 revealed to the Spanish ambassador that she knew her cousin did not wish her to succeed her. Nor was the Queen much more enamoured of Lady Mary Grey, a hunchbacked dwarf. Many people shared Elizabeth's antipathy towards the Grey sisters, and some argued that their father's treason in supporting Northumberland had rendered their claim to a place in the succession forfeit.

Next in the Suffolk line after the Grey sisters came Margaret, the only child of Eleanor Brandon, who was married to Henry, Lord Strange, later Earl of Derby. In Queen Mary's time, some people had viewed Margaret as a likely successor to the throne in view of the fact that, unlike the Grey family, she had not taken part in Northumberland's treacherous coup of 1553. Despite the fact that Margaret had no desire for a crown, Elizabeth insisted upon her coming often to court 'as one very near in blood to us', so as to keep an eye on her. Poor Margaret hated the court as much as she hated her home life with her quarrelsome husband, and never knew true happiness or peace of mind.

All the Suffolk claimants were tainted with a suspected stain of bastardy, for there had always been doubts as to the validity of Mary Tudor's union with the Duke of Suffolk, who had put away two previous wives by questionable processes.

Another possible Protestant claimant was Henry Hastings, 3rd Earl of Huntingdon, a descendant of Edward III. Like Margaret Strange, he had no wish to be England's king, although Queen Elizabeth would sometimes give his wife (as he told his brother-in-law Robert Dudley) 'a privy nip concerning myself' as a warning not to become too ambitious. He never did, avoiding 'conceiving any greatness of myself', and served her loyally.

Henry VIII had been at war with Scotland when the Act of Succession was passed, and at that time his ambition was to marry his son Edward to his young great-niece the Scots Queen, Mary Stuart, and so unite England and Scotland under English rule. The Scots resisted this violently, and therefore, when determining who was to succeed him, Henry passed over the heirs of his elder sister Margaret, who had married James IV of Scotland and was the grandmother of Mary Stuart. Hence, although many Catholics regarded Mary as the rightful Queen of England, or at least the claimant with the greatest right to succeed Elizabeth, she had no right to a place in the succession according to English law. Some took the view that a foreigner born out of the realm was automatically barred from succeeding to the throne, because such people were legally prohibited from inheriting property in England. Others argued that the Crown was exempt from such constraints.

Similarly passed over by Henry VIII was Lady Margaret Douglas,

Margaret Tudor's daughter by her second marriage to the Earl of Angus, and now the wife of Matthew Stewart, Earl of Lennox, by whom she had two sons, a strong point in her favour. However, doubts as to the validity of her parents' marriage meant that few regarded her as a strong contender for a place in the succession. Lady Margaret, however, was a very ambitious woman, not for herself, but for her elder son, Henry, Lord Darnley, who had been born in England. This alone, some felt, gave him a better title than Mary Stuart, a foreigner.

In 1561, the Scots ambassador observed to the Queen that, apart from Mary Stuart, 'none of all the others who had any interest were meet for the Crown, or yet worthy of it'. The Queen's response was non-committal. In fact, the subject of the succession was taboo with Elizabeth. From the first she made it clear that she had an abhorrence of naming an heir to succeed her. She had known what it was like to be the heir and to be the focus of conspiracy and rebellion, and there were threats enough to her security without that. If she acknowledged the right of any of these claimants to succeed, she once declared, she would be back in the Tower 'within a month'.

The answer, of course, was for her to marry and bear children, and de Feria was at hand to assist in this matter. Elizabeth had been so busy that he had seen her only once that January, coming out of her Privy Chamber. She had talked 'very gaily' to him, despite her cold, and, in response to his guarded query, informed him that the issue of her marriage would be raised in Parliament. He therefore decided to wait and see what transpired before laying Philip's proposal before her.

On Saturday, 4 February, the Commons drafted a formal petition to the Queen, asking her to marry as soon as possible in order to safeguard the succession. This petition was delivered to her two days later at Whitehall by a deputation from the House.

The petition reminded Elizabeth that it would be better for her 'and her kingdom if she would take a consort who might relieve her of those labours which are only fit for men', and the Speaker, Sir Thomas Gargrave, kneeling, candidly reminded her that, while princes are mortal, commonwealths are immortal. If she remained 'unmarried and, as it were, a vestal virgin', such a thing would be 'contrary to the public respects'.

When she heard his words, the Queen was plainly astonished at his boldness in broaching such a delicate issue, but she recovered herself and responded graciously, saying, 'In a matter most unpleasing, pleasing to me is the apparent goodwill of you and my people.' She stated that she had chosen to stay single despite being offered marriage by 'most potent princes', and that she considered she already had a husband and children. Showing them her coronation ring, she declared, as she was to do on many subsequent occasions: 'I am already bound unto a husband, which is the kingdom of England.' As for children, 'Every one of you, and as many as are Englishmen, are children and kinsmen to me.' She was gratified that the deputation had not named any potential husband, 'For that were most unbeseeming the majesty of an absolute princess, and unbeseeming your wisdom, who are subjects born.'

Elizabeth went on to assure her Commons that she would do as God directed her. She had never been inclined towards matrimony, but would not rule it out completely. If she did marry, she would not do anything to prejudice the commonwealth, but would choose a husband who 'would be as careful for the preservation of the realm as she was herself'. However, it was possible that it would 'please Almighty God to continue me still in the mind to live out of the state of marriage'.

As for the succession, the Queen promised that 'the realm shall not remain destitute of an heir', yet who that heir was to be she did not specify. If she remained single, she continued, she was certain 'that God would so direct mine and your counsels that ye shall not need to doubt of a successor, who may be more beneficial to the commonwealth than he who may be born of me, considering that the issue of the best princes many times degenerateth'. Her children might 'grow out of kind, and become perhaps ungracious'. She was implying that any son of her body might conspire to overthrow her, a mere woman, a thing which few among her patriarchal advisers would try to prevent. At best, pressure might be put upon her to abdicate in favour of that son. In 1561, she confided to the Scots ambassador her belief that 'Princes cannot like their children, those that should succeed unto them,' quoting many notable examples where there had been discord and strife between monarchs and their heirs. There is little evidence anyway that the young Elizabeth was particularly fond of children, although she was to become godmother to over one hundred of them. All things considered, she continued, she would prefer, for her part, to leave the matter of her successor to Providence, trusting that, with divine help 'an heir that may be a fit governor' would somehow materialise.

Concluding, she declared: 'In the end, this shall be for me sufficient, that a marble stone shall declare that a queen, having reigned such a time, lived and died a virgin.' Thus was born the legend of the Virgin Queen, upon which Elizabeth would capitalise to full advantage, and which would achieve cult status in the years to come.

A transcript of the Queen's speech was read out to the Commons on 10 February. Naturally, Parliament was startled and alarmed by Elizabeth's response: if she did not marry, there would be no heirs of her body to counteract the ever-present threats to her safety and security, and no satisfactory resolution to the succession question. The hoped-for religious settlement would be at risk, not to mention the lives of all her Protestant subjects. For a woman to reject marriage was seen as against the laws of nature, and most men concluded that their mistress was merely displaying an innate maidenly modesty, and would soon come to her senses when she realised the necessity for marriage. William Cecil's continual prayer would from henceforth be that 'God would send our mistress a husband, and by and by a son, that we may hope our posterity shall have a masculine succession'. He would repeatedly remind Elizabeth of his hope that God 'would direct Your Highness to procure a father for your children'. To Cecil, this petticoat government was an unnatural aberration; he longed to see a man in control of the government, and that could only be achieved once Elizabeth was married and preoccupied with her proper business of bearing children. Then her husband could rule in her name.

But the fact remained that, although Elizabeth was undoubtedly, as one councillor put it, 'the best marriage in her parish', she had no wish to marry. Politically, there were advantages to her remaining single. Her sister's unhappy example had exposed the dangers of espousing a foreign prince. Such a husband might offer protection against England's enemies, but he might also drain her resources in wars of his own. He might regard England as a mere satellite state of his own country, and – if he were a sovereign in his own right – he would certainly have to spend long periods out of the country. Moreover, the English were an insular, even xenophobic, nation, who had reacted adversely, indeed violently in some cases, to Queen Mary's Spanish match; they were unlikely to accept another foreign consort.

Of course, Elizabeth could always marry one of her own subjects, which was what the majority of Englishmen desired her to do. 'We are all of us in favour of one of our own countrymen in preference to a stranger,' wrote Roger Ascham, and Il Schifanoya reported how everyone 'agreed in wishing her to take an Englishman'. The main exceptions were Cecil, Arundel and the Duke of Norfolk, Elizabeth's cousin, who all foresaw greater advantages from a princely alliance.

However, the Queen had no desire to marry one of her subjects, predicting that to do so would cause dangerous rivalries at court and in the country. Factions would form, as in the Wars of the Roses, and the tensions thus created might even lead to civil war, as was to happen in Scotland within the decade. Furthermore, Elizabeth hesitated to demean her royal blood by marrying a commoner.

Above all, she did not want to lose her newly-gained freedom, having suffered constraints of one kind or other throughout her young life. Sixteenth-century husbands – even those married to queens regnant – were notoriously autocratic, and society regarded them as the masters in their homes. Wives were expected to be submissive and obedient, in honour of their marriage vows. A queen regnant was a novelty in that age, and stood in a virtually impossible position: placed by God in authority over her people, she was yet required to be subject to her husband. Queen Mary had reached an uneasy compromise in this respect, but was much resented by King Philip when she did not heed his advice or requests. Such a situation did not make for marital harmony, and Elizabeth was of a far more independent mind than her sister. Her formidable intellect and pride in her royal blood would have made it difficult for her to become the subordinate of any man. She meant to rule by herself, and had no intention of permitting any interference with her prerogative. If she married, both independence and prerogative would be under threat.

Privately, she was inclined towards a single existence. In 1559, she confided to a German envoy that 'she had found the celibate life so agreeable, and was so accustomed to it that she would rather go into a nunnery, or for that matter suffer death', than be forced to renounce it. The Imperial ambassador was informed by her that she would much prefer to be a 'beggarwoman and single, far rather than a queen and married'. On another occasion she stated that she took the issue of her marriage very seriously, it was a matter of earnest with her, and she could not marry as others did. She once told Parliament, 'If I were a milkmaid with a pail on my arm, whereby my private person might be little set by, I would not forsake that poor and single state to match with the greatest monarch.' She seems to have regarded marriage as a refuge for those who could not contain their lust: in 1576, she told Parliament that she held nothing against matrimony, nor would she 'judge amiss of such as, forced by necessity, cannot dispose themselves to another life'. She herself was determined not to give in to such fleshly weakness.

Writers have endlessly speculated that there was a more fundamental reason for her aversion to marriage. Robert Dudley later told a French ambassador that, from the age of eight, the Queen had declared that she would never marry. She had been eight when Henry VIII's fifth wife Katherine Howard had been executed for adultery, and this may have awakened a painful awareness of how her father had similarly killed her mother. When she was fifteen, the man who had sexually first aroused her in her early teens – Admiral Seymour – had gone to the block. It is possible that these events so traumatised her that she could only equate marriage with death. She herself told a Scots envoy in 1561 that certain events in her youth made it impossible for her to regard marriage with equanimity or equate it with security. She blamed this on the marital problems of her father and his sisters: 'Some say that this marriage was unlawful, some that one was a bastard, some other to and fro, as they favoured or misliked. So many doubts of marriage was in all hands that I stand [in] awe myself to enter into marriage, fearing the controversy.' In addition to this, the tragic connubial experiences of her sister Mary and the unhappy example of many marriages amongst the peerage cannot have failed to deter the Queen. In that age of arranged marriages, many well-born persons suffered in incompatible unions, and some, such as the Earls of Worcester, Derby and Shrewsbury, even separated from their wives. In each case Elizabeth would act as an unofficial marriage guidance counsellor, insisting – without success – upon reconciliation.

Another reason for her reluctance to marry may have been fear of childbirth. The whole business of childbearing was dangerous in the sixteenth century, and maternal mortality rates were high: two of Elizabeth's stepmothers, Jane Seymour and Katherine Parr, as well as her grandmother, Elizabeth of York, had succumbed to puerperal fever. Queen Mary had suffered the mortifying humiliation of two phantom pregnancies. Young brides, such as the late Duchess of Norfolk, could marry, conceive, give birth and die within the space of a year. The Queen's physician, Dr Huick, once warned her that childbirth might not be easy for her, and succeeded in scaring her profoundly. Time and again Elizabeth would flirt with the idea of marriage, only to shy away from the commitment at the last minute. It is true that there were often good political reasons for doing so, but it is possible that an inherent fear of childbirth was a factor.

It has also been suggested – as it was speculated in her own time – that Elizabeth was reluctant to marry because she knew that she could never bear children. The evidence for this is contradictory. Her ability to conceive was naturally the subject of intense, discreet diplomatic speculation and inquiry, and because of her reluctance to marry rumours abounded. In 1559 de Feria reported: 'If my spies do not lie, which I believe they do not, for a certain reason which they have recently given me, I understand she will not bear children.' In 1561, his successor wrote: 'The common opinion, confirmed by certain physicians, is that this woman is unhealthy, and it is believed certain that she will not bear children.' However, he had also heard other scurrilous rumours: there was 'no lack of people who say she already has some [children], but of this I have seen no trace, and do not believe it'. The Venetian ambassador informed the Doge that Elizabeth was barren, saying he had been told certain secrets about her that he did 'not dare to write'.

Thereafter, it became *de rigueur* for foreign emissaries to pursue the most delicate investigations in order to safeguard their masters' dynastic interests. Discreet inquiries were made of the royal chamberwomen, and the Spaniards regularly offered bribes to the Queen's laundress to divulge whether or not Her Majesty menstruated regularly. The woman reported that Elizabeth functioned perfectly normally as a woman, and thereafter King Philip always conducted diplomatic negotiations on the assumption that she would marry and produce heirs. He is unlikely to have done so had there been any good reason for believing otherwise.

Elizabeth herself seems to have fuelled the rumours. She once told the Earl of Sussex mysteriously that 'for her part, she hated the idea of marriage every day more, for reasons which she would not divulge to a twin soul, if she had one, much less to a living creature'. In 1566, the French ambassador's nephew quizzed one of the Queen's doctors on her ability to bear children. He told the doctor that Her Majesty had stated in the past that she understood from her physicians that she was barren, and he needed to know if this was true because, if it was, he would not wish the Queen to marry a member of the French royal house. The doctor stated that his mistress had been talking nonsense, and that she sometimes said such things out of caprice. If she did marry, he himself would answer for it that she was capable of bearing ten children, adding, 'There is not a man in the kingdom who knows her constitution better than I.'

In 1579, when Elizabeth was in her mid-forties, William Cecil himself closely questioned her physicians, laundresses and ladies as to whether she might still hope to bear children, and in a private memorandum he recorded: 'Considering the proportion of her body, having no impediment of smallness in stature, of largeness in body, nor no sickness nor lack of natural functions in those things that properly belong to the procreation of children, but contrariwise by judgement of physicians that know her estate in those things, and by the opinion of women, being more acquainted with Her Majesty's body', it could only be concluded that there was an overwhelming 'probability of her aptness to have children'. This investigation was also prompted by fears that bearing children so late in life would endanger the Queen's life. The report was not intended for public – or royal – consumption, and Cecil was apparently satisfied with the results.

But as the years passed, and the Queen remained childless, a lot of people came to believe she had indeed been infertile all along. Mary, Queen of Scots, many years later, claimed that Bess of Hardwick had informed her that Elizabeth was 'not like other women', but she had an ulterior motive for doing so, since she had quarrelled with Bess and wished to expose her to the Queen as a spiteful gossip; therefore we must not place too much weight on her allegation. A more reliable witness was Elizabeth's godson, Sir John Harington, who in the 1590s voiced the general and widespread viewpoint when he wrote: 'In mind, she hath ever had an aversion and (as many think) in body some indisposition to the act of marriage.' Elizabeth may well have confided to Harington the fact that she had a mental aversion to sex – although this is by no means certain – but he was purely speculating as to the physical indisposition. In fact, in her courtships, Elizabeth usually assumed that her marriage would be fruitful.

When she was dead, the playwright Ben Jonson – no admirer of hers – told a Scots friend, William Drummond of Hawthornden, whilst they were drinking wine together, that the Queen had 'had a membrane on her, which made her incapable of man, though for her delight she tried many'. His source for this information is unknown, and he was probably repeating mere gossip, or inventing it under the influence of alcohol.

Modern writers have speculated that the gossip had its basis in fact, and that Elizabeth either had an abnormally thick hymen or suffered from an hysterical condition that causes sexual penetration to be excruciatingly painful. Recently, the writer Michael Bloch has suggested that the Queen, like the Duchess of Windsor, was a victim of Androgen Insensitivity Syndrome. In such cases, sufferers are born with male XY chromosomes but, owing to the body's failure to produce male sex hormones, develop outwardly as females. However, they have no ovaries, and only a deformed womb and a shallow vagina. Of course, it is impossible for them to bear children or even, in some cases, achieve sexual intercourse. Adults tend to be tall, mannish, and straight-limbed with 'strident personalities', although they can appear to be very attractive women. Elizabeth, argues Mr Bloch, may well have suffered from AIS. However, unless one takes into account Ben Jonson's highly dubious testimony, there is no proof to support this or any other of these theories.

At the beginning of her reign, Sir Thomas Challoner warned Elizabeth: 'A young princess cannot be too wary what countenance of familiar demonstration she maketh.' In other words, she could not be too circumspect in her behaviour. But it was not long before fantastic tales of her alleged promiscuity abounded, particularly in the courts of Catholic princes, where she was sometimes reviled – much as her mother had been – as a virtual nymphomaniac. It was said that she refrained from marriage so as to gratify her lusts with numerous lovers. Unfortunately, Elizabeth made no secret of the fact that she was interested in sex, and demonstrated a vicarious pleasure in talking about it. This, along with her known partiality for handsome, virile, intelligent men, her notorious flirtatiousness and sometimes outrageous behaviour led many to believe that rumour did not lie and that she was not the Virgin Queen she claimed to be.

There were numerous stories that she had secretly borne children, although how she could have done so without people knowing of it, given the very public life she led, remained unexplained. The jealous Bess of Hardwick was fond of relaying to Mary, Queen of Scots all the nasty tales she had heard of Elizabeth, such as how she had been discovered often in bed with the Earl of Leicester, or how she had forced Sir Christopher Hatton to make love to her. Mary very rashly repeated all this in a letter to her cousin, in a deliberate attempt to get Bess into trouble. Luckily for Bess, Cecil intercepted the letter and ensured that the Queen never saw it. Bess later confessed to the Council that she had made up all the tales, and Hatton would swear to Sir John Harington, 'voluntarily and with vehement asseveration, that he never had any carnal knowledge of Her Majesty's body'.

Abroad, Catholic writers such as the English Jesuits, Nicholas Sanders and Robert Parsons and Cardinal William Allen, were the source of many of the scurrilous – and untrue – stories about Elizabeth's promiscuity.

In England, as we shall see, those who were caught spreading malicious gossip about the Queen were often punished by the authorities, for fear that ignorant people would believe and spread the rumours. As late as 1598, Edward Francis of Dorset was hauled before the justices for having said, in an attempt to persuade one Elizabeth Baylie to cohabit with him, 'that the best in England had done so, and had three bastards by noblemen of the court, and was herself base-born'.

In later years, the notorious sadist, Richard Topclyffe, who tortured prisoners in the Tower of London, boasted of having touched Elizabeth's breasts and seen her bare thighs. He was probably fantasising, although, as we shall see, on one occasion in old age, the Queen appeared to enjoy exposing her breasts to a French ambassador.

Yet Elizabeth was too much mistress of herself and too great a stateswoman to succumb to the temptations of illicit sex. She was a proud and normally dignified woman who was very conscious of her exalted status and strict about observing propriety, and it is hardly likely that she would have risked her reputation, or the possible security of her throne, for physical pleasure. There was no effective contraception in those days, and a pregnancy outside wedlock would have spelled ruin for her. The very fact that she took no pains to hide her love and admiration for certain men indicates that her relations with them were above reproach. There is no proof to support the gossip. In 1561, when the rumours were at their most rampant, Nils Guilderstern, Chancellor of Sweden, came to England to press the suit of his master, King Erik. Having observed Elizabeth at court, Guilderstern reported: 'I saw no signs of an immodest life, but I did see many signs of chastity, virginity and true modesty; so that I would stake my life itself that she is most chaste.'

This was a view that would be shared by many other ambassadors in the years to come. Most agreed that the rumours were 'but the spawn of envy and malice'. In 1571, the French envoy, de la Mothe Fénelon, informed the Queen of France that Elizabeth was 'good and virtuous', adding that the gossip could not be believed when one had experienced the ethos of the English court, where the Queen, who was watched 'with Argus eyes', both inspired and received such a degree of respect as to preclude any possibility of her being unchaste.

Another French ambassador, Michel de Castelnau, Sieur de la Mauvissière, having been acquainted with Elizabeth for a quarter of a century, stated: 'If attempts were made falsely to accuse her of love affairs, I can say with truth that these were sheer inventions of the malicious and of the ambassadorial staffs, to put off those who would have found an alliance with her useful.' Most Spanish ambassadors were hostile to the English Queen, but one, de Silva, admitted that he was never able to find any truth in the rumours about her virtue. Elizabeth herself had told him: 'I do not live in a corner. A thousand eyes see all I do, and calumny will not fasten on me for ever.' There was no question in the minds of most of the Queen's subjects that she was inviolably chaste. Years later, the Lord Chief Justice, the brilliant Francis Bacon, described her as 'certainly good and moral; and as such she desired to appear' and his sentiments were echoed by others who knew her well, such as William Cecil and Sir Francis Walsingham, successive Secretaries of State.

The Queen's much vaunted virginity was a matter, not of personal choice, but of state policy, and in many ways it cost her dear, condemning her to a lifetime of lonely isolation, emotional deprivation and enforced chastity. She did indeed make a virtue of what she saw to be a necessity, and the strain sometimes showed. She may have teased her lovers and allowed them certain liberties – she was undoubtedly of an amorous nature – but never more than that. It may well be that the sex act itself did frighten her in some way, that she was psychologically unable to give herself to a man. But even if this were true, it did not alter the fact that she felt more invincible in the persona of the Virgin Queen than she would have done as a married sovereign. To remain invincible, she must not only bear the name but also play the part with conviction. And that meant that illicit sexual intercourse was forever strictly out of the question, whatever her private feelings about it.

Many people believed, and some still do, that because Elizabeth loved courtship and flirtation she was sexually immoral, but in fact she lived a very circumscribed life – she was hardly ever alone, being (as she said herself) 'always surrounded by my Ladies of the Bedchamber and maids of honour', who slept in her room – and she valued herself and her honour highly: it would have been unthinkable for the Queen of England to become some man's plaything. 'My life is in the open, and I have so many witnesses,' she once said, having learned what was being said about her abroad. 'I cannot understand how so bad a judgement can have been formed of me.' She had, moreover, learned what happened to queens – and, for that matter, princesses – who were suspected of overstepping the bounds of morality, and it had been a grim lesson. Besides, while she remained unattainable, she remained in control of her relationships, and that was how she liked things to be.

Hardly anyone took Elizabeth at her word when she expressed her wish to stay single. Both Parliament and the Council would behave as if only the choice of husband was an issue, and foreign ambassadors would press the suits of their various masters with good hopes of success. Elizabeth played along with this game enthusiastically. She loved nothing better than masculine attention and flattery, and revelled in the rituals of courtship. So well did she play her part that most people were deceived into thinking that she had indeed changed her mind about remaining celibate, and that it was only a matter of time and choice before she gave herself in marriage. This view was given credence by Elizabeth's fondness for discussing her possible nuptials, or declaring that 'She was but human and not insensible to human emotions, and when it became a question of the weal of her kingdom, or it might be for other reasons, her heart and mind might change.' She became, it was said by a courtier, 'greedy of marriage proposals'. It would also prove advantageous to her to have European princes competing for her hand and England's friendship at a time when the country was weak and impoverished. While they believed they stood a chance of success, they would not think of making war or stirring up trouble.

The matter of the Queen's marriage was to dominate English political thinking and policy and provoke endless speculation for a quarter of a century, with many tortuous twists and turns along the way that would cause untold grief and anguish to Her Majesty's beleaguered advisers, most of whom were utterly perplexed by her contrary behaviour. Few, even Cecil, realised that she meant it when she said, as she did on numerous occasions, that she had no desire to marry.

A quarter of a century of queenly prevarication was initiated in February 1559, when Elizabeth received the first marriage proposal since her accesssion. De Feria at last obtained a private audience and informed the Queen of King Philip's hopes. He was disconcerted when she displayed no sense of the honour being done her, and even more so when she responded by delivering a coy speech about the virtues of remaining a virgin. Unimpressed, the ambassador retorted that, if she did not marry and produce an heir to sit on England's throne, the King of France would rise against her and place Mary Stuart there instead.

This was a red rag before a bull, and prompted a furious outburst from the Queen, in which she 'began to rave' against King Henry II, the Dauphin, Mary Stuart and the French and Scottish nations in general. So vehement was her anger that, having raged and stormed for a considerable time, she collapsed with fatigue into a chair, telling de Feria that she needed time to think about King Philip's proposal.

A few days later, she was more rational, although she did point out the objections that could be made against such a marriage. The King's marriage to her sister had placed herself and Philip within the forbidden degrees of affinity; although the Pope would hardly be likely to refuse Philip a dispensation, this would be controversial in England, for had not Henry VIII been so 'scrupulous' as to question the Pope's right to issue a dispensation allowing him to marry his brother's widow? An English court had declared that marriage invalid, and it was likely that the validity of a marriage between Elizabeth and her sister's widower would be similarly disputed. The Queen quoted the Book of Leviticus to de Feria to prove her point, saying that she could never accept a papal decree which contravened the Word of God. For these reasons, she went on, she could not marry her sister's husband without dishonouring her father's memory.

However, all was not lost. She would, she promised, lay the matter before Parliament and the Council, and in the meantime the ambassador could assure King Philip that, if she married at all, she would prefer to take him before all others.

For the next month she considered the matter, while de Feria grew daily more optimistic. But the Queen's councillors, when they heard of the proposal, were aghast that their mistress could even contemplate accepting it, and in heated discussions did their best to dissuade her from doing so. She assured them that she would do nothing prejudicial to England's interests: 'I am descended by father and mother of mere English blood, and not of Spain, as my sister was,' she told them. Nevertheless, it would not be politic to turn down King Philip with unflattering haste, because England still needed Spain's friendship, especially since a peace with France had not yet been concluded. For the time being, therefore, de Feria might continue to hope for a favourable answer.

3

'Disputes over Trifles'

Queen Elizabeth had from adolescence been imbued with the beliefs and teachings of the Cambridge reformers who tutored her, yet although she grew up in and professed the Protestant faith, she was no reformer herself; it was the traditional ritual and ceremony of religion, the glorious anthems and motets sung by her choristers, and the intellectual satisfaction of theological literature that appealed to her. She knew that literature well, informing Parliament in 1566 that 'I studied nothing but divinity till I came to the Crown.' Furthermore, in an age in which people were burned for their beliefs, she held surprisingly enlightened views. 'There is only one Jesus Christ,' she declared to one French ambassador, André Hurault, Sieur de Maisse. 'The rest is a dispute over trifles.'

Unlike her sister, she was no fanatic, and hated fanaticism in others, both Catholic and Protestant, just as she had little time for bishops and despised those hard-line Protestant divines who went about calling each other 'my brother in Christ'. She was not above keeping episcopal sees vacant in order to retain their revenues for the Crown.

For her, the arguments of theologians and divines were as 'ropes of sand or sea-slime leading to the Moon'. She told Parliament in 1590, 'I see many overbold with God Almighty, making too many subtle scannings of His blessed will, as lawyers do with human testaments. If I were not certain that mine were the true way to God's will, God forbid that I should live to prescribe it to you.' Early in her reign, she confided to de Feria that she 'differed very little' from Catholics in her beliefs, 'as she believed that God was in the sacrament of the Eucharist, and only dissented from three or four things in the mass'. This, however, was said at a time when she needed Spain's support. She was quite capable of denigrating the old faith, as in 1577 when she referred to it, in a letter to German Protestants, as 'the darkness and filth of popery'.

When she learned that King Philip was persecuting Protestants in the Spanish Netherlands, she wrote to ask him why it mattered to him if his subjects chose to go to the Devil in their own way. She shocked one of Philip's ambassadors by flippantly expressing her hope that she would be saved as well as the Bishop of Rome, as English Protestants called the Pope. Later in the reign, she refused to allow Sir Walter Raleigh's suspected atheism to be investigated, on the grounds that she enjoyed theological arguments with him.

Because of these attitudes, some people accused her of having no religion at all. One Spanish ambassador, de Quadra, observed: 'She is not comfortable with the Protestants, nor with the doctrines of the other side either, and gives ground for the assertion that she is an atheist.' Yet she read the Bible regularly, and at the end of her life averred, 'I have ever used to set the Last Judgement before mine eyes and go to rule as I shall be judged to answer before a higher Judge.' Her views on transubstantiation were perhaps expressed in a doggerel verse traditionally ascribed to her and first printed in Richard Baker's *Chronicle* in 1643:

> Christ was the Word that spake it,
> He took the bread and brake it,
> And what His words did make it,
> That I believe and take it.

What she also believed in was the strong hand of a divine Providence, guiding and watching over her and her kingdom. When England faced the great threat from Spain in the 1580s, Elizabeth told the French ambassador, de la Mothe Fénelon, 'I think that, at the worst, God has not yet decided that England shall cease to stand where she does, or at least that God has not given the power to overthrow her to those men who would like to undertake it.'

Sermons – one of the chief features of morning services in Protestant churches – were her particular bugbear, and woe betide those clergymen who preached for more than an hour. She had even less time for those who attempted to instruct her from the pulpit as she sat in the royal closet with its lattice window, which she might have open or shut, according to her mood. 'To your text, Mr Dean! To your text!' she would shout, or she would send a message to the preacher, warning him to desist from an offending theme. In 1565, Dr Nowell, Dean of St Paul's, attacked the recent dedication of a Catholic tract to the Queen, then spoke out against the idolatrous graven images – the crucifixes – which Elizabeth had insisted upon keeping in the royal chapels.

'Do not talk about that!' snapped the Queen, but the Dean ignored her. 'Leave that!' she bawled. 'It has nothing to do with your subject, and the matter is now threadbare.'

Another preacher, Bishop Aylmer, who protested about 'the vanity of decking the body too finely', was curtly told to change the subject. 'Perchance', commented the Queen's godson Harington, 'the Bishop hath never sought Her Majesty's wardrobe, or he would have chosen another text.'

In 1596, when Elizabeth attained the age of sixty-three, known in Tudor times as the grand climacteric year, which many could not hope to survive, Bishop Rudd was informed by the Archbishop of Canterbury that Her Majesty 'now is grown weary of the vanities of wit and eloquence wherewith her youth was formerly affected, and plain sermons which come home to her heart please her the best'. The Bishop thus chose for his text the prayer, 'O teach us to number our days, that we may incline our hearts unto wisdom,' and proceeded to discourse upon significant sacred numbers such as three for the Holy Trinity, seven for the Sabbath, then seven times nine for the grand climacteric year, sixty-three. By this time, the Queen was frowning. Panicking, Dr Rudd went on to refer to the Revelatory number 666, 'with which he could prove the Pope to be Antichrist'. When he had finished, Elizabeth leaned forward in her closet and tartly commented 'that he should have kept his arithmetic for himself. I see', she added, 'that the greatest clerics are not the wisest men.'

'Queen Elizabeth', remembered Godfrey Goodman, Bishop of Gloucester under James I, always insisted 'that she had rather speak to God herself, than hear another speaking of God. She seldom heard sermons, but only in Lent.' Those summoned to preach at court were instructed to cut their address to a minimum and to choose their text from a list of those approved by the bishops. Sir John Harington records that the Queen's mind was capable of wandering during sermons. She once congratulated a divine on preaching on a matter that would have offended her greatly had she been listening to him.

Yet there were more cogent reasons for Elizabeth's dislike of sermons: preaching offered a forum for men to air their opinions, which, given the religious climate of the times, could only lead to disputes and cause public unrest. Those extreme Protestants who would come to be known as Puritans were heartily disapproved of by Elizabeth, not only for their fanaticism, but also because they insisted upon a 'preaching ministry'. Most of her subjects applauded her stand against Puritanism, especially after 1585 when she quashed a Puritan Bill aimed at banning all sports and entertainments on Sundays. The Queen felt that her people had a right to spend their only day of rest enjoying themselves as they pleased, without interference from killjoys. She also refused to agree to the suggestion – again from a Puritan source – that heresy, adultery and blasphemy be made criminal offences. In her opinion, those things were matters of conscience, not of law.

Perhaps her most famous triumph over Puritanism came in the field of the arts. The Puritan authorities in several cities, especially London, held the theatre in especial odium, and made strenuous efforts to suppress play-going, as it drew people away from the churches. The Queen sympathised with the theatre-goers: she, too, hated sermons. When, in 1575, she discovered that the renowned Coventry cycle of mystery plays had been banned by the Puritan authorities in that city, she ordered them to be restored. The Puritans in London then began complaining that theatre-goers in the City helped to spread the plague that was endemic each summer. In 1583, the Corporation of London closed the theatres on the Surrey shore, but Elizabeth retaliated by forming her own company of players, who became known as The Queen's Men. The civic authorities backed down, but in 1597 they eventually persuaded the Council to agree to close down the theatres on the grounds that they were hotbeds of subversive propaganda against the government. When Elizabeth heard, she was furious, and the Council hastily rescinded the order. There were no further threats to the theatre in her reign.

The Queen particularly abhorred married clergy, especially bishops and archbishops. Time and again she refused to acknowledge the existence of their wives, and on several occasions she was so rude about Archbishop Matthew Parker's wife that the shocked primate 'was in horror to hear her'. In 1561 he wrote to Cecil: 'Her Majesty continueth very evil to the state of marriage in the clergy, and if I were not therein very stiff [i.e. in his views] would utterly and openly condemn and forbid it.' She had the septuagenarian Bishop of Ely brought before the Council to be rebuked for having taken a young woman as his second wife. His excuse was that he had married to avoid being tempted into fornication, but this cut no ice with the Queen, whose views were shared by many of her subjects.

Queen Mary had repealed Henry VIII's Act of Supremacy, and when Elizabeth succeeded to the throne England was technically a Catholic kingdom under the jurisdiction of the Pope. However, most people expected the royal supremacy to be restored by Parliament, just as some kind of Protestant religious settlement was anticipated. Since her accession, Elizabeth had given only hints as to her intentions regarding the crucial issue of religion, but those hints had led people to believe that England would once again become independent of the Catholic Church. As far as Elizabeth was concerned, there could only be one head of the Church in England, and that was the monarch. She believed she had been called by the Deity to bring about 'the according and unity of these people of the realm into a uniform order of religion, to the honour and glory of God, the establishing of the Church and the tranquillity of the realm'.

One of her chief concerns was that public worship should be conducted in the correct form, in English, and she was to insist – much to the disgust of her stricter Protestant subjects – upon retaining some forms of Catholic ritual. She kept candles as well as crucifixes in her private chapels and insisted that her clergy wore caps, copes and surplices; she nevertheless abandoned the more elaborate ceremonies and practices which smacked of papistry, such as belief in miracles, the system of indulgences, and the veneration of the Virgin Mary. Always sensitive to strong smells, she loathed the scent of incense in churches, and banned it. But the Puritans still found much to complain about in her practice of her religion.

Although the worship of saints was abhorrent to Protestants, she encouraged the popular cult of St George, who was revered as a national symbol and the patron of the Order of the Garter. She continued the Maundy ceremonies – a detailed miniature by the female artist Levina Teerlinc shows the Queen at a Maundy service at the beginning of her reign. Elizabeth also revived the custom of touching sufferers of the skin disease scrofula, 'the King's Evil', which her medieval predecessors had done for three centuries. She took her almost mystical role in this ritual very seriously, steeling herself to lay her hands on the infected places on the supplicants' bodies, in the hope of effecting a cure. She restricted her attendance at chapel to weekly visits on Sundays and during Lent, and she always wore black to church.

Although her reign saw a cruel persecution of Catholics, Elizabeth had no personal antipathy towards them. Despite the ever-harsher laws against Catholics, she welcomed some recusant noblemen at court and sometimes visited them in their houses; she employed Catholics, such as the composer William Byrd, in her household, and rejoiced when her Catholic subjects demonstrated their loyalty to her, as they often did. Once, on progress, a man ran to her litter shouting, '*Vivat Regina! Honi soit qui mal y pense!*' Turning to the Spanish ambassador, who was present, the Queen told him, 'This good man is a clergyman of the old religion.' On another occasion, during her visit in 1564 to the University of Cambridge, she watched a group of undergraduates perform a masque ridiculing the Catholic mass; when a character dressed as a dog appeared with the Host in its fangs, an offended Elizabeth rose and stalked out, 'using strong language'. The Puritans would later accuse her – with some justification – of being more partial to Catholics than she was to true Protestants like themselves.

The persecution for which her reign became notorious was prompted by political necessity, not religious fanaticism, as will be shown in later chapters. The priests who were executed had committed crimes against the state, and were perceived as a very real threat to national security. Queen Mary had ordered the burnings of over three hundred Protestants in three years; fewer Catholics were executed under Elizabeth, and only four people, all Anabaptists, were burned in the whole of her forty-five-year-long reign. Like most of her subjects, the Queen was horrified and repelled by reports of the mass burnings of heretics by the Inquisition in Spain. As far as she was concerned, a man's conscience was his own. According to Sir Francis Bacon, she lived by the maxim, 'Consciences are not to be forced', and she 'would not have any unnecessarily sifted to know what affection they had towards the old religion'. Her Majesty, he wrote, had no 'liking to make windows into men's hearts and secret thoughts'. All she wanted from her subjects was loyalty to herself and the state and outward conformity to her laws governing religion.

Parliament now moved towards passing the first of those laws. On 9 February 1559, a bill to restore the royal supremacy over the Church of England was introduced into the Commons, but it was flawed in many respects and, after much debate, was thrown out.

In Rome, on 16 February, Pope Paul IV published a Bull proclaiming that all rulers who supported heretical doctrines might be deposed by the faithful. This rendered England liable to attack from crusading Catholic powers, and increased English fears of a French attempt to place Mary Stuart on the throne. It also tested the allegiance of Elizabeth's Catholic subjects.

The Queen was insisting upon treading a middle road. The Protestant faith was to become the established religion of England, but her watchwords were to be caution, compromise and moderation. Care must be taken not to offend her Catholic allies in Europe, and no extreme measures were to be adopted. She herself was forced to compromise, when the Protestant bishops refused to agree to enforcing celibacy upon the clergy or allowing roods, crucifixes or candles in churches. And moderation itself was compromised when those Catholic bishops who opposed the new ideas were sent to the Tower. Meanwhile, confusion reigned throughout the land, and both Catholic and Protestant services were conducted in the churches.

The bishops and some MPs expressed doubts as to whether a woman could be Supreme Head of the Church, for St Paul had stated that no woman was permitted to act as apostle, shepherd, doctor or preacher. Eventually the Queen agreed to be styled Supreme Governor instead. On 18 March, an amended bill restoring the royal supremacy was passed by the Commons. The following week, the Queen decreed that Holy Communion should from henceforth be conducted according to the Book of Common Prayer that had been in force under Edward VI.

Meanwhile, Elizabeth had been considering how she should respond to King Philip's proposal of marriage. She had put off de Feria for a month, telling him that he should have 'no answer that was not a very good one', but his initial optimism was deflating daily now as he realised that her Protestant councillors were doing their best to dissuade the Queen from accepting his master.

There were also rivals for her hand, although de Feria did not know that yet. On 20 February, Count von Helfenstein arrived from Austria, sent by the Holy Roman Emperor, Ferdinand I, who was Philip's uncle. The Count's mission was ostensibly to present his master's congratulations to Elizabeth on her accession, but also to determine whether she might make a suitable wife for one of the Emperor's two younger sons.

Elizabeth received von Helfenstein most warmly on 25 February, and he quickly fell under the spell of her charm. To his master, he wrote ecstatically of her prudence, her dignity, her great-mindedness 'and all other heroic virtues'. It was not long before he was telling the Queen and her courtiers about the two archdukes, Ferdinand and Charles. 'There was no one there who did not prick up his ears and listen with great admiration and silent reverence when I spoke about the ages, the morals, the talents of Your Imperial Majesty's sons, as on these points frank and exhaustive inquiries were made of me. For many thought that one of them would soon become consort of the Queen, and rule her and England.' Elizabeth asked pointedly if von Helfenstein had anything private to say to her, but he remained noncommittal. The English courtiers might not know of Philip's proposal, which had been kept a secret, but he did, and his orders were not to do anything until he knew the outcome of that matter.

There was one crucial issue on which the Emperor had instructed him to report back, and that was Elizabeth's religion. The elder archduke, Ferdinand, was a very pious Catholic, and even if his younger brother was less staunch in the faith, there was no question of his turning heretic. The Count watched the Queen and carefully questioned her courtiers, reporting: 'I have observed nothing that deviates from the old Catholic creed, so there is hope that if they get a Catholic king, all religious questions may easily be settled by authority of the sovereign.' Nevertheless, he was not wholly deceived by the outward religious ceremonial at court, being unable 'clearly to fathom' what Elizabeth's intentions were regarding religion. 'She seems both to protect the Catholic religion and at the same time not entirely to condemn or outwardly reject the new Reformation.' He resolved therefore to wait and see what transpired.

On 14 March, when it was almost certain that the religious settlement and a peace treaty with France would soon be concluded, Elizabeth summoned de Feria to a private audience and explained that 'she could not marry Your Majesty because she is a heretic'. Besides, she had no wish to marry at all. It was her hope that the friendship between England and Spain would bring the same advantages as a marriage alliance would have done. When de Feria questioned her as to how she had reached her decision, she became 'so disturbed and excited' that he ended up assuring her that neither he nor King Philip regarded her as a heretic. He told her they could not believe that she would sanction the bills being debated by Parliament.

Elizabeth protested that she was a Protestant and could never change her views.

'My master will not change his religion for all the kingdoms in the world,' answered de Feria loftily.

'Then much less would he do it for a woman,' retorted the Queen.

De Feria had his own private theory as to the real reason for her rejection of Philip. He had been making discreet inquiries and had reached the conclusion, as he confided to his master, 'that she would have no children'. A mysterious entry in the Venetian Calendar of ambassador's dispatches states there were 'secret reasons' why Philip did not marry Elizabeth, and this may be a reference to de Feria's findings. But if so, why did Philip continue to make strenuous efforts to bring about a Habsburg match for the Queen, and talk of her having heirs, if he knew she was barren? It is perhaps unwise to place too much reliance upon the often prejudiced reports of ambassadors, some of which were based on little more than court gossip.

When Philip learned of Elizabeth's decision, he could feel only relief, but he wrote to her expressing his regret, saying that although he had desired the marriage, yet 'with good friendship we shall attain the same subject'.

But Spain, too, was moving towards a peace with France, and before the month of March had ended Philip, with most unflattering haste, had announced his impending marriage to Elisabeth of Valois, daughter of Henry II. When Elizabeth was told, she took the news amiably, giving 'little sighs, which bordered upon laughter' She imputed the failure of their marriage negotiations to Philip, fibbing that she had given no answer, and pretending to be piqued because he had not been prepared to wait for three or four months for her to do so; she declared he could not have been as deeply in love with her as de Feria would have had her believe. The ambassador received the distinct impression that she was laughing at him. Thus she saved face, although Philip's betrothal could not have pleased her more, for it meant that she would retain his friendship. De Feria was soon assuring her that his master, who was anxious in case Elizabeth felt slighted, would 'remain as good as a brother to her as before, and as such shall take very great interest in what concerns her, and will try to forward her affairs as if they were his own', even after Spain's new alliance with France. He would also 'render her any service in the matter of her marriage'.

Thereafter, Elizabeth's relations with de Feria were fraught, if only because of her capriciousness, her tendency to tease or mislead him, and her fondness for playing diplomatic games. 'In short', he wrote despairingly to Philip, 'what can be said here to Your Majesty is only that this country, after thirty years of a government such as Your Majesty knows, has fallen into the hands of a woman who is a daughter of the Devil, and the greatest scoundrels and heretics in the land.' It was with relief that de Feria received notice in March that he was to be recalled. His replacement would be a worldly churchman, Alvaro de Quadra, Bishop of Aquila, who arrived in London on 30 March, though de Feria would continue to act as ambassador until he left England in May.

Philip remained determined that Elizabeth, and therefore England, should be brought back into the Catholic fold, and preferably by a Habsburg marriage. He was aware by now of the Emperor's hopes, and resolved to further an alliance between Elizabeth and one of the archdukes.

On 11 April he sent a memorandum to de Feria, listing the advantages of such a match, and instructing the ambassador to press them home to the Queen as a matter of urgency. He was to say that, since neither archduke had a principality of his own to govern, either would be free to come and reside permanently in England. Both were eminently fitted to help her bear the burden of government, as well as being well-connected and backed by the full might of the Habsburg Empire. Thus allied, her prestige would be enhanced, both in the eyes of Europe and of her subjects, and few would dare rise against her. The price of all this would of course be Elizabeth's conversion to the Catholic faith and the surrender of her independence.

Early in April peace was concluded between England and France and France and Spain with the signing of the Treaty of Cateau-Cambrésis, after which Philip married Elisabeth of Valois. Under the terms of the treaty Calais was to remain in French hands for eight years, after which, if not before, Elizabeth felt certain that she would be in a position to recover it, which was one of her dearest hopes, and the one matter about which she constantly deluded herself. She was now in a stronger position politically, and felt more confident about proclaiming to the rest of Europe that England was once again to be a Protestant nation.

Over the Easter holidays, the Queen thrashed out the new settlement with her lords spiritual and temporal, and in the end managed to reach a compromise with the more puritanical reformers. Elizabeth was to have the title Supreme Governor of the Church of England, and an Act of Uniformity was to restore by law Edward VI's Book of Common Prayer of 1552. The mass was outlawed and all services were to be in English. Transubstantiation was denied; Anglican communicants were to 'feed on [Jesus Christ] in their hearts, with faith'. Church ornaments and vestments were to be subject to the Queen's own discretion. Every subject over sixteen was to be required to attend church on Sundays or be fined twelvepence for non-attendance. These fines would, of course, be paid mainly by Catholic recusants, who were not to be otherwise molested. In practice, in a few areas, some were subject to petty harrassment for attending or celebrating mass.

Elizabeth took time away from these negotiations on 23 April, when she dined with the Earl of Pembroke at his riverside mansion, Baynard's Castle, near Blackfriars, after which she

> took a boat and was rowed up and down on the River Thames; hundreds of boats and barges were rowing about her, and thousands of people were thronging at the waterside to look upon Her Majesty, for the trumpets blew, drums beat, flutes played, guns were discharged, and squibs hurled up into the air, as the Queen moved from place to place. And thus continued until ten of the clock at night, when the Queen departed home. By these means, showing herself so freely and condescendingly unto her people, she made herself dear and acceptable to them.

The Acts of Supremacy and Uniformity were passed on 29 April 1559, and received Elizabeth's approval on 8 May, making Protestantism the official religion of the state and establishing a form of worship that in essence still exists in England today.

Both Catholics and Calvinists would have liked the legislation to have gone further, in different directions, and bitterly criticised it, but the Queen was determined on following a middle road, which the majority of her subjects seem to have wanted. Although it offended radical and vocal minority groups, the Anglican settlement of 1559 was highly successful in that it offered a moderating stability in an age of violent religious change and debate. For the Queen, it was the house built upon the rock of true religion.

The newly established Church of England desperately needed a spiritual leader: the See of Canterbury had been vacant since the previous November. Elizabeth wanted Matthew Parker as her Archbishop, but Parker was reluctant to accept. An early reformist, he had been chaplain to Anne Boleyn and it was to him that the doomed Anne had entrusted her daughter's spiritual welfare. Parker had prospered under Henry VIII and Edward VI, becoming Vice-Chancellor of Cambridge University, but Mary had ordered him to be defrocked because he had taken a wife. Cecil had a high opinion of Parker and felt that he had the qualities needed to lead the new Church. He was firm, and he was diplomatic; he also held moderate views. Because of this, Elizabeth was prepared to overlook Parker's marriage, and offered him the primacy.

Parker was horrified. 'I would rather go to prison than accept,' he declared, but the Queen and Cecil were persistent. Nevertheless, it was not until August 1559 that Parker capitulated.

De Feria knew now that Elizabeth was bound ultimately for hell, and as a means of saving her and her subjects from eternal damnation, joined forces with the Imperial ambassador, von Helfenstein, in an attempt to arrange a marriage with one of the Austrian archdukes. The Emperor had just sent a portrait of the elder, Ferdinand, to his London embassy, and de Feria threw his weight behind the project, determined that Philip should take the credit for arranging the marriage.

The ambassador saw the Queen to discuss the matter, but she was delightfully evasive and left him fuming. On 18 April, he reported: 'To say the truth, I could not tell Your Majesty what this woman means to do with herself, and those who know her best know no more than I do.'

Meanwhile, the Emperor, having heard that Elizabeth had rejected Philip II as a husband, and also having learned of her heretical sympathies, had decided not to press the suit of the pious and bigoted Archduke Ferdinand, whom Elizabeth had privately dismissed as being 'fit only for praying for his own family'. Instead, the Emperor planned to put forward his younger son, Charles, as the most suitable husband for the Queen of England. There was some risk involved, naturally, and the Emperor confided to von Helfenstein that he would never have permitted Charles to place his immortal soul in such danger were it not for weighty political reasons. Underestimating Elizabeth's commitment to the Anglican settlement, Ferdinand was confident that marriage to Charles would bring about her conversion to Catholicism.

English diplomats, on the other hand, were rather too optimistic that Charles would turn Protestant after the wedding, having read misleading reports that his faith was not too deeply rooted. 'He is not a Philip', observed one, 'but better for us than a Philip.'

In May, the Emperor dispatched a second ambassador, Baron Caspar Breuner, to England. He arrived on the 26th and immediately sought the help of the Spanish ambassador. De Quadra perceived that the Baron was 'not the most crafty person in the world'. Two days later de Quadra accompanied him when he had his first audience with the Queen, whom they found watching some dancing in her Presence Chamber. 'Breathing a prayer to the Almighty', Breuner laid the Archduke's proposal of marriage before her.

Elizabeth betrayed no emotion. She thanked the Emperor for deeming her worthy of one of his sons, but reminded Breuner that, although her subjects were continually exhorting her to marry, she had 'never set her heart upon, nor wished to marry anyone in the world', although she might indeed change her mind, 'for she was but human and not insensible to human emotions and impulses'. Breuner, his hopes dashed, warned the Archduke that he would have to be patient, but added that, having seen the palaces and possessions of this Queen, he had no doubt that she would be 'well worth the trouble'.

De Quadra had taken the opportunity to speak to Cecil about the Austrian marriage plan, but found the Secretary unenthusiastic. The ambassador then saw the Queen and, resorting to desperate measures, hinted that Charles might be thinking of leaving the Catholic church. Elizabeth displayed a flicker of interest, then 'went back to her nonsense and said she would rather be a nun than marry, without knowing with whom, and on the faith of portrait painters'. She told de Quadra she had heard rumours that Charles had an abnormally large head: she dared not risk accepting a deformed husband. De Quadra attempted to reassure her on this point, but after much 'wasting of words', she declared that she would never marry unless it was 'to a man of worth whom she had seen and spoken to'.

Slyly, she suggested that Charles might come to England and be inspected; did de Quadra think he would agree to this? De Quadra gave his opinion that the Archduke might well come out of love for her, but it was doubtful if the Emperor would send his son on approval. Indeed, he was to refuse to do so: it would be too public a humiliation were Elizabeth to refuse Charles. Given the constraints and etiquette that governed European royal courtships, the Queen's request was unusual, to say the least.

'I do not know whether she is jesting, which is quite possible', de Quadra told Philip, 'but I really believe she would like to arrange for this visit in disguise.' The Emperor was to veto that idea also, on the grounds that it was undignified and contrary to the usual way of conducting royal courtships. The Archduke himself proved reluctant to visit Elizabeth unless the marriage was a foregone conclusion.

Breuner, having completed his mission, now withdrew to await a reply. On 29 May, the Austrian proposal was laid before senior councillors, Elizabeth vowing to heed their advice, but only on condition that she would be able to 'see and know the man who was to be her husband' before accepting any offer of marriage. Nevertheless, in subsequent meetings with Breuner, she remained adamant that she would not marry at all for the present. God, with whom all things were possible, might change her mind in the future. She hoped that the Emperor would respect her honesty.

Breuner, in despair, retorted that the Emperor would most likely be offended and upset, considering the warm welcome afforded von Helfenstein, but Elizabeth made the rejoinder that the Emperor was in too much of a hurry, and that she would write to him personally, explaining the situation. In the meantime, Breuner was welcome to stay on in England. The Baron took this as an encouraging sign, and during their next two meetings contrived to persuade Elizabeth to tell him whether there was any point in pursuing 'this marriage business'. If not, he would return to Vienna. Elizabeth, with infuriating complacency, told him to act as he thought best, although her manner suggested that she wanted him to stay. Throughout the next few days, she paid him a great deal of attention, flattered him and exercised her charm to devastating effect. But she would say nothing about the Archduke's proposal, and was now declaring that she had taken a vow not to marry anyone she had not seen, 'and will not trust portrait painters'. She recalled how King Philip had cursed both painters and ambassadors when he had first beheld Queen Mary; she, Elizabeth, would not give the Archduke any cause to curse in a like manner.

Breuner's chief concern was that the Queen might accept someone else as a husband. Early in April, Prince Erik of Sweden, who had been a suitor for her hand during Mary's reign, renewed his courtship, but his envoy committed a terrible *faux pas* by demanding from the Queen an answer to the proposal made before her accession. Elizabeth regally insisted that Erik propose again to her as queen, whereupon he obliged, dispatching a handsome gift of tapestries and ermines. On 6 May, Breuner worriedly reported that 'The Swedes have brought a likeness of their young King [*sic.*] with them and shown it to the Queen, who praised the portrait highly.' Unlike the Archduke, Erik was prone to sending the Queen letters containing passionate declarations of love, which greatly entertained her. However, she made it plain that he would have to leave his country to marry her, as she would not leave hers for any consideration in the world. It was not realistic for either to abandon their kingdoms, and in May, when the Swedish envoys had begun to outstay their welcome and were becoming the butt of courtly ridicule, Elizabeth turned Erik down. She had not, however, heard the last of him.

To add to Breuner's concern, ambassadors from the Duke of Saxony and Adolphus, Duke of Holstein, arrived in England around the same time with offers of marriage; these the Queen would also turn down after spinning out negotiations for as long as she decently could.

There were additionally English suitors competing for her hand, and by May two serious candidates had emerged.

The first, who had originally displayed an interest in Elizabeth – to her great amusement – while her sister was alive, was Henry FitzAlan, 12th Earl of Arundel, aged about forty-seven, a widower with married daughters and with no good looks, trim physique or courtly manners to commend him. He was 'a flighty man of no ability, rather silly and loutish', who had too good an opinion of his chances with the Queen. What he had to offer was his wealth – he lived in Henry VIII's magnificent Nonsuch Palace in Surrey, leased to him by the Queen – and a family lineage stretching back as far as the Norman conquest, although neither were sufficient compensation for his boorish stupidity. Nor did Elizabeth take his courtship seriously; she thought him a buffoon, although she hid it well and strung him along much as she did her other suitors.

The other candidate for her hand was the debonair diplomat, Sir William Pickering, who was five years Arundel's junior and had just returned that May from ambassadorial service abroad. As far back as December court gossips had linked his name to Elizabeth's. Pickering was the son of Henry VII's Knight Marshal, had studied under John Cheke at Cambridge, and had risen to prominence under Henry VIII. He had been a loyal supporter and friend of Elizabeth during Mary's reign, although in 1554 he had been obliged to escape abroad after being implicated in the rebellion led by his friend Sir Thomas Wyatt. Mary had later taken him back into favour and used him on diplomatic missions to the courts of France and Italy. Illness had prevented him from returning to England at the time of Elizabeth's accession, and as soon as he arrived at court, on Ascension Day, and was received by the Queen at a private audience – only granted to the most privileged – which lasted for four or five hours, there was intense speculation that she might marry him, many considering that he was the only possible match for her among her subjects. The next day she spent a further five hours alone with him, and soon afterwards allocated him chambers in Greenwich Palace. This was her way of rewarding an old friend whom she was glad to see again after an absence of several years.

Pickering was 'tall of stature, handsome', muscular and gallant, and although many women had succumbed to his charms, he had never married. One affair had produced a bastard daughter, Hester, whom he was to name his heiress. He had bought former ecclesiastical property, and owned a fine London house in St Andrews Underhill, where he maintained an extensive library, which was the envy of the Queen. He had no claim to noble ancestry, but he was popular at court and in the capital, and it was his hope that his personal attractions would induce the Queen to marry him. Certainly he was the most popular choice among his compatriots, who believed it likely that the Queen might indeed take him as her consort.

Without being given much encouragement by Elizabeth, who seems never to have seriously contemplated marrying Pickering, councillors and courtiers began to seek Sir William's favour, and his new-found importance went to his head. He began spending extravagantly in order to adopt the lifestyle of a future king consort: he gave himself airs and graces, spent large sums on sumptuous clothes, and entertained on a grand scale, dining apart from his guests, with music playing as his food was served – just as if he were royal. Much excitement was generated by his behaviour, with London bookmakers giving odds of 25–100 that he would soon be King, though he openly maintained that the Queen would never marry anyone. This could have been a diplomatic façade to disguise his private hopes and ambitions. De Feria, in his last dispatch from England, commented: 'If these things were not of such great importance and so lamentable, some of them would be very ridiculous.'

Not to be outdone, Arundel too began swaggering about the court, handing out lavish bribes of jewels worth £600 to the Queen's ladies, as an inducement to them to sing his praises to their mistress. But even the nervous Baron Breuner, who had Arundel constantly in his sights, realised that here was no serious threat to the Archduke's prospects. It was Arundel alone who 'entertains that hope'.

Naturally, some of the older nobility resented Pickering's pretensions, and Arundel was glad of any opportunity to belittle him. One day, as Sir William was ostentatiously making his way to the Chapel Royal through the inner sanctum of the Queen's apartments, Arundel barred his way, saying he was too lowly in rank to be there: as a mere knight he should not have ventured beyond the Presence Chamber. Pickering retorted that he knew as much, just as he knew that Arundel was 'an impudent, discourteous knave'. At that, Arundel challenged him to a duel, but Pickering declined to fight, pointing out that Arundel was the weaker man. A furious Arundel thereafter went about protesting that, if Elizabeth married Pickering, he, Arundel, would sell all his estates and live abroad.

During the spring of 1559, public attention was focused upon Arundel and Pickering. But there emerged at this time a third English suitor, who was to prove a more serious contender for the Queen's hand, and who was probably the only man she ever loved.

His name was Robert Dudley.

4

'Bonny Sweet Robin'

The first evidence that Queen Elizabeth was becoming emotionally involved with Robert Dudley appears in a dispatch from de Feria to King Philip dated 18 April 1559. 'During the last few days', he wrote,

> Lord Robert has come so much into favour that he does whatever he likes with affairs. It is even said that Her Majesty visits him in his chamber day and night. People talk of this so freely that they go so far as to say that his wife has a malady in one of her breasts, and that the Queen is only waiting for her to die to marry Lord Robert. I can assure Your Majesty that matters have reached such a pass that I have been brought to consider whether it would be well to approach Lord Robert on Your Majesty's behalf, promising him your help and favour and coming to terms with him.

It was essential that Dudley be made to see the advantages of a continuing friendship between England and Spain.

Others, too, saw what was going on between the Queen and her Master of Horse, and soon the gossip spread to the courts of Europe. Paolo Tiepolo, Venetian ambassador to the court of Philip II, reported to the Doge and Senate: 'Dudley is a very handsome young man, towards whom, in various ways, the Queen evinces such affection and inclination that many persons believe that, if his wife – who has been ailing for some time – were perchance to die, the Queen might easily take him for her husband.'

On 10 May, Il Schifanoya observed, 'My Lord Robert Dudley is in great favour and very intimate with Her Majesty. On this subject I ought to report the opinion of many, but I doubt whether my letters may not miscarry or be read, wherefore it is better to keep silence than to speak ill.' Clearly, the most scurrilous of rumours were already circulating about the affair, but that was hardly surprising, since Dudley was a married man. Many were scandalised that Elizabeth should show him such favour, not the least of them William Cecil, who saw in Dudley's ascendancy a threat to his own power. Already, Elizabeth was consulting Dudley on state affairs, and there are indications that he had influenced her to stand her ground against the bishops during the discussions that preceded the recent religious legislation. Certainly he was instrumental in the advancement of no less than twenty-seven of the higher clergy during the early years of the reign.

Naturally, de Feria was still cherishing hopes that the Habsburg marriage negotiations might bear fruit, but he admitted that it was not easy trying to negotiate anything with Elizabeth because she was so changeable. 'For my part I believe she will never make up her mind to anything that is good for her. Sometimes she appears to want to marry [the Archduke], and speaks like a woman who will only accept a great prince, and then they say she is in love with Lord Robert and never lets him leave her.' The ambassador suspected that Dudley might pose a far greater threat to the Habsburg negotiations than Arundel or Pickering ever had. Not that they were yet out of the running, for Elizabeth continued to flirt with both; she even timed her first interviews with Pickering to take place while Dudley was away hunting at Windsor.

Dudley's duties brought him into daily contact with her, and there were plenty of opportunities for their relationship to flourish. They rode out together most days since both of them shared a passion for hunting. He was cultivated, witty, charming and attractive: in fact, a stimulating companion. Elizabeth could relax in his company, and he, sharing the same mischievous sense of humour, knew well how to amuse her. He alone had the gift of teasing her without giving offence, and it was later said of him, by one of his friends, that he knew her 'better than any man'.

When she was with him, she was anything but discreet, making no secret of her affection for him. She spoke of him often and never missed a chance to praise his talents as a horseman or as an arranger of tournaments and courtly entertainments. She openly danced spirited galliards with him, leaping into the air 'after the Florentine style, with a high magnificence that astonished beholders'.

For someone who normally set a high value on the good opinion of her people, she appeared to care not a jot what they were thinking. But as she was to point out on several occasions, much of the more salacious gossip – such as the rumour that 'Lord Robert did swyve the Queen' – was unfounded, because she was attended round the clock by her ladies and maids-of-honour. Court etiquette was such that she was hardly ever alone, and there would have been very few opportunities for her to carry on a sexual relationship with Dudley without other people finding out. The few allegations that the affair had progressed this far were made only by hostile ambassadors who would believe anything of a Queen who had embraced heresy. Yet even de Quadra, whose spies were everywhere, could find no evidence of a sexual relationship and refused to believe the rumours.

On 23 April, the first St George's Day she celebrated as Queen, Elizabeth bestowed the Order of the Garter upon Dudley, and upon the three senior peers of the realm, the Duke of Norfolk – Dudley's great rival – the Marquess of Northampton and the Earl of Rutland. This caused bad feeling, for the three noblemen had for many years served their country in various capacities, while Dudley was the son and grandson of upstart traitors. His only qualifications for the honour were good looks and superb horsemanship.

Not long afterwards, Elizabeth granted him the 'capital mansion' known as the Dairy House at Kew, Knole Park in Kent, lands in Leicestershire and Yorkshire, and the first of several grants of money.

Before long, he was freely dispensing patronage to a growing clientele of his supporters at court, and although he had no official political role in the government, the Queen looked to him frequently for advice. 'In the Privy Chamber', wrote one of his opponents, 'next to Her Majesty's person, the most part are his creatures, as he calleth them; and the rest he so overruleth that nothing can pass but by his admission.' Elizabeth fondly tolerated this situation, but never permitted Dudley to forget who was mistress and who was servant; there is no evidence that she ever allowed his advice to override decisions taken by her ministers. Nevertheless, many at court were suspicious of his motives and resentful of his over-familiarity with the Queen. Norfolk reviled him as an upstart, and many of the older nobility agreed with him. A lot of people thought Dudley a self-seeker who was professing love for the Queen only to further his own ambitions.

Yet there can be little doubt that the love between Elizabeth and Dudley was genuine on both sides. It endured through many storms until death intervened. There is no escaping the sincerity in Dudley's letters, the warmth of his addresses, nor his obvious concern for her welfare. With others he was usually haughty and reserved, but in the Queen's company he was congeniality itself. He was attracted to redheads, and enjoyed a sexual rapport with the Queen. It is also true that his feelings for her were not entirely selfless, yet she too was not above using him for her own ends. She certainly found him attractive physically, for she 'always took personage in the way of affection'. She admired his nerve, his sense of adventure and his robust masculinity. She could not resist the challenge of taming such a charmer and making him her creature. To her, he represented all that a man should be; his presence uplifted her spirits, and she declared it was imperative that she see him every day. In letters, he referred to himself as her 'Eyes', a nickname she had bestowed on him, and to which he alluded in his signature cipher of two lines above two circles.

For Elizabeth, Robert Dudley had one supreme advantage over all her other male admirers. He could not offer her marriage. With him, she had the best of both worlds. With his wife safely living in the country – Amy Dudley came rarely to London, and her husband's duties gave him leisure to visit her only infrequently – the Queen could enjoy all the advantages of male companionship without having to commit herself either to marriage, the loss of her independence, or the surrender of her body. As a single woman she could remain in control of the relationship, whereas a wife was subject to her husband's will. She could also preserve her carefully nurtured image as the Virgin Queen.

We do not know if at this stage Dudley entertained hopes that he would ever marry Elizabeth. If the ambassadors spoke truth, and his wife was indeed ill with a disease in the breast, then he may have foreseen a time when he would be free to offer himself as a consort to the Queen – an irresistible prospect for an ambitious man. For the present, however, he was content to bask in her favour, enjoying the benefits it brought, and knowing that he must retain it if he wanted his present prosperity to endure. Without the Queen's affection, he would be at the mercy of the noble wolves who were waiting to devour him.

Baron Breuner was so concerned about Elizabeth's regard for Robert Dudley that he felt obliged to inform the Emperor of it. Ferdinand, fearful of allowing his son to marry a woman with loose morals, instructed the ambassador to discover whether there was any truth in the rumours that had now reached Vienna. Breuner sent an agent to make discreet enquiries of Elizabeth's ladies, who conceded that their mistress 'showed her liking for [Dudley] more markedly than is consistent with her reputation and dignity', but protested that she had 'certainly never been forgetful of her honour'.

But Breuner was in for an unpleasant surprise. On 5 June, with the help of William Cecil and Roger Ascham, the Queen drafted a tactful letter to the Emperor, turning down the Archduke's suit. She admitted that marriage to him would have enhanced her prestige in the eyes of Europe, and thanked Ferdinand for his care for her welfare, but explained that 'When we reflect upon the question of this marriage and eagerly ask our heart, we find that we have no wish to give up solitude and our single life, but prefer with God's help to abide therein of our free determination.'

The next day, in a splendid ceremony at Windsor, Dudley was

formally installed as a Knight of the Garter. Around the same time, de Quadra was telling King Philip and others that the Queen had given Dudley £12,000 to spend on himself; in fact, the money was to be spent on Irish horses for the royal stables.

Breuner was perplexed by Elizabeth's attitude towards himself: she had turned down the Archduke, yet she continued to show special favour towards Breuner. 'Although the Queen affects a certain strangeness, she is quite otherwise in conversation,' he told Ferdinand, and he began to hope that her rejection of Charles was not as final as it appeared to be. On 10 June, as the ambassador was being rowed along the Thames, enjoying the summer evening, the royal barge, followed by that belonging to the Lord Treasurer, glided alongside. The Queen was taking the air, and she invited Breuner to board the Treasurer's barge; then, as the two barges drifted along side by side, she played her lute for him.

Breuner was entranced, and even more so when he was invited to take breakfast with the Queen the next morning – a rare privilege. That evening, he was again a guest on her barge, a luxurious craft rowed by eight oarsmen and boasting a cabin adorned with an awning of crimson satin. Heraldic shields hung inside it, and the floor of the barge was strewn with fresh flowers. The Queen relaxed upon a cushion of cloth-of-gold. She was in a relaxed, teasing mood, 'very talkative and merry', and commanded Breuner to take the helm. Later, she 'of her own accord began to talk about the Archduke', asking many questions and giving the impression that she was still interested in him as a possible husband. However, she had not wavered in her resolve to see any suitor face to face before agreeing to marry him. When Breuner recited the arguments against this, she would not listen, and when he attempted to pin her down as to her intentions regarding Charles, she was maddeningly evasive. Yet so overcome was he at such signal tokens of her friendship and favour that he ended up assuring her that the Emperor would never break off the marriage negotiations.

Shortly afterwards, the court moved to Greenwich, the beautiful Thames-side palace where Elizabeth had been born, and here, on 2 July, in the Great Park, the City's trained bands enacted a series of military manoeuvres as the Queen watched from a gallery over the detached gatehouse, which stood on the site now occupied by the Palladian Queen's House. On 11 July, a tournament organised by Dudley took place, and he had also arranged a lavish picnic, which was served in several pavilions built 'of fine poles, decked with birch and all manner of the flowers of the field and garden, as roses, gilliflowers, lavender, marigolds and strewing herbs'. The summer entertainments also included masques commissioned by Dudley for the Queen's pleasure, and he and the Queen were to be seen out riding together nearly every day – so much so, indeed, that she had begun to neglect her state duties to be with him.

Whilst the court was at Greenwich, news arrived from France of the death of Henry II, who had been mortally wounded in a joust. The news caused consternation at the English court, because although Henry had promoted the claim of his daughter-in-law, Mary Stuart, to the English throne, he was too much of a realist to jeopardise the peace of Cateau-Cambrésis by attempting to place her there by force. His son, Francis II, who was proclaimed King on 10 July, was, however, a weak and surly youth who was very much under the dominance of his sinister mother, Catherine de' Medici, and his wife's powerful uncles, the Duke of Guise and the Cardinal of Lorraine, who were all staunch Catholics and virtually ruled France. What alarmed Elizabeth was that the Guises and the Queen Mother were universally known to be hostile towards her. Furthermore, Mary Stuart's mother, Mary of Guise, was acting as regent in Scotland, although she was not popular there because she was of the old faith, and Scotland was at that time undergoing, under the direction of the militant Calvinist, John Knox, a radical reformation that would result in the establishment of a more rigorous and austere Protestant church than could be found anywhere else in Europe.

The English government feared that a two-pronged attack on England might be attempted by the French and the Scots, who were supposed to be allies. Although their friendship had become somewhat strained of late, that might not necessarily be to England's advantage. There were French troops in Scotland, and if they gained the upper hand there, they might decide to invade England from the north. What Elizabeth's advisers could not foresee, however, was that France would soon be so torn apart by religious wars between Catholics and Huguenots (French Protestants) that she would have little inclination and insufficient resources to make war on England. Nor would the Scots be likely to support it, because many were in sympathy with the Huguenots and distrusted the Catholics who were in power in France. For the present, though, the Queen was sufficiently worried about her vulnerable situation to reconsider her position on marriage. If she could make mischief for the French, and so keep them occupied, she would, and when she heard that Francis II had boasted that he would have himself proclaimed King of England, she loudly declared, 'I will take a husband who will give the King of France some trouble, and do him more harm than he expects.' The man she had in mind was a thorn in the side of the French, James Hamilton, Earl of Arran, and he had been mooted as a husband for Elizabeth as far back as 1543 by Henry VIII.

Until Mary Stuart bore a child, Arran was heir to the Scottish throne, and the Protestant lords in Scotland were in favour of a match between him and Elizabeth since both were 'chief upholders of God's religion' and their marriage would unite England and Scotland.

Arran was more than willing to fall in with this plan. Until recently, he had been a refugee in Switzerland, having fled there from the French, who feared the threat he posed to Mary Stuart's throne. At the beginning of July, Elizabeth had organised his escape, sending her agent Thomas Randolph, an expert on Scottish affairs, with instructions to smuggle him secretly to England disguised as a merchant. Soon, people were beginning openly to wonder whether Arran might be in England, and de Quadra was in daily expectation of an announcement of the Queen's betrothal to the Earl, whom he believed was 'something more than a guest'. In fact, Elizabeth was using her rumoured interest in Arran merely as a weapon against the French, and he did not arrive in London until the end of August.

To complicate matters, Erik of Sweden was still pressing for an answer, and had sent to say that he was coming to do his wooing himself. The personable – and Protestant – Erik was regarded in diplomatic circles as a serious threat to the Habsburg and Arran marriage plans: 'This is the man that hath given us many sharp alarms in our camp,' stated Randolph. 'This is he that breaketh our sleep and tieth oft our tongues.'

But what Elizabeth really wanted, and needed, was the protection of the Emperor and King Philip against French aggression, and, backed by Cecil, she set out to obtain this by deliberately reviving the Habsburg marriage negotiations, and then dragging them out for as long as it pleased her.

Meanwhile, the Queen was spending the season in a high good humour. Every summer, unless the plague threatened, custom decreed that English monarchs go on a progress through parts of their kingdom, staying in the houses of the great and seeing, and being seen by, the people. Such progresses were not mere holidays, but public relations exercises designed to promote the popularity of the sovereign. Queen Elizabeth delighted in going on progress, as we shall see, and on 17 July 1559 set out on the first of many, which took her to Eltham Palace, Dartford, Cobham and Nonsuch Palace, where she was lavishly entertained for five days by Arundel, who still fancied his chances as one of her suitors. One of the banquets he gave in her honour went on until three in the morning. Another banquet was followed by a masque performed 'with drums, flutes, and all the music that could be, until midnight'. When Elizabeth left Nonsuch for Hampton Court on 10 August,

Arundel gave her a magnificent set of silver plate in a presentation cabinet. There were bets that she would announce their betrothal within a week or so, but those who laid them were to be disappointed.

It was during this progress that Elizabeth's relations with Dudley grew increasingly intense, and as their intimacy became more obvious, so too, proportionately, did the scandal surrounding their affair escalate. If Dudley had been unpopular before, he could now be accounted one of the most hated men in England. He was the target of envy and resentment, and his enemies, who affected to believe him capable of any villainy, however foul, made great political capital of his treacherous family background, the implication being that here was another of Northumberland's race, 'fleshed in conspiracy', poised to make his bid to rule England. So universal and enduring was the backbiting against him that even the Queen, when she was momentarily displeased with him, reminded him that his forbears 'had been traitors three descents'.

William Cecil was one of those who resented, distrusted and feared Dudley. He resented the hold he had upon the Queen, distrusted his ability to advise her on political matters, and feared the consequences of their affair. Dudley being a married man, his relationship with Elizabeth could only attract the worst kind of speculation. Were his wife to die of her rumoured illness, the Queen might marry him, and then – goodbye Cecil. Either way, the throne would be undermined and the public wellbeing threatened. Cecil could not bear to contemplate a future with Dudley in power. Already, factions were forming at court, for and against the favourite, and that was a bad sign. To safeguard his own future, and those of Elizabeth and her realm, Cecil began to work in earnest for the Habsburg marriage.

To be fair, although he had many admirable qualities, and his loyalty to the Queen was never in doubt, Robert Dudley had a talent for making enemies. His haughty manner, transparent ambition and two-faced hypocrisy – he was not above maligning his 'friends' behind their backs – put people off. Most courtiers resented the fact that now, if they desired an audience with the Queen, they must first be supplicants to Lord Robert, who could – and did – demand his price. He could also be devious, and he invariably worked behind the scenes to abort any marriage negotiations embarked upon by the Queen. Failing this, he would openly try to discredit his rivals in Elizabeth's eyes, or raise objections on the grounds that a marriage alliance would not be beneficial to England's interests. Most people, however, saw through this, and concluded, quite correctly, that Dudley was looking to his own interests. Were Elizabeth to marry, his ascendancy would be speedily overthrown.

It is a measure of her feelings for her 'bonny sweet Robin', as she addressed him in their intimate letters, that Elizabeth, who normally cared deeply what her subjects thought of her, turned a blind eye to the hatred they expressed towards her favourite. Nor did she encourage him to court popularity among her people – she was too jealous of her own popularity to wish to share it. In fact, it pleased her to have him so dependent upon her, for such dependency virtually guaranteed his fidelity.

One of those not so enamoured of Robert Dudley, who feared for Elizabeth's good name and reputation, was her former governess, Kat Ashley, who had once gone to the Tower for aiding and abetting her mistress in her clandestine love affair with Admiral Seymour, and had good reason to fear the consequences of what was going on now. That August, Mrs Ashley took it upon herself to remonstrate with the Queen, and, on her knees, 'implored her in God's name to marry and put an end to these disreputable rumours, telling Her Majesty that her behaviour towards the Master of the Horse occasioned much evil speaking'.

Rather offended, Elizabeth retorted that, if she had showed herself gracious to Dudley, 'he had deserved it for his honourable nature and dealings'. It was beyond her how anybody dared object to their friendship, 'seeing that she was always surrounded by her Ladies of the Bedchamber, who at all times could see whether there was anything dishonourable between her and her Master of the Horse'. However, she went on defiantly, 'If she had ever had the will, or had found pleasure in such a dishonourable life – from which, may God preserve her – she did not know of anyone who could forbid her; but she trusted in God that nobody would ever live to see her so commit herself.

Mrs Ashley replied that the rumours were very damaging to Her Majesty's reputation, and confided her fear that they might alienate the Queen's subjects, or even provoke a civil war. Elizabeth shrugged this off. She commended Ashley for the devotion which had prompted her to speak out, but stated that she could not take a husband without first weighing all the advantages and disadvantages.

In that case, answered Ashley, should not her mistress distance herself from Dudley? Elizabeth responded with some emotion, protesting that she needed to see him constantly because 'in this world she had so much sorrow and tribulation and so little joy'.

Mrs Ashley or someone else reported the Queen's words to Baron Breuner, who believed that Elizabeth was telling the truth. But even though her remarks were widely reported, the rumours continued to flourish. Breuner believed that Robert Dudley's constant presence at the Queen's side was to blame – that, and the fact that he had a wife, 'a fine lady from whom he has always had nothing but good', whom he rarely visited.

The Emperor, in Augsburg, having also heard the latest disturbing rumours besmirching Elizabeth's reputation had instructed Breuner to undertake discreet but stringent enquiries to determine whether there was any truth in them. On 6 August, the Baron reported back:

I have employed as my agent a certain Francis Borth, who is on very friendly terms with all the Ladies of the Bedchamber and all other persons who have been about the Queen and have brought her up since childhood. They all swear by all that is holy that Her Majesty has most certainly never been forgetful of her honour. Yet it is not without significance that Her Majesty shows her liking for Lord Robert more markedly than is consistent with her reputation and dignity.

Indeed, for someone who had confided to Breuner that she was so beset by duties that she had not had time to think of love, she was doing little to dispel the impression that she was falling in love, or was already in love, with Dudley.

Later that month, Erik of Sweden sailed for England to woo his queen, only to be driven back by storms in the North Sea. Elizabeth immediately pronounced these to be a sign that God was protecting her, but Erik was undeterred. Soon afterwards, he put to sea again, only to encounter another storm which damaged his ships and obliged him to return home, battered, yet determined not to give up. To console himself, he wrote Elizabeth a series of passionate letters in Latin, in which he told her that, although 'Fortune had been harder than steel and more cruel than Mars', and prevented him coming through stormy seas to claim her, he would, at the first opportunity, hasten through armies of foes to be at her side, because her 'most loving Erik' was 'bound by an eternal love towards her'. However, as he had state commitments to meet just at present, he would shortly be sending his brother to England in the hope of having 'a favourable answer' to his proposal.

On 28 August, the Earl of Arran secretly arrived in London, and was smuggled into Cecil's house at Westminster, where he was to lodge. On the following day, he was granted a private audience with the Queen at Hampton Court, and two days later left for Scotland, escorted by Thomas Randolph. The plan was that he should lead the rebel Protestant lords there against the Queen Regent's government, and thus divert the Scots and French from turning their ambitious eyes towards England; all talk of a marriage alliance with Elizabeth had been abandoned, as she apparently was not impressed by the Earl personally. Arran's story was eventually to end in tragedy: he became insane, and never enjoyed the power and prestige that should have been his birthright.

It now appeared that the only foreign contender for the Queen's hand with any chance of success was the Archduke Charles.

Late in August, Elizabeth removed to Windsor Castle, where she spent her days riding and hunting in the Great Park, with Dudley never far from her side. In the evenings, they would sit together on a window seat, laughing and talking, or would play music and sing – a gittern given by Dudley to Elizabeth is now in the British Museum. They seemed not to care about the gossip that followed such open displays of affection, gossip that proclaimed them, at best, to be in love, or, at worst, to be sexual partners. It was even whispered that the Queen was pregnant by Dudley, although time, of course, gave the lie to that particular rumour. Cecil warned Elizabeth of what was being said and begged her to be more discreet, only to have her laugh in his face.

It was now clear that Arundel and Pickering could no longer be taken seriously as contenders for the Queen's hand, although both were still squabbling about matters of precedence. Robert Dudley's meteoric rise had left them totally eclipsed, and they now retired from the contest defeated, although not before Pickering had warned de Quadra that 'he knew [the Queen] meant to die a maid'. He lived on, unmarried and in declining health, until 1575.

Elizabeth was enjoying herself hugely with so many men dancing attendance upon her. At one point that autumn, there were a dozen foreign ambassadors at court, all hoping to win her friendship through a royal betrothal. How they would fare, commented Cecil sourly, 'God knoweth, and not I.' De Quadra was equally perplexed by the Queen's mercurial moods: one day she affected to be indifferent to the Habsburg marriage, the next she was discussing it as a serious possibility. In exasperation, the ambassador wrote to de Feria: 'Your Lordship will see what a pretty business it is to have to treat with this woman, who I think must have a hundred thousand devils in her body, notwithstanding that she is forever telling me that she yearns to be a nun and to pass her time in a cell praying. With her, all is falsehood and vanity.'

Early in September, de Quadra was visited secretly by Lady Mary Sidney, Dudley's sister and Elizabeth's most favoured Lady of the Bedchamber, who told the Bishop that now was the time to revive the Archduke's suit. He should ignore Her Majesty's apparent reluctance to discuss it, 'as it is the custom for ladies here not to give their consent in such matters until they are teased into it'. But Elizabeth might now be prevailed upon to give an answer within a few days. The Council would certainly urge her to do so – they were tired of all the delays and prevarication. De Quadra should rest assured that she, Lady Mary, would never say such things if they were untrue; in fact, she was acting with the Queen's consent. Elizabeth would never raise the subject of the marriage of her own accord, but there was no doubt that she very much wanted the Archduke to visit England.

De Quadra, unable to believe all this, sought corroboration from Dudley, who assured him that his sister was not lying. In fact, he himself would do anything to please King Philip, who had saved his life by securing his release from the Tower in 1554. Sir Thomas Parry, Elizabeth's Treasurer, also confirmed what Lady Mary had said, stating that the Queen 'believed the marriage had now become necessary'.

De Quadra could understand this: he was well aware of the threat posed by the French, and Lady Mary had told him of a plot by Arundel to poison Elizabeth and Dudley at Nonsuch Palace in August, expressing her fears for her mistress's safety. In fact, there had been no plot; it was an invention of the Queen's, conveyed to the Bishop as a practical joke. The Queen had also been the instigator of Mary Sidney's nocturnal visit to him, which was intended to prompt him into reopening the Habsburg marriage negotiations, a subject Elizabeth did not feel she could raise openly with him.

On 10 September, Baron Breuner, briefed by de Quadra, took a barge down to Hampton Court, whither the Queen had travelled from Windsor. Having anticipated a warm welcome, he was dismayed to find her in no mood to receive him. However, three days later, when Elizabeth had come up to Whitehall, de Quadra found her more amenable, although she was still protesting that she had no desire to marry the Archduke or any other foreign prince; she would only consider marrying someone she had seen face to face. It would be better if Charles did not come to England, because she could not commit herself, even indirectly, to marrying him.

'We are wasting words,' complained de Quadra. Her Majesty should begin with the premise that she had to marry someone, since that could not now be avoided. Then she should invite the Archduke to visit her; he assured her that she would not be committing herself in any way. The Emperor was now amenable to the idea – he, too, was eager for the marriage to take place – provided that matters could be managed in such a way as to spare Charles any humiliation should the Queen turn him down. Elizabeth wavered, then was silent for a moment.

'Shall I speak plainly and tell you the truth?' she asked. 'I think that if the Emperor so desires me for a daughter, he would not be doing too much by sending his son here without so many safeguards. I do not hold myself of so small account that the Emperor need sacrifice any dignity in doing it.'

De Quadra reported: 'By these words and her manner of saying them, I understood that she made no difficulty as to the conclusion of the business, but only in the procedure to bring it about.' One thing was certain: Elizabeth absolutely refused to invite Charles to England – it was not fitting for a queen and maiden to summon anyone to be her husband; she would rather die a thousand deaths. The Emperor must take the initiative. De Quadra assured her that there should be no difficulty in arranging that. Soon, the Queen was admitting that she would be delighted to receive the Archduke. She inquired what languages he spoke, and talked to the ambassador 'in a vastly different mood from her other conversations about her not wishing to marry'. De Quadra thought he had won the day.

However, when he asked if the Archduke's visit should be public or private, Elizabeth panicked, saying she would not be pressed further. The Archduke must do as he thought fit – she did not wish to become involved, and he must understand that she had not invited him. She kept repeating that she was not committing herself to marrying him; in fact, she had still not decided whether to marry at all. De Quadra dismissed her behaviour as 'nothing but ceremony. I do not believe that Lady Sidney and Lord Robert could be mistaken, and the latter says he never thought the Queen would go so far.'

Word of what was afoot quickly circulated around the court, and it was soon being said that Elizabeth would be the Archduke's wife by Christmas, although, as de Quadra drily observed, 'As she is a woman, and a spirited and obstinate woman too, passion has to be considered.' In his opinion, Charles should come at once: having seen him, the Queen would be unlikely to turn him down. Nor would she risk giving offence to the Emperor by doing so. On 2 October, the Bishop wrote to Ferdinand, urging him to send his son without delay.

At Whitehall that autumn, Lord Robert complained that the rooms allocated him were too damp because they were near the river. The Queen obligingly offered him a suite of apartments next to her own on the first floor, and tongues began to wag even more furiously than before. 'People are ashamed at what is going on,' shuddered de Quadra, but he, like most others, was making assumptions he could not substantiate.

The Duke of Norfolk was, according to de Quadra, 'the chief of Lord Robert's enemies, who are all the principal people in the kingdom'. Thomas Howard saw Dudley's constant presence at the Queen's side as an obstacle to the successful conclusion of any marriage negotiations, and openly criticised Elizabeth's 'lightness and bad government', warning Dudley that, if he did not abandon his 'present pretensions and presumptions, he would not die in his bed'.

Howard was the son of the poet Surrey, and the grandson of the third Duke, who had been the Queen's great-uncle and also the most implacable of Northumberland's opponents. His grandson was the premier peer in England, indeed, the only Duke in the peerage, and by virtue of his birth he expected to enjoy the favour and patronage of the Queen, and to be among her closest advisers. But with Dudley constantly in the way, that was never likely to be. Worse still, rumour had it that the Queen meant, one day, to marry Dudley. 'The Duke and the rest of them cannot put up with his being king,' commented de Quadra. Even though Dudley was married, the thought had crossed the Bishop's mind that he might be seeking a means whereby he might be freed from his lady so that he could marry Elizabeth – which was exactly what Norfolk and others feared.

At the beginning of October, John, Duke of Finland, the 'very courteous and princely' brother and envoy of Erik of Sweden, arrived in England, with the express purpose of concluding a marriage between his besotted master and Queen Elizabeth. That Elizabeth had made it perfectly clear that she was not interested seemed to have made no impression on Erik. Although Sweden was not a wealthy country, he was a Protestant, and he imagined that that was reason enough for Elizabeth to want to marry him.

Courtesy demanded that the Queen extend a warm welcome to the brother of a fellow monarch, and Dudley was sent to greet Duke John at Colchester, but the latter interpreted this as a sign that his mission had already been successful, and it required a great deal of tactful diplomacy on the part of the courtiers before he could be persuaded otherwise. Thereafter he showed himself impressed by the customs of England, and with its Queen, who showed him both friendship and favour, finding much to commend in this educated young man; soon there were speculations that she would marry him instead of his brother. Dudley was affability itself to the Duke – on the 19th he hosted a court banquet in his honour – but he cannot have welcomed his presence in England.

Duke John was flamboyant, and lavish with his gifts – even if they did consist of counterfeit coin – and his behaviour made Baron Breuner's hackles rise, obliging the Queen to exercise considerable ingenuity in keeping the two men apart. However, she was gaining immense satisfaction from the situation, and was proving more than adept at handling them. She would give a little, appear to be promising much, and then withdraw at the right tactical moment, leaving all concerned perplexed and frustrated. Then, just as they were ready to give up, she would show herself eager once more. It was a game that required a finely-tuned sense of timing, but one that she relished. And while she was dangling hopes of success before her suitors, she remained her own woman, free and uncommitted, whilst retaining the friendship of those princes who lived in hope.

'Here is a great resort of wooers and controversy amongst lovers,' wrote Cecil to Sir Nicholas Throckmorton that autumn. 'I would Her Majesty had one, and the rest honourably satisfied,' he told Sir Ralph Sadler. Apart from the Archduke Charles and Erik of Sweden, there was the King of Denmark, whose envoy was posturing about the court in a crimson velvet doublet embroidered with a heart pierced by an arrow 'to demonstrate the King's love for the Queen of England'. Nobody took him seriously, nor the continuing suits of the dukes of Saxony and Holstein. 'Her Majesty,' wrote de Quadra, 'is charmed by so many loose and flighty fancies.' However, out of the ten or twelve ambassadors competing for her favour, only those of Austria or Sweden had realistic hopes of success. Both were 'courting at a most marvellous rate'. They were also, within a short time and despite Elizabeth's efforts, trading insults and ready to do violence upon each other. Alarmed, Elizabeth forbade them to come to court at the same time, 'to avoid their slashing each other in her presence'.

De Quadra was worried in case Elizabeth accepted Erik rather than the Archduke, but the chief threat to the Habsburg alliance was nearer at hand. As John Jewel, Bishop of Salisbury, said, she might act as if she meant to make a foreign match, but she was really 'thinking of an alliance nearer home'.

Early in November, the French ambassador, Antoine de Noailles, was amused to see the Queen, flanked by Bishop de Quadra and Duke John, the representatives of her two foremost suitors, sitting in the gallery at Whitehall, watching Dudley, the man widely rumoured to be her lover, and her cousin, Lord Hunsdon, take on all comers at a tournament. Dudley did well, and de Noailles noticed how much this pleased Elizabeth.

Breuner was despondent. Thanks to Dudley, it seemed, the Queen was no longer interested in marrying the Archduke. Sadly, the Baron told her that there was no point in him staying in England. Elizabeth took offence at this, and was 'worried and peevish the whole day, giving no one a gracious answer'. She was aware that, if Breuner left, Dudley would be blamed for it. 'It is generally stated', wrote Breuner, 'that it is his fault that the Queen does not marry.' De Quadra, too, was complaining that Dudley was 'slackening in our business'. The favourite was now so hated that, according to Breuner, it was 'a marvel that he has not been slain long ere this'. Many people at court deplored Dudley's influence over the Queen and were concerned that Elizabeth was casting away a brilliant marriage because of him.

During November, the Duke of Norfolk confronted Lord Robert, warning him that he would do all in his power to bring about the Habsburg marriage.

'He is neither a good Englishman, nor a loyal subject, who advises the Queen to marry a foreigner,' retorted Dudley haughtily, whereupon Norfolk stalked off in a temper, though he had the support of Arundel and many other nobles.

When de Quadra told Elizabeth that the Archduke might be on his way, since all her conditions had been met, she answered that she was not contemplating marriage at present, although she might change her mind when she saw Charles.

The Bishop angrily pointed out that she had all but invited the Archduke for inspection, but she airily justified this by claiming to have only wished to meet him and get to know him in case she decided to marry at some future time. De Quadra, simmering with anger, repeated what Mary Sidney had said. Elizabeth replied that members of her household often said such things, with the best of intentions, but had never done so on her authority. Afterwards, de Quadra realised he had been made to look a fool, and prepared for the collapse of the marriage negotiations he had worked so hard to bring to a successful conclusion. 'I do not pretend to understand Her Majesty', he wrote, 'and I have given up all hope in her affairs.'

He also faced the prospect of Elizabeth marrying Robert Dudley, which would, he was convinced, be a highly unsuitable match, even if one discounted the rumour, communicated by 'a certain person who is accustomed to give me veracious news' and reported by the Bishop to Philip on 13 November, that Dudley had 'sent to poison his wife. Certainly, all the Queen has done with us and with the Swedes, and will do with the rest in the matter of her marriage, is only keeping Lord Robert's enemies and the country engaged with words until this wicked deed of killing his wife is consummated.' If rumour spoke true, then Dudley's resort to murder was extremely short-sighted, since suspicion would be bound to attach to him, and the Queen could then consequently never marry him for fear of being implicated in the deed. But de Quadra clearly believed them both capable of such a crime, and he could foresee ruin staring them in the face if they dared to marry.

Nor were the rumours confined to England. Sir Thomas Challoner, the English ambassador to the court of King Philip at Brussels, was so shocked at hearing the 'most foul slander' against his mistress, that he wrote to warn Cecil of it, without giving any details, since it was too offensive to be committed to paper. Challoner stressed that he knew the rumours were false, but urged the Queen to be more discreet in her dealings with men and to marry soon, 'for without posterity of Her Highness, what hope is left unto us?'

On 24 November, the Queen appointed Dudley Lord Lieutenant and Constable of Windsor Castle. He was already advancing his friends and supporters to influential posts at court, and was promoting himself as the champion of Protestantism. As such, he was hostile to the Spanish and inclined to favour the French. In his opinion, the English government should be at the forefront of the Protestant revolution, and should abandon the alliance with Philip. Yet although he had been elected to Parliament in January 1559, he had no seat on the Council, and those that did resented him meddling in high politics. Some, according to de Quadra, even muttered that they wanted no more women ruling over them.

Nevertheless, many Englishmen, wishing to court the favour of the man they believed might one day be their king, acknowledged Dudley as the leader and inspiration of the radical religious reformers, and a great number of devotional tracts were dedicated to him. There is no doubt that he was sincere in his beliefs: 'I take Almighty God to be my record', he once wrote, 'I never altered my mind or thought from my youth touching my religion . . . I was ever from my cradle brought up in it.'

Around Dudley, a court faction had formed. Cecil, in a private memorandum, listed its members, who included Robert's brother-in-law, Sir Henry Sidney, his brother Ambrose Dudley, Sir James Croft, who had supported Elizabeth during Mary's reign, and John Appleyard, half-brother of Lady Dudley. Cecil was under the impression that his own position at court was becoming less and less secure as Dudley became more powerful. Ever cautious, he took care not to alienate Dudley, but behaved affably and courteously towards him. Behind the scenes, however, he was assiduously courting Norfolk, the favourite's bitter enemy, who had emerged as the leader of the anti-Dudley faction.

There were some ugly incidents. One ambassador wondered if England was so poor that none could be found to stab Dudley with a poniard, and it seems that there was a plot to kill him around this time, for two men – Sir William Drury, a soldier, and his brother Dru, a Gentleman of the Privy Chamber – were sent to the Tower for several months, charged with attempted murder. Whether there was any substance to the accusation is not clear, because it was Dudley himself who later secured their release. In December, Norfolk publicly accused him of interfering in state affairs, thus provoking a heated exchange between the two men. Dudley went straight to the Queen, and less than a week later, Norfolk found himself on the way north to serve as Lieutenant General on the Scottish border. This was no sinecure, because that month saw Elizabeth dispatching, in direct contravention of a treaty she had made with Mary of Guise, an English fleet to assist the Protestant lords in Scotland in their struggle against the Queen Mother and the French troops she had summoned to support her.

As Christmas approached, Queen and court indulged in a continual merry-go-round of balls, banquets, masques and hunting parties, Elizabeth ignoring the unsavoury things that were being said about her.

It was fortunate that the Archduke had not yet set out for England, for it was now obvious to de Quadra and Breuner that the Queen had lost interest in marrying him, and they concluded that she was merely using them 'and the other envoys who are sojourning here on matrimonial business'; they guessed that her real purpose in keeping them guessing had been to counteract the threat of French aggression and deceive her own subjects into thinking that she was serious about marrying. 'For as long as we are here, she can put off the vulgar mob who daily beg and implore her to marry, with the plea that she must have leisure to occupy herself with the requests of so many potentates, to the weal and advantage of her realm.'

In December, Breuner left England, having failed in his mission. He was no nearer to understanding Elizabeth now than he had been at the start, and he imputed her changeable behaviour to her youthful experiences, 'for sometimes she was regarded as legitimate, and at other times not. She has been brought up at court, then sent away, and to crown all she has even been held captive.' Having attained the throne, she could be compared to 'a peasant on whom a barony has been conferred', having become so puffed up with pride that she imagined she could indulge her every whim. 'But here she errs, for if she took my Lord Robert, she will incur so much enmity that she may one evening lay herself down as the Queen of England, and rise the next morning as plain Mistress Elizabeth.'

Yet it seemed that Elizabeth was indeed contemplating such a step. In January 1560, de Quadra reported that there was ill-feeling among the Queen's subjects at the prospect of her taking Dudley as her consort; he believed they would 'do something to set this crooked business straight. There is not a man who does not cry out on him as the Queen's ruin, and on her with indignation.' It was now believed by all that 'she will marry none but the favoured Robert'.

In March, there was talk that Dudley might attempt to have his marriage dissolved. Bishop de Quadra had heard him boasting that 'if he lives another year, he will be in a very different position from now. He is laying in a good stock of arms and is every day assuming a more masterful part in affairs. Every day he presumes more and more, and it is now said that he means to divorce his wife.' But, again, the rumours appear to have been baseless, for Dudley took no steps to have his marriage dissolved.

Early in the new year von Helfenstein returned to England in an attempt to revive the Habsburg marriage negotiations. The King of Bohemia and the Duke of Bavaria, vassals of the Emperor, both sent envoys urging the Queen to reconsider, and suggested to Charles that it might be better if he went and did his courting in person, but the Emperor, offended by Elizabeth's apparent indifference to the match, was now refusing to let his son go to England unless she made some commitment beforehand. A stalemate had been reached, and by February it was obvious that the marriage negotiations had collapsed. On the 19th de Quadra gave it as his opinion that the Queen's strategies would lead to her ruin, because without the support and friendship of the Habsburg monarchies, 'not only will the French despise her, but her own people as well, and she will be left helpless'.

In February, Elizabeth disposed of her other foreign suitor, who had just succeeded his father as King of Sweden. She wrote on the 25th to tell Erik that, despite being unable to doubt 'the zeal and love of your mind towards us, yet we are grieved that we cannot gratify Your Serene Highness with the same kind of affection'. She protested that she had 'never yet conceived a feeling of that kind affection towards anyone', and begged Erik 'to set a limit to your love, that it advance not beyond the laws of friendship'. She stated firmly that, 'if God ever direct our heart to consideration of marriage, we shall never choose any absent husband, how powerful or worthy a prince soever. I have always given to your brother the same answer, that we do not conceive in our heart to take a husband, but highly commend this single life, and hope that Your Serene Highness will no longer spend time in waiting for me.' In a postscript, she begged him to desist from coming to England, 'since nothing but expectation can happen to Your Serene Highness in that business, and we very greatly fear that your love, which is now so great, might be turned to another alien feeling, which to us would be very grievous'.

At first, Erik refused to take no for an answer, but as the weeks passed and the Queen showed no sign of relenting,, he reluctantly summoned Duke John home.

In England many were asking had the way been cleared for Robert Dudley?

5

'Presumptions of Evil'

In February 1560, the Duke of Norfolk reached an accommodation with the Protestant lords of Scotland that, in order to prevent the French troops called in by Mary of Guise from taking over that kingdom, Queen Elizabeth would take it under her protection for as long as its rightful Queen remained in France. Shortly afterwards, Elizabeth sent English ships to blockade the Firth of Forth and so prevent arms from France getting through to the Queen Regent's forces. Mary of Guise retaliated, and there was a disastrous confrontation at Leith, where the English were driven back with great loss of life.

Elizabeth was, not surprisingly, unpopular with the French at this time, and in April, Sir Nicholas Throckmorton, her ambassador in Paris, wrote to warn her of a 'pestilent and horrible device', a plot by the Guise faction to have her poisoned by an Italian called Stephano, 'a burly man with a black beard'. Cecil immediately drafted a memorandum with the heading 'Certain cautions for the Queen's apparel and diet', which was intended to help Elizabeth avoid any danger from poison. 'Do not accept gifts from strangers of perfume or scented gloves, or anything edible,' it warned.

De Quadra was impressed by the Queen's courage in the face of danger from both France and Scotland. Watching her putting her Neapolitan jennet through its paces with the London trained bands, he observed that she 'made a brave show, and bore herself gallantly'. At around this time, Pope Pius IV sent a letter to Elizabeth enjoining her to return to the Catholic fold, but she gave orders that his messenger was to proceed no further than Brussels. For the rest of her life she would turn a deaf ear to similar overtures from the Vatican.

On 11 June, Mary of Guise died of dropsy, and the French signified that they were ready to sue for peace. Elizabeth decided to send William Cecil to Scotland to negotiate a treaty with the Scots and French on terms advantageous to England. Throckmorton, hearing of her decision, was worried: without Cecil's restraining hand, the Queen might well do something rash. 'Who can or will stand fast against the Queen's arguments and doubtful devices? Who will speedily resolve the doubtful delays' in decision-making? Elizabeth was notorious already for not making up her mind. 'Who shall make despatch of anything?'

Cecil himself was reluctant to leave court. He suspected that Dudley had persuaded the Queen to send him to Scotland to get him out of the way, and he was convinced that, once he had left, Dudley would supplant him in the royal counsels. He confided to Throckmorton: 'My journey is to me very strange and diversely judged of. My friends think I am herein betrayed to be sent from the Queen's Majesty.' On another level, he would be relieved to be away from all the backbiting and intrigue at court, which wearied him. Yet when he left for Edinburgh, it was with a heavy heart, for he could see himself being ousted from power during his absence by a man who would surely bring England to speedy ruin, a man to whose name foul rumours were still attaching themselves.

In June 1560, old Mother Annie Dowe of Brentwood in Essex was fond of repeating to her ignorant cronies the latest gossip from London about the Queen and Dudley. The latter, she had heard, had given Her Majesty a red petticoat.

A friend, who had also heard rumours, retorted, 'Thinketh thou it was a petticoat? No, no, he gave her a child, I warrant thee.'

Annie Dowe gleefully repeated this gem of gossip in the next village.

'My Lord Robert and the Queen have played at legerdemain together', she said meaningfully, 'and he is the father of her child.'

The astonished villagers responded, 'Why, she hath no child yet.'

'No, she hath not', concluded Mother Dowe, 'they have put one to making.'

Her words were reported to the authorities and she was arrested, tried and, in August, sent to gaol. The local magistrates insisted that her case be tried *in camera*, in order to prevent her scandalous tales from reaching the public's ears. But it was too late: the stories were already circulating beyond Essex, and even ten years later there were persistent rumours that the Queen and Dudley had had a child. One man, Henry Hawkins, was punished for stating that 'My Lord Robert hath five children by the Queen, and she never goeth on progress but to be delivered.' By then, the authorities' patience was wearing thin; over the years many offenders had their ears cut off or suffered the same fate as Mother Dowe for spreading the slanders.

But even these harsh punishments did not silence the gossip, and ambassadors – particularly those from Spain – coming to England later in the reign heard these tales of royal bastards and believed them. One young man who appeared in Spain in the 1580s claimed to be the son of Elizabeth and Dudley, and King Philip went so far as to verify his claim; it was found to be fraudulent, but many were willing to believe in it, and some still do, even today, despite the evidence against its veracity.

On 2 July 1560, the war with Scotland was brought to an end by the signing of the Treaty of Edinburgh – for Cecil, a diplomatic triumph, achieved after weeks of tortuous bargaining. Under the terms of the treaty, the French agreed to withdraw from Scotland, leaving the government of that kingdom in the hands of the Scottish council, with the English and French undertaking not to interfere. In the name of Queen Mary, the French commissioners promised that she would renounce all claims to Elizabeth's throne and would cease to quarter the royal arms of England with her own. At last, the French had agreed to recognise Elizabeth as Queen of England. It did seem that a true foundation for peace had been arrived at, and that the threat of war had been removed. More importantly, Elizabeth's prestige had been much enhanced in the eyes of Europe. Cecil was well satisfied with what he had achieved.

Not so Elizabeth. In a series of letters to Edinburgh, she castigated him for not having secured the return of Calais, or for not forcing the French to reimburse the money she had spent fighting them in Scotland. Cecil's elation soon faded; he believed Dudley was behind her complaints and was out to discredit the Secretary. This might have been the case, but equally well Elizabeth had been pessimistic about the outcome of Cecil's mission, and may have been put out at being proved wrong.

Elizabeth was, in fact, enjoying the most glorious summer of her life. Freed from the threat of war, she now gave herself over to a season of revelry in the company of Dudley, neglecting her state duties in the process. At the end of July, she left Greenwich to go on progress, travelling by slow stages along the southern shores of the Thames and staying at great houses along the route. Dudley, as Master of the Horse, was much in evidence, but he was also to be seen at Elizabeth's side long after his official duties were done. They rode and hunted nearly every day, Elizabeth choosing the most spirited horses, and in the evenings there would be dancing and music-making. Whereas before she had flirted with other men besides Dudley, she now favoured him with all her attention to the point of being accused of being a wanton or an adulteress. The gossips reported that they spent whole days closeted alone together, and one courtier expostulated, 'Not a man in England but cries out at the top of his voice, this fellow is ruining the country with his vanity!'

There was, reported a Spanish envoy in Antwerp, much grudging on the part of the English nobles 'to see someone in such special favour, and the little regard the Queen hath for marriage'.

It was this 'little regard' that so worried Cecil: the related subjects of the Queen's marriage and the succession were never far from his mind, and even in Edinburgh, he took the trouble to write and express his hopes that 'God would direct your heart to procure a father for your children, and so shall the children of all your realm bless your seed.' Many of her subjects believed that Elizabeth was doing exactly as Cecil advised, but they deplored her choice.

At the end of July, after an absence of nearly two months, Cecil returned to court, expecting perhaps to receive a grateful welcome from his sovereign. But while his fellow councillors were warm in their congratulations, Elizabeth was cool and distant, and Dudley all-powerful and – contrary to his avowed principles – courting the goodwill and support of de Quadra, hoping to enlist Spanish support for himself in a bid to counter the Secretary's influence – all with the Queen's knowledge and approval. She had even declared that she wanted 'a swordsman' who would equal her 'scribes'.

Cecil realised with a sinking heart that he had been away too long. He apparently concluded that, during his absence, the relationship between the Queen and her favourite had undergone a fundamental change. Whatever he imagined this was alarmed him, but not so greatly as did the change in the Queen's attitude towards himself. She had shown no gratitude for his work in Edinburgh, and she had made it plain that she would not defray all his expenses, even though he was out of pocket on her account. Now, when he needed to consult her on state affairs, he would be told that she had gone out riding with Dudley. All the signs indicated that she meant to marry him, if he could be freed from his marriage.

Rumours of divorce – and worse – were still prevalent. A royal torchbearer was happily spreading a report of how the Queen, returning one evening from visiting Dudley at Kew, spoke warmly to her attendants of Dudley's praiseworthy qualities, and declared that she intended to bestow further honours on him. This led to speculation that he would have a dukedom conferred upon him, or that the Queen meant to marry him once he was free. It was all reported to the Privy Council and caused Cecil grave concern. He had no idea how far Elizabeth's relationship with Dudley had progressed and he could see her recklessly ruining her reputation and courting disaster.

The councillors debated the matter amongst themselves, deploring to a man the Queen's failure to marry one of her princely suitors. Some suggested that this was because she would brook no master; others believed she intended to use her marriage as a means of bargaining with her European neighbours; but most felt that it was of little use to contemplate a foreign marriage alliance, because they believed that Elizabeth had already decided to marry Dudley. The situation seemed so desperate that de Quadra expected a palace coup, and commented, 'The cry is, that they do not want any more women rulers, and this woman may therefore find herself and her favourite in prison any morning.'

Cecil, seeing his own career at an end, quickly became very depressed and, within a month, was seriously considering tendering his resignation, hinting as much in a letter to the Earl of Bedford. He planned to recall Sir Nicholas Throckmorton from Paris to replace himself as Secretary, and wrote to him, 'You must needs return. I dare not write that I might speak. God send Her Majesty understanding of what shall be her surety' – in other words, a prestigious foreign marriage alliance.

The Secretary also regaled Throckmorton and other English ambassadors abroad with a highly-coloured version of what was going on between the Queen and her favourite, intimating that it would be helpful if they could convey the disapproval of foreign governments, which might give Elizabeth pause for thought.

On 30 August, the court moved to Windsor. A week earlier, the Scottish Parliament had abolished the authority of the Roman Catholic Church and made the celebration of the mass in Scotland a capital offence. Instead, with the tacit approval of Queen Elizabeth, the Calvinist form of Protestantism became the official religion. The Scottish lords now hoped to consolidate their settlement by uniting Scotland with England through the marriage of Elizabeth to the Earl of Arran, notwithstanding the fact that Elizabeth had made it clear she was not interested in the match. The Scots were determined 'with tooth and nail' to bring it about, but before negotiations could proceed, something happened which brought state affairs in England to a near standstill.

Robert Dudley had never maintained a private establishment for himself and his wife. He had his house at Kew, given him by the Queen, but Elizabeth had made it clear that any reference to Amy Dudley was unpleasing to her, and was given to calling on her favourite un-announced, so Amy never came to Kew. Instead, she spent her time on long visits to the houses of relatives and friends.

Dudley and his wife had now been married for over eight years, but they rarely saw each other. The Queen insisted upon him being at court and he could only manage rare visits home. There is evidence that Amy made at least one visit to court, but it is unlikely that her presence was welcome. It was not unusual in those days for the wives of courtiers to remain in the country while their husbands served at court; it was possible for wives to reside at court, but the cost was enormous and the Queen discouraged the practice. She liked her male courtiers to dance attendance on her, not on their wives.

In the winter of 1558-9, Amy Dudley stayed with friends in Lincolnshire and Bury St Edmunds. In the spring, she travelled to Camberwell, south of London, to visit her mother's kinsfolk, the Scotts. Thereafter she seems to have stayed mainly at the house of William Hyde at Denchworth, near Abingdon, which still stands today, although it bears little resemblance to the house Amy knew. Dudley sent gifts to her there, all of which are listed in his account books: a hood, gold buttons, spices, venison, sewing silk, hosiery, a looking glass, and Holland cloth for ruffs. She was never in want of material things, and Dudley saw to it that her needs were provided for. Occasionally, he came himself to see her, although during 1560 those visits became less and less frequent.

We can deduce little of the relationship that existed between the couple from the records that remain. They had no children, nor is there any evidence that Amy was ever pregnant. Like most wives of her class, she diligently looked after matters of business concerning his lands and farms whilst her husband was away. She must have heard the gossip about his relationship with the Queen, but we do not know for certain how much it affected her.

Before midsummer 1560, Amy had moved again, for reasons that are obscure, this time to Cumnor Place, a house leased by Dudley's former steward, Anthony Forster, now the treasurer of his household and MP for Abingdon, from William Owen, the son of the late royal physician, Dr George Owen, who had served Henry VIII, Edward VI and Queen Mary. Mr Owen still lived in the house in his own apartments.

Situated near the road connecting Oxford with Abingdon, near a large village, Cumnor Place, which has long since disappeared, was a relatively small medieval house. Built of grey stone in the fourteenth century, it had once been part of a religious foundation, the summer retreat of the Abbots of Abingdon and an occasional sanatorium for its monks, and was a rambling, quadrangular building surrounding a central courtyard. Some accounts describe Cumnor Place as being a single-storeyed house, but at least three of its residents had rooms above the hall, so there must have been an upper floor. Set in pretty formal gardens, the building was in a good state of repair, thanks to the renovations made by Mr Forster – who later purchased it and is buried in the nearby church – and offered comfortable accommodation.

Amy brought with her some servants, as well as her personal maid,

Mrs Pirgo (or Pirto, or Pinto), and her companion, a Mrs Odingsells, the widowed sister of William Hyde, Amy's former host at Denchworth. Once they were all installed the house was rather crowded, for it also sheltered not only Mr and Mrs Forster (who was the niece of Lord Williams of Thame, who had been a friend to the Queen during Mary's reign) but also William Owen's elderly mother, Mrs Owen. Amy and Mrs Odingsells were assigned rooms in the west wing above the great hall, next to the apartment of Mrs Owen, whilst the Forsters had their own separate suite of rooms, as did Mr Owen. The Forsters, Hydes and Owens had long been acquainted with the Dudleys, were all related by marriage and were prominent in local society, into which they introduced Lady Dudley. Anthony Forster was a congenial host, being a cultivated and much-travelled man who loved music and could sing and play on the virginals with skill.

De Feria and de Quadra had both referred at different times to rumours that Amy Dudley was suffering from a 'malady in her breast' that was believed to be terminal. This may have been true, but all that we know for certain about her health is that, early in September 1560, she was very depressed. This depression could have been the result of hearing that her husband was only waiting for her to die so that he could marry the Queen, or it could have been caused by the knowledge that she herself was mortally sick.

The evidence for Amy's depression comes from two sources, the first being a statement by her maid, of which more later, and the second being the infamous tract *Leycester's Commonwealth*. This was a virulent attack on Dudley made by an anonymous Catholic writer in 1584, and was the chief source for most of the damaging – and often erroneous – stories that became attached to his name over the centuries, which are only now being refuted by modern scholars. *Leycester's Commonwealth* gives a highly embroidered account of the events of September 1560 that must be followed with caution. However, parts of what it recounts may be true, such as its claim that the Forsters and other members of the household at Cumnor Place were so concerned when they saw that Lady Dudley was 'sad and heavy' that they wrote to a Dr Bayly, the Queen's Professor of Physic at Oxford University, asking him to prescribe some medicine for her. Bayly refused absolutely to do so: he had heard the rumours, and, 'seeing the small need which the good lady had of physic, misdoubted (as he after reported) lest, if they poisoned her under the name of his potion, he might have been hanged for a cover of their sin'. In 1584, when *Leycester's Commonwealth* was published and quickly became notorious, Dr Bayly was still alive and renowned for his work, but he took no steps to deny that he had acted as the tract claimed. This indicates that the episode may indeed have happened, and, if so, it confirms just how widespread – and widely believed – was the gossip about the Queen and Dudley.

On Friday, 6 September, Bishop de Quadra arrived at Windsor Castle. On the 11th , he wrote for the Duchess of Parma, King Philip's sister, a report of what had taken place that weekend, but nowhere in it did he state the actual days on which the events he related occurred; however, it is possible to work out their chronology from the evidence in his report.

Saturday the 7th was Elizabeth's twenty-seventh birthday, and the ambassador hoped to be able to convey his master's congratulations, but she had something less felicitous to discuss. 'The Queen told me, on her return from hunting, that Lord Robert's wife was dead, or nearly so, and begged me to say nothing about it.' Her Majesty gave no details, and de Quadra seems to have assumed that Amy was dying of the breast cancer she had long been rumoured to have contracted. Because of the speculation that would naturally arise out of such a circumstance, it was natural for Elizabeth to enjoin de Quadra to silence.

On Sunday, the day after this interview, William Cecil dispensed with his usual caution and unburdened himself to de Quadra. That he should confide in the Catholic ambassador of Spain was unusual, and possibly significant, as will become clear shortly.

'After my conversation with the Queen', wrote the Bishop,

> I met the Secretary Cecil, whom I knew to be in disgrace. Lord Robert, I was aware, was endeavouring to deprive him of his place. With little difficulty I led him to the subject, and after my many protestations that I would keep secret what he was about to tell me, he said that the Queen was conducting herself in such a way that he was about to withdraw from her service. It was a bad sailor, he said, who did not make for port when he saw a storm coming, and for himself he perceived the manifest ruin impending over the Queen through her intimacy with Lord Robert. The Lord Robert had made himself master of the business of the state, and of the person of the Queen, to the extreme injury of the realm, with the intention of marrying her, and she herself was shutting herself up in the palace to the peril of her health and life.

What Cecil meant by this is not clear, since Elizabeth was out riding daily at this time – on her birthday, Dudley had reported that she was hunting with him every day from morning until night – but the Secretary may have been referring to the danger she was placing herself in by spending so many hours closeted alone with Dudley.

That the realm would tolerate the marriage, he said, he did not believe. He was therefore determined to retire into the country, although he supposed they would send him to the Tower before they would let him go. He implored me, for the love of God, to remonstrate with the Queen, to persuade her not utterly to throw herself away as she was doing, and to remember what she owed to herself and to her subjects.

Of Lord Robert, he said twice that he would be better in Paradise than here. He told me the Queen cared nothing for foreign princes. She did not believe she stood in any need of their support. She was deeply in debt, taking no thought how to clear herself, and she had ruined her credit in the City.

This was an exaggeration, but Cecil wanted to impress on de Quadra how Elizabeth was ruining herself and her realm for the love of her favourite.

Last of all, he said that they were thinking of destroying Lord Robert's wife. 'They had given out that she was ill' – did de Quadra at this point recall the Queen's conversation of the previous day? – 'but she was not ill at all, she was very well, and taking care not to be poisoned. God, he trusted, would never permit such a crime to be accomplished, or so wretched a conspiracy to prosper.'

At the very least, Cecil was stirring things up; at the worst, he was deliberately planting in the ambassador's fertile mind the notion that the Queen – whom he had served, and was to continue to serve, with loyalty and devotion – and her lover were plotting murder. The Secretary knew full well that his words would be reported and then repeated throughout the courts of Europe; the Queen and Dudley themselves would soon hear of them. If Cecil was so concerned about Elizabeth risking her reputation, he could not have done more to ruin it completely. But to de Quadra he appeared distraught, aware of his peril, and apparently bereft of his usual caution. In fact, what he was trying to do was bring the Queen to her senses, by fair means or foul. Not only his career, but the future of England and the Protestant settlement were at stake.

Cecil knew that, if Amy Dudley were to be murdered, her husband would be a free man; he also knew that the public outcry would be so great that Robert could never marry the Queen, since most people would believe he had killed his wife, even if he had not. And what Cecil wished to prevent was Dudley marrying the Queen. It was ironic that the one thing that could free the favourite for a royal marriage should be the same thing that would prevent him from achieving it.

De Quadra, having listened in astonishment to what the Secretary had to say, decided that there was no reason to disbelieve him, and undertook to raise these issues with the Queen, even though she had never taken his advice in the past. But before he had a chance to request an audience, events overtook him.

What was traditionally known as 'Our Lady's Fair' opened at Abingdon on Sunday, 8 September, and Amy Dudley gave all her servants permission to go. Indeed, she seemed unduly anxious that they should do so, for when some protested that it was not fitting to attend a fair on a Sunday, she sharply insisted that they obey her order. Nevertheless, Mrs Odingsells remained stubborn, declaring that it was unseemly for her to go to a place where she might have to rub shoulders with servants and ill-bred persons. Amy grew very angry at this, whereat Mrs Odingsells reasoned with her that, if she herself went to the fair, there would be no one at Cumnor Place with whom Amy could dine. Amy petulantly retorted that, as Mrs Odingsells was not a servant, she could do as she pleased; old Mrs Owen could bear her [Amy] company at dinner'. At this, Mrs Odingsells retired to her room and Amy's servants went off to Abingdon.

Around eleven a.m., dinner was served to Amy and Mrs Owen. The house was not otherwise deserted because, apart from Mrs Odingsells, Mrs Forster was also there at the time, and both these ladies had servants on duty. But the place was quiet, and everyone seems to have kept to their rooms or quarters.

When her servants returned to Cumnor Place late that afternoon, they were shocked and bewildered to find Amy Dudley's body at the foot of a shallow flight of stone steps that led from her rooms to the hall, with her neck broken. The author of *Leycester's Commonwealth* asserted much later that her head-dress and clothing were still in place and not disarranged, but this information appears nowhere in the contemporary records. The same author refers to the body being discovered at the foot of 'a pair of stairs', i.e. a staircase with a landing in the middle, which corroborates contemporary accounts.

A manservant, one Bowes, was dispatched at once to Windsor to convey the news to Dudley. The following morning, by a coincidence, he met on the way an important officer of Dudley's household, Thomas Blount, travelling in the opposite direction. Blount, whose tomb may still be seen in Kidderminster Church, was a distant relation of the Dudleys and had sometimes carried messages from husband to wife; he had been sent from Windsor that morning by Dudley on an errand to Cumnor Place.

When Bowes told him that their lady was dead 'by a fall from a pair of stairs', he did not turn back, but decided to continue his journey, proceeding at an unhurried pace and stopping for the night at an inn at Abingdon. He could have gone on to Cumnor but, as he later informed his master, he wished to discover 'what news went abroad in the country'.

At supper, he fell into conversation with the landlord, pretending to be a stranger en route for Gloucester, and inquiring 'what news was thereabout'. His host could talk of nothing but 'the great misfortune' which had taken place on the previous day less than a mile away. However, it was obvious that the man knew few details. Blount said he supposed that some members of Amy's household might be able to say what had happened, but the landlord replied that they would not, since they had all been away at the fair at the time she died, 'and none left with her'. He had heard how Amy had commanded them to go 'and would suffer none to tarry at home'.

Blount thought this sounded odd, but he kept his opinions to himself and asked the landlord for his views on what had happened, asking, 'What was the judgement of the people?'

'Some are disposed to say well, and some evil,' was the guarded reply. 'For myself, I judge it a very misfortune [i.e. accident] because it chanced at that honest gentleman's house: his great honesty doth much curb the evil thoughts of the people.' Blount realised that others might not be so charitable.

Meanwhile, Bowes had arrived at court on the morning of Monday 9 September, and, finding Dudley with the Queen, broke the news to them both. De Quadra recorded that Elizabeth was so shocked that she was almost speechless.

Dudley appeared genuinely bewildered at what had taken place. Learning from Bowes that Blount had gone on to Cumnor, he dispatched that evening a courier after the latter, with a letter for him and instructions to find out more details of his wife's death.

'Cousin Blount,' he wrote, 'the greatness and suddenness of the misfortune doth so perplex me until I do hear from you how the matter standeth, or how this evil should light upon me, considering what the malicious world will bruit, as I can take no rest. And, because I have no way to purge myself of the malicious talk that I know the wicked world will use, but one which is the very plain truth to be known, I do pray you, as you have loved me, and do tender me and my quietness, and as now my special trust is in you, that you will use all the devices and means you can possibly for learning of the truth, wherein have no respect to any living person.' He wanted a full inquiry into Amy's death, and he wanted it carried out by 'the discreetest and most substantial men, such as for their knowledge may be able to search thoroughly the bottom of the matter, and for their uprightness will earnestly and sincerely deal therein. As I would be sorry in my heart any such evil should be committed, so should it well appear to the world my innocency by my dealing in the matter.'

At the same time, Dudley sent another messenger to Norfolk, to inform his wife's relatives of her death. Amy's half-brother, John Appleyard, soon afterwards visited Cumnor Place to make his own enquiries.

On Tuesday, 11 September, de Quadra reported, in a postscript to his letter to the Duchess of Parma, that Elizabeth had ordered the news of Lady Dudley's death to be made public, the tragedy officially being attributed to accidental causes. The Queen then confided to the ambassador, in Italian, that Amy had broken her neck, adding, 'She must have fallen down a staircase.'

Anticipating what her subjects' reaction would be to the news, the Queen wasted no time in ordering an inquest to be held, and guessing that Dudley would be suspected of foul play, she immediately distanced herself from the tragedy and insisted that he leave court and go to his house at Kew, there to remain while he awaited the coroner's verdict.

Robert Dudley was devastated at what had happened, and fearful for his future. Like most people, he believed that Amy had been murdered, and although he exhibited few signs of grief at the loss of his wife, he was zealous in his efforts to uncover the truth surrounding her death, not only because he wished to see justice done, but also because he wished to clear himself – the prime suspect – of any complicity in it. To this end, he continued to insist that the most rigorous enquiries be made, knowing that the only way to exonerate himself would be in finding the real culprit.

But this was easier wished for than accomplished. On 10 September, Thomas Blount arrived at Cumnor Place to find not only his master's letter awaiting him, but also the coroner and his jury inspecting the scene of death. Blount told them of Dudley's earnest wish that they should carry out their investigation thoroughly and without respect of any person. He informed Lord Robert that the chosen jurymen seemed to be 'as wise and as able men, being but countrymen, as I ever saw. And for their true search I have good hope they will conceal no fault, if any be; for as they are wise, so are they, as I hear, part of them very enemies to Anthony Forster. God give them, with their wisdom, indifferency.' Already there were whispers that Forster had been Dudley's accomplice.

Blount then discussed the tragedy with the people living in the house. All he could report to Dudley was that they told the same story as the landlord, averring that her ladyship 'was so earnest to have her servants gone to the fair, that with any that made reason for tarrying at home she was very angry'. The quarrel with Mrs Odingsells was recounted, and it was clear that the servants felt that Amy's behaviour had been out of character. Blount wrote: 'Certainly, my lord, as little while as I have been here, I have heard divers tales of her that maketh me to judge her to be a strange woman of mind.'

Blount made a point of questioning Amy's maid, Mrs Pirgo, 'who doth dearly love her', and

in asking Pirgo what she might think of this matter, either chance or villainy, she saith by her faith that she doth judge very chance, and neither done by man or by herself. Lady Dudley was a good, virtuous gentlewoman, and daily would pray upon her knees, and at divers times Pirgo hath heard her pray to God to deliver her from desperation. Then, said I, she might have an evil toy in her mind.

In other words, she might have committed suicide.

'No, good Mr Blount', declared Pirgo, 'do not judge so of my words; if you should so gather, I am sorry I said so much. It passeth the judgement of man to say how it is.' Suicide, in those days, was regarded as a mortal sin leading to eternal damnation: truly the last refuge of the desperate. Blount seems to have felt that Pirgo was not denying that Amy had taken her own life, but regretting that she had confided in him. He himself apparently believed that suicide should not be ruled out, and he concluded his letter to Dudley by urging him to turn from sorrow to joy in his innocence, which fearless enquiry would soon reveal, and then 'malicious reports shall turn upon their backs'.

Whilst the coroner's investigation was being carried out, the Queen rarely appeared in public, but confined herself to her apartments, concealing her anxieties from her courtiers. On the few occasions when she did emerge, she appeared pale and agitated.

At Kew, Dudley fretted with anxiety, agitating helplessly over the coming coroner's verdict, while at a court throbbing with speculation his enemies drew the obvious conclusion and settled back to enjoy his discomfiture. Aware of what was being said about him – for he was allowed to receive visitors, among them his tailor come to fit him out in mourning – Dudley found the long hours of enforced idleness mental torture. His greatest fear was not that the finger of suspicion would be forever pointing at him, although that was bad enough, but that the Queen would decide never to admit him to her presence again. It was one thing to conduct an affair with a married man, but quite another to associate with one reputed to have murdered his wife.

Blount's letter reached Dudley on the 12th, and around the same time he received a surprise visit from William Cecil, who had been restored to the Queen's confidence almost as soon as the favourite was out of the palace door: it was natural that, at a time of crisis, Elizabeth should turn to her wise and reliable Secretary for advice and support. Cecil concealed his triumph well; he had come, he said, to offer his condolences on Lord Robert's sad loss, and he spent the visit murmuring the platitudes demanded at such times by convention and good manners.

Dudley was touched by Cecil's solicitude, and grateful for his apparent support, and soon afterwards he hastened to write to express his thanks for such kindness on the part of his rival and to enlist his help in asking the Queen if he could return to court:

> Sir, I thank you much for your being here, and the great friendship you have showed toward me I shall not forget. I am very loath to wish you here again, but I would be very glad to be with you. I pray you let me hear from you what you think best for me to do. If you doubt, I pray you, ask the question for the sooner you can advise me [to travel] thither, the more I shall thank you. I am sorry so sudden [a] chance should breed in me so great a change, for methinks I am here all this while, as it were, in a dream, and too far, too far from the place where I am bound to be. I pray you help him that sues to be at liberty out of so great a bondage. Forget me not, though you see me not, and I will remember you and fail you not.

Around the same time, Dudley wrote again to Thomas Blount, begging for news: 'Until I hear from you again how the matter falleth out in very truth, I cannot be quiet.' Then he wrote to the coroner's jury, urging them to do their duty without fear or favour.

On 13 September, Blount replied with the encouraging news that the jury, having taken great pains to uncover the truth, could find 'no presumptions of evil. And, if I judge aright, mine own opinion is much quieted.' Blount was now persuaded that 'only misfortune hath done it, and nothing else'. Dudley, anticipating the verdict, felt impelled to write to the foreman of the jury, Mr Smith, to see if he could glean any idea of how the official enquiry was progressing. Mr Smith's reply was non-committal.

Around this time Dudley received a sympathetic letter from the Earl of Huntingdon, his brother-in-law, who wrote: 'I understand by letters the death of your wife. I doubt not but long before this time you have considered what a happy hour it is which bringeth man from sorrow to joy, from mortality to immortality, from care and trouble to rest and quietness, and that the Lord above maketh all for the best to them that love Him.' These were conventional expressions of comfort for the bereaved, which may have expressed the family's view that Amy's death had been a merciful release from suffering.

Dudley's torment did not last long: a few days later the coroner pronounced a verdict of accidental death – we do not know the exact wording because no document relating to the inquest survives. The Queen's opinion, as expressed to a secretary, was that the verdict left no room for doubt, an opinion with which Cecil and others, including Robert's brother-in-law, Sir Henry Sidney, heartily concurred.

But for Dudley himself, this was not enough. He had hoped that the coroner's enquiry would expose Amy's murderer and thus clear his own name. Now, fearing that there was still room for others to draw malicious conclusions, he pressed for a second jury to be empanelled, so that the investigation could be continued. The Queen, however, whose relief was palpable, felt that one verdict was sufficient, especially since the coroner had acquitted Dudley from all responsibility for the tragedy. She did not hesitate to invite him back to Windsor, restoring him to full favour and making it clear that, as far as she was concerned, the matter was closed. As a mark of respect, she ordered the court into a month's mourning for Amy Dudley.

Others were not so certain of Dudley's innocence. While most people had been shocked at the news of his wife's death, many had not – given the rumours – been surprised. It was generally felt that the evidence laid before the coroner had been insufficient to exonerate the favourite from guilt, and that 'the very plain truth' remained to be exposed. On 17 September, a renowned Puritan minister, Thomas Lever, Rector of Coventry and Master of Sherborne Hospital, wrote to the Council to inform them that 'in these parts' the country was full of 'grievous and dangerous suspicions and muttering of the death of her which was the wife of my Lord Robert Dudley, and there must be an earnest searching and trying of the truth'.

This feeling persisted even after Dudley arranged a lavish ceremonial funeral for his late wife. Many had believed that her body had been buried with almost unseemly haste at the parish church near Cumnor Place, but there is no proof of this, as the church registers are lost. On 22 September, Amy's body was lying in state at Gloucester Hall in Oxford, and it was taken from there, on that day, and laid to rest beneath the choir of the Church of St Mary the Virgin in Oxford. The Queen sent her friend Lady Norris to represent her. Dudley did not attend, since custom decreed that the chief mourners at a funeral be of the same sex as the deceased. In 1584, in *Leycester's Commonwealth*, it was alleged that the preacher, in his sermon, referred to 'this lady so pitifully slain' but contemporary sources do not refer to this. In the twentieth century

Amy Dudley's coffin was exhumed and opened, but was found to contain only dust.

During the fraught days between her death and funeral, de Quadra had found it difficult to find out what was happening. Few courtiers would talk to him, and he heard only damning rumours and wild speculation, which led him to conclude, as did many other people, that the Queen had colluded in murder. 'Assuredly it is a matter full of shame and infamy. Likely enough a revolution may come of it. The Queen may be sent to the Tower, and they may make a king of the Earl of Huntingdon, who is a great heretic, calling in a party of France to help them.' It was obvious that if Elizabeth married Dudley now, she would launch herself on a headlong course to disaster. As for Dudley, rumour had condemned him of plotting to kill his wife even before Amy's death; predictably, few accepted that she had died of accidental causes.

How did Amy Dudley meet her death?

There is no dispute that she died as a result of a broken neck. She was found at the bottom of a staircase, and the obvious conclusion would have been that she had fallen down those stairs, and that her death was due, as Dudley's supporters asserted, to an act of God. Yet it was claimed at the time that the steps were too shallow to have caused a fatal injury, and this led many people to deduce that someone, with malice aforethought, broke her neck and then placed her body at the foot of the stairs to make her death appear accidental. Her husband, as we have seen, was the chief suspect.*

Leycester's Commonwealth openly accused Dudley of the murder, alleging that he hired an assassin to do the deed, and names this man as Richard Verney. Verney, who was Mrs Owen's nephew, had once been Dudley's page, and was staunchly loyal to him. *Leycester's Commonwealth* asserted that, by Lord Robert's 'commandment', Verney remained with her [Amy] that day [8 September] alone, with one man only, and had sent perforce all her servants from her to a market two miles off.' This was incorrect, as it was Amy herself who had sent her servants away, and they went to a fair. Nevertheless, the anonymous author claimed that

---

*Amy Dudley's half-brother, John Appleyard, would later let it be known that he possessed secret information about her death, but 'had for the Earl's sake covered the murder of his sister', hinting that Dudley, by then Earl of Leicester, was in some way implicated. But his motive was clearly the desire to profit financially, either from Dudley in return for remaining silent, or in the form of monetary rewards from the Earl's enemies. In 1567, suspected of fraud, Appleyard was committed to the Fleet Prison with orders to produce any relevant evidence concerning Lady Dudley's death, the Council having furnished him with a copy of the coroner's findings. Immediately, he backed down and stated he was fully satisfied that his sister's death had been an accident.

Verney, and the other man who was with him, could 'tell how she died.' Conveniently, Verney had since died himself, in London, raving incoherently about demons 'to a gentleman of worship of my acquaintance', and the mysterious accomplice was sent to prison for another offence and later murdered there because he had 'offered to publish' the truth about Amy's death.

It is impossible to check many of the details in this account since they are so vague. Verney's movements and whereabouts on 8 September cannot be traced. The only contemporary mention of him in connection with Dudley dates from the previous April, when the latter sent for Verney and Verney had to write and apologise for not being able to come. He added, 'I and mine shall always be to my best power advanced in any your affair or commandment where opportunity offereth.' It would be unwise to read too much of significance into these words.

It is, of course, possible that Verney's aunt Mrs Owen was privy to a murder plot; it was she with whom Amy dined on that day, and she who was the last recorded person to see Amy alive. Possibly Amy had already arranged to dine with Mrs Owen when she ordered her servants to go to the fair. Could Mrs Owen have persuaded her that there was a good reason why they should be alone? It is perhaps significant that there is no record of Amy being angry with Mrs Owen for staying at home.

Amy was certainly unusually anxious to be rid of her servants. Was she expecting a secret visitor? Could that visitor perhaps have been someone sent by her husband to discuss an annulment of their marriage? Such a development had been rumoured that year, and in view of the damage such rumours could do, it would have been natural for Robert to insist that Amy receive her visitor in private, with perhaps the discreet Mrs Owen present as a witness or chaperone. Or was Amy led to believe that a visitor was coming, when something more sinister was planned? On the other hand, one could also speculate that she was so depressed, and possibly so ill, that she was desperate for some peace and quiet with a sympathetic friend to whom she could confide her fears, without the constant presence of servants about her.

We should consider the behaviour of Mrs Odingsells, who stoutly refused to go to the fair, much to Amy's chagrin. Was she in league with those who sought to do Amy harm, or even with Mrs Owen? Had these two ladies, about whom we know very little, conspired to help an assassin? Was Mrs Odingsells deputed to let him in, while Mrs Owen kept Amy occupied at table, or with the game of backgammon that she was said to have been playing before she died? There are no answers to these questions, for they are mere speculation and theory.

If Amy was murdered before being laid at the foot of the stairs, how was it done? When Cumnor Place was converted into a gentleman's house after the Dissolution of the Monasteries, some building work was carried out and several doors were blocked up. There was a tale current after Amy's death that she had been persuaded – by whom is not clear – to lodge in a room that had a secret doorway behind the bedhead. It was through this doorway, it was claimed, that her murderer came into the room. Or perhaps the killer came upon her as she sat at table with Mrs Owen.

Some time after Amy's death, Anthony Forster was rewarded for good service by Robert Dudley, who gave him lands in fifteen counties, enabling Forster to purchase Cumnor Place and virtually rebuild it. Some believed, then and later, that Forster had been Dudley's accomplice in the murder, and that this was his reward, but there is no other evidence for this. When Forster died in 1572, Dudley bought the house from his heirs, having been given the option to do so in Forster's will. Why he should have wanted Cumnor, with its unpleasant associations, is not clear.

Several people, notably Blount, attributed Amy's death to suicide. She had been depressed and, according to her maid, in a state of near desperation before she met her end. Robert's neglect and his very public relationship with the Queen could have accounted for this, or Amy could have been in the last stages of breast cancer, suffering pain for which there was no palliative then, as well as the resulting emotional trauma. The theory that she took her own life is therefore a credible one, and would explain why she was so anxious to get her servants out of the house.

No one at the time thought to attribute Amy's death to natural causes, but since 1956, when a new theory was suggested by Professor Ian Aird, most modern historians have done so. Aird considered the possibility that Amy was suffering from breast cancer; the 'malady in one of her breasts' had first been referred to by de Quadra in April 1559. This disease, as it progresses, causes in about fifty per cent of sufferers a weakening of the bones due to cancerous deposits that break away from the original tumour and are carried through the bloodstream to settle on the bones, particularly the spine, which becomes unnaturally brittle. Thus, if Amy was in the last stages of the disease, even the slight exertion required to walk down a flight of stairs could have caused a spontaneous fracture of the vertebrae. However, if this theory is correct, it offers no explanation of Amy's unusual behaviour on the day of her death. Nor does the less commonly accepted modern theory, that she suffered from an aortic aneurism, the terminal enlargement of an artery from the heart, which causes pain and swelling in the chest, and mental aberrations – including depression or fits of anger – resulting from erratic blood-flow to the brain. Sudden slight pressure can cause the bursting of the aneurism, bringing instantaneous death. The resultant fall could, in Amy's case, have caused her neck to break.

Whether due to natural causes or not, Amy Dudley's death was certainly convenient, but not, ironically, for the person whom many supposed expected to benefit from it. Most people believed that her husband had killed her in order to marry the Queen, and thus far he had a motive for doing so. Yet even he, thick-skinned as he often was, could not have been so stupid as to think he would get away with it, and if she were indeed dying of cancer, he had no need to do anything. On the day before her death, the Queen told de Quadra that Lady Dudley was dead, or nearly so. If Elizabeth was involved in a murder plot, she was hardly likely to announce the death of the victim before she was certain that it had happened, or even refer to it — she was far too clever for that. Yet her announcement would make more sense if she had been told by Dudley that the end was near. The behaviour of the Queen and Dudley after the event suggests that they were both shocked and bewildered by the news, and both did their utmost to ensure that Amy's death was thoroughly and objectively investigated.

That Dudley's chief concern was to clear his own name is understandable, given what people were saying about him, and it proves that he was well aware of what the consequences would be, and what was at stake if a credible explanation was not arrived at. It was in his interests that his wife should die a natural death, and the evidence suggests that she might shortly have done so. He was hardly likely to have gone to the trouble of having her killed, or allowing her body to be left in such suspicious circumstances.

The Queen did not interfere in the coroner's enquiry, and if she appeared to be initiating a damage limitation exercise after the verdict, that was understandable, since tongues had not been stilled and were deeminq her guilty by association because of her intimacy with Dudley. If she had had any real wish to marry him now that he was free, it was unlikely that she would be able to do so and hold on to her throne. Some of her courtiers, knowing how she had so far shied away from marriage, were of the opinion that the news of Lady Dudley's death was not welcome to her, since Lord Robert might now begin to press his suit in earnest, and even though she loved him, she might not be prepared to surrender her independence. Such an impasse could only cause conflict, and the courtship dance that she had so perfected with her foreign suitors might not serve her so well when it came to a man with whom she was emotionally involved.

The fact remains that there is no factual evidence whatsoever to implicate either the Queen or Dudley in his wife's death. Neither gained anything but trouble and ill-fame from it, and the almost universal belief in his guilt was to bedevil Dudley until the end of his days.

One man did profit from the death of Amy Dudley, and that was William Cecil. He was swiftly restored to favour as soon as the news was known and his rival banished from court, and when he visited Dudley at Kew he did so in the comfortable knowledge that their positions had been reversed and that he now had the upper hand. In such circumstances he could afford to be magnanimous.

Of all those involved in the power struggle in 1560, Cecil was the one with the strongest motive for wishing Amy Dudley dead. He was a perceptive man, and he could foresee that if she died in suspicious circumstances, as many people expected her to do, then the finger of suspicion would point inexorably to her husband — as indeed it did. Cecil also knew that Elizabeth, who was very conservative at heart, would be unlikely to risk her popularity and her crown to marry a man whose reputation was so tainted.

In September 1560, Cecil had seen Dudley in the ascendant and his own future in ruins; he feared not only for his position, which he had attained only after years of hard work and loyalty to the Tudor dynasty, but also for the future of England and the Anglican Settlement. If the Queen married Dudley it would irrevocably weaken her tenure of the throne, and could even lead to her deposition, or, worse, a bid by foreign powers to replace her with the Catholic Mary Stuart. Cecil had tried to warn Elizabeth that she was plunging headlong into disaster, but she had not listened, and he was afraid for her, afraid that she would marry Dudley and so wreck everything that Cecil had struggled to achieve. It is not, therefore, inconceivable that it was William Cecil who decided upon a course that, although regrettable, would force Elizabeth to stop and think.

Cecil was a realist and a pragmatist. It is possible that, when he heard Dudley and the Queen giving out that Amy was very ill he decided to act quickly; it would be essential for people to believe that she had been murdered. Cecil was not a cruel man, and could have reasoned that, since she was dying of a painful disease, cutting short her sufferings could only be an act of mercy. Having laid his plans, he told de Quadra on the morning of 8 September that it was not true what Elizabeth and Dudley were saying: Amy Dudley was quite well. Then, knowing that his words would echo around Europe, he confided that Dudley was plotting to kill her, thus planting the seeds of suspicion before the deed was done. He begged the Bishop to dissuade Elizabeth from marrying Dudley, but of course, there would be no need for this, and nor did de Quadra get the opportunity.

It would have been easy for Cecil, with the co-operation of an accomplice at Cumnor Place – perhaps Mrs Owen or Mrs Odingsells – to invent a pretext to keep Amy at home on the afternoon of the 8th. Given her perilous state of health, it would have been the work of a moment for a hired assassin to break her neck and then lay her body at the bottom of the stairs. Cecil did not normally resort to violence, but he might have felt that such an act would have been more than justified by its beneficial consequences.

There is, of course, no direct evidence to support such a theory, but the fact remains that Cecil had a compelling motive for doing away with Amy, and was the person who profited most from her death. He himself, being a patriotic man, dedicated to the service of the state, would have said that it was his country and his Queen who had been the chief beneficiaries.

6

'Dishonourable and Naughty Reports'

Gossip about Dudley's alleged responsibility for the death of his wife spread rapidly, and in pulpits all over the country, preachers 'harped on it in a manner prejudicial to the honour and service of the Queen'.

Soon, it was the talk of Europe. From Paris on 10 October, Sir Nicholas Throckmorton wrote to Cecil that he had learned of the 'strange death' of Amy Dudley. In fact, the news was already being loudly bruited about the French court, with the most unfavourable conclusions being drawn, and in a private letter to the Marquess of Northampton, Throckmorton confided,

> I wish I were either dead or hence, that I might not hear the dishonourable and naughty reports that are made of the Queen, and the great joy among the French princes for the success they take it they are like to have in England – not letting to speak of the Queen and some others, that which every hair on my head stareth and my ears glow to hear. One laugheth at us, another threateneth, another revileth the Queen. Some let not to say, 'What religion is this, that a subject shall kill his wife, and the prince not only bear withal but marry with him?' If these slandrous bruits [rumours] be not slaked, or if they prove true, our reputation is gone forever, war follows, and utter subversion of the Queen and country.

Sir Nicholas said that his heart bled for his mistress, and he prayed that, for the sake of England's security and prestige, and the Queen's own reputation, she would not 'so foully forget herself' as to marry Dudley – a prayer echoed by English ambassadors at other courts.

Thomas Randolph wrote from Edinburgh that what he had heard 'so passioneth my heart that no grief I ever felt was like unto it'. By the end of October, weary of the malicious tongues of the French courtiers, Throckmorton thought fit to inform Cecil that it was generally accepted in France that Amy Dudley had been murdered by her husband; Mary Stuart herself had cattily commented, 'So the Queen of England is to marry her horse-keeper, who has killed his wife to make room for her!' Knowing that most people believed Elizabeth to have been an accomplice to murder, Throckmorton stressed 'how much it imports the Queen's honour to have the reports of Amy's death ceased', and warned: 'We begin already to be in derision and hatred for the bruit only, and nothing taken here more assured than our destruction; so, if it take place, God and religion, which be the fundaments, shall be out of estimation, the Queen our Sovereign discredited, condemned and neglected, our country ruined, undone and made prey.'

Similar damning conclusions were drawn elsewhere in Europe. Some people believed that Dudley had already married the Queen in secret. The Protestant princes of Germany were especially horrified, since they had looked to England as an ally and now saw Elizabeth apparently hell-bent upon self-destruction.

De Quadra informed Throckmorton, 'The Queen your mistress doth show that she hath honour but for a few in her realm, for no man will advise her to leave her folly.' No one had the courage to tell her that she should renounce Dudley. Although Elizabeth was aware of what was being said about them both, she felt nothing but indignation, which was apparent when Throckmorton sent his secretary, Robert Jones, to ask for advice from the Council as to how to counteract the rumours in France, and hopefully dissuade the Queen from marrying Dudley.

Jones thought Her Majesty looked 'not so heavy and well as she did by a great deal. Surely the matter of my Lord Robert doth much perplex her.' She told Jones that his visit was unnecessary, but he recklessly proceeded to try and convince her of the folly of marrying Dudley, only to have her round on him in a temper and declare, 'I have heard of this before!' When he tried to remind her how Dudley had been involved in Northumberland's conspiracy to set Lady Jane Grey on the throne seven years earlier, Elizabeth just laughed at him. In desperation, he revealed to her what was being said about her and Dudley in France, to which she responded spiritedly, 'The matter has been tried and found to be contrary to that which is reported.' Dudley had been at court when his wife died, and none of his people were present at the 'attempt at his wife's house; and it has fallen out as should neither touch my lord's honesty nor my honour'.

Elizabeth's reference to 'the attempt' has been seen as evidence that she did not accept the verdict of accidental death, or, worse, as a slip of the tongue that revealed guilty knowledge of Amy's murder. It could also have been an innocent, unthinking response to Jones's reports of French rumours, which assumed that an attempt on Amy's life had been made. It was, moreover, hardly accurate for the Queen to refer to 'his wife's house', but she was in a heated mood at the time and paying little attention to niceties of detail.

The rumours would not be stilled. It was said that the Queen was secretly betrothed to Dudley or that she was already expecting his child. Time proved these rumours false, but the story of Amy Dudley's death was continually embroidered and embellished, eventually passing into legend. Dudley's enemies made several attempts during the late sixteenth century to revive the scandal, with its details growing ever more lurid each time. Even in the reign of Elizabeth's successor a play performed in London would make reference to it, with the claim that 'the surest way to chain a woman's tongue is to break her neck; a politician did it'. Centuries later, the story would reach its apotheosis in Sir Walter Scott's highly fanciful novel, *Kenilworth*, which places Amy's death during Elizabeth's visit to Kenilworth Castle in 1575 and surrounds it with the most devious intrigues. Even today, tales are told of a clergyman being called to exorcise a pool at Cumnor which is allegedly haunted by the ghost of poor Amy Dudley.

In the middle of October, the court came out of mourning and speculation mounted as to whether Elizabeth would indeed marry Lord Robert. 'With these people, it is always wisest to think the worst,' de Quadra opined to the Duchess of Parma. Only the Earl of Sussex advocated the marriage; although he loathed and resented Dudley, he was desperately concerned about the succession, and felt that any husband was better than no husband for Elizabeth. However, no one else supported this view.

Rumour aside, if the Queen did decide to make Dudley her consort, she would be taking herself out of the European marriage market and abandoning her chance of making a match that would bring political and economic advantages to England; it might not, even now, be too late to revive plans for an alliance with either the Archduke Charles or the Earl of Arran, provided she dissociated herself from Dudley. More importantly, from her point of view, her marriage was the most advantageous asset she had, the means whereby she could keep other princes' goodwill and help maintain the balance of power in Europe.

There was also the question of Dudley's suitability as a husband; he had been vastly unpopular even before his wife's death, and were the Queen to marry a subject – which in itself could cause jealousy and faction fights amongst her courtiers, and even lead to civil war, given the strength of public feeling against the favourite – she would, in the eyes of the world, be degrading her royal rank.

Her cousin, the Duchess of Suffolk, had, after the execution of her husband in 1554, married her steward, Adrian Stokes, and suffered a humiliating loss of status as a result. Elizabeth was supremely conscious of her own royalty, and valued it too highly to debase it. Much as she loved Dudley, she was aware that his rank precluded him qualifying as a suitable consort.

Above all, there remained the risks she would incur by marrying him, and her oft-declared aversion to the married state. Single, she remained in control and kept the upper hand in their relationship; once married, their roles would be reversed, even though she was the Queen, and Elizabeth regarded any threat to her independence with horror. Moreover, if she did not marry Dudley, then she would prove the rumours false and dissociate herself from the scandal.

On a personal level, Elizabeth's feelings for Dudley had emerged unscathed from the scandal. When he returned to court, it was as if nothing had changed between them, and, far from being defeated by the rumours and gossip, Lord Robert was as self-confident and proud as before. The inquest had officially cleared his name, and now that he was a free man, he saw nothing improper in his courtship of the Queen. His behaviour gave rise to persistent reports that they would marry, which flourished side by side with speculation that a foreign marriage for Her Majesty was about to be announced. Elizabeth loved being at the centre of such intrigues, and was as usual non-committal and evasive on both issues.

Cecil, growing daily more confident, believed that there was little cause for concern. He was aware how much Elizabeth had struggled with her emotions during the past weeks, but he knew that her political judgement was as acute as ever, and that, although she would not renounce Dudley's company, it was now unlikely that she would marry him. Knowing that any implied criticism of Dudley would be unwelcome, Cecil had wisely refrained from burdening her with too much advice, but gave her time in which to reflect upon the available choices.

He also wrote warning Throckmorton to cease putting pressure upon her, as he had seen that attempts to convince her of Lord Robert's unsuitability as a consort only made her angry and more determined to favour and protect him. Katherine Ashley's husband had recently made derogatory remarks about Dudley, and Elizabeth, in a fit of temper, had banished him from court, whereupon Mrs Ashley had gone weeping to Dudley and persuaded him to sue for her husband's reinstatement.

Elizabeth was indeed torn, but she was also sensible of the duties and obligations of sovereignty, and when it came to reaching a decision, she compelled her head to rule her heart. It might not have been such a difficult decision: Dudley may have seemed to her infinitely more desirable and less of a threat as a married man than as a free one, and whilst Throckmorton and others agonised over the future, she had already made up her mind.

As early as 15 October, Cecil confided to de Quadra that the Queen had told him that she would not marry Dudley. In November, it was announced that she intended to raise him to the peerage; in fact, Dudley had badgered her to do so until she reluctantly gave in. The relevant Letters Patent were drawn up, but when it came to the ceremony of investiture, according to Robert Jones, the Queen astonished everyone, and shocked Dudley, by taking a knife and 'cutting [the papers] asunder', stating that she would not have another Dudley in the House of Lords since his family had been traitors for three generations. This was unlikely to have been an impulsive gesture, but one calculated to proclaim to the world – and to Dudley – that Elizabeth, aware of public opinion, meant to remain in control of her destiny and had made up her mind not to marry him.

Dudley glowered and begged her not to abuse him thus in front of her courtiers. She merely patted his cheek, saying teasingly, 'No, no, the bear and ragged staff are not so soon overthrown' – a reference to the heraldic crest borne by his father and brother as earls of Warwick. Talk of her action spread rapidly, and her courtiers were gleeful and exultant to see Dudley so discomfited. Some of his friends and supporters tried to persuade the Queen to abandon her scruples and marry him, but she made a 'pup with her lips' and declared that she would not marry a subject. When they objected that she could make her husband a king, she answered, 'No, that I will in no wise agree to.' She did intimate that she would create Dudley Earl of Leicester on Twelfth Night, but later changed her mind and decided it would be unwise for the time being.

Never again, when it came to the game of courtship, would Elizabeth allow her private feelings to undermine her good sense. She had realised, in good time, that if she abrogated her moral authority as queen, she would lose all respect and credibility, and even the throne itself. Thus the crisis passed, and before November was out, Robert Jones noticed that the gossip was dying a natural death. Dudley remained at the Queen's side, consort in all but name, but Elizabeth was firmly in control now. She had his constant presence, his loyalty and the stimulation of his company. It is tempting to conclude that she had perhaps never been serious about wanting more than that.

Meanwhile, another royal scandal was brewing. Although Elizabeth had refused to acknowledge her as such, according to Henry VIII's Act of

Thanks be to God for his indescribab

Succession, Lady Katherine Grey was next in line to the throne.

Katherine, the beauty of the Grey sisters, was now twenty. The Queen had never liked her, and had downgraded her and her sister Mary from their positions as ladies of the Bedchamber, to which they had been appointed by Queen Mary, to ladies of the Privy Chamber; Katherine's loud protests had availed her nothing. She was an ambitious young woman, and had enlisted the support of successive Spanish ambassadors, who saw in her a means to restore the Catholic faith to England. Although Katherine had been brought up as a Protestant, she had made a point of embracing the Catholic faith under Queen Mary, and after Elizabeth's accession, the Count de Feria had conceived a plan to marry her to King Philip's son, Don Carlos, stage a coup, and set her on the English throne, thereby uniting England and Spain under Spanish rule. It is not hard to see why Elizabeth regarded her kinswoman as a menace.

Before he left England, de Feria had enjoined Katherine not to marry, but to remain single until he could arrange a grand dynastic marriage for her. However, early in 1559, whilst staying with her mother at Hanworth in Middlesex as a guest of the Duchess of Somerset, widow of Edward VI's Lord Protector, Katherine had met and fallen in love with the Duchess's eldest son, Edward Seymour, Earl of Hertford. The Duchess of Suffolk, seeing this, suggested that they marry; already she was scheming against the time when her family's fortunes might be revived through another daughter's claim to the throne, and she realised that young Hertford would prove popular with the people, who revered his father's memory. Katherine, in the first flush of love, was only too happy to go along with her mother's plans.

There was one seemingly insurmountable barrier to the marriage: given her attitude towards those of her relatives who were near in blood to the throne, the Queen would hardly be likely to give her permission, and under an Act passed in 1536 by Henry VIII it was treason for persons of royal blood to marry without the consent of the sovereign. Lady Suffolk nevertheless resolved to petition the Queen, but she fell ill and died in November 1559, before being able to do so. Katherine was too frightened of the Queen to dare approach her on the matter; word of Spanish ambitions on her behalf had reached Elizabeth's ears, and Katherine was obliged to tread very warily.

Cecil, however, had found out about her affair with Hertford, and realised that their marriage would put paid to any Spanish intrigues. Thus he was prepared to give them his support.

Then came more damning, and unfounded, rumours that Katherine was going to marry the Earl of Arran with the intention of uniting the thrones of England and Scotland. At this point, Elizabeth realised that she dare not alienate her young cousin for fear of driving her into the arms of her enemies, so she restored her to her former position as Lady of the Bedchamber and went out of her way to be amiable to her – 'to keep her quiet', as de Quadra drily put it. 'She even talks about adopting her,' he added, noting that Katherine was now referred to as Her Majesty's 'daughter'. The Bishop had also heard gossip that credited Lady Katherine with yet another potentially dangerous suitor, the Earl of Huntingdon.

Katherine was not interested in any of these great matches; she was secretly meeting Hertford in private, escaping from under the Queen's nose to do so. His sister, Lady Jane Seymour, one of Elizabeth's maids of honour, was thrilled at the prospect of her brother marrying the heiress to the throne, and acted as go-between, accompanying Katherine on her nightly visits to her lover's house in Cannon Row, Westminster. And when the Earl came to Whitehall Palace, it was Lady Jane who contrived that they were alone together, giving up her own tiny bedchamber that led off the Maidens' Chamber. It was here that Hertford asked Katherine to marry him in secret. 'I like both you and your offer,' she answered. 'I am content to marry with you.'

One morning in late November or early December 1560, while the Queen was away hunting at Eltham in Kent, the lovers seized their opportunity. Having excused herself from accompanying the royal party by pleading toothache, Lady Katherine walked with Lady Jane along the banks of the Thames to Cannon Row, while Hertford dismissed all his servants for the day. Jane had arranged for a priest to come to the house and perform the ceremony, but he failed to turn up. Ever resourceful, she found another, said to have been a Catholic, and with only herself as witness, a ceremony of marriage took place. When the priest departed, Jane, 'perceiving them ready to go to bed', left the newlyweds alone for two hours before returning to walk back with Lady Katherine to Whitehall. On arrival, they joined the other courtiers for dinner, no one being any the wiser as to where they had been.

That November, Francis II, King of France developed a virulent ear infection. After weeks of agony he died on 6 December, and was succeeded by his ten-year-old brother, Charles IX. Real power, however, now lay in the hands of the new regent, the Queen Mother, Catherine de' Medici, and the Guises found themselves thrust into the background.

Mary Stuart was left a widow at only eighteen years old, and the question of her future had to be settled. She was devastated by her young husband's death, but there was no question but that she should remarry after a suitable period of mourning. In the meantime she had a country to rule, and it was not long before the Queen Mother, jealous of Mary's status and influence, was urging her to return to Scotland. Mary's Guise relations suggested several possible husbands, but Catherine vetoed them all, knowing that any one of these marriages would keep Mary in France.

In England, Elizabeth's cousin, Margaret Douglas, Countess of Lennox, heard the news of King Francis's death, and immediately conceived the idea of putting forward her son, Henry Stewart, Lord Darnley, as a likely consort for the Scottish Queen. Without telling Elizabeth, she sent Darnley to France to press his suit, but it was too soon for Mary, who was in no fit state to consider any future husband. Moreover, the Queen found out about Lady Lennox's intrigues, and when Darnley returned home she had them both placed under house arrest in London.

Elizabeth was naturally concerned about the change of government in France. Francis and Mary had repeatedly refused to ratify the Treaty of Edinburgh, and had continued to use the royal arms of England; relations between England and France had therefore become rather strained, but it soon became apparent that the new regime had neither the interest nor the resources to cause trouble for Elizabeth.

That December, death also claimed Elizabeth's Comptroller, the ageing Sir Thomas Parry. He had also held the lucrative office of Master of the Court of Wards, which Dudley coveted, but in January 1561, Elizabeth, with wise caution, bestowed it upon William Cecil. By March, the Earl of Bedford was able to comment, 'The great matters whereof the world was wont to talk are now asleep, having had some fits, both hot and cold.'

Dudley had certainly been feeling out in the cold. Cecil told. Throckmorton, 'Whatever reports or opinion be, I know surely that my Lord Robert hath more fear than hope, and so doth the Queen give him cause.' But Dudley had not given up all hope of marrying Elizabeth, and he actively set about increasing his following. He knew that the Queen had been most concerned about reaction in Spain to the recent scandal, yet he was also aware that Philip II had envisaged that she might marry a subject and that Philip would wish to remain on good terms with that subject in order to advance the Catholic cause in England. Dudley therefore decided to seek Philip's support for his marriage to the Queen. Elizabeth may well have agreed to this plan, or even suggested it, for different motives: she knew that, if the Catholic powers could be led to believe that she privately wished to restore the old faith in England, they would not agitate for her excommunication.

In January, Dudley sent his brother-in-law, Sir Henry Sidney, to convey to de Quadra his assurances that, if he married the Queen, the Catholic faith would be restored in England, and Dudley 'would thereafter serve and obey [King Philip] like one of his own vassals'. Sidney revealed to de Quadra that Elizabeth had tired of 'the tyranny of Cecil' and was anxious to 'put religion right'; he stressed 'how much inclined the Queen was to the marriage' and suggested that it would be helpful if King Philip could do his best to persuade her to reconsider her decision not to marry Dudley. This was a strange stance for a man who had already set himself up as the champion of the Protestant faith to adopt, but with Dudley ambition ruled all: he had not paused to consider the consequences to himself if his intrigues became public.

Although de Quadra had consistently taken the view that the scandal surrounding Dudley had made him a less than suitable candidate for the Queen's hand, he was nevertheless aware that, if they married, bitter faction fights would arise in the court amongst the ruling Protestant elite, which would ensure that the oppression of Catholics would no longer be a priority. However, he responded to Sidney's startling revelations with scepticism.

'What I have heard so far of this matter has been of such a character that I have hardly ventured to write two lines to His Majesty about it, nor have the Queen or Lord Robert said a word to me that I could write,' he said stiffly. 'I have no means of guessing the Queen's thoughts, and although my master is always anxious to be helpful, his advice has been consistently disregarded in the past.'

Sidney was obliged to concede this point, but protested that if de Quadra 'was satisfied about the death of Lord Robert's wife', he saw no reason why the Bishop should not report Dudley's assurances to King Philip, since, although the Queen and Dudley had indulged in 'a love affair, the object of it was marriage'. De Quadra pointed out that, although Dudley had been cleared of any involvement in his wife's death, many people did not believe he was innocent. Sidney agreed that this was the chief obstacle to the marriage, but stressed that he was sure Amy Dudley's death had been accidental – 'He had enquired with great care, and knew that public opinion held to the contrary.'

Sir Henry went on to acknowledge that not only the marriage of the Queen and Dudley, but also the relaxation of sanctions against the English Catholics would prove impossible without Philip's support. Once that was assured, 'things would be very different, and the Queen and Dudley would do all they could to restore religion without delay'.

Despite de Quadra's summing up of Sidney as an honest man, he could not but remember how Lady Sidney had hoodwinked him over the matter of the Archduke Charles, with Elizabeth's connivance, and he suspected that there was a hidden agenda behind this intrigue also. However, on 13 February, Sidney brought Dudley himself to a private interview with de Quadra, in which the favourite confirmed all that

Sidney had said, after which the ambassador was sufficiently convinced that a Dudley marriage would be in Catholic interests to say so to King Philip in his next dispatch.

Philip responded favourably to the plan, but he did not trust Elizabeth and insisted that de Quadra 'get it in writing with her signature' before matters were carried any further. The ambassador duly saw the Queen, but she was evasive when he said he was glad to hear that she was contemplating marrying Dudley.

'After much circumlocution, she said she wished to confess to me and tell me her secret in confession, which was that she was no angel, and did not deny that she had some affection for Lord Robert, for the many good qualities he possessed, but she certainly had never decided to marry him or anyone else, although she daily saw more clearly the necessity for her marriage, and to satisfy the English humour it was desirable that she should marry an Englishman.'

'What would King Philip think', she asked, with a twinkle in her eye, 'if I married one of my servitors?'

'My master would be pleased to hear of your marriage, whoever Your Majesty chooses, as it is important for the welfare of your kingdom,' de Quadra assured her. 'His Majesty, I feel sure, would be happy to hear of Lord Robert's good fortune. I have always understood that King Philip has a great affection for him, and generally holds him in high esteem.' De Quadra noted that Elizabeth 'seemed as pleased at this as her position allowed her to be'.

Cecil, however, was not pleased to find out what was going on. In March, he asked de Quadra to obtain from King Philip a letter supporting the Dudley marriage. The Queen, he explained, did not wish to do anything without the goodwill of her subjects, and would use the letter as an excuse to summon Parliament and lay the proposal before them. Cecil knew it was a foregone conclusion that Parliament would reject any candidate of Philip's out of hand, and de Quadra knew it too, and began to suspect that the whole episode had been a plot to discredit the Catholics. In the middle of April, his suspicions were apparently confirmed when he was accused of involvement in a Catholic conspiracy against the Queen; several notable recusants were arrested, and it was bruited abroad that King Philip had undertaken to support a Dudley marriage if Elizabeth would acknowledge the supremacy of the Pope over the English Church. Not surprisingly, this provoked a furore, but there was in fact precious little evidence that such a conspiracy had ever existed. In all likelihood, it had been the invention of Cecil, out to discredit Dudley and prevent him from marrying the Queen.

Cecil was so successful at stirring up anti-Catholic feeling at court during the following weeks that Dudley soon perceived that if his dealings with de Quadra became known, he might well face ruin. He realised now that his intrigue had been detected and that there could be no question of official Spanish backing for the marriage.

Although Elizabeth had assured de Quadra that she did not believe he had been involved in the alleged conspiracy, Cecil continued to make life difficult for the Bishop. His secretary was suborned into spying on him, his letters were intercepted and read, his visitors followed and watched, and he was accused of sending defamatory dispatches to Spain.

Dejected, Dudley asked his friends what he should do, and a few even advised him to go and live abroad. His spirits were vastly uplifted, however, when the Queen assigned to him a sumptuous apartment at Greenwich, next to her own, which prompted him – and, unfortunately, others – to speculate that she had done so in order to ensure that they could enjoy intimacy in private. To Dudley, it seemed in the summer of 1561 that he might yet achieve his ambition of being consort, even without Spanish help. By May he had abandoned his flirtation with the Catholics and henceforth remained a staunch advocate of Protestantism, proudly boasting that 'There is no man I know in this realm that hath showed a better mind to the furthering of true religion than I have done.'

There was more to this than met the eye, for by playing the religious zealot and patriot, Dudley hoped to proclaim himself an ideal consort for the Queen, whilst at the same time demonstrating that his influence could be every bit as beneficial as Cecil's. And to a degree he was successful: although Amy Dudley's death had not been forgotten, from around this time onwards, people ceased to regard him as a mere favourite, and statesmen like Cecil realised that it was in their interests to remain on good terms with him. However, Cecil never ceased to fear that Elizabeth might change her mind and marry Dudley, and from time to time was driven to employing subtle means to sabotage the latter's chances.

For her part, Elizabeth kept Dudley – and everyone else – guessing. One evening in June, de Quadra was a guest on the royal barge when the Queen attended a splendid water pageant on the Thames. 'She, Robert and I being alone on the galley, they began joking, which she likes to do much better than talking about business. They went so far with their jokes that Lord Robert told her that, if she liked, I could be the minister to perform the act of marriage, and she, nothing loath to hear it, said she was not sure whether I knew enough English.' The dignified Bishop was not amused by this, and after he had 'let them jest for a while' he stiffly pointed out that the Queen should extricate herself from the tyranny of William Cecil and her other advisers, and then restore the true religion. If she could accomplish this, she could marry

Dudley as soon as they pleased, because with King Philip's support, no one would dare oppose their union. Elizabeth, who could not afford to lose Philip's goodwill, affected to be interested in his suggestions.

That summer, most observers thought that the Queen's love for Dudley was 'as great as ever'. Although there were reports that Erik of Sweden was coming in person to renew his courtship, they believed that there was only one serious contender for Elizabeth's hand, although it was characteristic of Elizabeth to provoke Dudley by commenting, when shown a new portrait of Erik, that if the King was as handsome as his portrait, no one could resist him.

Secure in his love, she could deliver a cruel put-down. When, a few years later, Charles IX's ambassador informed her and Dudley that his master thought that they should marry and wished to meet Dudley, Elizabeth retorted, 'It would scarcely be honourable to send a groom to see so great a king.' Then she laughed, and said, 'I cannot do without my Lord Robert, for he is like my little dog, and whenever he comes into a room, everyone at once assumes that I myself am near.'

If Dudley grew tired of this treatment, he did not show it, nor for many years did he contemplate any alternative marriage. Elizabeth kept him bound to her by lavish patronage – she granted him a pension of £1000 per annum in October 1561 – lucrative offices, privileges, informal but real political influence, manifest signs of favour – and hope.

In March 1561, just after Lord Hertford had left on a diplomatic mission to France, Lady Katherine Grey had discovered herself to be pregnant. On 23 March, her friend and accomplice Lady Jane Seymour died, aged just twenty, probably of tuberculosis; the Queen ordered that she be buried in Westminster Abbey with great ceremony, but her passing left Katherine alone to face the consequences of her rash marriage.

To her husband, she wrote desperately, 'I am quick with child. I pray you therefore to return and declare how the matter standeth between us.' In the meantime, she had to put on a brave face and continue with her duties at court, praying that her condition would not show.

By July, however, this was a vain hope. That month, the Queen went on a progress through East Anglia, and Katherine was one of those chosen to attend her. By the time they reached Ipswich, she was in great distress at the suspicious glances of court matrons, and took the extraordinary liberty of seeking out Dudley in his bedchamber in the middle of the night, knowing that he was the one person who might be able to mitigate the Queen's wrath. Kneeling by his bed and weeping, she confessed all and begged him to help her. Dudley, realising that what she was telling him could have disastrous consequences for the succession, told her to leave. Distraught, she went to the room of an old family friend, Elizabeth Cavendish, Lady Saintlow – who had served Elizabeth as a lady in waiting since Mary's reign and became better known in later years as the formidable Bess of Hardwick – but met only with an angry tirade against her utter foolishness, and a refusal to incur the Queen's displeasure by becoming involved.

The next morning, Dudley informed the Queen of her cousin's crime, and thereafter Katherine was in deep disgrace. Elizabeth took the view that, apart from having placed the succession in jeopardy, her cousin's weakness in having succumbed to an affair of the heart made her an unsuitable heir to the throne. She also saw the affair as evidence of a conspiracy against the Crown, although there was never any proof of that. Cecil concluded that Katherine's illicit pregnancy was a sign that God was displeased at the prospect of a Grey claimant succeeding to the throne.

When the court returned to Whitehall in August, Katherine was imprisoned in the Tower and Lord Hertford was summoned home, admitted paternity of the child, and joined his wife there, being housed in a separate cell. They were not allowed to meet. On 24 September, Katherine gave birth to a son, Edward Seymour. News of the birth of a male claimant to the throne only made the Queen more incensed against the couple, for she feared that Katherine's ability to produce a son might make her a more attractive prospect as queen in the eyes of the people. In order to make it impossible for the infant to be set up as a rival claimant, Elizabeth ordered that a commission, headed by the Archbishop of Canterbury, should investigate the validity of the marriage.

The commissioners examined the prisoners separately and rigorously, demanding details of their 'infamous conversation' and evidence to substantiate their 'pretended marriage', but of course there was none. The only witness was dead and the priest could not be traced. Hertford had referred to Katherine as his wife in a deed of jointure, but she had lost it. In 1562, after months of investigations, the commission pronounced the union null and void and its issue illegitimate, and, for their 'undue and unlawful carnal copulation', the offending couple were sentenced to imprisonment in the Tower at the Queen's pleasure. Fortunately, Elizabeth had not demanded the full penalty for treason which the law provided for.

However, Katherine Grey's disgrace signalled the end of any hopes that she might have had of being designated Elizabeth's successor, and it strengthened the Queen's resolve never to name her heir: that September she told the new Scots ambassador, William Maitland of Lethington, that she thought it was unreasonable of her subjects 'to require me in my own life to set my winding sheet before my eye'.

Nevertheless, there was a certain amount of sympathy for Katherine; her marriage was regarded as valid, and it was felt that she and Lord Hertford had been too 'sharply handled'. Their supporters believed that, if the Queen had done her duty by marrying and producing an heir of her own, the proceedings against these young people would have been unnecessary.

7

'The Daughter of Debate'

Mary, Queen of Scots had since 1558 considered herself the rightful Queen of England; in fact, her chief preoccupation was her interest in the English succession, and she had therefore consistently refused to ratify the Treaty of Edinburgh, which denied her the right to be even 'second in the kingdom' as Elizabeth's heir. She had also declined to acknowledge Elizabeth's title as Queen of England, and continued to flaunt the English royal arms quartered with her own. It was because of this that in the summer of 1561 Elizabeth refused Mary a safe-conduct through England on her way home to Scotland. She later changed her mind, but by then Mary had taken ship from France and landed at Leith, the port of Edinburgh, on 19 August.

Mary's return to the kingdom she had not seen for twelve years perturbed Elizabeth in several ways. Apart from the dynastic threat posed by her cousin, who was regarded by many Catholics in Europe as having a better title to the English throne than Elizabeth, there was the possibility of religious conflict north of the border: Mary had told the Pope that she intended to restore the Catholic faith in her Scottish kingdom.

On a more personal level Elizabeth regarded Mary as her rival: younger than Elizabeth, and reputedly more beautiful, Mary's widowhood meant that the Queen of England was no longer the most desirable match in Europe. It was universally assumed that Mary must marry again, and her choice of husband was also a matter of concern to her cousin, who feared the arrival of a powerful foreign Catholic prince in the neighbouring kingdom. Above all, the near-proximity of the Catholic claimant to the throne posed a continuing threat to the Queen's security. These preoccupations, and the rivalry between the two female sovereigns, were to become the focal points of Anglo-Scots relations for the next quarter of a century.

*

Born in 1542, Mary had succeeded her father James V within a week of her birth. In order to escape Henry VIII's 'rough wooing' of her as a bride for his son, the future Edward VI, she was sent at the age of five to the French court, where she was educated with the children of Henry II, becoming betrothed to the Dauphin Francis. Her formative years were spent in a luxurious and stable environment, quite the opposite to that in which her cousin Elizabeth grew to maturity.

Mary's education followed traditional lines in many respects. She was imbued with a deep reverence for the Catholic faith, and taught the accomplishments then considered desirable in a well-born woman. Unlike Elizabeth, she was no bluestocking, preferring the bawdy satires of Rabelais, or courtly verse of Ronsard, to weightier works in Latin or Greek. She was brought up to speak and write French as if it were her native tongue, and was taught only a smattering of Italian, Spanish, and Latin, which she could understand but not write. When she returned to her native land, she could remember just enough Scots to carry on polite conversations with Sir Nicholas Throckmorton and John Knox, though she made efforts to improve her command of the language. Although Henry II had groomed Mary as the future Queen of France, Scotland and England, he had not thought fit to have her taught any English, and she did not learn it until well into adult life.

The Queen who returned to Scotland was to all intents and purposes an elegant and graceful Frenchwoman, able to compose stylish sonnets and produce exquisite needlework and embroideries, of which many examples still survive today; she was also an accomplished calligrapher. Always exquisitely dressed, she loved music, dancing, ballets and masques, and was an excellent horsewoman.

Having lived at the French court, she was quite worldly-wise, and there is no doubt that she was extremely attractive to men, which the dour John Knox referred to as 'some enchantment, whereby men are bewitched'. Despite her virtuous reputation, her romantic and impulsive nature led her, however innocently, to encourage men, and because she was a notoriously bad judge of character, this could sometimes have disastrous results: a few tried to take liberties, and others would later cause her worse grief. Moreover, although she was accomplished at exerting her famous charm over even the soberest of men, she found that the opposite sex were more than a match for her when it came to the business of ruling her kingdom. Her own ambassador to England, William Maitland of Lethington, told Thomas Randolph that Mary lacked the mature judgement and political experience of Elizabeth.

At six feet, Mary was exceptionally tall in an age when people were generally shorter than they are today. She was also slim, and had a very pale complexion, frizzy chestnut hair and brown eyes. Her slightly oriental features were somewhat marred by an over-long nose, inherited from her father. Graceful and dignified in her bearing, she was yet considered to be a most approachable monarch. She was kind and loyal to her friends, and her servants adored her.

Mary was an indomitable woman with strongly-held convictions and the courage to defend them, but she lacked practical experience in the art of government. Ever at the mercy of her emotions, she was subject to mood swings, and rarely hid her feelings. When things went well, she was buoyant with happiness, but setbacks or stress could plunge her into so lachrymose a depression that one English ambassador was driven to describe her as 'a sick, crazed woman'. The unkindness of others could reduce her to the point of collapse, and there were times when she spent days in bed recovering from nervous strain – which was regarded as very odd by many of her contemporaries. Unlike Elizabeth, Mary did not enjoy robust good physical health, but was intermittently ill, often with a mysterious pain in her side. It is possible that these ailments were of an hysterical origin.

For Mary, the kingdom of Scotland came as something of a culture shock after the refinement and luxury of the French court. Scotland was remote from the rest of Europe and had been largely by-passed by the civilising influence of the Renaissance. The climate was chilly and the nobility, who lived in primitive castles and peel towers, uncouth and violent. The religious settlement was strictly Calvinist, and despite the generally warm welcome she received from her subjects, Mary was soon being lectured by John Knox on the 'idolatry' of her masses, which she openly heard in the royal chapels. Knox, whose sermons made Mary weep with anger, feared that the Queen might try to effect a Counter Reformation, but the ruling Protestant clique were prepared to tolerate her Catholicism, having been snubbed – as they saw it – by Elizabeth's failure to marry Arran and ally herself with them. For her part, Mary did not understand the Scots people, nor did she perceive how much, after their struggle with her mother, they hated all things French. To many of them, she seemed a foreigner.

Nevertheless, she was willing to make compromises, and was soon announcing that there should be liberty of worship for all her subjects. Her conciliatory approach found favour with the Scots lords and before long she had established a strong following amongst them.

For the first few years of her reign, Mary's chief adviser was her older half-brother, James Stuart, whom she created Earl of Moray in 1562. Moray was one of King James V's numerous bastards, and had come to prominence as one of the Lords of the Congregation who had masterminded the Scottish Reformation of 1560. Despite this, Moray had vigorously taken the Queen's part against John Knox, by insisting on her right to hear mass in her private chapel, and for this she rewarded him with her confidence. Thereafter, until she married, she followed his guidance in ruling Scotland

Elizabeth's feelings towards Mary were ambivalent: on the one hand she saw her as a dangerous rival, and on the other she felt a great affinity with her as another female sovereign and as her cousin. Because of this, she decided that, if Mary showed herself willing to renounce her pretensions to the English throne, then she, Elizabeth, would be her friend. Although the Council advised against it, she insisted that she should meet with the Scots Queen, believing that, face to face, they would between themselves resolve the vexed question of the succession and possible misunderstandings over the Treaty of Edinburgh.

It was not long before Mary came to the same conclusion. She had cause to resent Elizabeth, who had done much to help establish the Protestant religion in her kingdom, but Mary also realised that friendly personal relations between herself and Elizabeth could only be advantageous. Her continued refusal to ratify the Treaty of Edinburgh stemmed partly from fear that renouncing the right to use the arms of England might prejudice her future chances of succeeding Elizabeth. Moray and the Scots lords advised her to come to an agreement with her cousin: in return for Mary's renunciation of her claim to the English throne, Elizabeth might be persuaded to recognise her as her heiress presumptive. When this was reported to Elizabeth, she characteristically hedged, whilst Cecil privately shuddered at the prospect of yet another female on the throne after the decease of its present impossible occupant.

Mary sent William Maitland to England with friendly greetings and instructions to ask Elizabeth if she would be prepared to revise the terms of the Treaty of Edinburgh. After a warm welcome, he wasted no time in asserting Mary's claim to be acknowledged as heiress presumptive to the English throne. Elizabeth did not hide her disappointment.

'I looked for another message from the Queen your sovereign,' she said. 'I have long enough been fed with fair words.' No, she went on, she would not meddle with the succession.

'When I am dead, they shall succeed that have most right,' she declared. 'If the Queen your sovereign be that person, I shall never hurt her; if another have better right, it were not reasonable to require me to do a manifest injury.' However, she conceded that she knew of no better title than Mary's, and that if she could avoid a public declaration of her intentions, which might prejudice her security since 'more people worship the rising than the setting sun', she had no objection to naming Mary as her successor. Nevertheless, Henry VIII's will and the Act of Succession might preclude her from doing so, and any claim Mary might make would have to be debated in Parliament. 'I am sworn, when I was married to the realm, not to alter the laws of it,' the Queen reminded Maitland. It would be better, she went on, if Mary tried to win the love of the English by showing herself a friendly neighbour; then they might be better disposed to regard her as the rightful heiress.

Even so, the matter was fraught with dangers.

'Think you that I could love my winding sheet, when, as examples show, princes cannot even love their children that are to succeed them?' Elizabeth concluded. 'I have good experience of myself in my sister's time, how desirous men were that I should be in place, and earnest to set me up. It is hard to bind princes by any security where hope is offered of a kingdom. If it became certainly known in the world who should succeed me, I would never think myself in sufficient security.'

This was quite unsatisfactory from Mary's point of view, but it was nevertheless a friendly and reasonable reception of her request, and it paved the way for more cordial dealings between the two queens.

On 17 September Elizabeth wrote again to Mary to demand the ratification of the treaty, but Maitland, during a second audience at which he was less conciliatory, warned her that if Mary was not named heiress to the crown, she might try to take it by force. He reminded Elizabeth that, 'Although Your Majesty takes yourself to be lawful, yet are ye not always so taken abroad in the world.' The Queen was so unnerved by this stark appraisal that Maitland was able to wring from her the assurance that she would review and alter the wording of the treaty. Cecil was naturally unhappy about this, since it had, after all, been his handiwork; he distrusted Mary for her Catholicism and her pretensions to the English throne, and he told Elizabeth so in candid terms, so that she was soon regretting having conceded so much.

By December, she was urging that she and Mary should meet soon to discuss their differences, and she wrote again to Mary, suggesting this. Mary responded warmly, expressing her delight at the prospect of seeing her 'dearest sister' face to face, and taxing Thomas Randolph minutely as to Elizabeth's 'health, exercise, diet and many more questions'. Gazing at her cousin's portrait, she 'said she wished that one of them was a man, so that their kingdoms could be united by marital alliance'.

'I think the Queen shall be able to do much with her [Mary] in religion if they once enter in a good familiarity,' Maitland told Cecil hopefully. What he did not express was his suspicion that Mary would be no match intellectually for Elizabeth, a fear shared by several of Mary's advisers. But such meetings were not arranged overnight, and there followed several months of letters and diplomatic negotiations, during which time the two queens grew increasingly impatient, so enthusiastic were they at the prospect of a personal encounter.

Maitland wrote to Cecil: 'I see my sovereign so transported with affection that she respects nothing so she may meet with her cousin, and needs no persuasion, but is a great deal more earnestly bent on it than her counsellors dare advise her.' Both the Scots and the English lords were loudly protesting at the expense of funding a state visit by Mary to England, and Elizabeth's advisers were warning her that the climate of political opinion in France, which was then strongly anti-Guise, was against the visit. But Elizabeth would not listen: in her opinion, much good could come out of a meeting with Mary, and that hope outweighed the risk of offending the French.

There were also compelling personal reasons underpinning Elizabeth's desire to see her cousin. Being inordinately vain, she was curious to see if Mary was as beautiful as reported, and also eager to find that she was not. Elizabeth was jealous of her reputation as the most desirable catch in Europe, and could not bear competition. When a German diplomat told her that Mary was reputed to be very lovely, she retorted that that could not be so as 'she herself was superior to the Queen of Scotland'.

In England, Elizabeth's popularity had survived the Dudley scandal. On 8 September 1561, when she arrived to take up residence at St James's Palace in London, ten thousand people turned out to see her, 'such was their gladness and affection for her'.

That autumn, Erik of Sweden again offered himself as a future consort for the Queen, but although she appeared to encourage him for a time, she only did so, according to de Quadra, to prevent him from switching his attentions to Mary, Queen of Scots. But it was not long before even this hitherto dauntless suitor lost interest and gave up. Seven years later Erik was to be deposed by Duke John of Finland, who would have him murdered in 1577.

Dudley's star was still in the ascendant. In November 1561, Elizabeth was observed, wearing a disguise, leaving Whitehall by a back exit to watch him take part in a shooting match. On 26 December, the Queen restored to his brother Ambrose Dudley the earldom of Warwick, once held by his father and late brother, together with Warwick Castle and huge tracts of land in the Midlands, while on 22 December, Dudley was admitted to membership of the Inner Temple of the Inns of Court, whom he had supported in a land dispute. Five days later he presided over a magnificent gathering in the great hall of the Temple, while on the next day, plays were performed there, all with a common theme, that the Queen should marry Dudley.

Dudley himself was still occasionally hopeful that this might come to pass, but the ambassador of the Duke of Saxony reported to his master that Elizabeth had told him 'that she had never thought of contracting a marriage with my Lord Robert, but she was more attached to him than to any of the others, because when she was deserted by everybody in the reign of her sister, not only did he never lessen in any degree his kindness and humble attention to her, but he even sold his possessions that he might assist her with money, and therefore she thought it was just that she should make some return for his good faith and constancy'.

Dudley wanted more than that. In January 1562, he again approached de Quadra with a plea that King Philip endorse his suit for Elizabeth's hand by a written recommendation. This time, he did not insult the Spaniards by pretending that his conversion to Catholicism would follow, but merely hinted that the French were offering him substantial bribes to use his influence with the Queen on their behalf. However, de Quadra was not to be fooled a second time. He smoothly replied that Her Majesty was already aware that King Philip was anxious to see her married and she knew too that he had high hopes of Dudley. Therefore a letter such as his lordship suggested would be quite unnecessary. As de Quadra saw it, the real stumbling block was the Queen's inability to reach a decision about her marriage; he himself would raise the matter with her again, if Dudley wished it.

Dudley did, and soon afterwards the Bishop was inquiring of the Queen whether she had made up her mind to marry.

'I am as free from any engagement as the day I was born,' she told him, adding that she had resolved never to accept any suitor she had not met, which meant, she realised, that she would have to marry an Englishman, 'in which case she thought she could find no person more fitting than Lord Robert'. What she wanted, she continued, were letters from friendly princes, including King Philip, recommending that she marry Dudley, so that her subjects could never accuse her of choosing him in order to satisfy her own desires. This, she said, was what Dudley himself wanted.

De Quadra was, unsurprisingly, suspicious of her motives, and 'in a joking way' he sidestepped her request and advised her not to hesitate any longer, but to satisfy Dudley without delay, because he knew that King Philip would be glad to hear of it. In reality, both de Quadra and King Philip knew that by marrying Dudley Elizabeth would be sacrificing both status and reputation, which would weaken her position and perhaps leave the way clear for a strong Catholic claimant – such as was now to be found just north of the border.

Around this time, Elizabeth restored to Dudley many of the lands once held by his father, giving him the means to maintain his position. Later in the year she granted him a lucrative licence to export woollen cloth free of duty. Once again, rumour had it that she meant to marry him, and by June it was common talk in London that they had secretly married at Baynard's Castle, the London residence of Dudley's friend, the Earl of Pembroke. The Queen found this all very amusing, and took pleasure in teasing de Quadra, telling him how her ladies had asked her if they were now to kiss Dudley's hand as well as hers. Dudley himself was going about openly saying that Elizabeth had indeed promised to marry him, 'but not this year'.

The Council accused de Quadra of spreading the story of the secret marriage, but he denied that he had done so, declaring that he was only sorry he could not inform anyone that the Queen was married.

By the spring of 1562, the Countess of Lennox and her son, Lord Darnley, had been released from house arrest in London and received back into favour by the Queen. But Lady Lennox was a woman of powerful ambitions, and it was not long before she resumed her intrigues to marry Darnley to Queen Mary, thereby uniting two claims to the English throne, a prospect that had already alarmed Elizabeth considerably. This time, however, the Countess went too far, for her plans hinted at the deposition of the Queen. Her plotting was soon uncovered, and for her suspected treasonable designs she was arrested and sent to the Tower.

In May, after months of frustrating negotiations, Mary sent Maitland back to England with instructions to procure an invitation for her to make the proposed state visit soon. Elizabeth told Maitland that there was now nothing to delay her meeting with his sovereign, whereupon a jubilant Mary wrote to the Duke of Guise, 'You can think how astonished others will be when they see us, the Queen of England and me, according so well!'

Unfortunately, a religious war between Catholics and Huguenots had just erupted in France, prompting Sir Nicholas Throckmorton and Robert Dudley to urge Elizabeth to offer full support for the oppressed Huguenots, who might in return be able to assist her towards the recovery of Calais, a fulfilment of one of her dearest dreams. Throckmorton warned her that a meeting with the Catholic Mary, a relation of the Guises, would be impolitic at this time.

Mary was dismayed when she heard that the project might be abandoned, but Elizabeth was reluctant to become embroiled in a foreign civil war and resolutely insisted on going ahead with the meeting, arguing that many benefits would result from it. Her Council, however, when ordered to finalise plans for the state visit, strongly advised her not to meet with Mary at present because to do so would only identify her with, and so strengthen, the Guise cause, bringing further suffering to the French Protestants who she should be succouring. But Elizabeth was obstinate. Unless Throckmorton advised her otherwise, she declared, 'go she would' to meet Mary, and that was an end to the matter.

Preparations for the visit were set in train, although unseasonably wet weather that rendered the roads impassable held things up. Not surprisingly, someone – Sir Henry Sidney – 'groaned and lamented' in an urgent letter to Throckmorton, pointing out that only he could dissuade the Queen from her disastrous purpose, and begging him to use his persuasive powers to good effect. But before Throckmorton could respond, the religious conflict in France ended in an uneasy peace on 25 June, and the way was left clear for the two queens to meet.

Two weeks later Elizabeth and Maitland discussed the final plans for Mary's visit, which would take place at York, or another northern city convenient to the Scots Queen, between 20 August and 20 September, and Maitland then hastened north to acquaint Mary with the details. In York, the civic authorities were already buying in vast stores of provisions to meet the needs of the two royal retinues, and plans were made for a series of tournaments, whilst courtiers on both sides of the border ordered new clothes, most of them grumbling at the expense.

Six days later, Throckmorton sent an urgent message to inform the English government that, despite Catherine de' Medici's efforts to preserve the peace, civil war had broken out again in France. This time Elizabeth knew she could not allow the Huguenot leaders, the Prince de Condé and Admiral de Coligny, to be thrown to the wolves without intervening to help them. She had been dismayed to hear that Mary was actively encouraging her Catholic relations to overthrow the Huguenots, and on 15 July, she reluctantly dispatched Sir Henry Sidney to Scotland to inform the Scots Queen that her visit must be postponed for a year. The effect on Mary, who had nurtured great hopes of the meeting, was to cause her to take to her bed and remain there weeping all day, only rallying when Sidney managed to convince her that Elizabeth was as disappointed as she was.

Unlike Elizabeth, Mary had definitely resolved to marry, preferably a powerful Catholic prince who would intimidate Elizabeth into revising the Treaty of Edinburgh in Mary's favour. Elizabeth was aware of her intentions, and they caused her the gravest concern, since the Queen of Scots' attraction lay not only in her present status, but also in her expected future inheritance. If Mary were to marry a prince of the royal houses of Spain, Austria or France, Elizabeth would have the Catholic threat brought right to her back doorstep, her chief fear being that Scotland might then be used as a springboard for an invasion of England.

Elizabeth had therefore decided to use her subtle powers of persuasion to influence Mary to take a less dangerous husband, one preferably of Elizabeth's own choosing. She had even suggested to Maitland that

Mary might marry a member of the English aristocracy, but he had dismissed that idea, saying that his sovereign would never consider any match that might diminish her reputation.

In fact, Mary had set her sights on Don Carlos, Philip II's heir, whom she had heard described at the French court as a brave and gallant prince, but who was, in reality, a sadistic degenerate who suffered epileptic fits. She was not interested in Charles IX – he was too young – nor in the Archduke Charles of Austria – he was too poor.

Elizabeth, of course, had no desire to see Mary married to the heir to Catholic Spain, and warned Mary that, if she went ahead with it, she, Elizabeth, would ever afterwards be her enemy. 'Consider well your steps,' was her advice; if Mary chose a husband agreeable to the English, Elizabeth would be her good friend for life.

Two months later, Elizabeth signed a treaty pledging her assistance to the Huguenots, who in return placed their port of Newhaven (later renamed Le Havre) in English hands as surety for the future restoration of Calais, which they hoped to wrest from their enemies.

Elizabeth's patriotic sentiments had been fired by the prospect of recovering Calais, and in October 1562, she gave orders for the mustering of a force of six thousand men, whose commander was to be Ambrose Dudley, Earl of Warwick; they were to sail to Newhaven and Dieppe and reinforce the Huguenot armies in the region.

However, before she could give the order for her soldiers to leave for France, the Queen fell so dangerously ill that her life was despaired of.

8

'Without a Certain Heir'

Smallpox was exceptionally virulent during the early years of Elizabeth's reign, and in the early 1560s reached epidemic form, seeming to single out 'aged folks and ladies': the Countess of Bedford and hundreds of lesser folk had recently succumbed to it. Smallpox was a dreaded disease, not only because it was life-threatening, but also because those who did survive it were often left horribly disfigured. Thomas Randolph described the early symptoms as being 'a pain in their heads that have it, and a soreness in their stomachs with a great cough'.

Queen Elizabeth was at Hampton Court when, on 10 October 1562, she first felt unwell. Believing, as many did then, that it would effect a cure, she immersed herself in a bath, then took a bracing walk outdoors; as a result, she caught a chill. Within hours, she had taken to her bed, running a high temperature.

Dr Burcot, a respected but irascible German physician, was summoned to examine her. He diagnosed smallpox, but there were no spots, and the Queen dismissed him for a fool. No eruptions appeared, which many believed betokened the onset of a serious attack, and a day or so later the fever grew worse. By 16 October she was very ill indeed, first becoming incapable of speech and then lapsing into an unconscious state in which she remained for twenty-four hours. The royal doctors, fearing that her death was imminent, sent urgently for Cecil to come down from London.

The next night, Elizabeth drifted in and out of consciousness as the crisis approached, and there was a hurried convening of an anxious Privy Council, whose members were all panic-stricken over the unresolved matter of the succession. If the Queen died, as most believed she would, who should succeed her? Over the next few days there were urgent discussions, with the councillors, according to de Quadra, divided in their opinions: extreme Protestants favoured Lady Katherine Grey, while moderates supported the Earl of Huntingdon, who had no near blood relationship to the Queen. The rest wanted the judiciary to determine the matter. Not one spoke in support of Mary, Queen of Scots. But a consensus was lacking, which hinted at deep divisions and boded ominously for the future.

As the court prepared to go into mourning, Lord Hunsdon persuaded a reluctant Dr Burcot – some said at the point of a dagger – to resume his treatment of the Queen. Following a curative measure first used by the Arabs and recommended by the English medieval physician John of Gaddesden, Burcot ordered that she be wrapped in red flannel, laid on a pallet beside the fire, and given a potion of his devising. Two hours later, Elizabeth was conscious and able to speak.

Fearfully, the councillors gathered around her bedside. She was aware that she was dangerously ill – 'Death possessed every joint of me,' she told a parliamentary delegation soon afterwards – and her chief concern was to make provision for the government of England after her death. Turning *in extremis* to the one man she felt she could trust, she commanded the councillors to appoint Robert Dudley Lord Protector of England, with the magnificent salary of £20,000 per annum. She also asked that his personal servant, Tamworth, who slept in his room, be given a large pension of £500 per annum. Many people thought, then as now, that this was to buy the silence of one who had stood guard while the Queen and Dudley were alone, but Elizabeth, anticipating that adverse conclusions would be drawn, declared 'that, although she loved and always had loved Lord Robert dearly, as God was her witness, nothing unseemly had ever passed between them'. It is hardly likely that one who believed she would shortly be facing divine judgement would have lied over such a matter.

Although the councillors were much dismayed by her commands, 'everything she asked was promised', for nobody wished to distress her with any arguments, since she was 'all but gone', but, according to de Quadra, 'it will not be fulfilled'. It was obvious that the appointment of Dudley as Lord Protector could only provoke a bitter power struggle.

Shortly afterwards, Dr Burcot entered the royal bedchamber with some medicine, and it was at this point that Elizabeth groaned as she noticed that the first red eruptions of smallpox had appeared on her hands.

'God's pestilence!' swore the doctor at his august patient. 'Which is better? To have a pox in the hand, or in the face, or in the heart and kill the whole body?' The spots, he told the anxiously hovering councillors, were a good sign, and indicated that the worst was over. Soon, the pustules would dry out, form scabs and fall off.

From then onwards, to the profound relief of the Council and her subjects at large, Elizabeth improved rapidly – Randolph wrote that she was in bed for six days only – but it had been a near thing, and her grateful subjects issued a coin to mark her recovery. Her brush with Death, 'the blind Fury with the abhorred shears', brought home to them as nothing else could that only her life, which could be snuffed out at any time, stood between peaceful, stable government and the uncertainties of a disputed succession, which could easily lead to civil war. The scare left both councillors and Members of Parliament determined to force the Queen to marry and provide the country with an heir without further dithering or fruitless prolonging of courtships and diplomatic negotiations.

Throughout her illness, Elizabeth had insisted that only her favourite ladies attend upon her, and none nursed her more devotedly than her friend, Lady Mary Sidney, wife of Sir Henry, and sister to Dudley. But while the Queen's pockmarks eventually faded, Lady Mary caught the dreaded smallpox and emerged from it so hideously scarred that she never appeared publicly at court again. Sir Henry Sidney was abroad throughout her illness, and later wrote, 'When I went to Newhaven, I left her a full, fair lady, in mine eyes at least the fairest, and when I returned, I found her as foul a lady as the smallpox could make her, which she did take by continual attendance on Her Majesty's most precious person. Now she lives solitary.'

Elizabeth remained friends with Mary Sidney, being truly sorry for her tragedy, and would visit her privately at Penshurst Place in Kent, the Sidney country seat. On the rare occasions when Mary could be persuaded to come to court, she remained in her apartment, and the Queen, abandoning royal precedent and etiquette, visited her there.

As for Dudley, who had very nearly become the ruler of England, on 20 October Elizabeth, having just settled on him a pension of £1000 per annum, finally made him a Privy Councillor; in order to preserve the peace, she bestowed the same honour upon his rival, Norfolk. Although the rivalry between the two men remained as intense as ever, they were now displaying in public a 'close intimacy'. As for Dudley, he was to prove a faithful and diligent councillor, attending more meetings than most right up to the end of his life.

By 25 October, Elizabeth had resumed her normal duties, but she was aware that certain demands would undoubtedly be made of her by Parliament: the mood in the country and the Council left her in little doubt of public feeling. She therefore tried to stall when it came to summoning Parliament, but her councillors were not prepared to suffer her delaying tactics. In November, weeping with rage, she had a furious confrontation with her former suitor Arundel, who stood his ground and defended the right of her lords to interfere in the matter of the succession, which touched the whole country. Later that month, Elizabeth, who needed the money that it could vote, had no choice but to summon Parliament.

When Elizabeth's second Parliament met on 12 January 1563, its members were determined to have the question of the succession settled once and for all. The matter was first raised when, during the opening ceremonies, Alexander Nowell, Dean of St Paul's, at Dudley's behest, castigated the Queen for failing to marry.

'Just as Queen Mary's marriage was a terrible plague to all England, so now the want of Queen Elizabeth's marriage and issue is like to prove as great a plague. If your parents had been of like mind, where had you been then?' he asked the Queen. 'Alack! What shall become of us?' Elizabeth never spoke a friendly word to him again.

But the Lords and Commons were unanimous in supporting Nowell, and soon afterwards agreed that lovingly-worded petitions from both Houses should be submitted to Her Majesty, urging her to marry or designate a successor, for 'thereby shall she strike a terror into her adversaries and replenish her subjects with immortal joy'. Cecil supported the petitions, but not openly – 'The matter is so deep I cannot reach into it,' he wrote. 'God send it a good issue!'

Both petitions were couched in humble terms, reminding Elizabeth of the terror felt by her subjects during her illness and warning her what might ensue if she died without naming her successor: 'the unspeakable miseries of civil wars, the perilous intermeddlings of foreign princes, with seditions, ambitions and factious subjects at home, the waste of noble houses, the slaughter of people, subversion of towns, unsurety of all men's possessions, lives and estates', attainders, treasons and a host of other calamities.

> We fear a faction of heretics in your realm, contentious and malicious Papists. From the Conquest to the present day, the realm was never left as now it is without a certain heir. If Your Highness could conceive or imagine the comfort, surety and delight that should happen to yourself by beholding an imp of your own, it would sufficiently satisfy to remove all manner of impediments and scruples.

Elizabeth always took the view that neither her marriage nor the succession were the business of her subjects, but matters for herself alone, yet she could not afford to alienate Parliament, and therefore resorted to deliberate obfuscation and procrastination. After dinner on 28 January, she graciously received the delegation from the Commons in the gallery at Whitehall Palace. The Speaker, on his knees, presented the Commons's petition, which she 'thankfully accepted' and then delivered 'an excellent oration' in which she assured him and his fellows that she was as worried as they were about the succession, and had been especially so since her illness. She won sympathy by confiding that the matter had occupied her mind constantly as she recuperated. 'Yet desired I not then life so much for my own safety as for yours.'

She laboured, she told them, under an intolerable burden. They were asking her to name a successor, but she could not wade into so deep a matter without weighty deliberation and was more concerned about choosing the right claimant. If her choice led to civil war, her subjects might lose their lives, 'but I hazard to lose both body and soul', she said, being responsible to God for her actions.

It was not their place, she admonished, to petition her on this matter, but she knew the difference between men who acted out of love and loyalty and those who were mischief-makers. She did not wish to hear them speak of her death, for she knew now, as well as before, that she was mortal. She would, she promised, take further advice, and then give them an answer.

'And so I assure you all', she concluded, 'that though after my death you may have many stepdames, yet shall you never have a more natural mother than I mean to be unto you all.'

Two days later she received the deputation from the Lords with their petition, in which they urged her to marry 'where it shall please you, to whom it shall please you, and as soon as it shall please you'. Even if she chose Robert Dudley, he would be better, they felt, than no husband at all. Failing this, they begged her to name her successor, since 'upon the death of princes the law dieth'. The Lords were anxious to have Mary Stuart's claim disposed of: they did not, 'as mere, natural Englishmen', wish to be 'subject to a foreign prince', and Mary was 'a stranger, who, by the laws of the realm, cannot inherit in England'. According to Sir Ralph Sadler, who served four Tudor sovereigns, 'the stones in the streets would rebel' at the prospect of Mary ruling England.

Displaying some irritation, the Queen told the delegation that she had made allowances for the Commons, where she had observed 'restless heads in whose brains the needless hammers beat with vain judgement', but she expected the Lords to know better than to press her on such weighty matters. It was not impossible that she would marry: 'The marks they saw on her face were not wrinkles, but the pits of smallpox, and although she might be old, God could send her children as He did to St Elisabeth, and they had better consider well what they were asking, as, if she declared a successor, it would cost much blood to England.'

Initially, both Lords and Commons were too impressed by her

graciousness and her powers of oratory to realise that Elizabeth had stalled again; they really believed that she would now take steps to resolve the matters of her marriage and the succession, when in fact she had promised nothing at all. Consequently, Parliament refrained from debating the succession, although by 12 February, the Commons were getting restive, and sent the Queen a humble reminder that they were waiting for an answer. But Elizabeth was biding her time until Parliament had voted the subsidy she wanted.

Parliament had by then proceeded to its other business, that of passing legislation to protect the Anglican Settlement of 1559. These Acts extended the Oath of Supremacy required from all in public life, and imposed penalties upon those who upheld the authority of the Pope and those who opposed the Church of England. In February, Convocation approved the restoration of the Thirty-Nine Articles of Henry VIII (in place of the Forty-Two Articles of Edward VI) in which were enshrined the Church's basic doctrines: these were finally approved by Parliament in 1571.

When, on 10 April, Parliament assembled for its closing ceremonies, the Queen, who had been voted her subsidy, attended and gave to the Lord Keeper, Sir Nicholas Bacon, a handwritten answer, composed by herself, to the petitions of the two Houses. Fuming over her subjects' temerity, she had written two earlier drafts which referred to the 'two huge scrolls' they had given her, but had amended this as her irritation subsided. In the final version she wrote:

If any here doubt that I am, as it were by vow or determination, bent never to trade that way of life [i.e. spinsterhood], let them put out that kind of heresy for your belief therein is awry. For though I can think it best for a private woman, yet do I strive with myself to think it not meet for a prince. And if I can bend my liking to your need, I will not resist such a mind. I hope I shall die in quiet with '*Nunc dimittis*', which cannot be without I see some glimpses of your following surety after my graved bones.

And that was that. Parliament was prorogued with what Elizabeth herself described as an 'answer answerless', a most unsatisfactory response to its carefully-drafted petitions.

By rejecting the claim of Mary Stuart to be Elizabeth's successor, the Lords were by implication endorsing that of Lady Katherine Grey, whom many supported. Lady Katherine and Lord Hertford had remained in the Tower since August 1561, but they had not been ill-treated. Katherine's apartment was hung with rich curtains and tapestries, and she was permitted such comforts as a Turkey carpet and a fine tester bed with a feather mattress. Delicacies were brought in for her table, and she was allowed to keep her pet dogs with her. All this had been arranged with the full knowledge and approval of the Queen, but what the Queen did not know was that Katherine's gaolers, feeling some sympathy for Katherine and her husband, had allowed the young couple to meet regularly and even share the feather mattress at night.

By the autumn of 1562 Katherine was pregnant again, and in the first week of February 1563, she gave birth to her second son, Thomas. This could not be concealed from Elizabeth, whose fury knew no bounds, and she gave orders that under no circumstances were Katherine and Lord Hertford to meet again. They never did, and Katherine spent the best part of the rest of her life weeping for her lost love

Hertford was hauled before the Court of Star Chamber, where he was found guilty of having compounded his original offence of having 'deflowered a virgin of the blood royal in the Queen's house' by having 'ravished her a second time'. He was fined £15,000, later commuted to £3000. As for Sir Edward Warner, the kindly Lieutenant of the Tower who had allowed the couple conjugal visits, he was dismissed from his post.

In the summer, when there were cases of plague within the Tower, the Queen sent both young people, heavily guarded, into the country, there to be kept separately under house arrest. There was no question now of Elizabeth acknowledging Katherine Grey as heiress to the throne, but later that year talk of a secret conspiracy to have her two sons legitimised prompted the Queen to bring her cousin back to the Tower, lest she become a focus for rebellion. As a near relative in blood, with two sons, she represented a very dangerous threat to Elizabeth's security. Thereafter she remained in the Tower, being allowed to leave it only for short visits under guard to the Lieutenant's house in Suffolk, Cockfield Hall. Hertford's piteous requests to visit her there met with firm refusals.

Lady Katherine Grey died of tuberculosis in 1568 at Cockfield Hall. The Queen paid for a ceremonial funeral in Salisbury Cathedral. Although she never forgave Katherine for her secret marriage, she no longer nourished animosity towards Lord Hertford, who was released from the Tower. He married twice more and lived to be an old man. As for his sons by Katherine, they were placed in the care of Cecil, who brought them up for a time with his own children.

In February 1563, scandal had also touched Mary Stuart, who, since her return to Scotland, had cherished a nostalgia for the court of France and employed as her secretary a young French courtier called Pierre de

Chastelard. Unwisely, Mary showed special favour to this gallant, but he soon grew too ardent in his behaviour towards his mistress, and could have seriously compromised her honour when he was discovered hiding under her bed by Scots lords who were jealous of his influence. They arrested him, and on 22 February had him executed.

After Queen Elizabeth had recovered from smallpox, Warwick's force had gone to France, where they had occupied Newhaven, but in March 1563 the capture of the Huguenot leaders and the murder of the Duke of Guise enabled Catherine de' Medici to bring the religious conflict to an end. The English troops were therefore technically redundant, but Elizabeth had invested her money in them in order to secure the return of Calais, and insisted that they remain in France to achieve this aim. However, with the country at peace, both Catholics and Protestants now united against the English invaders and laid siege to Newhaven. A terrible epidemic of plague swept through the English ranks and decimated their numbers. As the months went by, and the siege continued, it seemed increasingly likely that Calais was irretrievably lost.

During this time, Queen Mary consistently supported her 'dear sister, so tender a cousin and friend', having resisted all attempts by the Guise faction to draw her over to their side. On 2 November, Mary wrote to Elizabeth to express her relief that her cousin had recovered from her illness and that 'your beautiful face will lose none of its perfections'. Mary was still enthusiastic about meeting Elizabeth, and even more anxious to persuade her cousin to declare her her successor. Elizabeth wrote Mary affectionate letters of condolence on the death of the Duke of Guise, and after Parliament had been prorogued in April, she ordered the imprisonment of John Hales, a lawyer who wrote and circulated a pamphlet deriding Mary's claim to the throne and supporting that of Lady Katherine Grey. The Queen also temporarily banished his patron, Sir Nicholas Bacon, from court.

Maitland was still pressing for Mary to be acknowledged as heiress presumptive, but the problem of the succession was a complex one, as Elizabeth knew well. The succession was not a thing she could bestow as a gift, it was a right under the law, and there was, as we have seen, much dispute over whose claim was the strongest. For Parliament to accept Mary, Queen of Scots as Elizabeth's heir, Mary would have to demonstrate that she had English interests at heart, and her marriage plans so far had done little to reinforce this conviction. Elizabeth complained to Cecil that she was 'in such a labyrinth' with regard to the problem of Mary and the succession that she had no idea what course to follow, yet Cecil could not offer much comfort. Elizabeth knew he distrusted Mary because of her Catholicism, but he had also told her that if she excluded her cousin from the succession, the result would probably be war. Cecil's unwelcome advice was that Elizabeth should marry as soon as possible.

Unaware of his sadistic tendencies, Mary was still pursuing negotiations for a marriage to Don Carlos, which was seen in England as being directly opposed to English interests. Elizabeth's chief desire was to see Mary married to a loyal Englishman, and it was around this time that she first conceived the idea of proposing Robert Dudley as a husband for the Scots Queen. It seems that, initially, this was her way of paying him back for inciting Parliament to press her into marriage. Gradually she grew to like the idea and began to pursue it seriously.

It was not such a preposterous notion as it seemed. Dudley was the one man who could be trusted to promote England's welfare north of the Border; indebted to Elizabeth for his meteoric rise to power and an almost princely status, he would not be likely to forget the woman for whom he felt a genuine affection, if not love. Dudley was hungry for a crown and had a penchant for attractive redheads; by marrying him, Mary would remove herself from the European marriage market, and the threat of foreign interference in Scotland would recede. England and Scotland would draw closer together in friendship. As a Protestant, Dudley would be acceptable to the Calvinist lords and would hold the Scots Catholics in check. The drawback, of course, was that Elizabeth would have to give him up, but it seems that she had already decided to embrace celibacy, and, hard as renouncing him would be, she convinced herself she could do so if she knew that it was to her and England's advantage. Moreover, royal marriage negotiations took so long that their parting might be months, if not years, away.

Few people shared her view of the situation. Only Cecil, who perceived what good could result from the match and who, for reasons of his own, wanted Dudley out of the way, supported the plan. When, in the spring of 1563, Elizabeth first broached the matter to Maitland, quite suddenly in a private audience, saying that she was prepared to offer his Queen a husband 'in whom nature had implanted so many graces that, if she wished to marry, she would prefer him to all the princes in the world', an embarrassed Maitland guessed whom she was referring to and tried to pass the whole thing off as some royal joke. When, however, he saw that Elizabeth meant what she said, he stuttered 'that this was a great proof of the love she bore his Queen, that she was willing to give her a thing so dearly prized by herself', but he felt certain his sovereign would not wish to deprive her cousin of 'all the joy and solace she received from his company'. Elizabeth was not to be put off. It was unfortunate, she said, that the Earl of Warwick was not as handsome as his younger brother, for had this been so Queen Mary could have married Ambrose while she herself became the wife of Dudley. Maitland rejoined that Her Majesty ought to marry him anyway, 'and then when it should please God to call her to Himself, she could leave the Queen of Scots heiress to both her kingdom and her husband; that way, Lord Robert could hardly fail to have children by one or other of them'.

Cecil also praised Dudley to the skies, writing to Maitland that he was 'a nobleman of birth, void of all evil conditions that sometimes are heritable to princes, and in goodness of nature and richness of good gifts comparable to any prince born and, so it may be said with due reverence and without offence to princes, much better than a great sort now living. He is also dearly and singularly esteemed [Cecil had written "beloved" here, but crossed it out] of the Queen's Majesty, so as she can think no good turn or fortune greater than may be well bestowed upon him.' In Maitland's private opinion, the Queen's plan to foist her discarded lover – a commoner – upon Mary Stuart was little short of insulting, especially in view of his reputation as a former traitor and suspected wife murderer, and when the ambassador returned to Scotland he said nothing of Elizabeth's suggestion to Mary. But he had informed de Quadra of it, de Quadra informed King Philip, and before long the news had spread rapidly to Scotland and France. Everywhere it met with derision, and few believed that Elizabeth was serious.

Elizabeth was determinedly set on her course, and having made this resolution, she could afford to be generous to Lady Lennox. She ordered her release in the spring of 1563, making it conditional upon a promise that Lady Lennox would never again scheme to marry her son to the Queen of Scots. Furthermore, in June Elizabeth wrote to Queen Mary asking that an old attainder on the Earl of Lennox be reversed, so that he could return to his estates in Scotland.

Dudley was still riding the crest of success. In June, Elizabeth bestowed upon him Kenilworth Castle in Warwickshire, a huge medieval fortress that had been converted by John of Gaunt in the fourteenth century into a luxurious palace. Northumberland had briefly owned it, and Dudley had had his eye on it for some years. Now he would have a country seat of his own, just five miles south of Warwick Castle, the residence of his older brother Ambrose, and he wasted no time in drawing up elaborate plans for its improvement and renovation in order to make it a fit place to entertain the Queen. It would be ten years before Kenilworth was ready to receive her, and then it would be the most magnificent of all Elizabethan mansions.

Dudley enjoyed a standard of luxury tasted by few, yet he was still living beyond his means. His pride demanded that he make it known how munificently the Queen had enriched him, which led to him being besieged by those who craved his patronage. As a result of this the number of his clients and those beholden to him increased, affording him a substantial following. Sensitive about his lack of popularity and disinterested supporters, he was usually quick to revenge himself on those of his followers who failed to reciprocate his kindness, but steadfast and generous to those whose loyalty was genuine.

Ambrose Dudley, Earl of Warwick was still in Newhaven, trying to cope on insufficient funds with a plague-ridden army whose numbers were dwindling at an alarming rate. In July, Elizabeth agreed that he had no choice but to surrender Newhaven to the French, but during negotiations he was shot in the leg by an enemy musket. At the end of the month, having withdrawn from France with as much honour as he could salvage, Warwick returned home, but his leg would never fully heal, and he walked with a stick for the rest of his life. Lord Robert went down to Portsmouth to welcome his brother but the Queen sent a messenger after him to warn him that he was in danger of catching the plague from the returning troops. Dudley defied her, having found Ambrose in bed in some pain, and an angry Elizabeth commanded him to stay put in case he brought the contagion back to court.

Elizabeth was in no very good mood just then: she was furious with the French and humiliated over the loss of Newhaven. It seemed that Calais would never be recovered, and to make matters worse there was grumbling in England against the incompetence of women rulers. De Quadra reported that he had heard people blame the Queen for what had happened and say, 'God help England and send it a king.'

As Elizabeth feared, the returning soldiers had brought the plague to England. For the rest of the summer, it raged unchecked, claiming, in London alone, three thousand souls each week, and in the suburbs around the capital twenty thousand altogether. One of those who succumbed was Bishop de Quadra, who died in August, having been a source of trouble to Elizabeth to the last. His mischievous reports had done much to weaken the friendship between England and Spain.

That month, Elizabeth sent Thomas Randolph back to Scotland, with instructions to persuade Mary to allow Elizabeth to choose her a husband. He was to say that if Mary consented 'to content us and this our nation in her marriage', Elizabeth would be as a mother to her and would 'proceed to the inquisition of her right and title to be our next heir, and to further that which shall appear advantageous to her'. The only clue as to whom the chosen husband might be lay in the reference to 'some person of noble birth within our realm, yea, perchance such as she would hardly think we could agree unto'.

Mary, however, did not understand what was implied, and begged for clarification. Who, among the English aristocracy, would her 'good sister' regard as suitable? Randolph, who knew of Elizabeth's intentions, was praying he would not have to tell her, opining to Cecil that it was asking too much of her 'noble stomach' to debase her 'so low as to marry in place inferior to herself'. Fortunately for him, Elizabeth was still playing for time and, in the interests of retaining Mary's interest and preventing her from pursuing other marriage plans, kept her guessing for the next few months. Thus when Randolph went home, Mary was none the wiser.

In the autumn of 1563, Don Carlos fell seriously ill, and this appeared to signal the end of Mary Stuart's hopes of a Spanish marriage. Finding the right husband was, for the Scots Queen, a priority, not only for political and dynastic reasons – she, like Elizabeth, had no heir of her body – but also because she was unsuited to the single life. Thomas Randolph attributed her bouts of depression and crying to emotional frustration and unsatisfied desire.

Don Carlos's illness was more than convenient for Elizabeth, who had done everything she could behind the scenes to delay Mary from marrying until a safe husband could be found for her.

It was at this time that Elizabeth, mindful of her promise to Parliament, attempted to revive negotiations for her own marriage to the Archduke Charles. This appeared at first to be a forlorn hope, because, despite being reminded of the advantages of an alliance with 'such a Helen, accompanied by such a dowry and so much dignity', the Emperor was justifiably suspicious of Elizabeth's motives and would not have forgotten that she had formerly rejected his son. There was also the persistent gossip about Dudley. He now had apartments next to the Queen's in all the royal palaces; he was the host at most courtly entertainments; he kept state like a prince, and enjoyed vast power and influence.

In spite of these obstacles, Elizabeth expected the Archduke to make the first move towards reviving his courtship – it was unthinkable that she, a woman, should take the initiative. Cecil therefore wrote to one of his agents in Germany, who in turn approached the Duke of Wurttemberg, who in his turn sent a letter to the Emperor. Ferdinand consented to the reopening of negotiations, but proceeded with caution, as did Cecil, who made it clear that the Archduke must take matters slowly, since the Queen was much inclined to celibacy. She had acknowledged that the Archduke was the best foreign match for her, but she waxed alternately hot and cold over the matter.

In January 1564, the Duke of Wurttemberg, acting on the Emperor's behalf, sent an envoy, Ahasverus Allinga, to Windsor to discover the

Queen's true feelings about the marriage. Allinga was received by Elizabeth with just Cecil and two maids of honour present. The envoy and the Secretary praised the merits and advantages of the match, whereupon the Queen replied that they might save their breath, 'For she would never be induced by any appeals to reason but only by stern necessity, as she had already inwardly resolved that, if she ever married, it would be as Queen and not as Elizabeth.' She said she blamed the Emperor for the failure of the earlier negotiations: he had behaved like an old woman, refusing to allow his son to visit her in England. She insisted that she would never accept a suitor without seeing him first, and that the Archduke must make the first move towards reviving the courtship, for she herself could not do so 'without covering herself in ignominy'. She added that, for her part, she would far rather be a beggarwoman and single than a queen and married.

Not surprisingly, Allinga told Cecil afterwards that there was no point in pursuing the matter further, but Cecil was reassuring, saying the Queen had told him how much she had enjoyed her interview with him. Knowing her of old, he said, he believed she was by no means disinclined to the marriage. Much dissatisfied and confused, Allinga returned home.

By March 1564, it was obvious that Elizabeth could keep Mary guessing as to the identity of her suitor no longer. She therefore told Randolph he might now speak without using 'obscure terms', but when the time came to tell Mary who it was that Elizabeth wished her to marry, he hedged so much that she cut in incredulously, 'Now, Mr Randolph, doth your mistress in good earnest wish me to marry my Lord Robert?'

Randolph, cringing, admitted that it was. 'It pleased Her Grace to hear me with meetly good patience,' but she was in fact amazed and somewhat affronted by Elizabeth's plan, although remaining outwardly cordial. She was determined to be her own mistress, and certainly did not consider Dudley a fit mate for one whose previous husband had been the King of France and who was herself a reigning sovereign. Haughtily, she asked Randolph if this plan conformed to Elizabeth's promise 'to use me as her sister or daughter. Do you think that it may stand with my honour to marry a subject?' Randolph replied that no better man could be found, and that this marriage could bring good to her realm. Mary would only say that she would consider the matter in private.

She might have been more amenable to the offer of Dudley's hand if it had been accompanied by an undertaking from Elizabeth to declare her heiress presumptive to the English throne. Instead, she felt she was being made a fool of. Not for a minute did she believe that Elizabeth would really part with him – a view shared by many other people – although Elizabeth gave every appearance of being serious.

Mary's lack of enthusiasm for the marriage was shared by Dudley himself, who was panic-stricken at the prospect of leaving England for what he perceived to be a land of barbarians, and even more distraught at the thought of leaving Elizabeth, whom he still cherished some hopes of marrying. Yet Elizabeth was so insistent upon his co-operation that he had little choice but to acquiesce.

She now revived her plans for a meeting with Mary, suggesting that it should take place in the summer. Mary, however, had no desire to meet her cousin face to face just then, for she was secretly trying to re-open negotiations for her marriage to Don Carlos, and did not want to prejudice them by seeming to favour a match with Robert Dudley. She therefore declined the invitation, giving Elizabeth offence and causing a cooling in Anglo-Scots relations which lasted through the summer.

On 11 April, England and France signed the Treaty of Troyes, bringing hostilities between them to an end and placing Calais firmly beyond reach of recovery.

In June, Philip II sent a new ambassador to England, Don Diego de Guzman de Silva, who did much to foster good Anglo-Spanish relations. In the same month the Emperor Ferdinand died, and was succeeded by his eldest son, who was crowned as Maximilian II. These events brought talk of Elizabeth's marriage to the Archduke to a temporary standstill, but the new Emperor was more in favour of the match than his father had been, although anxious to ensure that his brother 'would not', as on the last occasion, suffer himself to be led by the nose'.

On 5 August, one of the most famous progresses of her reign brought Elizabeth to Cambridge, where she stayed for five days. Strikingly attired in a gown of black velvet slashed with rose, with a netted caul studded with pearls and gems and a feathered and bejewelled hat atop her red hair, the Queen entered the city preceded by trumpets and attended by a magnificent retinue. She was welcomed by Cecil in his capacity as Chancellor of the University and by the scholars, 'lowly kneeling', crying, '*Vivat Regina!*'

During the visit she enjoyed a full programme of ceremonies, entertainments and, as she had requested, 'all manner of scholastic exercises', mostly organised by Dudley, who, at Cecil's request, acted as Master of Ceremonies. Elizabeth was particularly impressed with the glories of King's College Chapel – 'the best in our realm' – and its choir. She visited most of the colleges, including Trinity, founded by her father, and St John's, founded by her great-grandmother, Lady Margaret

Beaufort. She attended lectures and Latin plays, listened to orations, addresses and disputations, received gifts of books, gloves and comfits (sweetmeats), and tried whenever possible to talk – in the mandatory Latin – to the scholars themselves. She made elegant speeches in that language, to great acclaim: in one she promised to build a new college – a promise never fulfilled in Cambridge, but in Oxford, where she founded Jesus College in 1571.

When the Public Orator openly praised her virginity, Elizabeth was touched, and replied, 'God's blessing on your heart, *there* continue.' As he extolled her other manifold virtues, she shook her head, bit her lips and fingers, and displayed uncharacteristic embarrassment.

When she 'cheerfully departed' from Cambridge on 10 August, a day later than planned, she said she would have stayed longer if 'provision of beer and ale could have been made' for the court.

After the progress had ended there were widespread rumours in London that the Queen would marry the Archduke and was about to dispatch an embassy to Vienna, ostensibly to offer formal condolences to Maximilian II on the death of his father, but in reality to conclude the marriage. In fact, Elizabeth was stalling yet again.

She still favoured the plan to marry Dudley to Mary Stuart, but the Earl of Lennox, who was finally permitted to return to Scotland that September, warned Randolph that there was no chance of this happening: 'He has not descended from a great old house, and his blood is spotted. I fear we shall not accept him.' If the English pressed the matter, the Scots would turn to his own son, Lord Darnley.

At Elizabeth's command, Cecil did press the matter, writing a sixteen-page justification of the marriage to Randolph, which averred that Mary would have with Dudley the promise of the English succession, subject, of course, to the consent of Parliament. But Mary wanted more concrete assurances than that, and was angered that something she felt should be hers by right should be offered her only with conditions attached to it.

She was concerned, however, that her disinclination to accept Dudley might mar friendly relations between the two countries, and in September, in order to emphasise her goodwill, she sent a seasoned diplomat, the urbane, charming and cultivated Sir James Melville, to England. Years later, in his memoirs, Melville wrote a lively account of this and later visits, which is a valuable, if not entirely reliable source for historians.

Elizabeth wasted no time in complaining to Melville about the offensive tone of one of Mary's recent letters. She withdrew from her purse and showed him a strong reply she had composed, informing him that she had not sent it because she felt it was too mild. Melville managed to convince her that Mary had meant no harm, and she happily tore up both letters.

Sir James's wit and polish had impressed Elizabeth at that first interview, and throughout the nine days of his stay she would summon him to attend her as often as possible, flirting with him and angling for compliments. His long years of service at the courts of France, Italy and Germany had made him proficient in languages, which meant that Elizabeth could show off her skills as a linguist. She also dressed to impress him, one day in the English style, a second in the French style, and a third in the Italian style. When she asked him which he preferred, 'I said the Italian dress, which pleased her well, for she delighted to show off her golden-coloured hair wearing a caul and bonnet, as they do in Italy. Her hair was more reddish than yellow, curled in appearance naturally.'

This prompted her to ask him what colour hair was considered best in his country. How did her hair compare with his queen's? Which of them was the fairest? Melville realised that future diplomatic relations between England and Scotland might depend on his answer, so he offered a tactful reply, giving it as his opinion that 'the fairness of them both was not their worst fault'; when pressed to say more, he pronounced that Elizabeth was the fairest Queen in England and Mary the fairest Queen in Scotland. But this was not enough for Elizabeth, who archly insisted that he make a choice. Deftly, he answered that 'they were both the fairest ladies of their courts, and that Her Majesty was white [in complexion], but our Queen was very lovely'.

'Who is the higher?' demanded Elizabeth, after a pause.

Melville said that Mary was.

'Then she is over-high', was the retort, 'for I am neither over-high nor over-low.'

'Then she asked what kind of exercises [Mary] used. I answered that when I was dispatched out of Scotland, the Queen was lately come from the Highland hunting; that when she had leisure from the affairs of her country, she read good books, the histories of divers countries, and sometimes would play upon the lute and virginals. [Elizabeth] asked if she played well.'

'Reasonably, for a queen,' Melville answered.

That evening, determined to show him that she herself had the edge when it came to music, Elizabeth arranged for her cousin, Lord Hunsdon, to bring Melville, seemingly by chance, to a gallery overlooking a chamber where she would be alone, playing the virginals. Hunsdon acted out this little charade, and when Melville, who was not fooled, commented on the excellence of Elizabeth's playing, she pretended she had not known he was there and, coming towards him and 'seeming to strike me with her left hand', alleged 'that she used not to play before men, but when she was solitary, to shun melancholy'. Chiding him for entering her chamber without leave, she asked how he came to be there. Gallantly, he excused himself, saying, 'I heard such melody as ravished me and drew me within the chamber, I wit not how.' Much pleased, the Queen sank down on a cushion, and when Melville knelt at her side, 'She gave me a cushion with her own hand to lay under my knee, which at first I refused, but she compelled me to take it.' When she asked who was now the better musician, herself or Mary, he conceded that she was.

To please her, he delayed his departure so that he could stay at court one more night and watch her dance. Predictably, Elizabeth asked if Mary danced as well as she. 'Not so high and disposedly,' was the flattering answer.

On 28 September, the final morning of his visit, Melville was present with other ambassadors when, at a splendid ceremony in the Presence Chamber at St James's Palace, Elizabeth at last raised Robert Dudley to the peerage. To make Queen Mary 'think the more of him', he was created Baron Denbigh and Earl of Leicester in the presence of a glittering throng of dignitaries and courtiers. It was a solemn occasion, with the new Earl, whose motto was to be *'Droit et loyal'*, conducting himself with the utmost gravity and dignity, so that Melville was shocked to see Elizabeth smilingly tickle the kneeling Robert's neck as she invested him with the collar of his earldom and his ermine-lined mantle. This was an act at odds with her repeated assertions that she looked upon Dudley as merely 'a brother and best friend'.

When the ceremony was over, Elizabeth spoke with Melville, asking, 'How like you my new creation?' Melville, knowing how unpopular the Dudley marriage was in Scotland, made a polite but noncommittal response, whereupon the Queen pointed at the young Lord Darnley, who was in attendance as her sword-bearer, saying, 'And yet ye like better of yonder long lad!'

Gazing distastefully at the effeminate-looking youth, Melville replied, 'No woman of spirit would make choice of such a man, that was liker a woman than a man, for he is very lusty, beardless and lady-faced.'

Elizabeth was at pains to prove to Melville how sincere she was in her desire to marry Leicester to Mary, and invited him, in the company of Leicester and Cecil, into her bedchamber, to show him her treasures. From a little cabinet she took a miniature of the Scots Queen and kissed it affectionately. Sir James noticed another object in the cabinet, wrapped in paper which was inscribed in her own hand 'My Lord's picture', but it took all his powers of persuasion to persuade Elizabeth to show him the miniature of Leicester that was within the paper. When he declared that this would be the perfect gift for his Queen, Elizabeth refused to part with it on the grounds that she had no copy.

'But Your Majesty has the original,' Melville protested jocularly, although he was privately coming round to the opinion that the Queen was beginning to regret ever offering Leicester to Mary. This was not surprising, as he had noticed that Elizabeth and Leicester were 'inseparable'.

Nor would she give him another of her treasures, a ruby 'as great as a tennis ball'. If Queen Mary followed her advice, she said, 'she would in process of time get all she had'. In the meantime, Elizabeth would send her a beautiful diamond.

Conversation between Melville and the Queen was not confined entirely to pleasantries. On one occasion they discussed Mary's marriage prospects, then Elizabeth told him 'that it was her own resolution at this moment to remain till her death a virgin queen, and that nothing would compel her to change her mind except the undutiful behaviour of the Queen her sister'. A perceptive Melville replied sadly, 'Madam, you need not tell me that. I know your stately stomach. You think if you were married, you would only be a queen of England, and now ye are king and queen both. You may not endure a commander.'

Sir James managed to speak in private with Leicester, who told him that he was not worthy to wipe the shoes of the Queen of Scots. He made it plain that he felt no enthusiasm for the marriage, and blamed the whole project on Cecil, 'his secret enemy', who wanted him out of the way.

During his stay, Melville had talked to many people at court and at the Spanish embassy, where opinion of the Queen was hostile, and formed his own views of Elizabeth. When he returned home, he would increase Mary's suspicions, and do no great service to Anglo-Scots relations, by telling her that her cousin was not a plain dealer but a great dissimulator. The only positive development arising from his visit was an agreement that commissioners from England and Scotland should meet at Berwick to discuss the Dudley marriage. Elizabeth had told Melville that 'if she had ever wanted to take a husband, she would have chosen Lord Robert, but, being determined to end her life in virginity, she wished that the Queen her sister should marry him, as meetest of all others. It would best remove out of her mind all fear and suspicion to be offended by usurpation before her death, being assured that he was so loving and trusty that he would never give his consent nor suffer such thing to be attempted during her time.'

Melville had played along with this, but he had also gone to the Spanish embassy in a vain attempt to revive the project to marry Mary to Don Carlos. Mary had virtually given up hope of this match, but she needed to be certain that it was moribund before looking elsewhere for a husband. It was: Don Carlos was now so mentally unstable that there was no question of his marrying anyone.

Never having seriously considered Robert Dudley as a consort, Mary had found herself pondering more and more the idea of marrying the young Lord Darnley. As the Lennoxes had pointed out, there were definite advantages to it: the union of two claims to the English throne, and the enlistment of the Catholic Lennox faction – which Mary believed to be more powerful than it actually was – on the side of the Crown. There was one problem: Darnley was still in England – he and his mother were living at court, having been refused permission to accompany Lennox to Scotland – and it was doubtful if Elizabeth would allow him, as her subject, to leave.

After confirming that there was no hope of the Spanish match, Melville, again on Mary's instructions, saw Lady Lennox to discuss the possibility of a marriage between his queen and Lord Darnley. She welcomed him warmly and showered him with presents for Mary, Moray and Maitland, 'for she was still in good hope that her son would speed better than the Earl of Leicester concerning the marriage of our Queen'.

Elizabeth, ever perceptive, had already sniffed an intrigue. She had regretted her earlier letter to Mary, asking for Lennox to be restored to his estates, and had written recently to her in an attempt to persuade her to refuse him entry, although Mary would not go back on her word.

When the English and Scots commissioners met at Berwick in November, relations became fraught. Mary's half-brother, the Earl of Moray, demanded to know precisely what Elizabeth meant to do for Mary in the event of her accepting Leicester, but failed to extract any sureties from the English lords, who would only repeat that there was no better way than this marriage to further Mary's claim to the succession. Tempers flared, and the Scots left the conference angry and insulted.

The following month, both Moray and Maitland wrote to Cecil to say that Mary would not consider marrying Leicester unless Elizabeth promised to settle the succession on her. To everyone's surprise, Elizabeth did nothing. She suspected now that Mary would never accept Leicester, and she also knew that Mary had hopes of marrying Darnley, for which she would have to be a suitor to Elizabeth, whose subject Darnley was. With the focus on Mary in the role of supplicant, Elizabeth would not lose face over her cousin's rejection of her own candidate. Anticipating this, Cecil, enthusiastically backed by a relieved Leicester, suggested that Darnley be allowed to visit his father in Scotland, in order to whet the Queen of Scots' appetite. According to Mary herself, Leicester even wrote to her to warn her that Elizabeth's plan for their marriage had been a mere ploy to discourage more dangerous suitors. As for Elizabeth, her enthusiasm for the project was waning, and, like Cecil, she had already begun to believe that a marriage between Mary and Darnley was less of a threat to England than one between Mary and a powerful Catholic prince because, having recently come to know him better, she took the view that Darnley was a harmless political lightweight. However, for tactical reasons she still would not allow him to go to Scotland.

Leicester, recently appointed Chancellor of the University of Oxford by the Queen, now renewed his courtship of her, having been at pains during the past months to demonstrate that his real future lay at her side, where he could serve her best. He had enlisted the aid of de Silva, the new Spanish ambassador, against her plan to marry him to Mary, and had also been active in promoting Lord Darnley as a suitor for the Scots Queen. It was now his belief that Elizabeth had devised the scheme to unite him with Mary as a test of his loyalty to herself; having, as he saw it, proved that loyalty, he saw no reason why he should not capitalise upon it.

Fears about the succession were revived in December when the Queen fell 'perilously sick' with gastro-enteritis. Fortunately, her recovery was speedy, but, as Cecil informed Throckmorton, 'For the time she made us sore afraid.' There was renewed pressure on her to marry, and Cecil invoked the aid of God, praying that He would 'lead by the hand some meet person to come and lay hand on her to her contentation'. Otherwise, he told Throckmorton, 'I assure you, as now things having in desperation, I have no comfort to live.'

Bishop John Jewel of Salisbury spoke for many when he wrote, 'O how wretched are we, who cannot tell under what sovereign we are to live! God will, I trust, long preserve Elizabeth to us in life and safety!'

9

'A Matter Dangerous to the Common Amity'

In the early months of 1565, Cecil had cause to hope that Elizabeth was seriously considering a foreign marriage. Not only was the Archduke expected to renew his suit, but there had also been a proposal, sent by Catherine de' Medici via her envoy, Paul de Foix, that the Queen marry Charles IX. The French Queen was determined to prevent at all costs an English alliance with the Habsburgs. Elizabeth was privately unenthusiastic: she was thirty-one and Charles only fourteen, and she told de Silva that she did not relish the world making fun of 'an old woman and a child' at the church door. Sir Thomas Smith, her ambassador in Paris, had informed her that the young King was likely to be tall, though with knobbly knees and ankles and badly-proportioned legs. He gabbled his words rapidly and, having a volatile nature, was liable to act impulsively. Moreover, he spoke not a word of English. Even the Queen's jester urged her not to marry him, for he was 'but a boy and a babe'.

Elizabeth told de Foix she feared she was too old to marry his master. She would rather die than be despised and abandoned by a younger husband, as her sister had been. Why, the age gap was so wide that people would say King Charles had married his mother!

Offended, de Foix intimated that the matter should end there, but Elizabeth still needed to keep the French friendly and prevent them from making a new alliance with the Scots. She also wished to show the Habsburgs that they were not the only contenders for her hand. Thus she embarked on her old game of stringing along her suitors with half-promises and hope. Her opening gambit was to fly into a temper and accuse the French King of having so little regard for her that he was prepared to drop his suit so precipitately. She had only wished to draw attention to the difficulties that might be faced, so that the French would understand why she could not give an answer at once.

She then wrote to Sir Thomas Smith in Paris, asking for his honest opinion of Charles. He reported that he thought the King would be a good husband for her, for he appeared 'tractable and wise for his years. I dare put myself in pledge to Your Highness that Your Majesty shall like him.'

Elizabeth told de Foix that she would have to consult with her nobles, many of whom were openly hostile to the match. Only Leicester seemed in favour of it, since he welcomed anything that diverted the Queen's mind from thoughts of the more feasible Habsburg marriage. Cecil said nothing, but he did not regard Elizabeth's interest in Charles as being serious. Most of her Council advised against the marriage, particularly the Earl of Sussex, who warned that Charles would follow 'French usage' and 'live with pretty girls' in France, rendering useless 'all hope of an heir'.

De Foix, ignorant of what was being said behind closed doors, sensed success and, when with the Queen went into eulogies about the precocity and unusual maturity of his sovereign. For the next five months Elizabeth enjoyed the pleasures of courtship, agreeing to exchange portraits and even discussing the prospect of King Charles paying her a secret visit. Primed by his mother, Charles announced that he was in love with the Queen of England, and played the part of an ardent suitor. Throughout this time, however, Elizabeth resisted all pressure from de Foix to give a definite answer, and privately considered whether she should instead marry the Archduke.

Throughout this time, Leicester continued warmly to support the French match, though Cecil and the Imperial envoys guessed, rightly, that this was a front to mask his own ambitions. It was obvious that he was encouraging the Queen to delay making a decision in order to prevent her from marrying anyone other than himself.

By February 1565, Thomas Randolph had worked tirelessly for a year and a half to bring to a successful conclusion the Queen's plan to marry Mary to Leicester, and was under the impression that Mary was at last coming round to the idea: she had hinted that, if the terms were favourable, she might accept the newly-created Earl, and a jubilant Randolph wrote immediately to his mistress to tell her the good news.

He was therefore bitterly disappointed when Cecil informed him that the Queen had just changed her mind and, at the request of Queen Mary and Lady Lennox, allowed Lord Darnley to go to Scotland, ostensibly on the pretext of having family business to attend to. Elizabeth was no fool, and knew perfectly well why he was going; many people believed, especially later, that, knowing more about Darnley's character than her cousin, she had allowed him to go on the premise that, if she gave Mary enough rope, she would hang herself.

On the three nights before Darnley's arrival there, spectral warriors were reportedly seen fighting in the streets of Edinburgh at midnight, which the superstitious took as a portent that something terrible was about to happen. Mary gave no credence to the tales, and when Darnley arrived in Edinburgh on 13 February, she extended to him a warm welcome.

His attraction for her was immediate and strong; Melville says she tried to control her feelings, but it was not long before she was so infatuated that she could not bear to be apart from Darnley. At nineteen, three years her junior, he was a physically attractive, curly-haired, well-mannered young man with various accomplishments; he wrote elegant letters, could play the lute expertly and excelled at athletics. Mary thought him 'the lustiest and best proportioned long man' she had ever seen. What was not yet apparent to her was that, beneath the courtly veneer, he was spoilt, petulant, self-indulgent, unstable, aggressive and at times grossly uncouth. Blind to everything but her feelings for him, Mary was ready to set aside all considerations of state and the common good, and unwilling to listen to those of her nobles who spoke out against the marriage or advised caution.

Without giving any hint of her intentions towards Darnley, Mary wrote twice to Elizabeth that February to urge that her claim to the succession be recognised. On 15 March, Randolph delivered the English Queen's reply, which was that if Mary, her good sister, consented to marry Leicester, she, Elizabeth, would advance him all the honour she could and would promote Mary's claim behind the scenes, but she could not allow her claim to be formally examined, nor would she publish it until such time as she herself was married or had made known her resolve to remain single – one or other of which she meant shortly to do. On hearing this, Mary 'wept her fill', using 'evil speech of the Queen's Majesty, alleging she abused her' and wasted her time.

By now, Mary was deeply involved with Darnley. When he became ill with measles, she was frantic in case he might die, and did not trouble to hide it. She even risked infection to visit and nurse him. When he recovered, she knew she wanted to marry him. According to Randolph, it was obvious what she had in mind, although many of her advisers expressed reservations. 'A great number wish him well, albeit others doubt him and deeplier consider what is fit for their country than a fair, jolly young man.' Moray and his followers took the poorest view, anticipating that Darnley's Catholicism would lead to 'the utter overthrow and subversion of them and their houses'.

Concerns were being expressed in England too about a queen's love affair. Leicester had taken the Spanish ambassador de Silva riding in Windsor Great Park early one morning, coming back on the path overlooked by the Queen's lodgings. Leicester's fool was in the party and he began to shout out, announcing Leicester's presence; when the Queen came to her window, de Silva was shocked to see that she was wearing a very revealing nightgown, and that she seemed unaware of her *déshabille* when she greeted the Earl. It was well-known at court that Leicester visited her in her chamber each morning whilst she was being dressed, and she had been seen to kiss him as he passed her her shift – that most basic of female undergarments.

Fuelled by such gossip, the feud between Leicester and Norfolk was still simmering. That March, an ugly incident occurred in the tennis court at Whitehall, where the two men were playing the game of royal (real) tennis with the Queen looking on. Dudley, 'being very hot and sweating, took her napkin out of her hand and wiped his face'. Shocked at such disrespect, Norfolk lost his temper, accused Leicester of being 'too saucy and swore that he would lay his racquet upon his face'. And he would have done so had not the Queen's strident order made him desist. Afterwards, it was Norfolk who felt the full brunt of her anger, not Leicester, which hardly improved matters between them.

That same month, Leicester continued his campaign for the Queen's hand by arranging for a company of players from Gray's Inn to perform at court before the Queen. The entertainment began with a supper hosted by himself, then, reported de Silva,

> there was a joust and a tourney on horseback. The challengers were the Earl of Essex, the Earl of Sussex and Lord Hunsdon. When this was ended we went to the Queen's rooms and descended to where all was prepared for the representation of a comedy in English. The plot was founded on the question of marriage, discussed between Juno and Diana, Juno advocating marriage and Diana chastity. Jupiter gave the verdict in favour of matrimony. The Queen turned to me and said, 'This is all against me.'

De Silva considered this 'very novel . . . After the comedy, there was a masquerade of satyrs, or wild gods, who danced with the ladies, and when this was finished there entered ten parties of twelve gentlemen each, the same who had fought in the foot tourney, and these, all armed as they were, danced with the ladies.'

On 15 April, Randolph reported that there was more than met the eye to the rumours that Mary meant to 'forsake all other offers' and marry Darnley. Moray's faction were closing ranks against the interloper, and

Mary, incited by Darnley and her Italian secretary, David Rizzio, was much vexed with them, flinging at her half-brother the accusation that 'he would set the crown on his own head'. A fatal rift between the two ensued, which would later have serious consequences.

On 18 April, Maitland arrived in London to inform Elizabeth that Mary had decided to marry Darnley. The Queen declared that she was astonished at this 'very strange and unlikely proposal' and much offended at that young man's disobedience – as her cousin and subject he needed her permission to marry. On 1 May, through the Council, she issued a formal warning to Mary that, if she went ahead with this marriage, it would be 'unmeet, unprofitable, and perilous to the amity between the queens and both realms'. If Mary desisted, she might take her pick of 'any other of the nobility in the whole realm'. Headed by Cecil, most Privy Councillors subscribed to this document; Leicester was a notable exception. Many English councillors thought that this display of outrage was a sham: opinion hardened that Elizabeth had engineered the whole affair in order to tempt Mary into making a disastrous marriage. Nevertheless the English official view was that Mary had chosen Darnley in order to strengthen her claim to the English crown, and by so doing now posed an even greater threat to Elizabeth's security than before; moreover, the English Catholics could only be encouraged by such a development.

Throckmorton was promptly sent north to fetch Darnley home and warn Mary that this union would have been 'a matter dangerous to the common amity'. The Queen had told him to 'stop or delay it as much as possible'; it apparently did not occur to her that Darnley might disobey her. Throckmorton arrived at the Scots court on 15 May, and saw for himself that Mary had been 'seized with love in ferventer passions than is comely for any mean personage'. Genuinely concerned, he urged her to show moderation, but without success: as Randolph noted, 'She doteth so much that some report she is bewitched. Shame is laid aside.'

Later, Throckmorton had a formal audience and registered Elizabeth's disapproval. In a royal temper Mary commanded him to tell Elizabeth that 'she did mind to use her own choice in marriage. She would no longer be fed with yea and nay.' The ambassador was so alarmed at the violence of her language that he sent a warning to Cecil.

Elizabeth was now resigned to the fact that Mary would never accept Leicester as a husband, and to save face she informed de Silva that Dudley himself had not consented to the marriage, though public opinion held that she herself could not give him up. As for Leicester, now that Elizabeth had abandoned the project, he presented himself as a suitor for the Queen's hand. He had more supporters than usual because many lords and courtiers were worried about her failure to provide for the succession.

Early in June, de Silva reported that Leicester believed the prize was within his grasp: 'It looks as if the Queen favours it also, and the French ambassador has been pointing out to her the objections to the Archduke's match, saying that he is very poor and other things of the same sort, to lead her away from the project.' De Silva expressed to the Earl of Sussex, a prominent member of the Privy Council, his opinion that Elizabeth might never marry, or, if she did, she would take none but Leicester. Sussex hated Leicester and ridiculed the very idea of his marrying the Queen: 'There is no one else but the Archduke whom she can marry,' he snapped.

Even Cecil, more fatalistic, and more sure now of his own position than he had been five years earlier, was bracing himself to accept Dudley as consort, even though, as he later noted in a private memorandum, it would bring the kingdom no benefits. On a personal level, Cecil, who had grown fond of his difficult mistress, was worried that Leicester would prove an unkind and jealous husband. But there was no gainsaying that the Earl was now, along with Norfolk, Sussex and Cecil himself, one of the four most powerful men in England.

Of these, Norfolk enjoyed the least influence. Although he was England's only duke, and therefore the premier peer, he was a bitter, frustrated man who felt that his talents had gone unrewarded. By the summer of 1565, he had come much under the influence of Sussex, both men sharing a mutual antipathy towards Leicester.

Thomas Ratcliffe, Earl of Sussex was related to the Queen through his Howard mother. Born in 1525, he had opted for a military career, and had recently completed a nine-year tour of duty as Lord Lieutenant of Ireland, a difficult job which he had carried out energetically, and at times brutally, but with little success. Sir Henry Sidney, Leicester's brother-in-law, had served under him, and had no very good opinion of Sussex's abilities, which gave Leicester ample ammunition to use against the Earl. This was perhaps somewhat unfair, since Sussex had done his best in an impossible situation, and had paid for it with his health and his nerves, which had been so shattered that he had asked to be recalled.

Sussex now saw his opportunity to form a faction of Leicester's enemies, and Norfolk proved his willing tool. They were joined by the lords Hunsdon and Howard of Effingham, the Queen's uncle. Within a short while Leicester had gathered his supporters in a rival faction, and by the summer both groups were strutting about the court and city, openly bearing arms.

*

Meanwhile, Throckmorton had demanded that Darnley and Lennox accompany him back to England forthwith, 'having failed in their duty by their arrogant and presumptuous attempts to enterprise such a matter without making Queen Elizabeth privy, being her subjects'. But he had not reckoned on a number of the Scots lords now being in favour of the match, nor on Elizabeth's lukewarm response to Moray's plea for support: she said she would only give it if his purpose was just to offer advice to his sovereign. As a sister monarch, she could not countenance rebellion against an anointed queen. Darnley refused to obey his sovereign – 'I find myself very well where I am, and so purpose to keep me' – and Throckmorton knew that it was too late to influence Mary: on 21 May he informed Elizabeth that 'This Queen is so far past in this matter with Lord Darnley as it is irrevocable.' He did, however, extract from Mary a promise that she would wait three months before making her final decision.

By now, Randolph and others had seen through Darnley, who was daily becoming more arrogant and was beginning to throw his weight about in a worrying way, and the envoy spoke for many when he voiced his concerns about Mary's headlong rush towards the altar. She had been bewitched, he concluded; she was 'so altered with affection towards Lord Darnley that she hath brought her honour in question, her estate in hazard, her country to be torn in pieces. I see also the amity between the countries like to be dissolved, and great mischiefs like to ensue.'

Queen Mary would hear no criticism of Darnley, and a gloomy Randolph lamented, 'Woe worth the time that ever the Lord Darnley set his foot in this country. What shall become of her, or what life with him she shall lead, I leave it to others to think.' He felt genuine pity for 'the lamentable estate of this poor Queen', seeing her so changed as to be almost unrecognisable: 'Her majesty is laid aside, her wits not what they were, her beauty other than it was, her cheer and countenance changed into I wot not what.'

Elizabeth rarely let her heart rule her head, especially when it came to matters matrimonial, but she sometimes found the pressure to marry, or even make a decision, intolerable. In May 1565, faced with a demand from the French for an immediate answer to King Charles's proposal, and knowing what response her advisers expected her to give, she burst into tears in Council, accusing Leicester, Cecil and Throckmorton of seeking her ruin by urging her to marry. The three men, shocked at her outburst, did their best to placate her, vowing that they would never force her to do anything against her will and assuring her of their loyalty.

At the end of June, realising she could not drag matters out any further, Elizabeth formally rejected Charles IX's suit on the grounds that he was too young for her: a husband could only be of use to her, she told de Foix, if he could provide her with a son. That, she made clear, was to be his chief function, since she had no intention of allowing him to usurp her control of her treasury, army or navy.

Fearing that Leicester would now seize his opportunity, Cecil, Norfolk and the Earl of Sussex used all the resources at their disposal to bring about the Habsburg match. Maximilian II's personal envoy, Adam Zwetkovich, had arrived in England in May, ostensibly to return the late Emperor's Garter insignia, but really to see if the Queen was in earnest about marrying the Archduke: another refusal would be too humiliating. He was also to make discreet enquiries as to the truth of rumours about the Queen and Leicester; if there was nothing in them, he might reopen negotiations.

So that the Emperor should be reassured that the English were serious this time, Norfolk demanded of Leicester that he support the marriage and abandon his own suit. Because Elizabeth seemed to be enthusiastic about the project for the time being, Leicester had no choice but to acquiesce, albeit unwillingly, and found himself appointed joint commissioner with Throckmorton to negotiate with Zwetkovich. If the Queen ever did marry the Archduke, Leicester stood to lose all precedence, influence and favour, and would be left to the mercy of his many enemies. The French, who had lost their chance of uniting by marriage with England against their enemy Spain, were naturally against the Habsburg match, and now did their best to persuade Elizabeth that she should marry Leicester. Much to the Earl's pique, the Queen seemed to prefer the Archduke, though it was hard for anyone to tell whether she was serious or not.

Leicester was despondent, and confided to de Silva that he believed Elizabeth would never marry him 'as she had made up her mind to wed some great prince, or at all events no subject of her own'. De Silva, however, who liked Leicester, was more optimistic, and reported to Philip II that 'Lord Robert's affair is not off.' His master responded by ordering him to collaborate with the Austrian envoys in bringing the Habsburg negotiations to a happy conclusion, whilst at the same time affecting to assist Leicester's cause, 'helping him in such a way that if ever his marriage to the Queen should come off, he will be bound to continue friendly'.

Zwetkovich was much encouraged by what he heard around the court. When he saw Elizabeth, he told her that the Archduke 'had a great desire to see her'. She was evasive, and rather dashed his hopes when she protested, 'I have never said to anybody that I would not marry the Earl of Leicester.' Zwetkovich assured her that Dudley was in fact 'the most important originator and warmest advocate' of her marriage to the Archduke.

'I would have stayed single', she declared, 'did not the crown of England compel me to marry to the profit of England.'

Then, appearing suddenly to view the idea of marriage with favour, she brought up the awkward subject of the malicious rumours about her relationship with Dudley: 'The House of Habsburg will find that I have always acted with due decorum.' Zwetkovich, however, wanted this corroborated, and was soon making 'diligent enquiries concerning the maiden honour and integrity of the Queen'. He was impressed to find that there was not a shred of evidence that she had ever been to the slightest degree promiscuous, and concluded that the rumours were but 'the spawn of envy and malice and hatred'. As for Leicester, he was 'loved by the most serene Queen with sincere and most chaste and most honourable love as a true brother'.

After two audiences, Zwetkovich could not, however, comprehend why Elizabeth was so changeable in her attitude to this splendid marriage offer. 'She is so nimble in her declining and threads in and out of the business in such a way that her most intimate favourites fail to understand her, and her intentions are therefore variously interpreted.' This may have been a ploy to manipulate the Austrians into offering highly advantageous terms, although during the summer the Queen's attitude to the marriage grew increasingly positive.

Zwetkovich, observing this with some relief, wondered if she might send an envoy incognito to Vienna to look at the Archduke, and he wrote to the Emperor warning him to ensure that Charles always looked his best and rode 'fiery steeds' to impress the English. Elizabeth rejected the idea; she was still insisting that she meet her suitor before deciding to accept him, and declared that she could not trust anyone else's eyes.

'I have already said this a thousand times', she said tetchily, 'and I am still, and ever will be, of the same mind.' She asked if Charles might secretly visit her in England, saying she did not wish to give him cause to curse portrait painters and ambassadors as King Philip had done when he first set eyes on Queen Mary. The Emperor, however, viewed this suggestion as 'entirely novel and unprecedented' amongst royalty, and insisted that, if Charles were to go to England, 'it would be with all befitting ceremony' and only after the marriage negotiations had reached a satisfactory conclusion. An argument over who should finance the Archduke's household then broke out, with Elizabeth saying it was the Emperor's responsibility and Maximilian insisting it was hers.

Then the Queen began to make difficulties over religion, insisting that she could never marry anyone of another faith, since two persons of different persuasions could never live peaceably in one house, and pointing out the awful consequences for her realm if it became divided on this issue, as it surely would be if the Archduke remained a Catholic.

Zwetkovich reminded her that she had always known that Charles was of the old faith, to which she replied that she had been given to understand that his beliefs were not deep-rooted and that he would be willing to change his opinions. Informed that he would not, she was about to abandon the whole project when Sussex intervened with a suggestion that the Archduke agree to accompany the Queen to Anglican services, whilst hearing mass in private. But the Emperor proved obdurate, and demanded that his brother and his Austrian household be allowed to hear mass in a public place. This was anathema to Elizabeth, who knew that her subjects would never tolerate it, and negotiations reached a deadlock, though both sides were still hopeful of achieving a compromise solution.

Early in the morning of 29 July 1565, despite her promise to Throckmorton, Mary, Queen of Scots married Lord Darnley at Holyrood Palace in Edinburgh. Within weeks of the lavish Catholic ceremony, the bridegroom had revealed himself for what he was – a weak-willed and dissolute bully. He had offended many of the Scottish courtiers with his arrogance, and Randolph reported, 'It is greatly to be feared that he can have no long life among these people.' Darnley wished to be crowned King Consort, but Moray successfully blocked that idea, and he had to be satisfied with the empty style 'King Henry' and the recognition of France, Spain and the Vatican.

The majority of the Scots lords had distrusted him because he was a Catholic, and realised quite soon that he was unfit to bear any form of political authority. They only tolerated him because he might be useful to them. Moray had by now made himself so unpopular with the Queen and her husband that a civil war seemed inevitable.

When told of Mary's marriage, Elizabeth raged that her cousin had broken her promises, accused her of subverting religion in her realm, and urged her most strongly to make her peace with Moray. But Mary, 'marvellous stout', would not. She meant to rule Scotland without interference, restore the Catholic faith, and pursue the rebel lords 'to the uttermost'. She would tolerate no interference from England.

In retaliation, Elizabeth consigned Lady Lennox once again to the Tower and offered aid to Moray, though since she had no wish to provoke a war, she only sent him a small sum of money. On 5 August, she urged Mary to be reconciled to her half-brother, but Mary outlawed him the following day and, later, imperiously informed Elizabeth, 'Her Majesty desires her good sister to meddle no further.' She then had Throckmorton arrested on the grounds that he had refused to accept a safe conduct from Darnley as King. Elizabeth was furious, and indeed, she had just cause to be offended. As his sovereign, she had had every right to recall Darnley, her subject, to England, but he had defied her. She believed Mary should have insisted he obey his queen, then negotiated with Elizabeth for the marriage; instead she had married him without her cousin's permission. It is no coincidence that Elizabeth's friendship towards Mary began to dissipate at this time. From now on, her antipathy and hostility towards her cousin would be more evident. The first sign of this was her willingness to treat with Moray.

Another dynastic crisis occurred that August. Although her sister was in disgrace, the Lady Mary Grey – known derisively to the courtiers as 'Crookback Mary' – had remained in the royal household as a maid of honour to the Queen, who wanted her under her eye. Mary was now twenty-five, had no beauty or intellect to speak of, and was rather old for marriage by the standards of her day; nor was it likely that Elizabeth would ever permit her to marry.

Frustrated of a match suitable to her status, the diminutive Mary fell in love with Her Majesty's Serjeant-Porter, one Thomas Keyes of Lewisham, a man twice as old as she and reputed to be the largest man in London. At nine o'clock one night, in his lodging by the watergate at Whitehall Palace, they were secretly married by a priest whose identity was never discovered. A few weeks later Mary confessed what she had done to the Queen, whose rage was terrible. She consigned Keyes to the Fleet Prison for three years, and only let him out on condition that he undertook never to see his wife again. The Queen did her best to have the marriage declared unlawful, but Bishop Grindal of London refused to co-operate, much to her chagrin.

Mary was sent to Chequers in Buckinghamshire – now the official country residence of the British Prime Minister – and placed under house arrest in the custody of a Mr William Hawtrey. After a time, she was transferred to the Greenwich home of Katherine Willoughby, Dowager Duchess of Suffolk, who treated her with kindness, confiding to Cecil, 'Lady Mary is so ashamed of her fault that I can scarcely get her to eat anything. I fear me she will die of her grief. A little comfort would do her good.' Despite her distress, Lady Mary remained defiant, continuing to sign her letters 'Mary Keyes'. She paid a price for her obstinacy: when her husband died in 1571, the Queen refused to allow her to wear mourning for him. She did, however, permit her to visit the court from time to time thereafter, although Mary's health had been broken by her sad experiences, and she availed herself of this privilege only very rarely.

In fact, the marriage posed no threat to Elizabeth: Keyes had no royal connections and no ambitions. There was never any suggestion that Lady Mary Grey coveted a crown. Neither had plotted treason. The draconian punishments meted out to them were an indication of how sensitive the Queen had become regarding the succession.

Elizabeth's bitterness at Lady Mary's perfidy was compounded by her grief at the death of her former governess, Katherine Ashley, who had brought her up since childhood and taken the place of the mother she had never known, standing by her in the darkest days of her youth. Ashley was replaced in her post by Mistress Eglionby of Shropshire, but for Elizabeth, life would never be the same again. She had lost a confidant, someone who loved her for herself and had dared to reprove her when she thought it necessary.

The dismal affair of Mary Grey and Mrs Ashley's death put Elizabeth quite out of temper, and that August Cecil recorded, 'The Queen seemed to be much offended with the Earl of Leicester.' The reason for this was not far to seek, for Dudley had begun a flirtation with Elizabeth's cousin and confidante, the beautiful, red-haired Lettice Knollys, who had been married four years before to Viscount Hereford and was 'one of the best looking ladies of the court'. She was the daughter of Sir Francis Knollys by Katherine Carey, whose mother, Mary Boleyn, had been sister to Elizabeth's mother, Anne Boleyn. Some people believed that Throckmorton had put Leicester up to the pretence of an affair in order to discover whether or not Elizabeth was serious in her intent to marry him. If not, then Throckmorton hoped to secure Leicester's support for the Habsburg marriage.

If this was true, it provoked only an adverse reaction for, in retaliation, a jealous Elizabeth began to show especial favour to one of Leicester's friends, Thomas Heneage, who had been a Gentleman of the Privy Chamber since 1560, and who was safely married. 'A young man of pleasant wit and bearing', who 'for his elegance of life and pleasantness of discourse [had been] born as it were for the court'. He was no intellectual or political lightweight either, since his talents eventually won him the important Household offices of Treasurer of the Chamber and, much later, Vice Chamberlain.

Leicester was angry at the attention shown to Heneage, and there were clashes between the two men. Then Leicester added fuel to the fire by asking permission 'to go to stay at my own place as other men'. Elizabeth refused to answer him, and sulked for three days. Then she summoned him to Windsor, where a violent quarrel took place, with Leicester accusing her of casting him aside for another, and Elizabeth flinging the same complaint back at him and declaring she was sorry for the time she had wasted on him – 'And so is every good subject!' commented Cecil to a friend. 'The Queen was in a great temper, and upbraided him with what had taken place with Heneage, and his flirting with the Viscountess, in very bitter words.'

She was also angry at reports that he had been high-handed with one of her servants, and publicly, before the whole court, she shouted at Leicester, 'God's death, my Lord, I have wished you well, but my favour is not so locked up for you that others shall not participate thereof. And if you think to rule here, I will take a course to see you forthcoming. I will have but one mistress and no master.' According to Sir Robert Naunton, who wrote a memoir of Elizabeth's court and recorded the incident, this 'so quailed my Lord of Leicester that his feigned humility was, long after, one of his best virtues'.

Suitably admonished, Leicester shut himself in his apartments for the next few days, whilst Heneage was sent quietly from the court. Then, against their better judgements, Cecil and Sussex persuaded the Queen and Leicester to make it up. Elizabeth summoned him to her presence and, both weeping, they were reconciled.

For Leicester, however, it was the end of an era in his life. His relationship with the Queen was changing: the heady passion of first love had gone, and with it his conviction that she would indeed eventually marry him. From now on, he would still love her, but it would come to be a deeper, more selfless love, almost like that of a long-wedded husband for his wife: a love, moreover, that would permit him to look elsewhere for the fulfilment he could not find with her.

Dudley's flirtation with Lettice soon fizzled out, but Heneage returned to Windsor: the Queen never could resist male admiration, and thereafter she continued to show him marked favour. Only when her interest had cooled into friendship did the Earl and Heneage become friends.

Heneage was not the only handsome man to captivate Elizabeth that summer. When her distant cousin, Thomas Butler, 10th Earl of Ormonde and Lord Treasurer of Ireland, visited court, she began singling him out. 'Black Tom', as he was known, was of an age with her, and had been reared at her father's court, where she may originally have become acquainted with him. He was attractive and admiring, and was often in her company during the next year. Leicester, however, knew there was nothing in it, and when the Archbishop of York dared to admonish the Queen for her friendship with Ormonde – provoking an outburst of Tudor temper – the Earl took her part.

Whilst she was at Windsor, the Queen spent most of her time riding and hunting. De Silva noted that she 'went so hard that she tired everybody out, and as for the ladies and courtiers who were with her, they were all put to shame. There was more work than pleasure in it for them.'

It was at Windsor also that, as Elizabeth strolled in the park with de Silva and an Italian envoy, the former, weary of her constant demands that the Archduke come and visit her, teased her by asking if she had noticed anyone she had not seen before in his own suite or that of the Imperial ambassador. Was she entertaining more than she knew?

The Queen was startled – and panic-stricken. At a loss for words, she searched frantically among the faces of the men following de Silva and was so obviously nonplussed that the ambassador burst out laughing. Elizabeth conceded the joke, calmed down, then announced that it might be no bad idea for the Archduke to visit her in such a way, if his dignity would allow it.

'I promise you plenty of princes have come to see me in that manner,' she divulged mysteriously.

After the Mary Grey affair, it seemed more imperative than ever that the Queen get herself an heir. On 14 August, Zwetkovich was sent home with a letter from the Queen to the Emperor, containing 'an honourable answer'. Zwetkovich was confident of a happy outcome, and Cecil had persuaded himself that 'the Queen's Majesty, thanked be God, is well-disposed towards marriage'. In a letter to Sir Thomas Smith in Paris, he reported, 'Common opinion is that the Archduke Charles will come, which – if he do and will accord with us in religion, and shall be allowable for his person to Her Majesty – then we shall see some success.'

He was dismayed therefore to learn that Philip of Spain was now doing his best to halt the negotiations on the grounds that the Archduke could not possibly marry a heretic queen. De Silva's opinion was that Elizabeth had no intention of marrying Charles anyway, maintaining that 'if any marriage at all is to result from all this, it will be Leicester's'.

Philip had already decided that he himself should be the instrument through which England should be returned to the Catholic fold, but the time was not yet right for fulfilling that sacred duty. In Philip's opinion, Mary, Queen of Scots was 'the sole gate through which religion can be restored in England; all the rest are closed'. This did not mean that he advocated the deposition of Elizabeth, which would be a scheme fraught with dangers. It would be far better, he believed, if Mary waited patiently until her peaceful succession to the English crown could be secured.

Moray and his rebel lords had retreated to Glasgow, whither Mary marched at the head of an army to capture them. On 6 October, the rebels fled to England, hoping to be succoured by Elizabeth. When she received Moray, she wore black, kept him on his knees, and castigated him publicly for rebelling against his anointed sovereign: 'We will not maintain any subject in any disobedience against the prince, for we know that Almighty God might justly recompense us with the like trouble in our own realm.' As for aid, none was to be forthcoming, although Moray might remain as an exile in England. When, in what became known as the 'Chaseabout Raid', Mary sent her troops to hunt any rebels out of Scotland, Elizabeth, who preferred peace to war, lifted no finger to help Moray, and Mary emerged victorious.

It was, however, an empty victory. The unruly Scots lords were proving difficult to control, Darnley was frequently drunk and, in the words of a courtier, 'wilful, haughty and vicious', and had been involved in street brawls in Edinburgh. Randolph reported that he was 'of an insolent, imperious nature, and thinks that he is never sufficiently honoured'. Mary's infatuation had died, and there were bitter 'jars' (quarrels) between the young couple. Whereas before Mary had turned to Maitland for advice, she now leaned upon her secretary, Rizzio. 'Seigneur Davie', as her courtiers sneeringly referred to him, was a native of Piedmont and had first come to her court in the train of the Savoyard ambassador in 1561. Mary had noticed his fine bass voice and had persuaded him to stay at her court as part of a vocal quartet. Later, she had made him her French secretary, and he had become friendly with Darnley. By June 1565, according to Randolph, Rizzio was 'he that works all'.

Now, however, Darnley grew resentful as he saw Rizzio's influence increasing daily and the Queen showing more and more favour to the man he regarded as an upstart Italian. In addition, those who craved favours or patronage from Mary had to bribe Rizzio in order to obtain an audience. Had he been a great nobleman, this would have been acceptable, but he was not, and he soon became the object of general hatred, derision and resentment. The Queen, miserable in her marriage and drawn to the lively Rizzio's company, failed to perceive that there was trouble brewing and that her ill-considered favouritism had caused it.

The exiled Protestant lords, however, summed up the situation very clearly, and resolved to return to Scotland with the aim of crushing Rizzio – and Darnley, too, if they were lucky. They had an ally in Maitland, who was jealous of the Italian who had supplanted him in the Queen's counsels, and even in Darnley himself, who was jealous for different reasons: he believed his wife to be having an affair with Rizzio, and the rebel lords were happy to let him think so. Darnley's resentment was festering because he had not been given the power he claimed was rightfully his, and also because Mary would not even discuss state affairs with him.

In December, it was announced that Queen Mary was pregnant. Her marriage was nevertheless a sham, since both partners avoided each other's company as often as possible. Darnley enjoyed himself, mostly at the hunt, whilst Mary attended to matters of state. And if she was lonely or needed someone to divert her, Rizzio was always there.

10

'Things Grievouser and Worse'

By November 1565, the 'great controversy' between Norfolk and
Leicester had reached epic proportions. Each faction had now
adopted a livery, purple being worn by Leicester's followers, and yellow
by the Norfolk-Sussex affinity. The young bloods in these factions were
only too prone to resort to violence and brawling in order to settle their
differences, and at one point the tension between the groups became so
threatening that Sussex protested to the Queen that his life was in
danger.

Elizabeth was well aware that the favour shown by her towards
Leicester was at the root of these troubles, and that he did not help
matters by boasting that he was 'a man that never did depend upon any
but merely Her Majesty'. She tried to defuse the tension by publicly
warning him, in the Presence Chamber, not to provoke jealousy by
displaying too much familiarity towards her.

She acted as mediator between the factions on this occasion, insisting
that all quarrels be put aside. From Ireland, Sidney wrote to Leicester, 'I
hear of a great reconcilement lately made with you.' However, he could
not see it lasting: 'There may be fairer semblances between you and
others, but trust not before trial, for in such trust is oft treason.' These
views were shared by many other people around the court, who could
sense the animosity beneath the surface courtesies.

De Foix noted that month that Leicester was still the chief contender
for the Queen's hand, and related how even his enemies felt it expedient
to feign friendship towards him. Norfolk was the one exception.

The Duke had an audience with the Queen early in December, in
which he seized his chance to promote the benefits of marriage and the
desirability of settling the succession question. He told Elizabeth that
most of her influential subjects wanted her to marry the Archduke
Charles. If they had appeared to endorse a marriage to Leicester, they

had only done so because they believed that that was where her heart lay, 'not because they really thought the match would be beneficial to the country or good for her own dignity'. Elizabeth listened politely to the Duke, but refused to commit herself to a definite answer. She agreed to his request to return to his estates and the interview came to an end.

Immediately afterwards, Norfolk sought out Leicester and warned him not to forget that he had promised the previous summer to abandon his pursuit of the Queen. Leicester forbore to take issue with him, and Norfolk went home, feeling he had done his sovereign and his country a service.

At Christmas, Leicester, confident of success this time, asked the Queen to marry him. As usual she hedged, teasing him that he would have to wait until Candlemas in February for an answer, although during the next few days she appeared to be seriously considering his proposal. The court was lively with speculation, while Leicester capitalised on his expected future role as consort, making more enemies in the process. De Foix swore privately to de Silva that Leicester 'had slept with the Queen on New Year's Night', but de Silva discounted this as nothing but an attempt to besmirch the Queen's reputation and thus wreck her chances of a Habsburg marriage.

However, there was another heated exchange between Leicester and Heneage on Twelfth Night, when the latter was chosen as 'King of the Bean' and allowed to preside over the court for the evening. In one game of wits, Heneage forced Leicester to ask the Queen which was the more difficult to erase from the mind – jealousy, or an evil opinion implanted by a wicked tale-teller.

'Lord Robert, being unable to refuse, obeyed. The Queen replied courteously that both were difficult to get rid of, but that, in her opinion, it was much more difficult to remove jealousy.' Leicester took this personally as implying that he had been deliberately unfaithful to her, and sent a message warning Heneage that he would 'castigate him with a stick' for his impertinence. Heneage retorted that 'this was not punishment for equals, and that if Lord Robert came to insult him, he would discover whether his sword could cut and thrust. The only answer Lord Robert gave was that this gentleman was not his equal and that he would postpone chastisement till he thought it time to do so.' The French ambassador reported that Heneage complained about this to the Queen, who was very vexed with Leicester, storming at him 'that if, by her favour, he had become insolent, he should soon reform, and that she would debase him just as she had raised him'. Leicester, 'in deep melancholy', spent the next four days shut up in his rooms, which had the desired effect, since the Queen's anger soon turned to forgiveness. It was shortly afterwards reported in Venice that she meant to make him a duke and marry him. Candlemas came and went, however, without any announcement being made, and it soon became clear that Elizabeth was employing her usual evasive strategy.

Norfolk was still determined to oust Leicester from favour. On the surface, the two men made an effort to be friendly, but their mutual animosity was obvious. Therefore, when the King of France, grateful for the Order of the Garter, decided in return to confer the Order of St Michael upon two of the Queen's subjects, the choice being hers, she nominated both Leicester and Norfolk, and the ceremony was fixed for 24 January.

Norfolk, resentful that Leicester was being so honoured, refused to attend, and only after great persuasion on the Queen's part did he agree to do so. On the day, he and Leicester, wearing robes of white and russet velvet garnished with lace, gold and silver, formally embraced in the 'great closet' at Whitehall and then proceeded to the chapel for the ceremony of investiture. Beneath the veneer of courtesy, hatred simmered. Nor did the Queen remain impressed with the honour conferred. After the French had bestowed the same insignia on Lord Darnley, she found out that the Order of St Michael had been indiscriminately awarded to so many men that it was completely devalued.

Shortly after the ceremony, having learned from Cecil that the favourite had ignored his promise not to press his suit, Norfolk sought out Leicester and insisted he abandon all thoughts of marrying the Queen. Instead, it was vital that he support the Habsburg project. Leicester agreed to do whatever he could providing it would not appear to Elizabeth that he was doing so out of distaste for her, since she might, 'womanlike, undo him'. True to his word, he went straight to her and urged her to marry soon for her own sake, for that of her country, and to stop others from accusing him of preventing it.

Shortly afterwards, whilst walking with de Silva in the Privy Garden at Whitehall, Elizabeth commended Leicester to the ambassador for his selflessness in urging her to marry for England's sake. In fact, it was not her affection for Leicester that was holding up the marriage negotiations, but the Emperor's refusal to agree with her conditions. When, in January, Maximilian had urged her to relax them, she dug her heels in, declaring it would cause 'a thousand inconveniences' if she married a man of a different religion.

Leicester's true feelings were shortly afterwards revealed when Elizabeth indulged in further flirtation with Ormonde, which this time angered Leicester. He quarrelled with the Queen, achieved nothing, and left court. Norfolk left too, remaining in the country until September.

Leicester had had enough. He was weary of strife and intrigue, and depressed at being blamed for Elizabeth's failure to marry. People thought he had great influence over her, but that was not the case. He was held responsible for the failures of government, but never for its successes, which were always attributed to the Queen. During his absence both Cecil and Throckmorton kept him up to date on state and court affairs, and he confided to Cecil that he despaired of the Queen ever making a good marriage; Throckmorton advised him to stay away from court in order to avoid being blamed for this. Indeed, he had no inclination to return, nor any appetite for the Queen's temper or the exhausting courtship dance she required him to take part in.

By February 1566, Lord Darnley, having heard that Rizzio now enjoyed confidential sessions with Mary in her private chamber and might be the father of her unborn child (a rumour still current in the early seventeenth century), could no longer live with the conviction that his wife was betraying him; nor could he suffer existing as a king with no power. He made it clear to those around him that he would be a crowned king regnant and nothing less, and that if he was helped to achieve this, he was prepared to support the Protestant Church in Scotland. He was fair game therefore for the unscrupulous Scots lords, who unanimously resented Rizzio's influence and wanted both him and Darnley out of the way. It appeared that the ailing Patrick, Lord Ruthven and the Earl of Morton were the leading conspirators, although the evidence strongly suggests that they were just a front to cover up the activities of the exiled Moray and his rebels, who were seeking a means to restore themselves to power.

The plotters were resolved to kill Rizzio in the Queen's presence: knowing that Mary was six months pregnant, they anticipated that the shock might harm her and her unborn child, in which case she would be incapacitated. With the lords' apparent support, Darnley envisaged himself invested with the crown matrimonial, or, if Mary died in childbirth set up as regent, or even king in her place. Whatever happened to her, he believed he would still rule Scotland, for even if she survived the coup with her sanity and her pregnancy unscathed, the conspirators had agreed that she would be shut up in Stirling Castle at his pleasure.

Darnley's fellow conspirators had other plans. They meant to represent to Mary when the time came that he alone had been the prime mover behind Rizzio's murder, and that he had also intended harm to herself, so provoking her into charging him with treason – for which the penalty was death. Thus, at a stroke, they would rid themselves of two unwelcome nuisances.

Thomas Randolph had his informants around the Scottish court, and on 13 February he reported to Leicester

> I know now for certain that this Queen repenteth her marriage, that she hateth the King and all his kin. I know that, if that take effect which is intended, David, with the consent of the King, shall have his throat cut within these ten days. Many things grievouser and worse are brought to my ears – yea, of things intended against Her Majesty's own person –

Leicester was not to repeat this. Nevertheless, Cecil and the Privy Council were aware that murder was being planned, and could have deduced that harm might come to the Scots Queen. Elizabeth was not informed until after the deed had been done: on 6 March Randolph asked Cecil to warn her of what was planned, but his letter did not reach London in time.

The conspirators had originally planned to carry out the murder on 12 March, but, guessing that Randolph had betrayed them, decided to act three days earlier just in case Elizabeth should intervene. On 9 March 1566, Lord Ruthven led a group of armed men into the Palace of Holyrood, just as Queen Mary, now six months pregnant, was dining in private with Lady Argyll and Rizzio, who had not removed his cap, as was expected of one in the presence of his sovereign. Suddenly, Darnley and other intruders, including a fully-armoured Ruthven, burst into the room, jostled the Queen aside, and laid hands on the Italian, who screamed, 'Justice! Justice! Save me, my lady!' as he clung to Mary's skirts. Armed men pulled him away and he was dragged into an adjoining chamber, where he was savagely murdered, his body pierced with fifty-six dagger wounds. Mary was forcibly restrained from trying to help him, and later claimed that one of the conspirators had aimed a loaded pistol at her distended stomach. When she remonstrated with Darnley, asking why he had done this 'wicked deed', he flung back at her that 'David had had more company of her body than he for the space of two months.'

In a state of shock, the Queen was confined to her rooms, but during the next two days she managed to convince her not very intelligent husband that the conspirators were planning to murder him next. Darnley, frightened out of his wits, betrayed the names of all who had taken part in the murder, and Mary immediately concluded that the plot had been aimed at her. At midnight on 11 March, the royal couple stole down some back stairs, escaped from the palace through the servants' quarters, and, taking horses, rode like the wind through the night for twenty-five miles until they reached Dunbar.

From there the Queen, determined to avenge Rizzio's murder, raised an army of 8000 men and marched back to Edinburgh, reoccupying the capital on 18 March. The conspirators, however, had already fled the city, seething with vengeful hatred at Darnley's perfidy. It was not long before Mary discovered the extent of Darnley's involvement in the plot against Rizzio, which brought to an abrupt end the brief reconciliation between husband and wife. From now on, they would be estranged, with Mary excluding Darnley from all state affairs. He remained at court, however, a sullen, dangerous nuisance, who was permanently under scrutiny in case he involve himself in any new conspiracy.

Elizabeth, when informed by Mary, in an emotional and graphic letter sent from Dunbar, of the murder of Rizzio and Darnley's involvement, expressed genuine horror at how Mary had been treated. Wearing a miniature of Mary suspended from a waist chain, she received de Silva and, during the course of an hour's discussion on the evils of what had happened, told him, 'Had I been in Queen Mary's place, I would have taken my husband's dagger and stabbed him with it.' Then, remembering to whom she was speaking, she quickly added that she would never do such a thing to the Archduke Charles.

When she returned to Edinburgh, Mary found Moray waiting to offer her his support. He had been impressed by her courage in handling a dangerous situation, and now he managed to convince her he was on her side. She reinstated him on her Council, and as her pregnancy advanced, he gradually established himself as the effective ruler of Scotland, which suited Elizabeth very well. The Scots lords wanted no further truck with Darnley, and treated him with ill-concealed contempt.

The dark events in Scotland inspired in Elizabeth a genuine concern for Mary, who had asked her to put their differences behind them, and for a time relations between the two Queens were much improved. There was a new exchange of letters between the cousins, Elizabeth playing the part of the older, wiser woman dispensing advice, and praying that God would sent Mary only short pains during childbirth and a happy outcome. 'I too', she declared, 'am big with desire for the good news.' A grateful Mary paid Elizabeth the honour of asking her to be godmother to the infant.

Tensions over the succession question seemed to have eased too, with Mary expressing her gratitude to her 'dearest sister' for her efforts to promote Mary's claim. In Mary's opinion, the Archduke Charles would be the perfect consort for her cousin, and she warmly endorsed the match.

The war of attrition between Elizabeth and Leicester lasted a mere two weeks: as usual, she could not do without him, and at the end of March, much 'misliking' his absence, she sent Mrs Dorothy, one of her ladies, to tell him of her 'affection to your hasty repair and Her Majesty's unkindness taken with your long absence'. On 1 April he appeared again at court, and there was a reconciliation of sorts, with Elizabeth declaring that never again would she permit him to leave her side.

Cecil, who had prayed that her affection for the favourite had run its course, tried again to reconcile himself to the idea that the Queen might marry Leicester, but naturally he was not happy about it, not only on his own account, but also because he believed that the marriage would bring few benefits to England. In April, he drew up a chart comparing Leicester and the Archduke, and in nearly every respect Leicester proved the less desirable: he was of common birth, and he would bring to the marriage 'nothing either in riches, estimation, power'; his marriage had been childless and he might prove sterile. This would be 'a carnal marriage', and such marriages began in pleasure and ended in sorrow. While the Archduke was 'honoured of all men', Leicester was 'hated of many, infamed by the death of his wife'. If he married Elizabeth, 'it will be thought that the slanderous speeches of the Queen with the Earl have been true'.

Cecil believed, as he often averred to his correspondents, that the rumours were not true; he also believed that, given time, Elizabeth would come to favour the Habsburg marriage, and he prayed that God would guide her to this, for otherwise her reign would prove troublesome and unquiet.

Leicester did not remain long at court. There was still a coolness between him and the Queen, and rumour had it that she meant to deprive him of the office of Master of the Horse. At the end of April she allowed him to visit his estates in Norfolk, but she did not take his absence kindly and wrote a stinging rebuke which has not survived. A shocked Leicester informed Throckmorton,

> I have received your [letter] and another from one whom it has always been my great comfort to hear from, but in such sort that I know not what to impute the difference to. If there is any cause found in me to deserve it, I am worthy of much worse, but as there is none living that can so uprightly keep themselves from error, in this far can I, in conscience, acquit myself: that I never wilfully offended. Foul faults have been found in some; my hope was that one only might have been forgiven – yea, forgotten – me. If many days' service and not a few years' proof have made trial of unremovable fidelity enough, what shall I think of all that past favour, which my first oversight [brings about] an utter casting off of all that was before?

He was so cast down that 'a cave in a corner of oblivion or a sepulchre for perpetual rest were the best homes I could wish to return to'.

Again, the Queen summoned him back, and wearily he went, but her purpose was reconciliation and it was not long before he was restored to high favour.

In May, Elizabeth agreed to send Cecil's brother-in-law, Thomas Dannett, to the Emperor in Augsburg, to say that, if he permitted the Archduke to come to England, nothing would be allowed to hinder his marriage to the Queen. But Maximilian was still sticking on the religious issue, and Elizabeth, who had planned to honour him with the Order of the Garter, decided to delay sending it until he proved more amenable.

Dannett also saw the Archduke himself in Vienna, and reported that he was courteous, affable, liberal, wise, popular and fond of outdoor sports; he had survived an attack of smallpox, but it had not marred his good looks. 'For a man', he was 'beautiful and well-faced, well-shaped, small in the waist and broad-breasted; he seemeth in his clothes well-thighed and well-legged.' Although 'a little round-shouldered', he sat erect in the saddle. The drawback was that he was so devout that he would probably never agree to change his religion. Dannett urged the Queen to 'wink at' Charles attending mass in private, but she obstinately refused. Dannett remained in Austria until August, hoping in vain that she would change her mind, but all he got was a request for a portrait.

The birth of a healthy son, James, after a long and painful labour, to Mary, Queen of Scots on 19 June in the fortified sanctuary of Edinburgh Castle immeasurably strengthened her claim to the English succession. Now her ambitions were not only for herself, but also for her son.

An apocryphal story, related decades later by Sir James Melville in his memoirs, relates how Elizabeth reacted to the birth. She was, he said, 'in great mirth, dancing after supper' on 23 June, when Cecil whispered the news to her, 'Whereupon she sank down disconsolately, bursting out to some of her ladies that the Queen of Scots was mother of a fair son, while she was but a barren stock.' Melville was not a witness of this episode, and claimed he had been told of it by friends at court, but he did not report it at the time, and there is no other contemporary account of it. All Melville told Mary of Elizabeth's reaction was that the birth of the Prince was 'grateful to Her Majesty'. In fact, Cecil had told her the news before Melville arrived, and de Silva reported that 'the Queen seemed glad of the birth of the infant'.

What Elizabeth certainly did tell Melville was that she was 'resolved to satisfy the Queen in that matter [of the succession], which she esteemed to belong most justly to her good sister, and that she wished from her heart that it should be that way decided'. The Prince's birth, she added, would prove a 'spur to the lawyers' to resolve the matter, which would be decided in the next session of Parliament. Of course, Mary was jubilant to hear this, and confidently expected to be formally acknowledged as Elizabeth's heir. According to Melville, Leicester, Pembroke, Norfolk and others all upheld Mary's claim to succeed Elizabeth.

Cecil knew that Mary was using every means in her power to bring Elizabeth to heel. One of his spies reported that summer that Mary had told her advisers that she hoped to win over the Catholic nobles in England in order to establish a power base in the shires, particularly in the north, where the old religion was deeply rooted. 'She meant to cause wars to be stirred in Ireland, whereby England might be kept occupied; then she would have an army in readiness, and herself with her army to enter England; and the day that she should enter, her title to be read and she proclaimed queen.' Cecil, who was sceptical about such reports being true, already knew that Mary had contacted English Catholics, and that she had been told by her agents that these people would rise in her favour. However, he believed that her ambitions were centred upon the succession only, not the throne. Informed of this, Elizabeth sent Sir Henry Killigrew to warn Mary not to solicit the support of English subjects for her claims to the succession.

For the present Mary had more pressing matters to attend to, not least of which was the establishment of stable government in Scotland. There was also the problem of her husband. Relations between Mary and Darnley were now frigid. They rarely ate together and never shared a bed, avoiding each other's company whenever possible. In August, the Earl of Bedford reported to the Council, 'It cannot for modesty, nor with the honour of a queen, be reported what she said of him.'

Darnley was threatening to live abroad, an embarrassing reproach to Mary, who was horrified at the idea. By October, Maitland was aware that she felt desperate at the prospect of being tied to him for life.

In August, Thomas Dannett returned in despair from Vienna. The Habsburg negotiations seemed to have reached a stalemate, and Elizabeth took pains to make it clear to the Emperor that this was nothing to do with Leicester, 'as none of us is more inclining and addicted towards this match than he is, neither doth any person more solicit us towards the same'.

In the autumn, Elizabeth decided to send Sussex to Vienna, ostensibly to invest the Emperor with the Garter, but really to persuade him to agree to her terms. She was now complaining about the paucity of 'the Archduke's dowry', and arguments about this and other matters delayed

Sussex's departure for several months. Maximilian was obliged to remind Elizabeth, 'It is the future wife who provides the husband with a dowry and gives him a wedding gift.' Her behaviour confirmed his suspicion that she saw it 'as profitable to create delays somewhere or somehow in order to gain an advantage'.

Elizabeth left Greenwich for her annual progress in August, travelling through Northamptonshire to the former Grey Friary in Stamford, having avoided staying with Cecil at his house nearby because his daughter had smallpox. She then moved to Oxfordshire, staying at the old palace of Woodstock, where she had been held under house arrest in Queen Mary's reign. From here, she rode out in her litter to meet the dons who had come to escort her into the City of Oxford, where she received a warm welcome from the mayor, aldermen and scholars, the latter shouting '*Vivat Regina!*'

She thanked them in Latin, then responded to a loyal address in Greek in that language before attending a service at Christ Church, in which a *Te Deum* was sung. There then followed a hectic schedule of tours of the colleges, public orations and disputations, sermons, lectures, debates and plays. Elizabeth particularly enjoyed the now lost *Palamon and Arcite* by Richard Edwards, despite the stage collapsing, killing three people and injuring five more. The Queen sent her own barber-surgeons to help the latter, and ordered that the rest of the performance be postponed until the next day, when she personally thanked Edwards for entertaining her so merrily.

At St John's College, Master Edmund Campion, the future Catholic martyr, told her, 'There is a God who serves Your Majesty, in what you do, in what you advise.' Laughing, Elizabeth turned to Leicester and said this referred to him. Leicester was Chancellor of the University, and this visit was in his honour, as her visit to Cambridge had honoured its Chancellor, Cecil.

On her last public appearance before her departure, the Queen made a speech she had composed herself in Latin, declaring that it was her wish that learning should prosper, which received loud applause. When she left Oxford, the students and university officials ran alongside her litter for two miles beyond the city. One, Anthony Wood, recalled, 'Her sweet, affable and noble carriage left such impressions in the minds of scholars that nothing but emulation was in their studies.'

There were plans during this progress for Elizabeth to visit Leicester's seat at Kenilworth Castle, but the gossip among the courtiers proclaimed that this betokened an imminent announcement of their betrothal, and this so alarmed Elizabeth that she decided not to go ahead with the visit. Leicester, however, persuaded her to change her mind, and so to Kenilworth she went, being impressed with all the improvements he had made to the castle.

Desperately short of money, Elizabeth had no choice but to summon Parliament that autumn, but much to her vexation this only led to the resurrection of the succession question, which was by now a highly sensitive issue between her and the general public. Recently there had been a spate of pamphlets published, favouring mainly the claims of Katherine and Mary Grey, and one MP, Mr Molyneux, dared to suggest that the earlier petitions to the Queen be revived. Those Privy Councillors who were present tried to silence him, but the Commons were determined that the matter be settled once and for all, and resolved that another petition be submitted to the Queen, subscribed to by both Commons and Lords.

Elizabeth, being apprised of this, ordered Cecil to assure Parliament that, 'by the word of a prince, she would marry', but for the present, 'touching the limitation of the succession, the perils be so great to her person that the time will not yet suffer to treat of it'. Both Commons and Lords were determined to go ahead, the former defiantly refusing to approve any subsidy until the Queen resolved the succession question.

Their royal mistress reacted furiously, and told de Silva she would never allow Parliament to meddle in such a matter. She needed the subsidy for the good of her people, and Parliament should vote it freely and graciously. The ambassador pointed out that, if she were to marry, she could spare herself all this aggravation. She replied that she was well aware of it, and intended to write to the Emperor within the week, 'signifying that her intention was to accept the marriage'. De Silva knew that this was a bluff, since Maximilian had not moderated his demands in any way and negotiations had remained in deadlock for months, but he said nothing.

On 21 October, a deputation from the Lords waited upon the Queen in the Privy Chamber to remind her of the need to provide for the future and beg her to decide upon a successor. Elizabeth, who had not wanted to receive them but had been prevailed upon by Leicester to do so, was angry with the Lords for supporting the Commons's subversive behaviour, and reminded them that the Commons would never have dared be so rebellious in her father's day. They, the Lords, could do as they pleased, and so would she.

Three days later the Lords took her at her word and united with the Commons. The Queen was so furious that she used strong words to Norfolk, snarling that he was little better than a traitor. When Pembroke tried to defend the Duke, she told him he talked like a swaggering soldier. Leicester was next. If all the world abandoned her, she cried, yet she had thought he would not have done so.

'I would die at your feet,' he swore.

'What has that to do with the matter?' she retorted.

Then it was Northampton's turn.

'Before you come mincing words with me about marriage,' she warned, 'you had better talk of the arguments which got you your scandalous divorce and a new wife!' And so saying, she flounced out of the council chamber to seek comfort from de Silva, whom she was now treating as her chief confidante. He reported that she was angriest with Leicester, and had asked him his opinion of such ingratitude from one to whom she had shown so much favour that even her honour had suffered. She was now determined to dismiss him and leave the way clear for the Archduke to come to England. Leicester and Pembroke were soon afterwards dismayed to find themselves banned from the Presence Chamber. The nobility, complained the Queen, were 'all against her'.

She might have said the same about the stiff-necked Commons, who were virtually refusing to attend to any government business until the Queen acceded to their demands. Elizabeth told de Silva, 'I do not know what these devils want!'

'It would be an affront to Your Majesty's dignity to adopt any compromise,' he advised.

But matters could not rest as they were, and Elizabeth knew it. She therefore summoned a delegation of thirty members from each House to Whitehall, but refused to allow the Speaker to accompany them, since she alone meant to do all the talking on this occasion. Barely containing her anger, she opened by accusing 'unbridled persons in the Commons' of plotting a 'traitorous trick', and then rehearsed all the old arguments against naming her successor, administering a stinging rebuke to the Lords for so rashly supporting the Commons in this nonsense.

> Was I not born in this realm? Were not my parents? Is not my kingdom here? Whom have I oppressed? Whom have I enriched to other's harm? How have I governed since my reign? I will be tried by envy itself. I need not to use many words, for my deeds do try me. I have sent word that I will marry, and I will never break the word of a prince said in a public place, for my honour's sake. And therefore I say again, I will marry as soon as I can conveniently, and I hope to have children, otherwise I would never marry.

Touching on the succession, she went on:

> None of you have been a second person in the realm as I have, or tasted of the practices against my sister – whom I would to God

Elizabeth I at her accession

'An air of dignified majesty pervades all her actions.'

Robert Dudley, Earl of Leicester, attr. to Steven van Meulen
'Lord Robert does whatever he likes with affairs.'

William Cecil, Lord Burghley

'No prince in Europe hath such a counsellor.'

Lord Darnley and Mary Queen of Scots

'The Queen of Scots is a dangerous person.'

Philip II of Spain and Mary

'Sometimes it is necessary for princes to do what displeases them.'

Lettice Knollys, Countess of Leicester

'One of the best-looking ladies of the court.'

Sir Christopher Hatton by Nicholas Hilliard

'One of the goodliest personages of England.'

Sir Francis Walsingham by John de Critz the Elder

He set himself 'to break the neck of all dangerous practices'.

were alive again! There are some now in the Commons who, in my sister's reign, had tried to involve me in their conspiracies. Were it not for my honour, their knavery should be known. I would never place my successor in that position.

The succession question was a difficult one, 'full of peril to the realm and myself. Kings were wont to honour philosophers, but I would honour as angels any with such piety that, when they were second in the realm, would not seek to be first.'

Firmly, she chided them for their impertinence: it was for her, the sovereign, 'your prince and head', to decide the succession, and it was 'monstrous that the feet should direct the head'. All she would say was that she would resolve the succession problem when she could do so without imperilling herself.

As for her mutinous subjects, she hoped the instigators of this trouble would repent and openly confess their fault.

As for my own part, I care not for death, for all men are mortal, and though I be a woman, yet I have as good a courage answerable to my place as ever my father had. I am your anointed Queen. I will never be by violence constrained to do anything. I thank God I am endowed with such qualities that if I were turned out of the realm in my petticoat, I were able to live in any place in Christendom.

The Lords might have been subdued by this tirade, but the Commons were less impressed. When Cecil read out his edited draft of the Queen's speech to the House, it was received in silence, and three days later there were more calls for a petition. By now, Elizabeth had had enough of this insubordination, and on 9 November, on her orders, Sir Francis Knollys 'declared the Queen's Majesty's express command to the House that they should proceed no further in their suit, but satisfy themselves with Her Majesty's promise to marry'.

This prompted an uproar: MPs made clear their resentment at Elizabeth's high-handed attitude, perceiving it as an attack on their 'accustomed lawful liberties', while she was furious at their attempts to infringe her prerogative. On 11 November, she summoned the Speaker and insisted he impress upon the Commons the fact 'that he had received special command from Her Highness that there should be no further talk of the matter'.

The Commons, however, would not be silenced. By the end of the month it had become obvious to Elizabeth that they had her in a corner, for they had still not voted her the money she badly needed, and it was unlikely they would do so whilst she remained uncooperative. She could either forgo her much-needed funds and dissolve Parliament, or she could give in. The original dispute over the succession was turning into a battle over the privileges of monarch and parliament, and she had no wish for a showdown over that sensitive issue. Wisely, she capitulated, conceding that members might have a free discussion on the succession question, and remitting one third of the subsidy she had asked for. The Commons were so overjoyed and gratified at this that they agreed to proceed at once to the money bill without debating the succession. But when Parliament tried to incorporate the Queen's promise to marry into the preamble to the bill, she took one outraged look at the draft presented for her approval, and scrawled in the margin, 'I know no reason why my private answers to the realm should serve for prologue to a subsidy book; neither do I understand why such audacity should be used to make, without my licence, an Act of my words!'

The preamble was discreetly removed, leaving in the draft just a brief reference to Parliament's pious wish that the succession question would be resolved in the future. This of course dashed the hopes of Mary Stuart, who had expected her claim to be ratified by Parliament.

On 2 January 1567, Elizabeth dissolved a chastened Parliament, sourly advising its members, 'Beware however you prove your prince's patience, as you have now done mine! Let this my discipline stand you in stead of sorer strokes, and let my comfort pluck up your dismayed spirits. A more loving prince towards you ye shall never have.'

She behaved as though she had won a contest, but Cecil pointed out that she had been rather the loser, passing her a memorandum in which he enumerated what had not been achieved: 'The succession not answered, the marriage not followed, dangers ensuing, general disorientations.'

In November 1566, Mary had discussed with her advisers ways of freeing herself from Darnley, but to little effect. The marriage could not be annulled because that would call into question the legitimacy of her son. Some lords wanted her to arrest Darnley on a charge of treason, but she was reluctant to do so because foreign ambassadors were already assembling at her court for the christening of Prince James. This sumptuous Catholic ceremony, the last of its kind in Scotland, took place on 17 December at Stirling Castle. Queen Elizabeth stood godmother, and was represented by the Earl of Bedford, who presented her gift of a golden font, intricately carved and vividly enamelled. It had, however, been made for a much smaller baby, and Elizabeth felt bound to apologise, explaining she had not realised how much young James would have grown. Darnley, simmering with resentment, refused to attend his son's baptism.

After the christening, Bedford conveyed another message from his mistress, which brought welcome news, for Elizabeth had promised to block any legislation prejudicial to Mary's succession in return for an undertaking that her cousin would refrain from pressing her claim while Elizabeth lived.

Mary had by now turned for support to James Hepburn, Earl of Bothwell, to whose castle at Dunbar she had fled after Rizzio's murder. He had rallied his followers and her other supporters there, and returned with her to Edinburgh in triumph. Bothwell was described by one of his contemporaries as 'a glorious, rash and hazardous young man', but his cultivated manner, acquired during a sojourn in France, masked a ruthless and unscrupulous character. He was a Protestant, and had recently married the virtuous Lady Jean Gordon. Lady Jean, however, could not offer him a crown, and it was his desire for this that now fuelled his pursuit of the Queen.

Already Bothwell was hated and resented by his peers for his favour with her, and Bedford reported 'His influence is such as David [Rizzio] was never more abhorred than he is now.'

On 24 December, the day on which Darnley took himself off to stay with his father, the Earl of Lennox, at Glasgow, Mary formally pardoned Rizzio's murderers. It was now obvious that she was looking for a way to rid herself of her husband, and she confided as much to Maitland at a conference of nobles held that month at Craigmillar Castle near Edinburgh.

'Madam, let us guide the matter among us, and Your Grace shall see nothing but good, and approved by Parliament,' he soothed.

'Nothing must be done to stain my honour and conscience,' insisted the Queen. Nevertheless it was during that same conference that Bothwell and other lords first conceived a plot to murder Darnley, though there is no evidence that Mary either knew of it or gave her consent to it.

During the winter, Darnley fell ill. It was given out that he was suffering from smallpox, but it seems more likely that he had syphilis. Whatever his illness was, it had a debilitating effect and he took to his bed.

At least now Mary was enjoying good relations with Elizabeth. 'Always have we commended the equity of our cause to you and have looked to you for friendship therein,' the Queen of Scots wrote that January to her cousin. But this fragile amity was soon to be irrevocably shattered.

On 20 January, fearful that he might stir up trouble in the west of the country, Mary visited her husband in Glasgow and persuaded him to return with her to Edinburgh. Her manner was solicitous and she promised that, when he was well again, she would live with him as his wife. In the capital Bothwell was waiting to greet them and conduct them to an old house in Kirk o' Field, where Darnley had chosen to lodge rather than going to Craigmillar Castle at Mary's suggestion. Reputedly situated in healthy air, the house stood on a small hill near the city wall overlooking the Cowgate, and was surrounded by pretty gardens. Today the University of Edinburgh Hall of the Senate stands on the site of the Prebendaries' Chamber, where Darnley was accommodated. Beneath this room was a bedroom for the Queen, who visited him often and sometimes stayed at the house during his illness.

Bothwell had met with Morton that January and Darnley's assassination had again been discussed, but neither lord would later admit to initiating the subject. Bothwell had also talked with his kinsman, James Hepburn, of murdering Darnley. Although there is no evidence that Mary knew what they were planning, her contemporaries would come to believe after her husband's death that she had lured Darnley to Edinburgh at Bothwell's suggestion.

On Darnley's first night in Edinburgh, Mary sat up with him, talking, playing cards and giving every appearance of being a loving wife. Darnley's father, the Earl of Lennox, would later say that when he visited his son he found him sadly altered, desperately in need of company and comfort, and obtaining solace from the Psalms.

On 8 February, Mary announced that she was at last willing to ratify the Treaty of Edinburgh, and the next day her envoy left for England. Mary had intended to spend that night at Kirk o' Field with Darnley, but then remembered that she had promised to attend a wedding masque at Holyrood Palace. She took a fond farewell of her husband, pressing into his hand a ring as a token of her love, and then left in a torchlit procession for the palace.

11

'A Dangerous Person'

At two o'clock in the morning, on 10 February 1567, a violent explosion shook the city of Edinburgh, bringing people running to Kirk o' Field. They found the house a smouldering heap of rubble, while in the orchard lay the dead bodies of Darnley, naked beneath his nightgown, and his valet, Taylor. Marks on their throats indicated that both had been strangled: certainly they were not killed by the explosion, which had perhaps been intended to destroy the evidence of murder. It was thought that Darnley, sensing that something was wrong, had left the house with his servant to investigate and been attacked outside. An elderly neighbour had heard him plead, 'Pity me, kinsmen, for the sake of Him who pitied all the world!' The first person who ran out into the street nearby after the explosion was Captain William Blackadder, Bothwell's man, who was promptly arrested but swore he had merely been sharing a drink with a friend in a neighbouring house.

When the news was brought to the Queen, who had been awakened by the blast, she expressed shock and horror, and vowed that her husband's murderers would be speedily 'discovered' and punished. She expressed her belief that the murderers' intention had been to assassinate her also: had she not decided to attend the masque at Holyrood, she too would have been murdered, and she wasted no time in penning letters to foreign courts announcing her 'miraculous' escape.

There was no doubt that Darnley had been murdered: many people had a motive for doing away with him, or stood to gain from his death. Chief among them was the Queen herself, who had long since ceased to love him and had discussed ways of ridding herself of him. She also regarded him as a dangerous liability, and had recently complained to Archbishop James Beaton that it was well known how her husband was plotting to kidnap their son and rule in his name.

Bothwell wanted Darnley dead so that he himself could marry the

Queen and rule Scotland. He was 'high in his own conceit, proud, vicious and vainglorious above measure, one who would attempt anything out of ambition', as one contemporary described him.

Then there were the other Scots lords, who hated Darnley, many still nursing a sense of betrayal over his treacherous behaviour to them after Rizzio's murder. The finger of suspicion even touched foreign princes with vested interests in Scotland: the Catholic champions, Philip II, Charles IX and the Pope, had no wish to see Catholicism besmirched by the scandals surrounding Darnley. Conversely, Queen Elizabeth was anxious to promote the ascendancy of the Protestant establishment in Scotland, as led by Moray, and Darnley was an obstacle to this.

But, for most people, in Scotland and elsewhere, the evidence pointed overwhelmingly to Bothwell – and, quite soon, to Mary.

On 24 February, having received from her agents in Scotland a far more sinister account of Darnley's murder than appeared in the official version that would shortly be sent to her, Elizabeth wrote to Mary from Whitehall with serious urgency. Instead of her usual '*Ma chère soeur*', she began,

> Madam: my ears have been so astounded and my heart so frightened to hear of the horrible and abominable murder of your former husband, our mutual cousin, that I have scarcely spirit to write; yet I cannot conceal that I grieve more for you than him. I should not do the office of a faithful cousin and friend if I did not urge you to preserve your honour, rather than look through your fingers at revenge on those who have done you that pleasure, as most people say. I exhort you, I counsel you, I beg you, to take this event so to heart that you will not fear to proceed even against your nearest. I write thus vehemently, not that I doubt, but for affection.

Catherine de' Medici commented to her circle that Mary was lucky to be rid of the young fool, but warned her former daughter-in-law that, if she did not immediately pursue and punish the murderers, France would deem her dishonoured and would become her enemy.

Mary, concerned to dissociate herself from the crime, ordered an inquiry, but the depositions of witnesses were extracted in often suspicious circumstances, even under torture. The Earl of Moray, who stood to gain power in Scotland if his half-sister were to be overthrown, was to retain control of all these documents and, therefore, they are unreliable as evidence. It is possible that Mary, whose health at the time was poor, was paralysed by indecision and reluctant to act against the man who, a week after Darnley's murder, was named in anonymous obscene public placards that appeared in Edinburgh as the chief suspect,

Bothwell.

Darnley's parents suffered anguish, not only as a result of their son's death, but also because the Queen seemed to be doing so little to bring the culprits to justice. Elizabeth released a distraught Lady Lennox from the Tower and placed her in the care of Sir Richard Sackville. De Silva reported that the Countess believed that Mary 'had some hand in the business' as an act of 'revenge for her Italian secretary'. The Earl of Lennox successfully pressured Mary into allowing a private indictment of Bothwell for the murder of Darnley, but after an insulting travesty of a trial, which intimidated witnesses were too frightened to attend, he was acquitted on 12 April.

On 24 April, Mary, again convalescent after an illness, was travelling back to Edinburgh after visiting her son at Stirling, when Bothwell, reckless with regard to his reputation or hers – and possibly with her consent and foreknowledge, for she turned down an offer to rescue her – abducted her and bore her off to Dunbar, where he 'ravished' her, thus ensuring that it was impossible for her to refuse to marry him.

Shortly after the abduction, Lord Grey arrived from England with orders to tell Mary that Elizabeth was 'greatly perplexed' because the Queen of Scots had failed to bring to justice her husband's murderers yet had showered favour upon 'such as have been by common fame most touched with the crime'. Mary, of course, was *incommunicado*, and the message was never delivered. When Elizabeth learned that Mary had surrendered herself to Bothwell, she was shocked.

On 3 June, the Church of Scotland denounced Bothwell as an adulterer with one of his wife's maids and granted her a divorce. This left him free to marry Mary, their Protestant nuptials taking place on 15 May at Holyrood Palace. Afterwards, Mary asserted that she had had no choice in the matter, but there were many who thought her conduct depraved, and were now convinced that she had connived with Bothwell to murder Darnley.

Elizabeth could only deplore her cousin's behaviour, which contrasted so unfavourably with her own at the time of Amy Dudley's death, and in a letter to Mary she wrote, 'Madam, it has been always held in friendship that prosperity provideth but adversity proveth friends, wherefore we comfort you with these few words.' She had learned of Mary's marriage, and,

> to be plain with you, our grief has not been small thereat: for how could a worse choice be made for your honour than in such haste to marry a subject who, besides other notorious lacks, public fame has charged with the murder of your late husband, besides touching yourself in some part, though we trust in that behalf falsely. And

with what peril have you married him, that hath another lawful wife, nor any children betwixt you legitimate!

Thus you see our opinion plainly, and we are heartily sorry we can conceive no better. We are earnestly bent to do everything in our power to procure the punishment of that murderer against any subject you have, how dear soever you should hold him, and next thereto to be careful how your son the Prince may be preserved to the comfort of you and your realm.

Elizabeth told Randolph that she 'had great misliking of the Queen's doing, which she doth so much detest that she is ashamed of her'. Yet there were other reasons for her disapproval of the marriage. Randolph had long since warned her that Bothwell was 'as mortal an enemy to our whole nation as any man alive', and she feared that, to gratify his ambition, he might incite Mary to become her enemy. Bedford was therefore instructed to 'comfort' any Scots lords who 'misliked Bothwell's greatness'.

Two days after the wedding, Mary was already regretting what she had done, for Bothwell was proving a stern husband, frowning on frivolous pleasures and displaying jealousy of the influence of any other lords. The French ambassador saw her looking very sad and heard her wishing for death; at one point she was calling for a knife with which to kill herself. He noticed also that, despite her mental anguish, she could not resist Bothwell's physical attraction.

The Scots lords found the marriage intolerable. Having just rid themselves of Rizzio and Darnley, they were in no mood to endure the ambitious and ruthless Bothwell as King of Scots, and they were soon preparing for an armed confrontation with him. This took place on 15 June at Carberry Hill. Very little blood was spilt, but at the end of the day Mary was in the custody of her nobles and Bothwell had fled back to Dunbar, whence he escaped to Denmark via the Orkneys. The lords assured the Queen that they intended no harm to the Crown, but she soon found herself under guard like a common felon.

Thus she was led weeping and mud-spattered back to Edinburgh, and here it became starkly apparent how her subjects now felt about her. As she rode through the packed streets, they reviled her as an adulteress and murderess, and screamed, 'Burn the whore! Kill her! Drown her!'

'I will hang and crucify them all,' she cried, but her humiliation was complete. Placards depicting her as a mermaid – a symbol for a prostitute – confronted her at every turn. It was clear that her reign was effectively over.

Two days after her degradation in Edinburgh, Mary was imprisoned in the fortress of Lochleven, which stood on an island in the middle of a lake in Kinross. She had nothing with her but the clothes she wore, and some weeks after her arrival she miscarried of twins, losing so much blood that she was obliged to rest in bed for some time. Meanwhile, Mary's lords were doing their best to whip up public opinion against her, and deciding how best to dispose of her.

Elizabeth, hearing of these events, was deeply concerned at the implications of the imprisonment of a queen by her subjects. Whatever Mary had done – and Elizabeth, deploring her behaviour, had little sympathy for her on a personal level – she was still an anointed sovereign, to whom 'by nature and law' her people owed loyalty and obedience, and their treatment of her was setting a dangerous precedent. It was unthinkable that a queen could be thus divested of her regal authority. Alarmingly, seditious ballads applauding Mary's deposition had begun to appear in England. For these reasons, Elizabeth was determined to fight for Mary's release.

On 20 June, one of Bothwell's servants was arrested and made to deliver to the Earl of Morton what later became known as the 'Casket Letters' – a collection of correspondence said to be between Mary and Bothwell which, if authentic, appeared to incriminate the Queen of being an accessory to murder. The lords responded by telling Mary she must choose between being put on trial, with the Casket Letters being offered as evidence, abdicating, or divorcing Bothwell. She refused to consider any of these options, asking only, according to her enemies, to be allowed to sail away on a boat with Bothwell to wherever fortune would take them. Meanwhile, the Pope, having heard about her recent behaviour, refused on 2 July to have anything further to do with her.

Early in July, Elizabeth sent Throckmorton back to Scotland to bring about a reconciliation between Mary and her peers and insist on her restoration. When that had been accomplished, he was to demand that Darnley's murderers be pursued and brought to trial. Above all, he was to ensure that Prince James, whose dynastic importance Elizabeth appreciated, was kept safe; if possible, the child should be brought to England to be reared under her protection. This was, Throckmorton told Leicester, 'the most dangerous legation in my life', and he took his time travelling north, only to be overtaken by a royal courier who commanded him, in the Queen's name, to make haste.

Public opinion in Scotland, fanned by John Knox, was violently opposed to Mary, and Throckmorton's intervention was greatly resented. He was denied access to her, and the lords were even talking of executing her and breaking off their alliance with England in favour of a new one with France if Elizabeth did not offer her support. All Throckmorton could do was send Mary a letter advising her to divorce

Bothwell. Mary refused, even though her situation was now desperate.

The lords, having refused to sanction James's removal to England, now decided that Queen Mary must be forced to abdicate in favour of her son. Weakened by her miscarriage, she was in no fit state to resist, yet on 24 July, when Lord Lindsay came to demand that she sign away her throne, she refused to do so, demanding to be heard by the Scots Parliament. Lindsay threatened that if she did not co-operate, he would cut her throat, at which she capitulated. Five days later her infant son was crowned James VI at Stirling, according to the Protestant rite. On the day of the coronation there were noisy celebrations at Lochleven, with Mary's captors going out of their way to insult her.

On 27 July, an outraged Elizabeth commanded Throckmorton to demand of the Scots, 'What warrant have they in Scripture to depose their Prince? Or what law find they written in any Christian monarchy, that subjects may arrest the person of their Prince, detain them captive and proceed to judge them? No such law is to be found in the whole civil law.' If Mary was deprived of her throne, she threatened, 'we will take plain part against them to revenge their sovereign, for an example to all posterity'.

In Throckmorton's opinion, expressed to Leicester, any attempt to rescue Mary would only lead to her being killed, though at the same time there is little doubt that, had not Elizabeth reacted as violently as she did to their treatment of Mary, the Scots lords might have executed her without more ado. Throckmorton was grateful for having been able to communicate to Mary how zealous Elizabeth was in her cause, 'which I am sure the poor lady doth believe'. But relations between Elizabeth and the men who should have been her Protestant allies were now, thanks to her interference, so frigid that war seemed a very real possibility.

Despite this danger, the Queen, supported only by Leicester, was resolved to pursue the matter to a successful conclusion in the face of pleas and warnings from Throckmorton and Cecil, who wanted to foster friendly relations with Moray and were alarmed at their mistress's obsession with bringing the Scots to heel. Not content with demanding Mary's release, she was now doing her best to subvert Moray's efforts to establish stable government, and deliberately snubbed the Earl by imperiously recalling Throckmorton, thereby demonstrating that she did not recognise his authority. It was no more than a gesture, however, for Moray was well entrenched in power, and few Scots wanted the disgraced Mary restored, as Throckmorton had tried to explain to Elizabeth. Nor did Moray take her displeasure too seriously: as he commented to Cecil, 'Although the Queen's Majesty, your mistress, outwardly seems not altogether to allow the present state, yet doubt I not but Her Highness in her heart likes it well enough.'

Nevertheless, on 11 August, the Queen, in a foul temper because of the pain caused by 'a crick in the neck', sent for Cecil and, in 'a great offensive speech', soundly berated him and his fellow councillors for not having thought of any way in which she could revenge the Queen of Scots's imprisonment and deliver her. As Cecil hedged, the Queen began shouting that she would declare war on the Scots, and he should warn Moray and his lords that if they kept Mary locked up, or touched her life or person, Elizabeth, as a prince, would not fail to revenge it to the uttermost. When Cecil tried to defend Moray, the Queen retorted that any person who was content to see a neighbouring prince unlawfully deposed must be less than dutifully minded towards his own sovereign. Cecil persisted, however, reminding her that, if she threatened the Scots with war, they might well carry out their threat to execute Mary.

A week later the Secretary, who knew that his mistress had no real intention of going to war with her neighbour, was nevertheless gloomily reflecting on how her behaviour was wrecking the fruits of his seven or eight years of successful diplomacy with Scotland. Although she was no longer talking of war, she was still loudly denouncing Moray. Cecil was aware of her motives, knowing that she did not wish people to think her prejudiced against her cousin and that she was fearful in case her own subjects might be emboldened by the example set in Scotland to do the same to her. When, on 22 August, Moray was appointed head of a council of regency, Elizabeth refused to recognise his authority, just as she would not acknowledge James VI as King of Scots. It was not until October that she calmed down and faced the fact that she could not change the situation in Scotland.

Elizabeth had sent Sussex to the Imperial court at Vienna in June to invest Maxmilian II with the Order of the Garter and to inspect the Archduke Charles. The reports he sent back were encouraging: Charles was tall with reddish-brown hair and beard, 'his face well-proportioned, amiable, and of a very good complexion; his countenance and speech cheerful, very courteous and not without some state; his body well-shaped, without deformity or blemish; his legs clean, well-proportioned and of sufficient bigness for his stature'. There was not 'any thing to be noted worthy misliking in his whole person'. A fluent speaker in four languages, of which German was his mother tongue, he was popular in his own country and reportedly wise, liberal and courageous. He excelled at hunting, riding, hawking and all the manly exercises, and Sussex praised his horsemanship fulsomely. He was intelligent, highly-educated, and very rich, living in 'great honour and state'.

The only remaining obstacle to the successful conclusion of the marriage negotiations was the religious issue, since Charles would not, even to please Elizabeth, renounce his faith. The Emperor was prepared to compromise: if the Queen would relent and allow his brother to attend mass in private while publicly accompanying her to Anglican services, the Archduke would undertake never to do anything to undermine the Church of England and would be ready to marry her at once. In October, Sussex wrote urging Elizabeth to accept this offer, commenting in a private note to Cecil, 'The universal opinion is, that if Her Majesty will not satisfy him for the use of his religion, she wanteth or meaneth never to proceed in the matter.'

Knowing this issue to be highly contentious, Elizabeth asked her councillors for their advice. Cecil and Norfolk were in favour of accepting the compromise, but Leicester, who believed the marriage would herald his ruin, Northampton, Pembroke and Knollys were against it. Yet, even though she realised she could not delay much longer in giving the Archduke an answer, the Queen could not make up her mind, and for several weeks opposing groups of councillors warred to bring her over to their point of view. In Vienna, Sussex was furious to hear that Leicester was using every means at his disposal – 'the like hath not been seen' – to sabotage the project, including instructing zealous Protestant preachers to inveigh against the Catholic Archduke from the pulpit.

At length, Leicester emerged victorious, for on 10 December Elizabeth brought eight years of negotiations to an end by writing to Sussex to say that it was against her conscience and her policy of religious uniformity to allow Charles to practise his religion in private. Even if she personally permitted it, it was unlikely that Parliament would, and she could not act without the consent of Parliament. This signified the end of the hopes of Cecil, Norfolk and Sussex, who all blamed Leicester for this dismal outcome and foresaw 'certain mischief' resulting from Elizabeth's continuing failure to marry. The Emperor was 'much appalled' and turned down Elizabeth's request that Charles visit her to discuss the religious issue – as she had known he would – while a despondent Sussex handed over the Garter and began his long journey home.

In reaching her decision, Elizabeth had, however, acted wisely in saving England from the threat of religious controversy and the possibility of rebellion or even civil war. She had not forgotten how violently the English people had reacted to the news that her sister intended to marry Philip of Spain, and she was also aware how much attitudes towards religion had hardened during the past decade. She wished to make it clear to her subjects that she would do nothing to forfeit their love and loyalty, and that she would never allow the laws of her country to be broken, even by her husband.

The collapse of the Habsburg marriage negotiations coincided with the beginning of a period of cooler relations between England and Spain, which was sparked by the rudeness of the outspoken John Man, Bishop of Gloucester, whom Elizabeth had sent as her ambassador to Spain, and who, once there, openly vilified the Catholic faith and the Pope, and warned his mistress to shun 'the powers of darkness'. After Elizabeth had recalled him, at Philip's insistence, in the spring of 1568, she sent no more ambassadors to the Spanish court. De Silva returned home at the same time, to be replaced by the aggressive Don Guerau de Spes, who was hostile to the English.

A serious conflict had also broken out in the Netherlands, where over the past few decades many of Philip's subjects, particularly in the northern provinces, had converted to the reformed faith, and there was growing resentment of their autocratic Catholic ruler. Catholic churches were desecrated and Imperial officials attacked. Threatened with a breakdown in law and order, Philip sent an army of 50,000 men under the command of the formidable Duke of Alva to crush the rebels. Having carried out its task with terrible efficiency, the army stayed put at Brussels, almost on Elizabeth's doorstep, thus causing the greatest consternation in England.

The Queen's sympathies were naturally with the Protestant rebels, whose leader, William the Silent, Prince of Orange, had fled to Germany, but she was reluctant to respond to their appeals for help because of the proximity of that huge Spanish garrison. There was widespread fear in England that it would be only a matter of time before Alva received orders to invade England: it was no secret that Philip still cherished hopes of Elizabeth's conversion to Catholicism, and there was always the possibility that he might decide to force the issue. It was therefore imperative that Elizabeth order a strengthening of England's navy – her only protection against the Spaniards.

By March 1568, relations between England and Scotland were noticeably warmer, with Moray and Cecil corresponding on a regular basis and Elizabeth suggesting to Moray that she petition the King of Denmark, who had shut Bothwell in prison, to send back his captive to Scotland to stand trial for Darnley's murder.

The following month, Elizabeth who had been casting covetous eyes at Mary's jewels, particularly a six-stringed loop of large pearls, arranged with Moray to buy them for 12,000 écus, outbidding Catherine de' Medici. When they arrived on 1 May, she could not contain her excitement, but showed them off to Leicester and Pembroke. The pearls featured thereafter in several state portraits of the Queen.

On 2 May, Mary escaped from Lochleven. George Douglas, the laird's brother, 'in fantasy of love with her', under cover of a May Day pageant arranged for a servant to steal the laird's keys and help the disguised prisoner to hasten to a waiting boat. Douglas then escorted Mary to Hamilton Palace, where she was joined by several lords and an army of 6000 men. As soon as she heard of this, Elizabeth sent a handwritten message of congratulation, offering help and support.

But it had not arrived when Mary's force suffered a crushing defeat at Langside on 13 May at the hands of Moray's troops, and she fled in panic from the battlefield knowing that all was lost. For three days she rode southwards, shaving her head to avoid recognition, and existing on a diet of milk and oatmeal. On 16 May, she escaped from Scotland and crossed the Solway Firth to Workington in Cumberland, hoping to obtain refuge in England and announcing that she had come to place herself under Elizabeth's protection. Bitter and vengeful, she was desperate for military aid so that she could crush her enemies for good.

The English authorities, however, were not sure how to receive her, and placed her under guard at Carlisle until instructions about what to do with their uninvited guest arrived from London. Her arrival posed a dilemma for the government that would exercise it for the next two decades.

The Queen insisted that Mary must be restored at once. Cecil argued that it was folly to assist a queen who had schemed and plotted against her for years and was, in every sense, her enemy and no political innocent. Mary should be sent back to Scotland immediately. Elizabeth protested that to do so would be to send her to her death – it was unthinkable that she should do such a thing.

It was difficult to determine what should be done with Mary, since every option open to Elizabeth carried its dangers. The last thing she wanted was to go to war with Scotland on Mary's behalf, and she felt it would be infinitely preferable if she could bring about a reconciliation between Mary and the Scots lords on terms favourable to England. It would be insane folly to send Mary abroad to France or Spain, yet if Elizabeth left her at liberty in England, she would be an inspiration to every Catholic malcontent in the kingdom. The Queen was aware that there were those of the old faith, at home and abroad, who regarded Mary as having a better title to the English throne than herself, especially in the Catholic north, where Mary had been cultivating support for years and where there was spontaneous rejoicing at her coming to England. Those who had met her were beguiled by her beauty and charm, and also by her powers of persuasion. It therefore required no great leap of the imagination to envisage her becoming a force for rebellion, or treason, and there was always the fearful possibility that King Philip might decide to divert that great army in the Netherlands to England in support of her claim.

In the end, Elizabeth decided that Mary must remain, not in prison, but in honourable custody as her 'guest', and under constant observation. 'Our good Queen has the wolf by the ears,' commented Archbishop Parker. Elizabeth sent Sir Francis Knollys to Carlisle to welcome Mary and take charge of her. He was to say that it would be impossible for Mary to be admitted to Her Majesty's presence 'by reason of the great slander of murder whereof she was not yet purged': until Mary had been formally cleared of Darnley's murder, Elizabeth, as an unmarried Queen, could not see her or welcome her to court. Mary wept when she heard this.

Elizabeth had made noises about wanting to recognise Mary as Queen of Scots and receive her as an equal, but she had been easily overridden by her councillors, who could not comprehend why she would contemplate replacing a friendly Protestant neighbouring administration with a Catholic queen who had never renounced her claim to be rightful sovereign of England. Elizabeth wrote to Mary explaining her decision: 'If you find it strange not to see me, you will see it would be malaise for me to receive you before your justification. But once honourably acquitted of this crime, I swear to you before God, that among all worldly pleasures [meeting you] will hold the first rank.' The French ambassador drily observed that, once the two queens were in each other's company, they would be at loggerheads within a week as their friendship turned to envy and jealousy. He believed Elizabeth would never let Mary come near her.

Having heard that Mary had no change of raiment, Elizabeth declared she would make good her wants, and sent with Knollys a parcel of clothing. To his mortification it contained 'two torn shifts, two pieces of black velvet, two pairs of shoes, and nothing else'. To cover up his embarrassment he told Mary that 'Her Highness's maid had mistaken and sent things necessary for a maidservant'. In fact, Elizabeth herself had selected the items, intending that Mary should understand she was dependent on English charity, and when Knollys failed to write of Mary's gratitude, she indignantly sent to ask if her cousin had liked the clothes she had sent her.

Mary was angered by this 'cold dealing', and on 13 June replied:

Remove, Madam, from your mind that I am come hither for the preservation of my life, but to clear my honour and obtain assistance to chastise my false accusers; not to answer them as their equal, but to accuse them before you. Being innocent as, God be thanked, I know I am, do you not wrong me by keeping me here, encouraging by that means my perfidious foes to continue their determined falsehoods? I neither can nor will answer their false accusations, although I will with pleasure justify myself to you voluntarily as friend to friend, but not in the form of a process with my subjects.

This could not be achieved, of course, unless Elizabeth agreed to see her, and in her frustration she veered from outbursts of anger to spells of passionate weeping, in which she complained of her 'evil usage'.

The Council was not impressed, and on 20 June backed Elizabeth in her refusal to receive Mary, declaring that the Queen could not 'suffer her to depart without a trial'. Of course, English courts had no jurisdiction over foreign princes, so Elizabeth ordered what amounted to a political inquiry – 'a trial of Mary's innocence' before what was in effect a tribunal, although it was not referred to as such. Its purposes were to determine whether Mary had been in any way guilty of Darnley's murder and whether she should be restored to her throne. Six earls were appointed to act as commissioners under the chairmanship of Norfolk, their function being to consider the evidence. The Queen announced that she herself would act as judge between Mary and her Scots subjects.

In a letter to Mary, asking her to proclaim her innocence, Elizabeth wrote, 'O Madam! There is no creature living who wishes to hear such a declaration more than I, or will more readily lend her ears to any answer that will acquit your honour.' Once Mary had been acquitted, she would – she promised – receive her at court.

By now, it had dawned on Mary that she was effectively a prisoner of her cousin. When told of the impending inquiry, she furiously protested that, as an absolute prince, she would have no other judge but God: 'I see how things frame evil for me. I have many enemies about the Queen, my good sister, such as do all they can to keep me from her at the solicitation of my rebellious subjects.' There was a good deal of truth in this, but Mary clung to the notion that the inquiry was Elizabeth's way of helping her regain her throne, especially when Elizabeth informed her that its real purpose was to examine Moray's conduct towards his sovereign, and assured her that judgement would not be given unless it was against him or his party.

On 20 June, the Council categorically advised Elizabeth against doing anything that might assist Mary's restoration. She refused to listen: she had given Mary her word, and would stand by it. Subjects had to be shown that they could not depose princes at will. But the strain was telling on her, and in one letter she begged Mary to 'have some consideration of me, instead of always thinking of yourself'.

In July, Mary was taken to Bolton Castle in Yorkshire, which was to be her lodging for the foreseeable future. It was sufficiently far from both Scotland and London to pose any great security risk. At Bolton she kept state like a queen and was allowed to indulge her passion for hunting, but she was constantly guarded. Sir Francis Knollys was her 'host', but had a difficult time coping with her tears and tantrums as she chafed against the restrictions upon her liberty.

There was by now a strong 'Queen's Party' in Scotland, and two members of it, Lord Herries and the Bishop of Ross, took it upon themselves to go to England and plead Mary's case. 'If Queen Mary will remit her case to be heard by me as her dear cousin and friend', Elizabeth told Herries, 'I will send for her rebels and know their answer why they deposed their queen. If they can allege some reason for doing so, which I think they cannot, then I will restore Queen Mary to her throne, on condition that she renounces her claim to England and abandons her league with France and the mass in Scotland.' These were tough terms, but the promise was implicit, and Mary was desperate. On 28 July, she agreed to 'submit her cause to Her Highness in thankful manner'. What she did not know was that all parties were determined that she should not speak in her own defence. Nor was she aware that, on 20 September, Elizabeth assured Moray that she did not mean to restore Mary, despite reports to the contrary. Armed with this knowledge, he agreed to attend.

The inquiry opened at York on 4 October. Elizabeth had ordered her commissioners to press for Mary's restoration on terms favourable to the English, but to her annoyance, there were endless intrigues and delays, and very little was achieved, although it became transparently clear that Moray's chief objective was to keep Mary out of Scotland. Provoked by Elizabeth's anger at his initial failure to make the 'rigorous accusations' he had assured her would prove Mary 'privy' to murder, and fortified by her reassurance that if his proofs were convincing there would be no question of her pressing for Mary's restoration, he at length revealed the existence of the Casket Letters. He intended, at the right psychological moment, to produce them in evidence against Mary – in fact, they were to constitute the chief evidence against her. But the question was asked then, and has been asked countless times since: were they forgeries?

The Casket Letters no longer exist, having disappeared in 1584, although copies of nine of them survive in various archives. The original documents comprised eight letters said to be from Mary to Bothwell, twelve transcriptions of French sonnets, a written but undated promise to marry Bothwell, signed by Mary, and two copies of their marriage contract. All were contained in a small silver-gilt box of about thirty centimetres in length, engraved with an F for Francis II, which may be the one now on display at Lennoxlove House in Scotland. According to the Earl of Morton, this casket had been found in a house in Potterow, Edinburgh, and since then controversy had raged over the authenticity of its contents. There were claims that, although the letters were genuine, the Scots lords had inserted incriminating passages into them. Some said the love letters had been written to Bothwell by another lady. None of these theories were put forward in Mary's defence. When Moray produced these contentious documents at the inquiry, he insisted that the letters purportedly written by Mary were in her handwriting. Mary denied this, but was never allowed to see them. Many modern historians believe therefore that the Casket Letters were forged in an attempt to convict her. If, however, they were authentic, then they were conclusive proof that she was guilty of complicity in Darnley's murder.

Norfolk did see the originals and was in no doubt as to who had written them; in fact, he was utterly appalled at their contents, writing to Elizabeth that they described 'such inordinate love between [Mary] and Bothwell, her loathsomeness and abhorring of her husband that was murdered, in such sort as every good and godly man cannot but detest and abhor the same'. The widowed Duke was therefore astonished at a suggestion made by William Maitland, on a hunting expedition, that he consider marrying Mary himself, especially since the terms of his appointment as chief commissioner forbade him from doing so on pain of death. Knollys thought the marriage might be a good way of keeping Mary under control, but Elizabeth, alerted by the French ambassador and Cecil's spies, most certainly did not, and sharply reproved Norfolk for even discussing such an idea.

'Should I seek to marry her, being so wicked a woman, such a notorious adulteress and murderer?' he protested.

> I love to sleep upon a safe pillow. I count myself, by Your Majesty's favour, as good a prince at home in my bowling alley at Norwich as she is, though she were in the midst of Scotland. And if I should go about to marry with her, knowing as I do that she pretendeth a title to Your Majesty's crown, Your Majesty might justly charge me with seeking your crown from your head.

At this, Elizabeth appeared outwardly mollified, and no more was said then about the marriage. However, a seed of ambition had been sown in Norfolk's mind.

When Elizabeth received copies of the Casket Letters, she claimed to be convinced that they were genuine, stating that they 'contained many matters very unmeet to be repeated before honest ears, and easily drawn to be apparent proof against the Queen'. Irritated by the lack of progress made by the commissioners, and suspicious of Norfolk's loyalties, Elizabeth adjourned the inquiry to Westminster and appointed Leicester, Cecil and other councillors - most of whom were no friends of Mary – as additional commissioners. Meanwhile, Cecil was urging that Mary be moved to the greater security of Tutbury Castle in the Protestant Midlands, but Elizabeth demurred, wishing to preserve the fiction that Mary was a royal guest and not a prisoner to be shunted from stronghold to stronghold. Even Leicester could not persuade her that Cecil spoke sense.

Although she accepted an English prayerbook, Mary remained a devout Catholic, and – in an effort to wipe out her unfortunate recent history – had told King Philip she would die for her faith. The new Spanish ambassador, Don Gerau de Spes, shared the concern of his master for Mary's welfare, and by 9 November had decided upon action, having contacted her known supporters in England. Overestimating the numbers of her partisans, a mistake made repeatedly by foreign Catholic powers in the years to come, de Spes believed that it would not be difficult to arrange Mary's escape, nor even a rebellion against Elizabeth, with the intent of deposing her and setting up Mary as queen in her place.

It appears that Mary was plotting against Elizabeth almost as soon as she arrived on English soil. She told Knollys she had no desire to cause any more trouble, yet both the Council and Moray, having censored and read all her correspondence, suspected she was not telling the truth. In September she had told the Queen of Spain that with Philip's help she would 'make ours the reigning religion' in England; Philip, however, was just then too shocked by her conduct seriously to contemplate forceful intervention on her behalf. It was probably the realisation that Mary would not scruple to intrigue against her that prompted Elizabeth to assure Moray that the tribunal would after all pronounce on Mary's guilt or innocence, on the basis of the proofs contained in the Casket Letters.

Elizabeth was at Hampton Court when the Westminster tribunal met on 25 November. On the following day Moray accused Bothwell of Darnley's murder and Mary of having guilty foreknowledge of it. Her commissioners demanded that she be allowed to reply to this charge herself. On 4 December Elizabeth agreed this was reasonable, but declared that 'for the better satisfaction of herself', Moray must first present his proofs. She then refused to allow Mary to give evidence in her own defence, even though her cousin was insisting vehemently that the Casket Letters were forgeries and claiming that it was easy to copy her handwriting. She had still not been allowed to see them. Elizabeth stated that it would be degrading for Mary to have to give evidence, but in reality she did not want her beautiful, appealing cousin winning hearts and minds by publicly protesting her innocence, for then it would be virtually impossible to present the Casket Letters as credible evidence.

On 6 December Mary's commissioners withdrew from the inquiry. It seems that even they were not wholly convinced of their mistress's innocence. On 7 December, Moray again accused Mary of murder and produced the Casket Letters, to sensational effect, with the result that the commissioners spent the next few days comparing the handwriting with authenticated samples of Mary's. Mary herself repeatedly begged to see copies of the Casket Letters, but her pleas were refused. The Queen pleaded with her several times to reply formally in writing to the accusations made against her, but she repeatedly refused to do so unless Elizabeth promised that the inquiry would bring in a verdict of not guilty. This, of course, was out of the question.

The English commissioners and Council unanimously accepted the Casket Letters as authentic, on the grounds that they contained information 'such as could hardly be invented or devised by any other than [Mary] herself, for that they discourse on some things which were unknown to any other than to herself and Bothwell'. They were divided, however, as to how to proceed against Mary. The last thing Elizabeth wanted was for her cousin to be proclaimed guilty of murder, but she did see the necessity for Mary to accept her deposition and live quietly in England as a private person for the rest of her life, and told Knollys to persuade Mary to agree to this. Another option was for Mary to rule Scotland as joint sovereign with James VI, with Moray acting as regent. Alternatively, Mary could remain titular Queen but live permanently in England while Moray ruled in her name.

On 14 December, Elizabeth summoned her councillors and nobility to Hampton Court to hear the commission's proceedings read out to them and inspect the Casket Letters. The peers expressed their gratitude to Elizabeth for letting them know the particulars of the inquiry, 'wherein they had seen such foul matters as they thought truly in their consciences that Her Majesty's position was justified'. Mary's crimes were now so apparent that she could never be received at court. However, she could not be declared guilty unless she had put forward a defence, and this she had consistently refused to do, unless it was to Elizabeth in person – which, again, was out of the question.

A week later Elizabeth, still upset by the impact of the Casket Letters, as well as by the death of her old tutor, Roger Ascham, sent the commissioners to give Mary a detailed report of the inquiry and a letter in which the Queen informed her that, 'As one Prince and near cousin regarding another, we are heartily sorry and dismayed to find such matter of your charge,' and giving Mary one last chance of stating her defence. Mary did not respond.

Given the strength of English public opinion against Mary, Elizabeth could not allow her to be declared innocent, yet neither did she want a queen to be subject to the judgement of a tribunal, and in January 1569, the commissioners delivered the only verdict possible – that nothing had been proved against Mary. Mary herself refused to acknowledge that they had the jurisdiction to deliver any verdict at all.

But Elizabeth dared not set her at liberty: she posed too great a threat, even as a prisoner, for already there were signs that Catholics in England were beginning to regard her as their figurehead. As for Mary, she seemed more interested now in claiming the English throne than in recovering the Scottish one.

'The Queen of Scots', Cecil warned Elizabeth, 'is, and always shall be, a dangerous person to your estate.'

12

'A Vain Crack of Words'

By the winter of 1568-9, Norfolk was becoming increasingly disaffected, and with Sussex out of the way as a result of his appointment as President of the Council of the North, he came under the influence of Elizabeth's former suitor, the Earl of Arundel. Along with several northern Catholic lords, including the Earls of Northumberland and Derby, both men wanted to see ousted from the Council Cecil and other 'heretic' hardliners, including Leicester, who was now championing the extreme Protestants who were referred to as Puritans.

Relations between England and Spain had suffered a further deterioration in November, when Cecil had masterminded the theft of £85,000 – loaned to Philip II by bankers in Genoa to pay the wages of Alva's soldiers – from Spanish ships in distress off Southampton. In January 1569, instead of returning the money to Spain, Elizabeth, who was short of funds, impudently confiscated it and declared she would repay the loan herself. For a time it was feared that a furious Philip might use this incident as an excuse to declare war on England, while Norfolk and Arundel, encouraged by de Spes, did their best to ensure that the blame for the rift with Spain was laid at Cecil's door, hoping to prompt his speedy overthrow and committal to the Tower.

Within weeks Leicester had entered into the conspiracy, fired by the knowledge that Cecil was still doing his utmost to prevent him from marrying the Queen – a prospect that was becoming increasingly unrealistic as the years went by. Despite their antipathy towards him, Norfolk and Arundel could not afford to reject his support, and for a time relations between the three men were relatively harmonious.

Far from declaring war, however, Philip merely ordered his troops in the Netherlands to seize English ships and property. His priority was to bring his Dutch subjects to heel before entering into any overt hostility with England.

In January 1569, Mary Stuart was moved to Tutbury, a grim, crumbling castle in Staffordshire, which she loathed, and placed in the care of George Talbot, Sixth Earl of Shrewsbury, who was to remain her custodian for the next fifteen years – underpaid and overburdened with the responsibility. His wife was the formidable Elizabeth Cavendish – known to history as 'Bess of Hardwick' – and although Bess clashed with the Queen on several occasions, Elizabeth trusted Shrewsbury implicitly. Mary got on fairly well with both of them, making gifts to Bess and charming the puritanical Shrewsbury with 'her eloquent tongue, discreet head, her stout courage and liberal heart'. The Council warned him not to 'allow her to gain rule over him, or practise for her escape'. Cecil in particular feared Mary's wiles, believing 'She is able, by her great wit and sugared eloquence, to win even such as before they shall come to her company shall have a great misliking.'

Elizabeth had no time for Mary as a person, only as a queen. She had a low opinion of her character, irritably observing to the French ambassador that there must be something 'divine about the speech and appearance of the Queen of Scots, in that one or the other obliges her very enemies to speak for her'.

Whilst in the Earl's care, Mary lived at one or other of his many houses in the Midlands: Tutbury, Wingfield, Chatsworth and Sheffield Castle. In 1569, Shrewsbury, who admitted that he was not unaffected by Mary's charm, recorded his impressions of her for posterity: 'Besides that she is a goodly personage, and yet in truth not comparable to our sovereign, she hath withal an alluring grace, a pretty Scottish accent, and a searching wit, clouded with mildness. Fame might move some to relieve her, and glory joined to gain might stir others to adventure much for her sake.' He could see what the sight of Mary 'might work in others. Her hair is black, and yet Knollys told me that she wears her hair in sundry colours.'

Encouraged by reports of worsening relations between England and Spain, Mary that January sent a message to de Spes, averring that she would rather die than resign the throne of Scotland, and promising that, 'if his master will help me, I shall be Queen of England in three months, and mass shall be said all over the country'. The message was duly conveyed by the ambassador, who urged Philip to step up his embargo on English goods in the Netherlands, a strategy that was doomed to failure, since too many mercantile interests were at stake.

It was Throckmorton, supported by Leicester, who revived the plan for a marriage between Mary and Norfolk, to be followed by her restoration to the Scottish throne, which would be conditional upon Mary agreeing to maintain the Protestant faith in Scotland and remaining an ally of England. Once Mary was married to Norfolk,

Elizabeth might be persuaded to recognise her as her successor, and with the succession settled, and Mary hopefully no longer a focus for Catholic rebels, friendly relations with Spain could be restored. The chief obstacle to this plan was Cecil, which was one more reason why the Norfolk-Arundel faction wanted him displaced. By now, they had been joined in their conspiracy against him by several other northern lords and the Spanish ambassador de Spes, who was ever ready to make mischief.

It appears that the scheme to marry Mary to Norfolk was devised without Elizabeth's knowledge, although the details were communicated to Mary in a letter signed by the noblemen concerned, even Leicester, who must have known that he was embarking upon a perilous course. However, the evidence suggests that Elizabeth, who was already suspicious of Norfolk, may have been aware of what was going on and was waiting to see what transpired before endorsing or condemning the project.

In February de Spes was approached by a Florentine banker, Roberto Ridolfi, who had been sent by Norfolk and Arundel to enlist Spanish support for their scheme; Ridolfi was instructed to tell the Spanish ambassador that they intended to establish a Catholic government in England as soon as they were in a position to do so. It appears that they hoped for some kind of backing from Alva, but when this proved not to be forthcoming, they began to realise that their plan to oust Cecil might prove abortive.

The prospect of failure made them desperate, and on Ash Wednesday, whilst attending her in her chamber as she ate her supper, Leicester dared to tell the Queen that most of her subjects were in despair because state affairs were being so badly managed by Master Secretary that either England must be endangered or Cecil must lose his head. Elizabeth erupted in fury at this, forbidding the Earl to say anything further against Cecil and making it clear that nothing could shake her loyalty to him.

Norfolk, who was also present, then entered the fray, disclosing to the Queen the fact that many lords shared Leicester's opinion of Cecil. Elizabeth was by now in a foul temper and shouted him down. However, when Norfolk remarked to Northampton in her hearing, 'Look how Lord Leicester is favoured and welcomed by the Queen when he endorses and approves the Secretary's opinions; but now that he quite rightly wishes to state his good reasons for opposing them, she looks ill on him, and wants to send him to the Tower. No, no! He will not go alone!' Elizabeth made no comment.

Leicester was so unnerved by this episode that he threatened Norfolk with exposure of his plot against Cecil to the Queen. But Cecil had now guessed what was afoot, and concluding that his future and even his life were in jeopardy, put himself out to be friendly towards Norfolk, taking care not to do anything to anger or provoke the Duke and his friends. He also embarked upon a campaign to win over Leicester, who was soon warning him to look out for himself. It was now very clear to those who had conspired against him that, with Elizabeth firmly behind him, Cecil was invincible.

In April, Mary was dismayed to learn that her supporters in Scotland had failed to reach any accommodation with Moray; deeply depressed, she lost her appetite and wept constantly. Elizabeth, however, was desperate to have her contentious cousin out of her kingdom, and was still hoping to negotiate Mary's return to her own land, although she would not send her back without her safety being guaranteed. Moray's strong resistance to Elizabeth's overtures on Mary's behalf did not improve her temper. Nevertheless, she persevered.

Mary had, however, discovered a potential escape route from her prison. Norfolk had at first dismissed the idea of marrying her as treason, but as the months went by he had given the matter deeper consideration: it seemed to him that, if her marriage to Bothwell could be annulled, it made sense for the Queen of Scots to marry a loyal English lord who could safeguard Queen Elizabeth's interests when Mary had been restored to her throne. Added to this, of course, he would gain a crown for himself. In May 1569, Mary was overjoyed to receive a formal proposal of marriage through the Bishop of Ross, which Elizabeth was supposed to have sanctioned, and by June, she and Norfolk were exchanging the kind of letters that could only betoken a courtship. Signing herself 'Your assured Mary', the former Scots queen sent 'My Norfolk' a cushion embroidered by herself, which showed a knife cutting down a green vine said to represent Elizabeth. Neither party cherished any romantic notions: this was a union of driving ambition.

Knowing that the Queen would be against their marriage, since she would anticipate that a man who was ambitious to be King of Scots could also covet the crown of England, the Duke attempted in June to canvass the backing of his old rival, Cecil, but Cecil, being deeply suspicious of Mary Stuart, warned Norfolk that the only way out of this tangle was to confess all to Elizabeth. Leicester, fearful of the consequences of his involvement, also confided in Cecil, who – though he may have recalled the recent conspiracy against himself – did not betray his confidence. None of the conspirators wanted to divulge the marriage plan to Elizabeth until they were certain they could convince her that it was to her advantage.

Norfolk was too fearful of Elizabeth's anger to take Cecil's advice, but someone talked, and by the end of July the Duke's proposed marriage to Mary Stuart was common knowledge at court. In fact, most councillors were in favour of it. The Queen, who had learned of the plan as she listened to her ladies gossiping, was not, for she feared a conspiracy against herself, and on 1 August, upon meeting him in the gardens at Richmond, she gave Norfolk the chance to make a clean breast of the whole affair by asking if there was any news from London, whence he had just arrived. The Duke, probably realising what she was hinting at, said that there was nothing.

'No?' asked the Queen, feigning astonishment. 'You come from London and can tell no news of a marriage?' Norfolk was saved from having to answer by the inadvertent arrival of Lady Clinton with some flowers for Elizabeth, and seized his opportunity to flee to Leicester's apartments. When the Earl returned there from hunting at Kingston, Norfolk asked what he thought he should do, whereupon Leicester offered to soften the Queen when occasion offered.

Supporters of the marriage were dismayed when, early in August, Moray finally informed Elizabeth that neither he nor the other Scottish lords would accept Mary back as their queen. This angered Elizabeth, who vowed that she would continue to work for Mary's restoration anyway, although the only way to force the issue was by going to war, which Moray knew she would wish to avoid at all costs.

On 5 August the court left for Oatlands on its annual summer progress, and on the 11th came to Loseley Park near Guildford, the seat of Sir William More, where the room in which the Queen slept is still on view. The next morning, as Elizabeth sat on a step by the front door, listening to one of More's children strumming a lute and singing, Leicester, kneeling beside her, raised the subject of Norfolk. Elizabeth promised to speak to the Duke within the next few days.

Two days later, at Farnham, Elizabeth invited Norfolk to dine in private with her – a rare honour – but during the meal, although she gave him every opportunity to do so, he could not find the courage to say anything about his proposed marriage to Mary Stuart. When they had finished, he recorded, 'she gave me a nip', saying 'she would wish me to take good heed to my pillow' – echoing his own words the previous summer. 'I was abashed at Her Majesty's speech, but I thought it not fit time nor place there to trouble her.' Even so, Elizabeth gave him several further chances to confess to her, and still he did not take them. He was determined to pursue the marriage project, confiding to a friend that 'before he lost that marriage, he would lose his life'.

In June, the Duke of Alva, acting on Philip's behalf, had made it quite clear to de Spes that Spain would not be going to war with England and that he was under no circumstances to enter into any conspiracy against

Queen Elizabeth or her government, but was to remain strictly neutral.

De Spes was an incurable intriguer, and on 8 August Alva was complaining to Philip that the ambassador would not obey instructions: he was now plotting with disaffected northern magnates to liberate Mary and make her Queen of England, and was also encouraging Norfolk to marry her.

The mood of the court on progress was tense. Elizabeth was on edge because she suspected treason, and maddened by thoughts of Mary Stuart's likely involvement, complaining to Bertrand de la Mothe Fénelon, the French ambassador, that, although she had acted the part of a good mother to her cousin, Mary had repaid her by involving herself in intrigues. A person 'who did not wish to treat her mother well deserved a wicked stepmother'. The ambassador expressed disbelief that anything sinister was afoot, but Elizabeth shook her head.

'I know the identity of the troublemakers well enough,' she declared, 'and I would like to cut off a few heads.'

At the Earl of Southampton's house in Titchfield in Hampshire in early September, she was in a savage mood, snapping and snarling at both Cecil and Leicester, and accusing them of plotting on Mary's behalf. Leicester fled to his bed, feigning illness. On the 6th, he begged the Queen to visit him, and when she was seated beside his bed, he told her that Norfolk still cherished dreams of marrying Mary.

Elizabeth commented that, if their marriage were allowed to take place, she herself would be a prisoner in the Tower within four months of the ceremony. Abjectly, Leicester begged forgiveness for his involvement in the earlier scheme, explaining that he had been convinced he was acting in her best interests. Worried about the state of his health, for she believed that he really was ill, the Queen readily pardoned him.

Norfolk, however, was another matter. That afternoon, Elizabeth summoned him to attend her in the great gallery, and in a royal temper, castigated him for his disloyalty and made him swear on his allegiance 'to deal no further with the Scottish cause'. Quaking, the Duke tried to make light of his plans by claiming he had only 'a very slight regard for Mary' and that he did not rate marrying her very highly. Elizabeth was unimpressed and made her disfavour so plain that Norfolk found himself shunned by most people at court, including Leicester. On 16 September he returned to London without leave, and defiantly continued his pursuit of Mary, having, he felt, become too deeply involved to withdraw with honour now. Deeply suspicious, the Queen sent a summons from Lord Sandys's house, The Vyne, near Basingstoke, ordering the Duke to return to court. Meanwhile, Cecil had arranged for de Spes to be placed under observation and his correspondence to be vetted; as a precaution, orders went out to loyal subjects in all areas of the country to prepare for any emergency.

On 23 September, Elizabeth returned to Windsor, where she learned that Norfolk, pleading that he had taken purgatives to cure an ague and was unable to venture outdoors, had ignored her summons and gone that day to Kenninghall, his stronghold in Norfolk. Alarmed, she concluded that his intention was to rouse his tenantry and affinity in rebellion against her, and on 25 September she sent him a categorical command to present himself at Windsor without delay. Again, he was too terrified to do so, despite Mary urging him, in a letter, to deal boldly with her cousin and be valiant.

It so happened that, at that time, another serious conspiracy against the Queen was brewing in the north of England, prompted by local feuds, resentment of royal interference in the region, a desire to restore the old faith as the official religion of the state, resentment of Cecil and other Protestant councillors, and – above all – anger at the Queen's failure to settle the succession upon the Queen of Scots. Norfolk had not initially been involved, but the Spanish ambassador had been active in inciting the rebels.

Elsewhere in England, most Catholics were loyal to Elizabeth, but the north had never entirely reconciled itself to the religious changes of the last few decades, and the great northern magnates, the Catholic earls of Northumberland and Westmorland, had begun to organise large gatherings of the local gentry, supposedly for field sports. Their real purpose was rebellion, and their plan was to murder all royal officials in the north and liberate Mary Stuart, with whom they had been in contact since the spring. Some merely wanted to oust Elizabeth's 'ill-disposed advisers', but others hoped to depose Elizabeth in favour of Mary. The King of France was involved, having promised aid to the rebels, and Roberto Ridolfi, the Florentine banker, was funding the enterprise. There is no doubt that this rebellion constituted the most dangerous threat to her throne that Elizabeth had encountered since her accession. It seemed as if eleven years of peace were about to be violently brought to an end.

Cecil and Elizabeth were aware almost from the first that the Catholic lords in the 'inly-working north' were preparing to revolt against her. What they could not risk was Norfolk raising the eastern counties and joining forces with them, which there is little doubt he was contemplating at that time. According to William Camden, 'All the whole court hung in suspense and fear, lest the Duke should break forth into rebellion, and it was determined, if he did so, to put the Queen of Scots to death.'

It soon became clear that Norfolk would obtain little support in East

Anglia. Nor did he make much effort to raise it, being too ill and demoralised to do so. His chief concern was to try and limit the damage and write to the Queen, begging that she would pardon him and excuse him from attending on her at Windsor. He knew, he continued, that he was 'a suspected person' and he feared being sent to the Tower of London – 'too great a terror for a true man'.

The Queen replied tartly that she did not mean 'to minister anything to you but as you should in truth deserve', and dispatched two further summonses, insisting that the Duke must travel to court even if he was ill, if need be in a litter. Cecil and other councillors wrote urging him to obey her.

At last Norfolk capitulated. He was aware of what was being planned in the north and, fearful of being implicated, sent a messenger to Westmorland to beg him to call off the rising: 'If not, it should cost me my head, for that I am going to court.'

On 3 October Norfolk was arrested on the way to Windsor. Cecil had assured him that, if he submitted to her, the Queen would not deal harshly with him, but ten days later, as he had feared, he was committed to the Tower. Elizabeth's rage was truly majestic, and she was resolved to make him suffer in return for the months of anxiety and worry he had caused her. At the same time, Throckmorton was questioned about his part in the conspiracy, and confined to his farmhouse at Carshalton in Surrey; Arundel and Pembroke were likewise placed under house arrest. Pembroke was quickly released, only to die the next year, while Arundel remained under guard at Nonsuch Palace until the following March, when he was released at Leicester's instigation.

On 16 October, Cecil warned Elizabeth that the real threat to her throne lay with Mary Stuart, and used this information to remind her where her duty lay.

> There are degrees of danger. If you would marry, it should be less; whilst you do not, it will increase. If her person be restrained, here or in Scotland, it will be less; if at liberty, greater. If found guilty of her husband's murder, she shall be less a person perilous; if passed over in silence the scar of the murder will wear out, and the danger greater.

Elizabeth announced in Council that she wanted Norfolk tried for treason, but Cecil did not consider the Duke's actions to be 'within the compass of treason. Whereupon I am bold to wish Your Majesty would show your intent only to inquire into the fact, and not to speak of it as treason.' In fact, there was scant evidence that Norfolk's intentions had been treasonable, and certainly not enough to convict him.

The Queen, however, was out for his blood, and threatened that, if the laws of England did not provide for the Duke's execution, she would proceed against him on her own authority. She was so overcome with anger that she fainted, which brought her councillors running with vinegar and burnt feathers.

As usual, when her rage had cooled, she realised that Cecil had been right: to proceed against Norfolk without recourse to law was tyranny, pure and simple, and she was no tyrant. Eventually, she conceded that the Duke might not have had treasonable intentions and agreed to leave him to cool his heels in the Tower for a time, whereupon Cecil suggested that she divert Norfolk from ideas of marrying Mary Stuart by finding another, more suitable, bride for him.

On 26 October, Elizabeth dispatched to Sir Henry Norris, her ambassador in Paris, an eight-page draft in which she had written down her version of recent events, which Norris was to communicate to Charles IX and Catherine de' Medici. Elizabeth insisted that, 'By our means only, [Mary's] life was saved in her captivity, and since her flying into our realm, she hath been honourably used and entertained and attended upon by noble personages, and such hath been our natural compassion towards her in this her affliction, that we utterly set apart all such just causes as she had given us of sundry offences, whereof some were notorious to the whole world.' Regarding the inquiry into Darnley's murder, 'such circumstances were produced to argue her guilty'. The Queen now wished, however, that she had not authorised the inquiry. She had been 'fully determined to see Mary restored', but then she had discovered 'a disordered, unhonourable and dangerous practice', which had been going on since the inquiry opened at York.

According to Elizabeth, her cousin had bombarded her 'with frequent letters, tears and messages', promising 'She would never seek nor use any means to be helped but by us, nor would attempt anything in our realm but by our advice.' Instead, she had intrigued behind Elizabeth's back to marry Norfolk. Contrary to what Mary's supporters had been spreading about, Elizabeth had 'never thought' of naming Mary as her successor. She was 'right sorry, yea, half ashamed, to have been thus misused by her, whom we have so benefited by saving of her life'. Norris should emphasise that Mary's complaints about the conditions she was held under were simply untrue.

In November, having learned of Norfolk's fate and received a promise of Spanish aid, the northern earls mobilised their rebel forces, numbering over 2500 men, and marched southwards, sacking Durham Cathedral and moving on towards their ultimate goal, Tutbury, where Mary Stuart was held – 'her whom the world believed to be the hidden cause of these troubles'. Elizabeth shared this view, and for the first time gave serious consideration to her councillors' exhortations that Mary be executed. She even allowed them to draw up a death warrant to be used if her cousin was discovered to be behind the rebellion, or in the event of its appearing likely to succeed.

There were simultaneous smaller risings in other northern districts. On 25 November, at the Queen's command, Mary was removed to Coventry in the Protestant Midlands, and the Earl of Huntingdon was appointed to assist Shrewsbury, who was ill, in his task of guarding her. All ports were closed and the militia placed on alert. Windsor was prepared for a siege.

Realising they had no hope of reaching Mary at Coventry, the rebel earls lost heart, for her liberation had been central to their plans. By 20 December the rising had collapsed, and the rebels were fleeing in all directions in order to escape the avenging royal army, 28,000 strong, sent northwards, under the command of Sussex at Elizabeth's order. Sussex pursued the leaders, Northumberland and Westmorland to the Scottish border, whence they escaped into Scotland. 'The vermin are fled to foreign cover,' observed Cecil on Christmas Day.

During the rising Elizabeth had displayed to the world a cool, fearless front, remaining at Windsor with Pembroke, now restored to favour and deputed to guard her in the event of a foreign invasion, and Leicester, who could lend her moral support. Her cousin, Lord Hunsdon, had been sent north to provide military backing to Sussex. When the rebels retreated and the danger was past, Leicester went home to Kenilworth for Christmas.

Perhaps the most worrying aspect of the Northern Rising had been Philip's willingness to support it, which demonstrated just how hostile he had become towards Elizabeth. He had also instructed Alva to send Mary Stuart 10,000 ducats. Urged on by Cecil, Elizabeth determined to show her subjects that any rebellion against her authority would be punished with the utmost severity. 'You are to proceed thereunto, for the terror of others, with expedition,' she commanded Sussex. 'Spare no offenders. We are in nothing moved to spare them.'

The Earl wasted no time in rounding up the lesser rebels and making an example of them. Reprisals were unusually savage, and no village was to be without at least one execution, 'the bodies to remain till they fall to pieces where they hang'. By 4 February 1570, between 600 and 750 commoners had been hanged and two hundred gentry had been deprived of their estates and goods, which were distributed to loyal noblemen; the Queen, however, thought it unfair that those who had helped to plan the revolt had escaped with their lives, while lesser men suffered the ultimate penalty.

Norfolk was degraded from the Order of the Garter, his achievements being removed from his stall at Windsor and, as custom demanded, kicked into the moat. From his prison cell, the Duke wrote to the Queen: 'Now I see how unpleasant this matter of the Scots Queen is to Your Majesty, I never intend to deal further herein.'

As for the ringleaders, Westmorland fled into exile in Flanders with the Countess of Northumberland, who deserved, according to Elizabeth, to be burnt at the stake for her involvement in the rebellion. The Earl of Northumberland managed to evade capture for several months, but in August 1570 he was captured by the Scots, handed over to the English, and put to death in York. Plans to execute Mary Stuart were quietly abandoned.

Yet no sooner had one northern rising been quelled, than another erupted, led by the powerful Lord Dacre, who was resentful of the erosion of his territorial influence in the north. This was ferociously suppressed within a week by Lord Hunsdon, who was afterwards warmly congratulated by the Queen upon his victory: 'I doubt much, my Harry', [she wrote], 'whether the victory given me more joyed me, or that you were by God appointed the instrument of my glory, and I assure you, for my country's good, the first might suffice, but for my heart's contentation, the second more pleased me. Your loving kinswoman, Elizabeth R.'

Elizabeth's position was now very much stronger, and in a happier frame of mind on 23 January 1570, she opened the Royal Exchange in London, built by Sir Thomas Gresham as a central trading place for the City's merchants and bankers. John Stow recorded: 'The Queen's Majesty, attended with her nobility, came from her house on the Strand, called Somerset House, and entered the City by Temple Bar, through Fleet Street, Cheapside, and so by the north side of the bourse [Exchange], through Threadneedle Street, to Sir Thomas Gresham's in Bishopsgate Street, where she dined. After dinner, Her Majesty, returning through Cornhill, entered the bourse on the south side, and after she had visited every part thereof above the ground, she caused the same bourse by an herald and trumpet to be proclaimed the Royal Exchange.'

On that same day, the Regent Moray was assassinated at Linlithgow by rival lords who feared he had ambitions to be king. When Elizabeth heard the news she shut herself in her chamber to contemplate the awful prospect of political turmoil north of the border. There was indeed chaos in Scotland, with William Maitland forming a faction dedicated to restoring Queen Mary. When news of this reached England, Mary rejoiced and tried to contact her son, James VI, but Elizabeth took steps to prevent her from doing so, realising that the majority of the Scots did not want their Queen back.

However, the kings of France and Spain were demanding that she seize this opportunity to restore Mary to the Scottish throne. In view of Mary's involvement in the recent plots and risings, Elizabeth would only consider it on the tightest conditions, the chief of which was Mary's long-desired ratification of the Treaty of Edinburgh.

The continuing problem of the Queen of Scots was greatly exacerbated when, on 25 February 1570, Pope Pius V, inspired by outdated reports of the Northern Rising, impulsively published a bull, 'Regnans in Excelsis', excommunicating Elizabeth, 'the pretended Queen of England, the serpent of wickedness'. The bull deprived her of her kingdom, absolved all true Catholics from their allegiance to her, and extended the anathema to all who continued to support her. This was effectively an incitement to Elizabeth's subjects and to foreign princes to rise against her in what would amount to a holy crusade. It also actively encouraged Mary Stuart's supporters to set her up in Elizabeth's place. Most sinister of all, it subverted the loyalty of Elizabeth's Catholic subjects and made every one of them a potential traitor to be regarded with suspicion. From now on, each one of them would face an agonising choice of loyalties, for it would no longer be possible to compromise on matters of conscience.

This led, in turn, to the hardening of attitudes on the part of English Protestants, who became more patriotic and ever more protective towards their Queen, their zealous loyalty prompting them to press increasingly for Mary Stuart's execution and for tougher laws against Catholics. The bull's ultimate effect was to turn Catholicism into a political rather than a religious issue in England, and because of this it failed in its purpose. Most English people ignored it; a man who nailed it to the door of the Bishop of London's palace in St Paul's Churchyard was arrested, tortured and executed. In the north, where the bull might once have been well received, Catholic power had been effectively crushed.

Nor did the great Catholic monarchies of Spain and France hasten to invade England. On the contrary, both Philip II and Charles IX angrily condemned the Pope for taking such hasty action without consulting them first. Elizabeth herself announced defiantly that no ship of Peter would ever enter any of her ports; otherwise she was dismissive, and the mainly Protestant Londoners echoed her feelings when they described it as 'a vain crack of words that made a noise only'.

Elizabeth had a concept of Church and State as equal partners in one body politic, and considered it her duty as sovereign to deal with all matters affecting that body politic on a political basis. After the bull, her policy was to treat Catholic intrigues as treason, or crimes against the state, rather than as heresy. Those Catholics who were condemned were not to be considered as martyrs for their faith, but traitors to their country.

The Queen had never demonstrated any personal animosity towards Catholics in general. So long as they conformed outwardly, she was not interested in their private beliefs. Only when those beliefs led to conspiracy would she invoke the law.

It was at this time that Cecil began organising an efficient espionage network that could detect conspirators, for there was a minority of English Catholics who were prepared to risk death for their loyalty to the Pope and for the woman they believed to be their true queen. These people referred to Mary as 'the Queen' and to Elizabeth as 'the Usurper', and believed it their duty to depose her.

In late April, Elizabeth's Council warned her that, if she forced Mary's restoration in Scotland, she would never feel safe in her kingdom, but the Queen refused to listen, having been threatened with war by the French if she did not keep her word. Soon afterwards, she sent Mary a list of stringent conditions that must be agreed to before she would consider helping her to regain her throne. Not only had Mary to ratify the Treaty of Edinburgh, but she also had to send her son James to England as a hostage for her good behaviour. Cecil warned the Queen that she was endangering her own person, but this provoked such a violent storm of tears and temper that the Secretary backed off. Sir Nicholas Bacon faced a similar tantrum when he insisted that it would be madness to contemplate freeing Mary. These outbursts appear, however, to have been staged for the benefit of the French ambassador.

Throughout the summer, to placate the French, Elizabeth maintained that she was working for Mary's restoration, when in fact she was employing her usual delaying tactics to keep Mary safely under lock and key. No one could guess her true feelings on the matter. When Leicester suggested that Mary be restored with only limited powers, the Queen accused him of being too friendly towards the Queen of Scots, whereupon he left court in a temper. But the spat was soon over, and he was back and reconciled with Elizabeth within days.

The Queen's irritability was exacerbated by the appearance of what was probably a varicose ulcer on her leg. It did not heal and she suffered a good deal of pain, but still insisted that she would go on progress as usual. Meanwhile her courtiers had to put up with her sulks and uncertain temper.

In June, as a token of goodwill, Mary sent Elizabeth a bureau with a lock engraved with a cipher used by the two Queens in the years before Mary's abdication. Fingering it, Elizabeth sighed, 'Would God that all things were in the same state they were in when this cipher was made betwixt us.' It was October before Mary agreed to Elizabeth's terms.

On 12 July, Lennox, Elizabeth's favoured candidate, was appointed Regent of Scotland until such time as his grandson the King came of age. The new Regent wasted no time in hanging the Catholic Archbishop Hamilton for complicity in the murder of Darnley, thus provoking more bitter feuds between the noble factions. Meanwhile, Elizabeth kept Lady Lennox at the English court as a hostage for Lennox's loyalty to herself.

Early in August, Cecil and Leicester managed to persuade the Queen that Norfolk, who was popular with the people and had been foolish rather than malicious in his offence, be taken from the Tower – where plague was rife – and placed under house arrest, on condition that he solemnly undertook never again to involve himself in the Queen of Scots's affairs. Norfolk promised, and was duly moved to his London mansion, the Charterhouse, near Smithfield.

Mary Stuart's presence in England and the recent plots and conspiracies against the Crown had lent urgency to the argument that Elizabeth should marry and produce an heir as soon as possible. The birth of a Protestant successor would go a long way towards neutralising Mary's claims, especially if the child were a son. Without that child, Elizabeth stood alone, unguarded against foreign invaders, traitors at home, and the constant fear of assassination. If she died childless, there would be no bar to Mary's succession, and all that Elizabeth had worked for would be overthrown.

Which was why, in August, although she was still 'as disgusted with marriage as ever', Elizabeth sent an envoy to the Emperor to try and revive the Habsburg marriage project. The Archduke was still single, but made it clear that he was no longer interested, and the Queen pretended indignation at his rejection of her. Shortly afterwards he married a Bavarian princess, and in later life became a fanatical persecutor of heretics until his death in 1590.

Then, in September, a new proposal of marriage arrived, this time from Charles IX's brother and heir, the nineteen-year-old Henry, Duke of Anjou. Charles and Catherine de' Medici hoped, by this project, to unite England and France in a defensive alliance against Spain. Elizabeth was interested, if only for the political advantages and much-needed friendship that prolonged negotiations with France could bring her, and Cecil began drawing up lists of the 'commodities' to be gained from the union, putting out feelers as to how serious the French were about it. To this end, he sent the fiercely Protestant Sir Francis Walsingham to Paris to act as Elizabeth's envoy.

Walsingham was nearing forty; he had been educated at Cambridge, Gray's Inn and Padua, and become an MP; later, he had come under the patronage of Cecil, who had offered him a post at court and later placed him in charge of his secret agents. Because of his swarthy complexion and black clothes, Elizabeth nicknamed Walsingham her 'Moor', and although she liked him and was an occasional guest at his house in Barn Elms in Surrey, she sometimes found him more than a match for her intellectually. He was a serious, disciplined and cultivated man with deep convictions and formidable abilities, and was drawn to Leicester because of their shared religious beliefs. He spoke four languages besides English, and was a skilful diplomat with a wide knowledge of international politics. As a Puritan, he had a special loathing for and distrust of Spain and the Queen of Scots. Elizabeth knew she could rely on him implicitly, and that he would carry out her orders, even if he disagreed with them. Her preservation was his ordained mission in life, and to that end he devoted his energies, his wealth and – ultimately – his health.

As usual, religion was to prove a major obstacle in the marriage negotiations, because Elizabeth was as insistent as ever that her husband should abide by her country's laws, and the priest-dominated Anjou was adamant that he would never abandon his faith. Elizabeth might well have felt revulsion for the match on personal grounds, because it was well known that Anjou was bisexually promiscuous: at this time he was notorious for being a womaniser, but he was also attracted to men, and in later years became a blatant transvestite, appearing at court balls in elaborate female costumes and with a painted face. A Venetian envoy observed, 'He is completely dominated by voluptuousness, covered with perfumes and essences. He wears a double row of rings, and pendants in his ears.' Although Anjou's mother, Catherine de' Medici, backed the marriage because she was ambitious for him to gain a crown, he himself was less than lukewarm about it. Nor did the puritanical Walsingham favour it.

In November, the Queen sent Leicester to summon Fénelon, the French ambassador, to an audience. She had dressed to impress, and was playing the coy virgin, saying how she regretted having stayed single for so long. Fénelon replied that he could help to alter that state of affairs and would deem it a great honour if he could bring about a marriage between herself and Anjou. The Queen protested that, at thirty-seven, she was too old for marriage, but nevertheless managed to convey the impression that she was eager for it. She did voice concern that Anjou was so much younger than she was, but laughed when Leicester quipped, 'So much the better for you!'

Soon afterwards Fénelon sounded out Leicester on the project, and was surprised to find that the Earl supported it. Armed with this and

Elizabeth's obvious interest, Fénelon informed Queen Catherine that the time was ripe for an official proposal.

Eleven years of peace and stable government, coupled with the provocative action of the Pope, had securely established Elizabeth in the affection and imagination of her people as an able, wise and gracious ruler, and that regard found its expression in November 1570, when her Accession Day was first celebrated throughout the kingdom as a public holiday. Prior to that year it seems to have been marked with just the ringing of church bells, but the English were now determined that the day should be 'a holiday that surpassed all the Pope's holy days'. In 1576, 17 November officially became one of the great holy days of the Church of England, veneration of the Virgin Queen, who was hailed as the English Judith or Deborah, having replaced the worship of the Virgin Mary that was now banned. Indeed, some Puritans feared that Elizabeth was being set up as an object of idolatry.

Accession Day was celebrated with prayers of thanksgiving for a sovereign who had delivered the land from popery. There were sermons, joyful peals of bells, nationwide festivities and the famous Accession Day jousts at Whitehall. Special prayer books incorporating a service composed by the Queen herself for use on the day were printed, and ballads and songs composed. Throughout England the Queen's subjects would drink to her health and prosperity, feast and light fireworks and bonfires, whilst royal ships at sea would 'shoot off' their guns.

Camden relates how, 'in testimony to their affectionate love' towards the Queen, her people continued to celebrate 'the sacred seventeenth day' until the end of her reign. After the Armada victory of 1588, the festivities continued until 19 November, which was, appropriately, St Elizabeth's Day. Nor did this observance cease with her death, for her successors encouraged its continuance in order to emphasise England's greatness, and Accession Day was celebrated right up until the eighteenth century.

The Whitehall jousts, customarily attended by the Queen herself, were the most splendid aspect of 'the Golden Day', as it was termed. Presided over by the Queen's Champion, Sir Henry Lee, until his retirement in 1590, when he was replaced by George Clifford, Earl of Cumberland, and attended by up to 12,000 spectators, they presented an opportunity for the young men of the court to display their knightly prowess in the lists and so win fame. The pageantry at these occasions was breathtaking, with contestants appearing in the most elaborate and inventive costumes, often on mythological themes. Each would present a gift to Elizabeth as she sat with her ladies in the gallery overlooking the tiltyard, which occupied the site known today as Horse Guards Parade.

Often the Queen would appear in the guise of Astraea, the virgin goddess of justice, or Cynthia, 'the lady of the sea', or Diana the huntress, Belphoebe, or, in later years, as Gloriana, the Faerie Queen. In these unearthly roles, the Queen would acknowledge the homage and devotion of her gallant knights. Her Champion, wearing her favour – Clifford was painted by Nicholas Hilliard in full costume with her glove attached to his hat – would then defend her honour against all comers in the jousts, and afterwards, the contestants' shields, adorned with intricate symbolic devices, would be hung in the Shield Gallery in Whitehall Palace. Thus were the ideals of chivalry – of which this was the last flowering in England – kept alive by the Queen and her courtiers.

13

'Gloriana'

'To be a king and wear a crown is more glorious to them that see it than it is a pleasure to them that bear it,' Queen Elizabeth once famously said. At the same time, she revelled in and jealously guarded the privileges of sovereignty: 'I am answerable to none for my actions otherwise than as I shall be disposed of my own free will, but to Almighty God alone.' God, she believed, had preserved her through many trials to bring her to the throne, and she was convinced that she reigned by his especial favour. In 1576, she told Parliament, 'And as for those rare and special benefits which many years have followed and accompanied me with happy reign, I attribute them to God alone. These seventeen years God hath both prospered and protected you with good success, under my direction, and I nothing doubt that the same maintaining hand will guide you still and bring you to the ripeness of perfection.'

As 'God's creature', a divinely-appointed queen, hallowed and sanctified at her coronation, Elizabeth believed that she alone was able to understand fully the complexities and mysteries of Church and State. 'Princes', she declared, 'transact business in a certain way, with a princely intelligence, such as private persons cannot imitate.' If she felt that anyone was encroaching upon this sacred privilege, she was quick to reprimand them. 'She was absolute and sovereign mistress,' remembered one courtier, Sir Robert Naunton. 'She is our god in Earth', declared Lord North, 'and if there be perfection in flesh and blood, undoubtedly it is in Her Majesty.'

What was more important to Elizabeth than anything, however, was that she reigned with her subjects' love. She proudly pointed out that she was 'mere English', as they were, and constantly proclaimed that she was as a mother to her people, and cared deeply for the 'safety and quietness of you all'. 'She is very much wedded to the people and thinks as they do,' observed one Spanish envoy. She had their interests at heart and her instinct told her what was best for them. A stickler for justice, she 'condescended' to 'the meaner sorts', received their petitions on a daily basis, and often stood up for their rights. Sir Walter Raleigh told James I that 'Queen Elizabeth would set the reason of a mean man before the authority of the greatest counsellor she had. She was Queen of the small as well as the great, and would hear their complaints.' Her affection for her subjects is evident in contemporary sources, where her most frequently repeated utterance is, 'Thank you, my good people.'

Sir John Harington, the Queen's godson, reveals how well she understood how to deal with her subjects:

> Her mind was oft-time like the gentle air that cometh from a westerly point in a summer's morn: 'twas sweet and refreshing to all around. Her speech did win all affections, and her subjects did try to show all love to her commands; for she would say her state did require her to command what she knew her people would willingly do from their own love to her. Herewith did she show her wisdom fully: for who did choose to lose her confidence, or who would withhold a show of love and obedience, when their sovereign said it was their own choice, and not her compulsion? Surely she did play her tables well to gain obedience thus, without constraint. Again, she could put forth such alterations, when obedience was lacking, as left no doubt whose daughter she was.

In an age of personal monarchy, it was important that the monarch was on show as often as possible, and Elizabeth ensured that she was highly visible, travelling on annual progresses, riding out frequently through the streets of London or being rowed in her state barge along the Thames.

She also thought it important to justify her actions to her subjects in a series of carefully composed speeches, many of them written by herself, printed pamphlets and proclamations. She was a gifted orator and actress who could speak 'extempore with many brilliant, choice and felicitous phrases', and who knew well how to manipulate her audience so that she had them eating out of her hand. 'Princes' own words be better printed in the hearers' memory than those spoken by her command,' she told Parliament. In the latter decades of her reign, her style of writing and public speaking became more florid, mannerist and extravagant, in keeping with the prevalent trend for Euphuism, a prose form invented by John Lyly in the earliest English novel, *Euphues, or the Anatomy of Wit*, and at which Elizabeth became one of the foremost exponents.

Few realised how subtly the Queen dealt with them. 'I have seen her smile – with great semblance of good liking to all around,' recorded Harington, 'and cause everyone to open his most inward thought to her; when, on a sudden, she would ponder in private on what had passed, write down all their opinions, draw them out as occasion required, and sometimes disprove to their faces what had been delivered a month before. She caught many poor fish, who little knew what snare was laid for them.'

Not for nothing was she Henry VIII's daughter: she expected instant obedience and respect, and would have her way 'as absolutely as her father'. 'Majesty', she declared, 'makes the people bow.' She was fond of talking about Henry, and even seems to have modelled some of her speeches on his. She liked to remind her councillors how much sterner her father had been, and when they had the temerity to challenge her views, she would thunder, 'Had I been born crested, not cloven, you would not speak thus to me!' In 1593, she acknowledged her debt to Henry VIII before Parliament, as one 'whom in the duty of a child I must regard, and to whom I must acknowledge myself far shallow'. Nevertheless, she admitted that her style of government was 'more moderate' and benign than Henry's had been.

Elizabeth's command of politics and statesmanship was as exceptional as her intelligence was formidable. She was astute, pragmatic, very hard-working, and never afraid to compromise. In the face of rebellion and war, she displayed remarkable courage. The coarse buccaneer, Sir John Perrot, her deputy in Ireland, once said of her, 'Lo! Now she is ready to be-piss herself for fear of the Spaniards!' but was later forced to revise his opinion and admit that she had 'an invincible mind, that showeth from whence she came'.

Elizabeth's chief concern was to provide England with stable, orderly government. She had the gift of knowing instinctively what was right for her kingdom, her priorities being to maintain the law and the established Church, avoid war and live within her means. She told her judges, whom she selected herself, that they must 'stand *pro veritate* (for truth) rather than *pro Regina* (for the Queen)'. She loved peace, and frequently offered to mediate between warring foreign powers. Not for nothing did James VI of Scotland describe her as 'one who in wisdom and felicity of government surpassed all princes since the days of Augustus'.

'There was never so wise woman born as Queen Elizabeth', wrote Cecil in tribute, 'for she spake and understood all languages, knew all estates and dispositions and princes, and particularly was so expert in the knowledge of her own realm as no counsellor she had could tell her what she knew not before.'

*

For all this, there still remained in Elizabethan society a deeply ingrained prejudice against female sovereigns in general. The unhappy example of Queen Mary seemed to confirm the general view that women were not born to rule. In 1558, in his *First Blast of the Trumpet against the Monstrous Regiment of Women*, John Knox wrote: 'I am assured that God hath revealed to some in this our age that it is more than a monster in nature that a woman should reign and bear empire over man.' Women, he asserted, were naturally weak, frail, impatient, feeble and foolish, the port and gate of the Devil, and insatiably covetous. The Swiss reformer John Calvin believed that the government of women was 'a deviation from the original and proper order of nature, to be ranked no less than slavery'.

A typical example of male prejudice occurred when a French envoy asked for the Council to be present at his audience with the Queen, implying that the matters of state he had come to discuss were beyond female understanding. Back came a furious answer from Her Majesty: 'The ambassador forgets himself in thinking us incapable of conceiving an answer to his message without the aid of our Council. It might be appropriate in France, where the King is young, but we are governing our realm better than the French are theirs.'

Elizabeth herself was no early feminist; she accepted the creed of her day, that women had serious limitations, speaking of herself as 'a woman wanting both wit and memory'. In a self-composed prayer, she thanked God 'for making me, though a weak woman, yet Thy instrument'. To combat prejudice and underline her position, she invariably referred to herself as a prince, comparing herself with kings and emperors, and with some success, for according to William Cecil, she was 'more than a man and, in truth, something less than a woman'. 'My experience in government', she told Henry IV of France at the end of her reign, 'has made me so stubborn as to believe that I am not ignorant of what becomes a king.'

'Although I may not be a lioness', she was fond of saying, 'I am a lion's cub, and inherit many of his qualities.' Her apologists felt bound to point out that her reign fulfilled one of the ancient prophecies of Merlin: 'Then shall a Royal Virgin reign, which shall stretch her white rod over the Belgic shore and the great Castile smite so sore withal that it shall make him shake and fall.' The 'great Castile' was, of course, Philip of Spain, whose kingdom incorporated that of Castile.

By exploiting 'my sexly weaknesses', Elizabeth converted them into the strengths she needed to survive in a man's world. She used her femininity to manipulate the men who served her and make them protective of her. Her calculated flirtatiousness kept her courtiers loyal, and by playing off one against the other, she preserved a balance of power at her court. She established the convention that, as sovereign, she was above normal social mores. She asserted before the Venetian ambassador, 'My sex cannot diminish my prestige.'

So effective was she as a ruler that she managed to overcome the prejudice, and her subjects came to regard her as one of their most successful monarchs. She was certainly one of the best loved.

Being a woman was to Elizabeth's advantage when it came to creating her own legend, because then she could assume the allegorical and mythological personae assigned her by chivalrous courtiers, writers and poets. She was the 'Rosa electa', the chosen rose, around whom a cult of adoration flourished, and who came to be regarded as little less than divine. By the end of her reign she was being referred to in Acts of Parliament as 'Her Sacred Majesty'. The composer John Dowland wrote a song entitled 'Vivat Eliza for an Ave Maria', which plainly showed how the worship of the Queen had replaced the people's need for a female deity in the post-Reformation years.

Elizabeth herself, making a virtue of a necessity, promoted the image and cult of the Virgin Queen who was wedded to her kingdom and people. She took for her personal emblems those symbols of virginity that had been associated in earlier times with the Virgin Mary: the rose, the moon, the ermine or the phoenix. She also, like Henry VII, made much of her alleged descent from King Arthur, whose legends were a dominant theme in the pageantry of her reign.

It was the poets and dramatists, however, who did most to promote the cult of Elizabeth. In his epic poem, The Faerie Queen (1596), Edmund Spenser referred to her as 'Gloriana' and 'Belphoebe'. William Shakespeare, Ben Jonson and Sir Walter Raleigh called her Cynthia or Diana, Diana being the virgin huntress, 'chaste and fair'. Other poets eulogised the Queen as Virgo, Pandora, Oriana, or 'England's Astraea, Albion's shining sun', while the Protestant establishment saw her as a new Judith or Deborah. Throughout her reign, poems, songs, ballads and madrigals sang her praises and called upon God to preserve her from her enemies, or commended her for her virtues and her chastity. No English sovereign, before or since, has so captured the imagination of his or her people or so roused their patriotic feelings.

As well as inspiring her subjects, Elizabeth could be infuriating, as her close advisers often found. A mistress of the subtle art of procrastination, she was marvellously adept at delaying and dissembling, and would usually shelve problems she could not immediately solve. Her courtiers, lacking her subtlety and not understanding her motives, because she did not normally disclose them, were driven mad by her behaviour, yet they were forced to concede, in the long run, that she had often served her country better by deferring decisions than by making them hastily. Whenever she could, she would play for time.

'It maketh me weary of my life,' Sir Thomas Smith, one of her secretaries of state, complained in 1574, when Elizabeth had been particularly difficult. 'The time passeth almost irrecuperable, the advantage lost, the charges continuing, nothing resolved. I neither can get the letters signed nor the letter already signed, but day by day, and hour by hour [it is] deferred until anon, noon and tomorrow.' And Cecil once fumed, 'The lack of a resolute answer from Her Majesty drives me to the wall.'

As she grew older, she became increasingly reluctant to sign any document. Her secretaries would therefore 'entertain her with some relation or speech, whereat she may take some pleasure' to take her mind off what she was doing.

One of the Queen's mottoes, appropriately, was '*Video Taceo*' – 'I see all and say nothing', and like her father, she kept her own counsel. 'For her own mind, what that really was I must leave, as a thing doubly inscrutable, both as she was a woman and a queen,' wrote the courtier Dudley Digges. She had learned early on that it was never wise to show one's hand. Harington recorded that 'Her wisest men and best councillors were oft sore troubled to know her will in matters of state, so covertly did she pass her judgement.' As princess and as queen she never knew what it was to feel secure: there was always the threat of poison or the assassin's dagger, and always enemies seeking to destroy her by one means or another. She knew she might never die peacefully in her bed.

Elizabeth could be resolute and tough when she had to be, and on two known occasions did not shrink from authorising the torture of offenders, which was officially illegal but, in her view, necessary in the interests of national security; in both cases, the victims were involved in plots against the Queen's life, but even so the gaolers in the Tower were aware that her anger would fall upon them if they exceeded their warrant. She hated executions and issued reprieves to condemned felons whenever possible, so long as justice had been seen to be done. She was, as Cecil called her, 'a very merciful lady'. She followed major trials with interest, and intervened if she felt it necessary.

She was in most respects a conservative, who respected the old medieval ideal of hierarchical order within the Christian universe, and cherished traditional notions of 'degree, priority and place'. 'Her Majesty loveth peace. Next, she loveth not change,' observed Sir Francis Bacon. One of her secretaries, Robert Beale, warned his successor to 'avoid being new-fangled and a bringer-in of new customs'.

Her councillors found her infuriatingly unpredictable. For all her common touch and geniality, she remained very much on her dignity, and woe betide those who stinted in their outward show of respect towards her or failed to show the proper humility in her presence. Etiquette required that anyone addressing the Queen should do so on bended knees and remain in that position until given leave to rise. No one might sit while she stood, and it was seen as great condescension on her part when, in later years, she permitted Cecil, aged and lame, to sit upon a stool in her presence.

One of the criticisms often levelled against her was that she was mean. In fact, having inherited huge debts from her sister, she was determined not only to clear them but also to live within her means. This meant making stringent economies that were often unpopular, but these measures kept England solvent at a time when most European countries were virtually bankrupt. Out of a relatively small annual income that rarely exceeded £300,000, she had to defray her own expenses as well as those of the court and the government. In achieving this within her budget, Elizabeth showed that she had inherited the financial acumen of her grandfather, Henry VII, for throughout her reign she managed to accomplish much with very limited resources.

She did not, however, stint on outward show, because in an age of personal monarchy, pomp and splendour were regarded as the visual evidence of power. 'We princes are set as it were upon stages in the sight and view of all the world,' observed the Queen. Therefore no expense was spared on court ceremonial, furnishings and entertainments, nor on the Queen's wardrobe, for these were all aspects of sovereignty designed to impress foreign ambassadors and visitors to the court. It had, indeed, been the policy of successive Tudor sovereigns to maintain a magnificent court that would not only impress but also overawe all who visited it.

In the midst of all this pomp and ceremony, Elizabeth could display a very human face, as when she tickled Dudley's neck as she created him Earl of Leicester. She had the common touch, and was no slave to convention. It was not unusual for her to interrupt solemn addresses and even sermons: she would order the speaker to be quiet if he had rambled on too long for her liking. Yet when it came to an oration she admired, she was quick to praise it, as when she affectionately put her hands around the neck of a new Speaker in the Commons who had delivered an eloquent opening speech. She was sorry, she told her ladies, 'she knew him no sooner'.

Sovereignty in the sixteenth century was still viewed as an almost mystical institution, and Elizabeth I participated wholeheartedly in its ceremonies. Since the thirteenth century monarchs had touched for the

King's Evil, laying their hands on scrofulous persons whom their touch was believed to cure. At Whitehall and on progress, Elizabeth would regularly 'press the sores and ulcers' of the afflicted 'boldly and without disgust', sincerely believing that she was doing some good.

Each year, just before Easter, clad in an apron and with a towel over her arm, she presided over the Royal Maundy ceremony, and, in imitation of Christ at the Last Supper, washed the feet of poor women (which had been well scrubbed beforehand by her almoners) before distributing to them lengths of cloth, fish, bread, cheese and wine. Tradition decreed that not only the towels and aprons be given to the beneficiaries but also the monarch's robe, but Elizabeth did not want the poor fighting over her gown, and initiated the custom of giving out Maundy money in red purses instead.

When it came to the government of her kingdom, Elizabeth was unusually blessed in her advisers and councillors, whom she selected herself for their loyalty, honesty and abilities, with almost unerring perspicacity. Although she told one ambassador, 'We do nothing without our Council, for nothing is so dangerous in state affairs as self-opinion,' it was she who, after sounding out all her councillors, took the major decisions, especially in the field of foreign policy, which was her prerogative. She did not feel bound to take her councillors' advice, and frequently shouted at them or banned them temporarily from court if they disagreed with her. Many were prepared to risk this minor punishment for the sake of putting their views across.

Nor did the Queen care if she inconvenienced her ministers, for she expected them to be as hard-working, efficient and devoted to duty as she was herself. If they were not, she would demand to know why; she missed nothing, and was an exacting mistress. When Lord Hunsdon outstayed leave from his official duties, the Queen raged to his son, 'God's wounds! We will set him by the feet and set another in his place if he dallies with us thus, for we will not be thus dallied withal.'

Harington records that she would keep Cecil with her

> till late at night discoursing alone, and then call out another at his departure, and try the depth of all around her sometime. Each displayed his wit in private. If any dissembled with her, or stood not well to her advisings, she did not let it go unheeded, and sometimes not unpunished.

After these night-time consultations, the Queen would be ready to return to business before the next dawn had broken. She seems to have needed very little sleep, and it would be no exaggeration to state that she was, in modern terms, a workaholic. Harington attests that on one occasion she wrote one letter whilst dictating another and listening to a query to which she gave a lucid answer.

Each day she held successive private consultations with her ministers, read letters and dispatches, wrote or dictated others, checked accounts and received petitions. She kept letters, memos and notes in a 'great pouch' hung about her waist, or in her bedroom, and threw them away when they were not needed. She rarely attended the daily Council meetings, knowing that her councillors would try to impose their opinions on her – although she was perfectly capable of arguing the point with them. She preferred to keep a tight rein on affairs from behind the scenes. In the early days of her reign, Cecil tried to prevent her from dealing with matters too weighty, in his opinion, for a woman to cope with, but as the years passed he conceived a deep respect for and trust in her, both as his sovereign and as a shrewd and clever woman.

In day to day matters, Elizabeth delegated the decision-making to her Council, taking the credit herself when things turned out well. If disaster struck, the councillors got the blame. According to Harington, Cecil would 'shed a-plenty tears on any miscarriage, well knowing the difficult part was, not so much to mend the matter itself, as his mistress's humour'. Her temper was notorious: she was not above boxing the Secretary's ears, throwing her slipper at Walsingham's face, or punching others who displeased her, and after flouncing out of a Council meeting in a rage, she would retire to her Privy Chamber and read until she had calmed down, which she invariably did after these outbursts. Nor was she reluctant to admit she was in the wrong, for she would hasten to make amends. Leicester said of her, 'God be thanked, her blasts be not the storms of other princes, though they be very sharp sometimes to those she loves the best.'

'When she smiled', wrote Harington, 'it was a pure sunshine that everyone did choose to bask in if they could, but anon came a storm from a sudden gathering of clouds, and the thunder fell in wondrous manner on all alike.' One French ambassador, having witnessed the royal temper, confided, 'When I see her enraged against any person whatever, I wish myself in Calcutta, fearing her anger like death itself.' As a young queen, in 1559, Elizabeth rebuked two of her servants so wrathfully that they claimed they would 'carry it to their graves'. A colleague ventured, on bended knees, to plead with his mistress 'to make them men again, who remain so amazed as nothing can breed any comfort in them'.

Cecil, as the adviser closest to the Queen, learned early on how to gauge her mood, as well as how to weather the storms of her anger. All her servants, he wrote, 'must sometimes bear the cross words, as I myself have had long experience'. For over thirty years he was her chief adviser and the greatest moderating influence on the Council. 'No prince in Europe', she once said, 'ever had such a councillor as I have had in him.'

The Queen favoured both the older aristocracy and the gentry, the 'new men' whose fortunes were founded on wealth, and picked her councillors for their abilities, as well as for their breeding. She expected the highest standards of personal service from them. Most of the men who served her were related to each other in some way, which gave the court a cohesive family atmosphere. Although Sir Robert Naunton accused her of fostering factions at court, the Sidney Papers make it clear that she 'used her wisdom in balancing the weights'.

Parliament, however, was less easily managed than the Council, to which it was subordinate. The Queen believed that, as sovereign, she had absolute authority over Parliament, but the Puritans in the Commons could be relied upon to oppose many measures, and both Houses were jealous of their powers and privileges, seeking constantly to extend them. Clashes between Queen and Parliament were therefore inevitable, and as we have seen, Elizabeth was on occasions forced to concede defeat. Whenever possible, she managed without Parliament. In the forty-five years of her reign, it sat for only ten sessions, which lasted in total just 140 weeks – less than three years. The Queen attended only the opening and closing state ceremonies, arriving by barge or on horseback and wearing her state robes and crown; she wrote her own speeches for these occasions. If the Commons or Lords wished to speak to her, they sent a delegation to wherever she was lodging. After they had addressed her on their knees, she would rise from the throne and bow or curtsey gracefully to them. Messengers brought her news of debates, and Cecil conveyed her wishes to both Houses.

'It is in me and my power to call Parliament', Elizabeth once reminded the Speaker; 'it is in my power to end and determine the same; it is in my power to dissent to any thing done in Parliaments.' Certain matters, such as the succession and her marriage, were considered by her to be inappropriate for discussion by Parliament, though Parliament increasingly thought otherwise.

In her foreign policy, Elizabeth sought to preserve England's stability and prosperity in a Europe dominated by the great Catholic powers of France and Spain. She achieved this by a policy of tortuous diplomacy that was not always understood by her own advisers. War was anathema to her because it threatened her kingdom's stability and her treasury. Unlike Philip II, she had no desire to found an empire, and in 1593 told Parliament,

It may be thought simplicity in me that all this time of my reign I have not sought to advance my territories and enlarge my dominions; for opportunity hath served me to do it. My mind was never to invade my neighbours, or to usurp over any. I am contented to reign over mine own, and to rule as a just prince.

Queen Elizabeth was a complex personality. A studious intellectual who would spend three hours a day reading history books if she could ('I suppose few that be no professors have read more,' she boasted to Parliament), and who to the end of her life would for recreation translate works by Tacitus, Boethius, Plutarch, Horace and Cicero, she could also spit and swear 'round, mouth-filling oaths', as was the habit of most great ladies of the age. Cecil once spirited away a book presented to the Queen by a Puritan, Mr Fuller, in which 'Her Gracious Majesty' was censured for swearing 'sometimes by that abominable idol, the mass, and often and grievously by God and by Christ, and by many parts of His glorified body, or by saints, faith and other forbidden things, and by Your Majesty's evil example and sufferance, the most part of your subjects do commonly swear and blaspheme, to God's unspeakable dishonour.' Elizabeth demanded to see the book, but with the connivance of one of her ladies it had fortunately been 'lost'.

Like her mother, the Queen revelled in jests, practical jokes and 'outwitting the wittiest'. She would laugh uproariously at the antics of the comic actor Richard Tarleton, and her female dwarf. Yet her table manners were perfect, and she ate and drank moderately, her preferred beverage being beer.

She herself could be very witty. When a French ambassador complained about her having kept him waiting six days for an audience, she sweetly retorted, 'It is true that the world was made in six days, but it was by God, to whose power the infirmity of man is not to be compared.'

She charmed men by her undoubted sex appeal and self-confidence, although one courtier claimed that her 'affections are not carved out of flint, but wrought out of virgin wax'. As the years went by, she took more and more extreme measures to recapture her lost youth, but her chivalrous courtiers continued to reassure her that she was the fairest lady at court, a fiction her inordinate vanity allowed her to swallow. 'She is a lady whom time hath surprised,' observed Sir Walter Raleigh.

Her chief passions were riding, in which she bore herself 'gallantly', hunting and dancing. A painting at Penshurst Place shows her dancing with a man thought to be Leicester; they are performing La Volta, a controversial dance in which the man lifts the woman and twirls her round with her feet swinging out, and which was universally condemned by preachers as the cause of much debauchery and even murders. Less controversial dances required a high degree of skill and grace, especially the galliards beloved by the Queen, in which dancers took five steps, leapt high in the air, then beat their feet together on landing. The Queen insisted on extra, more intricate steps being incorporated, which effectively prevented her less skilled courtiers from participating. As she grew older, she was more often than not a spectator at court dances, but her standards were rigorous. A French ambassador noted, 'When her maids dance, she follows the cadence with her head, hand and foot. She rebukes them if they do not dance to her liking, and without doubt she is mistress of the art.'

Elizabeth's preferred table games were cards and chess. She also enjoyed plays, jousts and the cruel sport of bear baiting, maintaining her own bear pit at Paris Garden on the south bank of the Thames.

The study of philosophy was another abiding interest. In 1593, upset over the French King Henry IV's conversion to Catholicism, Elizabeth spent twenty-six hours translating Boethius's *Consolations of Philosophy* into English, to calm her anger. Being 'indefatigably given to the study of learning', she kept up her scholarly interests and maintained her gift for languages throughout her life. 'I am more afraid of making a fault in my Latin than of the kings of Spain, France, Scotland, the whole House of Guise, and all their confederates,' she once declared. On another occasion she boasted that she was 'not afraid of a King of Spain who has been up to the age of twelve learning his alphabet'.

Elizabeth cared passionately about education, and involved herself in the life of both Eton College and Westminster School. In her desire for the middle and upper classes to become literate, she founded grammar schools, continuing the work begun by Edward VI. She also founded Jesus College, Oxford.

Music was another passion. As well as playing skilfully on the lute and virginals, the Queen 'composed ballets and music, and played and danced them'. She patronised Thomas Tallis and William Byrd, the greatest musicians of the age, and they both praised her singing voice. Her virginals, bearing the Boleyn arms, are preserved in the Victoria and Albert Museum.

Elizabeth's continued patronage of the astrologer and reputed wizard Dr John Dee certainly protected him from those who suspected him of forbidden practices and sought his ruin. Dee wrote in 1564 how the Queen 'in most heroical and princely wise did comfort me and encourage me in my studies philosophical and mathematical'. She continued to visit him at Mortlake – in 1575 he recorded that 'The Queen's Majesty with her most honourable Privy Council and other her lords and nobility visited my library.' She even offered Dee apartments at court, but he declined because he did not wish to interrupt his studies.

The Queen was fascinated, not only by Dee's scientific and esoteric work, but also by his predictions; being the product of a superstitious age, she took them seriously. In 1577 Dee predicted the founding of 'an incomparable British Empire', and it was his vision that inspired Elizabeth to encourage explorers such as Drake, Raleigh and Gilbert in their voyages of discovery and their attempts to establish English colonies in the New World. She consulted Dee on a wide variety of subjects: a new comet, toothache, some scientific puzzle, or the interpretation of a dream.

When moved to it, Elizabeth could be compassionate and kind. To her close friend, Lady Norris, 'mine own Crow', who had lost a beloved son in the Irish war, she sent this sensible advice: 'Harm not yourself for bootless [useless] help, but show a good example to comfort your dolorous yoke-fellow. Now that Nature's common work is done, and he that was born to die hath paid his tribute, let the Christian discretion stay the flux of your immoderate grieving, which hath instructed you that nothing of this kind hath happiness but by God's Divine Providence.' Two years later, after two more Norris sons had been killed in Ireland, the Queen wrote to the grieving parents, 'We couple you together from desire that all the comfort we wish you may reach you both in this bitter accident. We were loath to write at all, lest we should give you fresh occasion of sorrow, but could not forbear, knowing your religious obedience to Him whose strokes are unavoidable. We propose ourselves as an example, our loss being no less than yours.' When she heard of the death of the Earl of Huntingdon, she moved the whole court to Whitehall so that she herself could break the news to his widow.

Throughout her long life, Elizabeth enjoyed remarkably robust physical health, which permitted her to indulge in rigorous daily exercise. She ate abstemiously, lived to a good age and retained her faculties and her grip on the reins of government to the last. She expended a great deal of nervous energy, and displayed an extraordinary ability to remain standing for hours, much to the discomfiture of exhausted courtiers and foreign ambassadors.

The nervous ailments of her youth had probably resulted from stress, insecurity and the tragic events of her childhood. The traumatic shocks she suffered then, particularly on learning of the fate of her mother, may well have permanently damaged her nervous system. Some of these nervous problems abated on her accession, and only reappeared with the menopause. Thereafter, she was subject to anxiety states, hysterical episodes, obsessiveness and attacks of increasingly profound depression. She hated loud noise, and her intolerance of closed windows and people crowding her suggests she was also claustrophobic. She suffered intermittent panic attacks: once, whilst walking in procession to chapel, 'she was suddenly overcome with a shock of fear', according to the Spanish ambassador, and had to be helped back to her apartments.

These ailments were almost certainly neurotic. The stresses and strains of the responsibilities she carried, and her constant awareness of threats to her security would have overwhelmed a lesser person. Her contemporaries believed that by denying herself the fulfilment of marriage and children, she was living a life against nature. In Cecil's opinion, marriage and childbearing would have cured all her nervous complaints.

By the standards of her time, Elizabeth was a fastidious woman, and very fussy. She loathed certain smells, especially that of scented leather. When one courtier came into her presence in scented leather boots, she turned down the petition he submitted to her, wrinkling her nose, whereupon he quipped, 'Tut, tut, Madam, 'tis my suit that stinks!' The Queen at once relented. She was not so forbearing when it came to bad breath. After receiving one French envoy, she exclaimed, 'Good God! What shall I do if this man stay here, for I smell him an hour after he has gone!' Her words were reported back to the envoy, who at once betook himself back to France in shame.

Elizabeth also hated kitchen odours, which was unfortunate because her privy kitchen at Hampton Court was immediately beneath her apartments, and 'Her Majesty cannot sit quiet nor without ill savour.' Attempts to perfume the air with rosewater failed to disguise the smell, and in 1567 a new kitchen had to be built. It survives today, as a tea-room within the palace.

As she grew older, Elizabeth became plagued with headaches, which may have been migraines or caused by eye-strain, and rheumatism. 'An open ulcer, above the ankle' was first mentioned in July 1569 and on several occasions thereafter prevented her from walking: in 1570 she was obliged to travel in a litter whilst on progress. Although the ulcer had healed by 1571, the Queen was left with a slight limp, about which she was very sensitive. It did not, however, prevent her from taking the long, early morning walks in which she so delighted.

Although they were legion, her complaints were chronic rather than serious, and she refused on many occasions to give in to them. Like her father, she had an abhorrence of illness, and she could not bear people thinking she was ill. In 1577, she commanded Leicester to ask Cecil to send her some of the spa water from Buxton, where he was staying. When he did so, however, she would not drink it, on the grounds that 'It will not be of the goodness here it is there.' The real reason for her reluctance was that people were saying – with truth – that she had a 'sore leg', and that she would never admit to; in fact, she gave Leicester a dressing down for having written to Cecil.

The following year she suffered the 'grievous pangs and pains' of toothache, but because she 'doth not or will not think' that the offending tooth needed to be extracted, her doctors dared not suggest it. Various methods of relief were essayed, but all failed, and still the Queen would not 'submit to chirurgical instruments', despite the remonstrances of her Council. A heroic Bishop Aylmer of London, to demonstrate that it was not such a terrible process, offered to have one of his own decayed teeth pulled out in her presence. In December 1578, he underwent the operation, whereupon Elizabeth, after nine months of agony, finally allowed the doctors to take out her own tooth. After that, the subject of teeth became a taboo one with her, and she resolved to keep hers and suffer, rather than have them out as they decayed, for she had heard that King Philip had done so and now had to live on slops. This decision condemned her to years of intermittent pain from toothache, gum disease and resultant neuralgia in the face and neck. Contemporary sources refer to swellings in her cheeks which may have been abscesses. Her increasing preference for sugary confections, custards and puddings did not help matters, but she nevertheless succeeded in keeping some of her teeth, although a foreign observer who saw her in old age noticed that they were 'very yellow and unequal, and many of them are missing'.

Even in old age, the Queen would never admit she was unwell. In 1597, Cecil reported that she had 'a desperate ache in her right thumb, but will not be known of it, nor the gout it *cannot* be, nor *dare* not be, but to sign [documents] will not be endured'.

Her physicians were the best that could be found in an age in which a doctor might well hasten a patient's end by employing dubious and often dangerous treatments, but Elizabeth had little time for them and avoided consulting them if she could. Nor could she easily be persuaded to take any medicine, although she was fond of pressing sick courtiers to take herbal 'cordial broths' prepared to her own recipes, which she was convinced were excellent restoratives. The Queen could sometimes even be found spoon-feeding these homely and ancient remedies to her friends, and would boast that there was not an ailment that they could not cure. The only one of her recipes to survive is a cure for deafness, which she prescribed for Lord North: 'Bake a little loaf of bean flour and, being hot, rive it in halves, and into each half pour in three or four spoonfuls of bitter almonds, then clap both halves to both ears before going to bed, keep them close, and keep your head warm.' History does not record whether it worked.

The Queen deplored the contemporary fashion for purgatives, mainly on the grounds that those who took them were likely to take time off work, and forbade her maids to take them. In 1597, she banned two girls from her chamber for three days for disobeying her by 'taking of physic'.

The reasons for Elizabeth's reluctance to admit that she was ill were not far to seek. 'In another body, [illness was] no great matter, but [it was] much in a great princess.' It meant that people would think she was, to a degree, out of control; it meant giving in to human weakness, and as we have seen, Elizabeth enjoyed being regarded as more than human. Illness also betokened advancing age, which she would never admit to, and it threatened the image of eternal youth so central to the cult of the Virgin Queen.

In Tudor times, the royal image was all-important, much more so than today, for magnificence was regarded as being synonymous with power and greatness. The Tudor monarchs were renowned for their splendour, no less than their personal charm, and this found its most evident expression in their public dress and in the palaces they built and inhabited.

Elizabeth I's wardrobe, which was rumoured to contain more than three thousand gowns, became legendary during her lifetime, as her costumes grew ever more flamboyant and fantastic. The image of the godly Protestant virgin in sober black and white, so carefully cultivated by Elizabeth during her half-sister's reign, soon gave way to an altogether more colourful and showy image. The Queen's portraits invariably show her in dresses of silk, velvet, satin, taffeta or cloth of gold, encrusted with real gems, countless pearls and sumptuous embroidery in silver or gold thread whilst her starched ruffs and stiff gauze collars grew ever larger. Her favoured colours were black, white and silver, worn with transparent silver veils. Many gowns were embroidered with symbols and emblems such as roses, suns, rainbows, monsters, spiders, ears of wheat, mulberries, pomegranates or pansies, the flowers she loved best.

Some of Elizabeth's dresses and other items of clothing were presented to her as New Year gifts by her courtiers; some certainly remained unworn. These, with other discarded dresses and shoes, she gave away to her ladies. However, she certainly appreciated the many gifts of clothing from friends and courtiers: in 1575, having given the Queen a blue cloak embroidered with flowers and trimmed with carnation velvet, Bess of Hardwick was gratified to learn from a friend at court that 'Her Majesty never liked anything you gave her so well; the colour and strange trimming of the garment with the great cost bestowed upon it hath caused her to give out such good speeches of Your Ladyship as I never hear of better.'

As an unmarried woman, Elizabeth delighted in wearing low-cut necklines, right into old age, and on occasions wore her artificially-curled hair loose, although it was usually coiled up at the back. As she grew older and greyer, she took to wearing red wigs, which were copied by the ladies of the court. Many of her clothes were made by her tailor, Walter Fish, whilst Adam Bland supplied her with furs.

It took her ladies about two hours each morning to get the Queen ready. She had bathrooms with piped water in at least four of her palaces, as well as a portable bath that she took with her from palace to palace and used twice a year for medicinal purposes. It is therefore reasonable to suppose that Elizabeth bathed more often than most people in those days, which could be as little as three times a year. She cleaned her teeth with toothpicks of gold and enamel, and then buffed them to a shine with a tooth-cloth. In old age, she chewed constantly on sweets in the mistaken belief that they would sweeten her breath.

Beneath her clothes she wore fine linen shifts to protect her unwashable gowns from the damage caused by perspiration. These gowns came in pieces – stomacher, kirtle, sleeves, underskirt and collar or ruff – which were tied or buttoned together over whalebone corsets and the ever-widening farthingale, a stiff, hooped petticoat. Elizabeth had worn this type of garment since girlhood, but sometimes required hers to be modified by the royal farthingale-maker, John Bate, since they could cause the same problems as those experienced by Victorian ladies in crinolines three centuries later. In 1579, Mendoza, the Spanish ambassador, reported that he could not carry on a conversation with the Queen until she had moved her farthingale to one side and enabled him to 'get closer to her and speak without being overheard'. Yet Elizabeth never looked ridiculous: Sir John Hayward described her as having 'such state in her carriage as every motion of her seemed to bear majesty'.

Nearly every garment owned by Elizabeth was exquisitely made. Handkerchieves given her by Katherine Ashley were edged with gold and silver thread. At the beginning of her reign, the Queen had been presented with a pair of the new silk stockings from Italy, and had vowed that thereafter she would wear no other type. For much of her reign, her stockings were made by Henry Herne, or knitted by her ladies. A pair of silk stockings, reputedly Elizabeth's, are preserved at Hatfield House, along with a wide-brimmed straw hat and long-fingered gloves. The Queen's shoe-maker, Garrett Johnston, provided her with a new pair of shoes each week. In winter, her outdoor wear comprised cloaks or mantles, of which she had 198 in 1600.

In appearance, according to Sir John Hayward, Elizabeth was 'slender and straight; her hair was inclined to pale yellow, her forehead large and fair, her eyes lively and sweet, but short-sighted, her nose somewhat rising in the middle; her countenance was somewhat long, but yet of admirable beauty, in a most delightful composition of majesty and modesty'. Like many other women of her time, she used cosmetics to enhance her appearance, whitening her complexion with a lotion made from egg-whites, powdered egg-shell, alum, borax, poppy seeds and mill water, and scenting herself with marjoram or rose water. She would have her hair washed in lye, a mixture of wood-ash and water, which she kept in pots on her dressing table along with her looking glass and combs in jewelled cases.

Once dressed, she would deck herself with so many jewels that, when she stood in candlelight, they would glitter so much that they dazzled observers. In 1597, the French ambassador noted that she wore 'innumerable jewels, not only on her head, but also within her collar, about her arms and on her hands, with a very great quantity of pearls round her neck and on her bracelets. She had two bands, one on each arm, which were worth a great price.' Four years later, an Italian diplomat was impressed to see the Queen 'dressed all in white, with so many pearls, broideries and diamonds, that I am amazed how she could carry them'. A German visitor reported that everything she wore was 'studded with very large diamonds and other precious stones, and over her breast, which was bare, she wore a long filigree shawl, on which was set a hideous large black spider that looked as if it were natural and alive'.

Her collection of jewellery was extensive, arguably the best in Europe, and so renowned that even the Pope spoke covetously of it. By 1587, she had 628 pieces. Many had been inherited from her parents: she had Anne Boleyn's famous initial pendants, and an enormous sapphire encircled by rubies from Henry VIII, which was reset by her German jeweller, Master Spilman. Many other jewels were gifts, it being the custom for courtiers to present the Queen with costly trinkets or gifts of money each New Year and when she visited their houses. Sir Christopher Hatton gave her several beautiful sets of up to seven matched pieces. A considerable number of Elizabeth's other jewels had been looted from Spanish treasure ships. Yet more were probably designed and made for her by the goldsmith and miniaturist, Nicholas Hilliard. Several pieces were engraved with one of the Queen's mottoes, 'Semper Eadem' ('Always the same').

The Queen also owned nearly a dozen jewelled watches fashioned as crucifixes, flowers or pendants, as well as gem-encrusted bracelets, girdles, collars, pendants, earrings, armlets, buttons, pomanders and aglets (cord-tips). She had fans of ostrich feathers with jewelled handles, and several novelty pieces that held symbolic meanings, or were based on a pun, often a play on her name. Her favourite jewels were fashioned as ships or animals, while her pearls, the symbols of virginity, were magnificent, and included the long ropes formerly owned by Mary, Queen of Scots. Some of these pearls now rest in the Imperial State

Crown; the rest are missing. One of Elizabeth's rings, containing tiny portraits of herself and Anne Boleyn, is in the collection at Chequers. The Queen often gave away jewels as gifts to her councillors – Sir Thomas Heneage was given the exquisite Armada Jewel, a medallic portrait locket designed by Nicholas Hilliard and now in the Victoria and Albert Museum – while her god-children received some of the numerous cameos showing her in profile. The Queen's Wardrobe Books list several jewels 'lost from Her Majesty's back' on progress or elsewhere; often these were gold or diamond buttons, or a brooch in the form of a monster, which she mislaid at Wanstead in 1584. Sadly, her jewellery collection was dispersed after her death, and only a few pieces survive. 'Oh, those jewels!' lamented one MP in 1626. 'The pride and glory of this realm!'

Elizabeth put on her extravagant costumes chiefly for state occasions, court festivals, personal appearances, the receiving of ambassadors and official portraits. Her everyday dress was rather simpler – she once wore 'the same plain black dress three days running', and she was fond of spending her mornings in loose gowns edged with fur. Her clothes and jewels were her working clothes, the outward symbols of majesty, and essential for the preservation of the mythology of the Virgin Queen. No one else might aspire to such magnificence, which was why Elizabeth's costumes were more exaggerated than anyone else's.

Naturally, this drew criticism from the more puritanically-minded. One bishop dared, in a sermon preached at court, to castigate the Queen for indulging in the vanity of decking the body too finely. Afterwards, fuming at his temerity, she declared to her ladies, 'If the bishop hold more discourse on such matters, we will fit him for heaven, but he should walk thither without a staff, and leave his mantle behind him!'

The portraits of Elizabeth I have been the subject of several weighty books. Although there was a great demand for her portrait in the years after her accession, she was – according to Cecil – 'very unwilling to have a natural representation', and there was therefore a proliferation of poor likenesses. The very earliest portraits are half-lengths showing the Queen full-faced, wearing a French hood; only a few examples survive. She is also depicted full-face in her coronation portrait, formerly at Warwick Castle and now in the National Portrait Gallery. This painting on a wooden panel has been tree-ring dated to about 1600, and is probably a copy of a lost original which may have been the work of Levina Teerlinc, a Flemish woman artist who painted many miniatures for the Queen during the early years of her reign. Teerlinc is known to have painted a miniature of the Queen in coronation robes, which was copied around 1600 by Nicholas Hilliard.

By 1563, both Elizabeth and Cecil were becoming concerned about her being misrepresented: Sir Walter Raleigh later recorded that 'pictures of Queen Elizabeth made by unskilful and common painters were, by her own commandment, knocked in pieces and cast into the fire'. Cecil suggested that a good likeness of the Queen be made available for artists to copy, but Elizabeth did not like this idea, since there were, in her opinion, no artists good enough to produce such a prototype. It was not until later in the decade that Hans Eworth came into his own as a court painter, with his allegorical painting of the Queen triumphing over Juno, Minerva and Venus. Other portraits from the 1560s are rare, and in 1567 the Earl of Sussex told the Regent of the Netherlands that most of them 'did nothing resemble' their subject.

Around 1572, an unknown artist at last produced the portrait that was to be the model for every portrait of the Queen thereafter, the famous Darnley Portrait. At this time Elizabeth discovered that her goldsmith, Nicholas Hilliard, was also a talented portrait painter and miniaturist; he painted the equally renowned Phoenix and Pelican Portraits. Elizabeth was fascinated by Hilliard's talent, officially designated him 'Queen's Limner', and spent many happy hours discussing 'divers questions in art' with him. By now, however, she was approaching forty and sensitive about the lines on her face. At her insistence, Hilliard was obliged to paint her, as he recorded, 'in the open alley of a goodly garden, where no tree was near, nor any shadow at all'. She had told him 'that best to show oneself needed no shadow, but rather the open light'. What he produced was not so much a likeness as an icon of royalty, an idealised image adorned with a glittering costume.

Thereafter, the Queen began to take an increasing interest in how she was represented, insisting upon the trappings and appearance of majesty taking precedence over any attempt at realism. In all of these later portraits, Elizabeth's face appears as a smooth, ageless, expressionless mask. It was doubtless comforting to her subjects to observe that their Queen was an unchanging institution in an insecure world, someone to whom the normal laws of humanity seemed not to apply.

During the 1580s, when there was an increased demand for portraits of the Queen, the prolific Hilliard painted miniatures of her, which her courtiers delighted in wearing, whilst her serjeant-painter, George Gower, executed larger portraits, of which the most famous is the Armada Portrait, of which several versions exist. Another favoured painter was John Bettes. The pictures by these artists, with their attention to symbols and clothes and status, set the trend for the peculiarly English costume portrait, a genre which remained popular well into the next century.

In 1592, Marcus Gheeraerts painted the magnificent Ditchley

Portrait, the largest surviving full-length of Elizabeth, which shows her standing on a map of England, with her feet placed on Ditchley Park in Oxfordshire, the home of her Champion, Sir Henry Lee, who commissioned the work. The painting is full of symbolism, much of it yet to be fully understood, and it represents a high point in the portraiture of Queen Elizabeth. Although the face is similar to that in other state portraits, a discreet attempt has been made to convey an older woman.

Towards the end of the reign Marcus Gheeraerts the Younger, William Segar and Robert Peake continued the tradition begun by Hilliard. In a painting now at Sherborne Castle in Dorset, Peake portrayed the ageing Queen as a young woman being carried in a litter by her courtiers to a wedding at Blackfriars. Hilliard was still working for Elizabeth, and no less than twenty of his miniatures survive from the six years before her death: all portray what is now known as the Mask of Youth. The anonymous Rainbow Portrait at Hatfield House, painted around 1600 and, again, laden with symbolism, depicts Elizabeth as a nubile and beautiful sun goddess.

There are therefore few realistic portraits of Elizabeth I. In 1575, the Italian Federico Zuccaro painted companion portraits of Elizabeth and Leicester which are, sadly, now lost; his preliminary sketches convey a degree of realism. Medals of the 1590s depict the Queen in profile with sagging chin and cheeks, and there existed – 'to her great offence' – similar portraits, for in 1596, on Elizabeth's orders, the Council seized and destroyed a number of pictures that showed her looking old, frail and ill. With the succession question still unresolved, the government could not risk disseminating amongst her subjects any image of an ageing monarch. A miniature of the Queen, almost certainly painted from life by Isaac Oliver, who attempted to portray what he saw, was never finished, and is now in the Victoria and Albert Museum. The famous painting of a melancholy Elizabeth with Time and Death was painted posthumously, and is therefore perhaps the most lifelike one of her to survive. The ageing face is in stark contrast to Gheeraerts' pretty icon.

In sum, virtually all we have to show us what Elizabeth I looked like are stylised images. Painters throughout history have flattered and idealised royalty, but in her case this was a deception that was deliberately maintained over a period of forty-five years. One only has to compare the early photographs of Queen Victoria with the seemingly realistic portraits of her of the same date to realise what a vast difference there can be between the painted image and the harsh reality of the camera. With Elizabeth I, this difference would without a doubt have been far more dramatic.

14

'A Court at Once Gay, Decent and Superb'

Queen Elizabeth's pageant of royalty was played out against a backdrop of some of the most magnificent royal palaces in Europe, most of them situated near the River Thames for drainage purposes and also so that they could be reached by barge. Some were also connected to London by private roads reserved for the Queen's use, the most notable being the King's Road, which connected Chelsea, Richmond and Hampton Court, or the road which wound along the south bank of the Thames from Lambeth Palace to Greenwich and Eltham.

These palaces, no less than her clothing and the ceremonial that marked every aspect of her life, were the outward symbols of personal monarchy. In these palaces were displayed more than two thousand tapestries acquired by Henry VIII, of which only twenty-eight remain today at Hampton Court, and more acquired by his children, as well as a substantial collection of portraits and works of art.

The Tudor court was nomadic: around fifteen hundred persons might be in attendance at any one time, and sanitation facilities were primitive. Sir John Harington complained that 'Even in the goodliest and stateliest palaces of our realm, notwithstanding all our provisions of vaults, or sluices, or gates, or pains of poor folks in sweeping and scouring, yet still this same whoreson saucy stink!' The Queen herself used close stools with lids, which were emptied and cleaned by her maids, but a single large house of easement had to serve the needs of the rest of the court; it was hardly surprising that many people took to relieving themselves in the courtyard, or against the walls. Not until 1596 did Sir John Harington invent the water closet or 'jakes'; within a year Elizabeth had had one installed at Richmond.

Another problem was that local provisions were limited, and the presence of the court imposed a severe strain on local food resources. After a time, each palace had to be vacated so that it could be cleaned and sweetened, and its supplies replenished. Thus Elizabeth was constantly on the move between residences. While she and her heavier baggage travelled by barge wherever possible, her household and lighter effects went by road.

Splendid and luxurious though they were, the Queen's palaces were run, at her order, with rigorous economy, and woe betide her Clerk Comptroller if he did not keep within the annual budget of £40,000 for the maintenance of the royal household. The maintenance of all the Queen's houses came from the income generated from Crown rents. With the exception of Windsor, the Queen spent little on rebuilding or extending any of her houses – unlike her father. What funds were available went towards maintaining the outward trappings of her royal estate; the salaries of her household officials had not changed since Henry VIII's day.

As well as the royal palaces, the Queen had inherited sixty castles and fifty houses, many of which she sold or leased to her courtiers, such as the London Charterhouse, Durham House and Baynards Castle. Some she let fall into ruin, while others were maintained for use on progress. Somerset House on the Strand was regularly placed at the disposal of foreign visitors, although the Queen did stay there fourteen times during her reign. What was left of John of Gaunt's Savoy Palace was turned into a hospital, and the Priory of St John at Clerkenwell was converted into the office of the Master of the Revels. The Queen's wardrobe was kept in the Royal Wardrobe on St Andrew's Hill. Her chief residences, however, were her 'houses of access', the great palaces of the Thames valley.

Westminster Palace, the London residence of English sovereigns and the principal seat of government since the eleventh century, had burned down in 1512, and only ruined towers and vaults remained. Whitehall Palace opposite was therefore Elizabeth's chief residence, and the place she stayed in more than any other. It was a vast, sprawling range of buildings that occupied a site of twenty-three acres, and with two thousand rooms, most of them small and poky, was probably the largest palace in Europe. Originally known as York Place, the palace was once the London residence of the Archbishops of York, and had been given by Cardinal Wolsey to Henry VIII in the 1520s. Henry had enlarged and beautified it, and by Elizabeth's time it was renowned for its superb decorations, which were in the medieval rather than the Renaissance style. In the older parts, vivid murals survived from the thirteenth century, whilst in the more recent Privy Chamber, visitors were overawed by Holbein's huge masterpiece of the Tudor monarchs, Henry VII and Henry VIII, with their queens: as one observer put it, 'The King, as he stood there, majestic in his splendour, was so lifelike that the spectator felt abashed, annihilated in his presence.' Elizabeth I was fond of standing in front of this painting to receive visitors, in order to emphasise whose daughter she was.

'Glorious' Whitehall's spacious state rooms followed a typical pattern: the Great Hall gave on to the Guard Chamber, which led to the Presence Chamber, beyond which was the Privy Chamber, guarded by an usher of Black Rod, who would permit only the favoured few to enter. Here the Queen spent most of her working day; in the evenings she would relax by playing cards or chatting to her intimates. The Privy Chamber gave on to the Queen's private apartments, the *'sanctum sanctorum'*, to which only the most privileged had access: these comprised her withdrawing chamber and bedchamber and numerous small closets.

Persons who were suitably attired could gain admittance to the Great Hall, Guard Chamber and Presence Chamber, and might therefore see the Queen at official functions or as she processed to and from the Chapel Royal. When she was not in residence, parties of visitors were taken on guided tours of all the rooms, even her bedchamber, although some grumbled that 'all the fine tapestries are removed, so that nothing but the bare walls are to be seen'. When the Queen was in residence, the Great Hall was used for banquets, pageants and plays, although it was too small, and in 1581, the Queen had a new banqueting hall built next to Sermon Court, where sermons were preached to throngs of courtiers in the open air.

Elizabeth's bedroom overlooked the river. A German visitor, Paul Hentzner, noted in 1598 that her bed was 'ingeniously composed of woods of different colours, with quilts of silk, velvet, gold, silver and embroidery', its draperies being of Indian painted silk. There was a silver-topped table, a chair padded with cushions, and 'two little silver cabinets of exquisite work' in which the Queen kept writing materials. A jewellery chest 'ornamented all over with pearls' housed some of her bracelets and earrings. There was a gilded ceiling and 'a fine bathroom' next door. Hentzner noted that the bedroom was stuffy and dark, having only one small window. A private way led from the royal bedroom to the river gatehouse, where Elizabeth would board her barge sometimes in the evening to be rowed along the Thames, playing her lute as she went.

Outside the palace there was an orchard and 'a most large and princely garden', which featured a series of thirty-four painted columns topped with heraldic beasts, all gilded, encircling a sundial capable of telling the time in thirty different ways. The Queen always took a keen interest in her gardens, and liked them to be in bloom throughout the year: some were a riot of colour even in winter. The great tiltyard at Whitehall occupied the site of the present Horse Guards and was connected to the palace by a gallery which passed through the Holbein Gate (which spanned the main road into London) and joined the long Privy Gallery, which led to the rabbit warren of state apartments, which were all well-guarded. There was also a tennis court and a cockpit.

Windsor was another favoured residence, although Elizabeth tended to stay there only in the summer months, as the old castle was difficult to heat in winter. Here she built a stone terrace that ran beneath the windows of her apartments on the northern side of the Upper Ward, and it was on this terrace that the Queen enjoyed taking the air in the evenings, or would stride along briskly each morning 'to get up a heat'. Below it nestled a pretty garden, 'full of meanders and labyrinths'. In 1583, Elizabeth also built an indoor gallery, more than ninety feet long, where she could exercise in wet weather; this now houses the Royal Library, and the original Elizabethan fireplace survives largely intact, although the low Tudor ceiling was replaced in 1832. There are tales that Elizabeth's ghost has been seen here. Her other building works – a private chapel, a bridge and an outdoor banqueting pavilion – have long since disappeared. In 1567, she was planning to erect a worthy tomb over her father's vault in St George's Chapel, but the plan came to nothing.

In the Great Park, the Queen could indulge her passion for hunting, dressed in all her finery and outdistancing most of her courtiers. Never a squeamish woman, she did not shrink from killing stags 'with her own hand', using a crossbow, and she would watch unflinching whilst the greyhounds savaged their prey. The suffering of animals did not concern her: she once spared the life of a stag, but ordered that its ears be cut off as trophies. In later life, she and her ladies would sometimes shoot game from specially built stands north-east of the castle, although the Queen preferred to ride with the men whenever possible.

Her apartments at Windsor were luxurious. She slept in a huge, ornate bed 'covered with curious hangings of tapestry work' and rested her head on a cushion 'most curiously wrought by Her Majesty's own hands'. Bathrooms with running water had been installed, with walls and ceilings comprised entirely of mirrors. The Great Hall was a favoured setting for plays, banquets and recitals by the Children of the Chapel Royal. Paul Hentzner, touring Windsor Castle in 1598, was shown rooms containing the gold- and silver-bedecked state beds of Henry VIII and Anne Boleyn, French tapestries, and curiosities such as a unicorn's horn – possibly a narwhal's tusk.

Greenwich Palace, where Elizabeth had been born, was built around three courtyards but was smaller than most of the Queen's other palaces, although it was just as sumptuous, and was used for state occasions and ambassadorial receptions; foreign envoys, arriving by barge, were welcomed at the imposing riverside gatehouse, from which the Queen would also watch naval exercises and displays on the Thames and military reviews in the park, as in July 1559, on her first visit as Queen. From here she would wave farewell as her ships set off on their voyages of exploration. Benches painted with the royal arms were set up 'for Her Majesty to sit on in the garden'. Most rooms in the palace overlooked the river, and there were eighty feet of glass in the Presence Chamber windows. The hangings in the chapel were of gold damask, and there was a gilded alcove in which the Queen received Holy Communion.

After nearly dying of smallpox there in 1562, Elizabeth avoided her father's vast red-brick palace of Hampton Court in Surrey for a time, but she came to use it 'with great and plentiful cheer' for the great feasts of Easter or Whitsun, and sometimes Christmas, and as a setting in which to receive ambassadors and foreign princes, who were lavishly entertained and in whose honour plays were performed in Henry VIII's Great Hall with its splendid hammerbeam roof. Equally famous in its day was the throne room off Cloister Green Court known as the Paradise Chamber (demolished in the late seventeenth century with most of the Tudor royal apartments), which was shown to 'the well-dressed public' for a fee when the Queen was not in residence. Hentzner recorded that the Persian 'tapestries are garnished with gold, pearls and precious stones, not to mention the royal throne', which was upholstered in brown velvet and studded with three great diamonds, rubies and sapphires. One table twenty-eight feet long was covered with a pearl-edged surnap of velvet, while another table, made from Brazilian wood, was inlaid with silver. On this was displayed a gilt mirror, a draughts-board of ebony, a chessboard of ivory, and seven ivory and gold flutes which, when blown, reproduced various animal sounds. Also on display was a backgammon board with dice of solid silver and an impressive collection of musical instruments. Visitors were shown the Horn Room, north of the Great Hall, where the antlers of deer killed in the royal hunts were displayed.

Hampton Court was perhaps the most elaborately decorated of the Queen's palaces: 'All the walls shine with gold and silver,' reported Hentzner. 'Many of the splendid large rooms are embellished with masterly paintings, writing tables of mother-of-pearl, and musical instruments, of which Her Majesty is very fond.' There were fretwork ceilings with intersecting ribs and pendants picked out in gold, and all the palace woodwork was either gilded or brightly painted in red, yellow, blue or green. *Trompe l'oeil* decorations abounded. Despite such splendours, the Queen always maintained that Hampton Court was an uncomfortable and unhealthy place, and its chief use therefore was as a display piece.

The Queen took a personal interest in the gardens at Hampton Court, and gave orders for tobacco and potatoes, imported from the New World, to be planted there. In 1570, Henry VIII's stables were extended for her, with the addition of two barns and a coach house.

A little way up the river from Hampton Court, near Weybridge, was the miniature palace of Oatlands, 'a cheerful hunting box', where Henry VIII had married Katherine Howard in 1540. Elizabeth visited it on at least twenty occasions for the excellent hunting, and was fascinated by the huge colonies of rooks in the park. Nothing remains of Oatlands today, and a council housing estate occupies the site.

Richmond Palace had been the favourite residence of Elizabeth's grandfather, Henry VII, who had built it in the perpendicular style, but it was not until later in her reign that she came to appreciate its charm, spending time there each summer when the gardens and orchards were at their best. This was a fairytale palace, with numerous turrets and pinnacles crowned with bulbous domes surmounted by gold and silver weather vanes; it boasted fan-vaulted ceilings, vast oriel windows, a huge hall measuring a hundred by forty feet, which had murals of heroic English kings, and a network of galleries and loggias bisecting the beautiful gardens. These were a wonder in themselves, being filled with numerous flowers, herbs and over two hundred trees, whilst the orchards yielded peaches, apples, pears and damsons.

Eighteen kitchens kept the court supplied with food. Another attraction for the Queen was her grandfather's plumbing system, which piped pure spring water into the palace. She was also impressed by the absence of draughts, referring to Richmond as 'a warm nest for my old age'.

Another exquisite summer palace, 'which of all places she likes best', was Nonsuch in Surrey, a fantastic edifice built in the 1530s by Henry VIII in the Italian Renaissance style in emulation of the great French palaces of the Loire. Mary I had leased it to the Earl of Arundel, and although she was a frequent visitor, Elizabeth was not able to repossess it until his death in 1592. During her visits, she would be out riding or hunting every day in the park. When she received ambassadors at Nonsuch, it was in rooms adorned with furnishings and hangings brought over from nearby Hampton Court. There was no great hall, the palace being very small, and when the court was in residence a number of tents had to be set up in the grounds to accommodate all the guests. Nevertheless the state rooms were magnificent, there was a fine library, and in the inner courtyard there was an imposing white marble fountain and a clock tower. Nonsuch was famed for its novel octagonal towers, whilst its walls were of white stucco with a deep relief pattern picked out in gold on plaster, and there was a vast array of classical statuary in the picturesque grounds, where was to be found the famous Grove of Diana.

In London, St James's Palace, once favoured by Queen Mary, who had died there, was not so popular with Elizabeth, though she used it as her London base whenever Whitehall was being cleaned. Little remains of the Tudor Chapel Royal here, except for Elizabeth's coat of arms above the main door, supported by a carved lion and the red dragon of the Welsh Prince Cadwaladr, an emblem adopted by the Tudors. St James's had its own park and an artificial lake known as Rosamund's Pool.

Elizabeth hated the Tower of London. Her mother and various others close to her had died violently there, and she herself had terrifying memories of her imprisonment in 1554. She also detested the noises and smells which emanated from the royal menagerie within the Tower walls. It is hardly surprising therefore that she never used the state apartments there after the obligatory visit prior to her coronation. Nevertheless, her rooms in the royal palace were kept in readiness, and in 1598 Hentzner and another visitor, Thomas Platter, reported that the state apartments were hung with tapestries worked in silk, gold and silver thread, and furnished with grand beds and canopies of estate edged with seed pearls. One of the huge chairs made for the ageing Henry VIII, with its footstool, was on show, and several of Elizabeth's gowns were stored there, along with chests full of rich materials. The Queen's Parliament robes were kept at the Tower and aired every month. Her gowns were regularly sprinkled with scented powder to prevent them from becoming musty - twenty-four pounds of the stuff were used in 1584 alone.

When the court was in residence at Whitehall, the crown jewels were put on display at the Tower, but most of those from Elizabeth's time do not survive, having been melted down or dispersed under Oliver Cromwell.

The old medieval palace of Woodstock was another house avoided by Elizabeth, who had been kept under house arrest there for a year during Mary's reign. Only rarely did she spend a night there whilst on progress.

Queen Elizabeth's hunting lodge is preserved in Epping Forest; a picturesque legend claims that the Queen raced her palfrey up the stairs here, triumphant after learning of the defeat of the Spanish Armada. This hunting box had actually been built by Henry VIII as a stand from which to view the hunt. Elizabeth also used the decaying nursery palace of Eltham as a hunting lodge.

After her accession, Elizabeth spent little time at the palaces in which she had lived during her circumscribed youth. The oak tree at Hatfield House, beneath which she had learned of her accession, flourished until the nineteenth century, and its remains may be seen in the palace shop. The Queen sometimes stayed at Hatfield whilst on progress, but after her death most of the 'stately lodgings' of the Old Palace were demolished, leaving only the wing that survives today, much altered. Ashridge, Newhall and Hunsdon were leased, the latter two to the Earl of Sussex. The Queen visited Enfield Palace on her first progress, but returned infrequently thereafter. A fireplace from the palace is preserved in a house in Gentleman's Row, and carries the cipher E.R., with the Latin legend, 'Our only security is to serve God; aught else is vanity.' Elizabeth honoured nearby Elsynge more often, and it was kept in good repair; canvas shutters were attached to her windows, armorial stained glass installed in her bedroom, and fires were kept lit to prevent damp. In 1596 the Queen ordered 'toils set up, to shoot at buck after dinner' in the deer park. Nothing remains above ground of the two palaces at Enfield; the Jacobean Forty Hall occupies the site on which Elsynge once stood.

In fact, few of Elizabeth's palaces survive today. Whitehall burned down in 1698. Others did not survive the neglect of Oliver Cromwell's time, and those that did were too large or outdated for Georgian taste. Richmond was all but destroyed during the Commonwealth, and only the outer gatehouse now remains. Greenwich Palace, the royal apartments in the Tower and Nonsuch Palace were demolished in the late seventeenth century. The ruinous Woodstock was pulled down to make way for Blenheim Palace, whilst Somerset House has been completely rebuilt. One wing of Newhall survives, and the royal apartments at Windsor were extensively remodelled in the early nineteenth century. Very little remains today to testify to the lost splendours of the Tudor court.

The court itself was not only the seat of government but also the stage on which the Queen could make a magnificent display. It was also the cultural heart of England and a showcase for the arts, intended to impress foreign visitors. Elizabeth spent lavishly on her court, since she understood the political importance of visible wealth. Court taste in painting, music, costume and other decorative arts, which naturally reflected the tastes of the Queen, set trends that were followed in the great country houses.

Queen and court followed an almost unvarying annual routine. In the autumn, when the legal term began and Parliament might be sitting, the court would return to Whitehall, Elizabeth being received at the gates of London by the Mayor and aldermen in their best furred gowns, and processing through the streets, revelling in the acclaim of her subjects. The Accession Day tilts took place on 17 November, and the Queen usually kept Christmas at Whitehall or Hampton Court, with the twelve days of festivities reaching their climax on Twelfth Night, the Feast of the Epiphany, when gifts were exchanged and the Queen herself presented offerings of gold, frankincense and myrrh in the Chapel Royal. Elizabeth normally spent Christmas Day itself in prayer. Male courtiers were expected to remain at court for the revels, and few dared to sneak away to their families 'lest the Queen take offence'. Dancing and card games such as primero were the chief pastimes, and even the careful Elizabeth would indulge in a moderate wager. Fortunately, she was a lucky card player, although Ben Jonson, who never liked her, claimed – probably maliciously – that she cheated. There were also plays – as many as eleven were staged at court during the Christmas season, and more during Shrovetide.

Whilst she was in London, the Queen was frequently seen in public, going to dine at the houses of noblemen, attending weddings, watching bear baitings and enjoying military displays or river fêtes. Her state barge was kept moored at Paris Garden, on the Surrey shore of the Thames. Hentzner described it as having 'two splendid cabins, beautifully ornamented with glass windows, painting and gilding'. The Queen's cabin was luxurious with cushions of cloth of gold and a crimson velvet rug strewn with flower petals. The barge could move swiftly, and required twenty oarsmen to man it.

Early in the New Year Elizabeth would move to Oatlands, Greenwich, Nonsuch or Richmond, but would return to Whitehall in the spring for the rituals of Maundy Thursday and Easter. In April, she would go to Windsor for the Garter ceremonies on St George's Day. During the summer, Queen and court would go on progress, then spend the early autumn at Oatlands, Hampton Court, Windsor or Nonsuch before returning to Whitehall.

Elizabeth's daily routine varied. She was, she claimed, 'not a morning woman', and would not be seen in public until she had completed her lengthy toilette, although she was fond of taking a brisk walk before breakfast in her private gardens. Rarely was she seen in *déshabille*, although in 1578 Lord Shrewsbury's son encountered her hanging out of a window, listening unseen to people gossiping: 'My eye was full towards her; she showed to be greatly ashamed thereof, for that she was unready and in her nightstuff. So when she saw me after dinner, as she went to walk, she gave me a great fillip on the forehead and told the Lord Chamberlain how I had seen her that morning, and how much ashamed she was.'

On another occasion, when she was fully dressed, the Queen leaned out of her window and espied in her garden a melancholy Sir Edward Dyer, who had unsuccessfully importuned her for a post at court. In

Italian, Elizabeth asked him, 'What do you think about when you think of nothing?'

'Of a woman's promise,' he replied meaningfully.

'Anger makes dull men witty, but it keeps them poor,' retorted the Queen, then withdrew from the window before the impertinent Dyer had a chance to answer.

Because she normally kept late hours, working through the night, Elizabeth often slept late in the mornings. She was served breakfast – manchet bread, meat pottage, ale, beer or wine – in her bedchamber, then would work and play until dinner time, which was at eleven o'clock. 'Six or seven galliards of a morning, besides music and singing, were her ordinary exercise. First in the morning she spent some time at her devotions, then she betook herself to the dispatch of her civil affairs, reading letters, ordering answers, considering what should be brought before the Council, and consulting with her ministers. When she had thus wearied herself she would walk in a shady garden or pleasant gallery, without any other attendants than a few learned men, then she took coach and passed, in the sight of her people, to the neighbouring groves and fields, and sometimes would hunt and hawk; there was scarce a day but she employed some part of it in reading and study,' noted a courtier, Edmund Bohun, after observing the Queen at Richmond. Harington recalled that 'Her Highness was wont to soothe her ruffled temper with reading every morning. She did much admire Seneca's wholesome advisings, when the soul's quiet was flown away.'

In the afternoons the Queen might sleep a little; she was also prone to taking brief naps at other times. Supper was at five o'clock, then there would be entertainment until nine o'clock and the ceremony of Good Night in the Presence Chamber, after which light snacks were dispensed from the buttery. Then an usher would call, 'Have in for the night!' and an Esquire of the Body would clear the state rooms and the watch would begin its patrols of the palace precincts. Courtiers were expected to retire for the night at this point, although many did not.

Mention has already been made of the Queen's patronage of musicians and painters. She was also a great lover of pageants, masques and dramas, and many plays, including some written by William Shakespeare and Ben Jonson, were performed at her court, usually at an average cost of £400 each. Tradition has it that after a 1597 production of *The History of Henry IV, with the Humorous Conceits of Sir John Falstaff,* Elizabeth was so taken with the character of Falstaff that she asked Shakespeare to write a play in which Falstaff falls in love. The result was *The Merry Wives of Windsor,* said to have been hurriedly written in a fortnight, but much enjoyed by the Queen. *Twelfth Night* was also written for a performance at court in 1601.

Elizabeth was passionate about the theatre, and actively protected it from the Puritans who wanted it banned. In 1583, she formed her own theatre company, the Queen's Men, of whom her favourite performer was the comic actor, Richard Tarleton, whose antics could make her weep with laughter. At one performance she 'bade them take away the knave for making her laugh so excessively'.

The Queen also loved pageants, and sometimes took part in those staged in her Presence Chamber, although she always appeared as herself, and it was not difficult to persuade her to join in the dancing that invariably followed.

When Elizabeth entertained, she did so on a grand scale: her ceremonies and receptions were lavish and impressed visitors with their orderliness and solemnity: in 1601, one Italian envoy claimed he would never in any other place 'see a court which, for order, surpasses this one', which was 'at once gay, decent and superb'.

Elizabeth's was a very visible monarchy. Every Sunday she went in procession from the Chapel Royal to the Presence Chamber, and people crowded to see her, falling to their knees as she walked 'grandly' past; she often paused to speak to some of them. Lord Herbert of Cherbury remembered the first time that he, an aspiring young courtier, was present on one of these occasions: 'As soon as she saw me, she stopped, and swearing her usual oath, "God's death!", demanded, "Who is this?" Everybody there present looked upon me, but no man knew me until Sir James Croft, a [Gentleman] Pensioner, finding the Queen stayed, returned and told who I was, and that I had married Sir William Herbert's daughter. The Queen hereupon looked attentively at me and, swearing again her ordinary oath, said, "It is a pity he was married so young!", and thereupon gave her hand to kiss twice, both times gently clapping me on the cheek.'

A German visitor, Leopold von Wedel, witnessed the Sunday procession in 1584 and described how the Queen 'showed herself very gracious and accepted with a humble mien letters of supplication from both rich and poor. At her passing the people fell on their knees, and she said, "Thank you with all my heart." Then eight trumpets gave the signal for dinner.'

Wedel also noted the easy familiarity of the Queen's manner. 'She chatted and jested most amicably, and pointing with her finger at the face of one Captain Raleigh, told him there was a smut on it. She also offered to wipe it off with her handkerchief, but he anticipated her.' She was also fond of lounging on cushions on the floor of the gallery whilst conversing with her courtiers. At the same time, she could be impressively majestic. Thomas Platter recorded that when she emerged with her councillors and retinue from her Presence Chamber and looked out of a window in the adjoining gallery to behold her people in the courtyard below, 'They all knelt, and she spoke to them, "God bless my people." And they all cried in unison, "God save the Queen!" and they remained kneeling until she made them a sign with her hand to rise, which they did with the greatest possible reverence.'

In 1598, Hentzner was admitted with other members of the public to observe the elaborate preparations for the Queen's dinner: the table-cloth, salt cellar and food were borne in to the Presence Chamber, to the sound of trumpets and kettle drums, by servitors escorted by guards, preceded by an usher with a ceremonial rod. Each officer bowed solemnly three times to the empty throne under the canopy of estate, both on entering the room and on leaving it. Gentlemen stood in attendance about the table whilst the ladies in waiting set it, laying the cloth and placing the food on it. Then a maid of honour dressed in white silk entered with a lady in waiting, who carried a tasting fork; the latter gracefully prostrated herself three times in front of the table and empty chair, before respectfully approaching the table and rubbing the plates with bread and salt 'with as much awe as if the Queen had been present'. She then gave each guard 'the assay' – a taste of the food from each dish, to ensure that none of the food was poisoned, after which more maids of honour appeared and 'with particular solemnity, lifted the meat off the table and conveyed it into the Queen's inner and more private chamber, where, after she had chosen for herself, the rest goes to the ladies of the court'.

Elizabeth usually ate alone in her Privy Chamber, and had her own private kitchen where her food was prepared. Only on occasions of high ceremonial did she eat in public in the Presence Chamber, where the public were allowed in to watch from a gallery. At Christmas 1584, Wedel was privileged to watch the Queen eat, and noted that she was served by young men who brought meat and drink, offering them on their knees and remaining kneeling as she ate and drank. Behind her stood Lords Howard and Hertford and Sir Christopher Hatton. She chatted to them quite familiarly, although each one knelt when addressed and remained so until bidden to rise. Throughout the meal the royal musicians 'discoursed excellent music'. When it was finished, four servitors brought a silver bowl and towel, so that the Queen could wash her hands.

Although the Queen was never offered a choice of less than twenty dishes, she usually ate sparingly, preferring light meals of chicken or game, and as she grew older ordered thick soups or stews, since she could only chew meat with difficulty. Il Schifanoya claimed that, although the Queen was served with 'large and excellent joints, the delicacies and cleanliness customary in Italy were wanting'.

Elizabeth's main indulgences were rich cakes and sweetmeats, tarts and fritters, which ruined her teeth. She claimed to eat fish twice weekly, on Fridays and Wednesdays (which was designated an additional fish day during her reign in order to boost the fishing industry), but was often – at the enormous additional cost of £646 per annum – secretly served meat on these days, although she did, unlike most of her courtiers, observe various fast days.

The Queen's white manchet bread was made from wheat grown at Heston, reputedly the finest available, and she drank lightly brewed beer, eschewing stronger ales. John Clapham wrote, 'She was in her diet very temperate. The wine she drank was mingled with three parts water. Precise hours of refection she observed not, as never eating but when her appetite required it.' She herself attributed her robust health to the fact that she was 'not tied to hours of eating or sleeping, but following appetite'. Nor did she 'delight in belly cheer to please the taste'.

Her courtiers ate in the Great Hall, with the chief officers of the household sitting apart at the great functionaries' table. The ladies of the Privy Chamber were so encumbered by their farthingales that there was not room for them all on the benches and they were obliged to eat 'on the ground on the rushes', the floors being strewn with herbs and grasses in order to scent the air and cover up dirt.

Each nobleman or knight was entitled to bring his servants to court with him, so that the main kitchens had to supply free food, or 'bouche', for hundreds of people on a daily basis, the menu varying according to rank. There was, invariably, much waste, and the Board of Green Cloth, which controlled household expenditure, was powerless to check it. Household management and organisation were inefficient: if the Queen wanted a snack at midnight, the order was passed along a chain of officials, and she often had cause to complain that the food, when it eventually arrived, was cold. At Windsor the facilities were so archaic that her meals were cooked in a public oven in Peascod Street and carried half a mile to the castle. Towards the end of her life, the Queen felt she could take no more of such poor management and announced 'with very bitter words that she would cleanse the court', but 'it pleased God to take Her Majesty to His mercy' before her planned reforms could be carried out.

Foreigners were always impressed with the singing of the choristers of the Chapel Royal – thirty-two men and twelve boys – which seemed more divine than human. One Danish ambassador said that divine service at Greenwich was 'so melodiously sung and said, as a man half dead might thereby have been quickened', whilst a French envoy claimed, 'In all my travels in France, Italy and Spain, I never heard the like: a concert of music so excellent and sweet as cannot be expressed.'

The Queen was so fond of polyphonic church music that she overrode demands by Puritans that it be banned from services, thereby preserving a tradition that survives to this day in the anthems and hymns sung in churches. She also protected several Catholic singers and musicians in her household, among them William Byrd, from persecution, and even permitted Byrd to compose in Latin. Predictably, this gave the Puritans more cause to grumble, although it got them nowhere. When it came to music, Elizabeth was prepared to make compromises. However, when she complained on one occasion that the celebrated organist, Christopher Tye, was playing out of tune, 'he sent word that her ears were out of tune'.

The Queen also instituted seasons of free concerts at the Royal Exchange in London, so that even the poor could share in her love of music. At court, she maintained her own orchestra of thirty musicians.

Security around the Queen was tight. She was theoretically guarded by twenty honorary Serjeants-at-Arms, but was in fact protected by the Yeomen of the Guard, founded by Henry VII, and by a body of mounted Gentlemen Pensioners, founded by Henry VIII. The latter, whose captains included Sir Christopher Hatton and Sir Walter Raleigh, were famous for being invariably tall and good looking. Despite all these guards, the Queen's advisers feared that her security was inadequate and might be breached in an attempt on her life, of which there were several during her reign. Cecil feared poison rather than violence, and drew up a memorandum advising on 'Certain Cautions for the Queen's Apparel and Diet', warning her against suspect gifts of perfume, gloves and food. The Queen herself had a relaxed attitude towards her own safety, and was fond of taking risks, placing confidence in the love of her people – much to the dismay of her fraught ministers.

Although the royal household was large, and cost several hundred pounds a week to run, Elizabeth kept far fewer personal servants than her forebears: as well as her ladies, she had a couple of gentlemen of the Privy Chamber, ten grooms, and an Esquire of the Body who was responsible for guarding the Presence Chamber after the 'Good Night' ceremony. The Queen also employed the Greens, a family of jesters, Ippolita the Tartarian, 'our dearly beloved woman' dwarf, Thomasina, an Italian dwarf, and Monarcho, an Italian fool, who is mentioned by Shakespeare in *Love's Labour's Lost*. Then there were footmen of the Privy Chamber, and a little black boy who went about dressed in a jacket of black taffeta and gold tinsel above wide breeches.

The court was of a diverse character. Elizabeth ensured that it observed strict rules of decorum and etiquette, which set standards in manners for the rest of the country, and promoted the ideals of chivalry and gentlemanly conduct, as exemplified in Balthasar Castiglione's enormously popular book *The Courtier*. Castiglione asserted that the ideal courtier was a generous, witty sportsman who pursued his own advancement.

The Virgin Queen expected her courtiers to maintain high moral standards, and would not tolerate promiscuity, knowing that it would reflect badly upon her own reputation. Nevertheless, commentators such as John Chamberlain and John Aubrey both expressed moral outrage at the apparent prevalence at court of 'whoredom, swearing, ribaldry, atheism, dancing, carding, carousing, drunkenness, gluttony, quarrelling and suchlike inconveniences', sentiments echoed by many of Elizabeth's Puritan subjects. In fact, according to the contemporary chronicler, Raphael Holinshed, bad behaviour was 'utterly expelled out of the court, or else so qualified by the diligent endeavour of the chief officers of Her Grace's household, that seldom are such things seen there, without due reprehension and such severe correction as belongeth to those trespasses'. Scandals at court were relatively rare, and when they did occur they were sensational.

Elizabeth's courtiers found that the worst thing about the court was the frantic competition for places and preferment and the stresses this engendered. The nearer one was to the Queen, who was at the centre of a great web of patronage, the greater the rewards, which included court and government posts, knighthoods, peerages (very rare), monopolies on goods, annuities, pensions, wardships and loans. Several courtiers – notably Leicester – died in debt to the Queen, because although she would graciously extend the term of a loan, she rarely wrote off a debt. Nor was she extravagant in bestowing privileges and favours – she could not afford to be, so she kept everyone guessing and hoping.

There was much gossiping, backbiting and jostling for place, but violence was eschewed, Her Majesty having forbidden the use of swords, although they were allowed for decorative purposes, and the penalty for duelling was the severance of the right hand. Although the Queen sometimes preferred to turn a blind eye to breaches of these rules, the wise courtier learned that it was better to live on his wits. His part was to wait in galleries in feverish impatience, hoping for the chance to speak to the Queen as she passed, or for an *entrée* to her private apartments, where the chances of being noticed were much greater. This, of course, could result in no more than 'empty words, grinning scoff, watching nights and fawning days', as Harington put it. If he were lucky, he might, by bribes of gifts or money, secure the patronage of a great lord who had the royal ear, which was perhaps the quickest road to preferment. It was small wonder therefore that Elizabethan courtiers were prepared to go to astonishing lengths to gain their sovereign's attention in the hope of achieving what Harington called 'ambition's puffball'. Some young courtiers, it was claimed, wore an estate on their backs, just to get themselves noticed; others wore 'outlandish habiliments' based on foreign styles. Many ran up crippling debts in order to finance their sojourn at court.

Few courtiers achieved their desire to speak to the Queen in person, but for those who did, the best time to ask favours was, according to Harington, 'before the breakfasting covers are placed'. One should 'stand uncovered as Her Highness cometh forth her chamber, then kneel and say, "God save Your Majesty, I crave your ear at what hour may suit for your servant to meet your blessed countenance."' This usually had the desired effect, as did gifts of jewellery, unless the Queen was in a bad mood. Emerging flustered and sweating from an audience one day, Hatton warned Harington, 'If you have any suit today, I pray you put it aside. The sun does not shine.' And being asked for something she was unwilling to give was often enough in itself to 'make the Queen fall out with any man'. When she got wind that a petition was in the offing, she would often dismiss the suitor with off-putting remarks, such as 'Faugh! Thy boots stink!' Nor did the granting of a request mean that she would immediately translate promises into deeds: there were often interminable delays, and on occasions her promises were conveniently forgotten.

A 'plain northern woman', having heard what the Queen was like in this respect, once asked for her promise in writing.

'Why, have I not given you my word you shall have your suit?' asked an astonished Elizabeth, 'willing to be rid of her'.

'Alas, Madam', replied the woman forthrightly, 'they say your word is nothing if one have not your hand in it.' Normally, Elizabeth would have taken offence at such impertinence, but this time she just laughed, and the woman got her written word.

Many deplored the superficiality of a court that one wit described as 'a glittering misery, full of malice and spite'. Sir Walter Raleigh famously wrote, 'Go tell the court it glows and shines like rotten wood.' Corruption was rife, and the Queen powerless to stop it. Nor did it put off men on the make. Lord Willoughby was almost the only nobleman who stayed away on the grounds that he was 'none of the reptilia, and could not brook the obsequiousness and assiduity of the court'. Most were agreed, however, that 'there was very little in that place to make an honest man much to love it, or a wise man long to tarry in it, but only one, and that was the mistress of the place'.

Anyone of or above the rank of gentleman might attend the court, although, as Cecil said, a man without friends there 'was like a hop without a pole'. Most courtiers were related to each other or bound by ties of marriage or loyalty, so there was a distinct family atmosphere. This did not, however, prevent frauds, nor the forming of factions around favourites. For most of her reign Elizabeth was adept at keeping the peace between such factions; only in old age did she find it difficult to control them.

A number of prominent courtiers were related to the Queen on her mother's side, but although she looked after these kinsfolk, she did not promote or ennoble them unless they deserved it. She would not make her great-uncle, William Howard of Effingham, an earl because he was not wealthy enough, and her cousin Lord Hunsdon was on his deathbed before she decided to create him Earl of Wiltshire. This tetchy old man refused the honour, saying, 'Madam, since you counted me not worthy of this honour whilst I was living, I count myself unworthy now that I am dying.' In fact, Hunsdon, a plain-spoken soldier, had enjoyed the Queen's favour throughout his long life. Other Boleyn relatives who prospered in varying degrees under their illustrious cousin were the Knollyses, the Sackvilles, the Howards, the Staffords, the Fortescues and the Ashleys. The Queen was particularly close to her cousin Katherine Carey, who was the sister of Lord Hunsdon and the wife of Sir Francis Knollys. When Katherine died in 1569, Elizabeth was grief-stricken.

The Queen enjoyed a unique relationship with her courtiers, who vied to outdo each other in compliments to her: some even went so far as to rebuild their houses in the shape of the letter E in readiness for a royal visit. Most men who came to court conformed to her ideal: they were well-educated, cultivated, well-travelled, and spoke several different languages. They had the confidence born of wealth, and were ready to extend their patronage to artists and scholars. The Queen expected them to be well-dressed, laid down guide rules, and could react adversely if they were not obeyed. 'I do remember she spit on Sir Matthew's fringed cloth, and said the fool's wit was gone to rags,' wrote Harington. 'Heaven spare me from such jibing!'

Although the Queen's attempts to preserve the old social caste system resulted in much snobbery, courtiers were not discriminated against for their accents, which in many cases were rustic. Letters show that Hatton said 'axe' instead of 'ask', that Leicester was prone to saying 'hit' rather than 'it', and was also guilty of dropping his aitches, and that Raleigh spoke 'broad Devonshire'. From her own writings, we can assume that the Queen herself spoke in a polished London accent and drawled her vowels.

The Queen was what would nowadays be described as 'a man's woman': although she did have women friends, she generally resented the presence of women at her court, preferring to be the sole focus of her male courtiers' attentions; consequently, there were rarely more than thirty women at court, most of whom were the Queen's own attendants. There was no rule against courtiers bringing their wives there, but the practice was discouraged, and there was no provision for wives to receive free board and lodging. Very rarely did the Queen relax this rule.

Relations between Elizabeth and her male courtiers reflected the age-old ideals of courtly love, in which the lover pays hopeless court to his unattainable mistress, whom he worships from afar. Many letters from courtiers to the Queen read like love letters: this from Sir Christopher Hatton is typical: 'My spirit and soul agreeth with my body and life, that to serve you is a heaven, but to lack you is more than hell's torment.' When, in 1581, Lord Shrewsbury applied for permission to visit court, he wrote, 'I neither regard health, travel, time of year, or any other thing in respect of the sight of Her Majesty, my greatest comfort, and until her good pleasure may be such, I shall long as one with child, and think every absent hour a year.' When the Queen was sixty-three, Lord Norris, retiring from court due to illness, stated, 'My heart hath been more grieved with my absence from the presence of Her Majesty than my limbs have been pained with the gout; for the true joy of my heart consisteth more in Her Majesty's eyes than in all worldly things else.' The Queen revelled in – and expected – this attention, fishing for men's souls, as Hatton put it.

This was not all sycophancy or self-seeking, since Elizabeth did fascinate men. She was also very good at retaining their interest, keeping them guessing and hoping as to what her true intentions were. She could also be frustratingly unpredictable: teasing, playful and informal one moment, imperious and tart the next – in short, a great prima donna. Yet she also had an excellent sense of humour. When the Earl of Oxford broke wind when bowing before her, he was so ashamed that he went into self-imposed exile for seven years; upon his return, Elizabeth warmly received him, then said, with a mischievous twinkle, 'My Lord, I had forgot the fart.'

The nicknames she bestowed on those closest to her were a sign of affection: Leicester was her 'Eyes', Hatton her 'Lids', Cecil her 'Spirit' and Walsingham her 'Moor'. However, she would not allow others to be over-familiar with her. When, in 1582, a young buck, 'being more bold than well-mannered, did stand upon the carpet of the cloth of estate and did almost lean upon the cushions' of the throne, which was occupied by the Queen, she said nothing to the offender but loudly reprimanded the Lord Chamberlain for permitting such behaviour.

*

Elizabeth was always attended by seven Ladies of the Bedchamber, six maids of honour and four chamberers in her private apartments, and whenever she appeared in public, her ladies and maids would accompany her. She was rarely alone, as her women attended her day and night. Duties were on a roster basis, and the most senior ladies would wait on the Queen in her bedchamber, whilst the younger attendants would be on duty in the Privy Chamber. One lady's sole task was to strew fresh flower petals in Elizabeth's path. Maids of honour performed errands, waited on the Queen at table, bore her train and looked after her clothes and jewellery. All these women were paid only for the time they were on duty, and they could not absent themselves from court without leave from the Queen. Unfortunately, Elizabeth was sometimes unsympathetic to their needs or family commitments, and might refuse to allow them time off. If she was fond of a friend's company, she expected to have it indefinitely. Poor Katherine Carey died at court, away from her husband, because Elizabeth could not bear to let her go.

The Queen's ladies and maids were selected from amongst her relatives or from the families of courtiers. Because serving the Queen was often a springboard to a brilliant marriage, there was intense competition for places, and large sums often changed hands to ensure a girl was accepted; one father paid £1300. When Lady Leighton was thought to be resigning from her post, twelve applications to replace her were immediately submitted.

Like most male courtiers, the Queen's ladies were well-educated and well-read. Most studied, read the Bible or translated works by Latin or Greek authors. One of their tasks was to read aloud to their mistress from some of the many erudite books in her library. Indeed, books were to be found in most rooms in the royal palaces. As one observer noted, 'The stranger that entereth into the court of England shall rather imagine himself to come into some public school of the universities than into a prince's palace.'

The Queen's ladies and maids were also expected to be accomplished in needlework, music, dancing and riding, so that they could share in their mistress's interests and entertain her as required. Some ladies distilled cordials, medicines or perfumes, or made sweetmeats and preserves.

Elizabeth demanded high standards, and was extremely critical of any lapse. Lateness and slovenliness earned sharp reproofs, and discipline was strict, the Queen having no compunction about slapping or beating any girl who offended her, even for small offences. Her rages were truly terrible and justly feared, and she frequently 'swore out [against] such ungracious, flouting wenches', making her maids 'often cry and bewail in piteous sort'. On the other hand, she counted among her women some of her closest friends, and inspired in them selfless devotion.

When Bridget Manners joined the Queen's service in 1595, her uncle advised her:

> First, above all things not to forget to use daily prayers to Almighty God, then apply yourself wholly to the service of Her Majesty, with all meekness, love and obedience, wherein you must be diligent, secret and faithful. Generally be no meddler in the causes of others. Use much silence, for that becometh maids, especially of your calling. Your speech and endeavours must ever tend to the good of all and to the hurt of none. If you have grace to follow these rules, you shall find the benefit.

The Queen required all her female attendants to wear black and/or white, so that the vivid colours and embellishments of her own costume stood out dramatically. Woe betide the lady whose dress excelled the Queen's, as did one of Lady Mary Howard's gowns, which was so gorgeous that a jealous Elizabeth tried it on without its owner's permission, only to find it too short. She thereupon told Mary it was 'too fine' for her, and the hapless girl was obliged to lay away the dress until after the Queen's death.

Stabling was provided for the ladies' horses, whilst the maids, who were paid so little that they could not afford horses of their own, were allowed to borrow horses from the royal stables. Often, the Queen's women were the recipients of gifts from visiting dignitaries, and Elizabeth herself often passed on very costly and beautiful items of clothing to them.

Many of the Queen's ladies are known to history: her former nurse and governess, Blanche Parry – the longest serving of the Queen's women – and Katherine Ashley; Isabella Markham, who had attended Elizabeth during her imprisonment in the tower in 1554, and who would later marry John Harington and become the mother of the Queen's famous godson of the same name. Mary Radcliffe served Elizabeth for forty years and turned down all suitors to remain with her beloved mistress. Lady Mary Sidney, although ravaged by smallpox, remained very close to Elizabeth until her own death in 1586: she was the mother of the famous soldier and poet, Sir Philip Sidney, and was herself a very erudite woman. Philip's celebrated sister, another Mary, who was a poet herself and, according to Spenser, 'in her sex more wonderful and rare' than any riches, became a Lady of the Bedchamber on her marriage, aged fifteen, in 1576. It was not unusual for three generations of the same family to serve the Queen as maids of honour.

Anne Russell was the wife of Ambrose Dudley, Earl of Warwick and before her lavish marriage at Whitehall in 1565 had been lauded by poets for her virgin grace, her genius and her charming voice. In later years, Elizabeth became close to the Swedish Helena Ulsdotter, third wife of William Parr, Marquess of Northampton, who was forty years her senior. Helena was much at court, and when she remarried after Parr's death, the Queen allowed her to retain her title of Marchioness and the precedence it conferred, and granted her the old royal manor of Sheen in Surrey.

Although at the beginning of her reign Elizabeth had enjoined her ladies 'never to speak to her on business affairs', aspiring courtiers attempted – often successfully – to bribe them to carry petitions to their mistress, and this was often the ladies' most lucrative source of money. 'We worshipped no saints, but we prayed to ladies in the Queen's time,' quipped one court wit. According to Raleigh, these ladies were 'like witches, capable of doing great harm, but no good'. Sir Robert Sidney once importuned Lady Scudamore to pass on a letter requesting the post of Lord Warden of the Cinque Ports.

'Do you know the contents of it?' asked the Queen.

'No, Madam,' replied Lady Scudamore.

'Here is much ado about the Cinque Ports', muttered Elizabeth as she read the letter 'with two or three poohs!' Soon afterwards, she gave the post to Sidney's rival, Lord Cobham, whose claim had been put forward by another lady, Mistress Russell.

Much has been written about Elizabeth's attitude towards the romantic and sexual adventures of her maids of honour. Although it is fair to say that she became less tolerant of young people as she aged, it is unlikely that mere sexual envy was at the root of her notorious disapproval. Not only was she *in loco parentis* to these unmarried girls – some as young as fourteen – and the guardian of their honour, but their parents also hoped that their daughters would make advantageous marriages through being in the Queen's service, and everyone knew that a deflowered virgin was worthless in the marriage market. Elizabeth was furious if her maids attempted to arrange their own marriages without her consent – which amounted to a grossly offensive breach of etiquette, since the responsibility for arranging suitable marriages for her maids rested with her. She was also conscious that 'scandal and infamy' and the loss of a maid's reputation would reflect badly upon her own morals. Thus she was excessively severe with those who broke the rules.

We have already learned of the sad fates of Lady Katherine and Lady Mary Grey. Later in the reign Sir Walter Raleigh would suffer the Queen's wrath after seducing and then marrying one of her maids. When one maid, Mary Shelton, a Boleyn cousin, secretly married James

Scudamore, the Queen was 'liberal in blows and words' and Mary ended up with a broken finger; 'no one ever bought her husband more dearly'. Later Elizabeth apologised and appointed Mary a Gentlewoman of the Privy Chamber. Frances Vavasour incurred similar displeasure for the same offence, while her sister Anne, a 'drab' who secretly bore the Earl of Oxford's bastard in the Maidens' Chamber in 1581, was irrevocably disgraced, since her lover refused to marry her, although the Queen made him settle £2000 on the child, imprisoned him briefly in the Tower, then banished him from court.

In fact, the records show that Elizabeth was not against her maids marrying, provided they chose approved suitors. There is not a single example of her refusing an advantageous marriage for them, and eighteen of them were married to peers of the realm. Yet until such an opportunity presented itself, the Queen expected her maids to rejoice in their virginity, as she did. Harington records that she often asked her maids 'if they loved to think of marriage', and would 'much exhort all her women to remain in virgin state; the wise ones did conceal well their liking thereto, as knowing the Queen's judgement'.

Elizabeth also protected her women from marriages they did not want, as when, in 1583, Tsar Ivan the Terrible desired to marry Lady Mary Hastings in order to cement an Anglo-Russian alliance. Mary was terrified of being sent to Russia, with its barbaric customs, and the Queen refused to allow it, though for many years after that Mary was nicknamed 'the Tsarina of Muscovy'. On another occasion, the Queen, using 'many persuasions', tried to deter Lady Frances Howard from marrying the Earl of Hertford, because she believed that he did not really love and care for Frances. But faced with a girl besotted with love, the Queen 'in the end said she would not be against my desire', although she was ultimately proved right, for the marriage foundered, as did so many other aristocratic unions of the period.

The result of the Queen's strictures was that the maids of honour were too terrified of their mistress to confide in her when they fell in love – which happened frequently in a court peopled with men – and were frequently compelled to conduct their often innocent liaisons in furtive secrecy. Towards the end of the reign, as the Queen's intolerance increased in parity with the loosening of her grip on affairs, there were more and more illicit affairs involving her maids. Hence the 1590s were a decade of court scandals. When Elizabeth Vernon was rumoured to be pregnant by the Earl of Southampton, it was said that she had taken a fencing thrust 'under the girdle and swells upon it, yet she complains not of foul play, but says the Earl will justify it'. She was right, for he did marry her, but only just in time for the baby to be born legitimate. Elizabeth was so angry that she consigned the Earl and his new wife to the Fleet Prison for a fortnight. Mary Fitton, who had gone out dressed as a man to meet her lover, was also imprisoned for becoming an unmarried mother, and was exiled permanently from court. In 1591, Leicester's bastard son suffered a similar exile for merely kissing Mistress Cavendish.

Naturally, these young girls found it hard to repress their high spirits, and after a day of decorous behaviour, they would let off steam in the Maidens' or Coffer Chamber, their spartan dormitory – an unheated room below the rafters, under a leaking roof. Lesser servants slept behind a low partition at one end, so there was little privacy. The girls were meant to be under the supervision of the Mother of the Maids, but the holders of this post seem to have been fairly lax, and these night-time antics constantly aggravated older courtiers who slept nearby.

> The Lord Knollys had his lodging at court where some of the maids of honour used to frisk and hey about in the next room, to his extreme disquiet at nights, though he had often warned them of it. At last, he gets one to bolt their own back door, when they were all in one night in their revels, strips off his [night] shirt, and so with a pair of spectacles on his nose and Aretino in his hand, comes marching in at a postern door of his own chamber, reading, very gravely, full upon the faces of them. Now let the reader judge what a sad spectacle and pitiful sight these poor creatures endured, for he faced them and often traversed the room in this posture above an hour.

Often there were jealousies and quarrels in this all-female household, and although the Queen expected arguments to be patched up for her sake, she was not above playing off one protagonist against the other. Yet she often did show a very human face to her ladies, and was especially kind when any of them had suffered bereavement or family problems.

During her reign, Elizabeth I undertook twenty-five progresses through her kingdom, usually during the months of July and August, when plague could be rife in London. For her, a progress was an enjoyable holiday, a rest from the usual routine of state duties, and a chance to meet her people and win their hearts. She visited twenty counties, most of them in the south and west, and many towns; plans for a northern progress never came to fruition, and the farthest north the Queen travelled was Stafford. At each county boundary she would be welcomed by the local sheriff and his officers, and they would remain with her during her stay, while at each town she would be greeted by the mayor and aldermen in robes and regalia, who would hand her the ceremonial keys. Wherever she went, church bells rang out in celebration of her arrival.

Travel in the sixteenth century was not easy: most roads were poorly maintained, and some were little more than trackways that became waterlogged with rain. Carts and carriages could get stuck, and if it was wet – rain never deterred the Queen – everyone would be spattered with mud. Even on a good day, the court could only travel a distance of ten or twelve miles. When Elizabeth visited Bristol, she faced a 'long and dangerous journey', for the roads in the West Country were notoriously bad, and when she arrived she gave thanks to God for her preservation. In 1573, Cecil reported that she 'had a hard beginning of her progress in Kent and Sussex, where surely were more dangerous rocks and valleys and much worse ground than was in the Peak'.

The Queen travelled either on horseback, in an open, horse-drawn litter padded with cushions, or – from 1564, when this mode of transport was first introduced into England from Holland – in an uncomfortable, unsprung, twelve-wheeled coach of red leather studded with gilt nails, seating only two persons. Two empty litters accompanied her in case of accidents or them being required by her ladies. Behind Elizabeth stretched her retinue of about five hundred people and an endless procession of 2,400 horses and 400-600 carts laden with clothing and jewellery, provisions, household effects, state papers and tents for those servants who could not be accommodated in the houses they would visit.

Elizabeth's energy never flagged during these exhausting journeys, and she expected her courtiers to show the same enthusiasm. Most councillors resented the enormous expense involved – which Cecil estimated at around £2000 a year – and did their best to persuade the Queen to abandon her plans, but she persisted right up to the last year of her life. In 1601, when her courtiers were moaning about the prospect of yet another long progress, the sixty-eight-year-old Queen told 'the old to stay behind and the young and able go with her'.

In Elizabeth's opinion, going on progress saved on expenditure, since the cost of maintaining her court was being borne by her subjects, although she was careful never to exploit those who could not afford the expense, and the Exchequer and the Revels Office often contributed. But her officials resented the vast amount of preparation and upheaval that these progresses entailed, which mirrored the preparations for royal tours today. The Vice-Chamberlain would draw up the itinerary in consultation with the Queen, and would then make direct arrangements with civic dignitaries, sheriffs and potential hosts. Then the royal harbinger and two ushers of the Bedchamber would inspect the accommodation set aside for the Queen. The route would be decided and checked for safety and security. Then there was endless packing to be done.

The Queen began her progresses almost at the beginning of her reign, and undertook them roughly every two years during the 1560s. Their golden age was the 1570s, when their organisation had been brought to a fine art. Security dictated restrictions on progresses during the 1580s, but there was a revival in the 1590s when the ageing Queen seemed determined to prove that she was as sprightly as she had been in her youth.

There is no doubt that her progresses contributed to Elizabeth's popularity. A vast train of officials and servants, many colourfully attired, accompanied the court, and a splendid spectacle they made for the crowds who flocked to see the Queen along the way. The poor folk would drop to their knees and cry out, 'God save Your Majesty!' People were encouraged to come forward and speak with the Queen or hand her petitions, and everyone would be amazed at how accessible and friendly their sovereign could be.

A contemporary recorded:

> In her progress she was most easy to be approached; private persons and magistrates, country people and children came joyfully and without any fear to wait upon her. Her ears were then open to the complaints of the afflicted, and of those that had been in any way injured. She took with her own hand and read with the greatest goodness the petitions of the meanest rustics, and she would frequently assure them that she would take a particular care of their affairs; and she would ever be as good as her word. She was never angry with the uncourtly approach, never offended with the most impudent or importunate petitioner. Nor was there anything in the whole course of her reign that more won the hearts of the people than this, her wonderful condescension and strange sweetness.

On one occasion, an eager Serjeant Bendlowes of Huntingdon bellowed at Elizabeth's coachman, '"Stay thy cart, good fellow! Stay thy cart, that I may speak with the Queen!" Whereat Her Majesty laughed as [if] she had been tickled, although very graciously, as her manner is, she gave him great thanks and her hand to kiss.' It was not unknown for her to accept an impromptu invitation to go into a nearby house for some refreshments.

'She was received everywhere with great acclamations and signs of joy', wrote the Spanish ambassador in 1568, 'whereat she was extremely pleased, and told me so, giving me to understand how beloved she was by her subjects and how highly she esteemed this. She ordered her carriage sometimes to be taken where the crowd seemed thickest, and stood up and thanked the people.'

Royal visits to towns and cities invariably boosted trade and industry. When news came that Elizabeth was to visit a town, the inhabitants threw themselves into enthusiastic preparations:

> No sooner was pronounced the name,
> But babes in street 'gan leap;
> The youth, the aged, the rich, the poor,
> Came running all on heap,
> And clapping hands, and calling out,
> 'O blessed be the hour!
> Our Queen is coming to the town
> With princely train and power.'

Tapestries and painted cloths or green boughs would be hung at the windows, speeches prepared, streets cleaned of rubbish and sometimes newly gravelled, and a cup of silver gilt purchased as a gift for the Queen.

At Coventry in 1565, the Queen declared herself touched by a gift of £100 in gold coins in a cup.

'I have but few such gifts,' she said.

'If it pleases Your Grace', declared the mayor, 'there is a great deal more in it.' Elizabeth asked what he meant.

'It is the hearts of all your loving subjects,' was the reply.

'We thank you, Mr Mayor, it is a great deal more indeed,' agreed the Queen.

At Sandwich, in 1579, she paid the magistrates' wives a great compliment when, without employing a food taster, she sampled some of the 160 dishes they had prepared for her and even ordered some to be taken to her lodgings so that she could eat them later.

During these progresses the Queen made at least 240 overnight stops, some at her own manors, although it was more usual for her to seek the hospitality of her wealthier subjects or civic dignitaries. 'When it pleaseth her in the summer season to recreate herself abroad, or view the estates of the country, every nobleman's house is her palace,' observed the writer William Harrison. In total, she was the guest of over 150 different people.

The Queen herself was lodged 'for her best ease and liking, far from heat or noise', whilst lesser folk had to take pot luck with what was available, since very few houses had room for the entire court. Sometimes, she arrived late, causing her hosts to spend a small fortune in candle wax. The court could also consume alarming quantities of food. Such visits could last for days and financially cripple the host: in 1577, it cost Sir Nicholas Bacon £577 to entertain the Queen for four days at Gorhambury, near St Albans, while in 1591 Cecil was poorer by over £1000 after Elizabeth had stayed for ten days at Burghley House near Stamford.

In 1600, Sir Henry Lee, who had twice entertained the Queen, wrote to Cecil to say he had heard that 'Her Majesty threatens a progress,' and that she would be 'coming to my house, of which I would be most proud'; however, 'My estate without my undoing cannot bear it.' In that same year, the Earl of Lincoln, on receiving warning that the Queen was advancing on his Chelsea home, fled to the country, and when she arrived the house was locked. Naturally Elizabeth was much offended by this, and declared her firm intention of returning the following week to dine with the Earl. Cecil and Nottingham informed Lincoln that they would make all the arrangements, and then presented him with the bill, which shook him badly. Nevertheless most courtiers deemed a royal visit a signal honour and welcomed the chance to have the Queen stay as their guest, while towns competed to be placed on her itinerary. There were bitter complaints from would-be hosts who were passed by.

The entertainments laid on for the Queen at the great houses were lavish and varied. Hosts vied to outdo each other in offering novel and extravagant attractions. At Beddington Park in Surrey, Sir Francis Carew delayed the flowering of a cherry tree by covering it with a tent, so that out-of-season cherries – a fruit which symbolised virginity – might be served to the Queen. Another host concealed an orchestra in an artificial cave. There were pageants, fêtes, banquets, masques, plays, dances, acrobatics, firework displays, tableaux, songs, rustic pastimes and wonderful opportunities for hunting. Many entertainments had allegorical themes, often celebrating the Virgin Queen. Also popular were Greek and Roman myths peopled by gods and goddesses, nymphs and satyrs, as well as characters from the Arthurian legends, mermaids and fairies. Some of the plays and verses were commissioned from the best writers of the age, including George Gascoigne and John Lyly. The legendary entertainments at Kenilworth in 1575, of which more will be heard later, were the most magnificent and memorable – and expensive – of the reign.

The great men of the realm built spacious houses especially designed for entertaining the Queen whilst on progress. Such a one was Cecil's Theobalds in Essex, where he entertained his mistress thirteen times. Elizabeth advised on the design and asked that the state bedchamber be adorned with artificial trees and an astronomical clock on the ceiling. There were five galleries in which she could walk if the weather were inclement, or four gardens when it was fine. Sir Christopher Hatton modelled his great mansion at Holdenby on Theobalds, and it became the largest house in the kingdom after Hampton Court. There is little doubt that the Queen inspired him to build it, as it was dedicated to her. These houses cost so much that Cecil wrote to Hatton, 'God send us long to enjoy her, for whom we both meant to exceed our purse in these.' In fact, the Treasury defrayed some of the cost of building. Sadly, both houses were demolished after falling into decay during the Civil War.

It was virtually obligatory for hosts to provide the Queen with a series of costly gifts, which added considerably to the expense. At Kew in 1598, Lord Keeper Egerton gave her a jewelled fan and a diamond pendant on her arrival at his house, followed by a pair of virginals at dinner, and there was 'a fine gown and skirt' waiting for her in her bedchamber. Not content with this, she intimated she would also like a salt, spoon and fork of agate, which he readily gave her on parting. Hosts were also expected to give presents to the Queen's entourage, whilst pilfering by courtiers and servants was common, despite Elizabeth's insistence that their conduct be impeccable. Nevertheless, most of those who had entertained the Queen treasured the memories of her visit.

Elizabeth was usually in a carefree, holiday mood during her progresses: she was 'well pleased with all things' and 'made very merry', expressing 'an extreme delight' at what was done for her pleasure, however humble. She sat patiently through interminable speeches of welcome, never betraying any impatience, and expressed fulsome thanks for the smallest of gifts. She always found something to praise, as when she called St Mary Redcliffe in Bristol 'the finest and goodliest parish church in England'. Assisted by Cecil, she always did her homework before making such visits. She was, however, inclined to alter her travel plans at a moment's notice, thereby putting some of her hosts to considerable inconvenience and prompting many complaints. In 1582, Lord and Lady Norris were deeply upset when the Queen was obliged to cancel a visit to Rycote. For more fortunate gentlefolk, she was usually a congenial guest, although being served sour beer could provoke a black mood, and she was not above making adverse comments about defects in the accommodation.

Some hosts were completely overawed by the Queen's presence. Cecil's secretary, Michael Hicks, had prepared a well-rehearsed welcoming speech, but when Elizabeth arrived at his house, 'Her Majesty's royal presence and princely aspect did on a sudden so daunt all my senses and dazzle mine eyes, as I had use neither of speech nor memory.' The Queen could not understand why her host had been struck dumb, but 'in her princely favour, said it pleased her to like of my

house. I know I shall like the worse of myself as long as I live,' Hicks
added ruefully.

In order for her subjects to share in the delights of her progresses, the
Queen publicised them by having accounts printed after her return.
Such pamphlets were hugely popular, and served – as they were
intended to do – to enhance the legend of the Virgin Queen.

15

'The Axe Must Be the Next Warning'

On 25 February 1571, Elizabeth created Cecil First Baron Burghley in recognition of his services to the Crown. Her inner circle of advisers now comprised Burghley, Sussex, Leicester and Walsingham. While Cecil was shrewd and cautious, Leicester was impulsive and militant; he and Walsingham were natural allies because of their devotion to the Protestant cause, and were to become even closer after the death from pleurisy of Leicester's friend, Sir Nicholas Throckmorton, that same month.

However, while Burghley and Sussex supported a marriage between the Queen and the Duke of Anjou, Leicester did not, although he pretended otherwise. His colleagues were in no doubt that, in the wake of the papal interdict, England stood in dangerous isolation in Europe, and needed the friendship of a strong ally like France. The French, although they deplored Elizabeth's treatment of Mary Stuart, feared the Spanish presence in the Netherlands as much as did the English, and they saw the sense of joining with Elizabeth in a defensive alliance. Charles IX wanted support against the increasing threat of the Guises, and also hoped to deter the Queen from aiding his own Huguenot subjects.

Elizabeth, who, according to Leicester, was 'more bent to marriage than heretofore she hath been', could see the wisdom in this, and that February she sent her cousin Lord Buckhurst to Paris, ostensibly to congratulate Charles on his marriage, but chiefly secretly to inform the French that she 'thankfully accepted' their proposals and was ready to treat with them over the marriage. This news delighted King Charles, who wanted his unstable, ambitious and meddling brother safely out of the country before the Guises could get him into their clutches. The thankless task of negotiating the marriage was left to Walsingham, England's resident ambassador in Paris.

'If I be not much deceived', noted Burghley, 'Her Majesty is earnest in this.' If the marriage went ahead, 'the curious and dangerous question of the succession would in the minds of quiet subjects be buried – a happy funeral for all England'.

Yet from the first it was obvious that religion was going to be a major obstacle. Elizabeth insisted that Anjou convert to the Anglican faith, while he, a fervent Catholic who was influenced by the Papal Nuncio and the Cardinal of Lorraine, refused to violate his conscience even for the hope of a kingdom.

Anjou, who was unenthusiastic about the match, complained to his mother that he feared he would be universally ridiculed if he took such a notorious bride. When an anxious Catherine de' Medici asked Fénelon to make discreet inquiries at the English court in order to discover if the rumours were true, the ambassador reported back that he had heard nothing to justify them, and Anjou reluctantly had to agree to negotiations proceeding. It was not surprising that they speedily reached an impasse.

That same February saw the arrival in London of the Earl of Morton and other commissioners from James VI, come to make it clear to the Queen that the Scots did not want her to press for Mary Stuart's restoration. In fact, Elizabeth now had no intention of doing so, for since the Pope had issued the Bull of Excommunication, she had become far less enthusiastic about having a troublesome Catholic monarch as her near neighbour, although she affected to be offended by James's impertinence.

The realisation that Elizabeth would now do nothing to help her soon filtered through to Mary, who declared to her friend, the Bishop of Ross, that 'our good sister must pardon us if, seeing no further deliverance to be had at her hand', she looked to foreign princes for help. If intrigue could secure her liberation, and hopefully the crown of England, that was the course she was now obliged to take. Indeed, she was already involved in one of the most dangerous plots of Elizabeth's reign.

Since the collapse of the Northern Rising, nothing had been heard of Roberto Ridolfi, the Florentine banker who doubled as a papal agent, until in January 1571 he had written to Mary offering to act as her representative in the courts of Europe, where he would be well placed to stir up support for her. He had conceived a plan whereby the Catholic powers would invade England, overthrow Elizabeth, and set Mary and Norfolk up in her place; already, King Philip and the Pope had agreed in principle to support it. Now he needed the consent of Mary herself.

Mary, after obtaining the Pope's approval, was only too happy to give it: this was what she had been praying for. She told Ridolfi to inform her friends that, if they did invade England, they could expect the support of many influential lords, and provided him with credentials issued by herself to show King Philip, the Pope and the Duke of Alva.

Mary still cherished hopes of Norfolk. While he languished in the Tower, she had written to him to persuade him that they should still marry when it became possible: 'You have promised to be mine, and I yours. I believe the Queen of England and country should like of it. You promised you would not leave me.' Even Norfolk could not have believed now that Elizabeth would welcome such a marriage, and he had, on his release, promised the Queen that he would 'never deal in the cause of the marriage of the Queen of Scots'. However, as with many men before and after him, she continued to exert a fatal fascination for him.

On 8 February 1571, Mary wrote to Norfolk, outlining Ridolfi's plans and inviting him to join the conspiracy. The Duke had no desire to become involved, at great danger to himself, in what was undoubtedly high treason. He was also alarmed at Mary's insistence that he become a Catholic. By 10 March, however, Mary had worn down his resistance, and, driven by the hope of a crown, he met Ridolfi in secret and offered his help and support. When he refused to sign a written request for men and supplies to King Philip, Ridolfi simply forged his name on the document.

Two weeks later, Ridolfi left for Rome, where the Pope was pleased to bless his enterprise.

In April, Burghley's agents in Scotland reported that they had evidence that the Queen of Scots was corresponding with the Duke of Alva. This could only mean trouble, and Shrewsbury was instructed to keep careful watch on Mary's doings.

Confirmation of the government's fears came soon afterwards, when the Grand Duke of Tuscany, whose court Ridolfi had visited en route to Rome, wrote to warn Burghley that the banker was involved in a conspiracy concerning the Queen of Scots. After that, Shrewsbury closely questioned Mary about her involvement with foreign courts, but she denied all knowledge of what he was talking about. Nevertheless, he remained vigilant, since the government were hopeful that she would incriminate herself and thus give them an excuse to proceed against her.

When Parliament reassembled in May 1571, its priority was to pre-empt any Catholic plots and tighten national security, and three Acts were passed. From now on, it would be high treason to say that Elizabeth was not the lawful Queen of England, or to publish, write or say that she was a heretic, infidel, schismatic, tyrant or usurper. It would also be treason for anyone to bring a papal Bull into the realm. Crucifixes, rosaries and religious pictures were banned, and Catholics who had fled abroad were ordered to return within six months or forfeit all their possessions.

Life was becoming exceedingly difficult for English Catholics. Forbidden to practise their religion, they were fined if they did not attend Anglican services. They had to be careful how they spoke of the Queen, and, in the political climate following the papal interdict, many people regarded Catholics as little better than traitors because of their faith. Some did look to Mary Stuart for deliverance, although their numbers were not so great as King Philip, the Pope and Mary herself fondly supposed. In fact, the majority of English Catholics were loyal to Elizabeth.

At the end of June, Ridolfi was warmly received by Philip II in Madrid. By now, the details of the plot had been finalised: the Duke of Alva would invade England with 6000 Spanish troops from the Netherlands, and would then march on London and occupy it. Simultaneously, Norfolk would incite loyal English Catholics to rise up against Elizabeth, who would be seized by the Duke and either assassinated or held as a hostage for Mary's safety. Mary would be liberated and proclaimed Queen of England, then she and Norfolk would marry and in time reign as joint sovereigns over England and Scotland, to which kingdoms they would restore the Catholic faith.

There were fatal weaknesses in the scheme, the chief one being that Ridolfi, like most Catholics, vastly overestimated the number of English Catholics who would be willing to rise on Mary's behalf – he believed there would be 39,000. The Florentine banker had no real understanding of English politics or the English people, and Norfolk, who should have had both, was either too gullible or too blinded by ambition to point out the flaws.

It was left to the Duke of Alva to veto the plan. Alva, who had scathingly dismissed Ridolfi as 'that great chatterbox', was convinced that the invasion would fail, and that, if it did, it would do irrevocable harm to Catholicism in general as well as to Mary's cause, and might well cost her her life. He refused point blank to use his troops in the enterprise, knowing that without them, Philip was powerless to help the Queen of Scots. Throughout the summer, the other conspirators tried to persuade Alva to change his mind, but with no success.

Leicester was still riding high. In July, a court had finally overturned his 1554 conviction for treason and cleared his name. In future, his enemies would be unwise to call him a traitor. But although he remained closer to the Queen than anyone else, he now had rivals for her affections. His friend, Sir Thomas Heneage, still enjoyed Elizabeth's favour, and there was a newcomer on the court scene, Christopher Hatton.

Born around 1540, Hatton was the son of a Northamptonshire squire, and had been educated at Oxford and the Inner Temple, where Elizabeth is said to have watched him dancing in the masque *Gorboduc* in 1562. It was his elegant dancing and his dashing skill in the tiltyard that captivated her interest after Hatton had been appointed one of her Gentlemen Pensioners in 1564. Thereafter, he rose rapidly to favour, receiving grants of land and court offices, and becoming a Gentleman of the Privy Chamber in 1569 and MP for Northampton in 1571. In 1572 the Queen would appoint him Captain of the Gentlemen Pensioners, her personal bodyguard, which meant that his duties would keep him in constant attendance upon her.

By 1571, he had become one of Elizabeth's intimates and been given a nickname. Where Leicester was her 'Eyes', Hatton was her 'Lids'. Later she would call him her 'Mutton' or her 'Bellwether'.

Hatton was the ideal courtier. According to Naunton, he was 'tall and portionable', while Nicholas Hilliard called him 'one of the goodliest personages of England'. He was strikingly handsome with dark hair and eyes, but it was his robust masculine charms and his passionate address that endeared him to Elizabeth. When he wrote to her, it was as a lover, sometimes ending his letters with a pun: 'Adieu, most sweet Lady. All and EveR yours, your most happy bondman, Lids.'

Once, after being parted from her for only two days, he wrote:

> No death, no, not hell, shall ever win of me my consent so far to wrong myself again as to be absent from you one day. I lack that I live by. The more I find this lack, the further I go from you. To serve you is heaven, but to lack you is more than hell's torment. Would God I were with you but for one hour. My wits are overwrought with thoughts. I find myself amazed. Bear with me, my most dear, sweet Lady. Passion overcometh me. I can write no more. Love me, for I love you. Live for ever.

Hatton flattered his Queen with compliments and unusual gifts, and made love to her with his eyes. His whole life was dedicated to paying court to her, and unlike her other suitors, he remained unmarried for her sake, to her great gratification, although whether she knew that he found his sexual pleasures elsewhere and was the father of a bastard daughter is another matter.

Leicester was naturally jealous of Hatton, and tried to belittle him in the Queen's eyes. When she praised Hatton's dancing, Leicester told her he could send her a dancing master who could do far better.

'Pish!' she snorted, unimpressed. 'I will not see your man. It is his *trade*!'

Leicester was further discountenanced by her fondness for the dashing young Edward de Vere, Earl of Oxford, who had, like Hatton, commended himself to her by his skill at jousting. Something of a free spirit, Oxford was well-educated in the classics, skilled in dancing and playing the virginals, and a superb horseman – qualities guaranteed to endear him to the Queen, who also appreciated the young man's slender figure and hazel eyes.

Everyone expected the Earl to become one of the court's brightest stars, and Leicester's enemies fervently hoped that Oxford would displace the favourite. When Oxford married Anne Cecil, Burghley's daughter, at Westminster Abbey, the Queen attended and bestowed on him a nickname – her 'Boar'. However, he soon lost interest in his fifteen-year-old bride, and grew weary of life at court, indulging his passion for adventure overseas. Although the Queen 'delighteth more in his personage and his dancing and valiantness than any other', there was no likelihood of his ever achieving entry to her inner circle, since he could 'by no means be drawn to follow the court'. 'If it were not for his fickle head, he would pass any of them shortly,' observed a contemporary.

Until March 1571, only the Queen's inner circle had known about the proposed French marriage, and when, that month, she had informed the Council of her intention to marry the Duke of Anjou, her councillors had been pleasantly surprised. As Burghley put it, such a marriage would make 'the Pope's malice vanish away in smoke'. Remembering the fate of earlier marriage projects, however, the councillors were only cautiously optimistic, and one had caused great offence to the Queen when he tactlessly asked if the Duke were not too young to be her husband.

Soon afterwards, Catherine de' Medici sent a special envoy, Guido Cavalcanti, to England with a formal proposal of marriage from Anjou, a flattering portrait of him, and a list of demands: the Duke must be permitted to practise the Catholic faith, he was to be crowned King of England on the day after the wedding, and the English Exchequer was to pay him an annual income of £60,000 for life. Elizabeth made difficulties about all these conditions: she would not agree to the Duke being crowned, nor to granting him a life income, and while she conceded that he would not be compelled to attend Anglican services, she refused to allow him to attend mass, even in private.

Unsurprisingly, little progress was made during the spring and summer, and, worst still, reports reached the Queen that the Duke, encouraged by his friends, was reluctant to proceed and, having heard of her varicose ulcer, had even publicly referred to her as 'an old creature with a sore leg'. Queen Catherine officially apologised for her son's rudeness, but for some times afterwards Elizabeth, sensitive about growing old, took pains to dance in public before Fénelon. She hoped, she said pointedly, that Monsieur would have no cause to complain that he had been tricked into marrying a lame bride.

Yet the age gap did concern her, and she confided as much in private to her ladies, but when Lady Cobham advised her against pressing ahead with her marriage plans because of the 'great inequality' in age, the Queen was much affronted and retorted, 'There are but ten years between us!' Lady Cobham dared not contradict her.

Angered that Anjou was proving so reluctant a suitor, Elizabeth created more difficulties over the marriage contract, at one point even demanding the return of Calais as one of its conditions. Burghley warned Walsingham that she seemed to be deliberately insisting on terms to which the French would never agree. In Europe, diplomats were equally confused, and in Spain it was believed that Elizabeth would not go through with the marriage, since she was only pretending an interest in it to raise French support. 'She will no more marry Anjou than she will marry me!' commented the Duke de Feria.

On 7 June, the Venetian ambassador in Paris reported, 'It is the opinion of many that the negotiations will be successful.' Yet Anjou was still insisting he would change his religion for no one, and by July, Walsingham was very pessimistic. Burghley, knowing that public feeling was in favour of the marriage, tried to persuade Elizabeth to permit the Duke to at least attend mass in private, but she declared that her conscience would not permit her to sanction any Catholic service to be held in England. She failed to see, she continued disingenuously, why the Duke could not worship as an Anglican without hurt to his conscience.

Burghley despaired at Elizabeth's attitude. Marriage to a French prince seemed the only sure means of protecting herself and England from the malice of the Papacy and Spain, yet she seemed to be doing her best to wreck negotiations. Walsingham and Leicester, however, believing that Anjou was pretending to be a more zealous Catholic than he actually was, felt that the French would at length make concessions and that the Queen was justified in taking a stand. Burghley, bitterly disappointed at Leicester's defection, believed that the Earl's sole objective was to marry the Queen himself. Certainly he had secretly advised the French to stand firm on the matter of the mass.

In August, the Queen Mother of France sent another special envoy, Paul de Foix, to London, to add his pleas to Burghley's, but still Elizabeth was adamant that she would make no concessions. It now seemed that she was up to her usual game of playing for time, and stringing out negotiations without having any intention of reaching a happy conclusion. Realising this, Burghley wearily advised her on 31 August that he would instruct her Council to devise other means for her preservation, although 'How Your Majesty shall obtain remedies for your perils, I think is only in the knowledge of Almighty God.'

By September, when de Foix returned dejectedly to France, Leicester, who knew Elizabeth better than anyone, was forced to conclude, as he told Walsingham, that 'Her Majesty's heart is nothing inclined to marry at all, for the matter was ever brought to as many points as we could devise, and always she was bent to hold with the difficultest.' That month, it was reported by the Venetian ambassador in Paris that the Anjou marriage negotiations had foundered, although the 'good understanding' between England and France might yet lead to an alliance.

In view of the intelligence he had received about the Ridolfi conspiracy, Burghley advised the Queen that it would be unwise to go on progress as usual, but she would not listen. She even stayed at Norfolk's house at Walden in Essex on 24 August.

Two days later, at a time when it was obvious to most of the conspirators that Ridolfi's invasion plan was unworkable, the game was up for Norfolk when a suspicious courier reported him to the authorities for sending money and letters in cipher to Mary's friends in Scotland. The Queen's reaction was angry, and the Duke was arrested on a charge of high treason on 3 September, being 'quietly brought into the Tower without any trouble' at midnight on the 7th. On the following day, government agents found a bundle of incriminating letters in cipher hidden below the roof tiles of the Charterhouse, Norfolk's London residence.

In the meantime, news had arrived of the murder of the Regent Lennox on 4 September at Stirling Castle, in revenge for his hanging of Archbishop Hamilton. To Elizabeth's relief, he was replaced by her own candidate, the Earl of Mar.

By 11 October, after the Queen had signed an order for his servants to be tortured to make them give evidence, Norfolk had confessed to his part in the plot, although he strenuously denied that he had meant to harm the Queen. Those questioning him concluded that it was his 'foolish devotion to that woman' that had been his motivation. Later, he made a written confession of his crimes.

On 24 October, despite claiming diplomatic immunity, the Bishop of Ross, who had remained in England as Mary's official envoy after her imprisonment, was committed to the Tower, where, threatened with the rack, he revealed all he knew, which was sufficient to bring both

Mary and Norfolk to the block. He added, for good measure, that Mary was not fit to be a wife, since she had poisoned her first husband, been a party to the murder of the second, and married the murderer hoping he would be killed in battle. In Ross's opinion, she would probably have done away with Norfolk too.

'Lord, what a people are these!' exclaimed Dr Wilson, the Bishop's interrogator. 'What a queen, and what an ambassador!'

The Bishop's evidence led to the arrest of several noblemen who were suspected of having been Norfolk's associates, the Earls of Southampton and Arundel and Lords Cobham and Lumley. Arundel tried desperately to clear his name, but failed and spent the rest of his life under a cloud of royal displeasure. Southampton spent more than a year in the Tower. The Spanish ambassador was expelled from the country, but Ridolfi, the perpetrator of the plot, had fled safely abroad, and out of reach of Elizabeth's vengeance.

Elizabeth's attitude towards Mary hardened after the discovery of the Ridolfi Plot, and she ordered her cousin to be kept more securely and closely watched. Never again would she consider restoring Mary to the Scottish throne; on the contrary, she now realised that she could never set her cousin at liberty. She had incontrovertible proof that Mary would stop at nothing to gain her freedom and, if possible, Elizabeth's crown. Bitterly disillusioned, the Queen authorised Burghley to have the Casket Letters published, and herself finally recognised James VI as King of Scots.

When Mary was confronted with evidence incriminating her in the recent plot, all she would say was that she had been attempting to recover her Scottish throne, and those who asserted otherwise 'were false villains and lied in their throats'. She claimed never to have associated with Ridolfi, and had nothing to say of Norfolk, who was Elizabeth's subject and no business of hers.

Charles IX, hitherto Mary's champion, appeared now to be willing to abandon his former sister-in-law to whatever fate was in store for her. 'Alas, the poor fool will never cease until she loses her head. They will put her to death. It is her own fault and folly,' he observed.

This was exactly what Mary feared in the weeks after the plot was uncovered. The first indication of her disgrace came when an order arrived for the dismissal of several members of her household who had been implicated. Mary reacted with indignation to this 'extreme severity', but it served her no purpose.

When, after a while, it seemed that she was to be left unmolested, she had the temerity to write several times to Elizabeth, attempting to excuse herself. No replies were received, so Mary wrote a further letter, expressing herself in 'uncomely, passionate, ireful and vindictive speeches'. This provoked a furious response from the Queen, who told Mary to be grateful that she had not been treated more severely and left her in no doubt as to the peril in which she stood.

The implications of the Ridolfi Plot prompted Elizabeth and her government to the stark realisation that an alliance with France, preferably sealed with a marriage, should be concluded as a matter of urgency. The Queen was now ready to make concessions, and did her best to revive the moribund Anjou marriage project by making it known that she would allow the Duke to have mass celebrated in private. 'Her Majesty was never more earnestly bent to the marriage than now,' Burghley wrote.

Walsingham, however, advised against reopening negotiations, since Anjou would 'utterly refuse' the match, even if the Queen granted 'all that he desires'. The Duke now had his sights set on being elected King of Poland, and was also deeply involved with Mademoiselle de Châteauneuf, whom he was loath to leave, although there was talk of him marrying a Polish princess. If the Queen persisted, warned Walsingham, she would almost certainly face a humiliating public rejection.

Elizabeth did not give up. In December, with Burghley's backing, she sent the experienced Sir Thomas Smith to Paris to test the water; if there was no hope of marrying Anjou, then he was to work towards concluding a treaty of friendship and mutual support against the common enemies of both countries. Smith was convinced that a French marriage was necessary to Elizabeth's future security, though he realised that soon she would no longer be a desirable catch: she was not getting any younger, and at thirty-eight was losing her looks and her hair, and had resorted to wearing false hair pieces and wigs. 'The more hairy she is before, the more bald she is behind,' observed Smith to Burghley.

It was soon clear to the ambassador that, despite Anjou's mother pleading with him and weeping 'hot tears', the Duke was no longer interested in Elizabeth or the crown of England: 'Monsieur is here entangled, and has his religion fixed in Mlle. de Châteauneuf,' observed Smith wryly. Elizabeth affected to be offended by his behaviour, and with an air of pathos declared that, since her attempts to get a husband had caused her to be so ill-used, she hoped her subjects would understand why she preferred to remain single.

However, two days later, Catherine de' Medici, aware that France still needed Elizabeth's friendship, suggested that the Queen might yet make a French marriage, and offered her youngest son, Hercules-Francis, Duke of Alençon, as a replacement bridegroom. 'Without a marriage, she could not see any league or amity being so strong or so lasting,' and Alençon was 'a much less scrupulous fellow' when it came to religious convictions.

Smith understood at once the political advantages of the match, and agreed with Queen Catherine that, if the Queen 'be disposed to marry, I do not see where she shall marry so well. The marriage with this Duke is ten thousand times better than the other.' Alençon was known to be sympathetic towards the Huguenots, and was 'not so obstinate and forward, so papistical and (if I may say so) so foolish and restive like a mule as his brother was. He is the more moderate, the more flexible, and the better fellow.' He was also unlikely ever to ascend the throne of France, so would be able to live in England. Smith, however, professed himself at a loss to understand why, when it came to 'the getting of children', everyone at the French court insisted that Alençon was 'more apt than th'other', and left Elizabeth to draw her own conclusions.

Nevertheless, the Duke was only seventeen, less than half as old as Elizabeth, and his skin was badly marked after two childhood attacks of smallpox. He had been a weak child, and was undersized for his age. His mother proudly pointed out his sprouting beard to Smith, saying that it would cover some of the worst pockmarks, and added that he was 'vigorous and lusty'. Smith himself felt that pockmarks were 'no matter in a man'.

When Elizabeth was told of the proposal, she objected that Alençon was too young and too small. When Burghley insisted that the Duke was of the same height as himself, she retorted, 'Say rather the height of your grandson!' Walsingham, however, optimistic that the religious difficulties would not be insurmountable in this case, persuaded the Queen to press ahead with negotiations, and she agreed. She could never resist the delights of a courtship and anticipated that she could prolong this one indefinitely.

At New Year 1572, Leicester presented the Queen with a bejewelled bracelet in which was set a tiny timepiece – the first known wrist-watch. Yet despite the festivities of the season, the atmosphere at court was tense.

On 16 January 1572, Norfolk was tried before a jury of twenty-six peers in Westminster Hall and found guilty on thirteen counts of high treason, the verdict – as in most Tudor state trials – being a foregone conclusion. Lord Shrewsbury, presiding, wept as he condemned the Duke to hanging, drawing and quartering, the usual penalty for traitors, although, when the condemned was a peer, the sovereign invariably commuted the sentence to decapitation.

Norfolk was returned to his lodging in the Tower, where, watched by his guards day and night, he occupied himself by writing farewell letters and exhortations to his children; Elizabeth was graciously pleased to accede to his plea that Lord Burghley, his former friend, be appointed their guardian. When the Queen of Scots was told by Shrewsbury of Norfolk's condemnation, she wept pitifully.

The Duke's execution was set for 21 January, but Elizabeth could not bring herself to sign his death warrant. Not only was he the foremost peer in England, and popular with the people, but he was also her cousin, bound to her by 'nearness of blood'. She put off the moment while the days turned into weeks.

'The Queen's Majesty hath always been a merciful lady', sighed Burghley, 'and by mercy she hath taken more harm than justice, and yet she thinks she is more beloved in doing herself harm. God save her to His honour long among us.'

Early in February, Elizabeth was prevailed upon to sign the warrant, but on the night before the Duke's execution was due to take place, she sent for Burghley and, in great distress, rescinded the order; the spectators who turned up at Tower Hill the next morning had to watch the hangings of two common malefactors instead.

Her councillors could not understand her hesitation. 'God's will be fulfilled and aid Her Majesty to do herself good,' prayed Burghley, while Lord Hunsdon declared, 'The world knows her to be wise, and surely there cannot be a greater point of wisdom than for any to be careful of their own estate, and especially the preservation of their own life. How much more needful it is for Her Majesty to take heed, upon whose life depends the commonwealth, the utter ruin of the whole country, and the utter subversion of religion.'

The matter was left in abeyance during much of March 1572, because the Queen fell seriously ill with gastro-enteritis. Her doctors despaired of her life, and Leicester and Burghley spent three anxious days and nights keeping vigil at her bedside, while Leicester stood deputy for her at a Garter ceremony at which Burghley was admitted to the order. The rivalry between the two men was now no longer so intense: they visited each other socially, exchanged a friendly correspondence, and had established an amicable working relationship. Even though, politically, they were often on opposite sides, they shared a common bond in their devotion to the Queen, their loyalty to the state and the Protestant faith.

When Elizabeth recovered, she made light of her illness, saying it was merely the result of eating bad fish, but for her councillors it had raised once again the grim spectre of the unresolved succession and the knowledge that, if the Queen were to die now, England would be lost to foreign predators who would force Catholicism on its people. With this in mind, they persuaded Elizabeth to agree to summon Parliament as a matter of urgency, so that measures could be taken against Mary Stuart.

That month, the octogenarian Earl of Winchester died. His post of Lord High Treasurer was first offered to Leicester, who turned it down on the grounds that he did not have sufficient 'learning and knowledge'. It was therefore given to Burghley, who was doubtless relieved to lay down the onerous burden of the duties of Secretary of State. He was increasingly troubled by gout, and had such a bad attack in April that the Queen, fearing for his life, came hastening to his bedside.

That month, Elizabeth signed another warrant for Norfolk's execution, and again withdrew it. It now seemed possible that the Duke would not suffer the extreme penalty after all.

Public feeling against Mary Stuart was running high, for most of Elizabeth's subjects agreed with Walsingham in believing that 'So long as this devilish woman lives, neither Her Majesty must make account to continue in quiet possession of the crown, nor her faithful servants assure themselves of the safety of their lives.'

When Parliament met on 8 May 1572, the catalogue of Mary's misdeeds was read out to both Houses, who immediately demanded that she be put to death. One MP declared he feared to go to sleep after hearing how the Queen of Scots had murdered Darnley and plunged Scotland into chaos, and insisted that the Queen 'cut off her head and make no more ado about her'. Another member pointed out that 'Warning hath already been given her, and therefore the axe must be the next warning.'

The Lords and Commons arranged for a committee to be set up to determine Mary's fate. By 19 May, its members had come up with two alternative ways of proceeding. Either Mary could be attainted of treason and executed forthwith, or they could legislate to bar her from the succession and warn her that, if she plotted against Elizabeth again, she would be put to death.

Parliament was unanimously in favour of the former course, but the Queen insisted that it would be wiser to adopt the second, since honour would not permit her to attaint a foreign queen who was not subject to English law. It would also be very costly and would mean that Parliament would have to sit through the summer, when there was usually plague in London.

The Lords and Commons were past caring about that: they were out for Mary's blood. 'Many members shed tears for the Queen,' and even the convocation of bishops used many 'godly arguments' to persuade Elizabeth to agree to an attainder, pointing out that, if she did not put to death this husband murderer and arch-traitress, this Scottish Clytemnestra, she would offend God and her conscience. She should not think that 'threatening words of law' would deter Mary from plotting against her in future, nor prevent traitorous subjects from aiding her.

Intent upon having a favourable answer, Parliament submitted to the Queen a petition, which was described as 'the call and cry of all good subjects against the merciful nature of Her Majesty'. But Elizabeth had already made up her mind that she could not 'put to death the bird that, to escape the pursuit of the hawk, has fled to my feet for protection. Honour and conscience forbid!' Nor had she any desire to provoke armed retribution on the part of Mary's Catholic allies. On 28 May, she received the petition at the hands of a deputation from both Houses, but, in a speech that has not survived, managed to turn down their request with such skill that they ended up thanking her for the good opinion she had of them. Only the radical MP, Peter Wentworth, who regarded Mary as 'a notorious whore', was heard to mutter that Elizabeth deserved no thanks.

On 26 May, having been forced to take less drastic measures against Mary, Parliament drew up a Bill listing her offences and depriving her of her pretended claim to the throne. From henceforth, it would be an offence for anyone to proclaim or assert it. However, when the Bill was submitted to the Queen for the royal assent, she exercised her veto. It was now obvious that she meant to take no action whatsoever against her cousin, and her councillors despaired; their intelligence from abroad showed conclusively that King Philip and the Pope were set upon overthrowing her in Mary's favour.

It was probably around this time that Elizabeth wrote her famous sonnet about Mary, which was published in her lifetime by George Puttenham in his book, *The Art of Poesie*. This is an extract:

The Daughter of Debate, that eke discord doth sow,
Shall reap no gain where former rule hath taught still peace to grow.
No foreign banish'd wight shall anchor in this port;
Our realm it brooks no stranger's force, let them elsewhere resort.
Our rusty sword with rest shall first his edge employ,
To poll their tops that seek such change, and gape for joy.

Having spared Mary, Elizabeth was obliged to throw Norfolk to the wolves. Parliament had been agitating throughout for the law to take its course, and on 31 May the Queen capitulated and signed the Duke's death warrant. On the following day she paid a rare visit to the Tower to ensure that arrangements had been made in a seemly and proper fashion, although she did not see her prisoner.

At seven a.m. on 2 June, Norfolk was beheaded on Tower Hill, declaring to the watching crowds that he had never been a Papist and acknowledging the justness of the sentence of beheading. 'For men to suffer death in this place is no new thing,' he told them. 'Since the beginning of our most gracious Queen's reign I am the first, and God grant I may be the last.' Dignified in a black satin doublet, he refused a blindfold and died bravely, his head being 'at one chop cut off'. His body was buried before the altar of the Chapel of St Peter ad Vincula within the Tower, between those of his cousins, Anne Boleyn and Katherine Howard. Courtiers at Whitehall reported that the Queen was very melancholy all that day.

16

'Less Agreeable Things to Think About'

On 19 April 1572, England and France concluded the Treaty of Blois, under the terms of which they undertook to provide each other with military and naval assistance against their common enemies. These included Spain and the Protestant states of the Netherlands, although Elizabeth was still sending surreptitious aid to the latter, if only to discountenance Philip and Alva. The treaty meant that England was no longer isolated in Europe, and it also put an end to the French support of Mary Stuart. Its signing was celebrated at Whitehall with a sumptuous banquet arranged by Leicester, who boasted that it was 'the greatest that was in my remembrance'.

That spring, fearing that Mary would appeal to Spain for help, Catherine de' Medici again discussed with Sir Thomas Smith the necessity for a royal marriage to seal the alliance.

'Jesu!' sighed the Queen Mother. 'Doth not your mistress see plainly that she will always be in such danger till she marry? If she marry into some good house, who shall dare attempt aught against her?'

Smith, nodding agreement, replied that if the Queen had but one child, 'Then all these bold and troublesome titles of the Scotch Queen or others, that make such gaping for her death, would be clean choked up.'

'But why stop at one child? Why not five or six?' queried Catherine, who had borne ten.

'Would to God she had one!' retorted Smith, with feeling.

'No', disputed the Queen Mother, 'two boys, lest the one should die, and three or four daughters to make alliances with us again, and other princes to strengthen the realm.'

'Why then,' smiled Smith, 'you think that M. le Duc should speed?'

Catherine laughed. 'I desire it infinitely', she said, 'and I trust to see three or four at the least of my race, which would make me indeed not to spare sea and land to see Her Majesty and them.'

In June, the Queen Mother sent to London, as ambassador extraordinary, the Duke of Montmorency, with powers to ratify the Treaty of Blois and formally offer Alençon as a husband for the Queen. Elizabeth was a gracious hostess, entertaining the embassy lavishly and investing the Duke with the Order of the Garter, but she was noncommittal about the marriage proposal, citing her reservations about Alençon's age and appearance. When Montmorency left, she promised that she would consider the matter and give King Charles her answer within a month.

She then told Burghley to instruct Walsingham to submit a full report on Alençon. The response was initially favourable, with the ambassador describing the Duke as wise, stalwart, not so light-minded as most Frenchmen, and in religion 'easily to be reduced to the knowledge of the truth'. His notorious pockmarks, which many people had hastened to reassure the Queen were not as bad as rumour had it, were 'no great disfigurement on his face because they are rather thick than great and deep'. While his beard covered some of them, those on the 'blunt end of his nose are much to be disliked', although 'When I saw him at my last audience, he seemed to me to grow daily more handsome.' Nevertheless, 'The great impediment I find is the contentment of the eye. The gentleman is void of any good favour, besides the blemish of the smallpox. Now, when I weigh the same with the delicacy of Her Majesty's eye, I hardly think that there will ever grow any liking.' Burghley feared as much, and gave little credence to Fénelon's claim that he knew a doctor who could cure the Duke's pockmarks.

Throughout the next weeks Elizabeth considered the matter, blowing hot and then cold, the chief sticking point being Alençon's extreme youth. What concerned her most was 'the absurdity, that in general opinion of the world might grow'. On a more practical level, she also wondered whether the Duke's pockmarks might be sufficient excuse for her to demand the return of Calais as a condition of the marriage.

Then, in July, Catherine de' Medici sent Alençon's good friend, Monsieur de la Mole, to England, in the hope that he would be able to persuade Elizabeth to accept the Duke. De la Mole was a handsome, personable young man whose gallant charm was calculated to soften the Queen's heart. 'It seemeth the Queen Mother is come nearer to the matter than I hoped for,' observed Burghley.

Elizabeth, whilst she was not impervious to de la Mole's charms, did not trust Catherine de' Medici and was suspicious that the French were trying to manoeuvre her into joining them in a war against Alva in the Netherlands, they being as nervous as she was about the presence of a huge Spanish army on their doorstep. Charles wanted to set up Alençon as Regent of the Netherlands, but while this might have been to England's advantage in some respects, the prospect of a French army in the Netherlands was hardly more comforting to Elizabeth, who regarded the House of Valois as unstable and unreliable, than the presence of a Spanish one.

Meanwhile, in July 1572, Elizabeth, in holiday mood, set off on an extended progress through the Thames Valley and the Midlands. After staying at Theobalds with Burghley, she arrived on the 25th at Gorhambury, the recently completed Hertfordshire mansion of Lord Keeper Bacon, who warmly welcomed her with his bluestocking wife, Anne Cooke, and two scholarly sons, Anthony and Francis. The Queen was unimpressed by the size of the building.

'You have made your house too little for Your Lordship,' she commented.

'No, Madam,' replied Bacon, 'but Your Highness has made me too big for the house.'

At Coventry, the Recorder told Elizabeth that the people had 'a greedy taste for Your Majesty'. In August, she spent a week at Warwick, arriving with the Countess in an open coach so that the crowds could see her. After the town's Recorder, Mr Aglionby, had falteringly delivered a speech of welcome, Elizabeth put him at his ease.

'Come hither, little Recorder,' she said. 'It was told me you would be afraid to look upon me or to speak boldly, but you were not so afraid of me as I was of you.'

Local lads and maidens gave a display of country dancing in the courtyard of Warwick Castle, which the Queen watched from her window; 'It seemed Her Majesty was much delighted and made very merry.' At supper in the castle one night she insisted that M. de la Mole sit with her. Afterwards he listened appreciatively as she entertained the company by playing on the spinet. They had several private talks, and one evening he escorted her to a spectacular firework display and mock water battle arranged by the Earl and Countess, in which the Earl of Oxford took part, 'whereat the Queen took great pleasure'.

Unfortunately, the occasion was marred by sparks from the squibs and fireballs setting fire to four houses in the town and completely destroying one nearby which belonged to a Mr Henry Cowper. Elizabeth personally expressed her sympathy to him and his wife and organised a collection for them amongst her courtiers, which raised £25.63p.

Despite de la Mole's efforts, Elizabeth was unwilling to commit herself to accepting Alençon. She told Fénelon of her doubts and insisted she could not make up her mind until she had seen the Duke in person. The ambassador told her that the King and Queen Mother would be pleased to arrange a meeting, but only if she convinced them that she really did mean to marry. She replied that she must meet the Duke and be certain that they could love one another before giving an answer. Burghley, who, plagued by gout, had accompanied the progress in a litter, now began to doubt whether the marriage would ever take place.

By 22 August, the Queen had arrived at Kenilworth to be entertained by Leicester, who had arranged all kinds of 'princely sports'. But on 3 September, while she was out hunting one day, a messenger arrived with a dispatch from Walsingham in Paris that caused her to burst into tears, cancel all further entertainments and send de la Mole back to France. A Spanish agent in London informed Alva that she had 'sent all her musicians and minstrels home, and there are no more of the dances, farces and entertainments with which they have been amusing themselves lately, as they have some less agreeable things to think about'.

The events which took place in France from 24 August 1572 almost wrecked the Anglo-French alliance. On the occasion of the marriage of King Charles's sister, Marguerite de Valois, to the Protestant Henry, King of Navarre, the zealously Catholic Guise party, backed by Catherine de' Medici, tried to murder Admiral de Coligny, the Huguenot leader, who had incurred the Queen Mother's jealousy through his increasing influence over the King. The attempt failed, but it provoked riots and panic in Paris. On 24 August, St Bartholemew's Eve, Catherine, reluctantly backed by the King, gave the order for the Huguenots to be cleared from the capital. A bloodbath ensued, since the Catholics rose and slaughtered every Huguenot they could lay hands on, to the number of 3-4000. During the next four days, similar orgies of killing erupted in the provinces, bringing the total number of dead to around 10,000.

King Philip, hearing the news, in the privacy of his bedchamber danced for joy, and Mary Stuart stayed up all night celebrating, while the Pope expressed his satisfaction at the annihilation of so many heretics. But the Massacre of St Bartholemew, as it became known, profoundly shocked Protestants throughout Europe and provoked an outcry against the French government and Catholics in general. Huguenot refugees who had fled to England brought with them dreadful tales of atrocities, of rivers of blood in the streets and streams choked with bodies. Burghley was so appalled that words failed him, and Walsingham, who had hidden during the killings and barely escaped with his life, was profoundly shaken.

However, despite her outrage, and her conviction that the blame for the massacre should be laid at the door of the Queen Mother, Elizabeth knew she could not seek to avenge the slaughtered Huguenots because she dared not compromise the French alliance, which was so necessary to her and England's security. All she could do was express her deep shock and anger, whilst secretly sending arms to the Huguenots and using her diplomatic influence to protect them.

When, on 5 September, the French ambassador, Fénelon, requested an audience in order to impart to Elizabeth the official explanation for the massacre, which he referred to as an 'accident', Elizabeth kept him waiting for three days at Oxford. When he was finally admitted to her presence at Woodstock, he found the Queen and the entire court dressed in deepest mourning and standing in reproachful silence as he advanced to kiss the royal hand. With a stern countenance, Elizabeth led him to a window seat and said she hoped that King Charles would clear his name in the eyes of the world. Lying through his teeth, Fénelon explained that King Charles had uncovered a deadly Protestant plot aimed against himself and his family, and had had to act quickly to avoid assassination. However, it was not His Majesty's intention to persecute the Huguenots, nor to revoke his edicts of religious toleration.

Such provocation, Elizabeth pointed out, did not excuse widespread violence. She had wept, she said, when she read reports of the killings. However, because he was a monarch and a gentleman, she was bound to accept Charles's explanation, and was comforted by Fénelon's assurance that nothing was more important to His Majesty than the alliance with England. She hoped that, in the weeks to come, Charles would do everything in his power to make amends for so much blood so horribly shed, if only for his own honour, now blemished in the eyes of the world.

She would not, however, discuss the matter of her marriage to Alençon, even though the Duke had had nothing to do with the massacre and had spoken out against it.

'How should we think His Majesty's brother a fit husband for us, or how should we think that love may grow, continue and increase, which ought to be betwixt the husband and wife?' she demanded of Walsingham. For a time, therefore, negotiations were left in abeyance, although the French were desperate to revive them. When the Queen Mother suggested that Elizabeth meet with Alençon on neutral ground, perhaps in Jersey, the Queen declined. She would reach no decision, she declared, until she was satisfied that King Charles meant to treat his Huguenot subjects well in future.

In October, relations began to thaw somewhat when Charles IX sent a special envoy, the Sieur de la Mauvissière, to London to ask Elizabeth, an excommunicate, to be godmother to his new baby daughter. After much procrastination she agreed, even though the baby was to be baptised into the Catholic faith. However, she deemed it too dangerous for Leicester, a well-known champion of the Protestant faith, to go to France to represent her, and sent the Earl of Worcester instead with the gift of a gold salver, which was regrettably looted from his ship by pirates on the Channel.

Not surprisingly, the Massacre of St Bartholemew had provoked cries for Mary's head from those of Elizabeth's subjects who saw it as part of a Catholic plot. Elizabeth, however, did not want to provoke Philip or the Pope by executing Mary herself, so on 10 September, on her instructions, her councillors secretly requested the Earl of Mar to demand Mary's return to Scotland and there try her for the murder of Darnley, a trial that would almost certainly lead to Mary's execution. Mar, however, would only agree if English soldiers were present at the scaffold, and since this would implicate Elizabeth in Mary's death, the Queen was obliged to abandon the idea.

By October, when the crisis had passed, it was clear that there would be no repercussions from the massacre in England. It was as well for Mary, since when the Earl of Mar died that autumn, he was replaced as regent by the Earl of Morton, one of Mary's most implacable enemies.

At this time, Burghley attempted to revive England's trade with Spain and the Low Countries, which had been under an embargo since 1569, to the loss of both sides. Despite the state of cold war which existed between England and Spain, the pragmatic Alva could see that the restoration of trade would bring benefits to everyone, as well as a lessening of tension, but Philip was unconvinced.

'Sometimes, Sire, it is necessary for Princes to do what displeases them,' Alva pointed out. Still Philip could not bring himself to treat with the English, and it was not until March 1573 that the embargo was lifted.

After thirteen years, the relationship between Elizabeth and Leicester was no longer the passionate affair it had once been, although there were still scandalous rumours. Elizabeth and Leicester behaved, in fact, like a long-married couple, sharing interests and offering each other affection and support. Their mutual devotion and loyalty had fostered deep bonds that would never be severed, although it was at last becoming clear even to Leicester himself that she would never marry him. For a man in his position, this was difficult to accept, because like all his class, he greatly desired to have heirs to whom he could bequeath his vast wealth and title. On the surface, however, he played the part of adoring suitor, along with Hatton and Oxford.

Hatton, who was prone to expressing his resentment in tears or sulks, deeply resented the favour shown by the Queen towards Oxford, because he had recently apparently been given cause to believe that he himself stood higher in her affections than anyone else. His enemies claimed he had 'more recourse to Her Majesty in her Privy Chamber than reason would suffer, if she were so virtuous and well-inclined as some noiseth her', and there was probably some truth in this.

In fact, matters may have gone further than either of them intended. There is possible evidence for this in a letter written to Hatton in October 1572 by his friend, Edward Dyer, the poet, in whom he seems to have confided. Dyer wrote: 'Though, in the beginning, when Her Majesty sought you (after her good manner), she did bear with rugged dealing of yours until she had what she fancied; yet now, after satiety and fullness, it will hurt rather than help you. Never seem deeply to condemn her frailties, but rather joyfully commend such things as should be in her, as though they were in her indeed.'

There has been much conjecture as to what Dyer was referring. Had Elizabeth at last set aside her scruples and surrendered her much-vaunted virginity? Or had she, which is more likely, gone so far as to obtain sexual satisfaction while remaining, technically, a virgin? If it was Hatton's body that had drawn her, and she had surrendered in some way to him, it seems that she had regretted it, and wished him to behave towards her as if she were still the Virgin Queen. It has been claimed that Hatton's letters to her are platonic and do not support such a theory, but, as we have seen, they are intensely passionate. However, he himself later swore to Sir John Harington that he had never had any carnal knowledge of the Queen.

At the end of the year, the Queen moved to Hampton Court for the Christmas season and Shrovetide; on Twelfth Night, Leicester gave her two glittering collars set with precious stones. Soon afterwards, however, she fell out with Burghley for reasons that are not clear. Leicester offered to intercede for him, and fortunately encountered the Queen in a forgiving mood. 'I assure you I found Her Majesty as well disposed as ever', the Earl wrote, 'and so I trust it shall always continue. God be thanked, her blasts be not the storms of other princes, though they be very sharp sometimes to those she loves best. Every man must render to her their due, and the most bounden the most of all. You and I come in that rank, and I am witness to your honest zeal to perform as much as man can. Hold, and you can never fail.'

In May 1573, Shrewsbury's son reported to his father:

My Lord of Leicester is very much with Her Majesty, and she shows the same great good affection to him that she was wont. Of late, he has endeavoured to please her more than heretofore. There are two sisters now in the court that are very far in love with him, as they have been long: my Lady Sheffield and Frances Howard.

They (of like striving who shall love him better) are at great wars together and the Queen thinketh not well of them, and not the better of him. By this means, there are spies over him.

The indications are that Leicester and Douglas, Lady Sheffield had been romantically involved for months, if not years, but had kept their love secret for fear of incurring the Queen's wrath.

Lady Sheffield was now twenty-five and acclaimed a great beauty. She was the daughter of the recently dead William, Lord Howard of Effingham, the Queen's great-uncle and councillor, and had been married, whilst still very young, to Lord Sheffield, who had died in 1568, leaving Douglas a widow at twenty. Shortly afterwards, she had been appointed a Lady of the Bedchamber and had come to court, and some time after that had attracted Leicester's attention. It is possible that resentment of Hatton's influence with the Queen led Leicester to begin the affair.

The court gossips later alleged that it had even begun in Sheffield's lifetime, and had become adulterous during a visit by Leicester to Belvoir Castle. It was said that Sheffield had found a letter which incontrovertibly compromised the couple, but that, when he had ridden to London to petition Parliament for a divorce, Leicester had had him poisoned. No other evidence corroborates this tale, and as Leicester was invariably accused by his enemies of poisoning those about him, even such a friend as Throckmorton, little credence can be given to it.

In time, Douglas had indeed become Leicester's mistress, and was soon demanding marriage, though he repeatedly made it clear to her that his relationship with the Queen precluded such a commitment. In a letter to an unknown lady, whom internal evidence strongly suggests was Douglas, he explained his position and offered her two alternatives: she could either remain his mistress, or he would help her to find a suitable husband. Needless to say, neither was acceptable to the lady, even though she had been assured of his continuing affection: 'I have, as you know, long both liked and loved you. Albeit I have been and yet am a man frail, yet am I not void of conscience towards God, nor honest meaning toward my friend, and having made special choice of you to be one of the dearest to me, so much the more care must I have to discharge the office due to you.'

By the spring of 1573, people had begun to gossip about the affair, and rumour had it that in 1571 or 1572, Douglas had become pregnant by Leicester, and had given birth secretly at Dudley Castle, the home of her sister, who was married to Leicester's cousin, Edward, Lord Dudley. The baby was a girl, who died before she could be baptised. Douglas would later deny the rumours, but many believed them.

It was now becoming almost impossible to keep the liaison secret, and Douglas realised that her reputation would be ruined if the details were made public. She therefore put increased pressure upon Leicester to marry her, and may even have threatened to tell the Queen everything if he did not. Already, Elizabeth was becoming suspicious, although she was only aware as yet that there was rivalry between Douglas and another of her sisters, Frances, for Leicester's attentions.

In May, Leicester agreed that he and Douglas would marry secretly. The ceremony took place at a house at Esher, with at least three witnesses present. The bride was given away by one of Leicester's friends, and married with a diamond ring given to Leicester by the Earl of Pembroke. Although the validity of the marriage ceremony was later disputed and the parties behaved as if they were free agents, the evidence strongly suggests that it was entirely legal.

After his marriage, Leicester divided his time between the two women in his life, continuing as before at court with Elizabeth, whose suspicions seem to have been allayed, and secretly living with Douglas at Esher and Leicester House when he was away from court. He was well aware that his enemies would have seized any chance to discredit him, and in this case, he knew they could ruin him. Thus, when Douglas insisted that her servants serve her as a countess, he forbade it, in case word of it leaked out.

In July 1573, when Charles IX announced that his Huguenot subjects were free to follow their consciences with regard to religion, it seemed that there might be an end to religious strife in France. Following on from this, the French made new overtures to Elizabeth about the Alençon marriage, the Queen Mother claiming that peace had been made mainly for her sake. In fact, Alençon had urged his brother to it.

Since relations between England and Spain had improved, King Charles and the Queen Mother feared that Elizabeth might abandon them, and offered to allow Alençon to come to England without conditions. Perversely, Elizabeth's own enthusiasm had cooled, and she insisted that the Duke would have to promise not to take offence if she rejected him. Thus it went on for several months, while the French besought her for an answer and Elizabeth played for time.

On 7 September, Elizabeth was forty, rather too old to be contemplating marriage and motherhood in Tudor times. To mark the event, Leicester gave her a fan of white feathers with a handle of gold engraved with his emblem of the bear and hers of the lion.

In December that year Walsingham, who had been recalled from France, was appointed Chief Secretary of State in place of Burghley. His main responsibility was to be foreign affairs, and in this capacity he would concentrate his energies on bringing 'the bosom serpent' Mary, Queen of Scots to justice. He would also, at his own expense, progressively set up a superbly efficient and powerful network of spies, the best in Europe, that would enable him efficiently to counteract Catholic plots and preserve the Queen from harm.

By this time, Elizabeth was so enshrined in the affections of her subjects that the common purpose of the vast majority of them was her preservation. They realised that she was the sole bulwark that stood between England and its enemies, and their love for her was such that, when a Doncaster man dared slander her, the magistrates had to intervene to prevent him from being torn apart by the mob.

In Council, Walsingham was to enjoy the support of Leicester, who was now recognised as the leader of radical English Protestants, but he often clashed with the Queen, who at times fiercely resented his dictatorial manner and dogmatic views, although she admired his shrewdness and respected his advice — even if it was not always welcome. He was never afraid to speak his mind to her and she allowed him the freedom to criticise her, knowing that he had her interests at heart.

In March 1574, it was at last agreed that the Queen and Alençon should meet near Dover, but before this could come to pass, the Duke was implicated with Henry of Navarre in a series of intrigues against his brother, and was placed under house arrest at St Germain. The French continued to urge the marriage, to which Elizabeth responded by saying she thought it not unreasonable of her to expect that her husband should be a free man.

Then, on 30 May 1574, Charles IX died, probably of the congenital syphilis which was the scourge of the Valois. 'Well could he be spared, considering his bloody disposition,' commented the Queen. Charles was succeeded by his brother Anjou, who, hastily summoned from Poland, ascended the French throne as Henry III. He was known to be a fanatical, priest-ridden Catholic who was under the domination of the Guise party, and in England fears were expressed that he would end religious toleration in France and might even abandon any alliance with Elizabeth.

In response England moved closer to Spain, and diplomatic relations were restored in July when a new ambassador, Bernardino de Mendoza, arrived in London to be civilly received by the Queen. In August, the Treaty of Bristol brought about a cautious peace between England and Spain.

By this time, it had become evident that Henry III intended to follow the moderate policies of the Queen Mother, which came as a relief to the Protestant community in France. However, relations between Henry and Elizabeth were to remain cool, and when, later that year, she sent Lord North as ambassador to France, he was discourteously received by the King. He was also forced to watch with the Queen Mother as her two female dwarfs were dressed up to resemble Elizabeth; Catherine then asked Alençon, now released from confinement but kept under his mother's eye, what he thought of his intended. North was mortified, and when a furious Elizabeth made plain her displeasure, Catherine apologised, with the excuse that North's French was insufficient for him to have properly understood her joke, although no insult had been intended.

Shortly afterwards news reached England that Alençon had escaped his mother's surveillance and was now wandering aimlessly around Europe, a prey for any ill-intentioned princes. Elizabeth wasted no time in informing Catherine de' Medici that she would not marry the Duke in these circumstances.

The new Spanish ambassador, Mendoza, was as much of a troublemaker as his predecessors had been, and in September 1574 confidently reported that Elizabeth had borne Leicester a daughter who had been 'kept hidden, although there are bishops to witness'.

In fact, Mendoza may have been confused by court gossip about another birth, for a month earlier, on 7 August, Douglas Sheffield had borne Leicester a son, Robert, the Earl of Warwick and Sir Henry Lee standing as sponsors at the christening. Although the birth was not kept secret, and the Queen must have heard of it, there is no record of her expressing her displeasure. As far as she was concerned, the child was a bastard: had she known that its parents were married, her reaction might well have been stronger. In the circumstances, she presumably accepted that even the best of men could succumb to temptation, especially when she herself kept them at arm's length. Leicester was in a difficult position. He had long desired a son, but now that he had one he dared not acknowledge him as his heir, and would always refer to Robert as his 'base son' or 'the badge of my sin'.

In April, Elizabeth had sent troops to Edinburgh, where they had successfully crushed an attempt by Mary's supporters to take control of the castle and thereby put paid for ever to Mary's hopes of restoration. However, the presence of the Queen of Scots in England could only be prejudicial to the recent entente with Spain, and in 1574 Elizabeth tried to persuade the new regent of Scotland, Morton, to request Mary's return to Scotland to be tried for Darnley's murder. But even he, an

inveterate enemy of Mary, refused, and Elizabeth had to resign herself
to keeping Mary a prisoner in England.

By now, Scotland having abandoned her, Mary's sole ambition was to
ascend the throne of England. She saw herself as a champion of the
Catholic faith, overthrowing the heretic Elizabeth and restoring the true
religion. It was her mission in life, a crusade she would pursue to the
death. She had no scruples about what she was doing, and little grasp of
reality. 'I will not leave my prison save as Queen of England,' she once
declared, and events proved that she meant it.

Shrewsbury was so careful a guardian that escape was out of the
question, 'unless she could transform herself into a flea or a mouse'.
What she did manage to do, with the help of her attendants and friends
outside, was engage in a clandestine correspondence, with numerous
letters in cipher being smuggled out to the Pope, King Philip and others.
Thus she not only plotted ceaselessly against her cousin, but was able to
keep up with events outside her prison. She also managed to reward her
supporters and pay bribes with £12,000 she had saved from the income
from her dower lands in France. Elizabeth, when she heard of it, cut her
allowance from £52 to £30 per week in 1575.

Mary was now thirty-two and had been a prisoner for six years. She
spent her days reading, praying, conversing with her ladies, writing
letters, playing with her numerous pets, and doing beautiful embroidery.
From time to time she would send Elizabeth little gifts, such as a crimson
satin petticoat she had embroidered herself, or sweetmeats, or a wig. The
Council suspected her motives and feared that the gifts might be
poisoned, but Elizabeth accepted them nevertheless. They did not,
however, soften her attitude towards Mary, for Walsingham's agents had
intercepted enough of Mary's letters for Elizabeth to know that she was
only waiting for the day when she could supplant her cousin.

During 1574, Elizabeth had cause to believe that Darnley's mother, the
Countess of Lennox, had become reconciled to Mary. The Countess
denied it, but Elizabeth did not believe her and, hearing that the
Countess was travelling north, sent a message commanding her not to
attempt to visit her daughter-in-law.

Lady Lennox, accompanied by her younger son, Charles Stewart,
went instead to stay at Rufford Abbey near Chatsworth, where she was
visited by Bess of Hardwick, Shrewsbury's wife, with her young
daughter from an earlier marriage, Elizabeth Cavendish. With the
connivance of both matriarchs, the young couple were thrown together.
Then Charles fell ill, and tradition has it that Elizabeth Cavendish tended
him. Love flowered, and within a month the pair were married.

Since Charles was her cousin and subject, the Queen had every right to be consulted about his choice of bride, and when she discovered what had happened she exploded with rage and summoned both mothers to London, where they were sent to prison for a time as punishment for their presumption.

The following year, Elizabeth bore a daughter, Arbella Stewart. Both grandmothers would have preferred a son to further their ambitions, but it was not to be, for Charles died of tuberculosis in 1576 and Elizabeth followed him to the grave in 1582. But in Arbella, who was brought up by Lady Shrewsbury at Hardwick Hall, the Queen saw a new dynastic threat to her crown.

Nor was she the only threat, for from 1574 onwards highly-trained, committed, and often militant Catholic priests from the Jesuit seminaries in Europe began arriving in England to work undercover for the restoration of the old faith. Most of them hailed from the college at Douai in France, founded by a Catholic exile, the future Cardinal William Allen, in 1568, under the patronage of King Philip and the Pope. Here, priests were trained especially for the English mission, and in time, similar colleges were opened at Rome, Valladolid and Seville.

Many of these seminary priests were deeply devout and simply saw their task as providing spiritual comfort for beleaguered English Catholics, who were thus encouraged to remain true to their faith. Other priests undoubtedly did their best to undermine the English Church and state. The government did not distinguish between the two types, regarding all as traitors who deserved the severest punishments, and before long the word 'seminarist' was synonymous to all true Englishmen with 'conspirator' or 'traitor'.

By 1580, there were a hundred seminary priests in England, and their work had led to a noticeable increase in recusancy, a trend that justifiably alarmed the government. Even by the mid-1570s, there was talk in the seminaries of 'the Enterprise of England', in which King Philip would invade England and overthrow that 'she-devil' Elizabeth, replacing her with Mary Stuart, to whose cause most seminarists were committed. As usual, such talk did not take into account the realities of the political situation, but it was widespread enough for the English government to take it seriously, and many priests who were caught suffered torture to make them reveal what they knew, and often faced the terrible death reserved for traitors.

Given the activities of the seminarists, the ambitions of Mary Stuart, the hostility of King Philip and the Pope, the effects of the Bull of Excommunication, and her lack of an heir, Elizabeth could not feel secure on her throne. That she would remain there is a tribute to her political skill and tenacity, and the loyalty and abilities of her advisers.

17

'Princely Pleasures'

In January 1575, the leaders of the Protestant states of the Netherlands, in gratitude for her constant support, asked Elizabeth to accept the crown of Holland and Zeeland. Personally, she disliked the Dutch Protestants, and had disapproved of their hitherto republican sentiments: her help had been given purely with the intention of keeping Alva's army occupied. But although it was both flattering and tempting to be offered a crown, the Queen found herself confronting once again the same principles that had stayed her hand against Mary Stuart: Philip was an anointed king, the hereditary ruler of the Netherlands, and divinely appointed to rule there. If Elizabeth accepted the sovereignty, she would be supporting the rebels in the overthrow of a fellow monarch, even if she would be relieved to see the back of the Spanish presence in the Netherlands. It was an impossible dilemma, and she could not reach a decision. The eventual result was that the Dutch took offence at her prevarication and there was bitter criticism from her own subjects.

Nevertheless, by 1575 Elizabeth had cleared most of her debts, and with the restoration of trade with the Low Countries, England entered a period of economic prosperity. Friendlier relations with Spain had been established, and in April 1575, Henry III ended a year of tension when he requested a renewal of the Treaty of Blois, to which Elizabeth responded by honouring him with the Order of the Garter. Finally, Walsingham's spies had at last infiltrated Mary Stuart's household. For a while, it appeared that international affairs had stabilised.

On 17 May 1575, Matthew Parker, Elizabeth 's first and most tolerant Archbishop of Canterbury, died. In considering his replacement, Burghley made one of the greatest blunders of his career by nominating Edmund Grindal. Grindal turned out to be an unacceptably strict Puritan whose 'prophesyings' were, in the opinion of the Queen, seditious and subversive. His faults were not immediately apparent, but would become a matter of concern during the next two years.

Rather than strive in vain to keep the restless Earl of Oxford at court, Elizabeth gave her blessing in 1575 to him travelling abroad. He went first to Italy, where he squandered much of his inheritance. When he returned, he presented the Queen with a pair of embroidered gloves, but he would not return to court until she gave him an assurance that his wife would not be there. This was arranged, and the dissolute Earl was soon back in favour – so much so, that shortly afterwards the gossips were claiming that he and the Queen were lovers. In later years, it would even be said – without the slightest foundation – that the Earl of Southampton, who was born at this time, was their bastard child.

Another royal favourite was also causing a stir. In the spring of 1575, Christopher Hatton expressed a desire to acquire Ely Place in Holborn, the London residence of the bishops of Ely which had pleasant gardens. Elizabeth, pleased that Hatton would have a fine town house in which to entertain her, also saw this as a means of discountenancing its proprietor, Richard Cox, Bishop of Ely, with whom she had often clashed over religion. Cox was understandably reluctant to lease Ely Place to Hatton, resenting the appropriation by court 'harpies and wolves' of Church property, but the Queen was determined he should do so. She therefore instructed Lord North to write threatening the Bishop with interrogation by the Council for exploiting Church lands, an offence that could cost him his see and even lead to his being defrocked. Cox immediately yielded to the Queen's 'known clemency', and Ely Place passed to Hatton.

In the summer of 1575, the Queen went on her most famous progress of all, which culminated in the now legendary 'princely pleasures' at Kenilworth, where her host, Leicester, provided the most extravagant and costly entertainments of the reign over a period of ten days. Several eyewitness accounts survive, notably those by George Gascoigne, the playwright, and Robert Laneham, Leicester's gentleman-usher.

On this, her third visit to the castle, the Queen arrived on Saturday, 9 July, Leicester having ridden out to greet her seven miles away at Long Itchington, where he had entertained her to dinner in a sumptuous pavilion erected specially for the purpose. At eight o'clock in the evening, after an afternoon's hunting and a frantic search for some suitable ale for the Queen to drink on this very hot day, he escorted her up to the castle, which was illuminated by thousands of torches and candles. The pillars of the drawbridge were decorated with cornucopias of fruit and vines, to symbolise earthly bounty. On some were hung musical instruments, and on others armour, to remind the Queen that Leicester was ready to lay down his life for her.

When Elizabeth came to the outer gatehouse, her attention was focused on the lake, where there had just appeared 'a floating island, bright blazing with torches, on which were clad in silks the Lady of the Lake and two nymphs waiting on her, who made a speech to the Queen of the antiquity and owners of the castle', linking its history to the Arthurian legends and offering the castle to the Queen, who was heard to comment that she was under the impression that it was hers already.

Musicians played, and at the castle gate, a sybil clad in a white silk robe recited verses of welcome and prophesied that the Queen would enjoy long life, peace and prosperity. She was joined by a tall Oxford scholar dressed as 'Hercules the Porter', who performed a comic routine and affected to be put out by the noise and stamping made by the Queen's retinue. He was then prevailed upon to present to Her Majesty the keys to the castle. When she entered the Base Court to the sound of trumpets, she was greeted by gentlemen in the guise of King Arthur's knights, and as she was escorted to her apartments in the new tower called Leicester's Building, with its beautiful oriel windows, guns sounded a salute and fireworks exploded in the sky; the noise was heard twenty miles away. Fortunately, the Italian expert in pyrotechnics who had been hired for the occasion was persuaded not to carry out his original plan to shoot live dogs and cats into the air.

Leicester had made further improvements to Kenilworth since Elizabeth had last visited, and it was now one of the 'wonder houses' of the age, restored, not in Renaissance style like most Elizabethan houses, but in a medieval style in keeping with its twelfth-century structure. It had, wrote Laneham, 'every room so spacious, so well lighted and so high-roofed within, so glittering of glass a-nights by continual candle-fire and torchlight'. On the lake was a fountain with statues of naked nymphs that Laneham thought would 'inflame any mind after too long looking'. To the west was an extensive deer park and hunting chase. Leicester proudly wrote to Burghley, 'I assure you, I think Her Majesty never came to a place in her life she liked better or commended more, her own lodgings specially.'

It is said that, when the Queen pointed out to Leicester that she could not see the formal garden from her windows, he ordered a similar garden to be laid out below them overnight, engaging an army of workmen for the purpose. When Elizabeth looked out the next morning, there, to her astonishment and pleasure, was the new garden. Both gardens have gone now, as has most of the castle: only a ruin stands to bear mute witness to the former glories of Kenilworth.

On Sunday morning the Queen attended the parish church, and after dinner in John of Gaunt's magnificent great hall, was entertained by 'excellent music of sundry sweet instruments' and dancing. A second firework display took place that evening, continuing until midnight.

It was very hot the next day, and Elizabeth rested in her room, emerging late in the afternoon to go hunting. Four hours later, returning in a torchlit procession, she was surprised to encounter a 'wild man' who turned out to be George Gascoigne, who had been commissioned by Leicester to write the speeches and entertainments. On this occasion, Gascoigne was dressed in a costume of moss green with ivy leaves attached, and was accompanied by a player representing 'Echo'; the two of them engaged in a rhyming dialogue, and then the 'wild man' submitted to the Queen's authority by breaking a branch over his knee. Unfortunately, one half ricocheted and barely missed the head of the Queen's horse, causing it to rear in terror. But Elizabeth expertly calmed it.

'No hurt! No hurt!' she cried, as Gascoigne quaked with relief.

She was out hunting again on Tuesday, 12 July, and two days later attended a bear-baiting in the inner court of the castle, featuring thirteen bears against some small mastiffs. There were fireworks again that night, with some burning below the surface of the lake, and an Italian acrobat who was so agile that it seemed, according to Laneham, that his spine was made of lute-strings.

Bad weather put a stop to outdoor entertainment during the next two days, but on Sunday the 17th it was fine again, and after church the Queen was guest of honour at a country wedding feast or bride-ale in the castle courtyard. The rustic bridegroom, who had broken his leg playing football, arrived limping and wearing a tawny doublet of his father's, in the company of sixteen other men, all of whom had a try at tossing the quintain. This was followed by Morris dancing, after which spice cakes were served while the bride-cup, from which the newly-weds' health would be drunk, was borne by someone who appeared to be the local village idiot. Then came the bride, past her prime at thirty, ugly and foul-smelling, attended by a dozen bridesmaids. She was so puffed up at the prospect of dancing before the Queen that she gave herself airs and carried herself as if she were as pretty as her bridesmaids. After the dancing, the guests sat down to watch a pageant performed in the open air by a company of players from Coventry. The Queen, for whom such occasions as this were a novelty, watched the proceedings from her window, and requested that the pageant be performed again two days hence.

That evening, she graced an 'ambrosial banquet' with her presence, the table being laid with a thousand pieces of glass and silver and three hundred dishes being served by two hundred gentlemen. She only picked at her food, although she enjoyed the masque that was presented afterwards.

On Monday the 18th she knighted five gentlemen, including Burghley's son Thomas, and touched nine scrofulous persons for the King's Evil. It was very hot again, and she was obliged to keep to her chamber until five in the afternoon, when she went hunting. A water pageant was staged upon her return, for which had been built an eighteen-foot-long model of a mermaid and a twenty-four-foot-long dolphin, in which was concealed a consort of musicians and a singer representing the god Arion. The Lady of the Lake made another appearance, in company with the sea-god Triton and a villainous knight, Sir Bruce sans Pitee.

The Coventry pageant was repeated on the Tuesday, and on Wednesday, 20 July was to come the climax of the festivities, a richly-costumed mythological masque which Leicester had commissioned from George Gascoigne at 'incredible cost'. The story told how two goddesses, the virgin huntress, Diana, and the goddess of marriage, Juno, each tried to persuade a nymph, Zabeta – a near-anagram of the Queen's name – to follow their example. It ended with Juno warning Zabeta that she should not heed Diana, but should find more reason to marry like Juno. The underlying message was that Elizabeth should do likewise, and it was intended that in due course the company were to be left in no doubt as to whom she should marry. No one, of course, knew about Douglas Sheffield, who was not present during the royal visit, and it seems that, by this time, Leicester had tired of her and regarded himself as not legally bound in marriage.

Unfortunately for Leicester, it rained on that Wednesday, and, as the masque in which his message was to be delivered was to have been staged in a pavilion three miles away, it had to be abandoned, for the Queen remained indoors. The Earl was deeply disappointed: Elizabeth was due to leave on the following day, and he asked Gascoigne to write some farewell verses with a similar message.

On Thursday the 19th Elizabeth left Kenilworth, her courtiers declaring that they had never known anything to equal their experiences there. As she rode away, Gascoigne, in the guise of Sylvanus, sprang from a holly bush and walked and then ran beside her, declaiming his hastily composed doggerel, in which he described the heavy rain as the tears of the gods, weeping at her departure, and begged her to stay. When Elizabeth pulled up her palfrey, he cried breathlessly that she did not need to slow her pace, as he would run with her for twenty miles if need be to complete his tale. So the Queen rode away; Gascoigne, of course, could not keep up with her, and consequently, she never heard his verses.

Leicester and his household had worked very hard to ensure that the programme ran smoothly, and there was no doubt that the visit had been a great success and would never be forgotten by the courtiers or local people. Nor would Leicester's coffers ever recover from the huge expenditure. However, the purpose of it all, which was to convince the Queen that she should marry him, had been defeated by, of all things, the weather, and he knew that such a chance would never come again. It is no coincidence that, after Kenilworth, he began to seek comfort elsewhere.

From Kenilworth, the Queen, accompanied by Leicester and his talented young nephew, Philip Sidney, moved to the Earl of Essex's house at Chartley; the Earl was away in Ireland, but Elizabeth was made welcome by the Countess, who was her cousin, Lettice Knollys. Lettice had been a guest at Kenilworth, and although several courtiers guessed that she and Leicester were harbouring a secret passion for each other, the Queen remained oblivious to it.

After the progress, Philip Sidney came to court, and was soon afterwards appointed Standard Bearer to the Queen. Although he was the godson of Philip of Spain, he had been brought up in the Protestant faith and educated at Oxford, after which he had travelled in Europe, where he met and impressed many statesmen and scholars with his erudition, sense of chivalry and obvious ability. The Massacre of St Bartholemew had prompted him to call for the forming of a Protestant league of princes to counteract Catholic aggression, and in this, he was supported by his uncle, Leicester. Although Elizabeth was wary of Sidney's militant views, she began in 1575 to send him on routine diplomatic errands.

On 13 August, Elizabeth arrived in Worcester, her visit being intended to boost the declining woollen-cloth industry. Frantic preparations had been made on the orders of the city fathers: the gates were painted grey, with the arms of England mounted on them, and all the houses on the royal route had been lime-washed.

Ignoring the rain, Elizabeth came riding into the city and graciously accepted the mandatory silver-gilt cup. Soaking wet, she expressed delight at the laudatory verses of welcome and only when they were finished did she call for a cloak and hat. She then toured the cathedral, where her uncle, Arthur Tudor, Prince of Wales, lay entombed, and where she was entertained by a consort of cornets, sackbuts and voices. Afterwards, she went to her lodging in the bishop's palace. On Sunday, as the crowds roared themselves hoarse, she rode in an open coach to morning service in the cathedral, repeatedly calling, 'I thank you! I thank you all!' When she left the city two days later to dine with her cofferer nearby, she was escorted by local dignitaries to its boundaries. When the time came to say farewell, they made to dismount and kneel in the mud, but Elizabeth raised her hand, saying, 'I pray you, keep your horses and do not alight.' On her return to Worcester that evening, it was pouring again, but she remained on horseback, greeting the people with 'cheerful, princely countenance' and conversing with them.

After leaving Worcester, the Queen stayed for a few days with Sir Henry Lee at Woodstock, where she saw a play depicting the triumph of patriotism over love, before returning home.

By the end of 1575, Leicester had tired of Douglas Howard and was in hot pursuit of the Queen's cousin, Lettice Knollys, daughter of his friend and fellow councillor, Sir Francis Knollys, by Katherine Carey, and wife of Walter Devereux, Earl of Essex. Leicester and Lettice had enjoyed a brief flirtation in 1565, and if they thought that this time their relationship was a secret, they were much mistaken, for a Spanish agent reported in December: 'As the thing is publicly talked of in the streets, there is no objection to my writing openly about the great enmity that exists between the Earl of Leicester and the Earl of Essex in consequence, it is said, of the fact that, while Essex was in Ireland, his wife had two children by Leicester. Great discord is expected.'

Lettice was thirty-five and her portrait at Longleat, painted in 1585, bears witness to her sloe-eyed, seductive beauty. She had been married at twenty to Walter Devereux, then Earl of Hereford, and had lived thereafter mainly at Chartley, but although the couple had five children, it seems they were incompatible.

Essex headed a military expedition to Ireland in 1573, where he earned great renown for his courage and ruthlessness. He returned to England in November 1575, and it could not have been long before he heard the rumours about his wife and Leicester. Although many of them – including that reported by the Spaniard, which is the only source for the allegation that Lettice had borne Leicester two children – were probably wildly inaccurate, there can be little doubt that some were based on truth. For a knight to seduce the wife of another knight was a gross breach of the code of chivalry, and it was probably this that influenced Essex's decision to alter his will to the effect that, if he died while they were still young, his children were to be brought up under the guardianship of the Earl of Huntingdon, his most influential relation, whose wife was Leicester's sister. According to Sir Henry Sidney, who could not 'brook' the man, Essex was set to become the violent enemy of Leicester.

In July 1576, the Earl of Essex returned to duty in Ireland. His marriage was foundering and he had quarrelled with Leicester over Lettice. Two months later, when he and several other people fell ill with dysentery in Dublin Castle, he concluded that he had been poisoned with 'some evil' in his drink. Neither he nor anyone else at the time suggested that Leicester was responsible. After Essex died on 22 September, Sir Henry Sidney, the Lord Deputy of Ireland, ordered an immediate post-mortem, but, as he reported in detail to the Council, there was no evidence of foul play, nor did the doctors who had attended Essex believe that he had died of anything other than natural causes.

Essex was succeeded in his title by his nine-year-old son, Robert Devereux. The dying Earl had sent a message to the Queen hoping 'it will please Your Majesty to be as a mother to my children', especially his son, who would now be dependent on her. Elizabeth cancelled the debts the boy had inherited and gave his wardship to Lord Burghley, who had brought Robert up in his own household since the age of six. The young Essex was presented to the Queen that year at Cecil House in London. His mother, Lettice, had retired to her father's house near Oxford, her other children having, according to her husband's last wishes, been sent to live with the Earl and Countess of Huntingdon at Ashby-de-la-Zouche in Leicestershire.

Another boy who was much in Elizabeth's thoughts at this time was her fifteen-year-old godson, John Harington. His parents had served her well: Sir John Harington had been one of her father's courtiers and had later acted as an intermediary between Elizabeth and Admiral Thomas Seymour. In 1554, after Wyatt's rebellion, when Elizabeth was sent to the Tower, he and his wife, Isabella Markham, were both imprisoned on suspicion of being in league with her. Their loyalty was rewarded when Elizabeth came to the throne: Isabella was appointed a lady in waiting, and in 1561 the Queen stood godmother to the Haringtons' eldest son.

Young John was a bright, intelligent and creative boy, with a dry sense of humour that came to appeal to Elizabeth. Her first surviving letter to him dates from 1576, when he was still a schoolboy at Eton College. Obviously she thought it was time he started taking an interest in public affairs, for she enclosed a copy of her closing speech to Parliament, in which she had expressed her preference for the single life. She wrote:

> Boy Jack, I have made a clerk write fair my poor words for thine use, as it cannot be such striplings have entrance into Parliament assembly as yet. Ponder them in thy hours of leisure, and play with them till they enter thy understanding; so shall thou hereafter, perchance, find some good fruits hereof when thy godmother is out of remembrance. And I do this because thy father was ready to serve and love us in trouble and thrall.

Later on, Harington came to court, and his letters and published writings would become some of the richest sources of information about the Queen's later years.

During the past months, Elizabeth's relations with Archbishop Grindal had rapidly deteriorated. In the autumn of 1576, she summoned him before her and commanded him to ensure that all Puritan forms of worship were suppressed. Grindal, a Puritan himself, could not in his conscience obey her, and in the weeks that followed prepared a written defence of his objections.

In December he gave it to Leicester to submit to the Queen, but Elizabeth was most displeased by it. She barred the Archbishop from court, and all communication between them was conducted through Leicester. When the Earl, who was sympathetic towards the Archbishop's viewpoint, tried to suggest a compromise, neither Elizabeth nor Grindal would give way. Thus a deadlock was reached, which lasted until the following spring.

In May 1577, the Queen asked Archbishop Grindal one final time if he would prohibit Puritan practices within the Church. He refused, and begged to remind Her Majesty that she too was mortal and would have to answer for her actions at God's judgement seat. He declared that he would rather 'offend an earthly majesty than the heavenly majesty of God'. Mortified at his continuing defiance, Elizabeth placed the Archbishop under house arrest at Lambeth Palace, thus effectively preventing him from exercising his authority as Primate of England. She also ordered Burghley to command her bishops, in her name, to suppress all forms of Puritan worship.

In taking such a stand, the Queen was demonstrating that it was she, the Supreme Governor, and not the Archbishop, who was the ultimate authority in the Anglican Church. Even so, her councillors thought she was unfair to Grindal, and spoke up in his defence, urging her to treat him with greater moderation. If the Archbishop persisted in his stubborn attitude, she raged, he must be deprived of his See. In the event, thanks to the intercession of Leicester and others, he remained in office, but the Queen never again permitted him to carry out any of his archiepiscopal duties. For the next five years, therefore, the Church of England was effectively without a spiritual leader, and Elizabeth gave orders directly to her bishops. Her actions rebounded against her in the long run, however, for they only served to weaken the Church and give impetus to the Puritan movement.

Although Sir Christopher Hatton's enemies were of the opinion that his chief talents lay in dancing and jousting, Elizabeth recognised that he had real abilities that could be put to good use. He also shared her contempt for Puritanism and, anticipating that he would back her in her stand against Grindal's supporters, she knighted him, made him Vice-Chamberlain of her household, and appointed him to her Council on 11 November 1577.

In February 1576, Philip II had sent an envoy, the Sieur de Champigny, to Elizabeth to ask her, quite candidly, if she intended to give aid to his Protestant rebels in future. After keeping the envoy waiting for two weeks, she evaded giving him an answer, and complained instead that Philip had not written to her, which she found most hurtful. She added that Spain's attempt to establish absolute dominion in the Low Countries was intolerable to her; her beloved father would not have tolerated it, and she, though a woman, 'would know how to look to it'. However – and here she had smiled mischievously – she had a great personal liking for King Philip. Poor de Champigny withdrew in a state of bewildered perplexity.

Elizabeth was still keeping up the pretence that she was contemplating marrying the Duke of Alençon, if only to give Philip pause for thought, but by the spring of 1576, even she had to concede that the project was moribund. 'No one thing hath procured her so much hatred abroad as these wooing matters,' observed an exasperated Walsingham.

Elizabeth had by then decided to turn down the sovereignty of the Netherlands. When, in the summer, Spanish troops there mutinied and rioted over non-payment of their wages, their behaviour caused Dutch Catholics and Protestants to unite against a common enemy under the leadership of William of Orange. Later in the year, the rebels agreed at Ghent that they should elect their own assembly and fight for independence. Philip reacted angrily to this rebellion and appointed a new Regent, his half brother Don John of Austria, the most renowned soldier in Europe, who had commanded his forces at a recent naval victory over the Turks at Lepanto.

Elizabeth, whilst remaining outwardly friendly towards Philip, was still sending money to the rebels, while Leicester, possibly without her knowledge, had offered to support William of Orange with an English army if need be. The Dutch rebels, meanwhile, were urging that England and the Netherlands should combine their military forces to form a Protestant army with Elizabeth as its leader. The Queen rejected this proposal because she did not want to finance such a costly venture. She had already given the Dutch £20,000, and loaned them another £106,000 – almost half her annual income. Furthermore, she feared that, if she joined them in this war, she would risk losing her throne.

Elizabeth had offered to act as mediator between the Dutch and Don John of Austria, though in January 1577 the Dutch rejected this, being more interested in Leicester's offer of military assistance. However, when, later in the year, Don John offered them favourable terms for a peace, they wrote to the Earl to say that his help was no longer needed. This was perhaps as well, since Leicester had not served in a military capacity for over twenty years. He was now forty-four, 'high coloured and red-faced', and, having grown portly through good living, no longer even jousted. He was nevertheless bitterly disappointed not to have been given the chance to earn international renown as the armed champion of Protestantism.

'I am melancholy,' he wrote to a Dutch associate. 'I have almost neither face nor countenance to write to the Prince [William of Orange], his expectation being so greatly deceived.'

During the early months of 1577, Walsingham's spies gradually exposed a Catholic conspiracy masterminded by Don John of Austria, who, assisted by the Duke of Guise, was plotting to invade England with ten thousand troops, depose Elizabeth and return the kingdom to the Catholic fold. Don John then planned to marry Mary Stuart and rule jointly with her. Walsingham urged the Queen to take punitive measures against Mary, but once again she refused. She did, however, knight Walsingham that year for his services to the state. Fortunately, Don John was too preoccupied with affairs in the Netherlands to put into effect his plans for England.

In May, 1577, the Queen visited Gorhambury again. Mindful of his sovereign's remarks during her earlier stay in 1572, Lord Keeper Bacon had enlarged his house to twice its original size, and had added a Tuscan colonnade for good measure. The Queen was impressed by the changes and also by the lovely gardens and the 'noble' standard of living enjoyed by Bacon, who 'at every meal had his table strewed with sweet herbs and flowers'. Her Majesty stayed for five days, taking picnics in the little banqueting house in the orchard, or feasting on food prepared by twelve cooks specially brought from London. Although the Puritanical Lord Keeper considered courtly revels to be sinful, he swallowed his principles and laid out £20 for performers for his sovereign's sake. Altogether the visit cost him £577.

Gorhambury, like many other noble palaces of the age, is no more. It was a ruinous, ivy-shrouded shell by the end of the eighteenth century, and was pulled down soon afterwards.

The summer of 1577 brought with it a particularly bad outbreak of plague, which prevented the Queen from going on her usual progress. Instead she remained at Greenwich, although she is recorded as having spent two very pleasant days at Loseley House near Guildford in Surrey.

In June, Leicester, whose health was no longer so robust, travelled north to Buxton to take the waters. On the way he stayed as the guest of his friends the Earl and Countess of Shrewsbury. The Countess, Bess of Hardwick, was now back in favour after her spell in prison, and the Queen had already written in mischievous vein to warn her of Leicester's voracious appetite.

'We think it meet to prescribe unto you a diet which we mean in no case you shall exceed,' she advised, 'and that is to allow him by the day for his meat two ounces of flesh, referring the quality to yourselves, so as you exceed not the quantity, and for his drink the twentieth part of a pint of wine to comfort his stomach, and as much of St Anne's sacred water as he listeth to drink. On festival days, as is meet for a man of his quality, we can be content you shall enlarge his diet by allowing unto him for his dinner the shoulder of a wren, for his supper a leg of the same, besides his ordinary ounces.'

History does not record whether Bess attempted to follow the royal advice, but what is certain is that, while at Chatsworth, Leicester was presented to the Queen of Scots. Their conversation was limited mainly to pleasantries, although when Mary complained about her continuing confinement, Leicester expressed polite sympathy. Afterwards he wrote an account of the meeting for Burghley, which prompted the Lord Treasurer to ask the Queen if he might visit Mary himself. But she refused, having heard too often how her cousin's beauty and charm were capable of making the wisest men act foolishly.

Bess of Hardwick also produced her infant granddaughter, Arbella Stewart, for Leicester's inspection, hoping he would agree with her that Arbella's claim to the throne was better than Mary's and that he would try to persuade Elizabeth to name the child as her successor. Arbella was the great-granddaughter of Henry VII, and was being brought up in England in the Protestant faith, untainted by treason and scandal: in every respect she would be a better candidate than the Queen of Scots. Urged by her grandmother, Leicester could see that this was sound reasoning, and also perceived that there might be some advantage to himself in it. He was now resigned to the fact that he would never wear the crown matrimonial, but his ambition would be satisfied if his descendants were to occupy the throne of England. With this in mind, he suggested that Bess marry her granddaughter to his 'base son', a suggestion which the formidable matriarch accepted with alacrity, since the Earl, with his considerable influence and wide net of patronage, could do much for her and her family.

The Elizabethan age was one of discovery and geographical expansion. During the century before Elizabeth's accession, Spain had established colonies in the Americas and the Indies, whilst Portugal had colonised large parts of Africa and what is now Brazil. New trade routes meant wider markets and better opportunities for plunder, and there were several English privateers who, succumbing to the lure of adventure and easy spoils, ventured upon the high seas in a quest for riches, new markets for English goods, the chance to discountenance the Spaniards, or even the opportunity to found new colonies in the Queen's name.

Such a man was Francis Drake, a Devon mariner, who, on 24 May 1572, had sailed from Plymouth to the New World, his purpose being to exact retribution from the Spaniards, who had attacked and harried his ships during earlier voyages. Fifteen months later he returned from the Americas with a fabulous horde of treasure looted from Spanish ships. This was not the first time that English privateers had seized Spanish treasure, but it was the greatest haul.

News of Drake's booty and his colourful adventures soon reached the Queen, who was jubilant at the thought of how maddened King Philip would be by such blatant piracy, and fascinated by Drake's exploits. Overnight, he became famous throughout England, and notorious in Spain, where he was called 'El Draque' – the Dragon. Naturally, the Spaniards complained to Elizabeth, but while she was vaguely conciliatory, or affected to be concerned, she did nothing to stop these acts of piracy, and indeed benefited from them, since much of the looted treasure went into her coffers.

At the end of 1577, Francis Drake set off in his ship, the *Pelican*, on what was to be an epic world voyage. His priority, however, was not exploration but to harry the Spaniards, who had retaliated for his seizure of their treasure by attacking English ships. There was a great deal of public interest in the venture, and Walsingham arranged for Drake to be presented to the Queen before he left.

'Drake!' she greeted him effusively. 'So it is that I would be revenged on the King of Spain for divers injuries that I have received.' Drake answered that the most effective way to do this would be to prey on Philip's ships and settlements in the Indies, with which Elizabeth wholeheartedly agreed. Burghley, however, was not to be told about the expedition until it had sailed, since he felt it unwise to provoke the Spaniards any further. According to Drake, the Queen invested 1000 marks (nearly £665) in the voyage; other backers included Leicester, Walsingham and Hatton.

Just before Drake sailed, a royal messenger arrived bearing gifts from the Queen, an embroidered sea cap and a silk scarf on which she had stitched the words, 'The Lord guide and preserve thee until the end'.

Morton's regency in Scotland came to an abrupt end in March 1578, when the lords mounted a coup against him, which resulted in James VI, now nearly twelve, being declared of an age to assume personal rule.

On 4 April, Mary Stuart's husband, the Earl of Bothwell, died, mad and chained to a pillar in the dungeons of Dragsholm Castle in Denmark, where he had been held prisoner since soon after his flight from Scotland in 1567. The rigours of his imprisonment and the ever-present fear of imminent execution had unhinged his mind, although there were still those among Mary's supporters who claimed that, at the last, he had dictated a confession which cleared her of all complicity in Darnley's murder. This is unlikely, however, given his mental state at the time. Bothwell's mummified body may be seen today, under glass, at Faarevejle Church near Dragsholm.

18

'Frenzied Wooing'

In January 1578, news came that the Protestant Dutch armies had suffered a crushing defeat at the hands of Don John of Austria, which gave Elizabeth cause to point out to Leicester that she had been right all along about not wanting to involve England in a war it might lose. Instead, she now hoped to use her diplomatic influence with Philip II to bring about a settlement that was not only acceptable to both sides but also to English interests. Thanks to the provocation given to King Philip by English privateers and the help supplied to the Dutch by Elizabeth, the peace with Spain now seemed to be on a very precarious footing, and fears were expressed that Philip might yet invoke the Pope's interdict and make the rumoured Enterprise of England a reality.

Elizabeth had for some time been worried about reports that Alençon, now Duke of Anjou, was intending to meddle in the affairs of the Netherlands. The last thing she needed was the undermining of her negotiations for a peace that would safeguard England's security and economic prosperity, nor did she want any French military presence in the Netherlands. By the spring of 1578, when it had, to her relief, become clear that Anjou was acting without the backing of the French government, it occurred to her that the best way of controlling his activities to her advantage would be to revive negotiations for their marriage and a new treaty with France. She did not know it, but this was to be her last venture into the European marriage market.

The same idea had occurred to Anjou, whose ambition had found no outlet at the court of France, where he was regarded as a troublesome nuisance, and who still dreamed of a crown. This was why he had looked to find fame and glory in the Netherlands, though it now seemed unlikely he would achieve it without the backing of a powerful ruler such as the Queen of England. With her as his bride and the wealth of her kingdom behind him, matters would be very different. The evidence suggests that it was he who made the first approach: he certainly wrote to Elizabeth to assure her of his entire devotion and his willingness to be guided by her in all his doings. It was astonishing, he added, 'that after two years of absolute silence, he should wake up to her existence'. Elizabeth was gratified to hear from him and by the realisation that his letter gave her the perfect excuse to revive the courtship.

Walsingham, however, was not deceived by Anjou's flowery sentiments, believing that 'he entertaineth Her Majesty at this present only to abuse her', so that she would not protest when he marched at the head of an army into the Netherlands. Elizabeth was not pleased when she heard this, and instructed Leicester to inform Walsingham that it was not in the least surprising that Anjou should have fallen in love with her. He was, she asserted, only going to the Netherlands to give himself 'better means to step over hither'.

Since the death of her husband, Lettice, Countess of Essex, had struggled to pay her debts. Ambitious and still beautiful, she was determined not to waste her assets, and, being a confident, opportunistic woman, saw no reason why her lover, the Earl of Leicester, should not be persuaded to marry her. It is not known how much Lettice knew of the circumstances of Leicester's union with Douglas Sheffield, although it is clear that both she and the Earl regarded him as a free man.

When Lettice discovered that she was pregnant, Leicester, desperate for a legitimate heir, agreed to marry her; the ceremony took place secretly in the spring of 1578 at Kenilworth. He then purchased the house and manor of Wanstead in Essex so that he could visit Lettice there when his duties at court permitted. Their union was undoubtedly happy, for the Earl 'doted extremely upon marriage'.

After the wedding, Leicester came up to London to stay at Leicester House, giving out that he was ill and unable to come to court. He may, in fact, have been enjoying a brief honeymoon with Lettice, or the 'illness' may have been tactical, for the evidence suggests that, on 28 April, Elizabeth found out what he had done. Mendoza reported that,

> The Queen had fixed the 28th for my audience with her, but as she was walking in the garden that morning she found a letter which had been thrown into the doorway, which she took and read, and immediately came secretly to the house of the Earl of Leicester, who is ill here. She stayed there until ten o'clock at night, and sent word that she would not see me that day as she was unwell. I have not been able to learn the contents of the letter, and only know that it caused her to go to Leicester's at once.

There were two likely possibilities: either Leicester himself had written asking the Queen to visit him, giving good reasons why she should do so as a matter of great urgency, or someone else had found out about his marriage and had informed the Queen. Of course, her visit could have related to another matter entirely, but, given the circumstances and her behaviour afterwards, this is the likeliest version of events. If the letter had come from Leicester himself, it was in character for him to feign sickness in order to soften Elizabeth's heart and mitigate her anger.

In May, possibly prompted by Leicester's betrayal, the Queen sent an envoy to France to open negotiations for her marriage to Anjou. Around the same time, Leicester travelled north again to Buxton to take the waters, insisting he was still unwell. It may also have been politic for him to go away to give Elizabeth time to adjust to the situation and perhaps make her realise how lonely she would be if she cut him out of her life, as she may have threatened to do. Whatever the reason, he stayed away for more than two months, which was unusual, since the Queen normally hated to have him out of her sight.

While Leicester was away from court, Elizabeth took out her frustration on Hatton, apparently giving him to understand that she could not bear it if he were to betray her as Leicester had by marrying someone else, especially after he had sworn undying loyalty to her, who, if she were able, would leap at the chance of marrying him.

In perplexity, Hatton wrote to Leicester on 18 June:

> Since Your Lordship's departure, the Queen is found in continual and great melancholy; the cause thereof I can but guess at, notwithstanding that I bear and suffer the whole brunt of her mislike in generality. She dreameth of marriage that might seem injurious to her: making myself to be either the man, or a pattern of the matter. I defend that no man can tie himself or be tied to such inconvenience as not to marry by law of God or man, except by mutual consents on both parts the man and woman vow to marry each other, which I know she hath not done for any man, and therefore by any man's marriage she can receive no wrong. But, my Lord, I am not the man that should thus suddenly marry, for God knoweth, I never meant it.

In fact, Elizabeth seems to have been broken-hearted rather than angry at Leicester's desertion, and when, during the next week or so, she received from him several letters, which have not survived, Hatton was able to inform the Earl, on 28 June, that she had been overjoyed to have them 'because they chiefly recorded the testimony of your most loyal disposition from the beginning to this present time'. She was now impatient for Leicester's return, and thought 'your absence much drawn in too length, and especially in that place, supposing indeed that a shorter time would work as good effect with you, but yet [she] chargeth that you now go through according to your physician's opinion. For if now these waters work not a full good effect, Her Highness will never consent that you cumber yourself and her with such long journeys again.'

Subtly, Elizabeth had set the tone for her future relationship with Leicester: in return for his behaving towards her as if nothing had happened and continuing as her favourite, she was prepared to ignore his unfortunate marriage, as long as he put her needs first. Relieved to have got off so lightly, Leicester played along with this fantasy, but he soon found that there was a heavy price to pay, for Elizabeth, who had once been so affectionate towards her cousin Lettice, now developed an implacable hatred for her and behaved as if she did not exist. Aside from her marriage to Leicester, Lettice had offended the Queen by not seeking her permission to marry, which, as the widow of an earl, she was obliged to do.

Leicester, caught in a conflict of loyalty between two strong women, one his wife and one his queen, suddenly realised that his life, from now on, was going to be very complicated. In the interests of keeping the peace, therefore, he resolved to avoid any reference to his marriage.

Of course, his relationship with the Queen had to change. He remained close to her in a way no other favourite did: for example, he sat up all night soothing her when she had toothache, and he continued to give her expensive and original gifts, such as the gold clock he presented to her at New Year 1579. But they could no longer enjoy the intimate friendship of the past: there were fewer shared private jokes and affectionate personal messages. Instead, the Queen lost her temper with him more frequently or was more capricious when it came to granting favours. She also made such demands on his time that he had few opportunities to visit his wife, which was exactly what the Queen intended.

The discovery of Leicester's marriage put Elizabeth into a bad mood that lasted throughout the summer and drove her councillors to near despair. It was exacerbated by her having such painful toothache as to cause her whole face to be inflamed, and her long-suffering doctors spent hours debating with her 'how Her Majesty might be eased of the grief'. Depressed and in pain, she refused to make any decisions, snapped and snarled at her ministers and once shouted at Walsingham that he deserved to be hanged – in which case, he drily said later, he asked only that he could be tried by a Middlesex jury.

When the French ambassador spoke out against her treatment of the Queen of Scots, Elizabeth, who had just learned from Walsingham that Mary had been plotting with her Guise relatives again, hissed that her cousin was 'the worst woman in the world, whose head should have been cut off years ago, and who would never be free as long as she lived'.

Even in the face of pressing state business, the Queen sometimes refused to see her councillors at all, giving her toothache as an excuse. In the end, they defied her and insisted that she act to prevent Anjou from leading a French army into the Netherlands. Leicester, who now usually acted as spokesman for the Council to the Queen, spoke to her 'so plainly, so boldly and so faithfully against delays', and in a way that no other councillor would have dared, but to no avail. She told him to be silent. Nor would she speak even to Hatton. Leicester then tried the proven tactic of taking to his bed, feigning sickness in the hope that she would come hastening to his side, but even this did not work, and many wondered at the coolness in her attitude towards him. Nor did she intervene to prevent squabbles breaking out between Burghley and Leicester.

Then, on the morning of 9 August, Elizabeth finally woke to the realisation that Anjou was not playing games and might cause more trouble for her in the Netherlands than the Spanish ever had. She had, after all, delayed too long.

The Queen's progress that year took her to East Anglia, and was arranged at such short notice that there was a scramble by the worthies of the region to obtain new silks and velvets, which were soon sold out.

On 10 August, she visited Thetford, and stayed with the Catholic Mr Rookwood, the owner of nearby Euston Hall in Suffolk. The notorious sadist, Richard Topclyffe, who was later responsible for the torture of several Catholic priests, described Rookwood as a criminal and a 'blackguard. Nevertheless, her excellent Majesty gave Rookwood ordinary thanks for his bad house, and her fair hand to kiss.' During the visit someone had found a statue of the Virgin Mary in the house, which was brought into the hall and held up for Elizabeth to see. She ordered it to be burnt, which was done immediately, 'to the unspeakable joy of everyone'. After she had gone, Rookwood was arrested and imprisoned in Norwich gaol until his death twenty years later. His estates were declared forfeit to the Crown.

After a visit to Kenninghall where she lodged with Philip Howard, formerly Earl of Surrey, son of the executed Norfolk, who made her very welcome, the Queen paid a memorable visit to Norwich, arriving in 'her most dutiful city' on 16 August to a rapturous welcome, hundreds of people turning out to greet her.

She evinced great interest in children spinning and knitting worsteds, and in the craftsmen who demonstrated their weaving techniques for her on a stage near St Stephen's Church. At her insistence, time was made for local children to perform a pageant for her in the market place, in which the Queen was lauded as 'the Pearl of Grace, the Jewel of the World, her People's Whole Delight, the Paragon of Present Time, and Prince of Earthly Might'. They had been rehearsing for weeks, and although the Queen's schedule was tight, she did not want to disappoint them.

Whilst she was touring the cathedral, she received news that Anjou had invaded the Netherlands and concluded a treaty with the Protestant States, who had invited him to be their governor and conferred upon him the title 'Defender of the Liberties of the Low Countries against Spanish Tyranny'. Later, in her lodgings in the bishop's palace, Elizabeth exploded with anger, accusing all her ministers of allowing this to happen, and refusing to concede that she herself had done nothing to prevent it. Her immediate reaction was to send a message of support to King Philip, although her covert plan was to distract Anjou with hopes of marriage.

Meanwhile, the Norwich ceremonies continued. On Thursday the 21st, she watched another play with many magical special effects, including underground music, although before it ended the heavens opened and everyone hastened for shelter. There was a farce about fairies, written by Thomas Churchyard, a contemporary writer of poetry and prose, on the last day, 'frowning Friday', 22 August, before the Queen, alternately smiling and looking sad, took her leave of the city at seven o'clock in the evening, after knighting the mayor.

'I have laid upon my breast such good will, as I shall never forget Norwich,' she told the citizens, with a catch in her voice. Then she shook her riding whip and cried, 'Farewell, Norwich!' with tears in her eyes.

Her visit was the occasion of twenty-two Catholic recusants being committed to jail for refusing to recognise the Acts of Uniformity. However, several local Catholics who had undertaken to conform were knighted alongside leading Protestants by the Queen, one of whose purposes in visiting the region was to subvert Catholic influence and reinforce the people's loyalty. Churchyard noted that, wherever Elizabeth went in East Anglia, she 'made the crooked paths straight and drew the hearts of the people after her'.

The Knollys family had constantly objected to the fact that Leicester had married Lettice in secret, and Lettice was determined not to be abandoned as casually as Douglas Howard had been. She resented the fact that her husband was still in contact with Douglas and their son, and insisted that this other woman in his life must go.

Leicester, whose passion for Douglas had long since died, arranged to meet her in the gardens of Greenwich Palace, where, in the presence of two witnesses, he told her he was releasing her from all obligations to him. He offered her an annuity of £700 if she would deny all knowledge of their marriage and surrender to him custody of young Robert Dudley. In the only account of their meeting, written by Douglas a quarter of a century later, she stated that she burst into tears at this point and turned down his offer, at which he lost his temper and shouted at her that their marriage had never been lawful.

Why he should have reached this conclusion is puzzling. The marriage had been freely entered into and performed before witnesses, by a priest, and neither party were contracted elsewhere at the time. It had been consummated, and both partners were of sound mind.

Douglas asked for a short time to think, and then capitulated, fearing that otherwise Leicester would seek revenge on her for thwarting him. His parting advice to her was that she should find herself a husband, and before the year was up he had arranged for her to marry a rising courtier of noble blood, Sir Edward Stafford, whose wife, Rosetta Robsart, a relative of Amy, had recently died.

In 1604, Leicester's 'base son', then Sir Robert Dudley, applied to the Court of Star Chamber to determine whether or not his parents' marriage was valid. However, he was opposed by the powerful Sidney family, who had inherited the earldoms of Leicester and Warwick and had much to lose if Dudley won his case. The Sidneys enjoyed the favour of the new King, James I, who may have influenced the outcome, which was inconclusive. The issue of the legality of the 1573 ceremony was left undecided, whilst Dudley was condemned for trying to prove his legitimacy, and his evidence was impounded. What little remains suggests that the marriage was, indeed, valid.

In the nineteenth century, the question of its legality was again revived when Sir John Shelley-Sidney laid claim to the barony of de Lisle and Dudley, to which he would not have been entitled had Robert Dudley been legitimate and left direct heirs to inherit it. The House of Lords investigated the matter, and concluded that Sir John had not succeeded in establishing his right to the barony, on the grounds that the marriage of Robert Dudley's parents had indeed been valid. Leicester, however, for reasons of his own, preferred to think otherwise, and though he was fond of his son, he never, until he died, acknowledged his legitimacy.

The Earl now felt it incumbent upon him to arrange a second, more appropriate wedding ceremony in order to satisfy Lettice and her father.

This took place early in the morning of 21 September 1578, at his house at Wanstead, with members of the Knollys family and the Earls of Warwick and Pembroke present. Lettice, now noticeably pregnant, wore 'a loose gown'. Two years later, just to make sure that all was in order, the officiating priest was required by the bride's family to make a sworn statement that he had married the couple. The Queen was not told about this second ceremony, which was kept a closely guarded secret.

Two days afterwards, Elizabeth and her court arrived at Wanstead on their way back to London. They stayed for several days, and were royally and expensively entertained, although the new Countess was nowhere to be seen. Philip Sidney had been commissioned by Leicester to produce a pastoral masque, *The Lady of May*, in the Queen's honour; it portrayed a lady being courted by rival lovers, and Elizabeth had to decide which of them she should choose.

By the autumn, having been engaged in a secret correspondence with Anjou, the contents of which she confided to no one, Elizabeth was considering seriously the advantages of marrying him, among which she numbered the possibility of England and France uniting in renewed friendship to achieve a real peace in the Netherlands and the fact that she would be in a position to help the Huguenots in France. Burghley and Sussex were again in favour of the marriage, even if they did not really believe it would ever take place, while Leicester, who now had nothing to lose, was strongly against it on religious grounds, although given the fragility of his relationship with the Queen, he had to be very wary of upsetting her.

After Don John of Austria's death on 1 October, King Philip sent another army under the Duke of Parma to subjugate the Netherlands. Parma occupied the south, pushing back William of Orange's forces to Holland and Zeeland, which became formally known in 1579 as the United Provinces.

In November, Anjou, now back in France and desperate for someone to back his next foray into the Netherlands, sent his 'chief darling' and Master of the Wardrobe, Jean de Simier, Baron de St Marc, 'a most choice courtier, exquisitely skilled in love toys, pleasant conceits and court dalliances', to England to discuss the terms of the proposed marriage with Elizabeth and prepare her for the Duke's 'frenzied wooing'.

Simier was a dubious character, having just murdered his brother for having an affair with his wife, who had poisoned herself shortly before he sailed to England. Yet when he arrived on 5 January 1579 with an entourage of sixty gentlemen Elizabeth, who knew nothing of his background, was so taken with this 'perfect courtier', whom she nicknamed her 'Monkey' and called 'the most beautiful of her beasts', that anyone observing them together might have been forgiven for concluding that she meant to marry him rather than his master.

As soon as Simier arrived, laden with jewels worth 12,000 crowns as gifts for the English courtiers, negotiations began to proceed more smoothly, with Simier wooing the Queen with consummate skill on Anjou's behalf and Elizabeth responding like a skittish girl, never happier or better-humoured than when in his company. She gave a court ball in his honour, at which was presented a masque in which six ladies surrendered to six suitors. She summoned him to her side as often as she could, and frequently kept him with her until late at night. She treasured the gift he had brought her from Anjou, a miniature book with a gem-encrusted binding, and kept it with her at all times. In return, she gave Simier little mementoes to send to the Duke, including a miniature of herself and some gloves. One day, she declared, she hoped to give Monsieur many more fine and valuable things, but for now these must suffice.

Never before had any of her politically-motivated courtships generated such excitement, and as the winter months passed in a series of romantic interludes, her councillors and courtiers began to wonder if, this time, she really did mean to get married. 'It is a fine thing for an old woman like me to be thinking of marriage!' she told Mendoza teasingly.

'If Your Majesty will consent to marry me', wrote the eager bridegroom, 'you will restore a languishing life, which has existed only for the service of the most perfect goddess of the heavens.'

No longer did the age gap or Anjou's pockmarks seem important. Elizabeth replied to her suitor that she would have his words of love engraved in marble. She vowed eternal friendship and constancy, which 'is rare among royalty', and brazenly assured him she had never broken her word. Whenever Anjou's name was mentioned, reported Simier, her face would light up, and he had been told by her ladies that she never ceased talking about the Duke in private. She had also said she now believed there could be no greater happiness in the world than marriage, and wished that she had not wasted so much time.

However, closeted with Simier, she expressed doubts. Was his master interested in her for herself, or did he just want to be king? She could not rest until she knew, and she would only find out if the Duke paid her a personal visit.

When her councillors heard that Simier had gained access to the Queen's bedroom and, by her leave, appropriated her nightcap and handkerchief as 'trophies' for his master, and when they learned that the Queen had gone early one morning to Simier's lodging, so that he was obliged to receive her wearing only a jerkin, they began to have reservations about this method of courtship, which was condemned by some as 'an unmanlike, unprincelike, French kind of wooing'.

If Elizabeth was using her flirtation with Simier to make Leicester jealous, she succeeded spectacularly. Although the Earl was obliged to be outwardly friendly towards Simier and entertain him at court, his enmity was plain to all. Leicester, who may have found out about Simier's shady past, was heard to protest that the envoy was employing 'love potions and other unlawful acts' to procure the Queen for the Duke. Most people, unaware that Leicester was married, concluded that he was speaking out of pique because he still hoped to marry Elizabeth himself, but when the Queen's ladies, who also distrusted Simier, spoke out in his favour, Elizabeth answered scathingly, 'Dost thou think me so unlike myself and unmindful of my royal majesty that I would prefer my servant, whom I myself have raised, before the greatest prince of Christendom, in the honour of a husband?' After this, no one dared criticise Simier to her face.

'He has shown himself faithful to his master, and is sage and discreet beyond his years in the conduct of the case,' she wrote to Sir Amyas Paulet, her ambassador in Paris. 'We wish we had such a servant of whom we could make such good use.'

Behind the Queen's back, however, it was being whispered that Simier had won his way, not only to her heart, but also to her body.

In March 1579, Simier presented a draft marriage treaty to the Council. 'I have very good hope, but will wait to say more till the curtain is drawn, the candle out, and Monsieur in bed. Then I will speak with good assurance,' he wrote on 12 April. Some Englishmen were even ordering their wedding suits.

In London, however, they were betting 3-1 against the marriage, whilst many people objected to it on the grounds that Anjou was not only a Frenchman but also a Papist. The Puritans were vocal in their opposition, and many Anglican preachers were denouncing it from their pulpits. One even dared to predict, in front of the Queen, that 'marriages with foreigners would only result in ruin to the country'. Much affronted, Elizabeth stalked out in the middle of his sermon. Such opposition was offensive, not only to herself but also, more importantly, to the French, and she took steps to ban any texts that might support her subjects' objections.

At the end of that month, the Council debated the treaty, but its members were divided in opinion. Religion was a stumbling block because, although Anjou was no fanatic and might willingly have converted for Elizabeth's sake, he was now heir to the French throne and therefore required to remain a Catholic.

There was also the problem of the Queen's age. She was forty-five, and old, even by modern standards, to be contemplating having children. Elizabeth was herself concerned about this, and it was reported in foreign courts that she had consulted a panel of physicians, who had nevertheless assured her that all would be well. Lord Burghley pointed out to the Council that the Duchess of Savoy had borne a healthy prince at nearly fifty, and survived. The Queen, he went on, 'was a person of most pure complexion, of the largest and goodliest stature of well-shaped women, with all limbs set and proportioned in the best sort, and one whom, in the sight of all men, Nature cannot amend her shape in any part to make her more likely to conceive and bear children without peril'.

Prompted by concern for Elizabeth's safety, Burghley had carried out thorough inquiries to determine whether or not the business of getting heirs would put her at risk. Noting the results in a private memorandum, he wrote that she was well-formed and had 'no lack of functions in those things that properly belong to the procreation of children, but contrary-wise, by judgement of physicians that know her estate in those things, and by the opinion of women being most acquainted with Her Majesty's body'. These same doctors predicted that Elizabeth had at least six years left in which to bear children, and we may conclude from this that she had not ceased to menstruate. That did not mean, however, that she would, at her age, conceive a child, nor did it ensure that she would not die in childbirth, as happened to an estimated one in forty women in the sixteenth century.

While Burghley believed that sexual fulfilment and childbirth would help to cure the neuralgia Elizabeth suffered in her face and 'the dolours and infirmities as all physicians do usually impute to womankind for lack of marriage', and felt that the benefits of a royal marriage far outweighed the risks, Walsingham was more realistic, and spoke for the majority when he expressed his fear that motherhood would place the Queen in extreme peril.

The French ambassador shared Burghley's optimism. Her Majesty, he informed Catherine de' Medici, 'has never been more pretty or more beautiful. There is nothing old about her except her years.' Women born under her constellation were invariably fertile, and rarely died childless. It was commonplace in England for women of advanced age to bear children: his neighbour was a woman of fifty-six, and she was at present eight months pregnant.

Simier flounced out of the room in anger when he was told by the Council that they had rejected three of the marriage articles, namely, that Anjou be crowned immediately after the wedding, that he share jointly with the Queen the power to grant lands and church offices, and that Parliament should settle upon him an annual income of £60,000, payable until his children had reached their majority. Nor would the Council reach any decision on the treaty until Anjou had come to England and met the Queen.

Simier went straight to the Queen, who was walking in her Privy Garden and listened 'with much graciousness and many expressions of sorrow that her councillors disapproved of her marriage, which she desired so much'. According to Mendoza, she became 'very melancholy' and declared afterwards to her ladies, 'They need not think that it is going to end this way. I must get married.'

Mortified, Simier informed the Duke of these developments, but Anjou was conciliatory and said he would leave everything to the Queen's good judgement. Elizabeth, meanwhile, had become so distressed at her councillors' attitude that her ministers hurriedly backed down and hastily summoned her best-loved ladies to court to calm her.

In May, she was sufficiently restored to complain to the French that they were making too many demands: 'If they had to deal with a princess that either had some defect of body or nature, or lacking mental gifts, such a kind of strainable proceeding might have been tolerated. But considering how otherwise – our fortune laid aside – it hath pleased God to bestow His gifts upon us in good measure, which we do ascribe to the giver and not glory in as proceeding from ourselves (being no fit trumpet to set out our own praises), we may in true course of modesty think ourself worthy of as great a prince as Monsieur is without yielding to such hard conditions.'

Fortunately, Anjou had already instructed Simier not to insist on every condition being met, which was as well, since the Queen was now expressing 'such a strong desire to marry that not a councillor, whatever his opinion may be, dares to say a word against it'.

Throughout the spring and summer, Anjou had repeatedly sought an invitation to England to meet the Queen. Elizabeth wavered: on the one hand, she had Burghley and Sussex urging her to agree, and on the other, daily opposition from Leicester, who reportedly even prostrated himself at her feet and begged her not to go through with this marriage, and was suspected, on flimsy evidence, of being behind two abortive attempts to murder Simier. In the end, Burghley prevailed, but only after Elizabeth had 'deferred three whole days with an extreme regret and many tears before she would subscribe the passport, being induced thereunto and almost forced by those that have led this negotiation in despite of Leicester'.

In 1615, Elizabeth's biographer, William Camden, claimed that early in July, Simier, desperate to neutralise Leicester's malevolent influence, told the Queen that the Earl was married, at which Elizabeth 'grew into such a chafe that she commanded Leicester not to stir out of the Palace of Greenwich, and intended to have committed him to the Tower of London, which his enemies much desired. But the Earl of Sussex, though his greatest and deadliest adversary, dissuaded her. For he was of opinion that no man was to be troubled for lawful marriage, which estate amongst all men hath ever been held in honour and esteem.'

As we have seen, it is more probable that the Queen had found out about the marriage fourteen months earlier. Camden claims that she briefly confined Leicester to his rooms at court and then banished him to Wanstead, but at a time when foreign ambassadors were reporting every titbit of gossip from the English court, there is no mention of this episode in any other source. Leicester was certainly away from court and staying at Wanstead at this time, but he was not out of favour. Mendoza reported on 6 July that Anjou's passport 'was given against Leicester's wish, and he is so much offended that he has retired to a house of his five miles away, where the Queen has been to see him and where she remained two days because he feigned illness. She afterwards returned secretly to London.' Hence we may conclude that Camden's tale is apocryphal.

Elizabeth did, however, vent her rage on Lettice. When Lettice dared to appear at court sumptuously attired, as befitted a countess, and attended by a large train of servants, the Queen advanced upon her like an avenging angel and boxed her ears, shouting, 'As but one sun lights the East, so I shall have but one queen in England.' After such public humiliation, Lettice did not dare venture to court again for many years, nor would Elizabeth have allowed it, despite Leicester's frequent pleas.

On 8 July, the Council informed Simier that they had sanctioned a visit by Anjou. His brother, Henry III, objected that it might be unwise, but the Duke ignored him and went to England, heavily disguised, in the middle of August. In case nothing came of it, his visit was meant to be a secret between himself, the Queen and Simier, but most people at court knew of it, although they wisely kept up the pretence that they did not. To ensure secrecy, Simier was assigned a pavilion in the gardens of Greenwich Palace, where Anjou would lodge with him.

Mendoza reported that Elizabeth was 'burning with impatience for his coming, although her councillors have laid before her the difficulties which might arise. She is largely influenced by the idea that it should be known that her talents and beauty are so great that they have sufficed to cause him to come and visit her without any assurance that he will be her husband.'

On 17 July, Elizabeth had a narrow brush with death as she left Greenwich in her barge to visit Deptford in the company of the Earl of Lincoln and the French ambassador. John Stow recorded that a fowler, Thomas Appletree, 'with two or three children of Her Majesty's

Chapel, was rowing up and down the reach with a caliver, shooting at random, very rashly'. One shot passed within six feet of the Queen, piercing both arms of an oarsman and sending him toppling out of his seat, which 'forced him to cry and screech out piteously, supposing himself to be slain'. Elizabeth, unabashed, 'bid him be of good cheer, and said he would want of nothing that might be for his ease'.

On her orders, Appletree was condemned to be hanged, and four days later the gallows were set up at the water's edge where he had committed his crime. But Elizabeth merely meant to teach him a stern lesson, and 'when the hangman had put the rope around his neck, he was, by the Queen's most gracious pardon, delivered from execution'.

The Duke of Anjou arrived at Greenwich early in the morning of 17 August, and went directly to Simier's pavilion, where he woke him up and demanded to see the Queen. When Simier pointed out that she was still asleep, the eager Anjou had to be restrained from going to wake her up and kiss her hand. Instead, Simier sent her a note, to say he had put his exhausted master between two sheets. 'Would to God it was by your side.'

At sunset, Anjou dined with the Queen, who had stolen out of the palace with one of her ladies. Until their meeting, she had expected him to be a hideously disfigured, misshapen dwarf; instead, there now stood before her a mature and attractive man, whose pitted skin did not detract from his dark hair and eyes and witty gallantry, and it occurred to her that here was a very desirable husband indeed. 'I have never in my life seen a creature more agreeable to me,' she declared.

'The lady has with difficulty been able to entertain the Duke, being captivated, overcome with love,' the French ambassador reported to the Queen Mother. 'She told me she had never found a man whose nature and actions suited her better.'

'The Queen is delighted with Anjou, and he with her, as she has let out to some of her courtiers,' wrote Mendoza to King Philip. She had said 'that she was pleased to have known him, was much taken with his good parts, and admired him more than any man. She said that, for her part, she would not prevent his being her husband.' Philip, knowing that nothing definite had yet been decided, dismissed this as mere pretence.

But there was no mistaking the sexual chemistry between the royal lovers. The Duke, who possessed both charm and sex appeal, was an ardent suitor and Elizabeth responded with delight. She nicknamed him her 'Frog' and they exchanged gifts, made extravagant promises, and swore to love each other until death parted them. Several courtiers were aware of this love-play, among them Leicester, who was sickened and embarrassed by it.

But he could do nothing because officially, as Mendoza reported,

the councillors deny that Anjou is here, and in order not to offend the Queen, they shut their eyes and avoid going to court, so as not to appear to stand in the way of interviews with him, only attending the Council when they are obliged. It is said that if she marries before consulting her people, she may repent it. Leicester is much put out, and all the councillors are disgusted except Sussex. A close friend of Leicester tells me he is cursing the French, and is greatly incensed against Sussex.

Meanwhile, the talk in London was all of the French duke's ostentatious courtship of the Queen, which left many people, notably the Puritans, scandalised, and inspired the poet Edmund Spenser, under Leicester's patronage, to write a satire entitled *Mother Hubbard's Tale*. This was less than flattering to Simier, and caused Leicester such embarrassment when the Queen condemned it that he was obliged to dismiss Spenser from his household, although not before he had used his influence to obtain a post for him with Lord Grey in Ireland, where Spenser was to write his greatest work, *The Faerie Queen*, which was dedicated to Elizabeth.

Because the Duke was not supposed to be in England, Elizabeth's fascination for him was fuelled by the necessity for snatching moments together in private. She saw him whenever she could and hated being apart from him. On 23 August, she arranged for him to view a court ball from behind a tapestry, and then gave the game away by showing off outrageously for his benefit, joining in more dances than usual and waving and smiling in his direction. Her courtiers politely pretended not to notice. Elizabeth even denied to Mendoza that Anjou was in England, and when two of her ladies gossiped openly about him, she ordered them to stay in their chamber.

Two days later, Leicester, 'in great grief', sought an interview with Elizabeth, from which he emerged in a state of visible emotion. That evening, he and the Sidneys, who also opposed the marriage, held a conference at Pembroke's house, after which Leicester decided that he could take no more, and left court with his sister Mary Sidney. All he could hope for now was that 'Parliament would have something to say as to whether the Queen married or not.'

Anjou's visit was abruptly curtailed when news arrived from France that a close friend had been killed in a duel, and he had to make arrangements to leave the next day. The Queen placed a royal ship, the *Scout*, at his disposal.

Simier told Elizabeth that, on the last night of the visit, a sleepless

Anjou had kept him awake with his sighs and moans, and hauled him out of bed early to tell him about her 'divine beauties' and swear a thousand oaths that, without hope of ever seeing her again, he could not live another quarter of an hour. She was, confessed the Duke, 'the gaoler of his heart and mistress of his liberty'.

When Anjou left Greenwich on 29 August, 'the parting was very tender on both sides'. After he reached Dover, he wrote Elizabeth four letters; then he crossed the Channel and wrote three more from Boulogne to tell her that he was desolate without her, and could do nothing but wipe away his tears. He signed himself the most faithful and affectionate slave in the world, declaring that he kissed her feet from the coast of that comfortless sea. He enclosed with his letters 'a little flower of gold, with a frog thereon, and therein [a miniature of] Monsieur, and a little pearl pendant'.

Although Elizabeth behaved as if nothing had happened, privately she seems to have been in turmoil, which is apparent from some pensive lines composed by her at this time, entitled 'On Monsieur's Departure':

> I grieve, yet dare not show my discontent;
> I love, and yet am forced to seem to hate,
> I dote, but dare not what I meant;
> I seem stark mute, yet inwardly do prate.
> I am, and am not, freeze, and yet I burn,
> Since from myself my other self I turn.
> My care is like my shadow in the sun,
> Follows me flying, flies when I pursue it,
> Stands and lives by me, does what I have done.
> Oh, let me live with some more sweet content,
> Or die, and so forget what love e'er meant.

Anjou left Simier behind to finalise negotiations for the marriage treaty and keep Elizabeth happy. Yet opposition to the match was now stiffer than ever in England, especially in the capital, and even some courtiers were violently opposed to it. Philip Sidney, remembering the horrors of St Bartholemew's Eve, wrote Elizabeth an open but courteous letter of protest, reminding her how perfidious were the French Catholics and insisting that Anjou, whose mother was 'a Jezebel of our age', would be wholly unacceptable to her Protestant subjects, 'your chief, if not your sole, strength'. The Queen wept as she read it and castigated him soundly. He therefore felt it politic to stay away from court for a year, during which he wrote his celebrated work *Arcadia* whilst staying with his sister at Wilton House. Mendoza gleefully reported that he feared there would be a revolution in England if the

Queen married Anjou.

The French ambassador would have disagreed, for he witnessed the Queen's return to London that autumn, and was overwhelmed to see her looking 'more beautiful than ever, bedizened like the sun, and mounted on a fine Spanish horse, and with so many people before her that it was a marvellous thing. They did not merely honour her, but they worshipped her, kneeling on the ground, with a thousand blessings and joyful remarks.'

Yet the Queen's apparently unshakeable popularity was soon to be under threat. In September, a Norfolk gentleman and Puritan, John Stubbs, wrote a pamphlet with the wordy title, *The Discovery of a Gaping Gulf whereby England is like to be swallowed by another French marriage, if the Lord forbid not the banns by letting Her Majesty see the sin and punishment thereof.* The pamphlet was printed and published in London, and thereafter widely distributed throughout England, becoming very popular and helping to influence public opinion.

It is not hard to see why the government was angered by its contents, for it was written in such strong language as to give great offence to the Queen, and to the Duke of Anjou in particular, since it described the House of Valois as being rotten with disease and sealed with the marks of divine vengeance for its cruelties, and the Duke as being 'eaten by debauchery'. He was 'the old serpent himself in the form of a man, come a second time to seduce the English Eve and ruin the English paradise', and was 'not fit to look in at her great chamber door'. Stubbs also called into question the wisdom of the Queen bearing children at her age.

Elizabeth was incandescent with anger when she read the pamphlet, not only because it had incited her people to oppose her, but also because of the way in which it slandered and insulted her allies, the French. On 27 September, she issued a proclamation condemning it as lewd and seditious, confiscated all copies and had them burned, then sent a preacher to Paul's Cross to assure her subjects that she had no intention of changing her religion on her marriage: 'She had been brought up in Christ, so she would live and die in Christ.' Although 'the people seemed, with a shout, to give God thanks' for this, they showed resentment 'at the sharp and bitter speeches' against Stubbs, who was a popular man and respected for his integrity.

Informed of this, Elizabeth consulted her judges and ordered that he be arrested and hanged for sedition, along with his printer, one Singleton, and his publisher, William Page. However, as this was not a capital crime, the men were condemned instead to have their right hands cut off and be sent to prison. A judge and lawyer who questioned the legality of the sentence were summarily thrown into gaol.

The Queen showed her customary clemency by pardoning the

printer, on account of his great age, but told the French ambassador that she would rather lose one of her own hands than mitigate the sentence passed on Stubbs and Page. Both were taken from the Tower to a public scaffold in front of Whitehall Palace, where Stubbs made a speech protesting his loyalty to the Queen.

'Pray for me, now my calamity is at hand,' he punned bravely. The executioner then chopped off his right hand 'with a cleaver driven through the wrist with a beetle'.* After the stump had been cauterised with a hot iron, Stubbs took off his hat with his left hand and cried, 'God save Queen Elizabeth!' before he fainted. Page, in turn, raised his bleeding stump and said, 'I have left there a true Englishman's hand.' Then he bravely walked away with his guards without assistance. The huge crowd of spectators watched the proceedings in sympathetic and disapproving silence.

When the furore had died down, Elizabeth realised that, by acting impulsively and with uncharacteristic cruelty, she had outraged public opinion. After eighteen months, she released Stubbs and later received him at court; he became an MP in 1581.

Parliament was due to meet on 20 October to conclude the marriage treaty, but the Queen, concerned about public opinion and remembering that she had never yet forfeited the good will of her subjects, prorogued it for a month and asked her Council for advice.

This gave rise to heated discussions. With Walsingham absent, Leicester and Hatton mustered five other councillors who were against the marriage, while Burghley led four others in favour. Bearing in mind that the Queen 'seemeth not pleased with any person or with any argument appearing to mislike of the marriage', they agreed at length to ask her to 'open her mind' to them as to her own inclinations.

Elizabeth must already have realised that it would be folly to go ahead with this marriage in the face of such focused opposition from her councillors and subjects, but when, on 7 October, a deputation of four councillors waited on her to know 'the inclination of her mind', she burst into tears at the realisation that she would have to turn down her last chance of marriage and motherhood. She marvelled that 'her councillors should think it doubtful whether there could be any more surety for her and her realm than to have her marry and have a child to inherit and continue the line of Henry VIII'. It had been foolish of her to ask for their advice, she sobbed, but she had anticipated 'a universal request made to her to proceed in this marriage'; she had not wanted to hear of their doubts. At this point, she was too distressed to go on.

*A heavy hand tool used for pounding or beating.

With their tails between their legs, the deputation slunk off to report to their colleagues. The next day, they were back, to tell the Queen that the Council was ready to offer its wholehearted support 'in furtherance of the marriage, if so it shall please her', and to explain that they had been moved to a change of heart by her obvious desire to have issue and because she had made it plain that she wanted the Duke for a husband, and no one else. Elizabeth, who had recovered her composure, spoke sharply against those who had opposed the marriage, saying that, had it not been for their eloquence, the majority would have been content for it to proceed. She was finally prevailed upon to promise the Council an answer, but gave no hint of what this would be. All she would say was 'she thought it not meet to declare to us whether she would marry with Monsieur or no'.

Mendoza reported: 'She remained extremely sad after the conversation, and was so cross and melancholy that it was noted by everyone who approached her. She has been greatly alarmed by all this.'

When she next met her councillors, she was in a difficult mood, telling Walsingham that he had better be gone, since he was good for nothing but protecting Puritan interests. She was not on speaking terms with Leicester, and Knollys and Hatton also felt the sharp end of her tongue, the latter being banished from court for a week for having opposed the marriage.

Elizabeth knew now that, if she wished to retain the love of her subjects, she could never accept Anjou as a husband, although it was important that the marriage negotiations be prolonged in order to keep the French friendly and the Duke under control. So, on 10 November, attired in a veil adorned with fleurs-de-lys, the emblem of France, she summoned her Council and 'told them she had determined to marry and that they need say nothing more to her about it, but should at once discuss what was necessary for carrying it out'.

On 24 November, she agreed that she and Simier should sign the marriage articles, with the proviso that she be allowed two months in which to dispose her subjects, as represented by Parliament, to agree to the marriage, before concluding the treaty. If she was unable to do so, the agreement would be rendered null and void. The Queen knew that there was little likelihood of Parliament's approval and that this would give her an excuse to break off negotiations.

'You realise, my dearest,' Elizabeth wrote to Anjou, 'that the greatest difficulties lie in making our people rejoice and approve.

> The public practice of the Roman religion so sticks in their hearts. I beg you to consider this deeply, as a matter which is so hard for Englishmen to bear that it passes all imagination. For my part, I

confess there is no prince in the world to whom I think myself more bound, nor with whom I would rather pass the years of my life, both for your rare virtues and sweet nature. With my commendations to my dearest Frog.

In the words of the Archbishop of York, 'The French matter was dashed.'

At the end of November, Simier and his retinue returned to France, with an impressive escort and many fine gifts, but Elizabeth had not heard the last of him, for he sent her a stream of passionate letters tied with pink silk ribbon.

During that same month, Douglas Sheffield married Sir Edward Stafford, now England's ambassador in Paris. The Queen, who had heard about Douglas's involvement with Leicester, seized upon this as an opportunity to be revenged upon Lettice Knollys, and voiced fears that there might be an impediment to this new marriage because of the earlier ceremony in which Douglas had been allegedly married to Leicester. If that ceremony could be proved legal and binding, then the Queen had resolved to give Leicester an ultimatum: either have his union with Lettice annulled and honour Douglas with marriage, 'or rot in the Tower'.

Sussex, who was cousin to Douglas, was appointed to question her on the matter, but she was unable to produce witnesses to the 1573 ceremony or documentary evidence. Understandably, she now hated Leicester, and wanted nothing more to do with him.

The Queen, put out at being cheated of her revenge, was further incensed when, in December, Lettice Knollys presented Leicester with an heir – their first child had been stillborn late in 1578. The baby was christened Robert and given his father's title Baron Denbigh, but his parents invariably referred to him as their 'noble imp'. Given this, and his undisguised distaste for the Anjou marriage, it would be some time before Leicester was received back into favour.

At the close of the year, Simier wrote to Elizabeth, 'Be assured, on the faith of a Monkey, that your Frog lives in hope.' Around the same time, Elizabeth discussed the subject of her marriage with Mendoza and 'referred to it so tenderly as to make it clear how ardently she desired it'.

But already, the magic of the spell Simier had woven was wearing off, and Elizabeth was once again mistress of her destiny.

19

'Between Scylla and Charybdis'

Elizabeth entered the New Year of 1580 in a gloomy frame of mind, at odds with those councillors who had opposed her marriage, and 'not showing so much favour as formerly to the Earl of Leicester'. Yet before long she began to appreciate the reasoning behind his and others' objections, and when the French ambassador criticised him for placing obstacles such as religion in the way of the marriage, she snapped that he had only been doing his duty as a councillor. This did not, however, herald a return to their previous intimacy, for it was not until April that her manner towards Leicester began to thaw.

At the end of January, the deadline for Elizabeth's decision about her marriage passed without her making any move to conclude negotiations. According to Mendoza, Anjou, who knew better than to press for an answer, was doing his best to court favour with the English, having written to ask the Queen to release Stubbs and Page from prison, so that he might be seen as a merciful prince.

Late in February, Mendoza heard that Elizabeth had complained to Burghley that she was 'between Scylla and Charybdis'.

'I believe that Your Majesty is disinclined to marry, either of your own disposition, or by persuasion of others whom you trust,' Burghley had observed sagely. The Queen would neither confirm nor deny it, even when he pointed out that, if she did not intend to marry, she must 'undeceive Anjou at once'. Her actual intention was to 'keep him in correspondence' indefinitely, and she was not interested in her councillors' warnings that the French would not take kindly to being treated so shabbily. 'Those that trick princes trick themselves,' muttered Burghley.

Elizabeth defiantly followed her chosen course, sending the Duke a stream of undated letters in her untidy 'running hand'. In them, she skilfully implied that, although they should perhaps renounce each other, since her people would object to his celebrating mass, given more time, she might be able to convince her subjects of the benefits of the marriage. Again and again, she praised the 'firm rock' of his constancy, and repeatedly managed to blame the delays in negotiations on the French. 'Our souls are meant to be united,' she insisted – but the burning question was when?

She let it be known, particularly in the hearing of the French ambassador, that she was still in love with Anjou, and wore his frog jewel to prove it. She often tucked a pair of gloves he had given her into her belt, and ostentatiously took them out and kissed them a hundred times a day. Once, during a court ball, she made the ambassador listen while she read aloud every single letter the Duke had ever sent her, with such warmth and feeling that he gained the impression she was trying to score a point over those who had opposed the marriage.

It was all pretence, of course, intended to keep the French happy. Yet although Elizabeth had almost come to terms with the fact that she could never marry Anjou, her councillors were nevertheless kept guessing, and Walsingham sighed, 'I would to God Her Highness would resolve one way or the other touching the matter of her marriage.' To Sussex, he wrote: 'If Her Majesty be not already resolved, it will behove her to grow to some speedy resolution, for the entertaining of it doth breed her greater dishonour than I dare commit to paper, besides the danger she daily incurreth for not settling of her estate, which dependeth altogether on the marriage.'

In July, Elizabeth was still reproaching Leicester for having prevented her marriage, and although her outbursts were less frequent, they were nonetheless bitter. After one such tantrum, the Earl was heard to sigh, 'Better for me to sell my last lands than to fall into these harsh conditions.' The coldness between them made him irritable with his colleagues, so much so that he felt obliged to write to Burghley to apologise. It would be some time before harmony was restored between Elizabeth and her erstwhile favourite.

The eccentric Oxford was also out of favour, having announced his conversion to the Roman faith. To counterbalance the effect of this upon the Queen, he disclosed to her the names of other courtiers who were secret Catholics, which led to all of them being placed under house arrest. However, his revelations did Oxford little good, for his former friends now shunned him, as did Elizabeth, who not only disapproved of his behaviour, but had also learned of his involvement with one of her maids of honour, Anne Vavasour, a 'drab' with a tarnished reputation.

The following March, when Anne gave birth to a son, Oxford immediately admitted paternity and made provision for the baby. But

Elizabeth was not so easily mollified, being 'greatly grieved by the accident', and committed both Anne and her feckless lover to the Tower for several weeks.

The relative stability of the previous five years showed signs of crumbling when, in 1580, Pope Gregory XIII reissued his predecessor's bull against Elizabeth. During the summer, much to the alarm of the government, Jesuit priests from Rome began arriving in England. Their mission, which was to preserve and augment the Catholic faith, was headed by the radical priest Robert Parsons and the devout and inspirational figure of Father Edmund Campion, who would be largely responsible for the remarkable success of the Jesuit mission and the upsurge in Catholic resistance during the coming decade, not to mention the patriotic reaction which came in its wake.

The political situation was hardly encouraging. Mary Stuart had embarked upon a fresh round of plots against Elizabeth, this time in league with the Spanish ambassador, Mendoza, a dangerous association that was to last for the next three years. Relations with Scotland had cooled since James VI's assumption of power, for the young King had become increasingly involved with his mother's Guise relations for a time, and there were fears that Philip II would appropriate the Portuguese throne. With its strong navy and wealthy foreign territories, Portugal would further strengthen his empire and make him the richest monarch in history. In France, the wars of religion had broken out once more, preventing Elizabeth from looking to her ally for support, and England, once again, was vulnerable in her isolation.

In August, news arrived that Philip had annexed Portugal and been proclaimed its monarch. 'It will be hard to withstand the King of Spain now,' Elizabeth commented grimly. To counteract this new threat, she threw the weight of her support behind Don Antonio, the illegitimate Portuguese claimant, whose claim was far less sound than Philip's own. To further discountenance him, Elizabeth offered her support to Anjou in the Netherlands, and invited the French to send marriage commissioners to England as a matter of urgency.

To her dismay, the French did not respond, and it soon became clear that Anjou himself was more interested in becoming King of the Dutch than King of England. The Venetian ambassador in Paris had heard gossip that the Duke had become less ardent, remembering 'the advanced age and repulsive physical nature of the Queen'. In September, the Dutch rebels, weakened by a series of defeats by Parma, had offered Anjou the crown if he would help rid them of the Spaniards; it was now almost certain that, as a condition of the marriage, he would insist on military support from his future bride. Elizabeth reacted to this development with alarm: 'I think not myself well-used. If this matter comes to pass, God forbid that the banns of our nuptial feast shall be savoured with the source of our subjects' wealth,' she wrote. The marriage, she feared, would involve England in a costly war, 'considering that the Queen must of necessity be engaged in her husband's quarrel'. Anjou, ignoring her protests, accepted the proffered crown, and on 19 September was proclaimed Prince and Lord of the Netherlands.

On 26 September 1580, Francis Drake, in his ship, *Pelican*, now renamed the *Golden Hind*, dropped anchor at Southampton after a three-year voyage in which he had circumnavigated the world, the first captain to do so since Ferdinand Magellan's pioneering journey in 1519-22. As he disembarked, he inquired whether the Queen was still alive, and showed relief when he found that she was, for he needed her protection against the wrath of Spain, whose King would be demanding his head as punishment for wrecking Spanish trade and seizing £800,000 worth of Spanish treasure.

Far from treating him as a criminal, the Queen promptly invited Drake to Richmond Palace, where he entertained her for six happy hours with tales of his adventures. Amongst the treasures he had brought with him on packhorses was a crown set with five huge emeralds, which she was to wear in public on New Year's Day 1581. So pleased was Elizabeth with the great booty Drake had captured that she allowed him to keep a sizeable portion of it for himself. Her own share, amounting to £160,000, was placed in the Tower. None was returned to Spain, nor was Drake punished, despite Mendoza's near-hysterical protests and demands. Instead, by the Queen's command, the *Golden Hind* was moored on the Thames and exhibited to the public as a memorial to Drake's heroic voyage.

Thereafter, Drake was always welcome at court, and became a frequent visitor. Elizabeth received him affectionately and delighted in talking of his travels, while he brought her costly gifts, among them an exquisite diamond cross.

Elizabeth's position was becoming increasingly endangered, for from 1580 onwards Philip II was planning a military and naval offensive against England. In December of that year, asked by two anonymous English Catholic lords if it were lawful to kill the Queen, the Pope sanctioned the assassination of

that guilty woman who is the cause of so much intriguing to the Catholic faith and loss of so many million souls. There is no doubt that whoever sends her out of the world with the pious intention of doing God service, not only does not sin but gains merit. And so, if these English nobles decide to undertake so glorious a work, they do not commit any sin.

The Pope's pronouncement was soon universally known, much to the dismay of the English government, which was painfully aware that it would not survive the assassination of the Queen. Only her existence, it seemed, prevented Rome from triumphing in England.

Both Parliament and the Council had repeatedly urged the Queen to take stern punitive measures against the Catholic recusants and missionary priests. Although by nature she loathed bloodshed, and had hitherto preferred to act with moderation, she now recognised that her peril was such that harsher sanctions were called for. Even so, Parliament was dissatisfied with the new Statute of Recusancy which was passed on 18 March 1581, which raised fines for non-attendance at Anglican services to a steep £20 per month, imposed a penalty of a year in prison for those caught participating in the mass, and classed as traitors any who converted to the Roman faith. Furthermore, anyone uttering remarks defamatory to the Queen would, for a first offence, be put in the pillory, have both ears cut off, and be fined £200; death was the penalty for a second offence. It was also declared illegal for anyone to cast the Queen's horoscope or prophesy how long she would live or who her successor would be.

From now on, missionaries such as Campion and Parsons would be regarded as dangerous enemies of the state, but even so, there was no wide-scale persecution. During the next twenty years, no more than 250 Catholics would be executed or die in prison. There is, however, evidence that about ninety of these persons were tortured, and although the Queen did not personally sanction it in any of these cases, she must have known about it. Personally, she preferred to punish such offenders with imprisonment or fines.

It was therefore with some relief that in January 1581, the Queen learned that the French had agreed to send their commissioners to England. For the next few months, she would be absorbed in the elaborate preparations for their reception, not because she wished to marry Anjou, but because she realised the necessity for concluding a treaty of friendship with France.

Anjou, deeply in debt and running out of resources, was once again seeking to ally himself in marriage with Elizabeth. In April 1581, the long awaited, and very high-ranking, French commissioners finally arrived at Whitehall, their objective being to conclude the marriage, or, failing this, to persuade Elizabeth to support Anjou in the Netherlands.

On their arrival, the commissioners presented the Queen with a posy of fresh flowers picked for her by the Duke, and she wrote to thank him for 'the sweet flowers plucked by the hand with the little fingers, which I bless a million times, promising you that no present was ever carried so gracefully, for the leaves were still as green as when they were freshly picked, a vibrant token of your affection, and I hope there shall never be any cause for it to wither'.

Shimmering in a gown of gold tissue, Elizabeth entertained the envoys to a sumptuous banquet in a luxurious new pavilion, 330 feet long, with 292 glass windows, and a roof decorated with suns and gilded stars, which had been built by 375 men at a cost of £1,744. There followed more dinners, plays and masques, pageants, a bear-baiting, a 'triumph' in the tiltyard, a grand ball, and many conferences with the Council. Mendoza commented that the Queen was more interested in 'ostentation and details of no moment than in points of importance for the conclusion of a treaty'.

When at last she did get down to business, she abruptly informed the commissioners that she was still concerned about the age-gap between herself and the Duke. She also felt that, if she married him, it would give unwelcome encouragement to English Catholics. Nor did she wish to become involved in a war with Spain. She preferred, in fact, to make an alliance which did not involve marriage.

When the stunned commissioners explained falteringly that their brief did not empower them to do anything other than conclude a marriage treaty, Elizabeth showed herself immoveable. Hoping she might relent, they remained in London.

On 4 April the Queen went from Greenwich to board the *Golden Hind*, then in dock at Deptford, to dine with Francis Drake and, in defiance of King Philip, knight him in recognition of his epic world voyage. She also brought the French commissioners with her. The banquet served on board was 'finer than has ever been seen in England since the time of King Henry', and during it the Queen was relaxed and animated. For her entertainment, Drake's crew put on Red Indian dress and danced for her, and for four hours their captain reminisced about the voyage. Although many courtiers wilted with boredom, the Queen was captivated.

When Drake escorted her around the ship, telling him that King Philip had demanded he be put to death, she produced a sword, joking that she would use it 'to strike off his head', whilst teasingly wielding it in the air.

Because Elizabeth wished to emphasise to King Philip her defensive alliance with France, she turned to one of Anjou's envoys, the Seigneur de Marchaumont, and, handing over the sword, asked him to perform the dubbing ceremony for her. Thus it was that the short, stocky adventurer found himself kneeling on the deck before a Frenchman, while the Queen looked on, beaming approval.

Later, her purple and gold garter fell off, and as she bent down to readjust it, de Marchaumont asked if he might 'capture' the garter as a trophy for his master. The Queen protested that 'she had nothing else to keep her stocking up', but on her return to Greenwich she sent him the garter for Anjou.

The newly-knighted Drake presented his sovereign with a map of the voyage and 'a diary of everything that happened to him during the three years he was away'. Neither the log-book, nor the *Golden Hind*, survive today; the ship was rotting by 1599. By then, Drake was himself dead, and already a legend, occupying an enduring place in the affections and imagination of Elizabeth's subjects and successive generations for many centuries.

On 11 June, Elizabeth having had another apparent change of heart, the French commissioners were permitted to draw up a marriage treaty at Whitehall. However, the Queen insisted that it would have to be endorsed in person by Anjou himself, and thereupon the French delegation went home in disgruntled mood.

By the summer, Anjou was desperate, realising that he might soon have to abandon his ambitions in the Netherlands and return to a hostile France. Although Elizabeth sent him a loan of £30,000, it was not nearly enough, and in one of her letters she implied that she had changed her mind about marrying him: 'Though her body was hers, her soul was wholly dedicated to him.'

Nevertheless, when she heard that the Queen Mother was suggesting to Anjou that he marry a Spanish princess, Elizabeth sent a reluctant Walsingham to France with instructions to maintain the fiction that she did indeed mean to marry the Duke, whilst attempting to negotiate an alliance that did not necessarily involve marriage. This was to be no easy task, especially in view of the contradictory stream of instructions that would arrive from England, and it was not long before Walsingham, supported by Leicester and Hatton, was urging that the Queen forget about the marriage. This plea fell on deaf ears.

'I should repute it a great favour to be committed to the Tower, unless Her Majesty may grow more certain her resolutions there,' wrote Walsingham to Burghley. 'Instead of amity, I fear Her Highness shall receive enmity, and we, her ministers here, be greatly discomfited.'

Walsingham told Henry III that Elizabeth would be 'content to marry, so as the French King and his brother will devise how she will not be brought into a war therewith.' But there was no guarantee that, even were this condition to be fulfilled, she would go ahead with the marriage. 'When Her Majesty is pressed to marry', Walsingham grumbled to Burghley, 'she seemeth to affect a league, and when a league is proposed, then she liketh better of a marriage. And thereupon she is moved to consent to marriage, then hath she recourse to a league; when the motion for a league or any request is made for money, then Her Majesty returneth to marriage.'

Henry III and Catherine de' Medici, on the other hand, were insistent that any alliance would be dependent on the marriage taking place. They, like Elizabeth, were anxious to be rid of the Spanish presence in the Netherlands, and if they could get Elizabeth to fund the war there, so much the better.

After several weeks of negotiations, Walsingham told Elizabeth plainly that she would have to make up her mind: 'If you mean it not, then assure yourself it is one of the worst remedies you can use (howsoever Your Majesty conceiveth it that it may serve your turn).' If she prevaricated for much longer, she would lose the friendship of other princes. Elizabeth chose to take this to mean that Walsingham was in favour of her concluding the marriage, and when he returned to England, teased, 'Well, you knave, why have you so often spoken ill of him [Anjou]? You veer round like a weathercock!'

In July, Campion was arrested and imprisoned in the Tower. On the following day, he was taken to Leicester House and examined by Leicester and other councillors. According to a Milanese source, 'He answered them with such learning, prudence and gentleness as to draw praise from the earls, [who] greatly admired his virtue and learning, and said it was a pity he was a papist. They ordered that his heavy irons be removed and that the Keeper of the Tower should treat him more humanely, giving him a bed and other necessities.' This did not, however, prevent Campion from being racked three times to make him reveal the names of his associates and recant, both of which he steadfastly refused to do. After that, his fate was inevitable: he was hanged, and the Roman Catholic Church would later make him a saint.

It was inevitable that the new, draconian laws against Catholics would have repercussions, and in the autumn, Philip II threatened Elizabeth with war, Mendoza warning her that, if she did not heed his words, 'it would be necessary to see whether cannons would not make her hear them better'. She answered him levelly, 'without any passion, but as one would repeat the words of a farce, speaking very low'. If he thought to threaten and frighten her, she said quietly, she would put him 'into a place where he could not say a word'.

Capitalising on this situation, Anjou decided that it would benefit his cause, and his treasury, if he went to England again to woo Elizabeth in person. Leaving his troops in winter quarters, he landed after a perilous journey at Rye in Sussex on 31 October, and when he arrived at Richmond on 2 November, the Queen received him openly and affectionately, and placed a house near the palace at his disposal: Elizabeth had personally supervised the furnishing of it, and joked that he might recognise the bed. She also presented him with a golden key, which fitted every door in the palace, and a gem-encrusted arquebus, while he gave her a costly diamond ring.

Immediately, both slipped into their erstwhile roles of adoring lovers, Elizabeth whispering sweet nothings to her 'Prince Frog', her 'Little Moor', or her 'Little Italian', and telling him he was 'the most constant of all her lovers'. Mendoza noted that 'the Queen doth not attend to other matters but only to be together with the Duke in the chamber from morning till noon, and afterwards till two or three hours after sunset. I cannot tell what the devil they do.' Nothing was too good for 'Francis the Constant', and it was rumoured at court that every morning, as he lay in bed, the Queen visited him with a cup of broth. Anjou was heard to say that he longed day and night to be allowed into her bed to show her what a fine companion he could be. Elizabeth even went as far as to have the Duke escort her to a service in St Paul's Cathedral, in order to allay the fears of her subjects, and kissed him in full view of the congregation.

On 11 November, Mendoza informed Philip II that the French ambassador and all of Anjou's entourage 'look upon marriage as an established fact, but the English in general scoff at it, saying that he is only after money. It is certain that the Queen will do her best to avoid offending him, and to pledge him in the affairs of the Netherlands, in order to drive his brother into a rupture with Your Majesty, which is her great object, whilst she keeps her hands free and can stand by, looking on at the war.'

By now, Anjou was becoming concerned at Elizabeth's failure to make any public declaration of her intentions towards him. Mendoza heard that 'when the Queen and Anjou were alone together, she pledges herself to him to his heart's content, and as much as any woman could to a man, but she will not have anything said publicly'. She was also demanding of the French ambassador that Henry III help to support Anjou financially.

On 22 November, knowing that the Duke's patience was wearing thin, Elizabeth staged an astonishing charade for his benefit. According to Mendoza, as she walked with him in the gallery at Whitehall, with Leicester and Walsingham in attendance, the French ambassador entered and said that he wished to write to his master, from whom he had received orders to hear from the Queen's own lips her intention with regard to marrying his brother. She replied, 'You may write this to the King: that the Duke of Anjou shall be my husband,' and at the same moment she turned to Anjou and kissed him on the mouth, drawing a ring from her own hand and giving it to him as a pledge. Anjou gave her a ring of his in return, and shortly afterwards the Queen summoned her ladies and gentlemen from the Presence Chamber, repeating to them in a loud voice, in Anjou's presence, what she had previously said.

Her announcement caused a sensation both at home and abroad. When William of Orange was told that Elizabeth had publicly accepted Anjou as her husband, he ordered that the bells of Antwerp be rung in celebration. The Duke was 'extremely overjoyed', but Leicester and Hatton, along with many of the Queen's ladies, burst into tears. Camden wrote: 'The courtiers' minds were diversely affected; some leaped for joy, some were seized with admiration, and others were dejected with sorrow.' Burghley, bedridden with gout, exclaimed, 'Blessed be the Lord!' Later, Elizabeth would claim that 'the force of modest love in the midst of amorous discourse' had prompted her to say more than she had intended. Nevertheless, what she had just done, before witnesses, constituted a formal betrothal.

That night, she sat doubting and pensive among her ladies, who 'wailed and laid terrors before her, and did so vex her mind with argument' that she could not sleep. She tried to ignore her doubts, anticipating that the French King would refuse the terms submitted for his approval by her envoys, thus releasing her from her promise. If he did not, she would make additional, even more impossible, demands. And if that did not work, she could be certain that Parliament would veto the marriage.

The next morning, Elizabeth told Anjou that if she endured two more such nights, she would be in her grave, and that she had come to the conclusion that she could not marry him just at present: she must sacrifice her own happiness for the welfare of her subjects, even though her great affection for him was undiminished. The Duke professed himself sad and disappointed, but after he had had time to reflect, he resolved that, if he could not fund his Netherlands venture through marriage to the Queen, then he would make her pay to get rid of him.

Elizabeth's new understanding with the French prompted Philip II to extend, in November, an olive branch, saying he would forgive the

FRAÇOIS. de France Duc Daniou d'Alençon.
et de Brabant Fils du Roy Henry 2.ᶜ
1650. Montornū ex.

Francis, Duke of Alençon

'He seemed to grow daily more handsome.'

Sir Philip Sidney

'That inconsiderate fellow, Sidney'.

Sir Walter Raleigh

'The best-hated man of the world.'

Sir Francis Drake

'Drake! I would be revenged on the King of Spain.'

FRANCISCVS, DRAKE,

Elizabeth I; The Armada Portrait

'She is our God in Earth.'

Sir Robert Cecil

'The greatest councillor of England.'

Robert Devereux, Earl of Essex

'He carries his love and his hatred on his forehead.'

James VI of Scotland and I of England

'Succession? Who is he that dares meddle with it?'

Elizabeth I in old age

'There is no contentment to a young mind in an old body.'

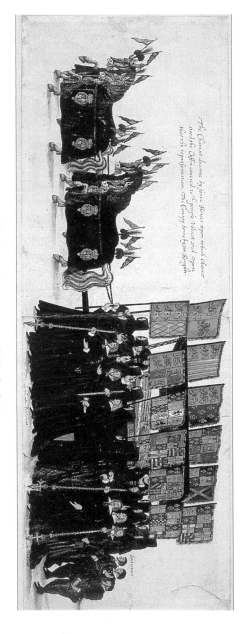

The funeral procession of Elizabeth I

'There was such a general sighing, groaning and weeping as the like hath not been seen.'

Queen's past offences against Spain, and offering to renew the old Anglo-Spanish alliance. This meant that Elizabeth stood in less danger than hitherto, although her government could not afford to relax its vigilance.

As Elizabeth had expected, Henry III received her list of terms with a 'sour countenance', swearing that it was outrageous for her to refuse to contribute a penny towards Anjou's venture in the Netherlands, and impossible for the French to agree to her demand that they promise to render military assistance should the Spaniards invade England. Not surprisingly, the King rejected the terms out of hand, and when Anjou learned what they were, he was heard to mutter something about 'the lightness of women and inconstancy of islanders'.

In December, Elizabeth, jubilant at having wriggled out of a difficult situation, told Anjou that, if it pleased him to depart for the Netherlands, she would send him a loan of £60,000 to finance a campaign against the Spaniards. He accepted this, and arranged to leave England on 20 December. Mendoza heard that Elizabeth danced for joy in the privacy of her bedchamber at the prospect of being rid of the Duke, and she told Sussex she hated the idea of marriage more every day.

However, Anjou was still at court at the end of December and showed no sign of budging, declaring to the Queen that he would rather die than leave England without marrying her. In alarm, she asked sharply 'whether he meant to threaten a poor old woman in her country', and said that from now on he must try to think of her as a sister, a remark which caused him to burst into such a torrent of weeping that she had to lend him her handkerchief.

By now, Elizabeth was desperate to be free of him. This time she had never had any intention of marrying him, and his insistence on continuing the pretence of courtship was imposing an embarrassing strain. Leicester suggested bribing him with £200,000 to leave, but the Queen was appalled at the thought of wasting so much money. She told Burghley to advise Anjou to leave before New Year, in order to avoid the expense of providing her with the customary gift, but this did not work. When, on 31 December, the Duke became difficult, reminding Elizabeth that she had pledged herself to him, she paid him £10,000 on account. Yet still he lingered, fearing, no doubt, that if he went abroad, he would not see any more money.

In the midst of her worries about Anjou, the Queen still had some consolation. That December, she was greatly taken with the charms of an impoverished Devon gentleman, Walter Raleigh, who had just arrived at court with dispatches from the Lord Deputy in Ireland, and it was not long before the newcomer had been asked to stay on permanently and added to her circle of favourites.

Raleigh had been born around 1552 and educated at Oxford; he was the great-nephew of her old governess Katherine Ashley. In his late teens he had fought with the Huguenots in France, and in 1578 had accompanied his half-brother, Sir Humphrey Gilbert, on a voyage of discovery, before securing a post under the Lord Deputy in Ireland.

He was a brilliant and versatile man: in his time he would be a soldier, adventurer, explorer, inventor, scientist, historian, philosopher, poet and scholar, and he also proved to be an eloquent orator and a competent politician and MP, who had a boundless capacity for hard work. He was fearless, daring and overpoweringly virile, being tall, dark and swarthy, with penetrating eyes and pointed beard. He had, wrote Sir Robert Naunton in his anecdotes of Elizabeth's court, 'a good presence in a handsome and well-compacted person'. Elizabeth was impressed by his intellectual skills, his forthright manner and candid views. 'True it is, he had gotten the Queen's ear at a trice, and she began to be taken with his elocution, and loved to hear his reasons to her demands. And the truth is, she took him for a kind of oracle, which netted them all.' Mimicking his broad Devon accent, she nicknamed him 'Warter'. He called her 'Cynthia', after the moon goddess, and in 1585 suggested that the English settlement on the Eastern seaboard of America be named Virginia in her honour.

The legend that Raleigh spread his cloak over a puddle in the Queen's path was first mentioned in Thomas Fuller's *Worthies of England*, written in the late seventeenth century; the incident is not recorded in any earlier source. Nevertheless, the gesture is in keeping with Raleigh's character and what we know of his relationship with Elizabeth.

Fuller also credits Raleigh with scoring a message with a diamond ring on a window in the palace where the Queen would be sure to see it:

Fain would I climb, yet fear I to fall.

Elizabeth is said to have scratched beneath it:

If thy heart fails thee, climb not at all.

In the course of his life, Raleigh was to write several books, including *A History of the World* (1614), political essays and much poetry, most of which has not survived because he refused to have it published. The lines written on the eve of his execution on a trumped-up charge in 1618, beginning 'Even such is time', are some of the most moving in the English language, while, of the Queen, he wrote:

Nature's wonder, Virtue's choice,
The only wonder of time's begetting . . .
O, eyes that pierce to the purest heart,
O, hands that hold the highest hearts in thrall,
O wit, that weighs the depths of all desert . . .
Love but thyself, and give me leave to serve thee.

Unfortunately, Raleigh was all too aware of his own qualities and gifts, and could be 'damnably proud', insufferably arrogant and contemptuous of those who had not succumbed to his charm. Their enmity did not bother him. He had a ruthless streak, had spent two spells in gaol in his youth, and when in Ireland was responsible for the massacre of six hundred Spanish mercenaries in Munster, after rebel troops had surrendered. He was also a notorious liar and a honey-tongued seducer. According to John Aubrey, Raleigh was spied having his way with a maid of honour up against a tree.

'Nay, sweet Walter! Oh, sweet Walter!' she protested weakly, but 'as the danger and the pleasure at the same time grew higher, she cried in ecstasy. She proved with child.'

Raleigh's rise to royal favour was spectacular, and it was not long before he was installed in Durham House on the Strand and appearing at court in expensive, dazzling dress; a pair of his gem-encrusted shoes cost 6000 crowns alone. He made other courtiers look, and feel, like poor relations.

Naturally, his meteoric rise provoked jealousy and hatred in the breast of Leicester, who resented the younger man's incursion on what he regarded as his territory. Hatton also voiced his concern that the new favourite was ousting him from his sovereign's affections in a letter enclosed in a miniature bucket, symbolising Raleigh's nickname, Warter. Elizabeth reassured him, saying that, 'If Princes were like gods (as they should be), they would suffer no element so to abound as to breed confusion. The beasts of the field were so dear unto her that she had bounded her banks so sure as no water or floods could be ever able to overthrow them.' And so that he should fear no drowning, she sent him a dove, 'that, together with the rainbow, brought the good tidings and the covenant that there should be no more destruction by water'. She was her Mutton's shepherd, and he should remember 'how dear her sheep was to her'.

In fact, Raleigh was never popular, mainly because of his conceit and his greed. 'He was commonly noted for using of bitter scoffs and reproachful taunts,' and his pride was 'above the greatest Lucifer that hath lived in our age'. 'He would lose a friend to coin a jest.' His enemies called him 'Jack the Upstart' or 'the Knave', and he was said to be 'the best hated man of the world, in court, city and country'. Perversely, he revelled in his unpopularity, deeming it the measure of his success.

Even the Queen was not blind to the unstable, reckless streak in him, and although she used his talents in many capacities, appointed him Captain of the Gentlemen Pensioners, and knighted him in 1585, she never conferred on him high political office nor admitted him to the Privy Council. He was too fond of 'perpetually differing' for the sake of it, and was 'insolent, extremely heated, a man that desires to be able to sway all men's fancies'. Instead, Elizabeth granted him lucrative offices and monopolies on goods. He therefore had sufficient wealth and leisure to indulge his passion for adventure, study and exploration.

John Harington, the Queen's godson, also made his court debut at this time, having completed his legal training at Lincoln's Inn. He was an immediate success, impressing people with his wit and conversational skills. Elizabeth herself was amused by his 'free speech', but she was probably not aware that he was recording for posterity a series of epigrams and anecdotes about herself and her court which would not be published for another two hundred years. There was a genuine affection between the Queen and her godson, and he never abused it by demanding favours or preferment.

It was the offer of a further £10,000, extended by Elizabeth after he had presented her with a New Year's gift of a jewelled anchor brooch, a symbol of constancy, that finally persuaded Anjou to leave England, which was as well, for the Queen was becoming so agitated about his presence at court that she could not sleep at night and even became feverish. On 7 February 1582, after saying a 'mournful' and tearful farewell to her at Canterbury, the Duke set sail from Sandwich, with an escort of three English warships, Leicester and other nobles accompanying him. The Earl had not wanted to go, but Elizabeth warned him that he would suffer if he did not respectfully treat the man 'she loved best in the world'. She was also relying on Leicester to convey a secret message to William of Orange, asking him to ensure that Anjou never returned to England. At the same time, unknown to the Queen, Sussex had requested William to detain Leicester in the Netherlands, though Elizabeth thwarted this by demanding Leicester's immediate return.

The Queen pretended to be grief-stricken at the loss of her lover, saying she could not lodge at Whitehall 'because the place gives cause of remembrance to her of him, with whom she so unwillingly parted'. She wept frequently, telling Leicester and Walsingham that she could not live another hour were it not for her hope of seeing Anjou again: he would, she promised, be back within six weeks, if the King of France was willing. She took to wearing at her girdle a tiny prayer book set with miniatures of herself and Anjou, a copy of which is now in the British Library. She declared to Mendoza that she would give a million pounds to have her Frog swimming in the Thames once more, and she continued to exchange affectionate letters with the Duke. He, in turn, kept up the pretence that they were to be married, and pressed her to name the date. Elizabeth knew it was in her interest to maintain this fiction, and kept it going for as long as possible. And it served its purpose, for she had kept Philip at bay with the threat of an Anglo-French alliance, and had also managed to avoid being involved in the war in the Netherlands.

On 10 February, Anjou docked at Flushing, fully intending to take up arms on behalf of the Dutch Protestants. Leicester, however, described the future conqueror to the Queen as looking like 'an old husk, run ashore, high and dry'; Elizabeth screamed at him for his insolence and mockery, and called him a traitor, like all his horrible family. As it turned out, Anjou found his liberty severely curtailed by the constraints imposed by his new subjects, and he was also hampered by his own incompetence. He ended up playing tennis and hunting while Parma took city after city and Elizabeth fumed impotently at the lack of support given by the rebels to the Duke and his own fatal inertia. 'My God, Monsieur, are you quite mad?' she thundered in one letter. 'You seem to believe that the means of keeping our friends is to weaken them!'

In January 1583, Anjou turned on the Dutch rebels who had imposed such intolerable constraints on him, and launched attacks on several of their cities. 'France never received so great a disgrace,' wrote an English envoy to Walsingham. In consequence of this, the Duke was obliged to leave the Netherlands and return to France, his ambitions in shreds, while Parma was able to consolidate his position. The Dutch, disillusioned with the French intervention, began to turn to William of Orange as their leader and their best hope of salvation against the Spanish threat.

Anjou's departure from England had signalled the end of Elizabeth's courting days, and she knew it. 'I am an old woman, to whom paternosters will suffice in place of nuptials,' she told her courtiers sadly. The Tudor line would end with her, and for the rest of her reign she would have to contend with the ever-present problem of the unresolved succession. Furthermore, she had lost perhaps her greatest bargaining counter: her hand in marriage. No longer was she 'the best match in her parish': she was ageing, and too old to bear children. All her councillors could hope for now was that she would outlive the Queen of Scots.

In May 1582, a Catholic conspiracy against Elizabeth involving the

Guises, the Pope, Philip of Spain and the Jesuits was hatched in Paris, its object being to place Mary Stuart on the English throne.

It was apparent by now to the government how successful the Jesuit missions to England had been, yet still the Queen would not sanction sterner measures against her Catholic subjects. 'Her Majesty is slow to believe that the great increase of Papists is a danger to the realm,' commented Leicester. 'The Lord of His mercy open her eyes!'

In October, Walsingham's spies seized a cipher letter written by the Queen of Scots, which indicated that she was involved in some new conspiracy. From then on, her correspondence was carefully vetted and her servants watched more closely.

By the spring of 1583, Mary Stuart and her Catholic allies had conceived a plan whereby she would be reinstated in Scotland as joint ruler with her son, James VI. The plan was doomed to failure because Mary herself was insisting that sovereign power devolve chiefly upon her, which would certainly be resisted by James. Nor would the Scots be likely to welcome a Catholic queen. However, Elizabeth, who was aware of what had been proposed, toyed with the idea, anxious to reach a settlement whereby the problem of the Queen of Scots could be solved without recourse to bloodshed. Mary herself believed that James's filial loyalty to the mother he had not seen since babyhood would ensure his co-operation in the plan, but although the young King declared that he desired her to be set at liberty, his chief concern was to preserve his own interests and position, not only in Scotland, but also with regard to the English succession.

Walsingham was still on Mary's trail. At this time, he found out that Sir Nicholas Throckmorton's nephew, Francis, a Catholic, was paying secret nocturnal visits to the French embassy. As he was known to be sympathetic to Mary's cause, the conclusion was correctly drawn that he was working as her agent. In fact he was in communication with the Duke of Guise and the Jesuits. However, Walsingham had little idea of what the object of this activity was at that time, and he therefore had Throckmorton and the French ambassador watched over the next six months.

In May, whilst staying at Theobalds, Elizabeth heeded the pleas of Burghley and Raleigh and, after 'bitter tears and speeches' at an emotionally charged audience, forgave Oxford for his liaison with Anne Vavasour and allowed him to return to court.

Philip Sidney was now high in the Queen's favour, and in 1583 she knighted him and sanctioned his marriage to Frances, only daughter and heiress of Sir Francis Walsingham, a match that was a source of great pride to Walsingham.

In July, Archbishop Grindal died, still in disgrace, and the Queen chose in his stead John Whitgift, formerly Bishop of Worcester, to be her third and last Archbishop of Canterbury. Whitgift, who became a personal friend, supported Elizabeth in her insistence on religious uniformity, and his consecration struck a blow at the Puritan movement, since he dealt with those who refused to conform with ruthless severity. A strict Protestant of Calvinist leanings, he was hard-working, dogmatic and inflexible, as well as being an astute politician – he was appointed a Privy Councillor in 1586 – and a religious disciplinarian. Thanks to Whitgift's influence, within ten years, Puritanism would lose its bite, and no longer pose a threat to the Anglican communion.

That July, Leicester found himself 'in great disgrace about his marriage', for he had presumed to refer to it 'more plainly than ever before' in the Queen's presence. He may even have dared take Elizabeth to task over her reaction to the recent elopement of Lettice's daughter, Lady Dorothy Devereux, with Thomas Perrot, son of Sir John Perrot, a future Lord Deputy of Ireland and reputed bastard of Henry VIII. The Perrots were a family of notorious adventurers, of whom the Queen did not approve. Sir John was to die in the Tower in 1592 under suspicion of treasonable dealings with Spain. Elizabeth had never liked him, nor did she consider his son a fit match for Essex's sister, who had moreover dared to marry without royal consent, for which the Queen predictably blamed the influence of Dorothy's mother. Elizabeth's wrath had been terrible to behold: she had banished Dorothy from court, clapped Perrot into the Fleet prison, and reviled Lettice as a 'she-wolf' whom she would expose in all the courts of Christendom for the bad woman she really was, even proving Leicester a cuckold. However, by the end of August, peace was restored, and the Earl was described as having 'grown lately in great favour with the Queen's Majesty, such as this ten years he was not like to outward show'.

Leicester lost his greatest enemy when Sussex died that year. Even on his deathbed in his house at Bermondsey, Sussex gave vent to his loathing for the favourite, and croaked to his fellow-councillors, 'I am now passing into another world, and must leave you to your fortunes and to the Queen's graces, but beware of the Gypsy, for he will be too hard for you all. You know not the beast so well as I do.' With Sussex gone, Leicester's opponents lost their voice; in future, attacks on him would come from more subtle, hidden enemies.

In fact, though, his power was waning. Elizabeth frequently ignored his advice, especially where the Netherlands were concerned. Leicester believed that England would not be safe until the Spaniards were expelled from the United Provinces, and he still favoured military intervention to accomplish this.

Leicester was now fifty, a corpulent, balding man with the ruddy colour that betokens high blood pressure. He was not well, and suffered intermittent stomach pains that may have been caused by advancing cancer; in vain did he eat a careful diet, and take the healing waters at Buxton. His poor health made him short-tempered and rather paranoid, perceiving criticism where there was none, and taking every man to be his enemy. His friends deplored the change in him, and one, John Aylmer, wrote, 'I have ever observed in you such a mild, courteous and amiable nature. I appeal from this Lord of Leicester unto mine old Lord of Leicester, who hath carried away the praise of all men.'

Leicester still occupied a special place in the Queen's heart, but he found it hard to compete with her younger favourites, Raleigh or even young Charles Blount, the twenty-year-old brother of Lord Mountjoy, who had recently visited Whitehall to see the Queen at dinner. Espying the attractive stranger, she had asked his name, at which he blushed. She beckoned him over and said, 'Fail you not to come to the court, and I will bethink myself how to do you good.' When Blount finished his training as a lawyer, he took her at her word, and was gratified to be admitted to her charmed circle of handsome male favourites.

In September, 1583, Elizabeth celebrated her fiftieth birthday; she had now reigned for nearly twenty-five years.

In October 1583, an insane young Catholic, John Somerville of Warwickshire, swayed by Jesuit propaganda, was arrested for bragging that he intended to march on London and shoot the Queen with a pistol and 'hoped to see her head on a pole, for she was a serpent and a viper'. He was thrown into Newgate prison and condemned to death, but hanged himself in his cell before the sentence could be carried out.

The publicity given to this event provoked an upsurge of national affection towards Elizabeth, and in November, the French ambassador reported that, when she travelled to Hampton Court, huge crowds of people knelt by the wayside, wishing her 'a thousand blessings and that the evil-disposed who meant to harm her be discovered and punished as they deserved'. The Queen made frequent stops to thank them for their loyalty, and told the ambassador 'she saw clearly that she was not disliked by all'.

20

'Practices at Home and Abroad'

In November 1583, Francis Throckmorton was arrested at his London house, a search of which revealed 'infamous pamphlets' and lists of papist lords and harbours where foreign ships could land in safety. More sinisterly, it became apparent that Mendoza was heavily involved in the plot, which surprised Walsingham, whose suspicions had centred upon the French ambassador, who, if he had been aware of what was going on, had managed to avoid being implicated.

Under torture in the Tower, Throckmorton gave nothing away, but after the Queen had authorised him to be racked a second time, his courage failed him: 'Now I have disclosed the secrets of her who was the dearest thing to me in the world,' he lamented. He revealed that the conspiracy's aim had been to prepare for King Philip's Enterprise of England, the object of which was to set Mary on the English throne. The Pope, the Guises and the Jesuits were involved, and there were to be four separate invasions, centred upon Scotland, Ireland, Sussex and Norfolk, co-ordinated by Catholic activists at home and abroad. Plans were so far advanced that all that remained to be done was stir up rebellion in England. Both Mary and Mendoza had been fully involved at every stage, but Walsingham had already guessed at Mary's complicity, for she had given herself away in several letters that had come under his scrutiny.

'All this shows that her intention was to lull us into security,' Elizabeth concluded, 'that we might the less seek to discover practices at home and abroad.'

The government were in no doubt that this was a very dangerous plot indeed, and set about hunting down the Catholic lords on Throckmorton's list. Some were committed to the Tower, but several had already fled abroad. The Queen was pressed to bring Mary to justice, for there was enough evidence to convict her, but she refused out of hand. She agreed, however, that Throckmorton be executed at Tyburn and that Mendoza be expelled in disgrace. His parting shot was that his master would avenge this insult with war. For the rest of Elizabeth's reign, Spain would never send another ambassador to England.

Both Parliament and the Council were in militant mood, fiercely protective of their queen, and urging that a 'final' policy towards Mary Stuart be settled. However, Elizabeth again baulked at this, and this time was backed by Leicester, who wanted Mary kept in honourable and comfortable captivity, a strategy dictated by self-interest, for if Mary ever ascended the throne of England, she would remember to whom she owed her life. Yet his was a lone voice, for most of his colleagues wanted Mary's head.

On 10 June 1584, the Duke of Anjou died of a fever at Château-Thierry in France. His death meant that there was now no direct Valois heir to the French throne, Henry III having no sons, and that the succession would pass to a cousin, Henry of Bourbon, the Huguenot King of Navarre.

Elizabeth was greatly grieved when she heard of Anjou's death, and wept in public every day for three weeks, leaving observers in no doubt that she had felt a genuine affection for her 'Frog'. The court was put into mourning, the Queen herself wearing black for six months. 'Melancholy doth possess us', wrote Walsingham to a friend, 'as both public and private causes are at stay for a season.'

To Catherine de' Medici, Elizabeth wrote:

> Your sorrow cannot exceed mine, although you are his mother. You have several other children, but for myself I find no consolation, if it be not death, in which I hope we shall be reunited. Madame, if you could see the image of my heart, you would see there the picture of a body without a soul, but I will not trouble you with sorrows, for you have too many of your own.

Not everybody was convinced of her sincerity. When Elizabeth told the French ambassador, 'I am a widow woman who has lost her husband,' he commented that she was 'a princess who knows how to transform herself as suits her best'.

Worse tidings were to come. Protestant communities in Europe were shocked shortly afterwards at the news that William of Orange had been assassinated on 10 July at Delft. It was obvious that Philip of Spain had been behind the killing, and this boded ill for Elizabeth, whose subjects were terrified that she might be next. Nothing stood now between her and Parma's great army in the Netherlands: the degenerate Henry III was too preoccupied in keeping the factions at his court from each other's throats, and Anjou was dead. Parma was advancing steadily, taking city after city, and Elizabeth believed that, once the Netherlands were subdued, as they would be if no leader could be found to replace William of Orange, Philip would set his sights on England. Something must therefore be done urgently to curb the activities of the Queen of Scots.

Mary Stuart was now forty-two, and sixteen years of captivity had had their effect on her former beauty and her health. Her hair was grey, she had put on weight, and she was plagued by rheumatism and a chronic pain in her side. Although she had been allowed to go several times to Buxton to bathe in the waters, this had not improved her symptoms.

In 1584, Mary's principal residence was Sheffield Castle, where she still lived under the guardianship of the Earl of Shrewsbury. From time to time she stayed at his other houses whilst Sheffield was cleansed. The Earl scrutinised all her correspondence, and whenever she went out to take the air, as she was permitted to do, he and a troop of guards accompanied her. In fact, there were guards everywhere, both inside and outside the castle, while at night, a watch was set in the surrounding town and villages. Every traveller was questioned as to his business in the district, and no one was allowed to enter the castle or communicate with Mary without written authorisation from the Council. She might only receive visitors under supervision.

Mary bitterly resented these restrictions, but she was nevertheless treated with the honour and deference due to a queen. She maintained her own household of forty-eight persons, selected her servants and paid their wages, Elizabeth defraying her food and fuel bills, which often amounted to over £1000 per annum, and she dined under a canopy of estate, being served two courses of sixteen dishes each at every main meal. She was allowed to indulge her passion for hunting, but rheumatism often prevented her from doing so; instead she worked with her ladies on exquisite embroideries, or played with her numerous lap-dogs and caged birds. She would never leave her prison, she told her friends, unless it was as Queen of England, and despite the risks, she continually intrigued to attain that, unheeding of the eyes that watched her every move. Over the years, it had become more and more difficult to correspond with her friends abroad, and now she had to rely on those members of her household who might be able to evade Walsingham's vigilance.

In August 1584, Walsingham decided to tighten the security net surrounding Mary; Shrewsbury had borne the burden of guarding her for many years and was inclined to be too lenient with her, and she was now transferred into the temporary care of Sir Ralph Sadler. The following month, after Walsingham had shown Elizabeth a letter which proved that her cousin was still plotting to depose her, Mary was removed from Sheffield to Wingfield in Staffordshire, and then, in January 1585, to the forbidding fortress of Tutbury. There would be fewer hunting jaunts there, and it would be far more difficult for her to smuggle out letters. However, she would still be able to retain her household, and although she protested at the move and complained that the castle was damp and cold, the accounts show that she was plentifully provided with food and fuel. Nor, it was pointed out to her, had she been 'so well entertained when she lived at her own will in her own country', where standards of living were far lower than in England.

But all this was not enough to ensure Elizabeth's safety, and by the autumn of 1584, public concern prompted the emergence of a movement among the English gentry and nobility to take more stringent precautions against threats to her throne. There was further alarm and indignation when a Jesuit, Father Creighton, was arrested by the Dutch authorities and found to be carrying a paper describing in detail plans for Philip's now notorious Enterprise of England.

Leicester, backed by several other privy councillors and probably the Queen, although she would later deny it, suggested the formation of a league of Protestant gentlemen, who would all swear an oath of association to take up arms on the Queen's behalf and destroy the Queen of Scots if she became involved, even unknowingly, in any plot against Her Majesty's life. This oath was to be called the Bond of Association, and when the idea was made public that October it so captured the public imagination that there was a huge response from thousands of gentlemen throughout the country, all clamouring to subscribe to the Bond and take the oath. They cared little whether or not they offended their Catholic neighbours, declaring that they would rather engage in a civil war than accept a papist monarch. At Burghley's instigation, the Bond of Association was shown to Mary Stuart, and it was thus made very clear to her that, if she continued her intrigues, her life would be in the gravest danger.

Mary, in the face of all the evidence to the contrary, protested that she knew nothing of any conspiracies against Elizabeth, and even added her signature to the Bond of Association; only two days later, however, she was writing to Philip of Spain urging him to press ahead with the Enterprise, even at the risk of peril to herself.

Elizabeth herself had an alarmingly careless attitude towards her own safety, and her male advisers could only deplore her feminine aversion to shedding blood in her own interests. Although she was immeasurably heartened by these new demonstrations of loyalty and affection, she was reluctant to sanction what amounted to lynch law, and declared she would not have anyone put to death 'for the fault of another' nor permit any legislation that would offend the consciences of her good subjects. Parliament took the same view, and insisted upon modifying the terms of the Bond of Association before enshrining it in law. Henceforth, any 'wicked person' suspected of plotting treason was to be put on trial before being 'pursued to death'.

In order to avoid the likelihood of having to bring Mary to trial under this new law, Elizabeth tried again to persuade James VI to agree to share his throne with his mother, but although the Scots King was anxious to ally himself with England, he made it very plain that he did not want his mother in Scotland stirring up trouble. Elizabeth saw to it that Mary was kept in ignorance of his betrayal for months to come.

In October, Leicester was viciously attacked in a pamphlet entitled *Leycester's Commonwealth*, which was widely circulated, and repeated every scurrilous and defamatory piece of gossip about him, past and present. It also made even more serious allegations that he was a serial murderer, extortioner and criminal. It was in fact such a masterpiece of character assassination, and so brilliantly written, that many people were convinced of its veracity. The Earl had never been popular, and the only people to speak out in his defence were Sir Philip Sidney and the Queen. Elizabeth banned the pamphlet, declaring that 'only the Devil himself' would believe such malicious lies, and writing to the Lord Mayor of London commending Leicester's 'good service, sincerity of religion and all other faithful dealings' and saying she took 'the abuse to be offered to her own self'.

Leycester's Commonwealth was almost certainly a piece of Jesuit propaganda, printed in Antwerp or Paris, but it differed from most such efforts in that it contained apparently authentic details. This lent it weight, and many believed it had been suppressed because it contained the truth. This fiction was maintained for the next three centuries, during which Leicester was vilified by most historians as an unscrupulous adventurer and wife-murderer, and it is only in our own time that the flaws in *Leycester's Commonwealth* have been exposed, revealing the Earl to have been a loyal servant of the Queen.

Leicester's enemies also suspected him of intending to play the part of his father Lord Protector Northumberland to Arbella Stewart's Lady Jane Grey, as a result of his plan to marry Arbella to his son.* Mary

---

*The son in question was now his heir, Lord Denbigh, since he had abandoned the idea of his base son as her putative husband. This arrangement suited Bess of Hardwick very well, a legitimate heir being far more desirable than a bastard.

Stuart thought that Bess of Hardwick's scheme to 'settle the crown of England on her little girl Arbella' was a 'vain hope', and wrote asking the French ambassador to ensure that Elizabeth knew what was afoot. Leicester, however, managed to convince the Queen that his prime motive for the match was to help cement good relations with Arbella's cousin, James VI.

Leicester and Elizabeth had reached the point in their relationship where they no longer regarded or wrote to each other as lovers, but as old friends, bound together by a quarter-century of shared experience and affection. Religion was a common bond, and was the dominant theme in many of Leicester's letters, such as this one, dated 1583, in which he sent the Queen

> thanks for your gracious remembrance. Your poor Eyes has no other way but prayer to offer for recompense, and that is that God will long, safely, healthfully and most happily preserve you here among us. This is the goodness of God, my sweet lady, that hath thus saved you against so many devils. Your Majesty only has been the maintainer and setter forth of His true religion against all policy and counsel of man, yet you see how He has served and kept you thereby. God grant you ever to cleave fast thereto.

They still quarrelled, though, and on one occasion Leicester told Hatton that he would not be attending a Council meeting because 'so many eyes are witnesses of my open and great disgrace delivered from Her Majesty's mouth'. Even after all these years, her verbal barbs could hurt him deeply, but he invariably forgave and forgot, and sometimes Elizabeth even apologised.

During 1584, Leicester brought his stepson, the eighteen-year-old Earl of Essex, to court, where almost immediately his 'goodly person, urbanity and innate courtesy won him the hearts of both Queen and people'. This was gratifying to the Earl, who hoped that Essex would supplant the insufferable Raleigh in the Queen's affections, but it would be some time before Elizabeth came to regard Essex as more than just a handsome and accomplished boy.

At the end of the year, yet another plot against Elizabeth was uncovered. A Welsh MP, Dr William Parry, hid in her garden at Richmond with the intention of assassinating her as she took the air, but when the Queen eventually appeared, he 'was so daunted with the majesty of her presence, in which he saw the image of her father, King Henry VIII, that his heart would not suffer his hand to execute that which he had resolved'.

There is some mystery as to his motive: Parry had travelled in Europe, and the Pope certainly believed that he was acting on Mary's behalf, as did her agent in Paris; yet Parry was also an English spy, working for Burghley, and on his return had told Elizabeth that he had posed as a would-be regicide in order to infiltrate papist circles. She rewarded him with a pension, but then Parry asked an associate if he would indeed be prepared to murder the Queen, and attracted attention by acting suspiciously before the abortive attempt on her life. He may, like John Somerville the previous year, have been unbalanced, yet, put on trial, he vigorously denied any evil intent.

The attempt provoked outrage, and the government were in no mood to give Parry the benefit of the doubt. 'It makes all my joints to tremble when I consider the loss of such a jewel,' wrote one MP. The Commons urged the Queen to let them devise some worse penalty than the terrible death already meted out to traitors, and there were more calls for Mary to be brought to justice. Elizabeth refused to take either course, although in February 1585 she agreed to send Parry to the gallows. Parliament passed a new law ordering all seminary priests to leave England within forty days or suffer the penalty for high treason, and Walsingham was paid to recruit more secret agents.

Although she thanked Parliament for its 'safe-keeping of my life, for which your care appears so manifest', Elizabeth remained apparently impervious to the danger of her isolated position and the threat of further assassination attempts. 'They are seeking to take my life', she told a delegation from the English colony in Newfoundland which had been founded in 1583, 'but it troubles me not. He who is on high has defended me until this hour, and will keep me still, for in Him I do trust.'

She would not modify her lifestyle, nor allow herself to be restricted by the greater security measures that were urged upon her. She showed herself in public as often as before, and when she went for country strolls with her courtiers, she would only permit the gentlemen to be 'slenderly weaponed'. And she would not listen to Leicester's suggestion that anyone with papist leanings be forbidden access to the court. Her councillors therefore existed in a state of permanent anxiety for her safety, although they could not but be impressed by her courage.

In March, James VI wrote to tell his mother that it would be impossible to ally himself with someone who was 'captive in a desert'. Mary was devastated by her son's betrayal, and anguished by the realisation that her last hope of negotiated freedom through diplomatic channels had gone.

'Alas!' she wailed in an emotional letter to Elizabeth. 'Was ever a sight so detestable and impious before God and man, as an only child despoiling his mother of her crown and royal estate?' She vowed she would abandon James. 'In all Christendom, I shall find enough of heirs who will have talons strong enough to grasp what I may put in their hand.' Yet in case her cousin took this to mean that Mary had designs on her throne, the Scots Queen hastened to reassure her that she abhorred 'more than any other in Christendom such detestable practices and horrible acts'. Privately, though, she had decided to bequeath her crown and her claim to the English succession to Philip of Spain.

Demands for Mary to be kept under stricter surveillance were met in April when Sir Amyas Paulet was appointed her new custodian. Paulet was nearing fifty, a staunch disciplinarian who was notorious for his strong Puritan views; when Mary learned of his appointment, she protested vehemently against it, not only because he was of 'no higher quality than a knight', but also on the grounds that he would be less tolerant than most of her religion, having treated her agents in Paris harshly during his time there as ambassador. But Elizabeth had chosen Paulet because he was 'towards God religious, towards us most faithful, by calling honourable, and by birth most noble'. His integrity and his unflinching loyalty to his sovereign had been demonstrated during his service as Governor of Jersey, and she could rely on him not to be moved by the Queen of Scots's wiles or her charm. He would indeed prove to be a diligent and strict custodian, never relaxing his vigilance nor swerving from his duty, and remaining maddeningly impervious to Mary's attempts to win him over.

Paulet wasted no time in imposing new 'rigours and alterations' into the household, and Mary soon realised that her life was going to be much more difficult under this new regime and that she was to be virtually isolated from the world. Sir Amyas scrutinised all her correspondence: nothing got past him, and letters from her friends abroad began to pile up on Walsingham's desk. Paulet would permit Mary no visitors, and strengthened the guard at the castle. Her servants were forbidden to walk on the walls, and when she went out she was accompanied by mounted soldiers carrying firearms, who prevented the local people from approaching her. Nor was she allowed to distribute alms to the poor, a rule she thought 'barbarous'.

There were few chinks in Paulet's security measures, but he had no solution to the risk posed by Mary's laundresses, who lived in the nearby village and visited the castle regularly. Unless he had them strip-searched each time, which was unthinkable to a man of his sensibilities, he could not be sure that they were not smuggling out messages. All he could do was place a close watch on them.

During 1585, relations between England and Spain deteriorated further. In May, in retaliation against English attacks on his ships, Philip ordered all English vessels in his ports to be seized and added to his own fleet at Lisbon, which he was preparing for a war he did not want but which he felt was his sacred duty. Three months later, at Nonsuch, Elizabeth made a treaty with the Dutch, who were now her sole allies, and in September she appointed Drake an admiral, provided him with a fleet of twenty-two ships and 2000 men, and dispatched him on a voyage to capture several of Spain's greatest naval bases in the Caribbean. Drake's mission was successful: he occupied Vigo on the coast of Spain and then sailed to the Indies and sacked Santo Domingo, Habana in Cuba and Cartagena, the capital of the Spanish Main.

Philip was deeply humiliated, but the Queen behaved as if it was nothing to do with her: Drake, she said blithely, 'careth not if I disavow him'. Her objectives, in this campaign of harassment, were to keep Philip fully occupied elsewhere, and at the same time demonstrate to him the might of England's naval power.

Leicester was visiting Nonsuch with the Queen when, at the end of July, he learned that his five-year-old son and heir, Lord Denbigh, had died at Wanstead after a short illness. Without asking permission to leave, he hastened to Wanstead to comfort his wife, leaving Hatton to apologise to the Queen for his abrupt departure. Elizabeth was saddened by the news, and sent Sir Henry Killigrew after the Earl with a message of sympathy.

His son's death had a devastating effect on Leicester. Ageing, sick and desolate, he contemplated retiring from public life. It was Hatton who, with his comforting letters, managed to dissuade him from doing so, and Cecil who would provide him and his 'poor wife' Lettice with a refuge at Theobalds, where they could grieve together. Then, within a month or so, would come the cheering knowledge that, after waiting so long, Leicester was to be given the military command he craved.

Under the terms of her treaty with the Dutch, Elizabeth had extended to them her protection and undertaken to send them an army of 6000 men and 1000 horse under the command of a general, who was also to act as her mouthpiece to their governing body, the States General. On 17 September, she reluctantly bowed to pressure and assigned this command to Leicester, whom she felt she could trust and who was enthusiastic about the venture. However, with his weakened health he was not the wisest choice, and, more pertinent, was the fact that it was thirty years since he had last engaged in active service. Warfare had changed since then, and his adversary, Parma, was one of the greatest generals of the age.

Moreover, when it came to it, Elizabeth could not face the prospect of parting from him. During the past year or so her moods had been more variable and her temper more volatile. Now she became clinging, and one night she besought Leicester 'with very pitiful words' not to go to the Netherlands and leave her, as she feared she would not live long. He found it impossible to reassure her, but a day or so later, she was cheerful again, although how long that would last was uncertain. Her behaviour suggests that at this time she was going through the menopause.

At the end of September, the Queen had Leicester woken at midnight with a message commanding him to 'forbear to proceed' in his preparations until further notice. In despair, he told Walsingham, 'I am weary of life and all.' In the morning, however, Elizabeth revoked her order, much to his relief, but in the days that followed she showed herself so morose and irritable at the prospect of his approaching departure that his heart sank.

She was also adamant that his role in the Netherlands be confined to that of Lieutenant General of her army, and nothing more, for she feared he would seek his 'own glory' rather than her 'true service'. Above all, he must never accept from the Dutch any title or role that would imply her acceptance of the sovereignty of the Netherlands, which she most certainly did not want.

Dejectedly, Leicester confided to Walsingham: 'Her Majesty will make trial of me how I love her and what will discourage me from her service, but resolved I am that no worldly respect shall draw me back from my faithful discharge of my duty towards her, though she shall show to hate me, as it goeth very near, for I find no love or favour at all.'

At Richmond in October, Elizabeth issued an open 'Declaration', twenty pages long, justifying her actions to King Philip and the world at large, and sent Sir Philip Sidney to the Netherlands, appointing him Governor of Flushing, one of two ports she had the right, by treaty, to garrison. She then dispatched an army which had cost her one half of her annual income.

On 8 December, Leicester left for the Netherlands, determined to rid England of the Spanish menace once and for all. He took with him a household of 170 persons, many of noble birth, as well as his wife, who insisted upon being attended by a bevy of ladies and taking a vast quantity of luggage, including furniture, clothing and carriages. When the Queen heard, she took 'great offence': after threatening to strip Leicester of his command, she changed her mind but affected to be no longer interested in preparations for the venture.

With Leicester went young Essex, appointed General of the Horse, a post that would keep him safely behind the lines. However, he excelled so well at the jousts in honour of Leicester's arrival that 'he gave all men great hope of his noble forwardness in arms'. When he arrived in Flushing on 10 December, Leicester received an ecstatic welcome from the Dutch, who hailed him as their saviour and honoured him for nearly three weeks with banquets, fireworks, processions, entertainments and tournaments.

Leicester was hoping to work out an offensive strategy for the defence of the Netherlands. However, he was to find it impossible to do so because Elizabeth, ever conscious of her purse, sent him insufficient supplies for his army. Moreover, as sovereign, she was painfully aware of the limitations of her sex and determined to remain firmly in control of the campaign, interfering at every opportunity. Leicester was not to take the offensive, nor 'hazard a battle without any great advantage'. He naturally resented this, and the further he travelled from her, the less notice he took of her injunctions.

It was the Dutch who caused the quarrel that followed. Disappointed that Elizabeth had declined to be their sovereign, they treated Leicester as a visiting prince, much to his gratification and the Queen's chagrin, and instead of leading a military campaign, he found himself at the centre of a royal progress round the country. Before very long, his hosts warmly invited him 'to declare himself chief head and Governor General'.

23

'The Tragical Execution'

Paulet's fears about security were allayed when, on Christmas Eve 1585, Mary Stuart, having been told that the Queen had heeded her complaints, was moved at Elizabeth's instigation from Tutbury to the absent Essex's fortified and moated house at Chartley, twelve miles away, where provision was made for her laundresses to live in.

'I cannot imagine how it may be possible for them to convey a piece of paper as big as my finger,' Paulet observed with satisfaction. Walsingham was not so sure, having had vast experience of Mary's ability to smuggle out messages, and it was at this time that he conceived the idea of using it to his advantage, in the hope that Mary would incriminate herself and give him the excuse he wanted to get rid of her once and for all.

Fate played into his hands that same month when a trainee Catholic priest, Gilbert Gifford, was arrested at Rye on his arrival from France and brought before Walsingham. Gifford, he learned, had been sent to England by Mary's friends in Paris with a view to re-establishing contact with her. Realising that his plans were known, the weak-willed Gifford was suborned into working for Walsingham instead, and was instructed to pass on the many letters from abroad that were waiting for Mary at the French embassy. Any replies she gave Gifford were to be brought directly to Walsingham, whose secretary, Thomas Phelippes, an expert in codes, would decipher, copy and reseal the letters and send them on to their destination. In this way, Walsingham could monitor all Mary's correspondence. Thus the trap was set.

Gifford was to inform Mary that he had organised a secret route whereby letters might be smuggled in and out of Chartley. Walsingham had discovered that Master Burton, the local brewer in Buxton, supplied the house regularly with beer in large barrels. It was Gifford's task to persuade the brewer, with the promise of substantial remuneration, to convey Mary's letters in a waterproof wooden box that was small enough to be slipped through the bung-hole of a barrel. The brewer, an 'honest man' who was sympathetic towards Mary, agreed, thinking he was doing her a service; he did not find out, until it was too late, that he had been used, and when Paulet let him in on the secret, he merely put up his prices, knowing that too much was at stake for his customer to protest.

Using this new channel of information, Gifford sent Mary a letter introducing himself, along with letters of credence from Thomas Morgan, her agent in Paris, and described the secret channel through which she might communicate with her friends overseas. To Mary, deprived of contact with them for so long, this was an answer to her prayers, and she responded enthusiastically to Gifford's plan, never suspecting that he was not what he seemed. Soon afterwards, she was delighted to receive twenty-one packets of letters from the French embassy, and set to work to answer them.

The only persons who knew about the framing of Mary were Walsingham, his assistants, Leicester and, almost certainly, Elizabeth, who at this time told the French ambassador, 'You have much secret communication with the Queen of Scotland, but believe me, I know all that goes on in my kingdom. I myself was a prisoner in the days of the Queen my sister, and am aware of the artifices that prisoners use to win over servants and obtain secret intelligence.' The evidence suggests that she not only knew and approved of what was going on, but followed developments closely.

When, on 5 February, Elizabeth learned from one of her ladies (who had heard it in a private letter) that Leicester had accepted the office of Supreme Governor of the Netherlands, and been inaugurated in this 'highest and supreme commandment' at a solemn ceremony at The Hague on 15 January, she exploded with such fury as her courtiers had never before witnessed.

'It is sufficient to make me infamous to all princes,' she raged, and she wrote castigating him for his

childish dealing. We could never have imagined, had we not seen it fall out, that a man raised up by ourself and extraordinarily favoured by us above any other subject of this land, would have in so contemptible a sort broken our commandment in a cause that so greatly touched our honour. Our express pleasure and command-ment is that, all delays and excuses laid apart, you do presently, upon the duty of your allegiance, obey and fulfil whatsoever the bearer shall direct you to do in our name. Whereof, fail you not, as you will answer the contrary at your uttermost peril.

Leicester was deeply upset by her reaction. He believed he had acted in her best interests, and although Elizabeth thought he had not dared to tell her what he had done, he had in fact sent one of the royal secretaries, Sir William Davison, to tell her. Davison, however, had been delayed by bad weather, and when he arrived on 13 February, he had been forestalled by others. Nor would the Queen listen to what he had to say, but lectured him 'in most bitter and hard terms'. 'At the least, I think she would never have so condemned any other man before she heard him,' Leicester observed bitterly.

Elizabeth was under immense strain as a result of the Netherlands war, and Walsingham noticed that she was becoming 'daily more unapt to bear any matter of weight'. In March, Warwick told Leicester that 'our mistress's extreme rage doth increase rather than in any way diminish. Her malice is great and unquenchable.' She was even withholding pay for Leicester's soldiers in order to teach him a lesson. Leicester tried to blame Davison for his acceptance of the governor generalship, saying Sir William had urged him to it, but the Queen did not believe this, and soon afterwards appointed Davison a councillor.

The Council was alarmed lest the Queen's anger should prompt her peremptorily to recall Leicester and thus expose the rift between them, for it was unthinkable that the Spaniards should see the English divided. They therefore exerted their combined talents to pacify the Queen and tried to make her understand why Leicester had apparently defied her; it was only after a messenger had brought her news that Leicester was ill that she grudgingly conceded that the Earl had acted in what he perceived to be her best interests.

On 14 March, in Leicester's presence, Sir Thomas Heneage informed the Dutch Council of State that the Earl would have to resign his office – 'matter enough to have broken any man's heart'. The Dutch wrote begging the Queen to reconsider, but it was Burghley's threat to resign that in the end moved her unwillingly to agree that Leicester might remain Governor General for the time being, provided it was made clear that in this respect he was not her deputy and that he remained aware of his subordinate position.

Leicester complied with these conditions. In April, when he celebrated St George's Day with a state banquet in Utrecht, an empty throne was set in the place of honour for the absent Queen, and food and drink were laid before it.

'The Queen is in very good terms with you,' Raleigh informed him after this, 'and, thanks be to God, well pacified, and you are again her Sweet Robin.' Exhausted and demoralised, the Earl wrote to

Walsingham, 'I am weary, indeed I am weary, Mr Secretary.'

In March 1586, Philip of Spain wrote to Pope Sixtus V, asking for the Church's blessing on the Enterprise of England. It was readily given, along with financial support. The planned invasion now assumed the nature of a crusade against the Infidel, a holy war that was to be fought on a grand scale.

On 20 May, Mary wrote to Mendoza, revealing her intention to 'cede and give, by will, my right to the succession of [the English] crown to your King your master, considering the obstinacy and perseverance of my son in heresy'. Philip, however, informed the Pope that he himself had no desire to add England to his already vast dominions, and had decided to resign any claim to the English succession to his daughter, the Infanta Isabella Clara Eugenia.

Late in May, Gifford sent Walsingham two letters from Mary Stuart: the first was to Mendoza, assuring the Spaniards of her support for the invasion and promising to enlist James VI's help. The second was to a supporter, Charles Paget, asking him to remind Philip II of the need for urgency in invading England. Paget's reply, which also arrived on Walsingham's desk, described how a priest, John Ballard, had recently arrived from France to orchestrate a Catholic rebellion against Elizabeth, timed to coincide with the Spanish invasion which was expected that summer.

Father Ballard was soon under the surveillance of Walsingham's spies. Like many other Catholics who had spent time abroad, this misguided priest had an exaggerated concept of the level of Catholic support for Mary in England. Full of zest for his mission, he visited a rich Catholic gentleman, Anthony Babington of Dethick, who had been a supporter of the Queen of Scots for two years. The handsome and zealous Babington was twenty-five, came from an old and respected Derbyshire family, and had once served in Shrewsbury's household as Mary's page. However, it was known to the authorities that the previous autumn he had been involved in a harebrained plot to assassinate the entire Council when it met in the Star Chamber.

In June, Ballard and Babington were overheard discussing King Philip's projected invasion and plotting the murder of the Queen, who was to be struck down either in her Presence Chamber, or while walking in the park, or riding in her coach. Babington undertook to do the deed himself, with the aid of six of his friends, who proved, like Babington himself, to be gently-born, idealistic young men blessed with very little common sense and carried away by chivalrous fervour inspired by the Queen of Scots.

Walsingham,   whilst   keeping   Babington   under   the   strictest surveillance, decided to turn his plotting to the government's advantage. It was fortunate that Thomas Morgan, Mary's Paris agent, had heard of Babington and had written to her commending his loyalty and pointing out that 'there be many means to remove the beast that troubles the world'. It was a simple matter for Walsingham to ensure that this letter reached Mary.

On 25 June, as he had expected, the Queen of Scots wrote to Babington, who replied on 6 July with an outline of his conspiracy, asking for her approval and advice. Addressing Mary as 'My dread Sovereign Lady and Queen', he told her that 'six noble gentlemen, all my private friends', would 'despatch the usurper' Elizabeth, while he himself would rescue Mary from Chartley, and then, with the help of the invading Spanish forces, set her on the throne of England. All Babington asked of Mary was that she would extend her protection to those who carried out 'that tragical execution' and reward them.

His letter was delivered to Chartley by Thomas Phelippes. Walsingham now waited in suspense to see how Mary would respond. On 9 July, he informed Leicester that something momentous was about to happen: 'Surely, if the matter be well handled, it will break the neck of all dangerous practices during Her Majesty's reign.'

On 10 July, Phelippes reported, 'You have now this Queen's answer to Babington, which I received yesternight.' However, this proved to be merely a brief note, in which Mary promised to write more fully within the next few days. 'We attend her very heart at the next,' observed Phelippes.

The letter that he and Walsingham had so eagerly awaited was written in code on 17 July by Mary's two secretaries, who transcribed it from notes in her own hand which she burnt immediately afterwards. The original letter does not survive, presumably having been destroyed by Babington, only the copy made by Phelippes, which was rushed with all speed to Walsingham, adorned with a sketch of a gallows drawn by Phelippes himself.

In this lengthy communication, Mary incriminated herself by endorsing the Babington plot and Elizabeth's murder: 'The affair being thus prepared, and forces in readiness both within and without the realm, then shall it be time to set the six gentlemen to work; taking order upon the accomplishment of their design, I may be suddenly transported out of this place.'

This letter was just what Walsingham wanted, for it enabled Mary to be dealt with under the 1585 Act of Association, and it is almost certain that, in order to discover the names of Babington's co-plotters, he forged a postscript to the 'bloody letter', asking for their names, before forwarding it to Babington on 29 July. Later, Mary's supporters would claim that Walsingham had forged other passages in the letter, particularly that endorsing Elizabeth's assassination; however, Mary's complicity is corroborated by Mendoza, who informed King Philip that she was fully acquainted with every aspect of the project.

By now, the conspirators were openly bragging of their enterprise and toasting its success in London inns. Babington had also commissioned a group portrait of himself and the future regicides 'as a memorial of so worthy an act'.

On 5 July, Elizabeth and James VI concluded the Treaty of Berwick, which provided for each monarch to help the other in the event of any invasion. This meant that Philip would not be able to invade England through its northern border. The news of her son's ultimate betrayal reached Mary just as Babington was asking her blessing on his plot; it caused her 'the greatest anguish, despair and grief' and gave impetus to her endorsement of the conspiracy.

During July, Leicester put it to Elizabeth that the surest way to winning the Dutch war would be for her to accept the sovereignty of the Netherlands. Horrified at the prospect of such a drain on her treasury, and fearful of provoking Philip too far, she reacted hysterically. Then, having calmed down, she wrote to him, rationally explaining her reluctance, and adding: 'Rob, I am afraid you will suppose by my wandering writings that a midsummer moon hath taken large possession of my brains this month, but you must take things as they come in my head, though order be left behind me . . . Now will I end, that do imagine I talk still with you, and therefore loathly say farewell, Eyes, though ever I pray God bless you from all harm, and save you from all your foes, with my million and legion thanks for all your pains and cares. As you know, ever the same, E.R.'

There was to be no more talk of her accepting the Dutch crown.

By August, Walsingham had gathered together most of the evidence he needed to bring the Queen of Scots to her death, and he now decided that it was not worth waiting for Babington to reply to Mary; he must strike now, before either of them got wind of what was going on and burned their correspondence, which Walsingham meant to produce in court.

On 4 August, Ballard was arrested and sent to the Tower, on the grounds that he was a Catholic priest. Learning of this through his friends, Babington panicked, seeking out one of his regicides, Savage, and telling him he should murder the Queen that very day. Savage, although ready to do so, pointed out that he would not be admitted to the court because he was too shabbily dressed, whereupon Babington gave him a ring, instructing him to sell it and use the proceeds to buy a new suit of clothes. But there was no time, and that evening Babington fled and went into hiding, at which point Elizabeth revealed to Burghley what had been going on and ordered him to issue a proclamation condemning the conspiracy. Copies of the painting of the conspirators were quickly made and distributed throughout the kingdom so that loyal subjects might identify the regicides: the hue and cry was on.

On 9 August, whilst Mary was out hunting near Chartley, Paulet had her belongings searched, impounding three chests full of letters, jewellery and money, which he forwarded to Walsingham. He apprehended her secretaries, Gilbert Curle and Claude Nau, and then rode out on to the moors, where he arrested Mary herself. In floods of tears, she was taken to a nearby house to compose herself before being brought back under guard to Chartley.

The Queen wrote to Paulet: 'Amyas, my most faithful and careful servant, God reward thee treblefold in the double for thy most troublesome charge so well discharged. Let your wicked murderess know how with heavy sorrow her vile deserts compelleth these orders, and bid her from me ask God forgiveness for her treacherous dealings towards the saviour of her life many a year, to the intolerable peril of my own.'

Elizabeth ordered that Mary's servants be dismissed and replaced with new ones chosen by Paulet; nor did she relent when she was informed that Mary was ill at the prospect of losing these friends.

Babington, his face 'sullied with the rind of green walnuts', was discovered lurking in St John's Wood north of London on 14 August, and taken to the Tower the next day. When news of the arrests was made public, the bells of London pealed out in jubilation and the citizens gave thanks, lit bonfires and held street parties. Elizabeth was deeply touched by these demonstrations of love and loyalty, and sent a moving letter of thanks to the City.

When Babington's house was searched, many seditious Catholic tracts were found, as well as prophecies of the Queen's death. By now, fourteen men were in custody, charged with high treason. Examined in the Tower by Burghley, Hatton and Lord Chancellor Bromley on 18 August, Babington, fearful of torture and naively believing that co-operation would lead to a pardon, confessed that he had plotted to assassinate the Queen, and made the first of seven detailed statements describing the conspiracy, in which he made no attempt to protect Mary or any of his collaborators. Curle and Nau confirmed that Walsingham's copy of Mary's fateful letter was identical with the original.

The Council now demanded that the Queen summon Parliament to deal with the Queen of Scots. Elizabeth tried to stall, knowing that the

Lords and Commons would insist on a trial and execution which she would have no choice but to sanction. Her advisers were implacable, pointing out that if the lesser conspirators, Babington and his friends, were to suffer the punishment the law demanded for their treason, then the chief conspirator, Mary, should not escape. On 9 September, with a heavy heart, Elizabeth capitulated and summoned Parliament.

On 13 September, Babington and his associates were put on trial. The verdict was a foregone conclusion, but the Queen insisted that the punishment usually meted out to traitors was insufficient in this case of 'horrible treason'. Burghley told Hatton, 'I told Her Majesty that, if the execution shall be duly and orderly executed by protracting the same both to the extremity of the pain and in the sight of the people, the manner of the death would be as terrible as any new device could be. But Her Majesty was not satisfied, but commanded me to declare it to the judge.'

The normal practice at such executions was for the executioner to ensure that the victims were dead before disembowelling them. In Burghley's opinion, ensuring that the lives – and agony – of Babington and the rest were prolonged for as long as possible would be a sufficiently awful punishment, and at length he won the Queen round to this view.

At his trial, although Babington admitted his guilt with 'a wonderful good grace', he insisted that it was Father Ballard who had been the instigator of the plot. Ballard, on the rack in the Tower, had admitted only that there had indeed been a conspiracy. The Queen had not wanted Mary Stuart's name mentioned during the trial, but when her commissioners pointed out to her that this would make nonsense of the evidence, she agreed that the references to Mary in the indictment and Babington's confessions could remain.

On 20 September, Babington, Ballard and five other conspirators were dragged on hurdles from Tower Hill to St Giles's Fields at Holborn, where a scaffold and a gallows 'of extraordinary height' had been set up. Here, in front of vast crowds, the condemned men suffered the full horrors of a traitor's death, Babington protesting to the end that he believed he had been engaged in 'a deed lawful and meritorious'. According to Camden, Ballard suffered first: he and the others 'hanged never a whit' before they were cut down and had 'their privities cut off and bowels taken out alive and seeing' before being beheaded and quartered. *In extremis*, Babington cried out, 'Spare me, Lord Jesus!' The people, whose mood had been vindictive, were revolted by the savagery they had witnessed and expressed such unexpected sympathy for the victims that, when the remaining seven conspirators were delivered to the executioner the next day, the Queen gave orders that the prisoners were to hang until they were dead before being disembowelled and quartered.

The executions gave rise to a flood of ballads and pamphlets, so that soon 'all England was acquainted with this horrible conspiracy' and not only the Council, but the people also were clamouring for Mary Stuart, the chief focus of the plot, to be tried and executed. Even now, however, Elizabeth wanted to spare Mary's life, if only because she could not countenance the execution of an anointed queen. She had hoped that the deaths of the conspirators would satisfy her subjects' thirst for blood and retribution, but, she realised, she was mistaken.

Her councillors pointed out that there were many good reasons for proceeding against Mary under the new statute. There was no doubt that Mary had plotted against her life, and evidence supporting this could be produced in court. James VI was unlikely to cause trouble, for he could only benefit from his mother's death. Mary's removal would clear the way for a Protestant heir who would be acceptable to the English people. It would also remove the chief focus for Catholic discontent and rebellion. The French had long since abandoned Mary, and King Philip could have no worse intentions towards Elizabeth than those he already cherished.

Above all, the Queen was urged to think of her people, who had become unsettled and fearful as a result of recent events and were now a prey to rumour-mongers, who were spreading alarming stories that Elizabeth had been killed, or that Parma had invaded Northumberland. To be on the safe side, the fleet was sent to patrol the coast, and people became more vigilant in hunting out papist priests.

The mounting sense of imminent catastrophe unsettled Paulet, who warned that he could not keep Mary secure at Chartley indefinitely, and urged that she be moved to another stronghold. The Council wanted her sent to the Tower, but the Queen was appalled at the prospect and flatly refused; she also raised objections to every other fortress they suggested, but at length, she was persuaded to agree to Mary being transferred to Fotheringhay, a medieval castle in Northamptonshire that had in the fifteenth century been the seat of the royal House of York. Mary was brought there on 25 September.

It was still by no means certain that Elizabeth would allow her cousin to be put on trial. While she conceded that there was every justification for it, she was aware that Mary's supporters would argue that the Queen of Scots was not only a foreigner who was not subject to English law, but an anointed sovereign, answerable to God alone for her actions. The question had already been put to a team of English lawyers, who had debated the matter in depth and now concluded that Elizabeth was within her rights to prosecute Mary under the statute of 1585.

The Queen realised that there was nothing more she could do to prevent the trial from going ahead. Reluctantly, she agreed to the appointing of thirty-six commissioners – Privy Councillors, peers and justices – who would consider the evidence and act as judges, and at the end of September these men began arriving at Fotheringhay. Among them were Burghley, Walsingham, Hatton and Paulet, as well as two Catholic lords, Montague and Lumley, to ensure impartiality.

On 10 October, a very concerned Leicester urged the Queen from the Netherlands to allow the law to take its course. 'It is most certain', he wrote to Walsingham, 'if you would have Her Majesty safe, it must be done, for justice doth crave it besides policy.' It was frustrating for him to be out of England at such a time, and he longed to return and use his influence with the Queen to make her understand what she must do.

On 11 October, the court assembled, but Mary refused to acknowledge its competence to try her, declaring that she was a twice anointed queen and not subject to the ordinary laws of England, and refusing to attend. Burghley was aware that this would dangerously compromise the trial, and urged her to reconsider.

'In England, under Her Majesty's jurisdiction, a free prince offending is subject to her laws,' he told Mary.

'I am no subject, and I would rather die a thousand deaths than acknowledge myself to be one!' she flared. In that case, Burghley warned, she would be tried in her absence. Hatton urged her to take advantage of the public platform a trial would afford her and clear herself of the charges against her, while Elizabeth herself wrote coldly to Mary: 'You have in various ways and manners attempted to take my life and bring my kingdom to destruction by bloodshed. It is my will that you answer the nobles and peers of the kingdom, as if I were myself present.'

At this, Mary capitulated, although she still refused to acknowledge the court's jurisdiction, and on 14 October, her trial began, the main charge being that she had entered into a treasonable conspiracy against the Queen's life.

Careful preparations had ensured that the proceedings would be conducted in a proper and lawful manner, but, as was usual in state trials of the period, Mary was permitted no counsel to aid her; instead, she conducted her own defence. Limping as a result of chronic rheumatism, she appeared before the commissioners, a tall, black-clad, 'big-made', middle-aged woman with a face 'full and fat, double-chinned and hazel-eyed', who confidently, passionately, even indignantly, denied all knowledge of the Babington Plot. Her crucial letter to Babington was, she claimed, a forgery; indeed, she had never received a single letter from him. As for sanctioning the murder of the Queen, 'I would never make shipwreck of my soul by compassing the death of my dearest sister,' she protested. All she had ever done during her captivity was to seek help to gain her freedom wherever it might be found.

Her eloquent defence was crushed, of course, by the weight of the evidence against her, which was irrefutable. Burghley concluded that her guilt was established beyond all doubt. The commissioners saw their duty clear, and were just about to pronounce Mary guilty when a messenger arrived with the Queen's command, issued in the middle of the night since Elizabeth had been unable to sleep, that the court be adjourned to London to reconvene in ten days' time.

The Lord Chancellor formally prorogued the court on 16 October, and the commissioners returned south. Mary was left to ponder her fate at Fotheringhay whilst they again examined the evidence in the Court of Star Chamber at Westminster, patiently enduring the Queen's constant interference. 'I would to God Her Majesty would be content to refer these things to them that can best judge of them, as other princes do,' fumed Walsingham. But the judges' conclusions remained the same as before and, with only one dissenting voice, they pronounced Mary guilty of being an accessory to the conspiracy and of imagining and compassing Her Majesty's destruction. Under the statute of 1585, these were offences punishable by death and disinheritance.

The court did not pronounce sentence; that would be a matter for the Queen and Parliament, which had to ratify the verdict.

The English had initially fought well in the Netherlands, earning even Parma's admiration. In September, they were victorious at the Battle of Zutphen, near Arnhem, at which Essex fought valiantly and was knighted by Leicester, and Sir Philip Sidney received a serious wound in the thigh, having lent his leg-armour to a friend who had none. Weak from loss of blood, he had ridden a mile to camp, 'not ceasing to speak of Her Majesty, being glad if his hurt and death might honour her'. Her Majesty, however, who since his return to court after his disgrace had been 'very apt upon every light occasion to find fault with him', considered that his wound could have been avoided, and that his chivalrous act had been misplaced. Her subjects, however, applauded it, and also loved to recount how, parched with thirst, Sidney refused the water that was offered him, insisting that it be given to a dying soldier nearby. 'Thy necessity is greater than mine,' he told the man.

At first, it was thought that Sidney would recover, and Elizabeth was moved to send him a heartening letter in her own hand. But his wound festered and he lingered in agony for twenty-six days before dying, a legend already at thirty-one years of age. It had been a tragic year for the Sidney family: Sir Henry Sidney had died that summer, followed by his wife, Elizabeth's old friend Lady Mary Sidney.

Court mourning was ordered for the dead hero and there were outpourings of grief, for Sidney had been popular and was regarded as the epitome of the chivalric ideal. His body was brought home in a ship with black sails, and given a state funeral in St Paul's Cathedral. The Queen, who was 'much afflicted with sorrow for the loss of her dear servant', did not attend.

After Zutphen, the tide had turned against Leicester's forces, not as a result of Spanish retaliation, but because of the Earl's ineptitude as a commander and his gift for antagonising both his allies and his men. Many of the latter deserted, and it became obvious that the venture was doomed to ignominious failure. Elizabeth wrote complaining of Leicester's shortcomings, to which he dejectedly replied, 'My trust is that the Lord hath not quite cast me out of your favour.' In fact, after a year apart, Elizabeth was sorely missing him, and was fearful that his health would be broken by a second winter of campaigning. Thus, when he asked for leave to come home, she willingly granted it.

Parliament assembled on 29 October, setting aside all other business to settle the fate of the Queen of Scots, 'a problem of great weight, great peril and dangerous consequence'. The Queen resolutely distanced herself from these proceedings and remained at Richmond, refusing to stay, as she usually did, at Whitehall. She told her courtiers that, 'being loath to hear so many foul and grievous matters revealed and ripped up, she had small pleasure to be there'.

Both Lords and Commons loudly demanded Mary's head, and unanimously ratified the commissioners' verdict on 'this daughter of sedition', resolving to petition the Queen that 'a just sentence might be followed by as just an execution'. This petition, which was presented to Elizabeth by a delegation of twenty peers and forty MPs at Richmond on 12 November, plunged her into an agony of indecision.

She stressed to them that, throughout the twenty-eight years of her reign, she had been free of malice towards Mary. 'I have had good experience and trial of this world,' she reminded them. 'I know what it is to be a subject, what to be a sovereign, what to have good neighbours, and sometimes meet evil willers. I have found treason in trust, seen great benefits little regarded.' She went on to say that she grieved that one of her own sex and kin should have plotted her death, and she had even written secretly to Mary promising that, if Mary confessed all, she would cover her shame and save her from reproach, but her cousin had continued to deny her guilt. Even now, though, if she truly repented, Elizabeth would be inclined to pardon her.

She desired to satisfy her people, yet it was plain to her audience that she might never bring herself to do so. 'I tell you that in this late Act of Parliament you have laid a hard hand on me, that I must give directions for her [Mary's] death, which cannot be but a most grievous and irksome burden to me. We princes are set on stages, in the sight and view of all the world. It behoveth us to be careful that our proceedings be just and honourable.' All she could say in conclusion was that she would pray and consider the matter, beseeching God to illuminate her understanding, for she knew delay was dangerous; however, she vowed 'inviolably' to do what was right and just. Her speech, according to Burghley, 'drew tears from many eyes'.

Two days later, she sent a message to Parliament by Hatton, asking if 'some other way' to deal with Mary could be found. But short of keeping Mary in solitary confinement for the rest of her life, to remain a focus for rebellion, there was no alternative but the death penalty.

Mary, meanwhile, appeared 'utterly void of all fear of harm', even when, on 16 November, Elizabeth sent a message warning her that she had been sentenced to death, that Parliament had petitioned to have the sentence carried out, and that she should prepare herself for her fate. Mary, officially informed of the sentence on the 19th, took the news courageously, showing neither fear nor repentance.

'I will confess nothing because I have nothing to confess,' she declared. Instead, she wrote to all her friends abroad, including the Pope and the Duke of Guise, proclaiming her innocence and declaring that she was about to die as a martyr for the Catholic faith. When Paulet tore down her canopy of estate, informing her that she was now a dead woman so far as the law was concerned, and therefore undeserving of the trappings of sovereignty, Mary simply hung a crucifix and pictures of Christ's passion in its place.

That same day, she wrote thanking Elizabeth for the 'happy tidings that I am to come to the end of my long and weary pilgrimage'. She asked only that her servants be present at her execution and that her body be buried in France. It was her wish to die in perfect charity with all persons, 'Yet, while abandoning this world and preparing myself for a better, I must remind you that one day you will have to answer for your charge, and for all those whom you doom, and I desire that my blood may be remembered in that time.'

Paulet, reading this letter, delayed sending it, fearing the effect it would have on Elizabeth. His fervent hope was that Mary would be executed before Christmas.

On 23 November, Leicester, accompanied by Essex, returned home. 'Never since I was born did I receive a more gracious welcome,' he wrote afterwards. Not only the Queen, but also Walsingham and Burghley expressed their pleasure at seeing him, for they all needed his help at this time. Although his influence on the Council had declined during his absence, Hatton and others having risen to political prominence, the Queen still valued his opinions highly, and needed his support more than ever now.

That evening, after a private supper with the Earl, Elizabeth sent a note to the Lord Chancellor stating she would publicly proclaim the sentence against the Queen of Scots. But the prospect deprived her of sleep that night.

At this time, the French ambassador arrived to plead for clemency for Mary. Elizabeth told him that matters had gone too far for that. 'This justice was done on a bad woman protected by bad men,' she told him severely. If she herself was to live, Mary must die.

The Queen's plea for some other way to be found of dealing with Mary had been laid before Parliament without evoking a single response. The Lords were asked if the execution should go ahead, at which every peer 'answered that they could find none other way of safety for her Majesty and the realm'. Having unanimously reaffirmed its sentence of execution, Parliament, on 24 November, sent another deputation to Richmond to urge the Queen, with many 'invincible reasons', to have it carried out, for the preservation of religion, the kingdom and her own life. As before, in her reply she was distracted and undecided.

> Since it is now resolved that my surety cannot be established without a princess's head, full grievous is the way that I, who have in my time pardoned so many rebels and winked at so many treasons, should now be forced to this proceeding against such a person. What, will my enemies not say, that for the safety of her life a maiden queen could be content to spill the blood even of her own kinswoman? I may therefore well complain that any man should think me given to cruelty, whereof I am so guiltless and innocent. Nay, I am so far from it that for mine own life I would not touch her. If other means might be found out, [I would take more pleasure] than in any other thing under the sun.

She concluded with a typically obscure statement:

> If I should say unto you that I mean not to grant your petition, by my faith I should say unto you more than perhaps I mean. And if I should say unto you I mean to grant your petition, I should then tell you more than is fit for you to know. I am not so void of judgement as not to see mine own peril, nor so careless as not to

weigh that my life daily is in hazard. But since so many have both written and spoken against me, I pray you to accept my thankfulness, to excuse my doubtfulness, and to take in good part my answer answerless.

Burghley remarked scathingly that this parliament would be known as 'a parliament of words', not deeds.

That evening, the Queen, having tremulously drafted a formal proclamation of the sentence on Mary, commanded the Lord Chancellor to read it out to Parliament. Her scrawl was so illegible that Burghley had to decipher it for Bromley, yet before the Lord Chancellor could publish it, he received a message from Elizabeth commanding him to stay his hand and adjourn Parliament for a week.

On the following day, the commissioners reassembled in the Star Chamber and formally condemned Mary to death. After that, Leicester, Burghley and others used all their powers of persuasion to compel Elizabeth to do what her people would expect of her. If she did not, they pointed out, she would lose all credibility, and men would say that the weakness of her sex was clouding her judgement.

When Parliament reassembled on 2 December, the proclamation of the sentence had been redrafted by the Queen and Burghley, and its publication on 4 December prompted an outburst of great public rejoicing, London being lit up by torches and bonfires, and echoing to the sound of bells and psalms. Yet the Queen had yet to sign the warrant for the execution, which was drafted by Walsingham that same day, and had in fact prorogued Parliament until 15 February, in order to give herself ten weeks in which to steel herself to it. Throughout that period, her councillors would do their utmost to force the reluctant Queen to face the inevitable and sign.

She was torn two ways, for the French and Scottish ambassadors were to be equally vigorous in trying to persuade Elizabeth to show mercy to Mary, and she was anxious not to offend either of these friendly neighbours. James VI wrote reminding her that 'King Henry VIII's reputation was never prejudged but in the beheading of his bedfellow,' a reference to Anne Boleyn which greatly offended her daughter. However, James was more concerned about his future interest in the succession than in saving his mother's life; he had heard that Mary had bequeathed her claim to Philip of Spain, and was determined to circumvent this. In his opinion, his mother was fit 'to meddle with nothing but prayer and serving of God', although he told Leicester that 'Honour constrains me to insist for her life.'

Public opinion in Scotland had, however, been influenced by the publication of the death sentence on Mary, who was now viewed with rising nationalist sympathy as something of a heroine; some lords had even threatened to declare war on England if she was executed, and James could not afford to ignore them, although he was not prepared to go so far on his mother's behalf – too much was at stake for that. He therefore made token protests, while telling his envoy, Sir Robert Melville, to say privately to the Queen, 'There is no sting in this death.'

Elizabeth faced the most agonising decision of her life. If she signed the warrant, she would be setting a precedent for condemning an anointed queen to death, and would also be spilling the blood of her kinswoman. To do this would court the opprobrium of the whole world, and might provoke the Catholic powers to vengeful retribution. Yet if she showed mercy, Mary would remain the focus of Catholic plotting for the rest of her life, to the great peril of Elizabeth and her kingdom. Elizabeth knew where her duty lay, but she did not want to be responsible for Mary's death.

For weeks she existed under the most profound stress, which affected her judgement and brought her close to a breakdown. Her scruples isolated her from her advisers, and she made excuse after excuse to the Council, using her well-tried delaying tactics to avoid having to make any decision.

Paulet could not delay sending Mary's letter to Elizabeth indefinitely, and it is known to have reached the Queen by 23 December, when a worried Leicester confided to Hatton that 'It hath wrought tears, but I trust shall do no further harm.' After this, Paulet forbade Mary to communicate with Elizabeth again.

At Christmas, the court moved to Greenwich, where the Queen agreed that Burghley should prepare a formal warrant from Walsingham's draft. Once this was done, it was given to Sir William Davison, recently appointed joint Secretary of State with Walsingham, for safe-keeping.

On 6 January, Melville suggested to the Queen that there would be no need to execute Mary if she formally renounced her claim to the succession in favour of her son, who, as a Protestant, would not become a focus for Catholic plots against Elizabeth. But Elizabeth saw the flaws in this immediately, and her anger flared.

'By God's passion, that were to cut my own throat!' she cried. 'I will not have a worse in his mother's place. No, by God! Your master shall never be in that place.' This angered Melville, who was unaware of her fear of the consequences of naming any successor, but he controlled his annoyance and urged her to delay the execution, even for a mere week.

'Not for an hour!' shouted the Queen in a passion, and stalked out of the room. She was also angered by a message from Henry III of France, who warned her he would deem it 'a personal affront' if she executed

Mary. That, she retorted, was 'the shortest way to make me despatch the cause of so much mischief'.

Nevertheless, her reluctance to sign the warrant was obvious to everyone. Her councillors had not yet worn her down, 'albeit indeed they are very extreme in this'. They even produced for her precedents from ancient Greece to justify the death of the person who had been at the centre of every conspiracy against her, and Burghley argued, 'Were it not more than time to remove that eyesore?' Davison feared Elizabeth would 'keep the course she held with the Duke of Norfolk, which is not to take her life unless extreme fear compel her'.

By January, the suspense had become intolerable; terrifying rumours, put about by the Council to harden the Queen's resolve, alleged that the Spaniards had invaded, London had been burned, and the Queen of Scots had escaped, causing such outbreaks of panic throughout the kingdom that many men were going about wearing armour, and guards were posted on major roads. It was at this time that the Council informed Elizabeth that they had arrested and questioned the French ambassador in connection with a suspected plot against her life. This may well have been an invention calculated to frighten her into signing the warrant – certainly no further action was taken against the ambassador – but true or not, it certainly swept away Elizabeth's scruples about provoking the French by executing Mary.

'Suffer or strike!' she declared in Latin, pacing restlessly up and down her apartments. 'In order not to be struck, strike!'

On 1 February, Elizabeth suddenly sent for the very efficient and respected Sir William Davison, who was deputising for an indisposed Walsingham. Two contradictory accounts of what happened next survive. According to a statement made later by Davison, Elizabeth told him that she was disturbed by reports of an attempt to liberate the Queen of Scots, and had therefore resolved to sign Mary's death warrant without further delay. Davison placed the document before the Queen, who read and signed it, saying that she wished the execution to take place as soon as possible in the Great Hall of Fotheringhay Castle, not in the courtyard. She instructed him to ask the acting Lord Chancellor, Sir Christopher Hatton, to append the Great Seal of England to the warrant, and then have it shown to Walsingham.

'The grief thereof will go near to kill him outright,' she jested grimly.

Her final instructions were that the warrant was to be sent to Fotheringhay with all speed and she 'would not hear any more thereof until it was done'.

Davison immediately showed the warrant to a relieved Burghley before taking it to Hatton, who attached the Great Seal, which validated the warrant so that it could be put into effect. The next day, the Queen sent word to Davison that he was not to lay the warrant before the Lord Chancellor until she had spoken with him again; when Davison told the Queen that it had already been sealed, she asked him, in some alarm, why he was in such a hurry. Fearing that she was about to change her mind, he asked Hatton's advice. On 3 February, both men went to Burghley, who at once called an emergency meeting of the Council, which debated whether or not to dispatch the warrant without further reference to the Queen. This resulted in a resolute Burghley taking it upon himself to insist that no councillor discuss the matter further with her until Mary was dead, in case Elizabeth thought up 'some new concept of interrupting and staying the court of justice'.

In order to spare Davison from taking the blame, all ten councillors present agreed that they would share the responsibility for what they were about to do. Burghley then drafted an order for the sentence to be carried out, which Davison copied and sent to Fotheringhay on 4 February with the warrant. His messenger was Robert Beale, clerk to the Council.

Elizabeth's version of events differed. She insisted that, after she had signed the warrant, she had commanded Davison not to disclose the fact, but when she learned that it had passed the Great Seal, she made him swear on his life not to let the warrant out of his hands until she had expressly authorised him to do so.

Davison might have been mistaken, but this is unlikely. It has been suggested, both by contemporary and more recent historians, that Burghley, realising that the Queen wanted someone else to take responsibility for Mary's death, chose Davison to be a scapegoat, but there is no proof of this. On the contrary, Burghley held a high opinion of Davison's abilities, asserting that he was capable of any office in the realm; he is hardly likely therefore to have regarded him as expendable. The only plausible explanation must be that Elizabeth herself had picked Davison to shoulder the responsibility – and the blame – for Mary's death. In her view, this would be morally justified under the Bond of Association.

What is undisputed is that, as Davison gathered up his papers and made to leave the room, the Queen detained him. Acting on the often-repeated advice of Leicester, Whitgift and others, she suggested that he ask Paulet, as a signatory of the Bond of Association, to ease her of her burden and quietly do away with Mary, so that Elizabeth could announce that Mary had died of natural causes and so avoid being held responsible for her death. Davison was horrified, asserting that Paulet would never consent to such an unworthy act, but when the Queen told him that wiser persons than he had suggested this, he reluctantly agreed to write to Paulet.

After the warrant had been dispatched, the unsuspecting Queen sent for Davison again and told him she had had a nightmare about Mary's execution. He asked her if she still wished it to go ahead. 'Her answer was yes, confirmed with a solemn oath in some vehemency,' but she added 'that it might have received a better form'. She asked if he had heard back from Paulet, but he had not.

Later that day a letter did arrive, but it was not the response the Queen desired, for although Paulet was one of those who was urging her to let the law take its course, he would not stoop to murder. 'My good livings and life are at Her Majesty's disposition', he wrote, 'but God forbid that I should make so foul a shipwreck of my conscience or leave so great a blot to my poor posterity as to shed blood without law or warrant.'

When she was shown his letter the next morning, Elizabeth complained about its 'daintiness' and wondered aloud why Paulet had ever subscribed to the Bond of Association. She 'blamed the niceness of those precise fellows who in words would do great things for her surety, but in deed perform nothing'.

Two days later, on 7 February, Elizabeth instructed Davison to write a 'sharp note' to Paulet, complaining of the fact that 'it was not already done'. Davison, realising that she was still hoping that Mary could be disposed of by covert means, insisted that Paulet required a warrant 'and not any private letter from me' as 'his direction in that behalf'. That was the end of the matter.

In fact, the warrant arrived at Fotheringhay that day, and in the evening, Paulet told Mary she must prepare to die at eight o'clock the following morning. She took the news well, and was quite cheerful at supper that evening. Afterwards, she wrote farewell letters and gave instructions for the disposal of her personal effects. She then spent several hours in prayer before falling asleep at about two o'clock in the morning.

When she awoke, the sun was shining; the 'very fair' weather was interpreted by Protestants as a sign that God approved of the execution. As she was made ready, Mary wept bitterly at the prospect of saying goodbye to her servants, but she had composed herself by the time she was summoned to the Great Hall.

At eight o'clock on Wednesday, 8 February 1587, escorted by the Sheriff of Northampton and attended by her ladies, her surgeon, her apothecary and the master of her household, Mary, Queen of Scots entered the Great Hall of Fotheringhay Castle, watched by three hundred spectators. Many were astonished to see that this almost legendary beauty was in fact a lame, plump middle-aged woman with a double chin. Her manner, however, was dignified and calm, and she had dressed herself with care for this, her last public appearance: 'On her head a dressing of lawn edged with bone lace; a pomander chain and an Agnus Dei; about her neck a crucifix of gold; and in her hand a crucifix of bone with a wooden cross, and a pair of beads at her girdle, with a medal in the end of them; a veil of lawn fastened to her caul, bowed out with wire, and edged round about with bone lace. A gown of black satin, printed, with long sleeves to the ground, set with buttons of jet and trimmed with pearl, and short sleeves of satin, cut with a pair of sleeves of purple velvet.'

As she approached the black-draped scaffold, strewn with straw, she turned to her ladies and said, 'Thou hast cause rather to joy than to mourn, for now shalt thou see Mary Stuart's troubles receive their long-expected end.'

The Protestant Dean of Peterborough was waiting on the scaffold to offer her consolation, but she refused: 'Mr Dean, trouble not yourself nor me, for know that I am settled in the ancient Catholic religion, and in defence thereof, by God's grace, I mind to spend my blood.' As he insisted on praying aloud, she read her Latin prayers in a louder voice, weeping as she did so.

Then the executioner and his assistant came forward to help her remove her outer garments, so as not to impede the axe. 'I was not wont to have my clothes plucked off by such grooms, nor did I ever put off my clothes before such a company,' she observed. But there was a ripple of comment amongst the onlookers when she took off her black gown to reveal a low-cut satin bodice and velvet petticoat of scarlet, the Catholic colour of martyrdom; by this, together with the religious ornaments she wore and carried, she proclaimed herself to be a martyr for the Catholic faith.

When the executioner knelt before Mary to beg forgiveness for what he must do, she gave it readily, saying, 'I hope you shall make an end of all my troubles.' With great fortitude, she knelt and laid her head on the block, repeating over and over, '*In manuas tuas, Domine, confide spiritum meum* (Into Thy hands, O Lord, I commend my spirit).' It took two blows of the axe to sever her head, and such was the trauma to the spinal cord that her lips continued to move for fifteen minutes afterwards.

As was the custom, the executioner lifted the head by its hair and cried, 'God save the Queen!' But on this occasion, as he did so, the lawn cap and red wig fell off, revealing grey hair 'polled very short', except for a lock by each ear. The face, too, seemed to have changed, having become virtually unrecognisable in death.

Orders had been given that the body was to be stripped and all the clothes burned, so that no relics should remain as objects of reverence for papists, but when the executioner stooped to pluck off her stockings, he found her little dog under her coat, which, being put from thence, went and laid himself down betwixt her head and body, and being besmeared with her blood, was caused to be washed, as were other things whereon any blood was. The executioners were dismissed with fees, not having any thing that was hers. Her body, with the head, was conveyed into the great chamber by the sheriff, where it was by the chirurgeon embalmed until its interment.

That afternoon, on Walsingham's orders, it was securely encased in lead and placed in a heavy coffin.

When news of the execution reached London, the people went wild with joy. Bells were rung in celebration, guns thundered a salute, bonfires were lit, and there were impromptu feasts in every street. The celebrations lasted for a week.

But the Queen did not rejoice: when news of Mary's execution was broken to her at nine a.m. on 9 February, her reaction was almost hysterical. According to Camden, 'Her countenance changed, her words faltered, and with excessive sorrow she was in a manner astonished, insomuch as she gave herself over to grief, putting herself into mourning weeds and shedding abundance of tears.' She erupted, not only in a torrent of weeping, but also in rage against those who had acted on her behalf and driven her to this. Her councillors and courtiers had expected recriminations, but nothing like this, and they quaked in fear at the terrible accusations that were hurled at them. Hatton was paralysed with apprehension; Walsingham fled home to Barn Elms and feigned illness; Burghley and Leicester were banished from the royal presence. A frightened Burghley wrote to Elizabeth several times, begging to be permitted to lay himself 'on the floor near Your Majesty's feet' to catch 'some drops of your mercy to quench my sorrowful, panting heart', and offering to resign, but his letters were simply marked 'Not received'.

Elizabeth was barely functioning, despite pleas from her councillors to 'give yourself to your natural food and sleep to maintain your health'. Yet although her grief and remorse were genuine, they were as much for herself as for her cousin, for she very much feared that God would punish her for Mary's execution, and she was also concerned about what would become of her international reputation when news of this terrible deed spread. Her chief preoccupation was to exonerate herself from blame. Therefore, after the worst outpourings of her misery had dried up, she deliberately affected to appear as ravaged as ever by emotion and regret, hoping thereby that her enemies would say that one so moved by the death of the Queen of Scots could not possibly have ordered it.

And of course there had to be a scapegoat, for she had to convince her fellow monarchs that her councillors were the ones responsible, not her. She insisted that the warrant should not have been submitted to the Council without her express authorisation, although Davison had quite correctly interpreted her signature on the document as implying just that. But in order to convince James VI that she was not guilty of his mother's death, the Queen accused poor Davison of having acted with impropriety; she refused to heed his explanations, and he was arrested on 14 February, tried in the Star Chamber, and sentenced to a heavy fine and imprisonment in the Tower during the Queen's pleasure. Elizabeth had wanted him hanged, but Burghley persuaded her that such vengeance smacked of tyranny: she must not think 'that her prerogative is above the law'. Beale, who had carried the warrant, was demoted to a junior post in York.

But the world at large was not deceived. 'It is very fine for the Queen of England now to give out that it was done without her wish, the contrary being so clearly the case,' observed Philip II, whose confessor was sternly reminding him that it was his duty to avenge Mary's death.

As Elizabeth had feared, Catholic Europe did indeed revile her for what she had done, and that revulsion expressed itself in virulent pamphlets and tracts, condemning her as a heretic and a Jezebel, and calling down the judgement of God upon her. The Pope called for a new crusade against her, and urged Philip of Spain, now ostentatiously mourning Mary, to invade England at the earliest opportunity. Since it was believed that Mary had bequeathed him her claim to the English succession, he would be justified in doing so. But despite papal efforts to establish otherwise, it soon became apparent that Mary had never actually made a new will naming Philip as her successor. A few Catholics in England, including Jesuit priests, nevertheless persisted in regarding Philip's daughter, the Infanta Isabella, as the rightful Queen of England. The lack of any will did not overly concern Philip, who felt that Mary's execution was sufficient to justify his planned invasion and seizure of the English crown.

To James VI, her 'dear brother', Elizabeth wrote a letter of sympathy, describing his mother's execution as a 'miserable accident which, far contrary to my meaning, hath befallen. I beseech you, that as God and many more know how innocent I am in this case, so you will believe me, that if I had bid aught, I would have abided by it. If I had meant it, I would never lay it on others' shoulders.'

James VI made the noises expected of a cruelly bereaved son, but could not afford to risk alienating Elizabeth, so did nothing beyond issuing a token protest. On 31 March, he declared to his angry nobles that he would not jeopardise the Anglo-Scots alliance by seeking to revenge his mother's death, and asserted his belief that Elizabeth's version of events was the true one.

Henry III officially condemned the execution, and there was fury against Elizabeth, 'this bastard and shameless harlot', in Paris, where the English ambassador was barred from the court and dared not show his face on the streets, where black-clad crowds clamoured for Mary's canonisation. But Henry III was faced with too many internal problems to contemplate war with England, and in the end he too lifted no finger against Elizabeth.

On 27 March, the Queen, still upset, commanded that the ten offending councillors appear before the Lord Chancellor, the Lord Chief Justice and Archbishop Whitgift to justify their actions. Burghley, on behalf of them all, protested that Davison had acted within his brief, and that they had all been driven by a desire for Her Majesty's safety. A week later, Walsingham noted that 'Our sharp humours continue here still. The Lord Treasurer remaineth still in disgrace, and behind my back Her Majesty giveth out very hard speeches of myself.' While Burghley was out of favour, his son Robert Cecil had an opportunity to prove his abilities, supporting Hatton, who, in recognition of his political skill, was sworn in as Lord Chancellor in April, Raleigh replacing him as Captain of the Guard. In May, a still distressed Elizabeth told the French ambassador that Mary's death 'will wring her heart as long as she lives'.

It was May before Burghley was allowed back to court, and even then the Queen 'entered into marvellous cruel speeches' with him, 'calling him traitor, false dissembler and wicked wretch, commanding him to avoid her presence – all about the death of the Scottish Queen'. The old man bided his time, and in June had his reward when Elizabeth invited herself to Theobalds for three weeks – the longest visit she ever spent with him, during which peace was restored and she recovered her equilibrium.

Leicester had also been forgiven, and he and Elizabeth were once again happily bickering about how England should react to the deteriorating situation in the Netherlands. That spring, Philip had ordered Parma to subjugate as much of the Provinces as possible, in order to create a springboard for the invasion of England, for which preparations had been stepped up, especially since April, when, with Elizabeth's authorisation, Drake had 'singed the King of Spain's beard' by burning thirty-seven Spanish ships in Cadiz harbour, impounding a hundred more at Cape St Vincent, and seizing a huge haul of Spanish treasure off the Azores; thanks to this action, the Armada was unable to set sail that year, but Drake's daring impertinence had made Philip all the more determined to crush the English once and for all. Leicester was all for armed intervention in the Netherlands, but the Queen was proving difficult.

After the initial furore over Mary's death had died down, Elizabeth rewarded Paulet by appointing him Chancellor of the Order of the Garter. By April, when it was clear that there were to be no immediate reprisals, heavenly or otherwise, she began to realise that Mary's death had been necessary and justified; above all, it had rid her of the threat of internal rebellion, for the Catholic cause had lost its focus and its claimant to the crown, and nothing now stood in the way of the succession of the Protestant James. Catholics abroad anticipated that their co-religionists in England would look to Philip as their saviour, but they greatly underestimated the loyalty and patriotism of Elizabeth's papist subjects, who identified Philip with the horrors of Mary Tudor's reign, and were as appalled as their mistress's Protestant subjects at the prospect of a Spaniard on the throne.

On 30 July, on the Queen's orders, Mary's coffin was at last taken from Fotheringhay for burial; with the coming of summer, it had become something of a health hazard, giving off such a bad smell that no one wished to enter the room where it was kept. It was brought to Peterborough Cathedral, where it was buried with royal honours and great pomp. In 1612, James I would give orders for his mother's body to be translated to Westminster Abbey, where it was laid to rest in a chapel opposite that in which Elizabeth then lay entombed.

22

'Eliza Triumphant'

Leicester, having got his way, sailed back to the Netherlands with 3000 new troops and a fleet of warships on 25 June 1587. Parma, playing for time, at once sued for peace, initiating months of tortuous negotiations.

On 29 July, the Pope signed a treaty with Spain, consenting to Philip nominating whoever he pleased as the ruler of England, so long as that person would agree to restore the Catholic faith. In September, Philip ordered Parma to assemble a fleet of barges for the coming invasion. Aware of the preparations being made, Elizabeth rested her hopes on the outcome of the peace talks, knowing that England was in no position to go to war, having no standing army and only a small navy.

Meanwhile, such serious differences had arisen between the English and their Dutch allies that it seemed the Netherlands might erupt in a civil war, and in the autumn, Leicester, whose own incompetence was largely to blame, advised the Queen that he could be of no further use there. She recalled him on 10 November. Before he left, he ordered a medal to be struck, bearing the legend, 'I reluctantly leave, not the flock, but the ungrateful ones'.

Back at court, he was dismayed to find that, although the Queen had received him graciously in public, she was much displeased with his failure to unite with her allies and check the Spanish advance. Unable to deal with her reproaches, he retreated to Wanstead, having relinquished the office of Master of the Horse, which he had held for nearly thirty years, and persuaded Elizabeth to bestow it on his stepson Essex.

During Leicester's second absence in the Netherlands, the young Earl of Essex had become closer to the Queen, using his newly-won power to the advantage of the stepfather who had groomed him to boost his own waning influence. Thanks to the affection between the two men, they never became rivals. Elizabeth was fascinated by the young Essex and kept him constantly by her, finding his company stimulating. He possessed all the attributes she most admired in men, even though she recognised that he lacked political acumen. All through the summer, he had been observed walking or riding with her, while in the evenings the pair of them could often be seen playing cards or listening to music 'until the birds sing in the morning'.

Essex came from a noble family: the blood of the Plantagenets ran in his veins, and he had adopted Leicester's strict Protestant faith. He was chivalrous, confident and open-handed. He wrote sonnets and stylish, lively letters, and acted well in court masques. In appearance, he was 'very tall', with reddish-brown hair and moustache, and elegantly-formed hands.

Women were susceptible to his charm, his masculinity and his athletic physique, and Elizabeth was no exception, even though she was thirty-three years his senior. This did not, however, preclude the young Earl from paying her extravagant compliments or acting as if he were lovestruck by her charms, which were the kind of attentions on which Elizabeth thrived. She had deliberately fostered the myth that her beauty was indestructible, but now she was becoming hard-pressed to maintain that fiction, having to resort to the increasing use of wigs and cosmetics. But in Essex's company, she appeared to have recovered her lost youth. However, she seems to have regarded him as the son she had never had rather than as a lover or suitor. There is certainly no evidence that she had any real sexual attraction to him, although it may be speculated that, in both looks and character, he reminded her of Thomas Seymour, who had awakened her youthful sexuality.

Yet there was a darker side to Essex. He could be moody, imperious, petulant and difficult, and, when his temper was roused, he tended to be rashly impulsive. He had little sense of self-discipline, and could 'conceal nothing. He carries his love and his hatred on his forehead.' He was 'soft to take offence and hard to lay it down'. A complex man, he appeared to rush through life, but he was also a dreamer who often inhabited a world of his own, being unaware even of what food he was eating and caring little whether his clothes made up a matching suit. He walked with a long stride, with his head aggressively thrust forward. He was as promiscuous as any other of the court gallants, but after casual sex would hasten to church to meditate on God for several hours. And while he loved the dazzle of the court, he often yearned to be at home in the quiet of Chartley. Since boyhood, he had been given to attacks of nervous prostration, during which he would lie in bed for days, hot, shaking and melancholy, unable to speak or think rationally.

The egotistical Essex was driven by ambition; he desired to be the leader of the swordsmen, the gallant young bucks of the court, but in order to enjoy their extravagant lifestyle, he needed money, and that was one thing he was never to have in plenty. He therefore lived beyond his means, existing in a permanent state of near-bankruptcy, from which the Queen, who could ill afford it, often did her best to bail him out.

The young Earl, full of restless energy, also cherished ambitions to achieve glory in a military sphere. Having been bequeathed Sir Philip Sidney's best sword, he saw himself as Sidney's successor, and was confident that he could lead men and inspire their devotion. There is no doubt that he did have some talent in this field, but he could also be very rash or take too much upon himself. 'No man was more ambitious of glory', observed Camden, 'and no man more careless of all things else.'

One person who resented Essex's rise was Raleigh, who had thought to replace the ailing Leicester in the Queen's affections, but whose star was now eclipsed by the new favourite. Raleigh became obsessively jealous, and determined to topple Essex from his present eminence. But when Essex was privileged to be invited into the royal bedchamber to speak with the Queen, Raleigh, on guard outside the door, could only simmer with rage and resentment.

On every possible occasion, he sought to injure his rival. Since her elopement, Essex's sister, Lady Dorothy Perrot, had been barred from the court. But when, in July, the Queen visited the Earl of Warwick's mansion, North Hall, during her progress, Lady Warwick, genuinely believing Elizabeth's anger to have cooled, invited Lady Dorothy to join the guests, along with Essex. Raleigh insinuated to the Queen that Essex had brought his sister because he thought he could get away with showing disrespect towards his sovereign. Elizabeth was so angry that she gave orders that Lady Dorothy was to keep to her room for the duration of the visit.

Mortified, Essex guessed who had been behind this, and after supper, as he sat alone with the Queen and Lady Warwick, with Raleigh eavesdropping outside the door, he defended his sister and accused Elizabeth of having acted hastily 'only to please that knave Raleigh, for whose sake I saw she would disgrace me in the eye of the world' – as he wrote to a friend afterwards.

Much riled, Elizabeth made it obvious that 'she could not endure anything to be spoken against Raleigh, and said there was no cause why I should disdain him. Her words did trouble me so much that, as near as I could, I did describe unto her what he had been and what he was.'

Essex asked her, 'What comfort can I have to give myself over to the service of a mistress that is in awe of such a man?' and spoke with 'grief and choler, as much against him as I could', hoping that Raleigh could hear him. But his complaints only served to irritate the Queen further, sparking a furious and undignified row in which she attacked the morals of his mother, Lady Leicester. This was too much for the volatile Essex, who shouted that he would not see his house disgraced and insisted he would send away his sister, even though it was almost midnight. As for himself, he told the Queen 'I had no joy to be in any place, but loath to be near about her, when I knew my affection so much thrown down, and such a wretch as Raleigh so highly esteemed of her.' Elizabeth did not answer him, but turned her back and spoke to Lady Warwick.

Furious at being ignored, Essex stamped out of the room, arranged for his sister to leave immediately, and then rode at once for Margate with the intention of sailing for the Netherlands, where he could immerse his wounded soul in war. 'A beautiful death is better than a disquiet life,' he declared.

But Elizabeth, guessing that he would do something rash, sent Lord Hunsdon's son, Robert Carey, galloping after him; catching up with the Earl at Sandwich, he persuaded him to return to North Hall, where he was reconciled with Her Majesty, despite continuing to complain of her 'extreme unkind dealing with me' – a complaint that would be heard many times in the years to come.

This set the pattern for their future relationship, which was to be volatile and passionate: their two strong personalities would clash, there would be bitter words followed by sulks, and then the Queen, who needed Essex's presence more than he needed hers, would capitulate. Essex certainly felt affection for his sovereign, but he knew his power over her, and never ceased to exploit it. He would not allow any woman, even the Queen herself, to rule him; in fact, he was to an alarming degree hostile towards, and contemptuous of, her authority, and detested his servile role, believing that a man like himself was far superior, not only in strength but in intellect. He might flatter the Queen, and play the ardent suitor, but he upbraided her with shocking impunity, and made it plain he resented her having the upper hand in the relationship. Clearly, he often found her to be a meddling, irritating and outdated old woman. The astonishing thing was that she, to the consternation of others, often let him get away with it. Some even wondered if she enjoyed having Essex ordering her about. But when it came to allowing him the political influence he did not merit, or the exercise of patronage which he would have exploited shamelessly, she drew a firm line. It was then that the sparks flew, for Essex believed, quite wrongly and contrary to all the testimony of older, sager men, that he could bully her into submission. Elizabeth knew this and was prepared.

On 21 December the Queen appointed Charles, Lord Howard of Effingham, Lieutenant General, Lord High Admiral and Commander of the English navy, and ordered the fleet to be put on standby. There was no doubt now that Philip would send his Armada soon; she had known his plans since November: the Armada of Spanish galleons was to defeat the English fleet and pave the way for Parma, who would immediately land in England with an army from the Netherlands. When Elizabeth had been deposed and the country secured, Philip himself would arrive to claim the crown for his daughter and the Catholic faith.

According to Holinshed, as the year 1588 approached, the English people remembered that astrologers and seers had predicted 'most wonderful and very extraordinary accidents' at this time, and were deeply fearful. But the Queen, who had had her own horoscope cast, was more optimistic.

On a practical level, she and her government had begun to brace themselves for war. Harbours and land defences were strengthened, eleven new ships were built, and old ones refurbished. A chain of beacons to signal the arrival of the invasion was being set up on hill-tops throughout the kingdom. Sailors and soldiers had been recruited, and arms and stores were being requisitioned. Even so, England was far from ready to face an invasion, and when it became clear that Philip's fleet was not ready either, and would probably not come until the following summer, the Queen, never one to waste money, commanded that her own ships be demobilised.

Although she possessed undoubted courage, Elizabeth certainly did not want a war: it was not in her nature to crave military glory, and she was appalled at the expense in both money and lives. If diplomacy could bring about a solution, she would take that course, and indeed she would continue to sue for peace right up until after the Armada had sailed.

Leicester had not been invited to court for Christmas, for Elizabeth was still angry with him, and when there was no word from her in January, he wrote begging her 'to behold with the eyes of your princely clemency my wretched and depressed state'. But he was cheered to learn of her loyal refusal to countenance an attempt by Lord Buckhurst to make him answer for the mismanagement of the Netherlands venture.

The looming reality of war prompted Elizabeth to send for Leicester, and throughout the early months of 1588 he was assiduous in his attendance at Council meetings, despite worsening ill health. More vociferous than the rest, he warned Elizabeth that diplomacy would not suffice: she must further strengthen her armed forces.

In April, Elizabeth ordered the refurbishment of twelve more ships and her government instituted a programme of intensive training for her fighting forces. Drake was in favour of sailing to Spain to sabotage Philip's fleet, but she would not allow it, being concerned that her own ships would be either damaged or lost when she most needed them. Any confrontation at sea, she said, must take place within sight of the shores of England, in order to remind her sailors what they were fighting for.

She was still hoping that it might never come to war. In April, she dispatched Dr Valentine Dale, her former ambassador to Paris, to Parma to sue for peace. The commissioners for both sides met to discuss the matter on 30 May, the very day on which the Spanish Armada of 130 ships, manned by 30,000 men under the command of the Duke of Medina Sidonia, set sail from Lisbon, bound for England. By then, the English fleet was already at battle-stations at Plymouth.

On board the Spanish ships were thousands of printed copies of a papal Bull blessing the enterprise, reaffirming Elizabeth's excommunication, and calling upon her subjects to depose her. These were to be distributed in England by the invading forces. However, when, late in June, Elizabeth's subjects learned of the existence of this Bull, they proved fiercely loyal.

In early June, Cardinal William Allen published a vicious attack on Elizabeth entitled *An Admonition to the Nobility and People of England*. In it, he referred to Henry VIII as the Queen's 'supposed father' and to Elizabeth as 'an incestuous bastard, begotten and born in sin of an infamous courtesan'. Elizabeth was angered and upset by these smears, and instructed Dr Dale to complain about them on her behalf to Parma. The Duke, however, said he had not read Allen's book and knew nothing of the new Bull. He was sorry for the bad feeling between his master and Queen Elizabeth, but as a soldier, he was bound to obey his orders. Even as late as 8 July, the Queen was writing to assure Parma that 'if any reasonable conditions of peace should be offered', she would not hesitate to accept them.

'For the love of Jesus Christ, Madam,' wrote the Lord Admiral, 'awake thoroughly and see the villainous treasons around you, against Your Majesty and your realm, and draw your forces round about you like a mighty prince to defend you. Truly, Madam, if you do so, there is no cause to fear. If you do not, there will be danger.'

On 17 July, Elizabeth brought the peace negotiations to a close.

The progress of the Spanish fleet had been impeded by storms, but on 19 July, what the Spaniards were referring to as the 'invincible' Armada was first sighted by the English off The Lizard. Legend has it that Drake was playing bowls on Plymouth Hoe at the time, but insisted he had time to finish the game before departing to vanquish the enemy.

As the chain of beacons flared, Elizabeth heard the news on the night of 22 July at Richmond, where the Council would meet daily in emergency session over the next few days. Robert Cecil was impressed by her calm response: 'It is a comfort to see how great magnanimity Her Majesty shows, who is not a whit dismayed.' She spoke stirring words of reassurance to Leicester, who 'spared not to blaze them abroad as a comfort to all'. The Queen's calm reaction was the result of knowing that everything possible had been done to make England ready to repel the invader, and that her navy, with its smaller, lighter and faster ships which sailed 'low and snug in the water', was, in the words of Effingham, 'the strongest that any prince in Christendom hath'.

A prayer of intercession, composed by the Queen, was read in churches. At court, a strange peace descended, for by Elizabeth's command, all squabbles between factions and feuding had ceased. Throughout the land, the nation waited, expectant and fearful.

Moving along the south coast, the stately Armada was making for the Netherlands, whence it would escort Parma's army to England. Waiting at Plymouth was the English fleet, 150 strong and flying the white and green colours of the Tudors from its masts. It was under the command of Admiral Lord Howard of Effingham, assisted by the much more experienced Sir Francis Drake; the Admiral, realising that his rank rather than his naval achievements had qualified him for his command, gallantly announced that he would 'yield ever unto them of greater experience'. Drake, in turn, behaved so 'lovingly and kindly' towards Effingham that he 'dispelled the fears about this doubtful union'.

The Admiral's flagship was the *Ark Royal*, formerly known as the *Ark Raleigh*, having been sold to the Queen by Raleigh the previous year. Effingham had been authorised by the Queen to conduct all engagements according to his own judgement. By contrast, Philip had written detailed – and sometimes unrealistic – instructions by which Medina-Sidonia was to abide.

Effingham put out to sea in pursuit of the Armada after nightfall on the 19th. There was a brief and inconclusive skirmish off Eddystone, near Plymouth, on Sunday, 21 July, followed two days later by a more vicious engagement near Portland, Dorset, in which several Spanish galleons were severely damaged. Two more were wrecked off the Isle of Wight on 25 July. The English fleet continued to shadow the Armada as it sailed east, neatly avoiding any further engagements by sailing out of range whenever the galleons prepared for battle.

Meanwhile, the shire levies had been mustered, and Leicester, who had just been appointed Lieutenant and Captain General of the Queen's Armies and Companies, had begun to assemble 4000 troops at Tilbury Fort in the Thames Estuary, ready to guard the eastern approach to London against Parma's forces. Already he had built a blockade of boats across the river.

The Queen was boldly insisting that she ride to the south coast to be at the head of her southern levies, ready to meet Parma when he came, a notion which horrified her advisers. To divert her, on 27 July, Leicester invited her to visit Tilbury and 'comfort' her army, assuring her that 'you shall, dear lady, behold as goodly, as loyal and as able men as any prince Christian can show you'; he himself would vouchsafe for the safety of her person, 'the most dainty and sacred thing we have in this world to care for, [so that] a man must tremble when he thinks of it'.

On that same day, the Armada anchored off Calais, not far from Dunkirk, where Parma was waiting with 16,000 troops to cross the Channel. The Dutch fleet was patrolling the sea nearby, hoping to prevent the Spanish from sailing.

The English followed the Armada to Calais, where at midnight on the 28th orders were given for five 'hell-burners', or fire-ships, packed with wood and pitch, to be sent amongst the towering galleons. The resulting inferno, fanned by high winds, caused panic and chaos, scattering the Spanish galleons and wrecking the crescent formation of the Armada, which was unable to regroup because of the winds. This meant that the little English ships would now be able to fight on more equal terms. As a result of this action, morale amongst Spanish forces was fatally weakened.

On 29 July, off Gravelines, Medina-Sidonia made heroic and not entirely unsuccessful efforts to re-form his ships before the two fleets engaged in what was to be the final battle. But the English, with greater numbers, now had the advantage, and they pressed it home. The Spaniards lost eleven ships and 2000 men, and the English just fifty men. The action was only abandoned when both sides ran out of ammunition.

Not yet knowing that the English had gained the upper hand, the Queen moved on 30 July to St James's Palace, where her security could be better assured than at Richmond, and which Lord Hunsdon, who had been designated responsible for the Queen's security when she was in the capital, immediately surrounded by a cordon of 2000 armed guards. However, Elizabeth was 'not a whit dismayed' at her peril.

It was at this time that the wind changed, forcing the Armada north-wards, off course, and scattering the remaining galleons. 'There was never anything pleased me better than seeing the enemy flying with a southerly wind northward,' wrote a jubilant Drake. Effingham ordered his ships to go after them, but they could not do much more damage because they had again run out of ammunition. In fact, they had no need to do anything further, for the wind – the 'Protestant' wind, as people were now calling it, taking it to be a sign from God – and terrible storms were bringing about more destruction than they could realistically have hoped to achieve themselves.

By 2 August, Lord Howard, having pursued the crippled remnants of the Armada as far north as the Firth of Forth, gave up and returned south, leaving the scattered and broken ships to make their difficult way around the coasts of Scotland, Ireland and Cornwall. 'Many of them will never see Spain again,' wrote one English sailor.

Although false reports of victory had prompted premature rejoicing in Spain, by 3 August, when Medina-Sidonia ordered his remaining few ships to return home, it was clear that the Spanish had suffered the most humiliating naval defeat in their history. They had lost two thirds of their men (many dying stranded on remote beaches of wounds and sickness, or slaughtered in Ireland by the Lord Deputy's men) and forty-four ships, and many more were so badly damaged that they would no longer be seaworthy. The English, on the other hand, had lost only a hundred men, and none of their ships. But Elizabeth was cautious. This 'tyrannical, proud and brainsick attempt' would be, she observed in a letter to James VI, 'the beginning, though not the end, of the ruin of that King [Philip]'.

The Spanish fleet might have been crippled, but there remained a very real threat from Parma and his army, who were poised to cross the Channel, and awaited only a favourable wind.

Expecting an invasion at any moment, Elizabeth, 'with a masculine spirit', resolved to accept Leicester's invitation and go to Tilbury to rally her troops, and thither she was rowed in her state barge from St James's Palace on 8 August. Her councillors had pleaded with her not to go, fearing her proximity to the expected invaders and raising a host of other objections, but she overrode them, and when she wrote informing Leicester of her determination to visit the camp, he replied, 'Good, sweet Queen, alter not your purpose if God give you good health. The lodging prepared for Your Majesty is a proper, sweet, cleanly house, the camp within a little mile of it, and your person as sure as at St James's.'

Escorted by Leicester, who walked bare-headed holding her bridle, and riding a large white gelding 'attired like an angel bright', the Queen appeared before her troops in the guise of 'some Amazonian empress' in a white velvet dress with a shining silver cuirass, and preceded by a page carrying her silver helmet on a white cushion and the Earl of Ormonde bearing the sword of state. Leicester had stage-managed the occasion brilliantly, incorporating much pageantry and spectacle. As the tent-flags and pennants fluttered in the breeze, and the drummers and pipers played, the Queen, with tears in her eyes, inspected the immaculate squadrons of foot soldiers, and the well-caparisoned, plumed cavalry, of which Essex was a commander, calling out 'God bless you all!' as many fell to their knees and cried aloud, 'Lord preserve our Queen!' As she passed, pikes and ensigns were lowered in respect. After a stirring service of intercession, she rode to Edward Ritchie's manor house at nearby Saffron Garden, where she stayed the night.

On the morning of 9 August, as she returned to the camp, there was a burst of spontaneous applause – 'the earth and air did sound like thunder' – and Elizabeth commented that she felt she was 'in the midst and heat of battle'. When the clamour had died down, the soldiers acted out a mock engagement, after which they paraded before her. Then, 'most bravely mounted on a most stately steed', and dressed as 'an armed Pallas' with her silver breastplate and a small silver and gold leader's truncheon in her hand, the Queen again touched their hearts by delivering the most rousing and famous speech of her reign.

'My loving people,' she cried,

we have been persuaded by some that are careful of our safety to take heed how we commit ourselves to armed multitudes, for fear of treachery; but I do assure you, I do not desire to live to distrust my faithful and loving people.

Let tyrants fear. I have always so behaved myself that, under God, I have placed my chiefest strength and safeguard in the loyal hearts and goodwill of my subjects, and therefore I am come amongst you, as you see, at this time, not for my recreation and disport, but being resolved in the midst and heat of the battle to live or die amongst you all, to lay down for my God and for my kingdom, and for my people, my honour and my blood, even in the dust.

I know I have the body of a weak and feeble woman, but I have the heart and stomach of a king, and of a king of England too, and think it foul scorn that Parma or Spain, or any prince of Europe, should dare invade the borders of my realm; to which, rather than any dishonour shall grow by me, I myself will take up arms, I myself will be your general, judge, and rewarder of every one of your virtues.

In the meantime, my Lieutenant General [Leicester] shall be in my stead, than whom never prince commanded a more noble or worthy subject, not doubting but, by your obedience to my general, by your concord in the camp and your valour in the field, we shall shortly have a famous victory over these enemies of God, of my kingdom, and of my people.

At the close of this 'most excellent oration', the assembled soldiers 'all at once a mighty shout or cry did give'. Dr Lionel Sharp, one of the Queen's chaplains, was commissioned by Leicester to take down the text of her speech, and it was read aloud again the next day, after the

Queen had left, to all those who had been out of earshot. Copies were widely circulated, and three decades later, Sharp gave the text to the Duke of Buckingham, whose son had it published in 1654. Leicester was convinced that Elizabeth's words 'had so inflamed the hearts of her good subjects, as I think the weakest among them is able to match the proudest Spaniard that dares land in England'.

At noon, as Elizabeth dined with Leicester in his tent, she received word that Parma was due to set sail. The Earl and his captains urged her to return to London for safety, but she protested that she could not in honour do so, having said she would fight and die with her people. Many were moved by her courage, but 'as night approached nigh' news arrived that the danger was past, for Parma had refused to venture his army without the backing of the Spanish navy, and Philip had, with a heavy heart, seen the wisdom of this.

He was, naturally, desolated by the defeat, and retreated into his palace of the Escorial near Madrid, seeking to find consolation and understanding in prayer. 'In spite of everything, His Majesty shows himself determined to carry on the war,' reported the Venetian ambassador. Philip told his confessor he would fight on and that he was hoping for a miracle from God, but if it was not forthcoming, 'I hope to die and go to him.' His people put on mourning clothes, and walked in the streets with heads bent in shame.

'The Duke of Parma is as a bear robbed of his whelps,' wrote Drake from Gravelines on 10 August. Making her way back to a triumphal welcome in London, secure in the knowledge that the Armada would not return, Elizabeth's first consideration was to decommission her ships and dismiss her forces, so that they could go home and bring in the harvest. Only when this had been done could she begin to celebrate England's great victory and her own triumph.

She had not 'lost her presence of mind for a single moment', reported the Venetian ambassador in Paris, 'nor neglected aught that was necessary for the occasion. Her acuteness in resolving the action, her courage in carrying it out, show her high-spirited desire of glory and her resolve to save her country and herself.'

According to Camden, her gratitude towards Leicester led her to have Letters Patent drawn up appointing him Lieutenant Governor of England and Ireland, a position that would invest him with more power than had ever been granted to an English subject. Burghley, Walsingham and Hatton, however, fearing the consequences of the favourite becoming a virtual viceroy, persuaded the Queen to change her mind, and it appears that Leicester never knew how well she wished to reward him.

Thanks to the thorough preparations made by the government, the intensive training and organisation of troops and resources, the skill of the English commanders, and of course the 'Protestant' wind, the mighty Armada had been vanquished, and England had achieved one of the greatest victories in her history.

The camp at Tilbury was disbanded on 17 August, when Leicester rode in triumph back to London 'with so many gentlemen as if he were a king', to be greeted by cheering crowds. On the 20th, the Lord Mayor and aldermen of London attended a packed service at St Paul's to give thanks for the victory.

At the beginning of September, most of the sailors were discharged; money was in desperately short supply and Elizabeth could not even afford to pay the remaining wages due to the men. Few had lost their lives during the fighting, but the poor provisioning of the ships and rations of sour beer had left thousands of sailors ill or dying of typhoid, scurvy or food poisoning in the streets of the Channel ports. Realising that no more money would be forthcoming from the Exchequer, Effingham, Drake and Sir John Hawkins themselves provided wine and arrowroot for their men. The Queen was furious to hear that other captains had squandered money apportioned for their men's wages, and was ever afterwards prejudiced against sea-captains, but the major blame for her sailors' plight was undoubtedly hers.

Great national celebrations of the victory were planned. On 26 August, Essex staged a triumphal military review at Whitehall, after which Elizabeth watched with Leicester from a window as the young Earl jousted against the Earl of Cumberland. Leicester, reported one of Mendoza's spies, had been dining every night with Elizabeth, and had fully regained his former position of power and prestige. But he was a sick man, exhausted by the stresses of the past weeks, and left immediately after the review for Buxton, hoping that the healing waters would restore him.

From Rycote in Oxfordshire, where they had often stayed together as guests of Lord and Lady Norris, he wrote to the Queen on 29 August:

> I most humbly beseech Your Majesty to pardon your old servant to be thus bold in sending to know how my gracious lady doth, and what ease of her late pain she finds, being the chiefest thing in the world I do pray for, for her to have good health and long life. For my own poor case, I continue still your medicine, and it amends much better than any other thing that hath been given me. Thus hoping to find a perfect cure at the bath, with the continuance of my wonted prayer for Your Majesty's most happy preservation, I humbly kiss your foot.
>
> From your old lodgings at Rycote this Thursday morning, by

Your Majesty's most faithful and obedient servant, R. Leicester.
P.S. Even as I had written this much, I received Your Majesty's token by young Tracy.

His plan was to proceed by slow stages towards Kenilworth, but on the way he was 'troubled with an ague' which turned into 'a continual burning fever', and was obliged to take to his bed at his hunting lodge in Cornbury Park, near Woodstock. Here he died at four o'clock in the morning on 4 September, with 'scarce any [one] left to close his eyelids'. Modern medical historians suggest the cause may have been stomach cancer. He was buried beside his little son in the Beauchamp Chapel in the Church of St Mary the Virgin at Warwick, where a fine effigy by Holtemans, portraying Leicester in a coronet and full armour, was later placed on his tomb.

'He was esteemed a most accomplished courtier, a cunning time-server, and respecter of his own advantages,' observed Camden. 'But whilst he preferred power and greatness before solid virtue, his detracting emulators found large matter to speak reproachfully of him, and even when he was in his most flourishing condition, spared not disgracefully to defame him by libels, not without some untruths. People talked openly in his commendation, but privately he was ill spoke of by the greater part.'

Even after his death the slanders continued. Although a post mortem produced no evidence of foul play the malicious Ben Jonson claimed, without any foundation, that Lettice had poisoned her husband with one of his own deadly potions in order to marry her lover, a tale that many believed, for few mourned his passing, not even the poet Spenser, his former protégé, who wrote dismissively:

> He now is dead, and all his glories gone.
> And all his greatness vapoured to nought.
> His name is worn already out of thought,
> Ne any poet seeks him to revive,
> Yet many poets honoured him alive.

'All men, so far as they durst, rejoiced no less outwardly at his death than for the victory lately obtained against the Spaniard,' wrote John Stow the antiquarian.

Elizabeth was griefstricken by the loss of Leicester, the man who for thirty years had been closer to her than any other, whom she called 'her brother and best friend'. In her hour of greatness, she was now plunged into personal sorrow. Walsingham wrote that she was unable to attend to state affairs 'by reason that she will not suffer anybody to have access unto her, being very much grieved with the death of the Lord Steward'. Mendoza's agent reported on 17 September, 'The Queen is sorry for his death, but no other person in the country. She was so grieved that for some days she shut herself in her chamber alone and refused to speak to anyone until the Treasurer and other councillors had the door broken open and entered to see her.' After that, according to Camden, she 'either patiently endured or politely dissembled' her grief.

When the Earl of Shrewsbury wrote congratulating her on her victory and condoling with her on her sad loss, she confided to this 'very good old man' that, 'Although we do accept and acknowledge your careful mind and good will, yet we desire rather to forbear the remembrance thereof as a thing whereof we can admit no comfort, otherwise by submitting our will to God's inevitable appointment, Who, notwith-standing His goodness by the former prosperous news, hath nevertheless been pleased to keep us in exercise by the loss of a personage so dear unto us.'

Sadly, she re-read Leicester's letter from Rycote, and then, inscribing it 'His last letter', laid it carefully in a little coffer that she kept by her bed. It was found there after her death, and now reposes in the Public Record Office at Kew.

In his will, Leicester left 'my most dear and gracious sovereign, whose creature under God I have been', a diamond and emerald pendant and a rope of six hundred beautiful pearls, but he had lived extravagantly and died virtually bankrupt, leaving his widow with debts of £50,000. Half was owed to the Queen, who now had her revenge on Lettice by exacting her dues: in October she ordered a detailed investigation of the late Earl's financial affairs, took back Kenilworth Castle and all his lands in Warwickshire, and ordered Lettice to auction the contents of his three main residences, Kenilworth, Wanstead and Leicester House. She had no sympathy for the grieving widow, and continued to behave as if Lettice did not exist. Although her marriage appears to have been happy – in his will, Leicester referred to Lettice as 'a faithful, loving, very obedient, careful wife' – the Countess, probably for financial security, remarried within a year: her third husband was Sir Christopher Blount, a friend of her son Essex.

The remaining part of Leicester's estate passed to his 'base son', Sir Robert Dudley, which many perceived as a tacit acknowledgement of the boy's legitimacy. However, Dudley was never able to prove this, and the earldom of Leicester passed to Leicester's sister's son, Robert Sidney. Leicester House on the Strand became the property of his stepson, who renamed it Essex House.

Leicester's death went virtually unnoticed, and certainly unmourned, in the national elation that followed the defeat of the Armada. Elizabeth had to put on a brave face in order to lead the people in their celebrations, but it was noticed, that autumn, that she was 'much aged and spent, and very melancholy'. When she sat for George Gower, for the famous Armada portrait, she wore Leicester's pearls, as she would in many subsequent portraits.

With Leicester gone, the task of organising the victory festivities fell to Hatton, Essex and Sir Henry Lee. A medal was struck, bearing the legend, 'God blew with His winds, and they were scattered', and proved hugely popular, while Sir Thomas Heneage commissioned Nicholas Hilliard to make the Armada Jewel, which was presented to the Queen, who later gave it back to Heneage. Freed from the fear of reprisals for Mary Stuart's death, Elizabeth released Sir William Davison from the Tower, remitting his fine the following year and, in 1594, making him a grant of land. She never employed him again, although she permitted him to draw his salary as Secretary up until her death.

On 12 November, the Queen moved her court to Somerset House. The public mood on 17 November, Accession Day, was especially jubilant, and the 19th, St Elizabeth's Day, was declared an additional public holiday to commemorate the victory, which that year was marked by services of thanksgiving, devotional processions, feasting, tilting, cock-fighting and bonfires.

Godfrey Goodman, the future Bishop of Gloucester, then a child of five living with his family in the Strand, later recalled how suddenly, that November,

> there came a report to us, much about five o'clock at night, very dark, that the Queen was gone to Council, and if you will see the Queen, you must come quickly. Then we all ran. When the court gates were set open, the Queen came out in great state. Then we cried, 'God save Your Majesty!' The Queen said unto us, 'You may well have a greater prince, but you may never have a more loving prince.' And so the Queen departed. This wrought such an impression upon us, for shows and pageants are ever best seen by torchlight, that all the way we did nothing but talk of what an admirable queen she was and how we would venture all our lives to do her service.

The culmination of the celebrations came on Sunday, 26 November, when the Queen, passing through railings hung with blue cloth behind which stood cheering people, came in an elaborate canopied chariot drawn by two white horses to St Paul's Cathedral to give public thanks for the greatest English victory since Agincourt and acknowledge her debt to God and to Providence. The enormous glittering procession that attended her was such as had not been seen since her coronation, and there were pageants, songs and ballads performed in the City of London in her honour as she passed.

At the west door of the cathedral, Elizabeth alighted from her chariot and fell to her knees, making 'her hearty prayers to God' before the huge crowds. Then she passed into the church, which was hung with the captured banners. Later, after the sermon had been preached, she read out a prayer she had herself composed, and addressed the congregation 'most Christianly', enjoining them to have gratitude for their glorious deliverance. They responded with a great shout, wishing her a long and happy life, to the confusion of her enemies.

The Queen then went in procession to the nearby bishop's palace, where she dined with the Bishop of London before returning, 'by a great light of torches', to Somerset House.

Elizabeth's reputation was never greater than at this time, making her the most respected monarch in Christendom. Even her enemies acknowledged her qualities, Pope Sixtus V declaring,

> She certainly is a great queen, and were she only a Catholic, she would be our dearly beloved daughter. Just look how well she governs! She is only a woman, only mistress of half an island, and yet she makes herself feared by Spain, by France, by the Empire, by all!

He jested that he wished he were free to marry her: 'What a wife she would make! What children we would have! They would have ruled the whole world.' He also praised the courage of Drake – 'What a great captain!'

It was a time for superlatives. In France and in Italy, as in Rome, Catholics honoured the Queen. Henry III lauded her valour, spirit and prudence, declaring that her victory 'would compare with the greatest feats of the most illustrious men of past times'. Even the Ottoman sultan sang her praises and made peace with Poland for her sake.

After 1588, the fame of the Virgin Queen spread far and wide, while in England, where her people basked in the reflected glow of victory, her legend grew, giving rise to a new cult figure, 'Eliza triumphant'. She was more convinced now than ever that God had destined her to rule her people, and that the victory was a signal manifestation of the divine will, and for the rest of her reign, writers and artists would portray the elements bowing to her authority. Her Catholic subjects had proved themselves loyal, and the threat of insurrection had receded, paving the way for more tolerance towards recusants in the future. The conviction of the Protestant majority that God and Providence had intervened in England's hour of need gave a new stability to the Anglican Church. Above all, there was a surge of national confidence, which led to the flowering of literature and the decorative arts known as the English Renaissance.

A Westminster schoolboy, John Sly, admirably expressed the mood of the English people when, in his text of Julius Caesar's works (now preserved at Oxford), he repeatedly scribbled the Queen's name, along with this couplet:

The rose is red, the leaves are green,
God save Elizabeth, our noble Queen!

23

'Great England's Glory'

After Leicester's death, Elizabeth turned to Essex, who rapidly assumed the role of chief favourite, moving into his stepfather's old apartments at court and being constantly in the Queen's company. Courtiers seeking patronage and favours thronged about him, for they had heard of his 'forwardness to pleasure his friends', and he was assiduous in using his influence with the Queen on their behalf. But if, as frequently happened, she turned down his requests, he would sulk, being 'a great resenter and weak dissembler of the least disgrace'. Elizabeth, whose patience he often strained, enjoined him to be content with his good fortune, but he did not cease his demands, and often threatened to retire from court and live in the country, knowing that she so needed his company that this might bring her to heel.

'She doth not contradict confidently', he would say, 'which they that know the minds of women say is a sign of yielding.' He thought to manipulate her, but constantly underestimated her formidable intellect and strength of will. However, such was her affection for him that she would invariably forgive him for minor transgressions: this, again, led him to believe that he could do as he pleased with impunity.

Unlike Leicester, he was popular with the people, whom he courted with 'affable gestures and open doors, making his table and his bed popularly places of audience to suitors'. The Queen soon grew jealous, wishing him to be dependent upon her alone for his success; she wanted no rivals for the people's affections.

Essex's old guardian Burghley tried to take the young man under his wing, but Essex was 'impatient of the slow progress he must needs have during the life and greatness of the Treasurer', and also resentful of the rising influence of Burghley's son, Robert Cecil. He desired to reach spectacular heights in the shortest time possible.

At fifty-five, Elizabeth was remarkably healthy. Her leg ulcer had healed and she was as energetic as ever, still dancing six galliards on some mornings, and walking, riding and hunting regularly. Age and victory had invested her with even greater dignity and presence, and when her people saw her pass by in her golden coach, she appeared to them 'like a goddess'. Essex was clever enough to defer to her as such, conveying to her overtly, and through the subtle symbolism beloved of the age, his love and devotion. 'I do confess that, as a man, I have been more subject to your natural beauty, than as a subject to the power of a king,' he told her. Naively, he thought that his influence would in future be unchallenged.

However, he was soon to be disabused of this notion, for in November 1588, the Queen's eye alighted again upon Sir Charles Blount, son of Lord Mountjoy, a scholarly youth with 'brown hair, a sweet face, a most neat composure, and tall in his person', whose skill in the joust brought him to her attention. Impressed, she 'sent him a golden queen from her set of chessmen', which he tied to his arm with a crimson ribbon. Observing it, the jealous Essex sneered, 'Now I perceive that every fool must have a favour.' The offended Blount challenged him to a duel in Marylebone Park, in which he slashed the Earl in the thigh and disarmed him.

Officially, Elizabeth took a hard line against duelling, but already she was becoming weary of Essex's high-handedness, and when she heard what had happened, she retorted, 'By God's blood, it was fit that someone or other should take him down and treat him better manners, otherwise there will be no rule in him.' She insisted, however, that she would not allow either man back to court until they had shaken hands, which they did, later becoming devoted friends, despite the fact that Blount remained in favour with the Queen.

Blount, who had fought in the Netherlands and against the Armada, was ambitious to go abroad to seek martial adventures, but Elizabeth would not hear of it, telling him, 'You will never leave it until you are knocked on the head, as that inconsiderate fellow Sidney was. You shall go when I send you. In the meanwhile, see you lodge in the court, where you may follow your books, read and discourse of the wars.' In 1589, she appointed him one of her Gentlemen Pensioners.

In December, Essex quarrelled fiercely with Raleigh, and challenged him to a duel, but the Council, in some alarm, forbade it. Despite their efforts at concealment, Elizabeth got to hear of it, and was 'troubled very much', but Essex was unconcerned. 'She takes pleasure in beholding such quarrels among her servants,' especially when they concerned herself, he informed the French ambassador.

By the spring of 1589, Essex was living well beyond his means and in debt for more than £23,000. When the Queen demanded immediate repayment for a loan, he reminded her that 'love and kindness' were more important than money. Relenting, she agreed to give him, in exchange for a manor, the right to all the customs on sweet wines imported into England during the next ten years, which would bring him a sizeable income at public expense.

That spring, determined to break Spain's naval strength for good and ensure that Philip would never be able to send another Armada against England, Elizabeth decided to dispatch Drake, Sir John Norris and Raleigh, with 150 ships and 20,000 men, on an expedition to Portugal to destroy the remnants of the enemy fleet and, in concert with a rebellion by Portuguese patriots, place Don Antonio, the illegitimate Portuguese pretender, on the throne.

Essex, hoping for rich pickings to clear his debt, was desperate to go, and when, early in April, the Queen, fearing his rashness, forbade it, he defied her and, slipping away from court without leave, rode determinedly to Falmouth, covering 220 miles in less than forty-eight hours. When Elizabeth learned what he had done, Essex was already at sea, having persuaded Sir Roger Williams to let him join his force. Enraged, she dispatched Knollys and Hunsdon in pinnaces to search the Channel for him, and when that proved fruitless, condemned Williams's behaviour in a furious letter to Drake:

> His offence is in so high a degree that the same deserveth to be punished by death. We command that you sequester him from all charge and service, and cause him to be safely kept until you know our further pleasure therein, as you will answer for the contrary at your peril, for as we have authority to rule, so we look to be obeyed. We straitly charge you that you do forthwith cause [Essex] to be sent hither in safe manner. Which, if you do not, you shall look to answer for the same to your smart, for these be no childish actions.

She also wrote to Essex, complaining of his 'sudden and undutiful departure from our presence and your place of attendance; you may easily conceive how offensive it is unto us. Our great favours bestowed on you without deserts hath drawn you thus to neglect and forget your duty.'

Her letters took two months to reach their destination, and Essex was still with the fleet when it reached Lisbon, where Drake launched an assault but was driven back thanks to the failure of the Portuguese to rise in revolt as planned. Then, ignoring Elizabeth's express orders, the English made for the Azores, hoping to intercept the Spanish treasure fleet, but were driven back home at the end of June by severe gales. Estimates vary, but between four and eleven thousand men had died of disease, and the Queen was the poorer by £49,000: the expedition had been an unmitigated disaster.

Elizabeth vented her anger on Drake, whom she would not entrust with another such expedition for some time, and also Norris. Raleigh and Essex had fought well at Lisbon, and Essex was now playing the part of a returning hero, but the Queen, aware that Raleigh had distinguished himself more, rewarded him with a medal. She even forgave Essex and Williams for their disobedience, dismissing Essex's headstrong behaviour as 'but a sally of youth', and peace was for a time restored, the court being given over to feasting, hunting and jousting and Essex growing 'every day more and more in Her Majesty's gracious conceit'.

But the toils in which she bound him only exacerbated his discontent, prompting him to begin writing secretly to James VI, while his sister, Penelope Rich, told the Scottish King that Essex was 'exceedingly weary, accounting it a thrall he now lives in', and wished for a change of monarch. James remained non-committal.

In July came the news that Henry III of France had been assassinated by a fanatical monk, in revenge for his murder of the Duke of Guise. Having no son, he was the last of the Valois dynasty, and was succeeded by his brother-in-law, the Protestant Henry of Navarre, who became Henry IV, the first king of the House of Bourbon.

Philip of Spain immediately put forward a Catholic pretender to the French throne, but Elizabeth, fearing the consequences of this, stood stoutly by the new king. Her dispatch of an army under the gallant Lord Willoughby to Normandy in October, and her continuing financial support over the next five years, undermined the opposition and helped to establish Henry firmly upon his throne.

Worn out with overwork, Sir Francis Walsingham died on 6 April 1590, having almost bankrupted himself in the Queen's service: he was buried at night in order to foil creditors who might impound his coffin. He had served Elizabeth faithfully, and with a rumoured fifty agents in the courts of Europe, had preserved her from the evil intentions of her Catholic enemies. He was much mourned in England, but 'it is good news here', commented Philip of Spain.

Elizabeth did not appoint anyone to co-ordinate Walsingham's spy network, nor did she immediately replace him; for the next six years, the Secretary's duties were shouldered by Robert Cecil, whose ability the Queen had come to recognise. Burghley had groomed his son to take over, and was much satisfied by his advancement.

Born in 1563, Robert Cecil had allegedly been dropped by a

nursemaid in infancy and consequently had a deformed back and was of short and stunted build. Naunton wrote: 'For his person, he was not much beholding to Nature, though somewhat for his face, which was his best part.' The Queen called him her 'Pigmy' or her 'Elf'. 'I mislike not the name only because she gives it,' Cecil commented, but in fact he resented it, being deeply sensitive about his deformity, of which his enemies cruelly made much.

Being delicate, he had been educated by tutors before going to Cambridge, after which he had served on diplomatic missions in France and the Netherlands, and been elected an MP in 1584. He had a quick intelligence and excellent powers of concentration. As well as being an astute politician he was a gifted administrator with a limitless capacity for hard work, who was often to be seen with 'his hands full of papers and head full of matter'. 'A courtier from his cradle', he had beautifully modulated speech, a charming manner and a good sense of humour. He was not devoid of cunning and was less principled than Burghley. Although she was never as close to him as to his father, the Queen trusted him implicitly.

It now seemed as if Elizabeth, by promoting the son of Burghley and the stepson of Leicester, was trying to recreate the court of her youth, but while Cecil was content to share the limelight with Essex, the latter, aware that he himself was relegated to the role of court favourite, was resentful of Cecil's political position and determined to undermine it. He saw no reason why he should not fulfil the dual role of favourite and chief political adviser, and never understood why Elizabeth would not allow such 'domestical greatness' to be invested in one man.

Essex's insistence on regarding Cecil as his rival led to the formation of the factions which were to dominate the last years of Elizabeth's reign and lead to so much squabbling, bribery and opportunism. Essex and his younger followers were avid for military glory and the continuance of the war with Spain, while the faction headed by Cecil and Burghley stood for peace and stability. From 1590 onwards, Essex began building an aristocratic following at court and in the country. Those who had been excluded from office by Cecil, as well as those who agreed that the war against Spain should be aggressively pursued, hastened to offer him their allegiance. He also courted the support of the London Puritans. Cecil, meanwhile, kept a vice-like grip on court appointments and political offices, and in Parliament his father led the House of Lords while he led the Commons.

The Queen, seeing her own generation of friends and councillors gradually disappearing, had to adjust to a court under the influence of a younger, less congenial generation, whose ideas and tastes were unlike her own, and who were becoming increasingly dismissive of the attitudes of their elders. She had also to keep the peace, and preserve a balance between the new factions that had sprung up, a taxing task for a woman moving towards old age.

That summer, the Queen's progress took her, amongst other places, to Bisham Abbey, where she was entertained by the daughters of Lady Russell, and to Mitcham, Surrey, where her host was Sir Julius Caesar, who presented her with 'a gown of cloth of silver, richly embroidered; a black network mantle with pure gold, a taffeta hat, white, with several flowers, and a jewel of gold set with rubies and diamonds. Her Majesty removed from my house after dinner, the 13 September, with exceeding good contentment.'

In reality it was a sad time for the Queen. During 1590, death took Ambrose Dudley, Earl of Warwick, Mary Stuart's former gaoler the Earl of Shrewsbury, and eighty-two-year-old Blanche Parry, Chief Gentlewoman of the Privy Chamber, who had served Elizabeth since her birth.

In the autumn, Elizabeth found out that, back in April, Essex had secretly married Walsingham's daughter and heiress, Frances, the widow of Sir Philip Sidney. The Queen, thinking Frances not good enough for him with no dowry or beauty to speak of, raged and sulked for two weeks before allowing herself to be persuaded that the Earl had only done what every other man of rank and wealth did, namely, married to beget heirs. Essex himself used every gallant trick in his repertoire to induce her to forgive him, and at length she began to relent.

On Accession Day, 17 November, a black-clad Essex entered the tiltyard at Whitehall in a funeral procession, to symbolise his disgrace, but it was soon obvious to all those watching that the Queen had forgiven him, although she would never agree to receiving Frances as his countess. Two days later he gave a splendid performance in the lists.

This was the last occasion on which the Queen's Champion, Sir Henry Lee, stage-managed the Accession Day jousts, and to mark it he put on a magnificent pageant of vestal virgins, set to music by John Dowland. Lee then retired to Ditchley Park in Oxfordshire with his mistress, the notorious Anne Vavasour.

Around this time the Queen's godson, Sir John Harington, foolishly circulated the manuscript of his bawdy translation of the twenty-eighth book of Ariosto's poem *Orlando Furioso* amongst the Queen's maids of honour. Elizabeth, demanding to know what book it was that was provoking such merriment, was shocked when she read it, and declared that it was an improper text for young maidens to read. The 'saucy poet' was severely reprimanded and commanded not to come to court again until he had translated Ariosto's entire work – a monumental commission which would take him the best part of a year.

*

During 1591, Essex came increasingly under the influence of Francis Bacon, one of the brilliant sons of the late Lord Keeper, whose elder brother Anthony had been working for the last ten years as one of Walsingham's agents in France and become a friend of Henry IV. Their mother had been Burghley's sister, but the Lord Treasurer had little time for his nephews, whom he suspected of working to undermine his own son's influence, and he had consistently refused to extend his patronage to them. This led to a bitter family rift, so it was not surprising that the Bacons should side with the opposing faction.

Francis Bacon was a thirty-year-old lawyer and MP of great erudition, who in his time would publish works of history, philosophy and legal theory. 'Of middling stature, his countenance had indented with age before he was old; his presence grave and comely,' wrote the seventeenth-century historian, Arthur Wilson. This future Lord Chancellor was cleverer than both Cecil and Essex, but the Queen never liked him and never appointed him to the high office he deserved. Both Francis and his elder brother Anthony were homosexual, and this may have had something to do with her aversion.

Francis Bacon quickly struck up a rapport with Essex, who soon perceived that, by obtaining advancement for his new friend, he could strike a blow at Cecil. The proud and calculating Bacon in turn saw in what he termed Essex's 'rare perfections and virtues' a means whereby he might use him to achieve political prominence and himself discomfit the Cecils. But it had already been noticed at court that, while Elizabeth might give Essex anything he wanted within reason for himself, she would not allow him to dispense patronage to anyone else, and that those who came to him looking for favours usually went away unsatisfied. It was obvious that she feared he might build up a large affinity of support.

The astute Bacon quickly sized up the situation and sent a letter offering Essex his candid advice, trying to make him see how he must appear to the Queen: 'A man of a nature not to be ruled; of an estate not founded on his greatness; of a popular reputation; of a military dependence: I demand whether there can be a more dangerous image than this represented to any monarch living, much more to a lady and of Her Majesty's apprehension.' He urged Essex to abandon his military ambitions in order to set the Queen's mind at rest, and seek advancement by peaceful means. It was sensible, sound advice, but the wilful Essex ignored it.

Nor did he do anything to allay Elizabeth's jealousy of his growing popularity. Not only was the Queen jealous of his rapport with the people, but she could not bear to see him paying attention to other women. Once, when she caught him flirting with Katherine Bridges and Elizabeth Russell, two of her ladies, she shouted at him in disgust, slapped Mistress Bridges (who later became Essex's mistress), and banished the girls from court for three days. But Essex himself could be jealous too: let the Queen smile upon a rival courtier, and there would be tantrums and sulks.

In May, Elizabeth spent ten days with Burghley at Theobalds, where the Cecil family staged a play in which it was intimated that she should formally appoint Robert, whom she knighted during her visit, to the secretaryship. She failed to take the hint, but three months later admitted him to the Privy Council. It was at this time also that the seventy-year-old Burghley, a martyr to gout, begged leave to retire. Elizabeth merely asked, in jest, if he wished to become a hermit, and refused to let him go on the grounds that he was 'the chief pillar of the welfare of England'.

During the summer, Raleigh, who as Captain of the Gentlemen Pensioners was sworn to protect the Queen's ladies and held a key to the Maidens' Chamber, secretly seduced, or was seduced by, the eldest of the maids of honour, Elizabeth (Bess) Throckmorton, daughter of Sir Nicholas. By July, she had conceived a child, but Bess was not like Raleigh's other conquests: she began to insist on marriage, although it was certain that the Queen would not have considered her a good enough match for him. That autumn, in great secrecy, Raleigh and Bess Throckmorton were married. Bess remained at court, attending to her duties and doing her best to conceal her pregnancy.

There were still rumbles over the succession, a taboo subject with the Queen which wise men avoided. Elizabeth had a greater aversion than ever now towards naming her successor, fearing that the factions at her court would be easy prey for would-be conspirators. As she grew older, she was apprehensive in case there were moves to replace her with a younger, preferably male, sovereign. Already, several of her courtiers were secretly ingratiating themselves with James of Scotland, the likeliest candidate for the succession. Therefore, that August, when the hot-headed Peter Wentworth, MP, impertinently published a tract entitled *A Pithy Exhortation to Her Majesty for Establishing the Succession* he was summarily clapped into prison.

That month, the Queen embarked on her greatest progress for years. She visited Farnham, then was the guest of Lord and Lady Montague at Cowdray Castle in Sussex, where her hostess was so overcome by the honour of having the Queen to stay that she threw herself into Elizabeth's arms and wept, 'O happy time! O joyful day!' Here the pageants and novelties in her honour were reminiscent of those staged at Kenilworth sixteen years before. One picnic was laid out on a table forty-eight yards long.

Afterwards, she proceeded to Petworth, Chichester, Titchfield,

Portsmouth and Southampton, before returning via Basing and Odiham to Elvetham, Hampshire, where the Earl of Hertford had excelled himself in an attempt to regain the royal favour that he had lost after his marriage to Lady Katherine Grey thirty years earlier. Three hundred workmen had enlarged and adorned the house and erected temporary buildings in the park to accommodate the court. A crescent-shaped lake had been specially dug on the lawn, with three ship-shaped islands with trees for masts, a fort and a Snail Mount, from which guns fired a salute at the Queen's arrival. It was beside this lake, seated under a green satin canopy, that Elizabeth watched a water pageant, whilst musicians in boats played for her. She stayed four days, during which time there were banquets, dances, games of volleyball (which the Queen 'graciously deigned' to watch for ninety minutes), fireworks, songs and allegorical entertainments. When she left, it was raining heavily, and one poet asked, 'How can summer stay when the sun departs?' The Queen told Hertford, from her coach, that she would never forget her visit. As she rode out of the park, she saw some musicians playing for her and, ignoring the rain, 'she stayed her coach', removed the mask she wore whilst travelling, and gave them 'great thanks'.

For months now, Henry IV had been sending Elizabeth urgent appeals for aid, for the Spaniards were fighting as allies with the Catholic French forces and had occupied parts of Brittany and Normandy. Elizabeth had stalled, not wishing to involve herself in another costly foreign war. Yet she had no desire to see another threatening Spanish army just the other side of the Channel, and that summer reluctantly consented to send 4000 men to Normandy, although she meant to spend no more money than was absolutely necessary.

Essex had been one of those who had repeatedly urged her to act, and eagerly requested command of her army, but she turned him down. He asked again, but the answer was still no. Even after he begged a third time, pleading with her for two hours, on his knees, with Burghley supporting his pleas, she remained adamant: he was 'too impetuous to be given the reins'. Only when Henry IV personally intervened did she reluctantly change her mind and say he might go after all, warning Henry that he would 'require the bridle rather than the spur'. Some believed she could not bear to let him go, nor the thought of him being killed.

Essex landed with his army in France in August and rode to meet King Henry at Compiègne, where he was received with great honour. It soon became clear that he regarded war as some superior sport: he revelled in his role of commander, exploiting his powers to the full. But he spent the first month doing virtually nothing, waiting for the King to reduce Noyon. Essex was supposed to be besieging Rouen, but could not do that without French assistance. He therefore entertained, held parades and went hawking in enemy territory, needlessly putting himself at risk and earning a rebuke from the Council. The Queen was in a fury of frustration at such a waste of time and money, and the fact that Essex did not see fit to inform her of his plans.

'Where he is, or what he doth, or what he is to do, we are ignorant!' she stormed, regretting that she had sent him. Exasperated she ordered him home.

'I see Your Majesty is content to ruin me,' he replied with equal heat. Burghley, suspecting that in reality she wanted to see him, commented: 'God forbid that private respects should overrule public.' The evidence indeed suggests that Elizabeth allowed her heart to override her head on this occasion.

Before Essex left France, he knighted twenty-four of his supporters against her express wishes, a rash act that appeared sinister to those who feared he was building up a power base for his own purposes. From Elizabeth's point of view, the Crown alone was the fount of honour, and to make new knights so indiscriminately could only debase her prerogative. Burghley tried to shield Essex from her wrath by not telling her what he had done, but she found out all the same, and commented ominously that 'His Lordship had done well to build his almshouses before he made his knights.'

Yet when Essex returned and exerted his charm, peace was restored, and after a few days, thanks to Burghley's influence, he was sent back to Rouen to rejoin his troops. From here, he wrote to the Queen:

> Most fair, most dear, and most excellent sovereign: the two windows of your Privy Chamber shall be the poles of my sphere, where, as long as Your Majesty will fix to have me, I am fixed and immoveable. While Your Majesty gives me leave to say I love you, my fortune is as my affection, unmatchable. If ever you deny me that liberty, you may end my life, but never shake my constancy, for it is not in your power, as great a queen as you are, to make me love you less.

The campaign ended in disaster. Essex took the town of Gournay – 'rather a jest than a victory' observed the Queen – but that was all. His army succumbed to disease, and morale was low, three thousand men died of illness or deserted, and his brother was killed in a skirmish. When Elizabeth complained of his lack of progress, Essex, ill with ague, wrote miserably to her, complaining that her unkindness had broken 'both my heart and my wits'. He had managed to salvage his honour by winning a friendly single combat with the Governor of Rouen, but this was small comfort. When the Queen ordered him to resign his command and return home, he blamed Burghley and Cecil, quite unfairly, for what had happened, believing that they had poisoned Elizabeth's mind against him.

In November 1591, the Queen visited Ely Place to see her faithful Hatton, who was very ill, administering to him 'cordial broths with her own hands'. He died shortly afterwards of kidney failure, owing her £56,000. Some said he had died of a broken heart because Elizabeth had hounded him to the grave, asking for repayment, but this is unlikely. His death plunged her again into grief: it seemed that all those to whom she had been close were being taken from her.

For a time, she was melancholy, obsessed with fearful thoughts of death, hating any word that reminded her of it. Once, when Lord North was acting as her carver, she asked him what was in the covered dish.

'Madam, it is a coffin,' he replied, 'coffin' being a contemporary word for a raised pie, but one that now moved the Queen to anger.

'Are you such a fool to give a pie such a name?' she shouted. Her reaction 'gave warning to the courtiers not to use any word that mentioned her death'.

Essex returned to England in January 1592. He had hoped to find that his application to be elected Chancellor of Oxford University had been approved, but was furious to learn that Cecil's candidate, Lord Buckhurst, had been chosen instead. Jealous complaints availed him nothing, so he decided belatedly to take Francis Bacon's advice and aim for high political office, with a view to breaking the hold on power enjoyed by the Cecils.

When, the following month, Anthony Bacon returned from France, Essex enlisted his support. Anthony was a difficult individual whose uncertain temper was aggravated by arthritis, yet he was more than willing to use his considerable talents in Essex's service. It was decided that he would help the Earl to build up his own intelligence network, hoping thereby to impress upon the Queen that, being so well informed, Essex deserved political credibility and must be taken seriously. Essex also began courting the favour of the Protestant Henry IV.

But it was not enough: he craved attention and excitement. By March, he was hanging irritably around the court, 'wholly inflamed with the desire to be doing somewhat', only to be told by Francis Bacon that he should be working towards becoming 'a great man in the state' rather than hankering after the military glory which constantly seemed to evade him. With so many of the Queen's advisers having died, there would surely now be an opening for him, and he should capitalise on this.

Bess Throckmorton had invented a pretext to secure leave of absence from court in February, and, seeking refuge in her brother's house, gave birth to a son in March. For some time now, her thickening figure had given rise to rumours at court, some of them pinpointing with deadly accuracy the father of her child. But Raleigh denied it, declaring, 'There is none on the face of the Earth I would be fastened unto.'

In April, Bess returned to court, where it could easily be observed that she had dramatically lost weight. The rumours became more insistent, until in May Raleigh's 'brutish offence' became known to the Queen, who, as one courtier wrote, was 'most fiercely incensed and threatens the most bitter punishment to both the offenders. S.W.R. will lose, it is thought, all his places and preferments at court, with the Queen's favour; such will be the end of his speedy rising, and now he must fall as low as he was high, at which the many may rejoice.'

Raleigh was away at sea, harrying Spanish ships at Panama, but he was 'speedily sent for and brought back' in the deepest disgrace, having committed the unforgivable crime of duping his sovereign, seducing a noble virgin committed to her care, and marrying without royal consent – the last two being punishable offences. Worse still was Elizabeth's bitter sense of betrayal, for Raleigh had for a decade been one of her chief favourites, and this marriage seemed to mock all his protestations of devotion to her.

In June, Elizabeth sent him and Bess to the Tower, where they were lodged in separate apartments. Raleigh was not strictly kept: he was allowed to walk in the gardens and probably managed to see his wife, but he was desperate to be free and did everything in his power to achieve that.

On 1 July, being told that Elizabeth was about to leave London to go on progress, he wrote to Cecil:

> My heart was never broken until this day that I hear the Queen goes so far off, whom I have followed so many years with so great love and desire in so many journeys, and am now left behind her in a dark prison all alone. While she was yet at hand, so that I might hear of her once in two or three days, my sorrows were less, but even now my heart is cast into the depths of misery. I that was wont to behold her riding like Alexander, hunting like Diana, walking like Venus, the gentle wind blowing her fair hair about her pure cheeks like a nymph; sometimes sitting in the shade like a goddess, sometimes singing like an angel, sometimes playing like Orpheus.

Behold the sorrow of this world! One amiss has bereaved me of all. She is gone in whom I trusted, and for me has not one thought of mercy. Yours, not worth any name or title, W.R.

Later that day, learning that the Queen's barge would be passing the Tower, he begged the Lieutenant, his cousin Sir George Carew, to row him out on the Thames so that he could see her and hopefully attract her attention, but the Lieutenant did not dare. Carew later reported to the Queen that Raleigh tried to kill himself at this point, and was only prevented from doing so by another official, who wrenched the dagger out of his grip, cutting his own hand in the process. Carew also warned Elizabeth that Raleigh would go insane if she did not forgive him, but she remained unmoved.

Raleigh was not to remain in the Tower for long. Early in August, a captured Spanish treasure ship was brought into Dartmouth carrying jewels worth £800,000. Most was appropriated by English sailors and local people, and when the Earl of Cumberland arrived to claim the Queen's share, there was a riot. Knowing that Raleigh was the only man capable of restoring order and ensuring that the treasure was fairly apportioned, the Queen agreed to his release. When he arrived at Dartmouth, he received a rapturous welcome from the sailors, but by then most of the jewels had disappeared. However, he managed to salvage Elizabeth's portion, but only at the expense of other investors, including himself.

Elizabeth allowed Raleigh to remain at liberty, but barred him from the court. Nor did her displeasure abate, for he was obliged to live quietly, 'like a fish cast on dry land', for the next five years at Sherborne Castle, the Devon property granted him by the Queen the previous January. Bess, who would prove a domineering wife, joined him there after her release in December.

A mysterious portrait by Marcus Gheeraerts the Younger in the National Maritime Museum is thought to illustrate Raleigh's disgrace. Recent cleaning has revealed that this portrait of a man was overpainted to look like Raleigh, and has also uncovered the tiny figure of a woman in the background, with her back turned to the sitter. She wears a coronet over her red hair and a chain of office around her neck, and holds a feather fan, and it would be reasonable to assume that this is the Queen herself, shunning Sir Walter in her displeasure. Essex was among the many who gloated over the fall of Raleigh, which removed one of his greatest rivals.

Whilst the Queen was on progress that summer, England experienced the worst visitation of the plague for many years. In order to avoid London, she travelled west to Sudeley Castle in Gloucestershire and then towards Bath. She had by now forgiven Harington for *Orlando Furioso*, and visited him at Kelston, near Bath, where he humbly presented her with a beautifully bound copy of his completed translation.

Elizabeth was in her element. One German visitor observed that she need not 'yield much to a girl of sixteen', either in looks or vigour. In September, she visited Oxford again, where she replied in extempore Latin to the loyal speeches made to her, watched the presentation of honorary degrees, and attended debates, sermons, lectures, dinners and three rather dull comedies. On the final day of her visit, she delivered a parting address, saying, 'If I had a thousand tongues instead of one, I would not be able to express my thanks.' Then, noticing that poor Burghley was having difficulty in standing, she broke off and ordered that a stool be brought. 'If I have always undertaken the care of your bodies, shall I neglect your minds?' she concluded. 'God forbid!'

On Shotover Hill, looking back on the city, she said, 'Farewell, farewell, dear Oxford! God bless thee and increase thy sons in number, holiness and virtue.' She then travelled to Rycote to stay with her old friends, Lord and Lady Nórris.

At New Year, the court was diverted with masques and other novelties. By February 1593, Essex's intelligence service was well established, and the Queen was so impressed with it that she at last appointed him a Privy Councillor, at the youthful age of twenty-seven. He could now play his part as a statesman, and he did it diligently, attending every Council meeting and co-operating with his rivals for the benefit of the state. 'His Lordship is become a new man', wrote a colleague, 'clean forsaking all his former youthful tricks, carrying himself with honourable gravity, and singularly liked for his speeches and judgement.' Where a knowledge of foreign affairs was concerned, there were few to match him. But being Essex, he was determined to exploit his position, and virtually bank-rupted himself in extending his patronage.

When the post of Attorney-General, which was in the Queen's gift, became vacant in April, he exerted his influence to secure it for Francis Bacon. But Bacon had recently challenged the granting of a subsidy to the Crown in Parliament, and Elizabeth was not at all pleased with him. When Essex put his name forward, she erupted in fury and barred Bacon from her presence.

For several months, Essex did all in his power to win her round, believing that 'there is not so much gotten of the Queen by earnestness as by often soliciting', yet despite all his arguments and pleas, she insisted that the irascible Sir Edward Coke, now Solicitor-General, was a better lawyer than Bacon, and remained 'stiff in her opinion', often being too busy or 'wayward' to discuss the matter. She told the importunate Earl that 'she would be advised by those that had more judgement in these things', and he told Bacon that, during one argument, 'She bade me go to bed if I could talk of nothing else. In passion I went away. Tomorrow I will go to her. On Thursday, I will write an expostulating letter.'

Philip of Spain had not abandoned his dream of conquering England for the Catholic faith and, having almost rebuilt his navy, 'breathed nothing but bloody revenge'. England stood again in danger of invasion, but a confident Elizabeth told Parliament,

> I fear not all his threatenings. His great preparations and mighty forces do not stir me. For though he come against me with a greater power than ever was, I doubt not but, God assisting me, I shall be able to defeat and overthrow him. For my cause is just, and it standeth upon a sure foundation – that I shall not fail, God assisting the quarrel of the righteous.

Parliament duly voted her a treble subsidy, for which she gave them 'as great thanks as ever prince gave to loving subjects'. When winds prevented the Spanish fleet from sailing that summer, Elizabeth put it down to the elements being in her favour, perceiving the workings of Divine Providence in such good fortune.

In July, Elizabeth was horrified to learn that her ally, Henry IV, in order to establish himself more securely on the French throne, had converted to the Roman Catholic faith, declaring that 'Paris is worth a mass.' She wrote to him: 'Ah, what griefs, what regret, what groanings I feel in my soul at the sound of such news! It is dangerous to do ill that good may come of it, yet I hope that sounder inspiration shall come to you.' Her fears were allayed when he reissued his edicts of religious tolerance, and she did not cease to support him in his conflict with Spain, the happy outcome of which could only benefit England.

That summer saw an even worse epidemic of plague than the previous year. The London theatres were closed, and, apart from brief visits to Sutton Place in Surrey, and Parham Park and Cowdray Park in Sussex, the Queen remained mainly at Windsor until Christmas. Here she celebrated her sixtieth birthday and spent her time translating Boethius, mostly in her own hand, in just twelve days. Her secretary informed her that, out of the twenty-five days between 10 October and 5 November,

> are to be taken four Sundays, three other holidays, and six days on which Your Majesty did ride abroad to take the air, and on those

days did forbear to translate, amounting together to thirteen days. Then remaineth but twelve days. Accounting two hours bestowed every day, the computation falleth out that in twenty-four hours Your Majesty began and ended your translation.

The manuscript survives, in a haphazard scrawl, with inconsistent spelling, and corrections by the Queen.

Winter came, and the Queen still prevaricated over appointing a new Attorney-General. Essex continued to importune her to choose Bacon, but she was determined to make her own choice; if she did not establish firm control over Essex, people would think that advancing age was diminishing her powers. So she ignored his tears of frustration, and endured when he stayed away from court in the hope that his absence would sway her. None of this made for a happy atmosphere, for when he returned she berated him with tirades and great oaths for leaving her. Then there would be an emotional reconciliation, and all would be well until the subject was raised again.

Early in 1594, Burghley begged the Queen to reach a decision as to who was to be Attorney-General. Essex had provoked him, asserting, 'I will spend all my power, might, authority and amity, and with tooth and nail defend and procure the same for Bacon.' And so the matter dragged on.

Elizabeth celebrated the New Year at Whitehall, watching a play and some dances until one o'clock in the morning from a luxurious high throne, with Essex, her 'wild horse', standing by. Anthony Standen, an elderly courtier, saw her often speak to the Earl and caress him 'in sweet and favourable manner', and gallantly remarked that 'she was as beautiful to my old sight as ever I saw her'. It had, however, been a stressful day, for Essex had uncovered a plot against the Queen, and the principal offender, someone very close to her, had just been arrested.

Roderigo Lopez was a Portuguese Jew, who had fled to England to escape the Inquisition in 1559, converted to Christianity, and set up a medical practice in London which had flourished. In time, he became senior doctor at St Bartholemew's Hospital, and men like Leicester, Walsingham and Essex became his patients. In 1586 he had been appointed chief physician to the Queen.

Because he was a Jew, Lopez was not popular: rumour credited him with having provided Leicester with poisons, and jealous rivals denigrated his undoubted skill as a physician. He had many enemies, among them Essex, whose spy he had refused to become and whose intimate physical shortcomings, confided to him as a doctor, he is said to have leaked. Elizabeth paid no attention to this and, thanks to her favour and his mounting wealth, Lopez could afford to ignore it also.

Essex was now the leader of the anti-Spanish, pro-war party at court. He had cultivated the Portuguese pretender, Don Antonio, then living in England, with a view to using him in intrigues against Spain. Knowing that King Philip wanted Don Antonio assassinated, Essex assigned Anthony Bacon to protect him, and it was Bacon who discovered that one Esteban Ferreira, a disaffected Portuguese supporter who had lost all in Don Antonio's cause, was not only living in Dr Lopez's house in Holborn, but was secretly in the pay of the Spaniards and conspiring against the pretender.

Essex informed the Queen of this, and she ordered Ferreira's arrest. Dr Lopez pleaded for his release, saying that Don Antonio had treated the man badly and that Ferreira had in fact been working for peace between England and Spain. but the Queen showed her 'dislike and disallowance' of this suggestion, and terminated the interview.

Two weeks later, another Portuguese connected with Dr Lopez, Gomez d'Avila, was arrested as a suspected spy at Sandwich. Ferreira warned Lopez that, if arrested, Gomez might incriminate them, and Lopez replied that he had thrice tried to prevent Gomez from coming to England. These letters were intercepted by Essex's spies.

Informed that Lopez had betrayed him, Ferreira swore that Lopez had been in the pay of Spain for years. Gomez, threatened with the rack, confessed that they had all been involved in a plot against Don Antonio. Another Portuguese, Tinoco, revealed to Essex under interrogation that the Jesuits in Spain had sent him to England to help Ferreira persuade Lopez to work for King Philip. Essex, almost paranoid where Spain was concerned, suspected that the subtext to these confessions was a plot against the Queen's life.

This led to Lopez's arrest on 1 January. He was confined in Essex House (formerly Leicester House), while his own house was searched. Nothing incriminating was found, and when he was examined by Burghley, Cecil and Essex, he gave convincing answers. Burghley and Cecil went to Hampton Court to tell the Queen they were certain that the man who had served her devotedly for years was innocent, and that the whole episode had been blown up out of proportion by Essex in an attempt to whip up popular support for a new offensive against Spain.

Essex was convinced otherwise, but when he went to the Queen, she accused him of acting out of malice, calling him 'a rash and temerarious youth to enter into the matter against the poor man, which he could not prove, but whose innocence she knew well enough'. Silencing him with a gesture, she dismissed him. He spent the next two days prostrate with fury and humiliation, then rallied, determined for honour's sake to prove that he was right and score a point against the Cecils. He had Lopez moved to the Tower and, hardly pausing to eat or sleep, interrogated the other suspects a second time. Under torture, or the threat of it, they insisted that the doctor was involved in the plot, and had agreed to poison the Queen for 50,000 crowns. This was the evidence which Essex was looking for, and on 28 January he wrote to Anthony Bacon: 'I have discovered a most dangerous and desperate treason. The point of conspiracy was Her Majesty's death. The executioner should have been Dr Lopez; the manner poison.'

His claim was lent credence by Tinoco's statement that, three years before, King Philip had sent Lopez a diamond and ruby ring. The Queen recalled that the doctor had offered her such a ring at that time, which she had refused. Lopez had firmly denied everything, but when faced with the Queen's testimony about the ring, admitted that in 1587, at Walsingham's behest, he had agreed to his name being used in a plot orchestrated by former ambassador Mendoza against Don Antonio, but only to deceive King Philip. Walsingham was of course dead, and could not corroborate this lame-sounding explanation, and it cost Lopez the support of the Cecils. There is, though, no reason to doubt that during Walsingham's lifetime Lopez acted for him as a secret agent. Indeed, papers discovered more recently in the Spanish archives substantiate his story and suggest he was indeed innocent, although the truth will probably never be fully known.

Worn down and terrified, the old man gave in, confessing to all kinds of improbable plots and sealing his fate. In February, he, Ferreira and Tinoco were arraigned for treason and sentenced to death. The people, outraged at this latest evidence of Spanish treachery, were in no doubt as to the guilt of the Jew and his accomplices, but the Queen was much troubled, fearing that her judges had convicted an innocent man simply to preserve Essex's honour: it would be four months before she could steel herself to sign Lopez's death warrant.

At Hampton Court, Elizabeth grew restless, wondering whether she might not be better off at Windsor. Several times she gave orders to pack in readiness for a move, and as many times changed her mind. After being summoned for the third time, the carter hired to transport Her Majesty's belongings was disgruntled to be sent away yet again.

'Now I see that the Queen is a woman as well as my wife,' he sighed, but Elizabeth had heard him through her window and put her head out, laughing.

'What a villain is this!' she cried, then sent him three gold coins to 'stop his mouth'. Soon afterwards, she decided to move to Nonsuch, where, on 26 March, she finally appointed Coke Attorney-General, much to the dismay of Essex, who interpreted this as a victory for the Cecils. However, he immediately suggested that Francis Bacon be given the vacated post of Solicitor-General. Elizabeth told him that she could not promote a man she disapproved of just because he, Essex, asked her to, whereupon he stalked off 'in passion, saying I would retire till I might be more graciously heard'. In fact, the Queen did not appoint a new Solicitor-General for eighteen months, during which time Essex relentlessly pursued his suit, precipitating endless quarrels and reconciliations. Bacon's mother felt that 'the Earl marred all by violent courses', but there were times when the Queen appeared to be wavering, as when she opined to Fulke Greville that 'Bacon begins to frame very well'. For both her and Essex, however, this was a test of whose will was the strongest, and neither were prepared to give in.

On 7 June, before a howling, jeering mob, Lopez and his alleged accomplices were hanged, drawn and quartered at Tyburn, Lopez protesting to the last that he loved his mistress better than Jesus Christ. The Queen, concerned at what Essex's power had wrought and still not wholly convinced of Lopez's guilt, returned some of the dead man's forfeited property to his widow and daughter, retaining only King Philip's ring, which she wore on her finger until she died.

It was a terrible summer. Rain fell ceaselessly, ruining the harvest, which in Tudor times meant a dearth that would inexorably lead to famine and inflated prices.

In July, Elizabeth gave Essex £4000 to defray his debts, saying, 'Look to thyself, good Essex, and be wise to help thyself without giving thy enemies advantage, and my hand shall be readier to help thee than any other.' Yet when it came to favours for his friends, she would give him nothing. He had, however, grown in prestige as a statesman, and also increased his popularity with the people. James VI was now his friend, and English ambassadors abroad would send him separate reports of international affairs. He employed four secretaries to deal with his correspondence, while his spies kept him supplied with confidential and often useful information.

There was one moment of panic, however. In Antwerp, an inflammatory book entitled *A Conference about the Next Succession to the Crown of England* had been printed, and its author, the Jesuit Robert Parsons, had dedicated it to 'the Most Noble Earl of Essex, for that no man is in more high and eminent dignity at this day in our realm'. The book discussed the claims of all Elizabeth's possible successors, and called on Essex to play the part of kingmaker on her death. Knowing Elizabeth's views on any speculation about the succession, Essex was highly embarrassed to have his name associated with such a subversive work, and by the suggestion that he should determine a matter that was strictly a question of royal prerogative, and was 'infinitely troubled'. When the Queen showed him the book, he greatly feared her reaction, but, much to his relief, she made little of it, realising that he had been the victim of a Catholic attempt to discredit him.

The following summer brought a return of the wet weather, and there was a second poor harvest, which resulted in a worse famine that winter. Many people died, and the buoyant mood that had marked the period after the Armada rapidly disintegrated.

In July 1595, four Spanish ships made a daring raid on Cornwall, burning Penzance and sacking the village of Mousehole. Alarmed by this, Queen and Council ordered that England's coastal defences be strengthened.

Elizabeth was still resisting intense pressure from Essex to appoint Francis Bacon Solicitor-General. Provoked beyond endurance, she screamed that she would 'seek all England for a solicitor' rather than accept the man, and in October, she slighted Bacon by appointing a little-known lawyer, Thomas Fleming, to the post. Essex was devastated, and unfairly blamed the Cecils who had in fact supported Bacon, but even he realised that there was no point in putting his friend forward for any other major offices, and by way of compensation, he made over to Bacon some property, which Bacon sold for £1800.

Accession Day, 17 November, was marked by the usual splendid jousts and celebrations at Whitehall. The Queen entertained the Dutch ambassador in the gallery, and discussed with him a new offensive against Spain whilst smiling and nodding to the watching crowd and the knights jousting below.

As usual Essex took centre stage in the tiltyard, but this year, in the evening, he put on an allegorical entertainment devised by Francis Bacon, in which three actors representing a soldier (Raleigh), a hunchbacked secretary (Cecil) and an aged hermit (Burghley) asked him 'to leave his vain following of love' for a goddess and choose a life either of experience, fame or contemplation. Then an actor dressed as his squire declared 'that this knight would never forsake his mistress's love, whose virtues made all his thoughts divine, whose wisdom taught him true policy, whose beauty and worth were at all times able to make him fit to command armies'. Here was a heavy hint, if ever there was one, but Elizabeth chose to ignore it.

The entertainment ended with Essex forsaking the goddess to devote himself to Love by serving his Queen; in his final speech, he made several vicious thrusts at the Cecils. 'My Lord of Essex's device is much commended in these late triumphs,' observed a spectator, but Elizabeth herself commented that, 'if she had thought there had been so much said of her, she would not have been there that night'.

Drake was now back in favour, and had suggested a further raid on Panama, in the hope of diverting King Philip and, of course, seizing more Spanish treasure, and the Queen agreed to this. But England's hero never came home: when his fleet returned, having achieved nothing, in the spring of 1596, it brought with it news of his death from dysentery on 29 January at Panama, where he was buried at sea.

By 1596, Cecil had become 'the greatest councillor of England, the Queen passing most of the day in private and secret conference with him'. Essex, however, was becoming bored with state duties, and people noticed that 'His Lordship is wearied and scorneth the dissembling courses of this place.' He was yearning for adventure and martial achievement.

His longings were to be fulfilled, for that spring Elizabeth, anticipating that Philip would send his new Armada in the summer, was preparing for an English expedition to destroy Philip's new fleet. She, Essex and Effingham were the chief investors, helping to provide 150 ships and 10,000 men. Elizabeth herself contributed £50,000.

The eager Essex was the obvious choice to command the expedition, but Elizabeth, as usual, was 'daily in a change of humour', even threatening to call off the whole thing. 'The Queen wrangles with our action for no cause but because it is in hand,' complained the Earl. 'I know I shall never do her service but against her will.' He had laboured hard to persuade her to agree to this enterprise, but if she continued to behave like this, he vowed he would 'become a monk upon an hour's warning'.

In March, the Queen, with poor grace, agreed to appoint Essex and Lord Howard of Effingham joint commanders, and Essex, in such a good mood that he had even set aside his enmity towards the Cecils, went happily off to Plymouth to take charge of the fleet and muster his men. Then, on 16 May, came a message: having heard the alarming news that a Spanish army had occupied Calais, the Queen required both Essex and Lord Howard to return to her presence, 'they being so dear unto her and such persons of note, as she could not allow of their going'. This caused an uproar, both at court and in Plymouth, but the Queen, who had worked herself into a frenzy of anxiety, ignored the protests. Essex had forced her to send this expedition against her will, she protested. Burghley tried to calm her, but matters were made worse when Raleigh, newly returned from a voyage to Guiana, suddenly appeared at court, begging forgiveness and asking to be appointed supreme commander above Essex and Howard.

When Elizabeth had recovered from these confrontations, she was persuaded that the expedition had the best chance of success if Essex and Howard were allowed to remain as joint commanders, and she reluctantly agreed to this, grudgingly appointing Raleigh Rear Admiral.

Essex was so relieved he made peace with Raleigh, telling him, 'This is the action and the time in which you and I shall both be taught to know and love one another.'

Soon, all was ready, and an anxious Elizabeth sent Fulke Greville to Plymouth with a farewell letter for Essex: 'I make this humble bill of request to Him that all makes and does, that with His benign hand He will shadow you so, as all harm may light beside you, and all that may be best hap to your share; that your return may make you better, and me gladder. Go you in God's blessed name.' There was also a humorous note from Cecil: 'The Queen says, because you are poor, she sends you five shillings.' Enclosed was a prayer composed by Elizabeth to be read aloud to her troops: 'May God speed the victory, with least loss of English blood.' This boosted morale tremendously, and Essex wrote, 'It would please Her Majesty well to see th'effect of her own words.'

Lord Hunsdon's death that spring had plunged his cousin the Queen into a melancholy mood. Around this time, she promoted Essex's friend, Sir Thomas Egerton, an excellent and experienced lawyer, to be Lord Keeper of the Great Seal, an office that was revived whenever there was no Lord Chancellor. His seals of office were handed to him by the Queen in a ceremony in the Privy Chamber. Elizabeth appeared in a gold satin gown edged with silver, and stood beneath her canopy of estate on a rich Turkey carpet. She observed to Egerton that she had begun with a Lord Keeper, Sir Nicholas Bacon – 'and he was a wise man, I tell you' – and would end with a Lord Keeper.

'God forbid, Madam,' cut in Burghley, who was present, seated in a chair because of his gout. 'I hope you shall bury four or five more.'

'No, this is the last,' said Elizabeth, and burst into tears at the prospect of encroaching mortality. The embarrassed Egerton hastily agreed that Bacon had indeed been a wise man, but Elizabeth only cried more loudly, 'clapping her hand to her heart'. Then, turning to go to her bedchamber, she paused, remembering that Burghley would have to be carried from the audience in his chair and said briskly, 'None of the Lord Treasurer's men will come to fetch him so long as I am here. Therefore I will be gone.'

When she reached the door, she remembered that Egerton had not taken the customary oath of allegiance required by his office, and, still weeping, cried, 'He will never be an honest man until he be sworn. Swear him! Swear him!'

On 3 June, Elizabeth formally appointed Cecil Secretary of State, a post he had filled in all but name since 1590. On the same day, the expedition sailed for Spain, where, the following month, Essex carried out a daring and highly successful raid on the rich port of Cadiz, 'the

Pearl of Andalusia', where some of Philip's ships were being kept in readiness for the invasion of England. Taken unawares, Spanish forces in the area could do little, and for two weeks, English troops ransacked and burned the town, mostly ignoring Essex's orders to spare its churches and religious houses. 'If any man had a desire to see Hell itself, it was then most lively figured,' observed Raleigh, who particularly distinguished himself during the fighting, although he was severely wounded in the leg and had to walk with a stick for some time afterwards. It was, in fact, he who had made some of the critical decisions that had ensured success, but as his rival Essex was determined to take all the credit himself, Raleigh's praises remained unsung. Predictably, the reconciliation between the two did not long survive Cadiz.

When Elizabeth received the first reports of the victory, she wrote to Essex, 'You have made me famous, dreadful and renowned, not more for your victory than for your courage. Let the army know I care not so much for being Queen, as that I am sovereign of such subjects.'

Flushed with success, Essex botched the ransoming of a Spanish merchant fleet trapped in the harbour; its owners decided to burn their ships rather than lose the twenty million ducats on board to the English. Undaunted, Essex decided that, rather than go on to attack Lisbon where the bulk of Philip's Armada lay, his forces should try to intercept the Spanish treasure fleet as it left port, bound for the Indies, but his colleagues overruled him, thereby depriving the English of the chance to seize thousands of pounds worth of booty. To make matters worse, Essex gave most of the loot from Cadiz to his men, rather than reserving it for the Queen.

Essex had at last achieved his ambition and proved himself a hero, and when he returned to England, sporting a newly-grown spade-shaped beard, it was to the acclaim of a grateful, adoring nation, who saw in him a second Drake or Scipio: 'He took a charter of the people's hearts which was never cancelled.' Preachers praised him as a champion of Protestantism, and spoke of his honour, justice and wisdom. There was no doubt that he was the most popular and important man in the kingdom.

24

'We Are Evil Served'

Elizabeth shared the public's jubilation over Cadiz, which further enhanced her reputation in Europe – the Venetians were now calling her 'the Queen of the Seas' – but she was more concerned about cost than glory, and when Essex returned she did not heap praises and thanks on him, as he expected, but sourly asked him to account for his expenditure, desiring to know what 'great profit and gain' she was to get on her investment. Essex was forced to admit what she already knew, that there was none; in fact, more money was needed to pay his men. Elizabeth snapped that she had known everyone but herself would make a profit, and reluctantly loaned Essex £2000 for wages, demanding that he pay it all back.

It was not only money that caused her irritation. She was also jealous of Essex's success and his all-too-evident popularity with her subjects. It made her feel insecure, for, given his instability, he could, under the influence of her enemies, prove dangerous when he commanded such support. She would not allow him to publish a pamphlet describing his heroic exploits, and when someone suggested that services of thanksgiving be held all over the country, she insisted that they take place in London only. She could not bear to hear people praising him, and made derogatory remarks in Council about his military strategies.

Essex bore it all patiently. 'I have a crabbed fortune that gives me no quiet', he wrote to Anthony Bacon, 'and the sour food I am fain still to digest may breed some humours. I assure you I am much distasted with the glorious greatness of a favourite.' But as it became clear to the Queen that it was not Essex's fault that the fleet had returned empty-handed, she softened somewhat, although when Burghley opposed a suggestion in Council that Essex should forfeit some of his profits from Cadiz, she berated him, shouting, 'My Lord Treasurer, either for fear or favour, you regard my Lord of Essex more than myself. You are a miscreant!

You are a coward!' Burghley had suffered such outbursts before, but they never failed to shake him, and he confided to Essex that he was between Scylla and Charybdis, 'daily decaying'. 'God be thanked!' said Anthony Bacon, who hated Burghley, though Essex wrote to the old man to express his sympathy. Nevertheless, his old rivalry with the Cecils had resurfaced, and was to become even stronger than before; the French ambassador noted that, 'It was a thing notorious to all the court; a man who was of the Lord Treasurer's party was sure to be among the enemies of the Earl.'

Essex now dominated both Queen and Council and was energetically involved in every aspect of state policy. The public regarded him with adulation as a near-legendary hero, and crowds gathered whenever he appeared. One poet referred to him at this time as 'Great England's glory and the world's wide wonder'. Of course, it went to his head, and Francis Bacon warned him that he must do his utmost not to trespass on the royal prerogative and assure the Queen of his utter loyalty. He should abandon martial pursuits and faction fights in favour of devoting himself to his conciliar duties, and should ask the Queen to appoint him to the vacant office of Lord Privy Seal, which carried 'a kind of superintendence over the Secretary'. But Essex, impulsive and headstrong as ever, was incapable of taking wise advice. Although he declared he had 'no ambition but Her Majesty's gracious favour and the reputation of well serving her', how could he, the renowned conqueror, ever confine himself to a civilian role?

Meanwhile, King Philip, indignant at the sack of Cadiz, declared his 'violent resolution' to be revenged upon the English, and ordered the building of more ships with the aim of sending an even greater Armada than in 1588.

For the third year running, there was excessive summer rainfall resulting in bad harvests and 'dearth'. Food prices were high and there was growing discontent and even rioting. Elizabeth ordered that her government bring in emergency measures to provide food for the poor, but that winter people were dying in the streets. Wednesdays and Fridays were declared fast days, when the wealthy were asked to forego their suppers, donating the money saved to the relief of their parish.

Discharged soldiers and sailors had swelled the labour market, and trade was going into a recession. There were fears that law and order were breaking down, and local JPs spoke out against the violent gangs of vagrants who terrorised many areas.

Sir John Harington was in disgrace yet again, not only because of his womanising, but for having written a book, *The Metamorphosis of Ajax*, the title of which was a pun on his new invention, the water closet or 'jakes'. Knowing that the Queen was fastidious about smells, he had presented her with a copy of the book, advising her to have his device installed in Richmond Palace. Elizabeth took offence, not because of the book's scatalogical detail, but because it contained witty and sometimes libellous references to several public figures, among them Leicester, whose memory she would not see sullied. She refused to grant Harington a licence to publish the book, but he defied her, and within a year it had sold out three editions. This resulted in him once more being banished from court.

Harington went to fight in Ireland, whence he wrote to Elizabeth, pleading for forgiveness. His cousin informed him, 'The Queen is minded to take you to her favour, but she sweareth that she believes you will make epigrams on her and on all her court. She hath been heard to say, "That merry poet, my godson, must not come to Greenwich till he hath grown sober and leaveth the ladies' sports and follies."'

Expecting the Spanish to invade in the summer, Essex put pressure on the Queen early in 1597 to send another expedition. She was amenable, but indecisive as to what form the attack should take and who should command it.

In February, when Essex gave out that he was ill, Elizabeth rushed to his bedside. This effected a miraculous recovery, which was, strangely, followed by a relapse, attributed by many to the Queen's insistence that he share command of the fleet with Raleigh. For a fortnight he lay in his chamber, while Elizabeth appeared agitated and the court buzzed with rumours of a quarrel. These were confirmed when the Queen announced, 'I shall break him of his will, and pull down his great heart.' She added that he must have inherited his obstinacy from his mother.

Essex was further angered by the Queen's refusal to appoint his friend, Sir Robert Sidney, to the wardenship of the Cinque Ports, which she bestowed on his enemy Lord Cobham. Bacon suggested that Essex make a tactical withdrawal from court, so he 'recovered' and announced that he was going to visit his estates in Wales. This prompted the Queen to send for him, and 'all was well again', Elizabeth having agreed to make him Lieutenant General and Admiral 'of our army and navy' and appoint him Master of the Ordnance. It was her firm hope that he would achieve a victory to parallel Cadiz without putting her to too much expense.

Since the Cecils supported the venture, Essex was disposed to set all jealousies aside, and in April invited them and Raleigh to a dinner at Essex House, where they all bound themselves in a pact of self-interested amity. At the beginning of June, Essex and the Cecils persuaded the Queen to restore Raleigh to favour. Summoning Sir Walter to her presence, she informed him that he might resume his duties as Captain of the Gentlemen Pensioners and come 'boldly to the Privy Chamber, as he was wont'. That evening, she graciously invited him to ride with her, but he was never to enjoy the same favour as before.

Late in June, Essex took his fond leave of the Queen, and rode to the coast to supervise the final preparations for the voyage. During the fortnight before he sailed, they exchanged affectionate letters, repeating their farewells, Essex addressing her as his 'most dear and most admired sovereign', and telling her that, since 'words be not able to interpret for me, then to your royal dear heart I appeal. I will strive to be worthy of so high a grace, and so blessed happiness. I am tied to Your Majesty by more ties than ever was subject to a prince.' The Queen sent him gifts and a portrait of herself for his cabin, and told him that, if things went badly, he should 'Remember that who doth their best shall never receive the blame, neither shall you find us so rigorous a judge.' He thanked her for her 'sweet letters, indited by the Spirit of spirits'.

Reports were coming in that the Spanish fleet was nearly ready to sail, but the weather was appalling, with rain and floods for the fourth summer running. After the English ships put out to sea on 10 July, a terrible gale raged for four days over southern England and forced them to flee back to port. Elizabeth, having seen her palace buffeted by the winds and heard rumours that Essex had been drowned, wept with joy and relief on learning he was safe, and Cecil wrote to him: 'The Queen is now so disposed to have us all love you, as she and I do talk every night like angels of you.'

Cecil also told Essex how Elizabeth had dealt with the impudent Polish ambassador, who, in a crowded Presence Chamber, and against all accepted protocol, had made a long and threatening oration to her in Latin, 'with such a countenance as in my life I never beheld'. Rising from the throne, a furious Queen berated him in perfect, extempore Latin for his insolence, in a speech that would pass into English folk-lore and be repeated for generations. If his king was responsible for his words, she hissed, he must be a youth and not a king by right of blood but by recent election.

'And as for you, although I perceive you have read many books to fortify your arguments, yet I believe you have not lighted upon the chapter that prescribeth the form to be used between kings and princes.' Had he not been protected by diplomatic immunity, she would have dealt with him 'in another style'.

Turning to her courtiers, she cried, 'God's death, my lords! I have been enforced this day to scour up my old Latin that hath lain long rusting.' Everyone burst out in admiring applause, and when Elizabeth told Cecil she wished Essex had been there to hear her, he assured her that he would write to him of it. Essex replied: 'I am sure Her Majesty is made of the same stuff of which the ancients believed the heroes to be formed, that is, her mind of gold, her body of brass.'

In August, its damaged ships repaired, the fleet sailed again for Spain, but because of further gales it was unable to reach Ferrol, where the Armada was in port. Elizabeth had told Essex that he might go in search of Spanish treasure, but only after he had wrecked Philip's navy, yet he now informed her that he was going off in pursuit of the West Indies treasure fleet. This was not what she had sent him for, and she replied frostily, 'When I see the admirable work of the eastern wind, so long to last beyond the custom of Nature, I see, as in a crystal, the right figure of my folly.' She warned him that 'this lunatic goddess make you not bold to heap more errors to our mercy. You vex me too much, with small regard for what I bid.' She expected his 'safe return'.

Essex, sailing towards the Azores, ignored this. When he arrived on 15 September, the Spanish fleet was expected at any moment, but whilst he searched for them, his own ships became scattered. Raleigh landed at the island of Fayal, and on his own initiative, took a town and seized a great haul of riches. Essex, furious at having been upstaged, accused Raleigh of disobeying orders and of attacking Fayal with the sole purpose of gaining honour and booty, without thought for his commanding officer. He even considered taking his captains' advice to bring Raleigh before a court martial and execute him: 'I would do it if he were my friend,' he declared fiercely. But Raleigh was persuaded to apologise, and the matter was dropped, though his reputation suffered as a result.

Essex now rashly decided to take the island of San Miguel. However, by diverting his ships there, he missed, by three hours, the treasure fleet, which passed unmolested with its cargo of £3,500,000 in silver bullion. Had the English seized the Spanish ships Philip would have been forced to sue for peace, but Essex had missed the opportunity, and had no choice but to return home empty-handed.

Learning that Essex's fleet was out of the way at the Azores, Philip ordered his Armada to sail, and on 13 October, as Essex was sailing homewards, 140 great galleons left Ferrol and made their stately way towards Falmouth, hoping to intercept and destroy the English fleet, which was in no state to resist. They would then occupy Falmouth and march on London. Southern England was placed on a state of alert, ready to repel the invasion, but by the end of October news had filtered through that the Spanish fleet had been wrecked and scattered by storms off Finisterre.

This disaster left Philip, who was a very sick man, prostrate with disappointment. He was bankrupt, his people were weary of this fruitless war, and he was now forced to face the fact that his great Enterprise of

England would have to be abandoned for ever.

On 26 October, Essex reached Plymouth, where he was alarmed to hear that 'the Spaniards were upon the coast'; some galleons had even been sighted off the Lizard. He hastily refitted his ships and sailed to meet the enemy, though it soon became clear that the crisis was past. When he returned to face Elizabeth, the failure of the 'Islands Voyage' was notorious, and he had little to offer her beyond a few merchant ships captured on the way home. More seriously, by his folly, he had left England dangerously exposed to invasion, and the Queen received him icily.

'I will never again let my fleet out of the Channel,' she had told Burghley, and she now accused Essex of having 'given the enemy leisure and courage to attempt us'. Elizabeth was also angry because Essex's popularity had been in no way diminished by his undutiful behaviour. Most people thought he had been plain unlucky, or held Raleigh responsible for the expedition's failure. England's hero, it seemed, could never be guilty of incompetence.

Essex was furious: he could not understand why she should criticise him. 'We have failed in nothing that God gave us means to do,' he wrote. 'We hope Her Majesty will think our painful days, careful nights, evil diet and many hazards deserve not to be measured by the event.' How could 'others that have sat warm at home descant upon us'? He did not try to excuse his failure, and withdrew from the court to sulk at Wanstead, which the Queen had returned to him. Dejectedly, he wrote to her:

> You have made me a stranger. I had rather retire my sick body and troubled mind into some place of rest than, living in your presence, to come now to be one of those that look upon you afar off. Of myself, it were folly to write that which you care not to know. I do carry the same heart I was wont, though now overcome with unkindness, as before I was conquered by beauty. From my bed, where I think I shall be buried for some days, this Sunday night, Your Majesty's servant, wounded, but not altered by your unkindness. R. Essex.

Essex's absence wrought, as usual, a change of heart in the Queen. After speaking affectionately of him to the Earl of Oxford, she wrote to him, inquiring after his health. Then she wrote again, implying that the time was now ripe for forgiveness.

Essex replied,

Most dear Lady, your kind and often sending is able either to preserve a sick man that were more than half dead to life again. Since I was first so happy as to know what love meant, I was never one day, nor one hour, free from hope and jealousy. If Your Majesty do, in the sweetness of your own heart, nourish the one and, in the justness of love, free me from the tyranny of the other, you shall ever make me happy. And so, wishing Your Majesty to be mistress of all that you wish most, I humbly kiss your fair hands.

Delighted by these words, Elizabeth invited Essex back to court for the Accession Day celebrations. He would not come, for by now he was nursing another grievance, having learned that, as a reward for his distinguished services against the Armada and at Cadiz, Elizabeth had created Lord Howard Earl of Nottingham, thus giving him, as Lord Admiral, precedence at court above himself who was only Master of the Horse. The jealous Essex felt that he alone deserved the credit for Cadiz, and therefore informed the Queen that he was too ill to move from Wanstead. This plunged her into so bad a mood that all her courtiers were praying for Essex's return, and Burghley and the new Lord Hunsdon wrote urging it, but in vain.

Accession Day, now called Queen's Day, came and passed without Essex. Burghley wrote again, reminding Essex that it had marked the start of the fortieth year of Elizabeth's reign, and Howard wrote too, in a spirit of friendship. By now, Essex was becoming weary of his self-imposed exile, and replied that he would come if Her Majesty asked him to. But Elizabeth had had enough, and declared that 'His duty ought to be sufficient to command him to court; a prince is not to be contended withal by a subject.'

She refused to discuss the matter further, saying she was too busy, having the French ambassador to entertain. Henry IV wanted to bring about a general peace between France, Spain and England, and had sent a special envoy, André Hurault, Sieur de Maisse, to sound out Elizabeth. This proved impossible, for she was prepared to discuss anything rather than a peace, having heard what proved to be unfounded rumours that Philip was planning yet another Armada the following spring. She was courtesy itself: she apologised for receiving him in her nightgown,* but said she was feeling wretched due to a boil on her face; she offered him a stool, and permitted him to remain covered in her presence. But she seemed distracted: 'All the time she spoke she would often rise from her chair and appear to be very impatient with what I was saying; she would complain that the fire was hurting her eyes, though there was a great

---

*What would now be called a dressing gown.

screen before it and she six or seven feet away, yet did she give orders to have it extinguished.' She told de Maisse she preferred to stand up at audiences, and mischievously added that she had often provoked weary envoys to complain of being kept on their feet. 'I rose when she did,' de Maisse recorded, 'and when she sat down again, so did I.'

On another occasion she suddenly claimed that Philip had plotted fifteen times to assassinate her.

'How the man must love me!' she laughed, then sighed, saying it was a pity they were so divided by religion. Her people were suffering as a result, and she loved her people, as they loved her. She would rather die than diminish by one iota their mutual love, but she feared for their future, since she stood on the brink of the grave. Then, seeing de Maisse's long face, she laughed again.

'No! No! I don't think I shall die as soon as all that! I am not so old, M. l'Ambassadeur, as you suppose.' Angling for a compliment, she said she was sorry that he, who had met so many great princes, should have come to see such a foolish old woman. She also spoke dismissively of her dancing and other accomplishments, 'so that she may give occasion to commend her'. When he duly praised her judgement and prudence, she answered 'that it was but natural that she should have some knowledge of the affairs of the world, being called thereto so young . . . When anyone speaks of her beauty, she says that she was never beautiful, although she had that reputation thirty years ago. Nevertheless, she speaks of her beauty as often as she can.'

De Maisse was amazed at the Queen's wardrobe. He learned that she had three thousand dresses. At his second audience on 15 December, she received him in a gown of silver gauze in the Italian style, edged with wide bands of gold lace. It had 'slashed sleeves lined with red taffeta', and was open in the front to display a white damask kirtle, beneath which was a chemise, both open to the waist, exposing 'the whole of her bosom', which was 'somewhat wrinkled'. Flustered with embarrassment, the poor man hardly knew where to look during the two-hour interview that followed. Whenever he looked at Elizabeth, he saw more than was seemly. To make matters worse, as she talked, 'she would open the front of this robe with her hands, as if she were too hot', so that he could see her stomach right down to the navel. She also wore a 'great reddish wig' with 'two great curls' down to her shoulders; it was laced with pearls and topped with a garland of rubies and pearls. De Maisse could only conclude that she was trying to bewitch him with her faded charms. 'So far as may be she keeps her dignity', but 'her face is very aged: it is long and thin, and her teeth are very yellow and irregular. Many of them are missing, so that one cannot understand her easily when she speaks.' However, 'It is not possible to see a woman of so fine and vigorous disposition both in mind and body.'

On 24 December, arriving for his final audience, de Maisse found Elizabeth listening to a pavane played on the spinet. They talked of many things, and he observed that 'One can say nothing to her on which she will not make some apt comment. She is a great princess who knows everything.' Despite his warm admiration for her, he had accomplished nothing, and feared that 'the English will do nothing in the business' of making peace with Spain.

The ambassador soon sensed the tension at court, and correctly surmised that it was due to Essex's absence. Elizabeth told him that, had Essex really failed in his duty during the Islands Voyage, she would have had him executed, but she had investigated the matter and was satisfied he was blameless.

Essex wanted Elizabeth to change the wording of Nottingham's patent, but she would not. He demanded to settle the matter by a duel, but Howard refused, claiming he was ill. Essex was now attending neither the Council nor Parliament in protest at the way Elizabeth had treated him, and the court was in an uproar, all business being held in suspension. Obviously, this situation could not continue, and on 28 December, on the advice of Cecil, the Queen appointed Essex Earl Marshal of England, an office in abeyance since the execution of Norfolk; this was a signal favour, having the added benefit of restoring Essex's precedence over Nottingham, and it brought about the desired effect. Peace was restored and 'the gallant Earl doth now show himself in public'. Nottingham, meanwhile, retired in a huff to his house at Chelsea.

In the euphoria of reconciliation, Elizabeth bowed to Essex's oft-repeated entreaties that she receive his mother Lettice at court, but she insisted that it would have to be in the privacy of her Privy Chamber. Several times the Countess had waited in the Privy Gallery to see the Queen as she passed, only to find that Her Majesty had gone by another route. Then she had been invited to a banquet the Queen was due to attend, only to learn that Elizabeth had changed her plans at the last minute. Now, however, she was, albeit frigidly, received in the Privy Chamber: she curtseyed, kissed the Queen's hand and breast, embraced her, and received a cool kiss in return, but it was not enough for her son, who now demanded that Elizabeth repeat the charade in the Presence Chamber. 'I do not wish to be importuned in these unpleasing matters,' the Queen snapped, and that was an end to the matter.

Early in 1598, de Maisse left England, dejected after being told by Essex that he was not interested in peace negotiations since he, unlike the Cecils, did not believe in the possibility of peace between Spain and

England. He had also informed the ambassador that the court was a prey to two evils, delay and inconstancy, 'and the cause is the sex of the sovereign'. It was true that the younger, masculine element at court were becoming restive under the governance of an ageing female sovereign, and some openly declared they would not submit to another female ruler.

Essex and many others who had a view to their future were already courting favour with James VI, but when Elizabeth discovered, early in 1598, that James, whom rumour declared might 'attempt to gather the fruit before it is ripe', had instructed his ambassadors in Europe to assert his claim to the English succession, she reprimanded him angrily: 'Look you not therefore without large amends. I may or will slupper up such indignities. I recommend you to a better mind and more advised conclusions.'

Generally, she was in good spirits, but Essex, under a 'great cloud' of gloom, had turned to ladies of the court for consolation. Both his wife and the Queen were unhappy at the rumours about his behaviour, and constant suspicion made Elizabeth depressed and vicious. Her maids were more than once reduced to tears after being unduly reprimanded, and when Elizabeth detected something going on between Essex and Lady Mary Howard, she became unbearable. Fortunately for everyone, Essex managed to convince her that her suspicions were groundless, and her good mood was restored.

Essex's friend, the long-haired dandy Henry Wriothesley, Earl of Southampton – famous for his patronage of Shakespeare – had for four years managed to conceal a clandestine affair with Elizabeth Vernon, one of the Queen's maids, but they wished to marry, and in February 1598, he asked Elizabeth's permission, which she refused. When he asked leave to travel abroad for two years, it was granted. He sailed for France on 10 February, leaving behind 'a very desolate gentlewoman, who have almost wept out her fairest eyes'.

Elizabeth Vernon had good cause to weep: she was pregnant. Fearing she would be ruined, she begged Essex to summon Southampton home. He did so, in the strictest secrecy, and arranged for the lovers to be married at Essex House, where Elizabeth Vernon stayed when Southampton returned to Paris.

Elizabeth celebrated St George's Day in April with a great feast for the Knights of the Garter. Soon afterwards, a German visitor, Paul Hentzner, saw her as she went in procession to chapel at Greenwich, and left a description for posterity: 'Next came the Queen, very majestic; her face oblong, fair, but wrinkled; her eyes small, jet-black and pleasant; her nose a little hooked; her lips narrow and her teeth black; her hair was of an auburn colour, but false; upon her head she had a small crown. Her bosom was uncovered, as all the English ladies have it till they marry. Her hands were slender, her fingers rather long, and her stature neither tall nor low; her air was stately, and her manner of speaking mild and obliging.'

As Her Majesty passed, 'she spoke very graciously, first to one, then to another, in English, French and Italian, for besides being well-skilled in Greek and Latin and the[se] languages, she is mistress of Spanish, Scotch and Dutch. Whoever speaks to her, it is kneeling; now and then she raises some with her hand. Wherever she turned her face, everybody fell down on their knees.'

In May, Henry IV made peace with Spain, which provoked Elizabeth to refer to him as 'the Antichrist of ingratitude'. Burghley urged her to make peace also with Philip, but Essex was violently opposed to it. He wanted to launch such an offensive against Spain as would crush her naval power for good. Burghley criticised Essex for breathing nothing but war, slaughter and blood. Elizabeth was torn between these two viewpoints, and had her work cut out to maintain a balance between them, which did little to preserve her good temper. On the whole, she agreed with the Cecils that it would be foolish to finance a war effort when there was no longer any danger of invasion.

Essex retaliated by publishing a pamphlet containing his views, appealing to the people to support him, and thereby incurred the anger of the Queen. As it turned out, Elizabeth did not sign the peace treaty because her allies the Dutch, who had regained more ground since Philip had switched his military ambitions to France, refused to back it. They had seen too much of the cruelty of the Spaniards to want them as their allies.

Then news came from Ireland that, amidst a deteriorating political situation, Elizabeth's Lord Deputy had died. She decided to replace him with Essex's uncle, Sir William Knollys, but when she announced this in Council on 1 July, Essex, wishing to have an influential enemy out of the way, argued that Sir George Carew, of the Cecil faction, was the better choice. When the Queen refused, Essex persisted, and there was a heated quarrel which led to Essex, with gross disrespect, deliberately turning his back on her.

'Go to the devil!' she shouted, and slapped him round the ears. 'Get you gone and be hanged!' This was too much for Essex, who reached for his sword and cried, 'I neither can nor will put up with so great an affront, nor would I have borne it from your father's hands.' Nottingham stepped between them before he could strike the Queen and, too late, Essex realised the enormity of what he had done.

Elizabeth stood in appalled silence. No one spoke. Then Essex stormed out of the room, uttering threats, and rode off to Wanstead, whence he wrote boldly to her:

> The intolerable wrong you have done both me and yourself not
> only broke all the laws of affection, but was done against the
> honour of your sex. I cannot think your mind so dishonourable but
> that you punish yourself for it, how little soever you care for me.
> But I desire, whatsoever falls out, that Your Majesty should be
> without excuse, you knowing yourself to be the cause, and all the
> world wondering at the effect. I was never proud till Your Majesty
> sought to make me too base. And now my despair shall be as my
> love was, without repentance. Wishing Your Majesty all comforts
> and joys in the world, and no greater punishment for your wrongs
> to me than to know the faith of him you have lost, and the baseness
> of those you shall keep.

Most people expected the Queen to order his arrest and
imprisonment in the Tower. Some anticipated that he would be
executed. But Elizabeth did nothing, nor did she refer to the incident
again.

The quarrel had been symptomatic of a subtle change in their
relationship. Each was growing tired of the other and finding it more
difficult to play their accustomed roles. Essex was weary of Elizabeth's
fickleness and tempests, while she was determined that he should be
governed by the same rules of behaviour as her other courtiers. She later
told the French ambassador that she was 'apprehensive, from the
impetuosity of his temper and his ambition, that he would precipitate
himself into destruction by some ill design', and she had advised him at
this time 'to content himself with pleasing her on all occasions, and not
to show such an insolent contempt for her as he did; but to take care not
to touch her sceptre, lest she should be obliged to punish him according
to the laws of England, and not according to her own, which he had
found too mild and favourable for him to fear any suffering from them'.
Her advice, she added with hindsight, did not prevent his ruin.

In mid-July, Knollys wrote begging his nephew Essex to 'Settle your
heart in a right course, your sovereign, your country and God's cause
never having more need of you than now. Remember, there is no
contesting between sovereignty and obedience.' When this had no
effect, Lord Keeper Egerton informed his friend, 'The difficulty, my
good Lord, is to conquer yourself. You are not so far gone but you may
well return.' Essex had embarrassed his supporters, 'ruined his honour
and reputation' and failed in his duty to his most gracious sovereign, so
he should 'humbly submit', for his country needed him.

Essex retorted,

If my country had at this time any need of my public service, Her Majesty would not have driven me into a private kind of life. I can never serve her as a villein or slave. When the vilest of all indignities are done unto me, doth religion force me to sue? I can neither yield myself to be guilty, or this imputation laid on me to be just. What, cannot princes err? Cannot subjects receive wrong? Pardon me, pardon me, my good Lord, I can never subscribe to those principles. I have received wrong, and I feel it.

And having uttered such dangerous and subversive sentiments, he continued to stand his ground.

The fact was, as Essex's friends were trying to tell him, that Elizabeth really did need him, for Burghley had fallen seriously ill. Now seventy-eight, he was white-haired and shrunken, but still in harness because the Queen, having relied heavily on him for over half a century, would not let him resign, even though she knew he was deaf, in constant pain with gout, and could barely hold a pen.

As he lay in bed in his house on the Strand, worn out with age and overwork, she visited him and affectionately spoon-fed him his meals. She also sent him medicines, writing, 'I do entreat Heaven daily for your longer life, else will my people and myself stand in need of cordial too. My comfort hath been in my people's happiness, and their happiness is thy discretion.' She told him she had no wish to live longer than she had him with her, a remark that made him weep. 'You are, in all things to me, Alpha and Omega,' she declared. So distraught was she at the prospect of losing him that she could attend to nothing. He was the last link with the ruling caste of her youth, all the others having died, and without him she knew she would be isolated amongst the rising new men, many of whom resented her or discounted her as a spent force.

When Cecil sent his father some game broth, he was too weak to lift it to his lips. Again, Elizabeth came to the rescue, and after she had gone, he dictated a letter to his son:

I pray you, diligently and effectually let Her Majesty understand how her singular kindness doth overcome my power to acquit it, who, though she will not be a mother, yet she showeth herself, by feeding me with her own princely hand, as a careful nurse; and if I may be weaned to feed myself, I shall be more ready to serve her on the Earth. If not, I hope to be, in Heaven, a servitor for her and God's Church. And so I thank you for your porridges.

P.S. Serve God by serving the Queen, for all other service is indeed bondage to the Devil.

Burghley died on 4 August 1598, Elizabeth took the news 'very grievously, shedding of tears', then she shut herself away to mourn in private. For months afterwards, she would break down at the mention of his name.

By the time of his death, Burghley was being called the father of his country. 'No prince in Europe hath such a counsellor,' Elizabeth had said. He had been, wrote Camden in tribute, 'a singular man for honesty, gravity, temperance, industry and justice. Hereunto was added a fluent and elegant speech, wisdom strengthened by experience and seasoned with exceeding moderation and most approved fidelity. In a word, the Queen was happy in so great a counsellor, and to his wholesome counsels the state of England for ever shall be beholden.'

The Queen ordered that, although Burghley was to be buried in St Martin's Church at Stamford, he should be honoured by a ceremonial funeral in Westminster Abbey. Among the five hundred black-cowled guests at the impressive ceremony, Essex 'carried the heaviest countenance', but this was attributed by most people to 'his own disfavour' rather than to grief over his enemy's passing. Even in her desolation, Elizabeth had declared that 'he hath played long upon her, and that she means to play a while upon him, and to stand so much upon her greatness as he hath done upon stomach'.

Death was taking not only the Queen's trusted friends but also her enemies. On 13 September, after fifty days of intense pain, Philip of Spain died, ravaged by a terrible disease that had reduced his body to a mass of putrefying, stinking sores. By his own orders, his lead coffin had been placed at his bedside before he died. He was succeeded by his less fanatical, twenty-year-old son, Philip III, who was to continue the war against England in a desultory fashion.

Two weeks after Burghley's death, serious news arrived from Ireland. A large English army under Sir Henry Bagenal had been ambushed at Yellow Ford by the forces of the rebel Irish under Hugh O'Neill, Second Earl of Tyrone, leaving over 1200 dead or wounded and the English-held territory from the north down to Dublin unprotected. This was the 'greatest loss and dishonour the Queen hath had in her time', and she knew she had to act quickly before it was too late to reverse the damage done.

Tyrone was a fighter of great stature and ability, who had once been loyal to the Queen but had turned traitor in 1595 and succeeded thereafter in uniting his countrymen against the occupying English. He wanted freedom of worship, the withdrawal of English troops from the province, and a say in the appointment of government officials. Many Irish looked to him as their saviour, and great numbers had deserted their English garrisons to join his rebels, while the Spaniards were in league with Tyrone, having for years used Ireland as a springboard for harrying England. On his deathbed Philip II had dictated a letter of congratulation and support to Tyrone as his last act of defiance towards Elizabeth. To control such a man, the Queen knew she must appoint a Lord Deputy of great reputation and ability, someone who could crush the rebel forces and effect a peace.

Essex had remained at Wanstead, still waiting for Elizabeth to apologise, but when he heard of Tyrone's victory, he wrote to the Queen offering his sword against the rebels and, without waiting for a reply, rushed off to Whitehall, only to find that she would not see him. Spluttering with rage, he wrote to her, 'I stay in this place for no other purpose but to attend your commandment.' Back came the terse reply: 'Tell the Earl that I value myself at as great a price as he values himself.'

Desperate for some military action, and worried in case he might miss out on the redistribution of Burghley's offices, Essex feigned illness, which had the desired effect. Elizabeth's heart melted and she sent a sympathetic message and her physician to attend him, which led to a speedy recovery and prompted the Earl to write a flattering letter of gratitude. Charmed, Elizabeth agreed to receive him. Because she was so gracious at their interview, Cecil and many others gained the impression that matters were 'very well settled again', but it was not so. When Essex demanded an apology, the Queen refused it, so he flounced back to Wanstead in a foul temper. In fact, she felt it was she who should have an apology, but Essex was not prepared to give her one. Neither would relent, so a deadlock was reached. Egerton and others advised Essex that it was his duty to submit to his sovereign, but he argued that her behaviour had made it impossible for him to do so. Even his election, in Buckhurst's place, as Chancellor of Oxford University did not lift his spirits.

Meanwhile, Elizabeth had sent a new commander, Sir Richard Bingham, to Ireland, but he had died soon after arriving in Dublin. Hearing of this, Essex again wrote to offer his services in the field, and this time the Queen accepted. Thus he came to court, and in a private interview they settled their differences. It is not known whether either apologised, but it may have been the Queen, for Egerton had showed her Essex's extraordinary letter of the previous July, and she had been much disturbed by it. Nor, after this, was she ever quite so affectionate towards him. Both retained a sense of injury, and this was to overlay their future dealings with each other.

Essex did not learn from his mistakes. Hoping to extend his following, he demanded from the Queen Burghley's old – and lucrative – office of Master of the Wards, but she told him she was thinking of retaining it herself. Essex stalked off in a temper, then sent her a letter of protest, in which he pointed out that none of her royal forebears had ever done such a thing. He told her she should think again, but this only stiffened her resolve, and the office remained unfilled.

Undaunted, Essex put himself forward as the new Lord Deputy of Ireland, insisting that he was the only man capable of conquering Tyrone, which everyone agreed would be no easy task. The Queen had proposed Charles Blount, now Lord Mountjoy, for the post, but neither he nor anyone else wanted it, and although she had reservations about giving it to Essex, she had no choice. Robert Markham, a courtier, wrote: 'If the Lord Deputy performs in the field what he hath promised in the Council, all will be well, but though the Queen hath granted forgiveness for his late demeanour in her presence, we know not what to think. She hath placed confidence in the man who so lately sought other treatment at her hands.'

The next two months saw Elizabeth and Essex wrangling over how his campaign should be conducted. He wanted the largest army ever sent to Ireland, and when she refused it, he sulked. 'How much soever Her Majesty despiseth me, she shall know she hath lost him who, for her sake, would have thought danger a sport and death a feast,' he raged. Already, he was having second thoughts about going to Ireland, yet 'his honour could not stand without undertaking it'.

In the end, his persistence got him what he wanted, the greatest army ever raised during Elizabeth's reign, comprising 16,000 infantry and 13,000 cavalry. 'By God', he told Harington, 'I will beat Tyrone in the field, for nothing worthy of Her Majesty's honour has [yet] been achieved.'

Meanwhile, Elizabeth Vernon was still living at Essex House. When the time came for her to be delivered, Essex sent her to stay with his sister, Lady Rich, who was just then engaged in an adulterous affair with Lord Mountjoy and was well versed in subterfuge. A daughter, Penelope, was born on 8 November.

Inevitably, the Queen found out, and ordered Southampton home at once. When he landed, he was arrested for having married without her consent, and committed for a short spell to the Fleet Prison. Essex was by then sheltering the Earl's wife and daughter at Essex House, and did his utmost to secure his friend's release. This did not make for harmony in his relations with the Queen.

He had also fallen out with Raleigh again. On Accession Day that year, Essex and his followers appeared in the tiltyard sporting orange tawny plumes, in an attempt to upstage Raleigh, whom Essex had learned intended to deck out his men in the same. Elizabeth was so disgusted at such petty behaviour that she left early, bringing the day's festivities to an abrupt end.

'To Ireland I go,' wrote Essex on 4 January, 1599. 'The Queen hath irrevocably decreed it.' Many would be pleased to have him out of the way because, as old age advanced, Elizabeth was finding it increasingly difficult to strike a balance between the rival factions at court, and to control Essex, whose 'greatness was now judged to depend as much on Her Majesty's fear of him as her love of him'.

But he faced no easy task. Most Englishmen had little understanding of the native Irish, accounting them savage tribesmen who had wilfully embraced their own form of Catholicism to undermine their English overlords. No Elizabethan Lord Deputy before him had succeeded in conquering them, and most English commanders found it impossible to apply their normal strategies to a land strewn with mountains and bogs, where guerrilla warfare was the norm.

Essex was dismissive of these difficulties, being confident that he would rout Tyrone and thus establish his supremacy in every respect over Cecil and Raleigh, whom he believed were working to undermine his influence. But he feared that, whilst he was away, his 'practising enemies' would poison the Queen's mind against him. 'I am armed on the breast but not on the back,' he told the Council, quite openly. It was this fear, more than any other consideration, that caused him, early in 1599, to have second thoughts about going to Ireland.

On Twelfth Night, Essex danced with the Queen before the visiting Danish ambassador. Elizabeth was at this time engrossed in translating the *Ars Poetica* of Virgil into English, and was still, at sixty-five, 'excellent disposed to hunting', going for long rides 'every second day'. That year, a German visitor, Thomas Platter, described her, certainly with exaggeration, as 'very youthful still in appearance, seeming no more than twenty years of age'.

It was gradually dawning on Essex that he had saddled himself with 'the hardest task that ever gentleman was set about'. On 1 March, we hear that 'new difficulties arise daily as touching the time of his abode, his entertainment, etc., upon which points he is so little satisfied that many times he makes it a question whether he should go or not'. And as the time for his departure loomed, he asked the Council to pity him rather than expect great victories.

Elizabeth was also having second thoughts about sending Essex to Ireland. His courage she did not doubt, but she had little faith in his judgement and stability, and nor, now, could she be sure of his loyalty. In February, she had been perturbed by the publication of Dr John Hayward's account of *The First Part of the Life and Reign of King Henry the Fourth*, which was dedicated to Essex. She was painfully aware that, since a performance of Shakespeare's *Richard II* in 1597, some of her subjects saw in Essex a second Henry of Bolingbroke, who might overthrow her as Henry had overthrown Richard. Aware that she was entrusting to Essex the greatest army she had ever raised, she declared herself offended by the book.

'Cannot this John Hayward be prosecuted for treason?' she asked Francis Bacon.

'Not, I think, for treason, Madam, but for felony,' he replied.

'How so?'

'He has stolen so many passages from Tacitus!' smiled Bacon. But Elizabeth was in no mood for jests.

'I suspect the worst,' she declared. 'I shall force the truth from him.' She even suggested the rack, though Bacon dissuaded her. Nevertheless, Hayward was arrested, condemned in the Star Chamber for having dared write of the deposition of a sovereign, and imprisoned in the Fleet for the rest of Elizabeth's reign.

Hoping that Essex would learn a lesson from this example, the Queen signed his commission on 12 March, giving him leave to return from Ireland when he thought fit. 'I have the best warrant that ever man had,' he observed.

The sun was shining on 27 March as a plainly-garbed Essex rode out of London at the head of his splendid army, cheered by the watching crowds, who cried, 'God bless Your Lordship!' Just beyond Islington, however, a thunderstorm broke, 'which some held an ominous prodigy'. Bacon wrote afterwards: 'I did plainly see his overthrow chained by destiny to that journey.'

With Essex rode Southampton (who was still, as far as the Queen was concerned, in disgrace), Mountjoy and John Harington, whom he would knight during the campaign; the Queen had vetoed him conferring any offices on the former two, fearing he would build up too great a military affinity. But Essex merely resolved to wait until he was safely in Ireland, and then appoint his friends to whatever offices he pleased.

His crossing was dogged by storms, and on 15 April, he arrived at Dublin, complaining of rheumatism. It had been agreed that he should advance on Ulster and attack Tyrone, but his Irish council urged him to wait until June, when the cattle would be fattened and there would be plenty of food for his army. Without informing Elizabeth, Essex decided, early in May, to march his army into Leinster and thence through Munster, to subdue the rebels in those provinces. Revelling in his power, he also set about creating thirty-eight new knights, despite having received from the Queen 'an express letter, all written with her own hand', commanding him not to; he also appointed Southampton

Master of the Horse, again in defiance of Elizabeth's wishes. When she wrote ordering him to revoke the appointment, he flatly refused on the grounds that it would encourage the rebels to see the English disunited.

June came, but although the cattle were fat, Essex made no move against Tyrone. So far, he had taken one small castle at Cahir. On the 28th, Elizabeth, furious at the delay, complained that she was 'nothing satisfied with the Earl of Essex's manner of proceeding, nor likes anything that is done, but says she allows him £1000 a day for going on progress'. Essex therefore marched his exhausted army back to Dublin, arriving on 11 July. He was ailing and in a temper, having learned that, behind his back, Cecil had been appointed Master of the Wards, and he complained to the Queen:

> Why do I talk of victory or success? Is it not known that from England I receive nothing but discomfort and soul's wounds. Is it not spoken in the army that Your Majesty's favour is diverted from me, and that already you do bode ill to me? This is the hand of him that did live your dearest, and will die Your Majesty's faithfullest, servant.

Elizabeth was unimpressed: she wanted deeds, not words. In a reply sent on 19 July, she pointed out:

> If you compare the time that is run on and the excessive charges that is spent, with the effect of anything wrought on this voyage, you must needs think that we, that have the eyes of foreign princes upon our actions, and have the hearts of people to comfort and cherish, who groan under the burden of continual levies and impositions, can little pleasure ourselves hitherto with anything that hath been effected. Whereunto we will add this one thing, that doth more displease us than any charge or expense, which is, that it must be the Queen of England's fortune (who hath held down the greatest enemy she had) to make a base bush kern to be accounted so famous a rebel as to be a person against whom so many thousands of foot and horse, besides all the force of the nobility of that kingdom, must be thought too little to be employed.

Whilst Tyrone was blazing his conquests throughout Christendom, Essex could only write letters boasting of his supposed prowess, when in fact he had squandered men, money and resources.

Again, Elizabeth commanded him to proceed to Ulster and deal with Tyrone as he had promised: 'When we call to mind the scandal it would be to our honour to leave that proud rebel unassailed, we must now plainly charge you, according to the duty you owe us, so to unite soundness of judgement to the zeal you have to do us service, and with all speed to pass thither in such order.'

During that summer there was talk that the Queen was showing signs of her age. She was not riding out in the park so often, and after a mile or two would complain 'of the uneasy going of her horse, and when she is taken down, her legs are so benumbed that she is unable to stand'. When Elizabeth, who greatly feared the consequences of people believing she had lost her grip on affairs, learned what was being said of her, she embarked on a vigorous campaign to counteract it, riding off on private excursions with fewer attendants than 'beseemed her estate', and hotly castigating Lord Hunsdon when he asked her if it was wise for one of her years to ride horseback all the way from Hampton Court to Nonsuch.

'My years!' she roared. 'Maids! To your horses quickly!' Nor would she speak to Hunsdon for the next two days. Soon afterwards, one courtier was able to report: 'Her Majesty, God be thanked, is in good health, and likes very well Nonsuch air. Here hath many rumours been bruited of her, very strange, without any reason, which troubled her a little.' But she did not relax her vigilance. After reading 'an intercepted letter, wherein the giving over of long voyages was noted to be a sign of age', she deliberately extended her progress.

By the time the Queen's letter arrived, in the third week of July, Essex was pursuing another fruitless foray into Leinster, to drive out minor rebels. Early in August he was obliged to return to Dublin after suffering a minor defeat at the hands of the Irish at Arklow, after which he sent his secretary, Henry Cuffe, to inform the Queen, not only that the Irish Council had advised him that it was now too late in the year to proceed against Tyrone, but that the weather in Ireland was appalling and that, of his 16,000 men, only 4000 were left, the rest having been killed, deserted, or died of disease.

Elizabeth was appalled, and incredulous at the advice given Essex; greatly agitated, she sent 2000 reinforcements, and on 10 August told him she expected to hear in his next letter that his offensive against Tyrone 'is begun and not in question'. She angrily charged him, on his allegiance, not to leave Ireland without her permission until he had 'reduced things in the north' and accomplished what he had been sent to do. He must stop wasting his resources on 'inferior rebels'. 'We require you to consider whether we have not great cause to think that your purpose is not to end the war,' she added perceptively.

Essex, ill with dysentery and kidney trouble, and demoralised, now baulked at facing Tyrone, knowing he faced almost certain defeat, but the Queen, in a further trenchant letter, insisted that he do so, adding that no good success ever attended a man who refused to heed sound advice. Her courtiers marvelled that 'Essex hath done so little,' whilst Francis Bacon, whose abilities Elizabeth was grudgingly coming to appreciate, warned her that leaving the Earl in Ireland and putting 'arms and power into his hands, may be a kind of temptation to make him prove unruly'. He urged her to recall Essex. Grimly, she thanked him for having given voice to her own suspicions.

Essex, his ego bruised by the Queen's stinging criticisms and complaints, was becoming obsessed with fears of what the Cecil faction were doing at home to undermine his influence. He had been dismayed to learn that his enemy, Lord Buckhurst, had been appointed Lord Treasurer in Burghley's stead. There was no doubt that the Queen was displeased with Essex, and this he imputed to the machinations of his enemies rather than his own behaviour. Suddenly, he knew what he must do. He had no business to be in Ireland, pursuing elusive military success; instead, he would return to England to safeguard his interests. He knew, with a mounting sense of despair, that, thanks to his incompetence, his army was in no fit state to conquer Tyrone, and at this point all good sense deserted him.

He now announced to his astonished colleagues that he intended to cross to Wales with 3000 men, gather reinforcements from his estates in the principality, and march on London to insist upon the removal of Cecil and his party, whose misgovernment and desire for peace was, he believed, responsible for the ruin of the kingdom. That accomplished, he would force the Queen to accept him as her chief minister. That it could be done, he was convinced, knowing that he had the love of the people and an army at his back. He stressed that he intended no harm to the Queen, and would personally justify his actions to her, hoping that the joy of seeing him would quell any displeasure on her part. Detached from reality as he was fast becoming, it did not occur to him that she might not welcome such an infringement on her prerogative.

Mountjoy and Southampton tried to warn Essex that what he was contemplating was sheer madness and could lead to civil war, but he would not listen. To ensure his safety, therefore, they urged him to leave his army in Ireland and take with him 'a competent number' of his officers and new knights to support him in his demands. But first, they insisted, honour required that he finish this business with Tyrone.

At the end of August, Essex finally left Dublin for Ulster, with a much depleted force, having written in melodramatic vein to the Queen, 'From a mind delighting in sorrow, from spirits wasted with travail, care and grief; from a heart torn in pieces with passion; from a man that hates himself and all things that keep him alive – what service can Your Majesty reap? Since my services past deserve no more than banishment and proscription into the most cursed of all countries, with what expectation shall I live longer?' The letter was signed, 'From Your Majesty's exiled servant, Essex.'

On 3 September, against the Queen's express orders, Essex, whose army was outnumbered 2-1, sent secretly to the rebel leader (with whom he had been in contact for at least a fortnight), first offering to settle their differences by personal combat, and then, after Tyrone had declined on the grounds that he was too old, asking for a parley and holding out hope of a pardon. Tyrone agreed, assuring Essex that, if he would listen to his advice, he would make him the greatest man in England. This only served to strengthen Essex's resolve, and he conceived the idea of enlisting Tyrone as his ally.

Tyrone came to the meeting with Essex to demand that the English leave Ireland to the Irish. On 7 September, the two leaders met on horseback at the Ford of Bellaclynth on the River Lagon, near Carrickmacross. What was discussed during the half-hour meeting is disputed, for Essex had unwisely omitted to bring any witnesses, and made Southampton order everyone out of earshot. However, three men hid themselves in nearby bushes and their evidence, which was later shown to the Queen, suggested that the Earl informed Tyrone of his plans and asked for his support. Essex's enemies believed he had suggested that Tyrone and he join forces with a view to deposing the Queen and setting up Essex as king, but this is unlikely, although Essex certainly did not inform Elizabeth of everything that had been discussed.

The meeting ended with both leaders fixing a truce, to be renewed every six weeks until May 1600. Under its terms, Tyrone would remain in possession of the territory he now held, and the English would establish no more forts or garrisons. The Irish leader now had all the time he needed to reinforce his army.

Although he had promised Tyrone that he would personally lay his demands before the Queen, Essex was under the impression that the rebel leader had in fact submitted to him, and was unaware of the extent of his humiliation. In case the Queen should complain about his failure to secure a military victory, he persuaded his officers to sign a document branding any campaign in Ulster as useless. Then he marched his weary army back to Dublin.

A week later, Elizabeth was told of the parley, but not of the terms of the truce, which Essex had not thought fit to tell her, and wrote urgently to her Lord Deputy, demanding to know what had been said: 'We never doubted but that Tyrone, whensoever he saw any force approach, would instantly offer a parley. It appeareth by your journal that you and the traitor spoke half an hour together without anybody's hearing, wherein, though we that trust you with a kingdom are far from mistrusting you with a traitor, yet we marvel you could carry it no better. If we had meant that Ireland should have been abandoned, then it was very superfluous to have sent over a personage such as yourself.' She reminded him that Tyrone had broken his word before – 'to trust this traitor on oath is to trust a devil' – and insisted that Essex take the field against him as planned. 'We absolutely command you to continue and perform that resolution,' she concluded.

Essex never received her letter. On 24 September, he suddenly announced he was leaving for England, and, taking a substantial number of followers, took ship half an hour later, in defiance of the Queen's orders and having, technically, abandoned his army. Elizabeth, and many other people, would interpret this as desertion. In six months, he had wasted £300,000 of public funds, and his campaign had been an unmitigated disaster.

At dawn on 28 September, having ridden hard for three days, he reached Westminster, where he discovered that the Queen was at Nonsuch. Leaving his escort in the capital, he crossed the Thames by the Lambeth ferry and galloped south at great speed in driving rain, arriving there at ten o'clock the next morning. Then he strode into the palace, caked with mud, marched through the Presence and Privy Chambers, and burst unannounced into the Queen's bedchamber.

25

'The Minion of Fortune'

Elizabeth had just left her bed, and her maids were about their work. It now took her a long time to put on her mask of youth, her wig, her fine clothes and her jewels, so that she could face the world looking her best. When Essex flung open her door and fell to his knees she was, according to Rowland Whyte, a courtier, 'newly up, her hair about her face' and her wrinkled face unpainted. Despite her shock and embarrassment, she did not lose her composure, but offered Essex her hand to kiss and 'had some private speech' with him, 'which seemed to give him great contentment'.

Elizabeth, having no idea of what was going on outside the palace, may well have concluded that her fears had become reality, and that Essex had come at the head of an army to depose or restrain her. Yet he seemed well-disposed, and with great presence of mind she dismissed him, promising they would talk further when they were both more presentable. He had no idea of her inner turmoil, nor of how grossly he had offended her: 'coming from Her Majesty to go shift himself in his chamber, he was very pleasant and thanked God that, though he had suffered much troubles and storms abroad, he found a sweet calm at home'.

The court was agog with speculation. ''Tis much wondered at here that he went so boldly to Her Majesty's presence, she not being ready and he so full of dirt and mire that his very face was full of it,' observed Whyte.

After Essex had gone, Elizabeth quickly completed her toilette, then summoned the four members of the Council who were at Nonsuch that day: Cecil, Hunsdon, Thomas, Lord North, and Sir William Knollys. At half past twelve, she saw Essex again, and for an hour and a half, 'all was well, and her usage very gracious towards him'. Later, at dinner, he was in high spirits, and entertained his friends and the ladies with tales of

Ireland. But Whyte sensed an underlying tension: 'As God help me, it is a very dangerous time here.'

In the afternoon, having ascertained from Cecil that there was no immediate danger of insurrection, Elizabeth summoned Essex once more, but this time 'he found her much changed in that small time, for she began to call him to question for his return, and was not satisfied in the manner of his coming away and leaving all things at so great hazard'. He responded by losing his temper and demanding to explain himself to the Council. The Queen 'appointed the lords to hear him, and so they went to Council in the afternoon', Elizabeth having retreated, in no very encouraging mood, to her apartments.

Essex was made to stand bare-headed before the Council table whilst Cecil accused him of disobeying Her Majesty's will, deserting his command, acting contrary to orders, making too many 'idle' knights, and intruding overboldly into the Queen's bedchamber. For five hours he sought to justify his actions before being informed that he was being dismissed so that the Council could adjourn to discuss the matter. After a debate lasting only fifteen minutes, the councillors recommended to the Queen that he be arrested.

That evening, at eleven o'clock, 'a commandment came from the Queen to my Lord of Essex, that he should keep [to] his chamber': he was to remain under house arrest until his conduct had been fully investigated. His enemies now closed in for the kill. Next morning, when the full Council, hastily summoned, was assembled, he was brought before it again, the clerks were sent out, and the doors were closed. He then underwent a further three hours of questioning, during which he conducted himself, for once, with 'gravity and discretion'. Informed of his answers, the Queen made no comment, merely saying she would think on the matter. But she was in an angry and vengeful mood. By now, the court was a-buzz with rumours, whilst the Queen and her councillors were still half-expecting the remnants of Essex's army to arrive and attempt a coup. When, by the morning of 1 October, it became clear that their fears were groundless, Elizabeth gave orders for Essex to be committed to the custody of his friend, Lord Keeper Egerton, to remain under house arrest during Her Majesty's pleasure at the latter's official residence, York House in the Strand. He was permitted only two servants and no visitors, not even his wife. No sooner had Essex been brought there than he fell sick – genuinely, this time.

Nobody, not even Cecil, believed that Elizabeth would keep him under lock and key for long.

Shortly afterwards, Harington received a message from Essex begging him to go to the Queen and show her his diary of the campaign, hoping that it would prove to her that Essex had done his best. Harington was reluctant to face her, for he feared she might have found out that he himself had visited Tyrone after the truce and been entertained to a 'merry dinner' with the rebels. It was as he had feared, for when he knelt before her, quaking, she bore down on him and, grabbing him by the girdle, shook him violently.

'By God's Son, I am no queen!' she thundered. 'That man is above me.' And 'she walked fastly to and fro', frowning at Harington. Tremulously, he handed her his journal, but, reading it impatiently, she was not impressed.

'By God's Son, you are all idle knaves, and the Lord Deputy worse, for wasting your time and our commands in such wise!' she swore. Terrified, he did his best to placate her, but 'her choler did outrun all reason', leaving all present in no doubt 'whose daughter she was'.

'Go home!' she bawled. Harington 'did not stay to be bidden twice', but rode off to Kelston as 'if all the Irish rebels had been at my heels'.

After a short interval, Harington sent his wife to plead his case with the Queen, instructing her to say, pointedly, that she kept her husband's love by showing her love for him. The analogy was not lost on Elizabeth, who replied, 'Go to, go to, mistress, you are wisely bent, I find; after such sort do I keep the goodwill of all my husbands, my good people; for if they did not rest assured of some special love towards them, they would not readily yield me such good obedience.' So saying, she agreed that Harington might return to court, but when he ventured to do so, she could not resist taking a dig at him.

'I came to court in the very heat and height of all displeasures,' he told Sir Anthony Standen, a friend.

After I had been there but an hour, I was threatened with the Fleet [prison]. I answered poetically that, coming so late into the land service, I hoped that I should not be pressed to serve in Her Majesty's fleet in Fleet Street. After three days, every man wondered to see me at liberty, but I had this good fortune, that after four or five days, the Queen had talked of me, and twice talked to me, though very briefly. At last she gave me a full-gracious audience in the Withdrawing Chamber at Whitehall, where, herself being accuser, judge and witness, I was cleared and graciously dismissed. What should I say? I seemed to myself, like St Paul, rapt into the third heaven, where he heard words not to be uttered by men; for neither must I utter what I then heard. Until I come to Heaven I shall never come before a statelier judge again, nor one that can temper majesty, wisdom, learning, choler and favour better than Her Highness did at that time.

In October, the truce expired and Tyrone re-armed. The Queen, whose wrath had increased rather than abated, blamed Essex and resolved to teach him a lesson. 'Such contempt ought to be publicly punished,' she told her Council. To the French ambassador, she declared her intention of showing Essex who held power in England. Had her own son committed a like fault, she asserted with passion, she would have him put in the highest tower in England. The world, however, did not realise the quality of her indignation, and looked daily for his release. Even the Council had recommended it several times, on the grounds that Essex had been incompetent rather than malicious, and that his offences did not merit such severity.

But 'Her Majesty's anger seems to be appeased in nothing'; months later, she confided to the French ambassador that she had not revealed to her councillors the full extent of Essex's disobedience, and although she did not elaborate further, such fragments of evidence as exist indicate she may have suspected the Earl of having been in league with Tyrone before he set out for Ireland, in which case, his offences were very serious indeed. It seems, however, that what she had learned was not sufficient to secure a conviction, for she remained unsure as to what she should do with him, and asked Francis Bacon, who wrote an account of their interview many years later, for his advice. Bacon, perceiving that Essex was ruined, had decided to abandon him in the interests of furthering his own career, and now pounced on this chance of ingratiating himself with the Queen. He told her that he thought Essex's offences serious. He would never, he advised, send him back to Ireland.

'Whensoever I send Essex back to Ireland, I will marry you! Claim it of me!' Elizabeth cried. She said she meant to bring Essex to justice, but how? Had he committed treason? Was it a cause for the Star Chamber? Bacon advised her that to proceed thus would be unsafe, since, although Essex had been incompetent, there was little evidence of deliberate misconduct or treason. Were he to be convicted on such flimsy proofs, his popularity was such that there would almost certainly be a massive public backlash; already, the people were criticising her for keeping him under arrest without charge. This was not what Elizabeth wanted to hear, and, with a venomous look, she indicated that the interview was over. However, when she had thought on what Bacon had said, a public trial did seem inappropriate and provocative.

At the Accession Day tilts on 17 November, Elizabeth appeared relaxed and unconcerned, presiding over the jousts for several hours. A week later, having announced that Mountjoy was to replace Essex as Lord Deputy of Ireland, she suddenly decided that she would make public account to her subjects for her treatment of Essex. It was then the custom, at the end of the legal term, for the Lord Keeper to deliver a speech to the people in the Court of Star Chamber, and the Queen resolved to make this the occasion for the sorry catalogue of Essex's offences to be read out, 'for the satisfaction of the world' and to suppress the 'dangerous libels cast abroad in court, city and country, to the great scandal of Her Majesty and her Council'.

When he received a summons to appear, Essex pleaded that he was too sick to attend, having 'the Irish flux', but Elizabeth did not believe him, so, on the afternoon of 28 November, accompanied by Lord Worcester and Lady Warwick, she had her bargemen row her to York House. What transpired there is unrecorded, and there is no evidence that she even saw Essex, who was said to be at death's door.

Nevertheless, on 29 November, before a solemn gathering of Privy Councillors, judges and laymen in the Star Chamber, Essex was accused of mismanaging the Irish campaign, squandering public funds to the tune of £300,000, making a dishonourable treaty with Tyrone and abandoning his command against the express orders of the Queen.

Bacon was not present, and when the Queen asked him why, he claimed he had been deterred by threats of violence and worse from the people, who were calling him a traitor for betraying his friend. She did not believe him, and refused to speak to him for weeks afterwards.

After Essex's offences had been published, the Star Chamber proceedings came to an end, and he remained in confinement, though many people thought it unfair 'to condemn a man unheard' without trial.

Throughout the weeks of his confinement, Essex had suffered greatly. He was in pain due to a stone in the kidney and recurring bouts of dysentery, he was allowed to see no one but his servants, he could not go out of doors, and his submissive letters to the Queen provoked no response, driving him to desperation. Even Harington, who bravely came to see him, dared not carry a letter to Elizabeth, for he had barely recovered her favour and had no wish to be 'wrecked on the Essex coast'. The people, however, had not lost faith in Essex, and their sympathy grew when it became known how critically ill he had become: laudatory pamphlets asserting his innocence were distributed in the streets; graffiti insulting the Queen and Cecil (who was blamed for poisoning her mind against Essex and had taken to going about with a bodyguard) appeared on the palace walls; and in pulpits throughout the land, preachers offered up prayers for this champion of the Protestant faith, urging Elizabeth to show clemency. Worst of all, 'traitorous monsters' (the Queen's words) had the temerity to make 'railing speeches and slanderous libels' against her. All this disturbed her greatly, for, having devoted her whole life to courting the love of her subjects, she could not bear to see evidence of their disaffection.

In early December, therefore, Elizabeth graciously allowed Lady Essex, who had stayed at court, conspicuously dressed in mourning, to visit her husband during the daytime, but he was so ill, both in body and spirit, that Frances concluded there was 'little hope of his recovery'. Whyte wrote, 'He is grown very ill and weak by grief, and craves nothing more than that he may quickly know what Her Majesty will do with him. He eats little, sleeps less, and only sustains life by continual drinking, which increases the rheum.'

Distressed to hear this, the Queen sent eight of her physicians to attend him, but their report was not encouraging: his liver was 'stopped and perished', and his intestines ulcerated. He could not walk, and had to be lifted so that his linen, soiled with black matter from his bowels, could be changed. All the doctors could prescribe were glisters (enemas) to cleanse his system. Elizabeth ordered that he be moved to Egerton's great bedchamber, and with tears in her eyes dispatched a messenger with some broth and a message bidding Essex comfort himself with it, and promising that, if she might with honour visit him, she would. She also conceded that, when he was better, he might take the air in the garden of York House.

Nevertheless, she had now seen enough evidence to suggest to her that his dealings with Tyrone had verged on the treasonable, and was still insisting that he be punished for his offences. Yet her anger was underlaid with sadness, and, as she told the French ambassador later, she was still hoping Essex might yet 'reform', for the sake of 'those good things' that were in him.

On 19 December, it was rumoured that Essex had died, and several church bells began tolling. On the door of Cecil's house, someone scrawled, 'Here lieth the Toad'. But when the Queen heard her chaplains praying for Essex, she bade them desist, for she had heard he was not dead, but had in fact recovered somewhat. A week later, he was sitting up in bed, and soon afterwards was taking his meals at table.

Elizabeth kept Christmas that year at Richmond; the court was crowded and merry, and the Queen appeared in good spirits, playing cards with Sackville and Cecil, and watching her ladies performing country dances in the Presence Chamber. There were also 'plays and Christmas pies' for her delectation. There was talk of Pembroke's heir, young William Herbert, becoming the new royal favourite, since 'he very discreetly follows the course of making love to the Queen', but he proved to be a dull, unambitious youth who preferred reading to jousting and was soon 'blamed for his weak pursuance of Her Majesty's favour. Want of spirit is laid to his charge, and that he is a melancholy companion.'

On Twelfth Night 1600, reported a Spanish agent, 'The Queen held a great feast, in which the Head of the Church of England and Ireland was to be seen in her old age dancing three or four galliards.'

Essex's sister, Lady Rich, had already incurred the Queen's displeasure with her incessant pleas on her brother's behalf. Before her lover Mountjoy left for Ireland on 7 February, he conferred with Southampton and Essex's friend Sir Charles Danvers as to how they might best help Essex. It was agreed that they would enlist the support of James VI by informing him that the Cecil faction was working to prevent his succession, and that his only hope of wearing the crown of England lay in the return to favour of Essex. If James would consider a show of armed strength to bring that about, Mountjoy would back him by bringing an army of 4-5000 men over from Ireland to force Elizabeth to agree to their demands. Since all three men were in secret contact with Essex, it is almost certain that he knew of, and had approved, this treasonable plan. But James diplomatically showed little interest in the proposal, and it was shelved.

By the end of January, Essex was well again, and, Elizabeth, stiffening in her resolve, announced to her councillors that she meant to have him publicly tried for treason on 8 February in the Star Chamber. Cecil and Bacon, fearful of public opinion, dissuaded her, suggesting instead that she secure his submission privately. At Cecil's suggestion, Essex wrote her a humble letter craving her forgiveness, beseeching her to let this cup pass from him. 'The tears in my heart hath quenched all the sparkles of pride that were in me,' he declared. Unwillingly, she cancelled the trial at the last minute.

On 3 March, Whyte noted that 'Her Majesty's displeasure is nothing lessened towards the Earl of Essex.' After representations by Egerton, who was finding his position intolerable, Elizabeth gave permission on 20 March for Essex to return under the supervision of a keeper, Sir Richard Berkeley, to live in Essex House, which had been stripped of its rich furnishings, but he was not allowed to leave it and was only permitted a few servants. Nor were his family allowed to live with him. He was still writing plaintive letters to the Queen, pleading to be restored to favour. 'God is witness how faithfully I vow to dedicate the rest of my life to Your Majesty,' he assured her.

Raleigh was fearful that Cecil was not taking a hard enough line with the Queen over Essex, and warned him,

> I am not wise enough to give you advice, but if you relent towards this tyrant, you will repent it when it shall be too late. His malice is fixed and will not evaporate by any [of] your mild courses. Lose not your advantage. If you do, I read your destiny. He will ever be

the canker of the Queen's estate and safety. I have seen the last of her good days, and all ours, after his liberty.

At that very moment, Essex was in correspondence with Mountjoy in Ireland, pleading with him to come to his aid with an army, even if James would not help him. But Mountjoy, having now himself seen the situation in Ireland, was less inclined to sympathise with Essex, and had rather more pressing matters to deal with, the chief of those being the overthrow of Tyrone. He therefore declared that, 'to satisfy my Lord of Essex's private ambition, he would not enter into an enterprise of that nature'. Essex wrote another beseeching letter to the Queen at this time, telling her he felt he had been 'thrown into a corner as a dead carcass'.

That spring, the Queen was very downcast, obviously torn two ways over Essex. When Lady Scrope, bringing her a letter from him, expressed the hope that Her Majesty would restore to favour one who with so much sorrow desired it, Elizabeth replied wistfully, 'Indeed, it was so.'

Public indignation at Essex's continuing imprisonment was mounting, with many believing he had not been brought to trial because there was 'want of matter to proceed against him'. To counteract this, on 5 June, at York House, Elizabeth had him brought before a commission of eighteen councillors, presided over by Lord Keeper Egerton. An invited audience of two hundred persons was present. This was not a formal court, but a tribunal invested with the power to mete out a punishment agreed beforehand by the Queen, who had devised the whole charade as a public relations exercise. Afterwards, many courtiers began to believe that she was paving the way for a reconciliation.

The proceedings lasted eleven hours. The prisoner, who understood very well what was required of him, was made to kneel before the board at which the lords sat, while the Attorney-General, Sir Edward Coke, read out a list of his 'delinquencies'. Chief of these was his gross contempt and disobedience, although it was made clear to him that his loyalty to the Queen was not in doubt. Then four lawyers for the Crown condemned his misdemeanours; Essex was astonished and hurt to see his erstwhile friend Bacon among them. Bacon had, in fact, begged to be excused, but the Queen had insisted on his being there.

Thanks to the intervention of Archbishop Whitgift, Essex was eventually permitted to lean on a chair-back and, as time wore on, to sit. After several hours of accusations, it was time for him publicly to apologise for his misdeeds and throw himself on the Queen's mercy, but at this point the Attorney-General took it upon himself to deliver a lengthy attack on the Earl, provoking Essex to heated retaliation. The dignified hearing quickly deteriorated into a slanging match, and only when Cecil intervened did the protagonists desist and Essex, in a passionate and moving speech, freely acknowledge his culpability and express his deep remorse at having offended the Queen. 'I would tear the heart out of my breast if ever a disloyal thought had entered it!' he cried.

The commissioners found Essex guilty on all counts, and Egerton told him that, had this been a normal court, he would have been condemned to a huge fine and perpetual imprisonment in the Tower, but since it was not, and since he had abjectly admitted his faults and begged for mercy, he might return to his house to await Her Majesty's pleasure. 'It was a most pitiful sight to see him that was the minion of Fortune, now unworthy of the least honour,' wrote Whyte, and many of the onlookers wept to see it.

Elizabeth ordered that he be dismissed from the Privy Council and deprived of his offices of Earl Marshal and Master of the Ordnance, allowing him to retain only that of Master of the Horse. She had considered releasing Essex, but both Cecil and Raleigh warned her that he was almost certain to start scheming again, so after the hearing he remained under house arrest at Essex House.

Three weeks later, the Queen decided to strip all those knighted by Essex of their knighthoods, sparking a terrible fuss, as many of the men quailed at the prospect of telling their wives they were 'Lady' no longer, just plain 'Mistress' again. Cecil intervened on their behalf, but it was some time before the Queen finally relented. Fortunately, news had come from Ireland that Mountjoy was proving himself a considerable strategist and was making headway against the rebels, which disposed the Queen to clemency.

During the summer, Elizabeth kept herself busy. She walked in Greenwich Park, rode her favourite horses, Grey Pool and Black Wilford, and danced in public on several occasions, hoping to prove that she was 'not so old as some would have her'. She was also entertained to dinner by her nobles on several occasions, practised archery at the butts, thrilled to the daredevil performance of a French tight-rope acrobat, and watched the baiting of some bears, a bull and an ape in the tiltyard.

On 15 June, she attended the wedding of a favourite maid of honour, Anne Russell, to William Herbert at Blackfriars. At a masque performed afterwards by eight ladies of the court in allegorical guise, Mary Fitton, another of her maids, invited Elizabeth to dance. The Queen asked her what her costume represented, whereupon Mary replied, 'Affection.'

'Affection!' sniffed the Queen, still keenly hurt by Essex's betrayal.

'Affection is false!' But she joined the dancing, nevertheless.

During August and September, she was hunting every day and, at sixty-seven, planning a long progress to Wiltshire and Farnham, prompting groans and protests from the older members of her household, 'but Her Majesty bid the old stay behind and the young and able to go with her'. Then she thought better of it and, with a very small train, went to Nonsuch instead, then Elvetham, and later to Oatlands, where she was reported to be 'very merry and well'. Thereafter, instead of going on progress, she spent days out, visiting Sir Francis Carew at Beddington Park, Archbishop Whitgift at Croydon Palace, and her New Forest hunting lodge.

Her moods were changeable. At Penshurst Place in Kent, she was in low spirits, and her host, Sir Robert Sidney, told Harington,

> She seemeth most pleased at what we did to please her. My son made her a fair speech, to which she did give most gracious reply. The women did dance before her, whilst the cornets did salute from the gallery, and she did eat two morsels of rich comfit cake and drank a small cordial from a gold cup. She doth wax weaker since the late troubles, and Burghley's death often draws tears from her goodly cheeks. She walketh out but little, meditates much alone, and sometimes writes in private to her best friends. At going upstairs, she called for a staff, and was much wearied in walking about the house, and said she wished to come another day. Six drums and trumpets waited in the court and sounded at her approach and departure.

That summer saw the seventh bad harvest in a row. For some time now, the Queen had been preoccupied with trying to solve her country's economic problems. Dearth and famine had given rise to widespread discontent and disorder, and there were angry rumblings about the dragging out of the costly war with Spain, which had curtailed much of England's trade. No longer could Elizabeth live within her means; instead, she was forced to sell off Crown lands, jewels and even Henry VIII's Great Seal, to pay her debts. Many of her courtiers relied on monopolies on goods and commodities to survive, but the abuse of this system led to bitter complaints from Parliament.

After the hearing in June, Bacon had written to apologise to Essex for his part in it, and had advised him to send two letters in succession, both composed by Bacon, begging the Queen's forgiveness. One read: 'Now, having heard the voice of Your Majesty's justice, I do humbly crave to hear your own proper and natural voice, or else that Your

Majesty in mercy will send me into another world. If Your Majesty will vouchsafe to let me once prostrate myself at your feet and behold your fair and gracious eyes, yea, though afterwards Your Majesty punish me, imprison me, or pronounce the sentence of death against me, Your Majesty is most merciful, and I shall be most happy.'

This worked to a degree. In July, Berkeley was dismissed, although Essex was commanded to keep to his house, and on 26 August, on Bacon's advice, the Queen set him at liberty. As he was forbidden, however, to come to court or hold any public office, he announced he would retire to the country. Both he and his friends were still hopeful that the Queen would forgive him, but in her opinion, he was not yet humble enough.

Essex was still deeply in debt, to the tune of £16,000; his creditors were growing restive, and he was counting on the Queen to renew his monopoly on sweet wines, which accounted for the lion's share of his income, when it expired at Michaelmas. Elizabeth was aware of his predicament, for he had written telling her of it, but when he began inundating her with a further barrage of flattering missives, she observed shrewdly to Bacon, 'My Lord of Essex has written me some very dutiful letters, and I have been moved by them, but' – and here she gave an ironic laugh – 'what I took for the abundance of the heart, I find to be only a suit for the farm of sweet wines.' Bacon pleaded with her 'not utterly to extinguish my Lord's desire to do her service', but she brushed him aside.

Unaware that she saw through him, Essex, having returned to London, was hoping she would agree to see him, and wrote again in desperation: 'Haste paper to that happy presence, whence only unhappy I am banished; kiss that fair, correcting hand which lays new plasters to my higher hurts, but to my greatest wound applieth nothing. Say thou comest from pining, languishing, despairing SX.' Elizabeth had consistently failed to reply to any of his letters, but to this one she sent a verbal message, 'that thankfulness was ever welcome and seldom came out of season, and that he did well so dutifully to acknowledge that what was done was so well meant'.

Michaelmas came and went, with no word from the Queen about his monopoly. There is evidence that the government had just found out about his dealings with Mountjoy, to whom he had recently sent a further request for help, with a view to launching an assault on the court.

'Corrupt bodies – the more you feed them, the more hurt you do them,' Elizabeth observed grimly. 'An unruly horse must be abated of his provender, that he may be the more easily and better managed.'

On 18 October, Essex made a final, despairing plea to her:

My soul cries out unto Your Majesty for grace, for access, and for an end of this exile. If Your Majesty grant this suit, you are most gracious. If this cannot be obtained, I must doubt whether that the means to preserve life, and the granted liberty, have been favours or punishments; for, till I may appear in your most gracious presence and kiss Your Majesty's fair, correcting hand, time itself is a perpetual night, and the whole world but a sepulchre unto Your Majesty's humblest vassal.

Late in October, the Queen announced that from henceforth the profits on sweet wines would be reserved to the Crown; perhaps she intended to restore them to him when he had sufficiently expiated his crimes, but for the present, Essex was ruined.

This, the culmination of months of ill-health, deep anxiety and strain, finally broke him. It would be no exaggeration to say that he lost his reason in consequence of this cruel blow, which coincided with Mountjoy's categoric refusal to help him. He was as a man possessed, raving with anger one moment and plunged into black melancholy another. Harington, who went to see him at this time, recorded that

ambition thwarted in its career doth speedily lead on to madness. He shifteth from sorrow and repentence to rage and rebellion so suddenly as well proveth him devoid of good reason or right mind. He uttereth strange words, bordering on such strange designs that made me hasten forth and leave his presence. His speeches of the Queen becometh no man who hath a healthy mind in a healthy body. He hath ill advisers and much evil hath sprung from this source. The Queen well knoweth how to humble the haughty spirit, the haughty spirit knoweth not how to yield, and the man's soul seemeth tossed to and fro, like the waves of a troubled sea.

One remark made by Essex was reported to Elizabeth: when someone, possibly Harington, referred to 'the Queen's conditions', he interrupted, shouting, 'Her conditions! Her conditions are as cankered and crooked as her carcass!' She never forgave him for this.

But his anger went beyond words. From now on, spurred on by the machinations of his clever and ambitious secretary, Henry Cuffe, who was the brains behind what was to come, he was in covert rebellion. He was paranoid, convinced that his misfortunes marked the success of a masterplan by his enemies to destroy him, and that Cecil was not only plotting to murder him, but was also conspiring with Philip III to set the Infanta Isabella on the throne. It was imperative that he warn the Queen of what was going on, so that she could rid herself of such treacherous ministers and be reconciled with himself, fully restoring him to favour. If she refused to listen, he would make her: Cuffe had convinced him the only way to get back into favour would be to force his way into her presence, backed by an army of his friends and those citizens who had so often expressed their love for him. Cuffe told him that honour demanded this of him: he must save his reputation.

Essex therefore began to gather around him disaffected peers such as the Earls of Southampton and Rutland, his staunch friends, who included Sir Charles Danvers, Essex's stepfather Christopher Blount, a Catholic recusant, Francis Tresham, Essex's secretary Henry Cuffe, his Welsh steward, Sir Gelli Meyrick, and even his sister, Lady Rich, who was Mountjoy's mistress. For good measure, Essex warned James VI of Cecil's imagined efforts to promote the claim of the Infanta, and urged him to insist that Elizabeth declare him her heir. James was disturbed by this, and responded in a coded message, which Essex ostentatiously carried with him at all times in a black pouch hung around his neck.

Soon, the conspirators were meeting, not only at Essex House, but also at Southampton's residence, Drury House. Essex was even contemplating breaking into the Queen's apartments, placing her under restraint, and ruling England in her name. Thanks to Cecil's agents, whose suspicions had been alerted by the number of swaggering young bucks converging on the Strand, the Secretary knew exactly what was going on, and was prepared to bide his time until Essex had woven enough rope with which to hang himself.

In November, the war in the Netherlands finally came to an end when an Anglo-Dutch army won a victory over the Spaniards at Nieuport. All that most people, including the Queen, wanted now was a safe, honourable peace with Spain.

Accession Day arrived, and there were the usual festivities at Whitehall. On this day also, Essex wrote his last surviving letter to Elizabeth, congratulating her on the forty-second anniversary of her accession and again begging to be forgiven: 'I sometimes think of running [in the tiltyard] and then remember what it will be to come into that presence, out of which both by your own voice I was commanded, and by your own hands thrust out.' Again, he received no answer.

By now, he had built up a wide affinity of support, which included, according to Camden, 'all swordmen, bold, confident fellows, men of broken fortunes, and such as saucily used their tongues in railing against all men'. Outcasts, social misfits, deserters from the army, Puritan preachers, Papists, adventurers, and all manner of malcontents found the door of Essex House open to them. Nearly all, even Essex's noble supporters, were desperately short of money, a disadvantage which they looked to the success of their revolt to remedy, and all were ready to be swept up in a fervour of misplaced patriotism. Even Mountjoy, learning of Lady Rich's involvement, now offered his assistance, should the rebellion prove successful.

At Christmas, Essex tried again to enlist the support of James VI against the Cecil faction, urging him 'to stop the malice, the wickedness and madness of these men, and to relieve my poor country, which groans under the burden'. The Queen, he asserted, was 'being led blindfold into her own extreme danger'. James agreed to send an ambassador to back Essex's complaints, but only after Essex had staged his coup.

Elizabeth kept Christmas at Whitehall; Cecil entertained her to dinner, and on 26 December there was dancing at court, she herself performing a coranto with a Mr Palmer. She also watched the eleven plays that were staged at court during the season.

During the early weeks of 1601, Essex finalised plans for his coup, which was planned for March, whilst his followers disseminated wild rumours of Catholic plots throughout London. It was decided that, once the City and the Tower had been secured, Essex would approach the Queen 'in such peace as not a dog would wag his tongue at him' and make her summon a Parliament, in which he would have Cecil, Raleigh and their associates impeached and himself named Lord Protector. Yet, although Essex had decreed that the Queen should not be harmed, according to Christopher Blount, 'if we had failed of our ends, we should, rather than have been disappointed, even have drawn blood from herself'.

One of Essex's friends, Sir Ferdinando Gorges, took fright and warned Raleigh of what was going on. Raleigh, in turn, alerted the Council, but Cecil was already prepared. At the beginning of February, he himself spread a rumour that Essex was about to be sent to the Tower. Hearing this, Essex realised there was no time to lose.

His sense of urgency deepened when, on the morning of 7 February, a messenger arrived from the Queen to demand that he present himself before the Council immediately. His friends warned him not to go, as he would be arrested, and urged him to act without delay. He briefly considered fleeing, but could not bring himself to abandon his hopes of glory, nor his public, for he felt sure they would rise on his behalf. He therefore dispatched the royal messenger with a message that he was 'in bed and all in a sweat' after playing tennis, and could not attend the Council. Then he summoned three hundred of his followers and told them that, since he had just discovered that Cecil and Raleigh were planning his assassination, the rising would take place on the morrow. The Queen, he insisted, must not be harmed.

Later that day, in order to rouse the populace of London, Essex's friend, Sir Gelli Meyrick, paid a reluctant Shakespeare and his company of actors, the Lord Chamberlain's Men, forty shillings to stage a production of the inflammatory *Richard II*, with its banned abdication scene, at the Globe Theatre in Southwark.

Cecil was also preparing for a confrontation: he summoned levies from the nearby shires, instructed the London preachers to tell the citizens to remain indoors on the morrow, and arranged for the guard to be doubled at Whitehall. Danvers, who had been watching the palace, warned Essex that his plans were known, and warned him to escape while he could. Essex refused to listen.

On the next day, the 8th, he staged his coup. As he gathered his friends and supporters and two hundred soldiers in the courtyard of Essex House, there was so much noise and commotion that the Queen, hearing of it, sent Lord Keeper Egerton, the Lord Chief Justice, Sir John Popham, the Earl of Worcester and Sir William Knollys to find out the cause of it and insist that Essex come and explain himself to the Council. Essex invited them into his library, but the crowd swarmed up the stairs behind them, crying, 'Kill them! Kill them!', drowning the lords' injunctions to disarm. Essex locked the four councillors in the library, and left with his by now unruly following for the City on foot.

Wearing his normal clothes rather than armour to signify his peaceful intent, and carrying just a sword, he marched through Temple Bar into Fleet Street, crying, 'For the Queen! For the Queen! The crown of England is sold to the Spaniard! A plot is laid for my life!' But he had overestimated his popularity and credibility: far from flocking to his side, the astonished citizens remained indoors and even tried, unsuccessfully, to prevent him forcing his way through Ludgate, which had been locked against his coming. By the time he reached St Paul's Cathedral, he was forced to face the fact that there would be no popular rising in his favour. As he turned into Cheapside, his face was 'almost molten with sweat' and suffused with fear. When he reached the house of the Sheriff of London, Thomas Smyth, who had offered his support, he was perspiring so much that he asked for a clean shirt. But already, his followers were deserting him, covering their faces with their cloaks, and Smyth, regretting having ever got involved in such a madcap scheme, escaped out of the back door to summon the Mayor, who was busy obeying the Queen's injunction to summon all the citizens to arms.

Meanwhile, heralds had ridden abroad proclaiming Essex a traitor, and government troops had begun erecting a barricade of coaches across the road that led from Charing Cross to Whitehall. Many citizens had hurried to the palace, one remarking that there was 'such a hurly burly at the court as I never saw'. A force under Sir John Leveson occupied

Ludgate, and every one of London's seven gates was locked.

Around two o'clock in the afternoon, realising that all was lost, Essex abandoned his remaining followers and fled to Queenhithe, where he took a barge back to his house, only to find that Gorges had released his hostages and returned with them to Whitehall. Realising his predicament, Essex locked himself in and burned dozens of incriminating papers as well as his black pouch containing the Scottish King's message. But it was not long before the Queen's soldiers, under the command of Lord Admiral Nottingham, came and surrounded his house and trained their cannon upon it, demanding he give himself up.

Essex clambered up on to the roof and brandished his sword. 'I would sooner fly to Heaven!' he cried. Nottingham replied, very well then, he would blow the house up. Essex had no choice but to come out, just after ten in the evening, and surrender his sword. He asked only that his chaplain, Abdy Ashton, remain with him. Before long, eighty-five rebels had been rounded up and taken into custody.

During the rebellion, Elizabeth had remained coolly in control and displayed remarkable courage, giving orders to Cecil and never doubting her people's loyalty. She took her meals as usual, stating that God had placed her on her throne and He would preserve her on it, and would not allow the normal routine of the day to be disrupted. At one stage, she received a false report that the City had gone over to Essex, but was no more disturbed by this 'than she would have been to hear of a fray in Fleet Street'. 'She would have gone out in person to see what any rebel of them all durst do against her, had not her councillors, with much ado, stayed her.' Nottingham spoke admiringly of the way she had placed her reliance on God: 'I beheld Her Majesty with most princely fortitude stand up like the Lord's Anointed and offer in person to face the boldest traitor in the field, relying on God's almighty providence, which had heretofore maintained her.' Cecil spoke for many when he gave thanks for 'the joy of Her Majesty's preservation'.

Having demonstrated that she was still in authoritative control of her realm, the Queen expressly ordered that Essex and Southampton be taken that night under guard to Lambeth Palace rather than the Tower, 'because the night was dark and the river not passable under [London] Bridge'. But on the next tide, at three o'clock the next morning, they were rowed to the Tower, closely followed by Rutland, Danvers, Blount and several others of gentle birth. Elizabeth would not retire to bed until she had been assured that her orders had been carried out. Cuffe and other rebels were thrown into the common gaols.

On 9 February, the Queen told the French ambassador that Essex, that 'shameless ingrate, had at last revealed what had long been in his

mind'. She had indulged him too long, she confessed, and with
mounting passion, spoke scornfully about Essex parading himself
through the City, making vain speeches and retreating shamefully. Had
he reached Whitehall, she declared, she had been resolved to go out and
face him, 'in order to know which of the two of them ruled'.

After the rising had collapsed, however, the strain told. Harington
noticed that Elizabeth was 'much wasted' and could not be bothered to
put on all her finery.

> She disregardeth every costly dish that cometh to the table, and
> taketh little but manchet and pottage. Every new message from the
> City doth disturb her, and she frowns on all the ladies. I must not
> say much, but the many evil plots and designs hath overcome all
> Her Highness's sweet temper. She walks much in her chamber, and
> stamps with her feet at ill news, and thrusts her rusty sword at times
> into the arras [tapestry] in great rage. But the dangers are over, and
> yet she always has a sword by her table. And so disordered is all
> order, that Her Highness hath worn but one change of raiment for
> many days, and swears much at those that cause her griefs, to the
> no small discomfiture of all about her.

As Elizabeth wanted the chief offenders brought to trial without
delay, the Council began examining them, uncovering the full details of
the doomed plot. On 13 February, in the Star Chamber, these were
made public. Four days later, indictments against Essex, Southampton
and many others were laid, and it was decided that the two principals
should be tried two days hence. Bacon was one of those chosen to act
for the Crown, and had no qualms now about doing so. The Queen was
prepared to overlook Mountjoy's involvement, in view of his successes
in Ireland, and also refrained from complaining to James VI about his
support of Essex.

Elizabeth's resolve to make an end of Essex was strengthened on 12
February, when one of his followers, a Captain Lea, who had served as
his messenger to Tyrone – and in 1597 had presented Elizabeth with the
severed head of an Irish rebel, much to her disgust – was arrested in the
palace kitchen on his way to the chamber where she supped with her
ladies, his intention being to force her at knife-point to issue a warrant
for Essex's release. Lea was tried at Newgate on 14 February, and hanged
at Tyburn the following day.

On 19 February, Essex and Southampton were tried by their peers at
Westminster Hall, Buckhurst presiding as Lord High Steward. They
were accused of plotting to deprive the Queen of her crown and life,

imprisoning the councillors of the realm, inciting the Londoners to rebellion with false tales, and resisting the Queen's soldiers sent to arrest them. As Essex looked on smiling, Sir Edward Coke, Francis Bacon and Sir John Popham presented a devastating case for the Crown, Coke accusing him of aspiring to be 'Robert, the first of his name, King of England'. Bacon's defection was, to Essex, 'the unkindest cut of all', but Bacon pointed out to the court, 'I loved my Lord of Essex as long as he continued a dutiful subject. I have spent more hours to make him a good subject to Her Majesty than I have about my own business.'

Essex, dressed in black and very much in control of himself, pleaded not guilty, as did Southampton, and boldly did his best to refute the charges, arguing heatedly with his accusers. He insisted that Raleigh had tried to murder him, but Raleigh, summoned as a witness, stoutly denied it. When Essex insisted that his chief intention had been to petition the Queen to impeach Cecil, whose loyalty was false, Bacon retorted that it was hardly usual for petitioners to approach Her Majesty armed and guarded, nor for them to 'run together in numbers. Will any man be so simple to take this as less than treason?' When Cecil demanded to know where Essex had learned that he was plotting to set the Infanta on the throne, Essex was forced to admit that this slander was based on a chance remark of Cecil's, made two years before, and taken out of context. 'You have a wolf's head in a sheep's garment. God be thanked, we know you now,' commented Cecil, vindicated.

The verdict was a foregone conclusion, the peers having asked the advice of senior judges beforehand, and taken into account the wishes of the Queen: after an hour's debate, they found Essex guilty of high treason, whereupon Buckhurst sentenced him to the appalling barbarities of a traitor's death – a sentence which, in the case of a peer of the realm, was invariably commuted by the monarch to simple beheading.

After being sentenced, Essex, who remained calm, dignified, and unmoved by the terrible fate awaiting him, was allowed to address the court: 'I think it fitting that my poor quarters, which have done Her Majesty service in divers parts of the world, should now at the last be sacrificed and disposed at Her Majesty's pleasure.' He asked for mercy for Southampton, but said he would not 'fawningly beg' for it for himself, and, looking at the peers, added, 'Although you have condemned me in a court of judgement, yet in the court of your conscience, ye would absolve me, who have intended no harm against the prince.' The condemned were generally expected to express humble submission, and Essex's speech was reckoned by many of those present to be unfittingly arrogant for one on the brink of Divine Judgement, and whose guilt was so manifest.

Southampton, who declared he had been led away by love for Essex, was also condemned to death, but the Queen was merciful, and later commuted his punishment to life imprisonment in the Tower. After her death, he was released by James I.

Many people at court believed that, if Essex begged the Queen for mercy, she would spare his life, but Essex remained true to his word and proudly refrained from making any 'cringing submission'. Despite the efforts of the Dean of Norwich, who had been sent to him by the Council, he would not acknowledge his guilt. Even had he done so, he would have posed too great a threat to the Queen's security to be allowed to live. On the day after the trial, without her usual prevarication, Elizabeth signed his death warrant in a firm hand; it may still be seen in the British Library.

On 21 February, Cecil, Nottingham, Egerton and Buckhurst were requested to attend on Essex in the Tower. His chaplain, having conjured up a terrifying vision of the punishment that awaited him in Hell if he did not own up to his sins, had succeeded where the Dean had failed and, in an agony of remorse, Essex had asked to make a full confession of his crimes in the presence of the Council. With great humility, he declared he was 'the greatest, most vilest and most unthankful traitor that has ever been in the land', and admitted that 'the Queen could never be safe as long as he lived'. He then rehearsed all his misdeeds, implicating most of his friends, and even his own sister, without a qualm. He asked to see Henry Cuffe, and when the secretary was brought in, accused him of being the author 'of all these my disloyal courses into which I have fallen'.

Lady Essex had written begging Cecil to intercede with the Queen for her husband's life, saying that if he died, 'I shall never wish to breathe one hour after'. Cecil was in fact grieved to see Essex brought so low, but the Queen was implacable. Later, she told the French ambassador that, had she been able to spare Essex's life without endangering the security of the realm, she would have done so, but 'he himself had recognised that he was unworthy of it'. She did, however, grant Essex's request for a private execution.

On 23 February, having been delayed to give the prisoner time to make his confession, Essex's death warrant was delivered to the Lieutenant of the Tower, but the Queen sent a message after it, ordering that the execution be postponed until the next day.

Shrove Tuesday fell on 24 February; the Queen attended the customary banquet at court, and watched a performance of one of Shakespeare's plays. That night, she sent a message commanding the Lieutenant of the Tower to proceed with Essex's execution on the morrow, ordering that two executioners be summoned to despatch the prisoner: 'If one faint, the other may perform it to him, on whose soul God have mercy.' Then she retired to the privacy of her apartments and remained there throughout the following day.

There is a legend, often repeated, that Elizabeth had once, in happier times, given Essex a ring, saying that, if ever he was in trouble, he was to send it to her and she would help him. A gold ring with a sardonynx cameo of the Queen, said to be this one, is in the Chapter House Museum in Westminster Abbey. In the seventeenth century, it was claimed that, whilst in the Tower, Essex leaned out of his window and entrusted the ring to a boy, telling him to take it to Lady Scrope and ask her to give it to the Queen; however, the boy mistakenly gave it to Lady Scrope's sister, the Countess of Nottingham, wife of Essex's rival, the Admiral, who, out of malice, made her keep the ring to herself. The story went that she only revealed its existence to the Queen when she herself was on her deathbed in 1603, whereupon Elizabeth is said to have told her bitterly, 'May God forgive you, Madam, but I never can.'

The story is a fabrication. It is first referred to in 1620 in John Webster's *The Devil's Law Case*, and later recounted in detail in *The Secret History of the Most Renowned Queen Elizabeth and the Earl of Essex, by a Person of Quality*, a work of fiction published in 1695. Camden, Elizabeth's usually well-informed biographer, knew of the tale, and condemned it as false, and this is borne out by the fact that Elizabeth, who did attend the death-bed of her great friend, Lady Nottingham, was so devastated with grief at her death that her own health was fatally undermined.

During the night of 24 February, Essex prepared for death, apologising to his guards for having no means of rewarding them, 'for I have nothing left but that which I must pay to the Queen tomorrow in the morning'.

In the early hours of the 25th, a select company of lords, knights and aldermen arrived at the Tower. They had been invited to watch the execution, and took their seats around the scaffold, which had been built in the courtyard of the Tower in front of the Chapel of St Peter ad Vincula. When Raleigh appeared, being required, as Captain of the Gentlemen Pensioners, to attend, there was a frisson of disapproval, for it was known that he had been Essex's enemy, and several people, seeing him position himself near the block, accused him of having come to gloat. He therefore withdrew to the armoury in the nearby White Tower, and watched the proceedings from a window. Later, he claimed he had been moved to tears.

Supported by three clergymen, Essex was brought to the scaffold just before eight o'clock; he was dressed in a black velvet gown over a doublet and breeches of black satin, and wore a black felt hat. Having ascended the steps, he took off his hat and bowed to the spectators. It was traditional for the condemned person to make a last speech before departing the world, and Essex's was abject in tone; 'he acknowledged, with thankfulness to God, that he was justly spewed out of the realm'. Then he continued:

> My sins are more in number than the hairs on my head. I have bestowed my youth in wantonness, lust and uncleanness; I have been puffed up with pride, vanity and love of this wicked world's pleasures. For all which, I humbly beseech my Saviour Christ to be a mediator to the eternal Majesty for my pardon, especially for this my last sin, this great, this bloody, this crying, this infectious sin, whereby so many for love of me have been drawn to offend God, to offend their sovereign, to offend the world. I beseech God to forgive it us, and to forgive it me – most wretched of all.

He begged God to preserve the Queen, 'whose death I protest I never meant, nor violence to her person', and he asked those present 'to join your souls with me in prayer'. He ended by asking God to forgive his enemies.

His speech over, he removed his gown and ruff, and knelt by the block. A clergyman begged him not to be overcome by the fear of death, whereupon he commented that several times in battle he had 'felt the weakness of the flesh, and therefore in this great conflict desired God to assist and strengthen him'. Looking towards the sky, he prayed fervently for the estates of the realm, and recited the Lord's Prayer. The executioner then knelt, as was customary, and begged his forgiveness for what he was about to do. He readily gave it, then repeated the Creed after a clergyman. Rising, he took off his doublet to reveal a long-sleeved scarlet waistcoat, then bowed to the low block and laid himself down over it, saying he would be ready when he stretched out his arms. Many spectators were weeping by now.

'Lord, be merciful to Thy prostrate servant!' Essex prayed, and twisted his head sideways on the block. 'Lord, into Thy hands I commend my spirit.' A clergyman enjoined him to recite the 51st Psalm, but after two verses, he cried, 'Executioner, strike home!' and flung out his arms, still praying aloud. It took three strokes to sever his head, but he was probably killed by the first, since his body did not move after it. Then the headsman lifted the head by its long hair and shouted, 'God save the Queen!'

*

Of the other conspirators, Blount, Danvers, Meyrick and Cuffe were executed. Otherwise, the Queen, on Cecil's advice, was disposed to be merciful. Some forty-nine were imprisoned or fined – some of whom would become involved in the Gunpowder Plot of 1605 – while Lady Rich and thirty others were allowed to go free. Lady Essex remarried twice, and Lettice Knollys, Blount's widow, lived to the age of ninety-four. Anthony Bacon, broken by the loss of his old friend, died three months after the rebellion. His brother Francis was rewarded by the Queen for his services with a grant of £12,000.

Essex's passing was mourned by many of the common people, who commemorated his deeds in popular ballads such as _Essex's Last Good Night_, and _Sweet England's pride is gone, well-a-day, well-a-day_, but the Queen, who had sent him to his death yet grieved for him on a personal level, had no doubt that he had deserved it, and that England was a more stable and secure state without him.

26

'The Sun Setteth At Last'

Elizabeth never showed any sign of regret for having executed Essex. As far as she was concerned, she had been justified in doing so. Yet she remembered him with sadness, and for the rest of her life wore a ring he had given her.

With Essex dead, the most powerful man in England was Cecil, that able and consummate statesman. However, he was not popular, and the people blamed him and Raleigh for Essex's death. 'Little Cecil trips up and down, he rules both court and crown,' ran a contemporary rhyme. This was not strictly true, for, although the public thought otherwise, the Queen remained firmly in control of affairs. 'I know not one man in this kingdom that will bestow six words of argument, if she deny it,' Cecil testified. The only man who would have done so was dead, and there was at last an unusual peace at court which not even Raleigh's pretensions could ruffle. Elizabeth knew he was jealous of Cecil's power, but was also aware that his 'bloody pride' would ensure he was never a serious rival.

In March 1601, Cecil began paving the way for James VI's succession, and his own continuance in office, by instituting a private correspondence with the Scots King, which was to be conducted in the strictest secrecy, Cecil insisting that James could expect nothing from him that was prejudicial to Elizabeth's estate. If James would accept his advice and guidance, however, he could rest assured that the crown would pass peacefully to him when the time came. James was only too pleased to co-operate.

In May, he sent envoys to Elizabeth to request that she openly acknowledge him her heir, but, as Cecil informed England's ambassador in Edinburgh, 'Her Majesty gave nothing but negative answers, the matter being of so sour a nature to the Queen.' By now, she had a pathological aversion to any discussion of the succession question, and even the news that the Scottish King, angry at her response, was doing his best to enlist foreign support for his claim, did not encourage her to settle the matter. Hence, relations between herself and James were tense for the rest of the reign; once, she informed him that she knew that all was in readiness for her funeral. Nevertheless, it is clear from her letters that she favoured him above all others as her successor. What she dared not do was acknowledge him openly as such. Yet she told Harington in private that 'they were great fools that did not know that the line of Scotland must needs be next heirs'.

For months after Essex's death, Elizabeth was weary and sad, suffering bouts of depression that drove her to seek sanctuary in her darkened bedchamber, where she would give way to fits of weeping. Drained of energy, she grew careless and forgetful when attending to state affairs. The last two years had broken her spirit, and there were few left of her generation to understand her terrible isolation. That summer, she confessed to the French ambassador that 'she was tired of life, for nothing now contented her or gave her any enjoyment'. She referred to Essex 'with sighs and almost with tears', but insisted that he had not heeded her warnings and had brought his own doom upon himself. 'Those who touch the sceptre of princes deserve no pity,' she declared.

In consequence of her mood, 'the court was very much neglected, and in effect the people were generally weary of an old woman's government'. After the fall of Essex, Elizabeth's popularity had declined, despite government efforts to set the record straight. 'To this day', wrote Camden in the next reign, 'there are but few that thought [Essex's] a capital crime.' The country was burdened by economic hardship, the war with Spain still dragged on interminably, and a need for change was making itself felt. Elizabeth was criticised, somewhat unfairly, for making savage cuts in her expenditure, by courtiers who could not meet the rising cost of living and looked to her successor to remedy matters. Bribery and corruption were now endemic at court, and the Queen was powerless to stamp them out. 'Now the wit of the fox is everywhere on foot, so as hardly a faithful or virtuous man may be found,' she complained.

In August, Elizabeth received the antiquary William Lambarde, Keeper of the Records in the Tower, who had come to present her with a copy of his catalogue of the documents in his care. Elizabeth showed great interest, reading some aloud and telling him 'that she would be a scholar in her age and thought it no scorn to learn during her life'. But when she turned to the papers documenting the reign of Richard II, it was obvious that Essex's rebellion was still on her mind, for she turned to Lambarde and said, 'I am Richard II; know ye not that? He that will forget God will also forget his benefactors. This tragedy was played forty times in open streets and houses.' Lambarde was in no doubt as to what she was referring. But she dismissed him graciously, saying, 'Farewell, good and honest Lambarde.' He died two weeks later.

The Queen's progress that summer took her to Reading and then into Hampshire, where she stayed with the Marquess of Winchester at Basing before moving on to Lord Sandys's mansion, The Vyne, where she entertained Marshal Biron, the French ambassador, in whose honour she had the house adorned with plate and hangings brought from Hampton Court and the Tower. She was heard to boast that none of her predecessors had ever, during a progress and at a subject's house, 'royally entertained an ambassador'.

Biron's associate, the Duc de Sully, was much impressed by Elizabeth's acute insight into matters of state:

> I was convinced this great Queen was truly worthy of that high reputation she had acquired. She said many things which appeared to me so just and sensible that I was filled with astonishment and admiration. It is not unusual to behold princes form great designs, but to regulate the conduct of them, to foresee and guard against all obstacles in such a manner that, when they happen, nothing more will be necessary than to apply the remedies prepared long before – this is what few princes are capable of. I cannot bestow praises upon the Queen of England that would be equal to the merit which I discovered in her in this short time, both as to the qualities of the heart and the understanding.

It was during this progress that Elizabeth's courtiers, noticing that the handsome young Irish Earl of Clanricarde bore a passing resemblance to Essex, tried to bring him to the Queen's notice in order to revive her spirits, but she betrayed no interest whatsoever in him, and made it clear that anything that reminded her of Essex only brought her pain.

On returning to London, she visited the Middle Temple, where, in the great hall, which had been built using timbers from the *Golden Hind*, she presided over a banquet at a table which is still there today, and watched a performance of Shakespeare's *Twelfth Night*.

The thirteenth and last Parliament of Elizabeth's reign met in October in a surly mood, being determined to break the wretched system of monopolies that was causing such financial distress to many.* When the

---

*Monopolies were royal grants bestowing the sole right to make or sell consumer goods such as salt or starch, but these privileges were frequently and scandalously abused by their holders, and there was much ill feeling against the system.

Queen went in state to open Parliament, few offered the customary greeting, 'God save Your Majesty'. There was momentary alarm when, as she addressed the assembly, weighted down in her heavy robes and crown, she suddenly swayed, prompting several gentlemen to rush forward and catch her before she sank to the ground. She recovered, however, and the ceremony proceeded as planned.

After she had left the Parliament house, the antechamber was so full there was 'little room to pass, [and] she moved her hand to have more room, whereupon one of the gentlemen ushers said, "Back, masters, make room." And one answered stoutly behind, "If you will hang us we can make no more room," which the Queen seemed not to hear, though she lifted up her head and looked that way towards him that spoke.'

To add to the problems of dearth and famine, the population of England had increased considerably during Elizabeth's reign. The practice of enclosing common land only added to the burgeoning numbers of the destitute, who would once have been cared for by monks and nuns, but the Dissolution of the Monasteries in the 1530s had dispossessed many in the religious life, placing an added burden upon the state. By the end of Elizabeth's reign, beggars had become a serious problem.

In 1598, Parliament had passed the famous Poor Law Act, which was published in November 1601, consigning beggars to the care of their native parishes, who were bound by law to provide relief for them. Each city or corporate town was to have its poor house – later known as the workhouse – and the system was to be paid for by local taxation.

The Commons, determined to end the abuse of monopolies, were resolved to block a subsidy Bill until the Queen had agreed to the passing of an Act limiting her powers to grant them. Before they could do so, and in order to avoid a dispute over the royal prerogative, Elizabeth issued a proclamation announcing that she would put an end to the present system immediately. There was a jubilant response to this in the House, with members weeping with emotion and fervently echoing 'Amen!' when the Speaker, John Croke, offered up a prayer for Her Majesty's preservation.

Parliament decided to send a deputation to the Queen to express her subjects' deepest gratitude and joy. When it came to choosing which MPs were to go, there were cries of 'All! All! All!', prompting Elizabeth to send word that although space was limited, she would be pleased to see them all. 150 members accepted her invitation.

On 30 November, she received them enthroned in the Council Chamber at Whitehall, where she proved that the old magic could still have its effect by making what would ever afterwards be known as her 'golden speech', and would, in effect, be her farewell words to her beloved people. The MPs knelt before her and the Speaker, who headed the delegation, began to express their gratitude, but the Queen was determined to have her say.

'Mr Speaker,' she said,

> we perceive your coming is to present thanks unto us. Know that I accept them with no less joy than your loves can have desired to offer such a present. I do assure you, there is no prince that loves his subjects better. There is no jewel, be it of never so rich a price, which I set before this jewel: I mean your love. For I do more esteem it than any treasure or riches, for those we know how to prize; but loyalty, love and thanks – I account them invaluable; and though God hath raised me high, yet this I account the glory of my crown, that I have reigned with your loves. This makes me that I do not so much rejoice that God hath made me to be a queen, as to be a queen over so thankful a people and to be the means under God to conserve you in safety and to preserve you from danger.

Bidding them rise, for she had more to say to them, she thanked them for making her aware of her people's resentment of the system of monopolies.

> Mr Speaker, you give me thanks, but I am more to thank you, and I charge you, thank them of the Lower House from me that I take it exceeding grateful that the knowledge of these things have come unto me from them; for, had I not received knowledge from you, I might have fallen into the lapse of an error, only for want of true information. That my grants shall be made grievances to my people, and oppressions be privileged under colour of our patents, our princely dignity shall not suffer. Yea, when I heard it, I could give no rest unto my thoughts until I had reformed it, and those abusers of my bounty shall know I will not suffer it.
>
> Of myself, I must say this: I never was any greedy, scraping grasper, nor a strict, fast-holding prince, nor yet a waster; my heart was never set upon any worldly goods, but only for my subjects' good. What you do bestow on me, I will not hoard up, but receive it to bestow on you again; yea, mine own properties I account yours, to be expended for your good, and your eyes shall see the bestowing of it.

She assured them that she did not 'desire to live longer days, than that I may see your prosperity, and that is my only desire. Since I was Queen, yet did I never put my pen to any grant, but that upon pretext or semblance made unto me that it was both good and beneficial to the subjects in general, though a private profit to some of my ancient servants who deserved well.' If they had abused the system, she prayed

God will not lay their offence to my charge. To be a king and wear a crown is more glorious to them that see it than it is a pleasure to them that bear it. And for my own part, were it not for conscience's sake to discharge the duty that God hath laid upon me, and to maintain His glory and keep you in safety, in mine own disposition I should be willing to resign the place I hold to any other, and glad to be free of the glory with the labours; for it is not my desire to live nor reign longer than my life and reign shall be for your good. And though you have had and may have many mightier and wiser princes sitting in this seat, yet you never had nor shall have any that will love you better.

I was never so much enticed with the glorious name of a king, or royal authority of a queen, as delighted that God hath made me His instrument to maintain His truth and glory, and to defend this kingdom from peril, dishonour, tyranny and oppression. I speak it to give God the praise, as a testimony before you, and not to attribute anything to myself; for I – O Lord, what am I? – O what can I do that I should speak for any glory? God forbid!

And thus concluding, she invited every delegate forward to kiss her hand, then rose from her throne and left the chamber to the sound of trumpets.

Her speech, it was unanimously agreed, had never been bettered; one MP said it was worthy to have been written in gold. Moreover, her magnanimous and prompt assent to Parliament's wishes restored her flagging popularity, enshrined her in her people's affections more than ever before, and inspired the Commons to vote her an unprecedented quadruple subsidy without one dissenting voice.

When Elizabeth dissolved Parliament on 19 December, the Speaker reminded the Lords and Commons that England, alone in Europe, had known stable government throughout the Queen's reign, and he thanked her on their behalf for 'the happy and quiet and most sweet and comfortable peace we have long enjoyed and, blessed be God and Your Majesty, do still enjoy.'

Elizabeth replied that they should go home and tell their people 'that your sovereign is more careful of your conservation than of herself, and will daily crave of God that they who wish you best may never wish in vain'.

*

It was an unusually quiet Christmas, with so few people at court that the guards 'were not troubled to keep the doors at plays and pastimes'. Yet there was to be cause for celebration, for on 24 December Mountjoy had achieved a great victory over Tyrone at Kinsale, leaving 1200 rebels dead on the field. Tyrone himself had escaped, but the commander of the Spanish army that had arrived the previous autumn to assist him had given up his cause for lost and sued for peace. On 2 January 1602, the Spaniards surrendered to Mountjoy and sailed back to Spain. The English were now in control of Ireland.

This was, wrote the Queen, 'one of the most acceptable incidents that hath befallen us'; she would have preferred the Spaniards to have been killed, but that was a minor detail. Mountjoy's offences had been forgotten; already, Elizabeth was writing regular and affectionate letters to him, signing herself 'Your loving sovereign'. Once, after he had complained she was treating him like a scullion, she responded with a lengthy and supportive letter in her own hand, but began with the greeting, 'Mistress Kitchen Maid . . .' Now, after his victory, she wrote, 'We have forgotten to praise your humility, that, after having been a queen's kitchen maid, you have not disdained to be a traitor's scullion. God bless you with perseverance.'

In June 1602, it seemed as if the great seafaring age of Drake was about to flourish once more, when a small fleet under Sir Richard Leveson captured a great Portuguese carrack, laden with treasure, despite its being protected by eleven galleys and 10,000 troops. But an expedition sent by the Queen to plunder the Spanish coast returned empty-handed. These were to be the last major maritime ventures of the reign.

There was an epidemic of smallpox in 1602, which claimed many lives, but the Queen was nevertheless planning a long progress to Bristol. However, the weather was again wet and stormy, and she was persuaded that entertaining her would cause hardship to her people, who had already suffered seven years of famine. In the event, the weather improved and the harvest was a good one, signalling the end of the period of dearth. Trade began to revive, and the people's spirits with it.

In August, Elizabeth announced that she was in better health than for the past twelve years. In a single day, she rode ten miles on horseback, then went hunting. She arrived home shattered, but took care to go for a long walk on the following day, lest her courtiers guessed she had been exhausted by her activities. At this time, Cecil presented her with a jewel set with rubies and topazes to match 'the life of her eyes and the colour of her lips'; it was still the fashion for men to maintain the fiction that she was some eternally youthful goddess of beauty.

That month, Elizabeth left Greenwich for Chiswick, then visited Lord Keeper Egerton at Harefield Park in Middlesex, where, despite constant rain, she was lavishly entertained and lauded as 'the best housewife in all this company'. There were banquets, masques, musical interludes, a rustic feast, allegorical pageants and a lottery which was rigged so that the Queen would win the prize. Printed pamphlets describing the festivities were on sale days later and avidly bought by the public. Because of the rain and the smallpox, however, the progress was curtailed, and the Queen settled for a time at Oatlands.

In September, she celebrated her sixty-ninth birthday, and was observed by the Duke of Stettin walking in the garden at Oatlands 'as briskly as though she were eighteen years old'. He was told she had been 'never so gallant many years, nor so set upon jollity'. Lord Worcester informed Lord Shrewsbury, 'We are frolic here at court; much dancing in the Privy Chamber of country dances before the Queen's Majesty, who is exceedingly pleased therewith.' Only rarely did she herself dance in public nowadays, although she was occasionally espied in her private apartments, dancing to pipe and tabor when she thought she was not observed.

That September, Fulke Greville informed Lady Shrewsbury, 'The best news I can yet write Your Ladyship is of the Queen's health and disposition of body, which I assure you is excellent good. I have not seen her every way better disposed these many years.'

Her sense of humour was still lively. She noticed that the Countess of Derby was wearing a locket containing Cecil's portrait, and, snatching it away, laughingly tied it on his shoe, then his elbow, so that all could see it. He took it in good part, commissioned some verses about it, and had them set to music and sung to the Queen, who was much amused. She could be alarmingly familiar with her subjects. When an Englishman who had lived abroad for some years was brought before her, kneeling, she 'took him by the hair and made him rise, and pretended to give him a box on the ears'.

Yet there were signs that her memory was failing. On 8 October she moved to Greenwich, where, four days later, some courtiers arrived to pay their respects to her. Although she could remember their names, she had to be reminded of the offices she herself had bestowed upon them. She was finding it harder to concentrate on state business, and this was exacerbated by failing eyesight. Cecil warned the Clerk of the Council that he must read out letters to her.

On 17 November, Elizabeth celebrated Accession Day at Whitehall 'with the ordinary solemnity and as great an applause of multitudes as if they had never seen her before'. Her fool, Garret, rode into the tiltyard on a pony the size of a dog, and 'had good audience with Her Majesty and made her very merry'. On 6 December, she dined with Cecil at his new house on the Strand, and afterwards watched a 'pretty dialogue' between a maid, a widow and a wife on the respective advantages each enjoyed; predictably, the virgin was deemed the most fortunate. When the Queen left, she appeared 'marvellously well contented, but at her departure she strained her foot'. We hear no more of this, so it cannot have been serious. Later in the month she was entertained by both Hunsdon and Nottingham at their London houses.

Around this time, a deep depression descended on Elizabeth, who was beginning to realise that she would not win this constant battle with advancing age. It became obvious to all that time was running out for her. Harington, up for Christmas, was shocked at the change in her, and wrote to his wife:

> Our dear Queen, my royal godmother and this state's most natural mother, doth now bear show of human infirmity; too fast for that evil which we shall get by her death, and too slow for that good which she shall get by her releasement from pains and misery. I find some less mindful of what they are soon to lose, than of what they may perchance get hereafter. Now, I cannot blot from my memory's table the goodness of our Sovereign Lady to me: her affection to my mother, her bettering the state of my father's fortune, her watching over my youth, her liking to my free speech and admiration of my little learning and poesy, which I did so much cultivate on her command. To turn aside from her condition with tearless eyes would stain and foul the spring and fount of gratitude.

Because the Queen was 'in most pitiable state', and hardly eating anything, he tried to cheer her by reading out some of his humorous verses, but although she managed a weak smile, she bade him desist, saying, 'When thou dost feel creeping time at thy gate, these fooleries will please thee less. I am past my relish for such matters.'

Harington was startled when she asked him if he had ever met Tyrone. 'I replied with reverence that I had seen him with the Lord Deputy [Essex]; she looked up with much grief and choler in her countenance saying, "Oh, yes, now it mindeth me that you was one that saw this man elsewhere."' But she was very distressed by the lapse, and 'dropped a tear and smote her bosom'. Harington was concerned about the implications of her failing memory. 'But who shall say, Your Highness hath forgotten?' he asked his wife.

The Queen kept Christmas at Whitehall with her former accustomed splendour, and seemed in better spirits. 'The court hath flourished more than ordinary. Besides much dancing, bear-baiting and many plays, there hath been great golden play' – Cecil lost £800 at cards. Then came further heartening news from Ireland: Tyrone had offered to surrender if the Queen would spare his life. Mountjoy urged her to accept this condition, and so bring the Irish war to an end.

Although Elizabeth refused to name her successor, speculation on the matter had increased as she grew older. Most people wanted James of Scotland because he was a Protestant and a married man with two sons. Despite their affection for, and admiration of, Elizabeth, few members of the nobility and gentry desired another female sovereign: the feeling still persisted that it was shameful for men to be subject to a woman's rule. It was also feared that 'we shall never enjoy another queen like this'. As for the claims of the Infanta Isabella or any of the other European descendants of John of Gaunt, such as the Dukes of Braganza and Parma, nobody in England took them seriously, nor was Philip III sufficiently interested to pursue them.

Of the English claimants, most people discounted the claims of Katherine Grey's son, whose legitimacy was questionable, nor were they interested in Arbella Stewart, mainly on account of her sex.

Arbella had come to court in 1587, but Elizabeth, offended by the girl's arrogance, had promptly sent her home to her grandmother, Bess of Hardwick, with whom she had lived ever since. She was now twenty-eight, neurotic and unstable, and still unmarried. She hated Bess, who was a harsh and critical guardian, and by the end of 1602 was so desperate to escape from what she regarded as a prison, that she sent a message to Lord Hertford, Katherine Grey's widower, offering herself as a bride for his grandson. Hertford, who had recently been in trouble for attempting to have his marriage to Katherine declared valid, informed the Council at once, knowing that on no account would Elizabeth have permitted these two young people, in whom flowed the blood royal of England, to marry each other.

When a royal deputation came to question Arbella, an enraged Bess, who had known nothing of her granddaughter's scheme, could hardly refrain from beating the girl; instead, she lashed out with her tongue. She also wrote to Elizabeth, assuring her that she had been 'altogether ignorant' of Arbella's 'vain doings' and pleading to be relieved of the responsibility of the girl, adding, 'I cannot now assure myself of her as I have done.' But Elizabeth insisted that Arbella must remain with her grandmother, who must make a better effort to control her. Two months later, Arbella was caught trying to run away, but Elizabeth was by then beyond such concerns.

Yet although her people of all classes were united in their anxiety as to what would happen after Elizabeth's death, the succession remained a taboo subject. 'Succession!' exclaimed one gentleman. 'What is he that dare meddle with it?'

On 17 January 1603, Elizabeth, who was looking 'very well', dined with Lord Thomas Howard, her 'good Thomas', younger son of the executed Norfolk, at the Charterhouse, and created him Lord Howard de Walden. Four days later, on the advice of Dr John Dee, who had cast Elizabeth's horoscope and warned her not to remain at Whitehall, the court moved from Whitehall to Richmond, 'her warm winter box', stopping on the way at Putney so that the Queen could have dinner with a clothier, John Lacy, whom she had known for years. The weather was wet and colder than it had been for years, with a sharp north-easterly wind, but the Queen insisted on wearing 'summer-like garments' and refused to put on her furs. Thomas, Lord Burghley, warned his brother Cecil that Her Majesty should accept 'that she is old and have more care of herself, and that there is no contentment to a young mind in an old body'.

During the journey to Richmond, Nottingham, riding beside the royal litter, presumed upon Elizabeth's familiar manner towards him and asked her bluntly if she would name her successor. She answered, 'My seat hath been the seat of kings, and I will have no rascal to succeed me; and who should succeed me but a king?' Nottingham, and others, took this to mean that she wanted James VI to succeed her, but she would neither confirm nor deny it.

On 6 February, the Queen, now suffering badly from rheumatism, made her last public appearance when she received Giovanni Scaramelli, an envoy from Venice, the first ever to be sent to England during her reign. Seated on a dais, surrounded by her courtiers, she was wearing an outdated, full-skirted, low-necked gown of silver and white taffeta edged with gold, and was laden with pearls and jewels, with her hair 'of a light colour never made by Nature' and an imperial crown on her head. Scaramelli noticed in her face traces of her 'past, but never quite lost, beauty'. When he bent to kiss the hem of her dress, she raised him and extended her hand to be kissed.

'Welcome to England, Mr Secretary,' she said in Italian. 'It is high time that the Republic sent to visit a Queen who has always honoured it on every possible occasion.' She rebuked the Doge and his predecessors for not having acknowledged her existence for forty-five years, and said she was aware that it was not her sex that 'has brought me this demerit, for my sex cannot diminish my prestige, nor offend those who treat me as other princes are treated'. Aware that she had pulled off a brilliant diplomatic coup by overcoming the prejudices of the Doge, who had hitherto been fearful of offending the Papacy, the ambassador accepted her reproaches in good part, and expressed his delight at finding her 'in excellent health', pausing to give her a chance to agree with him, but she ignored this and angled instead for another compliment, saying, 'I do not know if I have spoken Italian well; still, I think so, for I learnt it when a child, and believe I have not forgotten it.'

Ten days later, after much bullying on Cecil's part, the Queen wrote to Mountjoy, agreeing that he might accept Tyrone's submission and offer him a pardon, on the strictest terms. She might be an old, 'forlorn' woman, but she was going to end her reign with this final triumph.

In the middle of February, Elizabeth's cousin and closest woman friend, the Countess of Nottingham, who had been the late Lord Hunsdon's daughter, died at Richmond. The Queen was present at the deathbed, and her grief was such that she ordered a state funeral and sank into a deep depression from which she never recovered. At the same time, her coronation ring, which had become painfully embedded in the swollen flesh of her finger, had to be sawn off – an act that symbolised to her the breaking of a sacred bond, the marriage of a queen to her people. She knew her own death could not be far off, and wrote sadly to Henry IV of France, 'All the fabric of my reign, little by little, is beginning to fail.'

On 26 February, when the French ambassador, de Beaumont, requested an audience, the Queen asked him to wait a few days on account of the death of Lady Nottingham, 'for which she has wept extremely and shown an uncommon concern'. Nor did she appear again in public. 'She has suddenly withdrawn into herself, she who was wont to live so gaily, especially in these last years of her life,' observed Scaramelli.

There arrived at court at this time the Queen's cousin, Robert Carey, youngest son of the late Lord Hunsdon and brother to Lady Nottingham. Being a relative, he was admitted one Saturday night to the private apartments, where he found Elizabeth

> in one of her withdrawing chambers, sitting low upon her cushions. She called me to her. I kissed her hand and told her it was my chiefest happiness to see her in safety and in health, which I wished might long continue. She took me by the hand and wrung it hard, and said, 'No, Robin, I am not well,' and then discoursed with me of her indisposition, and that her heart had been sad and heavy for ten or twelve days; and in her discourse she fetched not so few as forty or fifty great sighs. I was grieved at the first to see her in such plight, for in all my lifetime before I never knew her fetch a sigh but when the Queen of Scots was beheaded.

The next day would be Sunday, and

> she gave command that the Great Closet should be prepared for her to go to chapel the next morning. The next day, all things being in readiness, we long expected her coming. After eleven o'clock, one of the grooms came out and bade make ready for the Private Closet; she would not go to the Great. There we stayed long for her coming, but at last she had cushions laid for her in the Privy Chamber, hard by the Closet door, and there she heard service. From that day forwards, she grew worse and worse.

The main trouble seemed to be slight swellings – probably ulcers – in the throat, accompanied by a cold. By the beginning of March, a fever had developed, and she could not sleep or swallow food easily. On 9 March, according to de Beaumont, 'she felt a great heat in her stomach and a continual thirst, which obliged her every moment to take something to abate it, and to prevent the hard and dry phlegm from choking her. She has been obstinate in refusing everything prescribed by her physicians during her illness.' These problems, which may have been symptomatic of influenza or tonsillitis, were exacerbated by her depression, although when her courtiers asked what the matter was, she told them 'she knew nothing in the world worthy to trouble her'.

Cecil, realising that the Queen might die, knew that it would fall to him to ensure James VI's peaceful and unchallenged succession to the throne. At the end of February, he ordered Robert Carey to hold himself in readiness to take the news of his accession to the Scottish monarch the moment the Queen ceased to breathe.

On 11 March, the Queen rallied for a day, then had a relapse, descending into 'a heavy dullness, with a frowardness familiar to old age'. She was, according to de Beaumont, 'so full of chagrin and so weary of life that, notwithstanding all the importunities of her councillors and physicians to consent to the use of proper remedies for her relief, she would not take one'. With a flash of her old spirit, she told Cecil and Whitgift, who had begged her on their knees to do as her physicians recommended, 'that she knew her own strength and constitution better than they, and that she was not in such danger as they imagine'. Nor would she eat anything, but spent her days lying on the floor on cushions, lost in 'unremovable melancholy' and unwilling to speak to anyone. It was obvious that she had lost the will to live.

'The Queen grew worse and worse, because she would be so, none about her being able to persuade her to go to bed,' recorded Robert Carey.

Cecil insisted, 'Your Majesty, to content the people, you must go to bed.' But she retorted, 'Little man, the word "must" is not to be used to princes. If your father had lived, you durst not had said so, but ye know that I must die, and that makes thee so presumptuous.'

Her throat felt as if it were closing up. Nottingham came to see her: having retired from court to mourn his wife, he had returned to cheer the Queen. He told her to have courage, but she said, 'My Lord, I am tied with a chain of iron around my neck. I am tied, I am tied, and the case is altered with me.' She complained of 'a heat in her breasts and a dryness in her mouth, which kept her from sleep frequently, to her disgust'. This suggests that she had now developed either bronchitis or pneumonia.

Nottingham tried also to get her to retire to bed, but she refused, telling him, 'If you were in the habit of seeing such things in your bed as I do when in mine, you would not persuade me to go there.' She added that 'she had a premonition that, if she once lay down, she would never rise'.

One day, she had herself lifted into a low chair. When she found herself unable to rise from it, she commanded her attendants to help her to her feet. Once in that position, by a supreme effort of will and a determination to defy mortality, she remained there unmoving for fifteen hours, watched by her appalled yet helpless courtiers. At length, fainting with exhaustion, she was helped back on to her cushions, where she remained for a further four days.

By 18 March, her condition had deteriorated alarmingly; de Beaumont reported that she 'appeared already in a manner insensible, not speaking sometimes for two or three hours, and within the last two days for above four and twenty, holding her finger continually in her mouth, with her eyes open and fixed to the ground, where she sat upon cushions without rising or resting herself, and was greatly emaciated by her long watching and fasting'. She had now been lying there, in her day clothes, for nearly three weeks.

On 19 March, she was so ill that Carey wrote informing James VI that she would not last more than three days; already, he had posted horses along the Great North Road, ready for his breakneck ride to Scotland. On the following day, Cecil sent James a draft copy of the proclamation that would be read out on his accession. All James hoped for now was that Elizabeth would not linger, 'insensible and stupid, unfit to rule and govern a kingdom'.

In order to avoid any public demonstrations or panic, Cecil vetoed the publication of any bulletins on the Queen's health, but the French ambassador deliberately spread word of her condition. 'Her Majesty's life is absolutely despaired of,' reported Scaramelli. 'For the last ten days she has become quite silly [i.e. pitiable]. London is all in arms for fear of

the Catholics. Every house and everybody is in movement and alarm.'
Camden recorded that, 'as the report now grew daily stronger and
stronger that her sickness increased upon her', it was astonishing to
behold with what speed the Puritans, Papists, ambitious persons and
flatterers posted night and day, by sea and land, to Scotland, to adore the
rising sun and gain his favour'.

At last, on 21 March, 'what by fair means, what by force',
Nottingham persuaded Elizabeth to go to bed. After lying there for
some hours, an abscess or ulcer in her throat burst and she declared she
felt better, and asked for some of her restorative broth to be made.
Scaramelli reported that rose water and currants were also placed on a
table by her bedside, 'but soon after she began to lose her speech, and
from that time ate nothing, but lay on one side, without speaking or
looking upon any person, though she directed some meditations to be
read to her'. Archbishop Whitgift and her own chaplains were from
then on in constant attendance on her, whilst her musicians played softly
in the background to soothe her.

Her councillors knew she could not last much longer. On the 23rd,
her chaplain Dr Parry held a special service of intercession in the royal
chapel, offering such fervent prayers for Her Majesty 'that he left few dry
eyes'. The diarist John Manningham learned in the Privy Chamber that
the Queen

> hath been in a manner speechless for two or three days, very
> pensive and silent, yet she always had her proper senses and
> memory, and yesterday signified [to Dr Parry], by the lifting of her
> hand and eyes to Heaven, that she believed that faith which she had
> caused to be professed, and looked faithfully to be saved by Christ's
> merits and mercy only, and by no other means. She took great
> delight in hearing prayers, would often at the name of Jesus lift up
> her hands and eyes to Heaven. She would not hear the Archbishop
> speak of hope in her longer life, but when he prayed or spoke of
> Heaven and those joys, she would hug his hand.
>
> It seems she might have lived if she would have used means, but
> she would not be persuaded, and princes must not be forced. Her
> physicians said she had the body of a firm and perfect constitution,
> likely to have lived many years.

That day, Nottingham, Egerton and Cecil asked Elizabeth to name her
successor, but she was beyond speech. Instead – as was afterwards alleged
– she used her hands and fingers to make the sign of a crown above her
head, which they took to mean that she wanted King James to succeed
her.

Scaramelli, returning to Richmond 'found all the palace, outside and in, full of an extraordinary crowd, almost in uproar and on the tiptoe of expectation'. It was now known that the end could not be far off.

At six o'clock, feeling her strength ebbing away, the Queen signed for Whitgift to come and to pray at her bedside. Robert Carey was one of those kneeling in the bedchamber on this solemn occasion, and was moved to tears by what Whitgift's arrival portended.

> Her Majesty lay upon her back, with one hand in the bed and the other without. The Archbishop kneeled down beside her and examined her first of her faith; and she so punctually answered all his questions, by lifting up her eyes and holding up her hand, as it was a comfort to all the beholders. Then the good man told her plainly what she was and what she was come to: though she had been long a great Queen here upon Earth, yet shortly she was to yield an account of her stewardship to the King of Kings. After this, he began to pray, and all that were by did answer him.

Whitgift remained at her bedside, holding her hand and offering her spiritual comfort until his knees ached, but as he made to rise, blessing the Queen, she gestured to him to kneel again and continue praying. He did so for another 'long half hour', but still Elizabeth would not let him go. So he prayed for half an hour more, 'with earnest cries to God for her soul's health, which he uttered with that fervency of spirit, as the Queen, to all our sight, much rejoiced thereat, and gave testimony to us all of her Christian and comfortable end. By this time it grew late, and everyone departed, all but her women who attended her.'

Around ten o'clock that evening, with heavy rain pattering against the windows, Elizabeth turned her face to the wall and fell into a deep sleep from which she would never wake. With Dr Parry, who 'sent his prayers before her soul', and her old friends Lady Warwick and Lady Scrope by her side, she passed to eternal rest, 'mildly like a lamb, easily, like a ripe apple from a tree', shortly before three o'clock in the morning of Thursday, 24 March, 'as the most resplendent sun setteth at last in a western cloud'.

Epilogue

As soon as she realised that her mistress had died, Lady Scrope, as prearranged, removed a sapphire ring from the late Queen's finger and dropped it through a window to her brother, Robert Carey, who was waiting below, ready saddled to ride to Scotland. King James knew that, when he received that ring, he would be King of England in truth.

Later that morning, the accession of King James I was proclaimed at Whitehall and in Cheapside. There was 'no great shouting', and Manningham felt that 'the sorrow for Her Majesty's departure was so deep in many hearts, they could not so suddenly show any great joy'. Nevertheless, that evening saw some muted celebrations, as bonfires were lit and bells rung in honour of a new king, a new dynasty, and a new era. Slowly, it was beginning to dawn on people that the great Elizabethan age was over.

Three days later, Carey arrived in Edinburgh, just as the King had retired for the night. Muddied and dusty as he was after his long ride, he fell to his knees and saluted James as King of England, Scotland, Ireland and France. Then he gave him Queen Elizabeth's ring.

At Richmond, now virtually deserted after the court had returned to London, 'The Queen's body was left in a manner alone a day or two after her death, and mean persons had access to it.' No post mortem was carried out, and it was left to three of her ladies to prepare the corpse for burial. Then it was embalmed, wrapped in cere-cloth and 'enshrined in lead'.

After five days, the coffin was taken at night, on a barge lit by torches, to Whitehall, where it lay in state in a withdrawing chamber, attended round the clock by many lords and ladies. It was then moved to Westminster Hall, where it lay 'all hung with mourning; and so, in accordance with ancient custom, it will remain, until the King gives orders for her funeral'.

On 28 April, more than a month after her death, Elizabeth's body was taken in procession to Westminster Abbey. It was an impressive occasion: the hearse was drawn by four horses hung with black velvet, and surmounted by a life-sized wax effigy of the late Queen, dressed in her state robes and crown, an orb and sceptre in its hands; over it was a canopy of estate supported by six earls. It was followed by her riderless palfrey led by Elizabeth's Master of Horse, and the Marchioness of Northampton, who as the senior noblewoman acted as chief mourner and led the peeresses of the realm in their nun-like mourning hoods and cloaks, and a thousand other black-clad people: lords, councillors, gentlemen, courtiers, heralds, and servants, as well as 276 poor persons. The Lord Mayor and his brethren were there, as were the Children of the Chapel Royal, and in the rear marched Raleigh with the Gentlemen Pensioners, their halberds pointed downwards. The solemnity was overlaid with gorgeous pageantry as colourful banners and standards fluttered in the breeze and trumpets sounded.

Thousands lined the funeral route: Stow says that 'Westminster was surcharged with multitudes of all sorts of people in their streets, houses, windows, leads and gutters, that came to see the obsequy, and when they beheld her statue lying upon the coffin, there was such a general sighing, groaning and weeping as the like hath not been seen or known in the memory of man, neither doth any history mention any people, time or state to make like lamentation for the death of their sovereign.'

With Whitgift officiating, Elizabeth I was buried in the north aisle of the Henry VII Chapel in the Abbey; after her coffin had been placed above that of her sister Mary in the vault, the chief officers of her household, as was customary, broke their white staves of office and cast them down on the coffin, to symbolise the termination of their allegiance. The vault was then sealed.

James I ordered a magnificent tomb to be erected to his predecessor's memory. It was designed by Maximilian Colt, at a cost of £765, and was completed in 1606. Colt's white marble effigy of the Queen portrays an old woman, and it has been conjectured that he may have worked from a death mask. The effigy was painted by Nicholas Hilliard and gilded by John de Critz, although all traces of colour and gilding have long since disappeared. A Latin inscription on the tomb would have pleased Elizabeth greatly, for it describes her as 'The mother of this her country, the nurse of religion and learning; for perfect skill of very many languages, for glorious endowments, as well of mind as of body, a prince incomparable.'

For forty-five years, 'though beset by divers nations', Elizabeth had given her country peace and stable government – her greatest gift to her people. During that time, England had risen from an impoverished nation to become one of the greatest powers in Europe. Bolstered by the fame of her seamen, her navy was respected and feared on the high seas, and not for nothing had Elizabeth been lauded as 'the Queen of the Sea, the North Star'.

The Queen had also brought unity to her people by effecting a religious compromise that has lasted until this day, and making herself an enduring focus for their loyalty. She had enjoyed a unique relationship with her subjects, which was never seen before and has never been seen since. Few queens have ever been so loved. Under her rule, her people grew ever more confident in the belief that they were a chosen nation, protected by Divine Providence, and this confidence gave rise, in the years after the Armada, to the flowering of the English Renaissance.

Of course, there had been failures. A careful housekeeper, she had striven throughout her reign to live within her means, but towards the end, even she had been defeated by economic forces, and she died £400,000 in debt. Ireland was not fully subdued, Calais remained in French hands, and the English had so far been unable successfully to found a permanent colony in the New World. Yet, under Elizabeth, England had defeated the might of Spain, won the respect of the rest of Europe, and established a lasting peace with Scotland through the union of the crowns. Elizabeth had also been extremely fortunate in her advisers, which was due in part to her having an uncanny ability to choose those men of the greatest merit as her chief servants.

By constantly shelving or avoiding problems, such as the royal finances, the resurgence of Puritanism, or Parliament's attempts to limit the royal prerogative, Elizabeth passed on to her successor the potential for future conflict, but she had managed as best she could, even when she had been beset on all sides by seemingly insurmountable threats and concerns.

Many of her contemporaries bore witness to her abilities. Lord Burghley had said of her, 'She was the wisest woman that ever was, for she understood the interests and dispositions of all the princes in her time, and was so perfect in the knowledge of her own realm, that no councillor she had could tell her anything she did not know before.'

'Our blessed Queen was more than a man', wrote Cecil, 'and, in troth, something less than a woman.' Then he added wistfully, 'I wish I waited now in her Presence Chamber, with ease at my foot and rest in my bed.' Life under James was less easy than he had imagined it would be.

Yet it was not until some years later that most people came to realise what they had lost. 'When we had had experience of a Scottish government, the Queen did seem to revive,' recalled Godfrey Goodman, Bishop of Gloucester. 'Then was her memory much magnified: such ringing of bells, such public joy and sermons in commemoration of her, the picture of her tomb painted in many churches, and in effect more solemnity and joy in memory of her coronation than was for the coming of King James.' Within a generation of her death, the unity she had fostered in her realm would have disappeared, a casualty of an unavoidable clash between Crown and Parliament. Then, people would look back on the reign of Good Queen Bess with nostalgia, and the legends would become embellished and pass into popular folk-lore: Drake playing bowls before the Armada, Raleigh spreading his cloak for Elizabeth to walk on, Elizabeth herself playing at the marriage game and giving rise to centuries of speculation.

The most fitting epitaph to this extraordinary woman is to be found in the pages of Camden's biography: 'No oblivion shall ever bury the glory of her name; for her happy and renowned memory still liveth and shall for ever live in the minds of men.'

A Note on Sources

The source from which each quotation is taken will in many cases be clear from the text or the Bibliography. Where a quote is unattributed, it will in every case have been drawn from one of the many collections of contemporary documents, the chief of which are:

Acts of the Privy Council
Archaeologia
Calendar of the MSS at Hatfield House
Calendar of the MSS at Longleat
Calendars of State Papers, Foreign and Domestic
The Cecil Papers
Collection of State Papers relating to the Reign of Elizabeth, edited by
    William Murdin
The Devereux Papers
The Dudley Papers
The Egerton Papers
Simonds D'Ewes: *Journals of all the Parliaments during the Reign of Queen
    Elizabeth*
N. Fourdinier: *Amy Robsart*
Lives and Letters of the Devereux Earls of Essex
Memoirs of the Reign of Elizabeth, edited by Thomas Birch
Sir Robert Naunton: *Fragmenta Regalia*
Original letters: several collections
Proceedings and Ordinances of the Privy Council
Progresses and Public Processions of Elizabeth I, edited by J. Nichols
Queen Elizabeth and Some Foreigners, edited by Victor von Klarwill
Queen Elizabeth and her Times, edited by Thomas Wright
The Rolls of Parliament
T. Rymer: *Foedera*

The Sidney Papers
State Papers: various collections

Full details of these and the many other works consulted are listed in the
Bibliography

Bibliography

Primary Sources

Acts of the Privy Council of England (32 vols., ed. John Roche Dasent, HMSO, 1890–1918)

Allen, Cardinal William: *Letters and Memorials* (ed. T.F. Knox, 1882)

L'Ambassade de France en Angleterre sous Henri IV, 1598–1605 (4 vols., ed. Laffleur de Kermaingant, 1886–95)

Anecdotes and Traditions Illustrative of Early English History and Literature (ed. W.J. Thomas, Camden Society, 1839)

The Antiquarian Repertory: A Miscellany intended to Preserve and Illustrate several Valuable Remains of Old Times (4 vols., ed. Stephen Perlin and Francis Blyth, 1775–84; ed. F. Grose and T. Astle, 1808)

Archaeologia, or Miscellaneous Tracts relating to Antiquity (102 vols., Society of Antiquaries of London, 1773–1969)

'Archives of the English Tournament' (ed. Sidney Anglo, *Journal of the Society of Archivists*, 2, 1960)

Ascham, Roger: *English Works* (ed. W.A. Wright, 1904)

Ascham, Roger: *Opera* (1703)

Aubrey, John: *Brief Lives* (ed. Andrew Clark, 1898; ed. Anthony Powell, 1949, and Oliver Lawson Dick, 1962)

Bacon, Sir Francis: *Collected Works* (ed. J. Spedding, R.L. Ellis and D.D. Heath, 1857–74)

The Bardon Papers: Documents Relating to the Imprisonment and Trial of Mary, Queen of Scots (ed. Conyers Read, Camden Society, 3rd Series, XVII, 1909)

Barthlet, J.: *The Pedigree of Heretics (1566)*

Brantôme, Sieur de: *Oeuvres Complètes* (1823)

Buchanan, George: *Detection of the Doings of Mary, Queen of Scots* (1572)

The Cabala sive scrinia Sacra: Mysteries of State and Government in Letters of Illustrious Persons (1654, 1691)

Calendar of Carew MSS, 1575–1588 (ed. J.S. Brewer and W. Bullen, 1868)

Calendar of Letters, Despatches and State Papers relating to Negotiations between England and Spain, preserved in the Archives at Simancas and Elsewhere (17 vols., ed. G.A. Bergenroth, P. de Goyangos, Garrett Mattingly, R. Tyler etc., HMSO, 1862–1965)

Calendar of the Manuscripts of the Marquess of Bath at Longleat (Historical Manuscripts commission, 1904–1980)

Calendar of the MSS of the Marquess of Salisbury. . . preserved at Hatfield House (18 vols., Historical Manuscripts Commission, 1883-1940)

Calendar of Patent Rolls: Elizabeth I (Public Record Office)

Calendar of the Pepys MSS in Magdalene College, Cambridge (Historical Manuscripts Commission)

Calendar of State Papers: Domestic Series: Edward VI, Mary, and Elizabeth, 1547–1580, 1581–90, 1591–1603 (12 vols., ed. Robert Lemon and M.A.E. Green, 1856–72)

Calendar of State Papers: Foreign Series, Elizabeth 1 (23 vols., ed. Joseph Stevenson and W.B. Turnbull etc., 1863–1950)

Calendar of State Papers: Ireland (11 vols., ed. H.C. Hamilton and R.P. Mahaffy, 1860–1912)

Calendar of State Papers and Manuscripts existing in the Archives and Collections of Milan, Vol. 1 1385–1618 (ed. A.B. Hinds, 1912)

Calendar of State Papers and Manuscripts relating to English Affairs preserved in the Archives of Venice and in the other Libraries of Northern Italy 7 vols., ed. Rawdon Brown etc., HMSO, 1864–1947)

Calendar of State Papers relating to Border Affairs (ed. Joseph Bain, 1894–6)

Calendar of State Papers relating to English Affairs, preserved principally at Rome in the Vatican Archives and Library, 1558–78 (ed. J.M. Rigg, 1916–26)

Calendar of State Papers relating to Scotland, 1509–1589 (ed. M.J. Thorpe, 1858)

Calendar of State Papers: Scotland, 1547–1603 (12 vols., ed. Joseph Bain, W.K. Boyd and M.S. Guiseppi, 1898–1952)

Calendar of State Papers: Spanish, Elizabethan, 1558–1603 (4 vols., ed. M.A.S. Hume, 1892–9)

Camden, William: *Annales Rerum Anglicarum et Hibernicarum Regnante Elizabetha* (1615; 3 vols., tr. Thomas Hearne, 1717; tr. H. Norton, 1630, 1688; also published as *Annals of the Reign of Queen Elizabeth* in 'The Complete History of England' ed. White Kennett, 1706)

Camden, William: *Britannia* (ed. R. Gough, 1789)

Camden, William: *The History of the Most Renowned and Virtuous Princess*

Elizabeth, late Queen of England (1630); later published as *The History of the Most Renowned and Victorious Princess Elizabeth* (1675)

Carey, Sir Robert: *Memoirs of the Life of Robert Carey, written by Himself* (ed. John Boyle, 1759; ed. Sir Walter Scott, 1808; ed. G.H. Powell, 1905)

Carleton, Dudley: *Memorials of Affairs of State in the Reigns of Queen Elizabeth and King James 1* (3 vols,1725)

Castelnau, Michel de: *Memoires de Michel de Castelnau, Seigneur de la Mauvissière* (3 vols, ed. L. Laboureur, 1731)

Castiglione, Balthasar. *The Courtier* (tr. G. Bull, 1967)

The Cecil Papers: A Collection of State Papers Relating to Affairs from the Year 1552 to 1570, left by William Cecil, Lord Burghley, at Hatfield House (15 vols., ed. Samuel Haynes and William Murdin, 1740–59)

Cecil, Sir Robert: *Letters from Sir Robert Cecil to Sir George Carew* (ed John Maclean, Camden Society, LXXXVIII, 1864)

Chamberlain, John: *Letters* (ed. Sarah Williams, Camden Society, LXXIX 1861; 2 vols., ed. N.E. McClure, American Philosophical Society, Vol. XII, 1939)

Chettle, Henry: *The Order and Proceeding at the Funeral of Elizabeth* (1603)

Churchyard, Thomas: *The Service of Sir John Norris in Brittany in 1591* (1602)

Clapham, John: *Elizabeth of England: Observations concerning the Life and Reign of Queen Elizabeth* (ed. E.P. Read and Conyers Read, 1951; Pennsylvania University Press, 1951)

Clifford, Lady Anne: *Diary* (ed. V. Sackville West, 1923)

Colección de Documentos ineditos para la Historia de España (112 vols., 1842–95, and the *Nueva Colección*, 6 vols., 1892 catalogued by J. Paz, 1930–1)

A Collection of Ordinances and Regulations for the Government of the Royal Household, made in Divers Reigns (Society of Antiquaries of London, 1790)

A Collection of State Papers relating to Affairs in the Reign of Queen Elizabeth, 1571–96 (ed. William Murdin, 1759)

A Complete Collection of State Trials (ed. D. Thom, William Cobbett, and T.B. Rowel I, 1809–98; reissued 1972)

Correspondance de Philippe 11 (5 vols., ed. L.P. Gachard, 1848–79)

The Correspondence of King James VI with Sir Robert Cecil and Others in England during the Reign of Queen Elizabeth (ed. J. Bruce, Camden Society, LXXVIII, 1861)

Correspondentie van Robert Dudley, graaf van Leycester (3 vols, ed. H. Brugmans, 1931)

Cotton MSS (British Library)

The Devereux Papers (Collection of the Marquess of Bath, Longleat House) (ed. P. Broughton, Camden Miscellany XIII, 1924)

Diary of Philip Julius, Duke of Stettin, Pomerania, through England in 1602 (ed. Gottfried von Bulow and Walter Powell, Transactions of the Royal Historical Society, 2nd Series, VI, 1892)

Digges, Dudley: *The Compleat Ambassador* (1655; contains many documents relating to the Duke of Anjou's courtship of Elizabeth I)

Documents from Simancas relating to the Reign of Queen Elizabeth (ed. Tomas Gonzalez, tr. and ed. Spencer Hall, 1865)

Dudley Carleton to John Chamberlain: Jacobean Letters, 1603–1624 (ed. M. Lee, 1972)

The Dudley Papers (Collection of the Marquess of Bath, Longleat House)

The Edmondes Papers (ed. G.G. Butler, Roxburghe Club, 1973)

The Egerton Papers (ed. J.Payne Collier, Camden Society, XXII, 1840)

Elizabeth and Mary Stuart (ed. F.A. Mumby, 1914)

Elizabeth I: *A Book of Devotions composed by H.M. Elizabeth R.* (ed. J.P. Hodges and Adam Fox, 1977)

England as seen by Foreigners in the Days of Elizabeth and James I (ed. W.B. Rye, 1865)

D' Ewes, Sir Simonds: *The Journals of all the Parliaments during the Reign of Queen Elizabeth* (revised and published by Paul Bowes, 1682, 1693)

The Foljambe Papers (Historical Manuscripts Commission, 15th report, Appendix, Part V, 1987)

Fourdinier, N.: *Amy Robsart, the Wife of Lord Robert Dudley, the Favourite of Queen Elizabeth I. Her Life, Ancestry and the True Cause of her Tragic Death* (MS. MC5/29, Norfolk Record Office)

Foxe, John: *Acts and Monuments of the Church* (1563; 8 vols., ed. G. Townshend and S.R. Cattley, 1837–41)

Fuller, Thomas: *The Church History of Britain* (1665)

Fuller, Thomas: *The Worthies of England* (1662; ed. P. Nuttall, 1890)

A Full View of the Public Transactions in the Reign of Queen Elizabeth (ed. P. Forbes, 1740–41)

Gascoigne, George: *The Princely Pleasures at the Court at Kenilworth* (1575)

The Girlhood of Queen Elizabeth (ed. F.A. Mumby, 1909)

Gleanings after Time (includes 'An Elizabethan Schoolboy and his Book' by A.M. Bell; ed. G.L. Apperson, 1907)

Golding, A.: *A Confutation of the Pope's Bull against Elizabeth* (1572)

Goodman, Dr. Godfrey, Bishop of Gloucester: *The Court of James the First* (ed. J.S. Brewer, 1839)

Grafton, Richard: *Abridgement of the Chronicles of England* (1563)

Greville, Fulke: *The Life of the Renowned Sir Philip Sidney* (1652; ed. N. Smith, 1907)

Greyfriars Chronicle (ed. J. Nichols, Camden Society, Old Series, XLXIV, 1852)

Grindal Edmund: *Remains* (ed. W. Nicholson, Parker Society, 1847)

Guide to the Manuscripts preserved in the Public Record Office (2 vols., ed. M. G. Guiseppi; 2 vols. 1923–4)

The Hamilton Papers (ed. J. Bain, 1890–92)

The Hardwick Papers: Miscellaneous State Papers, 1501–1726 (2 vols., ed. Philip Yorke, 2nd Earl of Hardwicke, 1778)

Harington, Sir John: *Letters and Epigrams* (ed. N.E. McClure, 1930)

Harington, Sir John: *A New Discourse of a Stale Subject called the Metamorphosis of Ajax* (1596; ed. Elizabeth Story, 1962)

Harington, Sir John: *Nugae Antiquae, Being a Miscellaneous Collection of Original Papers in Prose and Verse, Written in the Reigns of Henry VIII, Queen Mary, Elizabeth, King James, etc.* (3 vols., ed. Rev. Henry Harington, 1769–79; 2 vols., ed. Thomas Park, 1804)

Harington, Sir John: *A Tract on the Succession to the Crown* (1602; ed. C.R. Markham, Roxburghe Club, 1880)

Harleian MSS (British Library)

Harleian Miscellany (1746; 10 vols, ed. T. Park 1808–13)

Harrison, William: *An Historical Description of England* (4 vols., 1908)

Hayward, Sir John: *Annals of the First Four Years of the Reign of Elizabeth* (ed. John Bruce, Camden Society, VII, 1840)

Hayward, Sir John: *The First Part of the Life and Reign of King Henry IV* (1599)

Hearne, Thomas: *Remarks and Collections* (Oxford Historical Society, 1898)

Hearne, Thomas: *Syllogue Epistolarum* (1716)

Hentzner, Paul: *A Journey into England in the Year 1598* (tr. Horace Walpole, 1757; 1881–2)

Hentzner, Paul: *Travels in England* (1889)

Heywood, Thomas: *England's Elizabeth* (Harleian Miscellany, X, 1813)

Hilliard, Nicholas: *The Art of Limning* (Walpole Society, 1912)

Historical Collections of the Last Four Parliaments of Queen Elizabeth (ed. Heywood Townshend, 1680)

History of Queen Elizabeth, Amy Robsart and the Earl of Leicester (ed. F.J. Burgoyne, 1904)

Hoby, Sir Thomas: *The Book of the Courtier* (1561)

Holinshed, Raphael: *Chronicles of England, Scotland and Ireland* (1577; 6 vols., ed. Henry Ellis, 1807–8)

Illustrations of British History in the Reigns of Henry VIII, Edward VI, Mary, Elizabeth and James 1 (3 vols., ed. E. Lodge, 1838)

Intimate Letters of England's Queens (ed. Margaret Sanders, 1957)

Jonson, Ben: *Conversations with William Drummond* (Shakespeare Society
     1842)
Journals of the House of Commons (ed. Vardon and May, 1803)
Journals of the House of Lords (1846)

The Kenilworth Festivities (ed. F.J. Furnivall, New Shakespeare Society,
     1890)

Laneham, R.: *A Letter, wherein part of the Entertainment unto the Queen's
     Majesty at Kenilworth Castle in Warwickshire in this Summer's Progress,
     1575, is signified* (1575)
Lansdowne MSS (British Library)
Leti, Gregorio: *Historia o vero vita di Elizabetta, regina d'Inghilterra* (sur-
     vives only in an abridged French translation published as *La Vie
     d'Elisabeth, Reine d'Angleterre, traduite d'Italien* (1692; 1696)
The Letter Books of Sir Amias Paulet (ed. John Morris, 1874)
'A Letter from Robert, Earl of Leicester, to a Lady' (ed. Conyers Read
     Huntington Library Quarterly, April, 1936)
The Letters of Queen Elizabeth (ed. G.B. Harrison, 1935 and 1968)
The Letters of Queen Elizabeth and James VI of Scotland (ed. John Bruce,
     Camden Society, XLVI, 1849)
Letters of Royal and Illustrious Ladies (ed. M.A.E. Wood, 1846)
Lettres de Catherine de Medicis (10 vols, ed. H. Ferrière-Percy, 1880–1909)
Lettres de Marie Stuart (ed. A. Teulet, 1859)
Lettres, Instructions et mémoires de Marie Stuart, Reine d'Ecosse (7 vols., ed.
     Prince A. Labanoff, 1844)
*The Leycester Correspondence: Correspondence of Robert Dudley, Earl of
     Leicester, during his Government of the Low Countries, 1585–6* (ed. John
     Bruce, Camden Society, XXVII, 1844)
Leycester's Commonwealth (ed. F.J. Burgoyne, 1904)
De Lisle and Dudley MSS at Penshurst (Historical Manuscripts
     Commission, Report, 1934–46) (Now in the Kent County Archive
     Office at Maidstone)
Lives and Letters of the Devereux, Earls of Essex (2 vols., ed. Walter
     Bourchier Devereux, 1853)
The Loseley MSS (ed. A.J. Kempe, 1825)
'Lost from Her Majesty's Back' (ed. Janet Arnold, The Costume
     Society,1980)

Machyn, Henry: *The Diary of Henry Machyn, Citizen and Merchant Tailor
     of London, from A.D. 1550 to A.D. 1563* (ed. J.G. Nichols, Camden
     Society, XLII, 1848)
Maisse, André Hurault, Sieur de: *A Journal of all that was Accomplished by M.*

de Maisse, *Ambassador in England from King Henry IV to Queen Elizabeth, 1597* (tr. and ed. G.B. Harrison and R.A. Jones, London, 1931)

Manningham, John: *Diary* (ed. John Bruce and W. Tite, Camden Society, 1858)

Melville, Sir James, of Halhill: *Memoirs of his own Life, 1549–93* (ed. Thomas Thomson, Bannatyne Club, 1829, and A. Francis Steuart, 1929)

Memorials of the Rebellion of 1569 (ed. Cuthbert Sharpe, 1840)

Memoirs of the Life and Times of Sir Christopher Hatton (ed. N.H. Nicholas, 1847)

Memoirs of the Reign of Queen Elizabeth (2 vols., ed. Thomas Birch, 1754) (drawn chiefly from the Bacon MSS in Lambeth Palace Library)

Merbury, C.: *A Brief Discourse on Royal Monarchy etc.* (1581)

Monarchs and the Muse: Poems by Monarchs and Princes of England, Scotland and Wales (ed. Sally Purcell, 1972)

Moryson, F.: *An Itinerary* (4 vols., 1907)

La Mothe Fénelon, Bertrand de Salaignac de: *Correspondance Diplomatique* (7 vols., Bannatyne Club, 1838–40)

Naunton, Sir Robert: *Fragmenta Regalia, or Observations on the Late Queen Elizabeth, Her Times and Her Favourites* (1653; Harleian Miscellany II, 1744; ed. Edward Arber, 1870, 1896)

Newdigate, Lady: *Gossip from a Muniment Room* (1898)

Notes of Conversations with Ben Jonson by William Drummond of Hawthornden (ed. G.B. Harrison and R.F. Patterson, 1923)

Original Letters Illustrative of British History (11 vols., ed. Henry Ellis, 3rd Series, 1824–1846)

Original Letters relative to the English Reformation (ed. H. Robinson, Parker Society, 1846–7)

Parker, Matthew: *Correspondence, 1535–75* (ed. J. Bruce and T.T. Perowne, Parker Society, 1853)

Parsons, Robert: *A Conference about the Next Succession to the Crown of England* (1594)

Peck, Francis: *Desiderata Curiosa* (2 vols., 1732–5; 2 vols., ed. T. Evans, 1779)

Perlin, E.: *Déscription d'Angleterre et d' Écosse* (1558)

The Poems of Queen Elizabeth (ed. Leicester Bradner, 1964)

Proceedings and Ordinances of the Privy Council of England (ed. H. Nicholas, Records Commissioners, 1834–7)

The Progresses and Public Processions of Queen Elizabeth (3 vols, ed. J. Nichols, 1823)

Queen Elizabeth and some Foreigners (ed. Victor von Klarwill; tr. T.N Nash, 1928)

Queen Elizabeth and her Times (2 vols., ed. Thomas Wright, London 1838)

The Queen's Majesty's Passage through the City of London to Westminster the Day before her Coronation (ed. James M. Osborn, 1960; ed. J.E. Neale, 1960)

Raleigh, Sir Walter: *The History of the World* (1614, 1677)

Raleigh, Sir Walter: *Letters* (ed. E. Edwards, 1868)

Raleigh, Sir Walter: *Poems* (ed. Agnes Latham, 1929)

Raleigh, Sir Walter: *Works* (8 vols., 1829)

Relations Politiques de France . . . avec l'Ecosse (5 vols, ed. A. Teulet, 1862)

Rélations Politiques des Pays Bas et de l'Angleterre sous la Règne de Philippe II, 1555–79 (11 vols., ed. Kervyn de Lettenhove etc., 1882–1900)

Rotuli Parliamentorum (The Rolls of Parliament) (7 vols., ed. J. Strachey etc., Records Commissioners, 1767–1832)

Royal MSS (British Library)

MSS of the Duke of Rutland at Belvoir Castle (Historical Manuscripts Commission, 12th Report, Appendix, Part IV, 1888)

Rymer, Thomas: *Foedera* (20 vols., 1704–35 ed. T. Hardy, Records Commissioners, 1816–69)

The Sadler Papers (2 vols., ed. A. Clifford, 1809)

Sanders, Nicholas: *De Origine ac Progressu Schismatis Anglicani* 1585; ed. D. Lewis and printed as *The Rise and Growth of the Anglican Schism*, 1877)

The Sayings of Queen Elizabeth (ed. F. Chamberlin, 1923)

Secret Correspondence of Sir Robert Cecil and James I (ed. Lord Hales, 1766)

The Secret History of the Most Renowned Queen Elizabeth and the Earl of Essex. By a Person of Quality (1695)

The Sidney Papers: Letters and Memorials of State (2 vols., ed. Arthur Collins, 1746)

Sidney, Sir Philip: *Works* (4 vols., ed. A. Feuillerat, 1922–26)

The Somers Tracts (13 vols., ed. Sir Walter Scott, 1809–15)

State Papers, Foreign Series, Elizabeth I, 1589–90 (ed. R.B. Wernham, 1964)

State Papers relating to the Defeat of the Spanish Armada (ed. J.K. Laughton, Navy Record Society, 1894)

The Statutes, A.D. 1235–1770 (HMSO 1950)

Statutes of the Realm (11 vols., Records Commissioners, 1810–28)

Stow, John *The Annals of England, or a General Chronicle of England* (1592; ed. E Howes, 1631)

Stow, John: *The Chronicles of England, from Brutus unto this Present Year of*

Christ (1580; 1605)

Stow, John: *A Survey of London* (2 vols., ed. C.L. Kingsford, 1908; ed. Henry Morley, 1994.)

Stubbs, John: *A Gaping Gulf, with Letters and other Relevant Documents* (ed. Lloyd E. Berry, 1968)

Strype, John: *Annals of the Reformation* (4 vols., 1820–40)

Strype, John: *Ecclesiastical Memorials* (3 vols., 1721–33; 1822; 1823)

Thomas Platter's Travels in England, 1599 (ed. Clare Williams, 1937)

Tomkyns, J.: *A Sermon preached on the 26th day of May 1584* (1584)

Tothill, R.: *The Passage of our Most Dread Sovereign Lady, Queen Elizabeth through the City of London to Westminster* (1559)

Tudor Royal Proclamations (3 vols., ed. P.L. Hughes and J.F. Larkin, 1964–9)

Tudor and Stuart Proclamations (2 vols., ed. R. Steele, 1910)

Tudor Tracts (ed. A.F. Pollard, 1903)

Unton, Sir Henry: *Correspondence* (ed. Joseph Stevenson, Roxburghe Club 1848)

Walsingham, Sir Francis: *Journal, 1570–83* (ed. C.T. Martin, Camden Miscellany, IV, 1871)

Wilbraham, Sir Robert: *Journal* (Camden Miscellany, X, 1902)

Wilson, Thomas: *The State of England, Anno Domino 1600* (ed. F.J. Fisher, Camden Miscellany, CVI, 3rd Series, LII 1936)

Wriothesley, Charles, Windsor Herald: *A Chronicle of England in the Reigns of the Tudors, from 1485 to 1559* (1581; 2 vols., ed. William Douglas Hamilton, Camden Society, 2nd Series, X, XX, 1875–7)

The Zurich Letters (ed. H. Robinson, Parker Society, 1842)

Secondary Sources

Abbot, Edwin A.: *Bacon and Essex* (1877)

Abbot, Edwin A.: *Francis Bacon* (1885)

Adams, Simon: 'Faction, Clientage and Party, 1550–1603' (*History Today*, XXXII, 1982)

Adlard, George: *Amye Robsart and the Earl of Leicester* (1870)

Aikin, Lucy: *Memoirs of the Court and Times of Queen Elizabeth* (1818)

Aird, Ian: 'The Death of Amy Robsart: Accident, Suicide or Murder – or Disease?' (*English Historical Review*, 1956)

Andrews, K.R.: *English Privateering Voyages 1588–95* (Hakluyt Society, 1959)

Arber, E.(ed.): *An English Garland* (1877–96)

Armstrong Davison, M.H.: *The Casket Letters* (1965)

Arnold, Janet: *Queen Elizabeth's Wardrobe Unlock'd* (1988)

Ashdown, Dulcie M.: *Ladies in Waiting* (1976)

Auerbach, Erna: *Nicholas Hilliard* (1961)

Auerbach, Erna: 'Portraits of Queen Elizabeth I' (*Burlington Magazine*, 1953)

Auerbach, Erna: *Tudor Artists* (1954)

Axton, M.: *The Queen's Two Bodies: Drama and the Elizabethan Succession* (1977)

Bagwell, Richard: *Ireland under the Tudors* (1885)

Bainton, R.: *The Reformation in the Sixteenth Century* (1953)

Bassnett, Susan: *Elizabeth I: A Feminist Perspective* (1988)

Bayne, C.G.: 'The Coronation of Queen Elizabeth' (*English Historical Review*, XII, 1907)

Beckinsale, B.W.: *Burleigh, Tudor Statesman* (1967)

Beckinsale, B.W.: *Elizabeth I* (1963)

Bekker, E.: *Elisabeth und Leicester* (Giessener Studien, V, 1890)

Benson, E.F.: *Sir Francis Drake* (1927)

Bindoff, S.T., Hurstfield, J. and Williams, C.H. (eds.): *Elizabethan Government and Society* (1961)

Bindoff, S.T.: *Tudor England* (1950)

Black, J.B.: *Elizabeth and Henry IV* (1913)

Black, J.B.: *The Reign of Elizabeth* (1959)

Bloch, M.: *Les Rois Thaumaturges* (1924)

Bloch, Michael: *The Duchess of Windsor* (1996)

Boas, F.S.: *University Drama in the Tudor Age* (1913)

Boyd, M.C.: *Elizabethan Music and Musical Criticism* (1940)

Bradbrook, Muriel: *Drama as Offering: The Princely Pleasures of Kenilworth* (Rice Institute, XLVI, 1960)

Bradford, C.A.: *Blanche Parry* (1935)

Bradford, C.A.: *Helena, Marchioness of Northampton* (1936)

Bradley, E.T.: *The Life of the Lady Arabella Stuart* (1869)

Bromley, J.S. and Kossman, E.H.: *Britain and the Netherlands* (1961)

Brook, V.J.K.: *Whitgift and the English Church* (1957)

Brooke, Iris: *English Costume in the Age of Elizabeth* (1950)

Brookes, E. St. John: *Sir Christopher Hatton, Queen Elizabeth's Favourite* (1946)

Brushfield, T.N.: *The History of Durham House* (Devon Association, XXV)

Buxton, John: *Elizabethan Taste* (1965)

Buxton, John: *Sir Philip Sidney and the English Renaissance* (1966)

Chamberlin, Frederick: *Elizabeth and Leicester* (1939)

Chamberlin, Frederick: *The Private Character of Queen Elizabeth* (1921)

Chambers, E.K.: *'The Court' in Shakespeare's England* (1925)

Chambers, E.K.: *The Elizabethan Stage* (4 vols., 1923)

Chambers, E.K.: *Sir Henry Lee* (1930)

Chantelauze, M.R.: *Marie Stuart, sa Procès et son Exécution* (1876)

Chapman, F.: *Ancient Royal Palaces in or near London* (1902)

Chapman, H.W.: *Two Tudor Portraits* (1960)

Christy, M.: 'Queen Elizabeth's Visit to Tilbury in 1588' (*English Historical Review*, 34, 1919)

Clark, G.N.: *The Wealth of England, 1496 to 1720* (1946)

Collins, A.J: 'The Progress of Queen Elizabeth to Tilbury, 1588' (*British Museum Quarterly*, X, 1936)

Collinson, P.: *The Elizabethan Puritan Movement* (1967)

Cook, Greville: 'Queen Elizabeth and her Court Musicians' (*Musical Times*, 79, 1918)

Cowan, S.: *The Last Days of Mary Stuart (incorporating a translation of the Journal of Burgoyne)* (1907)

Creighton, Mandell: *Queen Elizabeth* (1899)

Cross, C.: *The Puritan Earl: Henry Hastings, Third Earl of Huntingdon* (1966)

Cust, L.: *Notes on the Authentic Portraits of Mary, Queen of Scots* (1903)

Davenport, C.: *English Embroidered Book bindings* (1899)

Dawley, A.: *John Whitgift and the Reformation* (1955)

Dawson, Giles E. and Kennedy-Skipton, Laetitia: *Elizabethan Handwriting: A Guide to the Reading of Documents and MSS* (1968)

Dent, John: *The Quest for Nonsuch* (1962)

Dewar, Mary: *Sir Thomas Smith: A Tudor Intellectual in Office* (1964)

Dictionary of National Biography (22 vols., ed. L. Stephen and S. Lee, 1885–1909)

Dimmock, Arthur: 'The Conspiracy of Dr Lopez' (*English Historical Review*, July, 1894)

Dodd, A.H.: *Life in Elizabethan England* (1961)

Dorsten, J.A. Van and Strong, Roy: *Leicester's Triumph* (1964)

Dowsing, James: *Forgotten Tudor Palaces in the London Area* (undated)

Dunlop, I.: *Palaces and Progresses of Elizabeth I* (1962)

Dutton, Ralph: *English Court Life from Henry VII to George II* (1963)

Eccles, Audrey: *Obstetrics and Gynaeocology in Tudor and Stuart England* (1982)

Edwards, Edward: *The Life of Sir Walter Raleigh, together with his Letters* (1868)

Edwards, R. and Ramsey, L.G.G. (eds.): *The Tudor Age* (1956)
Elton, G.R.: *England under the Tudors* (1955)
Elton, G.R.: *The Parliament of England, 1559–1581* (1986)
Elton, G.R.: *The Tudor Constitution* (1960)
Emmison, F.G.: *Tudor Secretary* (1961)
Erickson, Carolly: *The First Elizabeth* (1983)
Evans, Joan: *English Jewellery from the 5th Century A.D. to 1800* (1921)
Evans, Joan: *A History of Jewellery, 1100–1870* (1953)

Fairbank, A. and Wolpe, B.: *Renaissance Handwriting* (1960)
Falls. C.: *Elizabeth's Irish Wars* (1950)
Falls. C.: *Mountjoy: Elizabethan General* (1955)
la Ferriére, C.F.H. de: *Les Projects de Marriage de la Reine Elisabeth* (1882)
Finch, Peter J.: *John Dee: The World of an Elizabethan Magus* (1972)
Firth, C.H.: *The Ballad History of the Late Tudors* (Transactions of the
    Royal Historical Society, 3rd Series III, 1909)
Fisher, F.J. (ed.): *Essays on the Economic and Social History of Tudor and
    Stuart England* (1961)
Fleming, David Hay: *Mary, Queen of Scots: From her Birth to her Flight into
    England* (1898)
Fox Bourne, H.R.: *Sir Philip Sidney* (1891)
Fraser, Antonia: *Mary, Queen of Scots* (1969)
Freedman, Sylvia: *Poor Penelope: Lady Penelope Rich, an Elizabethan
    Woman* (1983)
Froude, J.A.: *A History of England from the Fall of Wolsey to the Defeat of
    the Armada* (12 vols., 1856–70)
Furnivall, F.J.: *Shakespeare and Mary Fitton* (1897)

Gaunt, William: *Court Painting in England* (1980)
Gardiner, D.: *English Girlhood at School* (1929)
Gee, Henry: *The Elizabethan Prayer Book and Ornaments* (1902)
Geyl, P.: *The Revolt of the Netherlands, 1555–1609* (1932)
Goodall, W.: *An Examination of the Letters said to be written by Mary,
    Queen of Scots to James, Earl of Bothwell* (2 vols., 1754)
Grew, J.H.: *Elisabeth d'Angleterre dans la Litterature Française* (1932)
Grun, Bernard: *The Timetables of History* (1991)

Hadfield, A.M.: *Time to Finish the Game* (1964)
Haigh, Christopher: *Elizabeth I* (1988)
Haigh, Christopher (ed.): *The Reign of Elizabeth I* (1984)
Hale, H.M.: 'The English Historic Portrait: Document and Myth'
    (*Proceedings of the British Academy*, 1963)
Hampden, John (ed.): *Francis Drake, Privateer* (1972)

Handover, P.M.:*The Second Cecil: The Rise to Power, 1563 to 1604 of Sir Robert Cecil* (1959)

Harrison, G.B.: *The Life and Death of Robert Devereux, Earl of Essex* (1937)

Haynes, Alan: 'The Islands Voyage' (*History Today*, XXV, 1975)

Haynes, Alan: *Robert Cecil, Earl of Salisbury (1989)*

Haynes, Alan: 'Supplying the Elizabethan Court' (*History Today* XXVIII, 1978)

Haynes, Alan: *The White Bear: The Elizabethan Earl of Leicester (1987)*

Headlam Wells, Robin: *Spenser's Faerie Queen and the Cult of Elizabeth* (1983)

Hearne, Karen (ed.): *Dynasties: Painting in Tudor and Jacobean England 1530–1630* (1995)

Henry, L.W.: *The Earl of Essex and Ireland* (British Institute of Historical Research, XXXII, 1959)

Henry, L.W.: 'The Earl of Essex as Strategist and Military Organiser 1596–97' (*English Historical Review*, LXVIII, 1953)

Hibbert, Christopher: *The Court at Windsor* (1964)

Hibbert, Christopher: *The Tower of London* (1971)

Hibbert, Christopher: *The Virgin Queen: The Personal History of Elizabeth I* (1992 edn.)

Hosack, J.: *Mary, Queen of Scots and Her Accusers.*(2 vols., 1870–74)

Hotson, Leslie:*Queen Elizabeth's Entertainment at Mitcham* (1953)

Howard, Philip: *The Royal Palaces* (1960)

Howarth, David: *The Voyage of the Armada.*(1981)

Hughes, P.: *The Reformation in England, Vol. 3* (1950–56)

Hume, M.A.S.: *The Courtships of Queen Elizabeth* (1898, 1904)

Hume, M.A.S.: *Treason and Plot* (1901)

Hurstfield, J.: *Elizabeth I and the Unity of England* (1960)

Hurstfield, J.: *Freedom, Corruption and Government in Elizabethan England* (1973)

Hurstfield, Joel: *The Queen's Wards* (1958)

Jackson, E.: 'Amye Robsart' (*Wiltshire Archaeological Magazine*, XVII, 1898)

Jardine, David: *Criminal Trials, Vol. I* (1832)

Jardine, David: *A Reading on the Use of Torture in the Criminal Laws of England* (1837)

Jebb, S.: *Life of Robert, Earl of Leicester* (1727)

Jenkins, Elizabeth: *Elizabeth the Great* (1958)

Jenkins, G.: 'Ways and Means in Elizabethan Propaganda' (*History*, 1941)

Johnson, Paul: *Elizabeth I: A Study in Power and Intellect* (1974)

Kendrick, T.D.: *British Antiquity* (1950)
Kenny, R.W.: *Elizabeth's Admiral* (1970)
Kingsford, C.L.: 'Essex House, formerly Leicester House and Exeter Inn' (*Antiquaries Journal, Archaeologia*, LXXIII, 1–54, Oxford, 1923)

Lacey, Robert: *Robert, Earl of Essex: An Elizabethan Icarus* (1971)
Lacey, Robert: *Sir Walter Raleigh* (1973)
Lamont-Brown, R.: *Royal Murder Mysteries* (1990)
Law, Ernest: *The History of Hampton Court Palace* (1890)
Leader, J.D.: *Mary, Queen of Scots in Captivity* (1880)
Lee, A.G.: *The Son of Leicester* (1964)
Lees-Milne, J.: *Tudor Renaissance* (1951)
Lever, T.: *The Herberts of Wilton* (1967)
Levine, M.: *The Early Elizabethan Succession Question, 1558–68* (1966)
Levine, M.: *Tudor Dynastic Problems, 1460–1571* (1973)
Lewis, Michael:, *The Spanish Armada* (1951, 1960)
Lloyd-Howell, A.:*The Rouen Campaign, 1590–92* (1973)
Long, J.H.(ed.): *Music in English Renaissance Drama* (1968)
Luke, Mary M.: *A Crown for Elizabeth* (1971)

MacCaffrey, Wallace: 'Elizabethan Politics: The First Decade, 1558–1568' (*Past and Present*, April, 1963)
MacCaffrey, Wallace: *The Making of the Elizabethan Regime* (1968)
MacDonald, H.: *Portraits in Prose* (1946)
MacNalty, Arthur S.: *Elizabeth Tudor: The Lonely Queen* (1954)
Mahon, R.H.: *Mary, Queen of Scots* (1924)
Marshall, Rosalind K.: *Elizabeth I* (1991)
Mattingly, Garrett: *The Defeat of the Spanish Armada* (1959)
du Maurier, Daphne: *The Golden Lads* (The Bacon brothers) (1975)
Mercer, Derek (ed.): *Chronicle of the Royal Family* (1991)
Meyer, C.S.: *Elizabeth I and the Religious Settlement of 1559* (1960)
Meyer, A.O.: *England and the Catholic Church under Queen Elizabeth* (tr. J.R. McKee, 1916)
Meyer, E.H.: *English Chamber Music* (1946)
Montagu, W.: *Court and Society from Elizabeth to Anne* (2 vols.,1864)
Morley, H. (ed.): *Ireland under Elizabeth and James I* (1890)
Morris, C.: *The Tudors* (1955)
Mumby, F.A.: *The Fall of Mary Stuart* (1921)

Neale, J.E.: 'The Accession of Queen Elizabeth' (*History Today*, May, 1953)
Neale, J.E.: 'The Elizabethan Acts of Supremacy and Uniformity' (*English Historical Review*, 1950)

Neale, J.E.: *The Elizabethan House of Commons* (1949)
Neale, J.E.: *Elizabeth I and her Parliaments*, Vol. 1: 1559–1581 (1953) Vol. 11: 1584–1601 (1957)
Neale, J.E.: *Essays in Elizabethan History* (1958)
Neale, J.E.: 'Parliament and the Succession Question in 1562/3 and 1566' (*English Historical Review*, 1921)
Neale, J.E.: *Queen Elizabeth I* (1934; revised edn.1965)
Neale, J.E.: 'Sayings of Queen Elizabeth' (*History*, X, October 1925)
Neale, J.E.: 'Sir Nicholas Throckmorton's Advice to Queen Elizabeth' (*English Historical Review*, LXV, 1950)
Needham, R. and Webster, A.: *Somerset House, Past and Present* (1905)
Nicholas, N.H.: *The Life of William Davison* (1823)

Orwell, G. and Reynolds, R.: *British Pamphleteers* (1948)
Osborne, June: *Entertaining Elizabeth I: The Progresses and Great Houses of her Time (1989)*
The Oxford Book of Royal Anecdotes (ed. E. Longford, 1989)

Paston-Williams, Sarah: *The Art of Dining* (1993)
Peck, D.C.: 'Government Suppression of English Catholic Books: The Case of "Leicester's Commonwealth"' (*Library Quarterly*, XLII, 2, 1977)
Percival, Rachel and Allen: *The Court of Elizabeth I* (1976)
Perry, Maria: *The Word of a Prince: A Life of Elizabeth I* (1990)
Picard, B.L.: *The Tower and the Traitors* (1961)
Plowden, Alison: *Elizabethan England* (1982)
Plowden, Alison: *Elizabeth Regina, 1588–1603* (1980)
Plowden, Alison: *Marriage with my Kingdom: The Courtships of Elizabeth I* (1977)
Plowden, Alison: *Two Queens in One Isle* (1984)
Pollen, J.H.: *The English Catholics in the Reign of Queen Elizabeth* (1920)
Pollen, J.H.: *Mary, Queen of Scots and the Babington Plot* (Scottish Historical Society, 3rd Series, 111, 1922)
Porter, H.C.: *Reformation and Reaction in Tudor Cambridge* (1958)
Prior, T.M.: *The Royal Studs of the Sixteenth and Seventeenth Centuries* (1935)

Quinn, D.B.: *Raleigh and the British Empire* (1947)

Rait, R.S. and Cameron, J.: *King James's Secret* (1927)
Read, Conyers: *Lord Burghley and Queen Elizabeth* (1960)
Read, Conyers: *Mr. Secretary Cecil and Queen Elizabeth* (1955)
Read, Conyers: *Mr. Secretary Walsingham and the Policy of Queen Elizabeth*

(3 vols.,925; reprinted 1967)

Read, Conyers: *The Tudors: Personalities and Politics in Sixteenth Century England* (1936)

Read, R.R.: *The Rebellion of the Earls, 1569* (Transactions of the Royal Historical Society, 2nd Series, XX, 1906)

Reese, M.M.: *The Royal Office of Master of the Horse* (1976)

Rice, G.P.: *The Public Speaking of Queen Elizabeth* (1951)

Rich, E.E.: 'The Population of Elizabethan England' (*Economic History Review*, 1949)

Richardson, A.: *The Lovers of Queen Elizabeth* (1907)

Ridley, Jasper: *Elizabeth I* (1987)

Robinson, Agnes M.F.: 'Queen Elizabeth and the Valois Princes' (*English Historical Review*, 11, 1887)

Rosenberg, Eleanor: *Leicester, Patron of Letters* (1955)

Roulstone, M.: *The Royal House of Tudor* (1974)

Rowse, A.L.: *An Elizabethan Garland* (1953)

Rowse, A.L.: *The Elizabethan Renaissance: The Life of the Society* (1971)

Rowse, A.L.: 'Elizabeth's Coronation' (*History Today*, III, 1953)

Rowse, A.L.: *The England of Elizabeth* (1950)

Rowse, A.L.: *The Expansion of Elizabethan England* (1955)

Rowse, A.L. and Harrison, G.B.: *Queen Elizabeth and her Subjects* (1955)

Rowse, A.L.: *Raleigh and the Throckmortons* (1962)

Rowse, A.L.: *Shakespeare's Southampton* (1965)

Rowse, A.L.: *The Tower of London in the History of the Nation* (1972)

Rowse, A.L.: *Windsor Castle in the History of the Nation* (1974)

The Royal Encyclopaedia (ed. Ronald Allison and Sarah Riddell, 1991)

Rye, W.B.:, *England as seen by Foreigners* (1865)

Rye, W.B.: *The Murder of Amy Robsart* (1885)

Scarisbrick, Diana: *Tudor and Jacobean Jewellery* (1995)

Seymour, William: *An English Family in the Shadow of the Tudors* (1972)

Simpson, A.: *The Wealth of the Gentry, 1540–1640* (1961)

Simpson, R.: *Edmund Campion* (1896)

Sitwell, Edith: *The Queen and the Hive* (1963)

Smith, A.G.R.: *The Government of Elizabethan England* (1967)

Smith, Lacey Baldwin: *The Elizabethan Epic* (1966)

Smith, Lacey Baldwin: *Elizabeth Tudor: Portrait of a Queen* (1976)

Soden, Geoffrey: *Godfrey Goodman, Bishop of Gloucester, 1583–1656* (1953)

Somerset, Anne: *Elizabeth I* (1991)

Spedding, James: *The Letters and Life of Francis Bacon* (2 vols., 1890)

Stafford, Helen G.: *James VI of Scotland and the Throne of England* (1940)

Starkey, David (ed.): *The English Court from the Wars of the Roses to the*

Civil War (1987)

Stebbings, W., *Sir Walter Raleigh* (1899)

Strachey, Lytton: *Elizabeth and Essex* (1928)

Strickland, Agnes: *Life of Queen Elizabeth* (1906)

Strong, Roy: *Artists of the Tudor Court* (1983)

Strong, Roy: *The Cult of Elizabeth* (1977)

Strong, Roy and, Oman, Julia Trevelyan: *Elizabeth R* (1971)

Strong, Roy: *The English Icon: Elizabethan and Jacobean Portraiture* (1969)

Strong, Roy: 'Federigo Zuccaro's Visit to England in 1575' (*Journal of the Warburg and Courtauld Institutes*, 1959)

Strong, Roy: *Gloriana: The Portraits of Queen Elizabeth 1* (1987)

Strong, Roy: 'The Popular Celebration of the Accession Day of Queen Elizabeth I' (*Journal of the Warburg and Courtauld Institutes*, 1947)

Strong Roy: *Portraits of Queen Elizabeth I (1963)*

Strong, Roy: *Splendour at Court* (1973)

Strong, Roy: *Tudor and Jacobean Portraits* (2 vols., HMSO, 1969)

Sugden, John: *Sir Francis Drake* (1990)

Summerson, John: *The Building of Theobalds* (*Archaeologia*, CVII, 1954)

Tanner, Lawrence E.: *The History and Treasures of Westminster Abbey* (1953)

Taylor, W.F.: *The Charterhouse of London (1912)*

Tenison, E.M.: *Elizabethan England*, I to XIIA (1933–61)

Thompson, G.S.: *Lords Lieutenant in the Sixteenth Century* (1923)

Thompson, J.V.P.: *The Supreme Governor* (1940)

Thurley, Simon: *The Royal Palaces of Tudor England* (1993)

Tighe, R.R. and Davis, J.E.: *Annals of Windsor, Being a History of the Castle and Town* (1858)

Tillyard, E.M.W.: *The Elizabethan World Picture* (1944)

Tillyard, E.M.W.: *Shakespeare's History Plays* (1944)

Tudor and Stuart Portraits (The Weiss Gallery, 1995)

Turton, Godfrey: *The Dragon's Breed: The Story of the Tudors, from Earliest Times to 1603* (1969)

Wallace, M.W.: *Philip Sidney* (1915)

Wallace, W.M.: *Sir Walter Raleigh* (1959)

Waldman, Milton: *Elizabeth and Leicester* (1945)

Walpole, Horace: *Anecdotes of Painting in England* (1876)

Waterhouse, E.: *Painting in Britain, 1530–1790* (1953)

Waters, D.W. 'The Elizabethan Navy and the Armada Campaign' (*Mariner's Mirror*, 1949)

Welsford, Enid: *The Court Masque* (1927)

Wernham, R.B.: *Before the Armada: The Growth of English Foreign Policy*

1485–1588 (1966)

Wernham, W.B.: 'Queen Elizabeth and the Portugal Expedition of 1589' (*English Historical Review*, 1951)

Westminster Abbey: *Official Guide* (various edns.)

White, F.O.: *Lives of the Elizabethan Bishops* (1898)

Wiesener, L.: *La Jeunesse d'Elisabeth d'Angleterre* (1878; 2 vols., tr C.M. Yonge, 1879)

Williams, E. Carleton: *Bess of Hardwick* (1959)

Williams, Neville: *All the Queen's Men* (1972)

Williams, Neville: 'The Coronation of Queen Elizabeth I' (*Quarterly Review*, 597, 1953)

Williams, Neville: *Elizabeth I, Queen of England* (1967)

Williams, Neville: *The Life and Times of Elizabeth I* (1972)

Williams, Neville: *Thomas Howard, 4th Duke of Norfolk* (1964)

William, P. 'The Fall of Essex' (*History Today*, 1957)

Williams, Penry: *Life in Tudor England* (1964)

Williamson, Hugh Ross,: *Historical Enigmas* (1974)

Williamson, J.A.: *The Age of Drake* (1960)

Wilson, C.: *Queen Elizabeth and the Revolt of the Netherlands* (1970)

Wilson, Derek: *Sweet Robin: A Biography of Robert Dudley, Earl of Leicester, 1533–1588* (1981)

Wilson, E.C.: *England's Eliza* (1939)

Wilson, J.D.: *Life in Shakespeare's England* (1911)

Wilson, Jean: *Entertainments for Elizabeth* (1980)

Wilson, Jean: 'The Harefield Entertainment and the Cult of Elizabeth I' (*Antiquaries Journal*, LXVI, 1986)

Wilson, V.A.: *Queen Elizabeth's Maids of Honour* (1922)

Woodfill, W.L.: *Musicians in English Society from Elizabeth to Charles I* (1953)

Woodworth, W.: *A Purveyance for the Royal Household under Queen Elizabeth* (Transactions of the American Philosophical Society, 35, 1945–6)

Wormald, Jenny: *Mary, Queen of Scots: A Study in Failure* (1988)

Wright, W.B.: *Middle Class Culture in Elizabethan England* (1935)

Yates, F.A.: *Astraea: The Imperial Theme in the Sixteenth Century* (1975)

Yates, F.A.: 'Elizabethan Chivalry: The Romance of the Accession Day Tilts' (*Journal of the Warburg and Courtauld Institutes*, 1947)

Yates, F.A.: 'Queen Elizabeth as Astraea' (*Journal of the Warburg and Courtauld Institutes*, 1947)

Young, Alan: *Tudor and Jacobean Tournaments* (1987)

Youngs, F.A.: *The Proclamations of the Tudor Queens* (1976)

Zweig, Stefan: *The Queen of Scots* (1935)

Genealogical Tables

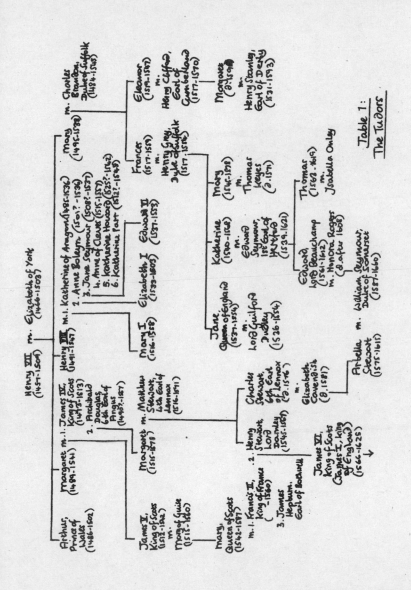

Table 1:
The Tudors

Table 2: The Boleyn and Howard Connections.

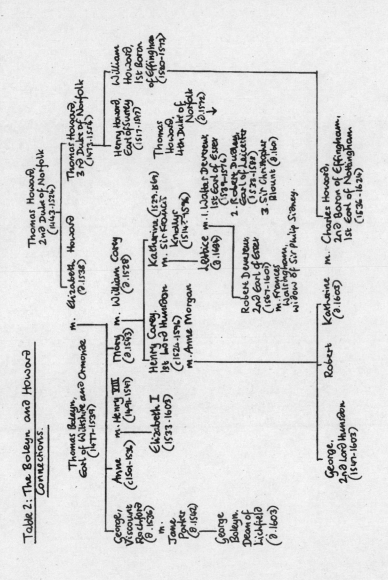

Table 3:
The Dudleys

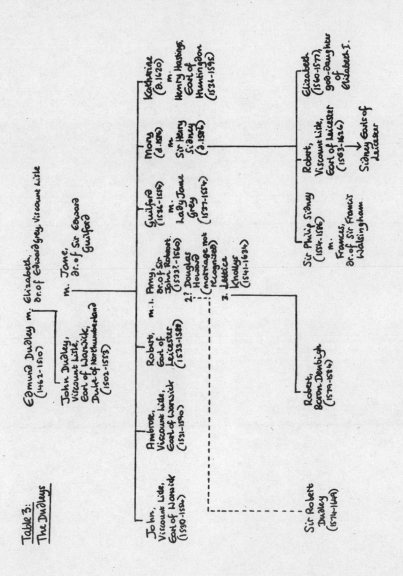

Edmund Dudley m. Elizabeth,
(1462-1510)   Dr. of Edward grey, Viscount Lisle

m. Jane,
Dr. of Sir Edward
Guilford

John Dudley,
Viscount Lisle,
Earl of Warwick,
Duke of Northumberland
(1502-1553)

John,
Viscount Lisle,
Earl of Warwick
(1530-1554)

Ambrose,
Viscount Lisle,
Earl of Warwick
(1531-1590)

Robert,
Earl of
Leicester
(1533-1588)

Guilford
(1536-1554)
m.
Lady Jane
Grey
(1537-1554)

Mary
(d. 1586)
m.
Sir Henry
Sidney
(d. 1586)

Katherine
(b. 1620)
m.
Henry Hastings,
Earl of
Huntingdon
(1536-1595)

m. 1. Amy,
Dr. of Sir
John Robsart
(1532?-1560)

2.? Douglas Howard
(marriage not
recognised)

3. Lettice
Knollys
(1541-1634)

Robert,
Baron Denbigh
(1579-1584)

Sir Robert
Dudley
(1574-1649)

Sir Philip Sidney
(1554-1586)
m.
Frances,
Dr. of Sir Francis
Walsingham

Robert,
Viscount Lisle,
Earl of Leicester
(1563-1626)
→ Sidney Earls of
Leicester

Elizabeth,
(1560-1577),
god-daughter of
Elizabeth I.

Index

Abingdon, Berks. 94–5, 98–9
Accession Day 217–18, 247, 398 406, 420,
    430, 439, 450, 459, 476
Adolphus, Duke of Holstein 67, 84
Aglionby, Mr, Recorder of Coventry 286
Aird, Professor Iain 106
Albert V, Duke of Bavaria 88
Alençon, Duke of (see Francis of Valois)
Allen, William, Cardinal 296, 389
Allinga, Ahasverus 145–6
Alva, Duke of (see Ferdinand de Toledo)
Angus, Earl of (see Douglas)
Anjou, Dukes of (see Henry; Francis)
Antonio of Portugal, Don 333, 403,
    417–18
Antwerp, Flanders 33, 92, 340, 353, 419
Appletree, Thomas 323–4
Appleyard, John 86, 100 104n
Apprentices, Statute of 1563 9
Argyll, Lady (see Stewart, Jane)
Ariosto, Ludovico 6
Arklow, Ireland 443
Armada, Battle of the Spanish, 1588 217
    238, 246, 382, 384, 388–400, 420,
    425, 430, 487–8
Armada Jewel, the 237, 398
Arnhem, Netherlands 370
Arran, Earl of (see Hamilton, James)
Arthur, King 223, 299
Arundel, Earl of (see FitzAlan)
Ascham, Roger 13–14, 18, 45, 73, 200
Ashby-de-la-Zouche, Leics. 304
Ashley, John 24, 113, 256
Ashley, Katherine, 15, 24, 78, 113, 164–5,

    235, 256, 259, 342
Ashridge, Herts. 247
Ashton, Dr Abdy 462
Association, Act of, 1585 370
Aubrey, John 254, 343
Augsburg, Austria 176
Avila, Gomez d' 417
Aylmer, John, Bishop of London 56, 233,
    348, 399
Azores 382, 403, 428

Babington, Sir Anthony, of Dethick
    363–7, 369
Bacon, Anthony 286, 407, 411, 418, 425,
    468
Bacon, Sir Francis 51, 59, 224, 286, 407,
    411, 414, 416, 418–20, 425, 441, 444,
    450–51, 453–4, 456–7, 463–4, 468
Bacon, Sir Nicholas, Lord Keeper 23, 41,
    139, 141, 214, 266, 286, 307, 407, 422
Bagenal, Sir Henry 437
Baker, Richard 55
Ballard, Father John 363, 365, 367
Barn Elms, Surrey 216, 380
Basing, Hants. 409, 471
Bate, John 235
Bath, City of 414
Bavaria, Duke of (see Albert V)
Baylie, Elizabeth 50
Bayly, Dr 95
Baynard's Castle, Blackfriars, London 63,
    130, 241
Beale, Robert 224, 377, 381
Beaton, James, Archbishop of Glasgow 185

Beaufort, Lady Margaret 148
Beaufort, M. de 480–82
Bedington Park, Surrey 266, 456
Bedford, Countess of 134
Bedford, Earl of (see Russell, Francis)
Bedingfield, Sir Henry 28
Belvoir Castle, Leics. 291
Bendlowes, Sergeant 264
Berkeley, Sir Richard 453, 457
Bermondsey, London 347
Bertie, Peregrine, Lord Willoughby
    d'Eresby 255, 404
Berwick, Northumberland 151–2
Berwick, Treaty of, 1586 365
Bess of Hardwick (see Cavendish,
    Elizabeth)
Bethune, Maximilien de, Duke of Sully
    471
Bettes, John 238
Bingham, Sir Richard 438
Biron, Marshal 471
Bisham Abbey, Berks. 406
Blackadder, Captain William 185
Blackfriars, London 239, 455
Bland, Adam 235
Blenheim Palace, Oxon. 247
Bloch, Michael 49
Blois, Treaty of, 1572 284–5, 297
Blount, Sir Charles, later Lord Mountjoy
    348, 402, 439, 441, 444, 450, 453–5,
    457–60, 463, 475, 478, 480
Blount, Sir Christopher 397, 459–60, 462,
    468
Blount, Thomas 98–102, 106
Boccaccio, Giovanni 6
Bohemia, King of (see Maximilian II)
Bohun, Edmond 349
Boleyn, Anne, Queen of England, 2, 4,
    11–13, 16, 18, 25, 36, 39, 64, 165, 230
    236–7, 243, 246, 256, 283, 374
Boleyn, Mary 23–4, 165
Bolton Castle, Yorks. 196–7
Bond of Association 1584 352–3, 377–8
Bonner, Edmund, Bishop of London 26
Borth, Francis 79
Bothwell, Earl of (see Hepburn, James)
Boulogne, Francis 326
Bourke, Richard, Earl of Clanricarde 471
Bowes, Mr 98–9
Branganza, Duke of (see Theodosius II)

Brandon, Charles, Duke of Suffolk 42
Brandon, Eleanor, Countess of
    Cumberland 41–2
Brandon, Frances, Duchess of Suffolk, 41,
    113
Breuner, Baron Caspar 65–8, 73–4, 78–9,
    81, 84, 87
Bridges, Katherine 407–8
Bristol, City of 6, 263, 267, 475
Bristol, Treaty of, 1574, 293
British Library and Museum, London 80,
    345, 465
Bromley, Sir Thomas, Lord Chancellor
    366, 373–4
Browne, Anthony, 1st Viscount Montague
    369, 408
Brussels, Flanders 26, 85, 89, 193
Buckingham, 2nd Duke of (George
    Villiers) 394
Buckhurst, Lord (see Sackville, Thomas)
Burcot, Dr 134–5
Burghley House, Stamford 19, 266)
Burghley, Lord (see Cecil, William)
Burton, Master 360–61
Bury St Edmunds, Suffolk 94
Butler, Thomas, 10th Earl of Ormonde
    166, 171, 392
Buxton, Derbyshire 232, 307, 313, 348,
    351, 360, 395
Byrd, William 7, 58, 230, 253

Cadiz, Spain 382, 422–6, 430
Cadwaladr, Prince of Wales 246
Caesar, Sir Julius 406
Cahir, Ireland 442
Calais, France 2, 25, 62, 91, 131, 133, 141,
    144, 147, 275, 391, 421, 487
Calvin, John 222
Camberwell, London 94
Cambridge, City of 147–8
Cambridge, University of 13, 18, 54, 58,
    64, 67, 147–8, 178, 215, 405,
Camden, William 208, 322–3, 340, 367,
    380, 386, 394, 396–7, 437, 466, 470,
    483, 488
Campion, Father (St) Edmund 178, 333,
    335, 338
Canterbury, City of 344
Cape St Vincent 382
Carberry Hill, Battle of, 1567 188

Carew, Sir Francis 266, 456

Carew, Sir George 413, 434

Carey, Eleanor, Lady Scrope 454, 466, 484–5

Carey, George, 2nd Lord Hunsdon 430, 443, 477

Carey, Henry, 1st Lord Hunsdon 24, 84, 135, 149, 157, 159, 211–12, 226, 256, 280, 387, 391, 403, 422, 480

Carey, Katherine, Countess of Nottingham 466, 480, 482

Carey, Katherine, Lady Knollys 23, 165, 256, 258, 303

Carey, Robert 387, 480–82, 484–5

Carlisle, City of 194–5

Carlos, Don, Infante of Spain, son of Philip II 42, 115, 132–3, 142, 145, 147, 152

Carrickmacross, Ireland 445

Carshalton, Surrey 209

Cartagena, Carribean 357

Casket Letters, The 189, 197–200, 277

Castelnau, Michel de, Sieur de la Mauvissière 51, 288

Castiglione, Balthasar 6–7, 254

Cateau-Cambrésis, Treaty of, 1559 62, 75

Cavalcanti, Guido 274

Cavendish, Elizabeth, Countess of Lennox 295–6

Cavendish, Elizabeth (Bess of Hardwick), Lady Saintlow, Countess of Shrewsbury 48, 50, 122, 203, 234, 295–6, 308, 353 & n, 476, 478

Cavendish, Mistress 262

Cecil, Anne, Countess of Oxford 274

Cecil House, Strand, London 304, 436

Cecil, Sir Robert 382, 390, 401, 404–5, 407–8, 411–12, 417–18, 420–2, 425–7, 432, 434, 436, 438, 440, 442, 444, 447–8, 451–3, 455, 458–62, 464–5, 468–9, 475–83, 487

Cecil, Sir Thomas, later 2nd Lord Burghley 301, 479

Cecil, William, 1st Lord Burghley 18–23, 25, 29, 39, 45, 48, 50–52, 57, 64–5, 71, 73, 77, 79–80, 84–6, 89–93, 96–7, 101–3, 108–9, 111, 113–15, 117–20, 122, 127–8, 134, 141–3, 145–8, 150–55, 158–9, 164, 166–7, 171–3, 175–9, 181–2, 190–94, 198–9, 201–5,
207–11, 214–16, 221–2, 224–8, 232, 237–8, 253, 256–7, 263, 266–7, 269, 271, 274–81, 285–7, 290, 292, 299, 301, 304, 308, 315, 318, 321–2, 328, 331, 337–8, 340–41, 346, 352, 355, 357, 362, 366–7, 369–90, 372, 374–7, 380–82, 394, 401, 404–5, 407–8, 410–11, 416–18, 420–22, 424–6, 429, 432, 434, 436–8, 456, 487

Challoner, Sir Thomas 49, 85

Chamberlain, John 254

Champigny, Sieur de 306

Charles of Habsburg, Archduke of Austria 60, 62, 64–6, 71, 73–4, 80–82, 84–5, 87–8, 112, 118, 133, 145–6, 148, 154–5, 158–9, 161–3, 166–7, 169, 174–7, 191–2, 215

Charles V, Holy Roman Emperor, King of Spain 12

Charles IX, King of France 116, 121, 133, 154–5, 160, 171, 186, 208, 210, 213, 215, 269, 277, 285–8, 292, 293

Charterhouse, The, Smithfield, London 27, 215, 241, 276, 479

Chartley, Staffs. 302–3, 360, 364, 366, 368, 385

Chastelard, Pierre de 140–41

Châteauneuf, Mlle. de 278

Château-Thierry, France 350

Chatsworth, Derbyshire 203, 295, 308

Cheke, John 18, 67

Cheke, Mary 18

Chelsea Palace, London 13–14, 240, 266, 432

Chequers, Bucks. 164, 237

Chichester, Sussex 408

Chiswick, London 476

Christopher, Duke of Wurttemberg 145

Churchyard, Thomas 316

Civil War, The 267

Clanricarde, Earl of (see Bourke, Richard)

Clapham, John 18–19, 252

Clifford, George, Earl of Cumberland 217–18, 395, 413

Clifford, Margaret, Lady Strange, Countess of Derby 42

Clinton, Henry, Lord, later Earl of Lincoln 266, 323

Clinton, Lady 206

Cobham, Kent 76

Cobham, Lady 275
Cobham, Lord 260, 277, 426
Cockfield Hall, Suffolk 140
Coke, Sir Edward 414, 418, 454 464
Colchester, Essex 83
Colet, John, Dean of St Paul's
Coligny, Admiral Gaspard de 132, 287
Colt, Maximilian 486
Compiègne, France 409
Condé, Prince de (see Louis I)
Cooke, Anne, Lady Bacon 286
Cooke, Sir Anthony 18
Cooke, Mildred, Lady Burghley 18
Cornbury Park,Oxon. 396
Cosimo I, Grand Duke of Tuscany 271
Coventry, City of 57, 211, 265, 286,
    300–301
Cowdray Castle, Sussex 408, 415
Cowper, Henry 286
Cox, Dr Richard, Bishop of Ely 41, 57,
    298
Craigmillar Castle, Edinburgh 183–4
Creighton, Father 352
Critz, John de 486
Croft, Sir James 86, 250
Croke, John 472–4
Cromwell, Oliver 246–7
Croydon Palace, Surrey 456
Cuffe, Henry 443, 458–9, 462, 465 468
Cumberland, Earl of (see Clifford, George)
Cumnor Place, Berks. 94–5, 90–100, 103,
    105–6, 109, 112
Curle, Gilbert 366

Dacre, Leonard, Lord 212
Dairy House, the, Kew 72, 92–3, 100–101,
    108, 267
Dale, Dr Valentine 389
Dannett, Thomas 176–7
Danvers, Sir Charles 453, 459, 461–2, 468
Darnley, Lord (see Stewart, Henry)
Dartford, Kent 76
Dartmouth, Devon 413
Davison, Sir William 362, 375–8, 381–2,
    398
Dee, Dr John 22, 33, 230–31, 479
Delft, Netherlands 350
Denchworth, Berks. 94–5
Denmark, King of (see Frederick II)
Deptford, Kent 323, 336

Derby, Countess of 476
Derby, Earls of (see Stanley)
Devereux, Dorothy, Lady Perrot 347,
    386–7
Devereux, Penelope, Lady Rich 404, 439,
    453, 459–60, 468
Devereux, Robert, 2nd Earl of Essex 304,
    347, 354, 358, 360, 370, 372, 384–7,
    395, 397–8, 401–12, 414–30, 432–71,
    477
Devereux, Walter, Viscount Hereford, 1st
    Earl of Essex 157, 165, 302–4, 312,
    314
Dieppe, France 133
Digges, Dudley 224
Dissolution of the Monasteries 3, 106, 472
Ditchley Park, Oxon. 238–9, 406
Doncaster, Yorks. 293
Dorothy, Mrs 175
Douai, France 296
Douglas, Archibald, Earl of Angus 43
Douglas, George 194
Douglas, James, Earl of Morton 172, 184,
    189, 198, 270, 289, 294, 309
Douglas, Margaret, Countess of Lennox
    42–3, 117, 131, 143, 152, 155, 163,
    187, 215, 295–6
Dover, Kent 293, 326
Dowe, Annie, of Brentwood 90
Dowland, John 7, 223
Drake, Sir Francis, 9, 231, 309, 334, 336–7,
    357, 382, 388–91, 394–5, 399, 403–4,
    420–21, 423, 475, 488
Dragsholm Castle, Denmark 310
Drummond, William of Hawthornden 49
Drury, Dru 86
Drury House, London 459
Drury, Sir William 86
Dublin, Ireland 303, 437–8, 441–2, 444–5
Dudley, Ambrose, Earl of Warwick 22, 86,
    129, 133, 141–3, 144, 260, 286, 294,
    318, 362, 386, 406
Dudley Castle, Worcs. 291
Dudley, Edmund 22
Dudley, Edward, Lord 291
Dudley, Lord Guilford 15
Dudley, John, Earl of Warwick, Duke of
    Northumberland 13, 15–16, 20–22,
    42, 77, 83, 111, 114, 353
Dudley, John, Earl of Warwick 20, 114

Dudley, Mary, Lady Sidney 22, 80–82, 85,
118, 136, 259, 325, 371, 397
Dudley, Robert, Baron Denbigh 330,
353&n, 357, 396
Dudley, Robert, Earl of Leicester 13,
20–22, 27, 31, 33, 36, 39, 42, 46, 50,
69–75, 77–88, 90–108, 110–114,
117–22, 129–30, 135–6, 142–8,
150–3, 155, 157–62, 165–6, 169–75,
178–80, 190, 192, 199, 202–7, 211,
215–16, 227, 229, 232–3, 239, 256,
262, 269, 272–6, 279–81, 284, 287,
289–94, 298–303, 305, 307–9, 311–18,
320, 322–5, 328–32, 337–41, 344–8,
350, 352–5, 357–9, 361–3, 365,
369–74, 377, 380, 382, 384–5, 388,
390–92, 394–8, 401, 405, 416, 426
Dudley, Sir Robert 262, 294, 308, 317,
353n, 397
Dunbar, Scotland 173–4, 183, 187–8
Dunkirk, Flanders 391
Durham Cathedral 210
Durham House, Strand, London 241, 343
Dyer, Sir Edward 248–9, 290
Dymoke, Sir Edward 39

Eddystone, Devon 390
Edinburgh, Castle and City of 90–92, 110,
156, 174, 176, 184–8, 198, 294, 469
485
Edinburgh, Treaty of, 1560 91, 117, 124,
127, 132, 184, 213–14
Edward III, King of England 42
Edward VI King of England 2, 4, 13–15,
18–20, 41–2, 60, 63–4, 94, 125, 139,
230
Edwards, Richard 178
Egerton, Sir Thomas, Lord Keeper 267,
422, 435, 438, 448, 450, 452–5, 461,
465, 476, 483
Eglionby, Mrs 165
Elisabeth of Valois, Queen of Spain 61–2
Elizabeth I, Queen of England:
accession 1, 11, 16, 18
accomplishments and interests 7, 14, 229–
31, 249–50, 253, 415–6, 431–2
appearance 16, 235–6, 414, 431, 433–4,
447
Armada speech 393–4
birth 4

character 17, 229, 231
clothes and jewellery 18, 32–3, 234–7,
431
coronation 33–40
court and ceremonial 240–42, 247–62,
405–6, 433–4, 470, 477–8
death 484–5
early life to 1558 9–10, 12–16
financial matters 40, 225
foreign policy and relations;
France 25, 40, 62, 75, 89, 91, 116–17,
131, 133, 141, 144, 147, 214, 228,
269, 284, 287–9, 292–4, 297, 333,
336, 382, 399, 404, 409–10, 430, 434
Netherlands 193, 202, 284, 297, 306–7,
311, 333–4, 341, 345, 347, 350–51,
357–9, 361–2, 365, 370–71, 382–4,
434, 459
Ireland 434, 437–8, 440–46, 450, 454,
475
Italy 339, 479–80
The Papacy 25, 89, 213, 296, 333–5,
346, 349, 381, 384, 399
Scotland 75–6, 79, 89–91, 93, 159–60,
167, 190–91, 193, 212–13, 270, 276,
294, 333, 365, 381–2, 469–70
Spain 24–5, 193, 202, 206–8, 228, 284,
292–4, 296–7, 306, 309, 311, 333–4,
336, 338, 340–41, 346, 349–50,
356–7, 363, 365, 381–4, 388–95,
398–9, 403–4, 409, 415, 420, 420–25,
427–31, 434, 459, 475
funeral and tomb 485–6
health and illnesses 17–18, 133–6, 153,
214, 231–4, 401–2, 432, 443, 470,
475–7, 479–83
household 7, 20, 24, 164–5, 253
marriage projects:
Philip of Spain 24–6, 30, 32–3, 43, 52–3,
59–61
Erik of Sweden 50, 66–7, 76, 79, 83–4,
88, 121, 129
Archduke Ferdinand 30, 60, 62, 64
Archduke Charles 60, 62, 64–6, 71,
73–4, 80–82, 84–5, 87–8, 112, 118,
133, 145–6, 148, 154–5, 158–9,
161–3, 166–7, 169, 174–7, 191–2, 215
Arundel 67–9, 71, 76–7, 80
Pickering 67–9, 71, 80
Arran 75–6, 79, 93, 112, 115, 126

Henry of Anjou 215–16, 269–70, 274–6
Francis of Alençon 278–9, 284–, 292–4,
   306, 311–16, 318–27, 329–41, 345,
   350–51
marriage speculation 45–7, 80, 84, 93,
   107, 112–13, 345
palaces (see also separate entries) 240–47
portraits 30–40, 237–9, 413
progresses 76–7, 91, 121, 147–8, 178–9,
   206–8, 262–8, 276, 286–7, 298–303,
   307, 315–16, 318, 406, 408–9,
   413–14, 471, 475–6
as Queen 10, 22–4, 26, 29–30, 219–28,
   293, 348, 352–3, 399–400, 487–8
relations with Cecil/Burghley 18–20,
   22–3, 29, 90, 92–3, 102, 108, 113,
   159, 204–5, 227–8, 269, 290–92, 382,
   424–5, 436–7
relations with Essex 304, 384–7, 401–2,
   405–11, 414–17, 419–30, 432–6,
   438–69
relations with Dudley/Leicester 20–22,
   69–75, 77–80, 82, 84–8, 90–93, 96–8,
   100–01, 103, 112–14, 117–21, 129–31,
   147, 156–9, 165–6, 169–72, 174–6,
   202, 272–4, 279, 289–90, 292, 294,
   308, 312–14, 322–3, 330–32, 347–8,
   353–4, 357–8, 361–3, 365, 372–3,
   382, 384, 388, 394–8
relations with Mary, Queen of Scots 124,
   127–9, 131–3, 141–2, 144–6, 148–53,
   155–8, 163–4, 174, 176–7, 182–3,
   186–91, 194–201, 203–5, 207, 211,
   214–15, 277–8, 289, 295, 314–15,
   333, 346, 349–50, 352, 355, 360–61,
   364, 366–70, 371–8, 380–81, 383
relations with Parliament 40–41, 136–9,
   179–82, 228, 271, 281–2, 328, 335,
   355, 371–4, 415, 471–4
religious matters 26, 30–31, 40, 43–5,
   54–9, 63–4, 213–14, 297–8, 305, 316,
   335–6, 347
rumours and scandal 49–52, 72–3, 78–80,
   85, 90–92, 103–4, 107, 110–12
sexual matters 18, 47–9, 290, 321
and the succession 40–43, 114–15, 296,
   308, 345, 408, 433, 478–9
other references 3–6, 9, 26–8, 31, 99,
   115–17, 121–3, 131, 140, 143, 164,
   206, 208–12, 217–18, 273, 289–81,
   298, 304–5, 323–4, 342–4, 346,
   354–5, 412–13, 418, 422, 426
Elizabeth of York, Queen of England 12,
   47
Elsynge Palace, Enfield, Herts. 247
Eltham Palace, Kent 76, 116, 240, 246
Elvetham, Hants. 409, 456
Ely, Bishop of (see Cox, Richard)
Ely Place, Holborn, London 298, 411
Enfield Palace, Herts. 247
Epping Forest, Essex 246
Erik XIV, King of Sweden 50, 66–7, 76,
   79, 83–4, 88, 121, 129
Erskine, John, Earl of Mar 276, 289
Escorial Palace, Madrid 394
Esher, Surrey 292
Essex, Earls of (see Devereux)
Essex House, London (formerly Leicester
   House) 397, 417, 426, 433, 439, 453,
   455, 459, 461–2
Eton College, Berks. 230, 304
Euston Hall, Suffolk 315
Eworth, Hans 7, 238

Faarevejle Church, Dragsholm, Denmark
   310
Falmouth, Devon 403, 428
Farnese, Alexander, Duke of Parma 318,
   333, 345, 351, 357, 368, 370, 382,
   384, 388–94
Farnham, Surrey 206, 408, 456
Fayal, Island of 428
Feckenham, Richard, Abbot of
   Westminster 38, 40–41
Fénelon, Bertrand de Salaignac de la
   Mothe 51, 55, 207, 214, 216, 270,
   275, 286, 288
Ferdinand of Habsburg, Archduke of
   Austria 30, 60, 62, 64
Ferdinand I, Holy Roman Emperor 60,
   62, 64–6, 73–4, 76, 79, 81–2, 88, 145,
   147–8
Ferdinand de Toledo, Duke of Alva 193,
   202, 204, 206–7, 271–2, 284–5, 287,
   289, 297
Feria, Count of (see Figueroa)
Ferreira, Esteban 417–19
Ferrol, Spain 428
Figueroa, Don Gomez Suarez de, Count
   de Feria 3, 24–8, 30, 32–3, 40, 42–3,

47, 52–3, 60–62, 64, 68, 70, 71, 95,
115, 275
Fish, Walter 235
Fitton, Mary 262, 455
FitzAlan, Henry, 12th Earl of Arundel 23,
45, 67–8, 71, 76–7, 80, 81, 85, 136,
202, 204, 209, 245, 277
Fleet Prison, London 104n, 164, 262, 347,
441, 449
Fleming, Thomas 420
Flushing, Netherlands 345, 358–9
Foix, Paul de 154–5, 160, 169–70, 275–6
Forster, Anthony, MP 94–5, 100, 106
Forster, Mrs 95, 98
Fortescue family 256
Forty Hall, Enfield, Herts. 247
Fotheringhay, Northants. 368–70, 376,
378, 383
Francis, Edward, of Dorset 50
Francis II, King of France 25, 40, 53, 75,
116–17, 125, 146, 197
Francis of Valois, Duke of Alençon, later
Duke of Anjou 278–9, 284–8, 292–4,
306, 311–16, 318–27, 329–41, 345,
350–51
Frederick II, King of Denmark 84, 193
Fuller, Mr 229
Fuller, Thomas 342

Gargrave, Sir Thomas 43
Garret the Fool 476
Gascoigne, George 266, 298, 300–01
Genoa, Italy 202
George IV, King of Great Britain 39
Gheeraerts, Marcus, the Younger 239, 413
Gifford, Gilbert 360–61
Gilbert, Sir Humphrey 231, 342
Glasgow, City of 167, 183
Globe Theatre, Southwark, London 6, 461
Gloucester, City of 99
Gloucester Hall, Oxford 103
Goodman, Godfrey, Bishop of Gloucester
56, 398, 488
Gordon, Jean, Countess of Bothwell 183,
187
Gorges, Sir Ferdinando 460, 462
Gorhambury, St Albans, Herts. 266, 286,
307
Gournay, France 410
Gower, George 238, 398

Gravelines, Flanders 391, 394
Gray's Inn, London 157, 216
Green family, jesters 253
Greenwich Palace, Kent 21, 67, 74–5, 91,
120, 178, 240, 243–4, 247–8, 252,
307, 317, 322–4, 326, 336–7, 375,
433, 455, 476
Gregory XIII, Pope 333–5, 346, 349, 355
Gresham, Sir Thomas 212
Greville, Fulke 419, 422, 476
Grey, Lady Jane, Queen of England 2,
15–16, 20, 41, 111, 353
Grey, Lady Katherine 41–2, 115–16,
121–3, 134, 139–41, 179, 260, 409,
478
Grey, Lady Mary 41–2, 115, 164–5, 167,
179, 260
Grey of Wilton, Lord 187, 325
Grindal, Edmund, Bishop of London,
Archbishop of Canterbury 164,
297–8, 305–6, 347
Grindal, William 13
Guiana, Africa 421
Guilderstern, Nils, Chancellor of Sweden
50
Guise, Charles de, Cardinal of Lorraine 75,
89, 116, 230, 269–70, 293, 315, 333,
346, 349
Guise, Francis, Duke of 75, 89, 116, 131,
141
Guise, Henry, Duke of 230, 269, 293, 307,
315, 333, 346, 349, 372, 404
Guzman, Alonso Perez de, Duke of
Medina Sidonia 389–92

Habana, Cuba 357
The Hague, Netherlands 361
Hales, John 141
Hamilton, James, Earl of Arran 75–6, 79,
93, 112, 115, 126
Hamilton, John, Archbishop of St
Andrews 215, 276
Hamilton Palace, Scotland 194
Hampton Court Palace, Surrey 76, 79, 81,
134, 199–200, 232, 240, 244–5, 248,
267, 290, 348, 419, 443, 471
Hanworth, Middlesex 115
Hardwick Hall, Derbyshire 296
Harefield Park, Middlesex 476
Harington, Sir John (father) 259, 304

Harington, Sir John (son) 48–50, 56, 220–21, 224, 226–7, 240, 249, 254–6, 259, 290, 304–5, 344, 406, 414, 425–6, 439, 441, 448–9, 451, 456, 458, 463, 477

Harington, Lady 449, 477

Harrison, William 265

Hastings, Henry, 3rd Earl of Huntingdon 42, 102, 104, 135, 211, 231, 303–4

Hastings, Lady Mary 261

Hatfield House, Herts. 1, 12, 18, 20–22, 24, 26, 235, 239, 246–7

Hatton, Sir Christopher 50, 236, 251, 253, 255–7, 267, 272–4, 289–90, 298, 305–6, 309, 313–15, 328–9, 337, 340, 343, 354, 357, 366–7, 369, 372–3, 376–7, 380, 382, 394, 398, 411

Hawkins, Henry 90

Hawkins, Sir John 9, 395

Hawtrey, William 164

Hayward, Sir John 27, 235, 440–41

Heath, Nicholas, Archbishop of York 1, 31, 34

Helfenstein, Count von 60, 64, 66, 88

Heneage, Sir Thomas 165–6, 170, 237, 272, 362, 398

Henry IV, King of England 440–41

Henry VII, King of England 11, 22, 67, 223, 225, 241, 245, 253, 308, 486

Henry VIII, King of England 2–4, 11–13, 15, 18, 22, 25, 29, 36, 38, 41–2, 46, 53, 57, 64, 67, 75, 94, 114–15, 125, 127, 139, 148, 221, 236, 240–46, 253, 304, 328, 336, 347, 354, 374, 389, 456

Henry II, King of France 3, 25, 52–3, 61, 75, 125

Henry of Bourbon, King of Navarre, later Henry IV, King of France 222, 230, 287, 293, 350, 404, 407, 409, 411, 415, 430, 434, 480

Henry, Duke of Anjou, later Henry III, King of France 215–16, 269–70, 274–6, 278–9, 293–4, 297, 323, 337–41, 344, 350, 375, 382, 399, 404

Hentzner, Paul 242–4, 246, 248, 251, 433–4

Hepburn, James, Earl of Bothwell 183–90, 193, 197–200, 205, 310

Hepburn, James 184

Herbert, Edward, Lord, of Cherbury 250

Herbert, Henry, 2nd Earl of Pembroke 292, 318, 325, 452

Herbert, William, 1st Earl of Pembroke 23, 27, 63, 130, 177, 179–80, 192–3, 209, 211

Herbert, William, 3rd Earl of Pembroke 452, 455

Herbert, Sir William 250

Hercules-Francis, Duke of Alençon (see Francis of Valois)

Hereford, Viscount (see Devereux, Walter)

Herne, Henry 235

Herries, Lord 197

Heston, Middlesex 252

Hicks, Michael 267–8

Hilliard, Nicholas 7, 218, 236–9, 273, 398, 486

Hilton, Joan 33

Holbein, Hans 7, 241, 243

Holdenby, Northants. 267

Holinshed, Raphael 254, 388

Holtemans, Master 396

Holyrood Palace, Edinburgh 163, 173, 184–5, 187

Howard, Charles, 2nd Baron of Effingham, 1st Earl of Nottingham 251, 256, 266, 387–92, 395, 421, 430, 432, 434, 462, 465–6, 477, 479, 482–3

Howard, Douglas, Lady Sheffield 290–92, 294, 301, 303, 312, 316–17, 330

Howard, Elizabeth, Countess of Wiltshire 11–12

Howard, Lady Frances 261, 290, 292

Howard, Henry, Earl of Surrey 83

Howard, Katherine, Queen of England 13, 46, 245, 283

Howard, Lady Mary 259, 433

Howard, Philip, Earl of Surrey 315

Howard, Thomas, 3rd Duke of Norfolk 83

Howard, Thomas, 4th Duke of Norfolk 45, 72, 82–3, 85–6, 89, 136, 157, 159, 161, 169–71, 179, 192, 196, 198–9, 202–10, 212, 215, 270–72, 276–7, 279–83, 315, 376, 479

Howard, Thomas, 1st Baron de Walden 256, 479

Howard, William, 1st Baron of Effingham 39, 159, 256, 291

Huicke, Dr 47

Hunsdon, Essex 247

Hunsdon, Lords (see Carey)
Huntingdon Earl of (see Hastings, Henry)
Hurault, André, Sieur de Maisse 54, 236, 430–33
Hyde, William 94–5

Ippolita the Tartarian 253
Ipswich, Suffolk 121
Isabella Clara Eugenia, Infanta of Spain 363, 381, 458–9, 478
Islands Voyage, the, 1597 427–9
Isle of Wight, Hants. 390
Ivan IV the Terrible, Tsar of Muscovy 261

James IV, King of Scotland 42
James V, King of Scotland 125–6
James VI and I, King of Scotland and England 56, 176, 182, 187, 189–91, 200, 212, 214–15, 220–21, 230, 270, 277, 309, 317, 333, 346, 353–6, 363, 365, 368, 374–5, 381–3, 392, 404, 408, 419, 433, 453–4, 459–60, 463, 465, 469–70, 478–9, 481–3, 485–8
Jersey, Channel Islands 288, 356
Jesus College, Oxford 148, 230
Jewel, John, Bishop of Salisbury 84, 153
John of Austria, Don 306–7, 311, 318
John, Duke of Finland 83–4, 88, 129
John Frederick II, Duke of Saxony 67, 84, 129
John of Gaddesden 135
John of Gaunt, Duke of Lancaster 143, 241, 299, 478
Johnston, Garrett 235
Jones, Robert 111, 114
Jonson, Ben 49, 223, 248–9, 396

Katherine of Aragon, Queen of England 2, 11–12, 25
Kelston, Somerset 414, 449
Kenilworth Castle, Warwicks. 112, 143, 178–9, 211, 266, 287, 298–302, 312, 396–7
Kenninghall, Norfolk 208, 315
Kew, Surrey (see also the Dairy House, Kew)
Keyes, Thomas, of Lewisham 164
Kidderminster Church, Worcs. 98
Killigrew, Sir Henry 177, 357
King's College Chapel, Cambridge 147

Kingston, Surrey 206
Kinsale, Battle of, 1601 475
Kirk o'Field, Edinburgh 184–5
Knole Park, Kent 72
Knollys, Sir Francis 23–24, 165, 181, 192, 195, 197–200, 203, 256, 262, 303, 316–18, 329
Knollys, Lettice (Laetitia), Countess of Essex and Leicester 24, 165–6, 302–4, 312, 314, 316–18, 323, 330, 347, 357–8, 396–7, 403, 432, 468
Knollys, Sir William 256, 434–5, 447, 461
Knox, John 75, 125–6, 189, 222

Lacy, John 479
Lambarde, William 470–71
Lambeth Palace, London 240, 305, 462
Laneham, Robert 298–9
Langside, Battle of, 1568 194
Lea, Captain 463
Lee, Sir Henry 217, 239, 266, 294, 303, 398, 406
Le Havre (Newhaven), France 133, 136, 141, 144
Leicester, Earls of (see Dudley, Robert; Sidney Earls of Leicester; Sidney, Sir Robert)
Leicester House, London (afterwards Essex House) 292, 312, 338, 397, 417
Leighton, Lady 258
Leith, Edinburgh, Scotland 89, 124
Lennox, Earls of (see Stewart)
Lennox, Countess of (see Douglas, Margaret)
Lennoxlove House, Scotland 197
Lesley, John, Bishop of Ross 197, 205, 270, 276–7
Lever, Thomas, Rector of Coventry 103
Leveson, Sir John 461
Leveson, Sir Richard 475
Leycester's Commonwealth 95, 98, 103–4, 353
Lincoln, Earl of (see Clinton, Henry)
Lincoln's Inn, London 344
Lindsay, Patrick, Lord 190
Linlithgow, Scotland 212
Lisbon, Portugal 357, 389, 403, 423
Lizard, the, Cornwall 389, 429
Lochleven Castle, Kinross, Scotland 188–90, 194

London, Bishop of (see Aylmer, John)
London, City of 1, 3, 5–6, 26–7, 33–8, 57, 62, 68, 73, 76, 117, 131, 134, 148, 157, 212, 220, 240, 247–8, 272, 276, 285, 291, 307, 320, 325, 349, 353, 365–6, 374, 380, 390, 395, 398–9, 415–16, 428, 444, 457, 460–63, 477, 485–6
Long Itchington, Warwicks. 298
Longleat House, Wilts. 303
Lopez, Dr Roderigo 416–19
Lord Chamberlain's Men, company of actors 461
Lorraine, Cardinal of (see Guise, Charles de)
Loseley Park, Guildford, Surrey 206, 307
Louis I, Prince de Condé 132
Lumley, John, Lord 277, 369
Lyly, John 220, 266

Machiavelli, Niccolo 6
Madrid, Spain 272
Magellan, Ferdinand 334
Maisse, Sieur de (see Hurault, André)
Maitland, William, of Lethington 122, 125, 127–8, 131–2, 142–3, 152, 157, 168, 177, 183, 198, 212
Man, John, Bishop of Gloucester 193
Manners, Bridget 259
Manners, Henry, Earl of Rutland 72
Manners, Roger, Earl of Rutland 459, 462
Manningham, John 483, 485
Mantua, Duke of 31
Mar, Earl of (see Erskine, John)
Marchaumont, Seigneur de 336–7
Margaret of Habsburg, Duchess of Parma 96, 100, 112, 238
Margate, Kent 387
Marguerite de Valois, Queen of Navarre 287
Markham, Isabella, Lady Harington 259, 304
Markham, Robert 439
Marlowe, Christopher 7
Mary of Guise, Queen of Scotland 75, 79, 87, 89
Mary I, Queen of England 1–4, 15–16, 19–20, 23–6, 29–30, 31–2, 36, 40–42, 45–7, 53, 57, 59, 64, 66–7, 86, 94–5, 115, 122, 137, 162, 178, 222, 225, 245–6, 383
Mary, Queen of Scots 25, 30, 32–3, 40, 42–3, 48, 50, 53, 59, 75–6, 89, 91, 108, 111, 116–17, 124–9, 131–3, 135, 139–53, 155–8, 160, 163–4, 167–8, 172–4, 176–7 182–91, 193–201, 203–8, 210–16, 236, 269–72, 276–8, 281–2, 284, 287, 289, 293–6, 297, 308, 310, 315, 333, 345–6, 349–53, 355–6, 360–61, 363–83, 398, 406, 480
Marylebone Park, London 402
Maximilian II, Holy Roman Emperor, King of Bohemia 88, 147–8, 161–2, 171, 176, 178–9, 191–2, 215
Medici, Catherine de', Queen of France 51, 75, 116–17, 132, 141, 154–5, 186, 193, 210, 215–16, 270, 274–5, 278–9, 284–8, 292–4, 321, 324, 337–8, 350
Medina Sidonia, Duke of (see Guzman, Alonso)
Melville, Sir James 148–152, 156, 176–7
Melville, Sir Robert 374–5
Mendoza, Bernardino de 235, 293–4, 312, 319, 322–6, 329–31, 333–4, 336, 338–9, 341, 345, 349–50, 363, 365, 395, 397, 418
Meyrick, Sir Gelli 459, 461, 468
Mitcham, Surrey 406
Mole, M. de la 285–7
Molyneux, Mr, MP 179
Monarcho the Fool 253
Montague, Lady 408
Montague, Lord (see Browne, Anthony)
Montmorency, Duke of 285
Moray, Earl of (see Stuart, James)
More, Sir William 206
Morgan, Thomas 361, 364
Morley, Thomas 7
Mortlake, Surrey 22, 230
Morton, Earl of (see Douglas, James)
Mountjoy, Lords (see Blount)
Mousehole, Cornwall 420

National Maritime Museum, London 413
National Portrait Gallery, London 40, 237
Nau, Claude 366
Naunton, Sir Robert 21, 166, 219, 228, 273, 342, 405
Neville, Charles, Earl of Westmorland 208–12

Newfoundland, colony of, America 355
Newgate Prison, London 348, 463
Newhall, Essex 247
Newhaven, France (see Le Havre)
Neiuport, Flanders 459
Noailles, Antoine de 84
Nonsuch Palace, Surrey 67, 76, 81, 209, 245–8, 357, 418, 443, 446–7, 456
Norfolk, Duchesses of 38, 47
Norfolk, Dukes of (see also Howard, Thomas) 11
Norris, Sir Henry, later Lord Norris 210, 231, 257, 267, 395, 414
Norris, Sir John 403–4
Norris, Margery, Lady 103, 231, 267, 395, 414
North Hall 386–7
North, Thomas, Lord 27, 219, 233, 295, 298, 411, 447
Northern Rising, the, 1569 208–13, 270
Northampton, Marquess of (see Parr, William)
Northampton, Sheriff of 378
Northumberland, Countess of 212
Northumberland, Duke of (see Dudley, John)
Northumberland, Earl of (see Percy, Thomas)
Norwich, City of 6, 315–16
Norwich, Dean of 465
Nottingham, Countess of (see Carey, Katherine)
Nottingham, Earl of (see Howard, Charles)
Nowell, Alexander, Dean of St Paul's 55, 137
Noyon, France 410

Oatlands Palace, Weybridge, Surrey 206, 245, 248, 456, 476
Odiham, Hants. 409
Odingsells, Mrs 95, 98, 105, 109
Oglethorpe, Owen, Bishop of Carlisle 31, 34, 38
Oliver, Isaac 239
O'Neill, Hugh, 2nd Earl of Tyrone 437–46, 449–52, 454, 463, 475, 477–8, 480
Orkney Islands, Scotland 188
Ormonde, Earl of (see Butler, Thomas)
Owen, Dr George 94

Owen, Mrs 95, 98, 104–6, 109
Owen, William 94–5
Oxford, City of 94, 178, 288, 304, 414
Oxford, University of 95, 148, 153, 178, 273, 302, 400, 411, 414, 438

Padua, Italy 216
Page, William 327–8, 331
Paget, Charles 363
Palmer, Mr 460
Panama, South America 412, 420–21
Parham Park, Sussex 415
Paris, France 89, 93, 110, 154–5, 167, 210, 215, 269, 275–6, 278, 287, 320, 330, 333, 346, 353, 355–6, 360–61, 364, 382, 389, 394, 415, 433
Paris Garden, London 230, 248
Parker, Matthew, Archbishop of Canterbury 57, 64, 122, 195, 297
Parma, Duchess of (see Margaret of Habsburg)
Parma, Dukes of (see Farnese, Alexander; Ranuccio I)
Parr, Katherine, Queen of England 13–15, 23, 47
Parr, William, Marquess of Northampton 23, 72, 110, 180, 192, 204, 260
Parry, Blanche 24, 259, 406
Parry, Sir Thomas 24, 81, 117
Parry, Dr 483–4
Parry, Dr William 354–5
Parsons, Father Robert 50, 333, 335, 419
Paul IV, Pope 59
Paulet, Sir Amyas 320, 356, 360–61, 366, 368–9, 372, 375, 377–8, 383
Paulet, William, 1st Marquess of Winchester 23, 281
Paulet, William, 4th Marquess of Winchester 471
Peake, Robert 239
Pembroke, Earls of (see Herbert)
Penshurst Place, Kent 22, 136, 229, 456
Penzance, Cornwall 420
Percy, Thomas, Earl of Northumberland 202, 208, 210–12
Perrot, Sir John 221, 347
Perrot, Sir Thomas 347
Peterborough Cathedral 383
Peterborough, Dean of (Dr Fletcher) 379
Petworth, Sussex 408

Phelippes, Thomas 360, 364
Philip II, King of Spain 2–3, 16, 20, 24–6,
    30, 32–3, 40–41, 43, 46, 48, 52–3, 55,
    60–62, 64–6, 70, 74, 76, 81, 85–6, 91,
    96, 117–19, 130, 143, 147, 161–2,
    167, 186, 192–3, 195, 202–3, 206–7,
    211, 213, 222, 228, 230, 233, 270–72,
    282, 284, 287, 289, 296–7,302, 306,
    309, 311, 316, 318, 324, 333–4, 336,
    338–40, 345–6, 349–52, 356–8, 363,
    365, 368, 374, 381–2, 384, 388–9,
    392, 394, 403–4, 415,417–21, 423,
    425, 428, 430–31, 434, 437–8
Philip III, King of Spain 437, 458, 478
Pickering, Hester 68
Pickering, Sir William 67–9, 71, 80
Piedmont, Italy 168
Pirgo, Jane 95, 101
Pius IV, Pope 89
Pius V, Pope 213, 217, 270–72, 274, 282,
    287, 289, 295–6, 311
Platter, Thomas 246, 250, 440
Plymouth, Devon 309, 389–90, 421–2, 429
Pole, Reginald, Cardinal, Archbishop of
    Canterbury 31
Poor Law Act 1598 472
Popham, Sir John 461, 464
Portland, Dorset 390
Portsmouth, Hants. 144, 409
Public Record Office, Kew 397
Putney, Surrey 479
Puttenham, George 282

Quadra, Alvaro de, Bishop of Aquila 55,
    62, 65, 72, 74, 76, 80–82, 84–89,
    92–3, 95–8, 100, 107–8, 111–12, 114,
    116–20, 129–31, 134, 143–4
Queen's House, the, Greenwich 74
Queen's Men, the, company of players 57,
    250

Rabelais, Francis 125
Radcliffe, Mary 259
Raleig'ı, Sir Walter 9, 55, 220, 223, 229,
    231, 238, 250, 253, 255–6, 260,
    341–4, 346, 348, 354, 362, 382,
    386–7, 390, 402–4, 408, 412–13,
    420–23, 426–9, 439–40, 453–5, 460,
    464, 466, 469, 486, 488
Randolph, Thomas 76, 79, 110, 125, 128,

    134, 136, 144–6, 148, 155–8, 160,
    163, 168, 173, 188
Ranuccio I, Duke of Parma 478
Ratcliffe, Thomas, Earl of Sussex 39, 48,
    112, 155, 157–9, 161, 166, 169,
    177–8, 191–2, 202, 211, 238, 247,
    269, 318, 322–3, 325, 330, 347
Reading, Berks. 471
Recusancy, Statute of, 1581 335
Rich, Lady (see Devereux, Penelope)
Richard II, King of England 441, 461, 470
Richmond Palace, Surrey 206, 240, 245,
    247–8, 334, 339, 354, 358, 371, 373,
    389, 391, 426, 452, 479–80, 483, 485
Ridolfi, Roberto 204, 208, 270–72, 276–8
Ritchie, Edward 393
Rizzio, David 157, 168, 172–4, 183, 186,
    188
Robsart, Amy, Lady Dudley 20–21, 73,
    85–7, 93–112, 118, 317
Robsart, Sir John 20
Robsart, Rosetta 317
Rome, Italy 271, 296, 333, 399
Ronsard, Pierre 125
Rookwood, Mr 315
Ross, Bishop of (see Lesley, John)
Rouen, France 410–11
Royal Exchange, London 212, 253
Royal Wardrobe, St Andrew's Hill,
    London 241
Rudd, Anthony, Bishop of St David's 56
Rufford Abbey, Derbyshire 295
Russell, Anne, later Countess of Pembroke
    455
Russell, Anne, Countess of Warwick 260,
    286, 386–7, 451, 484
Russell, Elizabeth 408
Russell, Francis, Earl of Bedford 93, 117,
    177, 182–3, 188
Russell, Lady 406
Ruthven, Patrick, Lord 172–3
Rutland, Earls of (see Manners)
Rycote, Oxon. 267, 395–7, 414
Rye, Sussex 339, 360

Sackville, Sir Richard 187, 256
Sackville, Thomas, Lord Buckhurst, later
    Earl of Dorset 256, 269, 388, 411,
    438, 444, 452, 463–5
Sadler, Sir Ralph 84, 138, 352

Saffron Garden, Essex 393
St Bartholemew's Eve Massacre, 1572 287–9, 302, 326
St Bartholemew's Hospital, London 416
St George's Chapel, Windsor 243
St Giles's Fields, Holborn 367
St James's Palace, London 129, 150, 246, 391–2
St John's Priory, Clerkenwell 241
St John's Wood, London 366
St Mary, Church of, Stamford 437
St Mary Redcliffe, Church of, Bristol 267
St Mary the Virgin, Church of, Oxford 103
St Mary the Virgin, Church of, Warwick 396
St Paul's Cathedral, London 6, 37, 213, 327, 339, 371, 395, 399, 461
St Peter ad Vincula, Chapel of, Tower of London 283, 466
Salisbury Cathedral, Wilts. 140
Sanders, Nicholas 50
Sandwich, Kent 265, 344, 387, 417
Sandys, Edwin, Archbishop of York 330
Sandys, Lord 207, 471
San Miguel, Island of 428
San Quentin, Battle of, 1557 20
Santa Domingo, Caribbean 357
Savage, Mr 365
Savoy, Duchess of 321
Savoy Palace, London 241
Saxony, Duke of (see John Frederick II)
Scaramelli, Giovanni 479–80, 482–3
Schifanoya, Il 31, 45, 70, 251
Scott, Sir Walter 112
Scrope, Lady (see Carey, Eleanor)
Scudamore, Sir James 260–61
Scudamore, Lady (see Shelton, Mary)
Segar, William 239
Seville, Spain 296
Seymour, Edward, Baron Beauchamp 122, 478
Seymour, Edward, Duke of Somerset, Lord Protector 14–15, 19, 115
Seymour, Edward, Earl of Hertford 115–16, 121–3, 139–40, 251, 261, 409, 478
Seymour, Jane, Queen of England 2, 12, 47
Seymour, Lady Jane 116, 121

Seymour, Thomas, Lord Sudeley 14–15, 46, 78, 304, 385
Seymour, Thomas 140
Seymour, William, later Duke of Somerset
Shakespeare, William 6–7, 223, 249, 253, 433, 441, 461, 465, 471
Sharp, Dr Lionel 393–4
Sheen Manor, Surrey 260
Sheffield Castle, Yorks. 203, 351–2
Sheffield, John, Lord 291
Sheffield, Lady (see Howard, Douglas)
Shelley-Sidney, Sir John 317
Shelton, Mary, Lady Scudamore 260–61
Sherborne Castle, Dorset 239, 413
Shrewsbury, Earls of (see Talbot)
Sidney Earls of Leicester 317
Sidney, Sir Henry 22, 86, 103, 117–19, 132, 136, 159, 169, 303, 325, 370
Sidney, Lady (see Dudley, Mary)
Sidney, Sir Philip 259, 302, 318, 325–6, 346, 353, 358, 370–71, 386, 402, 406
Sidney, Sir Robert, later Earl of Leicester 260, 317, 397, 426, 456
Silva, Don Diego de Guzman de 51, 147, 153–4, 157–8, 161, 166–7, 170–71, 174, 176, 179–80, 187, 193
Simier, Jean de, Baron de St Marc 318–26, 329–30
Singleton, Mr 327–8
Sixtus V, Pope 363, 372, 381, 384, 399
Sly, John 400
Smith, Mr 102
Smith, Sir Thomas 154–5, 167, 224, 278–9, 284
Smyth, Thomas 461
Somers, Will 33
Somerset, Duchess of (see Stanhope, Anne)
Somerset, Edward, Earl of Worcester 451, 461, 476
Somerset House, Strand, London 28, 212, 241, 247, 398–9
Somerset, William, Earl of Worcester 47, 289
Somerville, John 348, 355
Southampton, Earls of (see Wriothesley)
Southampton, Hants. 202, 334, 409
Spenser, Edmund 7, 223, 325, 396
Spes, Don Guerau de 193, 199, 202–4, 206–7, 277
Spilman, Master 236

Stafford family 256
Stafford, Sir Edward 317, 330
Stafford, Staffs. 262
Stamford, Lincs. 19, 178
Standen, Sir Anthony 416, 449
Stanhope, Anne, Duchess of Somerset 115
Stanley, Edward, Earl of Derby 23, 202
Stanley, Henry, Lord Strange, Earl of
    Derby 42, 47
Stephano, Signor 89
Stettin, Duke of 476
Stewart, Arbella 296, 308, 353&n, 354, 478
Stewart, Charles, 6th Earl of Lennox 295-6
Stewart, Henry, Lord Darnley 43, 117,
    131, 143, 150, 152-3, 155-60, 163,
    168, 171-4, 177, 182-9, 193, 195-6,
    198-9, 210, 215, 281, 289, 294-5, 310
Stewart, Jane, Countess of Argyll 173
Stewart, Matthew, 4th Earl of Lennox 43,
    143, 148, 152, 159, 183-4, 187, 215,
    276
Stirling Castle, Scotland 172, 182, 187,
    190, 276
Stokes, Adrian 113
Stow, John 212, 323, 396, 486
Strange, Lady (see Clifford, Margaret)
Strange, Lord (see Stanley)
Stuart, James, Earl of Moray 126-7, 152,
    156-7, 160, 163-4, 167-8, 172, 174,
    186, 190-91, 193-4, 197-200, 205-6,
    212
Stubbs, John 327-8, 331
Stubbs, Philip 6, 9
Succession, Act of, 1544 4, 15, 41-2,
    114-15, 127
Sudeley Castle, Gloucs. 413
Suffolk, Dowager Duchess of (see
    Willoughby, Katherine)
Suffolk, Duchess of (see Brandon, Frances)
Suffolk, Duke of (see Brandon)
Sully, Duke of (see Bethune, Maximilien
    de)
Supremacy, Act of, 1534 57
Supremacy, Act of, 1559 59, 63
Surrey, Earls of (see also Howard, Henry)
    11
Sussex, Earl of (see Ratcliffe, Thomas)
Sutton Place, Surrey 415
Syderstone, Norfolk 20
Talbot, Francis, 5th Earl of Shrewsbury 23,
47
Talbot, George, 6th Earl of Shrewsbury
    203, 211, 257, 271, 279-80, 290, 308,
    351, 363, 397, 406
Talbot, Gilbert, 7th Earl of Shrewsbury
    248, 290, 476
Tallis, Thomas 7, 230
Tamworth, Mr 135
Tarleton, Richard 229, 250
Taylor, Mr 185
Teerlinc, Levina 58, 237
Temple, Inns of, London 129, 273, 471
Theobalds, Essex 266-7, 286, 346, 357,
    382, 408
Theodosius II, Duke of Braganza 478
Thetford, Norfolk 315
Thomasina, royal dwarf 253
Throckmorton, Elizabeth, Lady Raleigh
    260, 408, 412-13
Throckmorton, Francis 346, 349-50
Throckmorton, Sir Nicholas 23, 84, 89-90,
    93, 110-11, 113-14, 117, 125, 131-2,
    153, 158, 160-1, 163, 165, 172, 175,
    189-90, 203, 209, 269, 291, 346, 408
Tiepolo, Paolo 70
Tilbury, Essex 390-95
Tinoco, Senor 417-19
Titchfield, Hants. 207, 408
Toothe, William 33
Topclyffe, Richard 50, 315
Tothill, Richard 38
Tower of London 6, 12, 16, 20-21, 27-8,
    34-5, 43, 50, 81, 86, 104, 122, 131,
    139-40, 163, 187, 202, 204, 207,
    209-10, 215, 224, 246-7, 261, 271,
    276-7, 279-80, 282-3, 304, 323, 328,
    330, 333-4, 337-8, 347, 349, 365-8,
    381, 398, 412-13, 418, 435, 455, 460,
    462, 465-6, 470
Tracy, Mr 396
Tresham, Francis 459
Troyes, Treaty of, 1564 147
Tudor, Arthur, Prince of Wales 11, 302
Tudor, Margaret, Queen of Scotland 42-3
Tudor, Mary, Duchess of Suffolk 15, 41-2
Tuscany, Grand Duke of (see Cosimo I)
Tutbury Castle, Staffs. 199, 203, 210, 352,
    360
Tyburn, London 350, 419, 463
Tye, Christopher 253